THE OXFORD HANDBOOK OF

AMERICAN LITERARY NATURALISM

THE OXFORD HANDBOOK OF

AMERICAN LITERARY NATURALISM

Edited by

KEITH NEWLIN

OXFORD
UNIVERSITY PRESS

Oxford University Press, Inc., publishes works that further
Oxford University's objective of excellence
in research, scholarship, and education.

Oxford   New York
Auckland   Cape Town   Dar es Salaam   Hong Kong   Karachi
Kuala Lumpur   Madrid   Melbourne   Mexico City   Nairobi
New Delhi   Shanghai   Taipei   Toronto

With offices in
Argentina   Austria   Brazil   Chile   Czech Republic   France   Greece
Guatemala   Hungary   Italy   Japan   Poland   Portugal   Singapore
South Korea   Switzerland   Thailand   Turkey   Ukraine   Vietnam

Published by Oxford University Press, Inc.
198 Madison Avenue, New York, New York 10016

www.oup.com

Oxford is a registered trademark of Oxford University Press

Library of Congress Cataloging-in-Publication Data
The Oxford handbook of American literary naturalism / edited by Keith Newlin.
p.   cm.
Includes bibliographical references and index.
ISBN 978-0-19-536893-2
1. American literature—History and criticism—Handbooks, manuals, etc.
2. Naturalism in literature—Handbooks, manuals, etc. I. Newlin, Keith.
PS169.N38O94   2011
810.9′36—dc22   2010015398

1 3 5 7 9 8 6 4 2
Printed in the United States of America
on acid-free paper

Contents

....

Contributors ix

Introduction: The Naturalistic Imagination and the Aesthetics of Excess 3
Keith Newlin

PART I CONTEXTS

1. Romancing the Machine: American Naturalism in Transatlantic
   Context 21
   Zena Meadowsong

2. The Response to Power in American Literary Naturalism: Visions and
   Revisions that Transformed a Narrative Mode 37
   Richard Lehan

3. Nature in Naturalism 52
   Bert Bender

PART II NATURALISM AND GENRE

4. Defining American Literary Naturalism 71
   Eric Carl Link

5. Sand in Your Mouth: Naturalism and Other Genres 92
   June Howard

6. The Documentary Strategies of Naturalism 104
   Keith Newlin

PART III THE SCIENTIFIC AND PHILOSOPHIC BACKGROUND

7. Determinism, Free Will, and Moral Responsibility
   in American Literary Naturalism 121
   Ian F. Roberts

8. "First Principles of Morals": Evolutionary Morality and American
   Naturalism 139
   Rick Armstrong

9. Naturalism and Religion 154
   Steven Frye

10. Things Fall Apart: Degeneration and Atavism in American Literary
    Naturalism 172
    Gina M. Rossetti

11. American Literary Naturalism and Psychology 182
    Stephen C. Brennan

12. American Naturalism and Modern Evolutionary Psychology 203
    Jeff P. Turpin

PART IV NATURALIST TENSIONS

13. Women Writers and Naturalism 223
    Donna M. Campbell

14. American Literary Naturalism and Sexuality 241
    Linda Kornasky

15. African American Writers and Naturalism 257
    John Dudley

16. Race and Naturalism in the Short Fiction of Norris,
    Crane, and London 274
    Jeanne Campbell Reesman

17. Naturalism and Commodity Culture 291
    Mary E. Papke

18. Naturalism and Class 307
    Jude Davies

19. The Grotesque City, the City of Excess, and the City of Exile 322
    James R. Giles

20. Naturalism and Crime 339
    Gary Scharnhorst

PART V   NATURALISM AND THE MARKETPLACE

21. Naturalist Authors and the American Literary Marketplace 357
    Charles Johanningsmeier

22. Consolation, Affirmation, and Convention: The Popular Reception of
    American Naturalist Texts 373
    Carol S. Loranger

23. Editing Naturalism 389
    Kevin J. Hayes

24. Refashioning American Literary Naturalism: Critical Trends at the
    Turn of the Twenty-First Century 404
    Christophe Den Tandt

PART VI   NATURALISM AND THE OTHER ARTS

25. Sad Endings and Negative Heroes: The Naturalist Tradition in
    American Drama 427
    Robert M. Dowling

26. Naturalism and Poetry 445
    Chris Beyers

27. Naturalism and the Visual Arts 463
    Donald Pizer

28. American Literary Naturalism and Film Noir 483
    Jeff Jaeckle

Index 499

Contributors

RICK ARMSTRONG is Assistant Professor of English at Kingsborough Community College of the City University of New York. He has presented papers at conferences of the Modern Language Association, the Midwest Modern Language Association, the American Literature Association, and the New York College English Association.

BERT BENDER, Emeritus Professor of American Literature at Arizona State University, now lives in Atascadero, California. His books include *Sea-Brothers: The Tradition of American Sea Fiction from Moby-Dick to the Present*; *The Descent of Love: Darwin and the Theory of Sexual Selection in American Fiction, 1871–1926*; *Evolution and "the Sex Problem": American Narratives during the Eclipse of Darwinism*; and a memoir, *Catching the Ebb: Drift-Fishing for a Life in Cook Inlet*.

CHRIS BEYERS is Professor of English at Assumption College. He is the author of *A History of Free Verse* and numerous essays on poetry and poetics, including the chapter "Augustan American Verse" in *The Oxford Handbook of Early American Literature*.

STEPHEN C. BRENNAN is Professor of English at Louisiana State University in Shreveport. He is coauthor of *Irving Babbitt* and has published numerous essays on literary naturalism in *Studies in American Fiction*, *American Literary Realism*, *Dreiser Studies*, and other journals. He is currently coeditor of *Studies in American Naturalism*.

DONNA M. CAMPBELL is Associate Professor of English at Washington State University. She is the author of *Resisting Regionalism: Gender and Naturalism in American Fiction, 1885–1915*, and her articles on late nineteenth- and early twentieth-century authors have appeared in *Studies in American Fiction*, *Legacy*, *American Literary Realism*, *Studies in American Naturalism*, and *The Cambridge Companion to Kate Chopin*. Her current project is a book on American women writers of naturalism.

JUDE DAVIES is Professor of American Literature and Culture at the University of Winchester. He is author of several articles on Theodore Dreiser and edited *Theodore Dreiser's Political Writings*. His previous books include *Diana, A Cultural History: Gender, Race, Nation and the People's Princess* and, as coauthor, *Gender, Ethnicity, and Sexuality in Contemporary American Film* and, as coeditor, *Issues in Americanization and Culture*.

CHRISTOPHE DEN TANDT teaches literature in English and cultural theory at the Université Libre de Bruxelles. He is the author of *The Urban Sublime in American*

Literary Naturalism and of articles on U.S. literature, popular culture (music, crime fiction), and postmodernist theory. His current research focuses on the theoretical groundings of contemporary realism (literature, film, television).

ROBERT M. DOWLING is Associate Professor of English at Central Connecticut State University. He is the author of *Slumming in New York: From the Waterfront to Mythic Harlem* and the two-volume *Critical Companion to Eugene O'Neill: A Literary Reference to His Life and Work*. His latest projects include a forthcoming critical anthology on Eugene O'Neill's early bohemian and radical influences, coedited with Eileen Herrmann, and *Eugene O'Neill: The Contemporary Reviews*, a compendium of reviews of O'Neill's books and plays, coedited with Jackson R. Bryer.

JOHN DUDLEY is Associate Professor of English at the University of South Dakota. The author of *A Man's Game: Masculinity and the Anti-Aesthetics of American Literary Naturalism*, he is currently working on a study of African American literature and culture between 1890 and 1928, with an emphasis on the role of music, aesthetics, and material culture in developing notions of racial identity.

STEVEN FRYE is Professor of English at California State University, Bakersfield. He is the author of *Historiography and Narrative Design in the American Romance* and *Understanding Cormac McCarthy*, editor of *Critical Insights: Poe's Tales* and *Critical Insights: Poe's Poetry*, as well as the author of numerous articles on the American novel in journals such as *American Studies, Studies in American Naturalism*, and *American Literary Realism*. In addition, he is associate editor of *ALN: The American Literary Naturalism Newsletter*.

JAMES R. GILES is Distinguished Professor Emeritus at Northern Illinois University. He is the author of nine books and the coeditor of eight others, including *The Spaces of Violence, Violence in the Contemporary American Novel: An End to Innocence, The Naturalistic Inner-City Novel in America: Encounters with the Fat Man, Approaches to Teaching the Works of Louise Erdrich* (coedited), and six volumes of the *Dictionary of Literary Biography* (all coedited with Wanda H. Giles). He has also published approximately thirty articles and short stories, the most recent in *Studies in American Naturalism* and *A Companion to Twentieth-Century United States Fiction*.

KEVIN J. HAYES, Professor of English at the University of Central Oklahoma, is the author of *Stephen Crane*, which forms part of the Writers and Their Work series published by Northcote House in association with the British Council. He is the editor of the Bedford edition of Crane's *Maggie: A Girl of the Streets* and of *Henry James: The Contemporary Reviews*. For six years, he served as Bibliography Editor for *Documentary Editing*. For his work, the Association for Documentary Editing presented him with its Distinguished Service Award.

JUNE HOWARD is Arthur F. Thurnau Professor and Professor of English, American Culture, and Women's Studies at the University of Michigan, Ann Arbor. She is the author of *Form and History in American Literary Naturalism* and, more recently, of *Publishing the Family*, a microhistorical study of an unusual episode in literary history: the serial publication in Harper's *Bazar* of a collaborative novel by twelve authors, including Henry James. She is currently working on a book-length study of literary regionalism.

JEFF JAECKLE teaches courses on literature and film at Portland Community College. His essays on American literary naturalism and Hollywood film have appeared in *Dreiser Studies, Quarterly Review of Film and Video, ALN: The American Literary Naturalism Newsletter*, and MLA's forthcoming *Approaches to Teaching the Works of Jack London*. He is the editor of the forthcoming anthology *Film Dialogue*.

CHARLES JOHANNINGSMEIER is Professor of English at the University of Nebraska at Omaha. He is the author of *Fiction and the American Literary Marketplace: The Role of Newspaper Syndicates, 1860–1900*, as well as of numerous articles about the history and reception of fictions published in American periodicals during the late nineteenth and early twentieth centuries.

LINDA KORNASKY, Professor of English at Angelo State University, has published articles on Edith Wharton, Ellen Glasgow, Kate Chopin, and other American women naturalist writers in *American Literary Realism, Mississippi Quarterly, ALN: The American Literary Naturalism Newsletter*, and elsewhere. She is currently working on a book about naturalism in Southern women's fiction from the 1890s to the 1930s.

RICHARD LEHAN, Emeritus Professor of English at UCLA, has written many books and essays on modern literary movements. His most recent books include *The City in Literature, Realism and Naturalism: The Novel in an Age of Transition*, and *Literary Modernism and Beyond: The Extended Vision and the Realms of the Text*. He is at present completing another book, tentatively entitled "Quest West," involving the idea of romantic destiny and the transformation of American historical ideals as the country moved west.

ERIC CARL LINK is Professor of American literature at the University of Memphis. The author of *The Vast and Terrible Drama: American Literary Naturalism in the Late Nineteenth Century* and *Neutral Ground: New Traditionalism and the American Romance Controversy* (coauthored with G. R. Thompson), his most recent book is *Understanding Philip K. Dick*. He is also the founder and editor of *ALN: The American Literary Naturalism Newsletter*.

CAROL S. LORANGER is Associate Professor and Chair of the Department of English Language and Literatures at Wright State University, where she has taught American literature and literary theory since 1993. She is book review editor for *Studies in American Naturalism* and has focused her scholarship on such groundbreaking and controversial American writers as William S. Burroughs, Thomas Pynchon, Stephen Crane, and Theodore Dreiser. She is a member of the governing committee for the Dayton Literary Peace Prize and serves on its University Consortium and Lifetime Achievement subcommittees.

ZENA MEADOWSONG is Assistant Professor of English Literature at Rowan University. She has contributed essays on literary naturalism to *Studies in American Naturalism* and *Nineteenth-Century Literature* and is currently at work on a book project, "Mechanization and the Making of the Modern Novel: Naturalism, Modernism, Postmodernism," which focuses on the relationship between the historical process of mechanization and the novel form, connecting narrative experimentation in the late nineteenth-century naturalist novel to the development of twentieth-century modernism and postmodernism.

KEITH NEWLIN is Professor and Chair of the Department of English at the University of North Carolina Wilmington. The author or editor of twelve books, recent volumes include *Hamlin Garland, A Life* and, as editor, *A Summer to Be, A Memoir by the Daughter of Hamlin Garland* and *A Theodore Dreiser Encyclopedia*. At present he is the coeditor of *Studies in American Naturalism*.

MARY E. PAPKE is Professor of English at the University of Tennessee. She is the author of *Verging on the Abyss: The Social Fiction of Kate Chopin and Edith Wharton* and *Susan Glaspell: A Research and Production Sourcebook*, and the editor of *Twisted from the Ordinary: Essays on American Literary Naturalism*. In addition, she has published essays on feminist theory, postmodern women writers, the unpublished drama of Evelyn Scott, the political theatre of Sean O'Casey, and Marxist literary criticism in early twentieth-century America, among other topics.

DONALD PIZER, Pierce Butler Professor of English Emeritus at Tulane University, has published widely on late nineteenth- and early twentieth-century American literature. His recent books include *American Naturalism and the Jews: Garland, Norris, Dreiser, Wharton, and Cather* and editions of Hamlin Garland's early radical writing and of Dreiser's interviews and letters.

JEANNE CAMPBELL REESMAN is Professor of English at the University of Texas at San Antonio, where she has also served as Graduate Dean and Director of English, Classics, Philosophy and Communication. She has published numerous monographs, collections, textbooks, and editions from Oxford, Macmillan, Stanford, University of Pennsylvania, Norton, and Éditions Phébus (Paris), among them her critical biography, *Jack London's Racial Lives*, and *Jack London, Photographer*, coedited with Sara S. Hodson and Philip Adam, a collection of London's historic photographs.

IAN F. ROBERTS teaches nineteenth-century literature, literary theory, and literature and science at Missouri Western State University. He also chairs the Literature and Science Area for the American Culture Association.

GINA M. ROSSETTI is Associate Professor of English at Saint Xavier University in Chicago, where she teaches late nineteenth- and early twentieth-century American literature. She is the author of *Imagining the Primitive in Naturalist and Modernist Literature* as well as the author of "It's a Family Affair: Nativism and Ethnic Panic in Jack London's *The Valley of the Moon*," which will appear in MLA's *Approaches to*

Teaching the Works of Jack London. She is also a member of the advisory board for the Jack London Society.

GARY SCHARNHORST is Distinguished Professor of English at the University of New Mexico, the author or editor of more than thirty-five books, a five-time recipient of Fulbright teaching fellowships to Germany, and editor of *American Literary Realism* and editor in alternating years of *American Literary Scholarship*.

JEFF P. TURPIN is a literary Darwinist who recently received his Ph.D. in English from the University of Texas at San Antonio. His minor concentrations include cognitive and evolutionary psychologies, modernism, and minority literature. He resides in rural Texas and currently works as a self-employed archeologist.

THE OXFORD HANDBOOK OF

AMERICAN LITERARY
NATURALISM

INTRODUCTION: THE NATURALISTIC IMAGINATION AND THE AESTHETICS OF EXCESS

KEITH NEWLIN

DESPITE the premature sounding of its death-knell in the 1959 anthology *What Was Naturalism?* American literary naturalism remains a vibrant and active field. Since 1980, more than two dozen books about the subject have appeared, and articles about its principal authors—Stephen Crane, Frank Norris, Theodore Dreiser, and Jack London—continue to be published in the leading journals. More important, the traditional conception of naturalism as a movement occurring between 1890 and 1915 and focusing on deterministic depictions of humanity as the passive pawns of an indifferent world has, in recent years, undergone considerable shifting. A raft of articles and books have appeared that trace the continuing presence of naturalism in authors as diverse as Kate Chopin, Edith Wharton, Upton Sinclair, Ernest Hemingway, John Steinbeck, Richard Wright, Joyce Carol Oates, Cormac McCarthy, and Don DeLillo. Scholars have traced naturalism's evolution into urban fictions that depict people's circumscribed possibilities or compel them to act in obsessive, repetitive, or compulsive behaviors; scholars have also been drawn to unveiling the culture that shaped naturalism's key texts.

While Lars Ahnebrink's *The Beginnings of Naturalism in American Fiction* (1950) charted the influence of Zola upon Hamlin Garland, Frank Norris, and Stephen Crane, the first book to map the broad contours of the movement was Charles C. Walcutt's *American Literary Naturalism: A Divided Stream* (1956). Walcutt's contention that naturalism can be divided into two "streams"—one optimistic and idealistic and leading to "progressivism and social radicalism," the other pessimistic and deterministic and leading to a mechanistic account of human behavior—proved tremendously influential for subsequent critics and prompted a host of revisions and reconceptualizations that are ongoing today. Since Walcutt's pioneering study, which is still unsurpassed in terms of scope, a steady stream of books on naturalism has poured forth. With few exceptions, most are either "thesis books"—volumes that mount an argument and trace its development though individual chapters on selected writers or texts—or collections of critical essays on authors or texts. The most important of these are two books by Donald Pizer: *Realism and Naturalism in Nineteenth-Century American Literature* (1966; rev. 1984) and *Twentieth-Century American Literary Naturalism: An Interpretation* (1982). The former book collects a number of Pizer's essays which, collectively, offer a vision of naturalism distinct from Walcutt's, one that identifies naturalism as "a movement characterized by similarities in material and method, not by philosophical coherence" (110), an interpretation Pizer extends to the twentieth century in which he argues, in chapters on Farrell, Dos Passos, Steinbeck, Mailer, Styron, and Bellow, that naturalism retained its relevance by responding to "the preoccupations of particular moments of modern American life" and discovering "appropriate forms for doing so" (*Twentieth-Century* vii).

Drawing on this foundational work by Walcutt and Pizer, other scholars have extended, modified, and challenged these interpretations of naturalism. The following titles suggest the range of recent books devoted to the movement: June Howard, *Form and History in American Literary Naturalism* (1985); Walter Benn Michaels, *The Gold Standard and the Logic of Naturalism* (1987); Lee Clark Mitchell, *Determined Fictions: American Literary Naturalism* (1989); Paul Civello, *American Literary Naturalism and Its Twentieth-Century Transformations* (1994); James Giles, *The Naturalistic Inner-City Novel in America: Encounters with the Fat Man* (1995); Donna Campbell, *Resisting Regionalism: Gender and Naturalism in American Fiction, 1885–1915* (1997); Eric Carl Link, *The Vast and Terrible Drama: American Literary Naturalism in the Late Nineteenth Century* (2004); Jennifer Fleissner, *Women, Compulsion, Modernity: The Moment of American Naturalism* (2004); and John Dudley, *A Man's Game: Masculinity and the Anti-Aesthetics of American Literary Naturalism* (2004).

What's clear from even a cursory glance at these titles is that each generation reinterprets the genre according to the critical theories and cultural concerns of its time. What's also clear is that thesis-driven books necessarily exclude elements of the movement that don't support an individual book's argument; similarly, while collections of essays about naturalist authors contain much that is provocative and enlightening, they too offer only a partial picture of the scope of naturalism. *The Oxford Handbook of American Literary Naturalism* differs from these volumes in that it is the first book to treat the subject topically and thematically in essays that attempt to present the best of current thinking about the genre. In part I, contributors explore the contexts that prompted the origins of the genre, from literary naturalism's origin in the writings of Émile Zola to the influence of Herbert Spencer and Charles Darwin, whose writings inflamed the imaginations of American writers. Essays in part II consider the problem of definition and the interconnections with other genres. Part III examines the scientific and philosophical background, with contributors exploring the response of writers to the problem of free will versus determinism and the effect of Darwin and Spencer on depictions of morality and the role of religion as well as their influence on the representation of characters' psychological motivations. In part IV, contributors explore current tensions in critical approaches to naturalism—the role of women and African American writers, depictions of sexuality, the problem of race, the critique of commodity culture and class, and the continuing presence of naturalism in twentieth- and twenty-first-century fiction. Part V considers the role of the marketplace in the development of naturalism as well as the popular and critical response. And essays in part VI conclude the volume by exploring the influence of naturalism in other arts.

THE NATURALISTIC IMAGINATION

The foregoing suggests that naturalism is an adaptive genre, changing its contours over the course of time as new ideas arise and as new writers (and critics) respond to those ideas and to the work of the writers before them. It is useful to conceive of the naturalist novel as primarily a novel of ideas, functioning like the Blob in the 1958 science fiction movie of the same title—absorbing everything it can to propel the idea—and this capacity for absorption explains not only the varied plots and philosophies contained in naturalism but also the prevalence of the narrative strategies of realism, documentation, sensation, sentiment, and romance; the occurrence of stereotyped characters and dialogue; the role of chance and coincidence; and especially the frequency of sensation and didactic exposition.

Naturalism's receptivity to adaptation reveals its similarity to another genre, melodrama, and exploring naturalism as a version of melodrama is a useful way of understanding its many anomalies and inconsistencies. Scholars typically conceive of naturalism as a version of realism, as a genre that grafts realistic detail onto a necessitarian ideology. When naturalistic fictions seem to depart from the realistic paradigm, usually through the inclusion of sensational effects, sentimental scenes, stilted dialogue, and improbable coincidences, critics often disparage such departures as instances of flawed technique or defective artistry. But these "flaws"—in fact, the narrative strategies of melodrama—provided the naturalists with an effective means through which to articulate the impingement of Darwinian and Spencerian thought upon such social issues as land speculation and poverty, marital infidelity and the double standard, political corruption and labor agitation, and sexual deviance and crime. Like melodrama, and unlike realism, naturalism conspicuously employs such emotive effects to promote the acceptance of a thesis, and this melodramatic vision is registered clearly and unmistakably in the literature of naturalism.

Naturalism in general shares with melodrama a tendency to focus on the universal and to depict the type rather than the individual to illuminate the abstraction that the plots and characters are contrived to illustrate. Like melodrama and unlike realism, naturalism is an essentially didactic literature with a thesis to prove, whether it be economic determinism, the latent atavism of human beings, or the inescapable force of heredity. The naturalist tends to share with the melodramatist a belief in the ultimate intelligibility of the world and of the discoverability of the forces that shape it. This shared belief encourages each to communicate a vision of human beings caught up in a welter of discreet events that combine to direct and prescribe their actions. Such a vision is an essential characteristic of both the melodramatic and naturalistic imaginations, and it accounts for the frequent intrusion of sensational scenes, improbable coincidences, and stilted rhetoric into fictions that are often derided as merely aesthetically flawed versions of realism.

What I am suggesting, then, is a way of reading naturalism that does not see it primarily in terms of evolutionary and deterministic philosophy applied to realism but rather in terms of popular narrative strategies, derived from melodrama, enlisted in support of a propagandistic cause.[1] London, Norris, Dreiser and other naturalists were writers with an agenda. Compelled by their acceptance of Herbert Spencer's evolutionary synthesis, outraged by the privations they witnessed on the farms and in the cities, and persuaded by the implications of advances in science, these writers employed the narrative devices of melodrama as an efficacious means to convince readers of the truth of their theses and to elicit sympathy for their protagonists or even, as in the case of Hamlin Garland, Upton Sinclair, and London, to prompt readers to take action to redress social imbalance. Although he deplored the genre's unflattering portrait of human beings and its tendency to exaggerate for effect, Malcolm Cowley appreciated the didactic strain that runs throughout these fictions. "Their books are full of little essays or sermons addressed to the reader; in fact they suggest a naturalistic system of ethics complete with its vices and virtues," he wrote in 1947. "Most of the characters presented sympathetically in naturalistic novels are either the victors over moral codes which they defy . . . or else victims of the economic struggle" (438).

Modern criticism has been quick to condemn the didacticism and sensationalism inherent in naturalistic fiction partly because the aesthetic yardstick by which most critics measure these fictions privileges organic integrations of theme and character, symbol and ambiguity, irony and narrative restraint. When a novel displays stereotyped characters, sentimental language or sensational scenes, as do Garland's *Main-Travelled Roads* (1891), Norris's *McTeague* (1899), and London's *The Sea-Wolf* (1904), critics have typically dismissed these elements as inept and derivative or as examples of authorial pandering to an audience hungering for romance. Thus Ronald Martin notes the power of Norris's "melodramatic realism" to "affect the reader's deepest feelings and fears," but he denounces these effects as Norris's "artistic failings" (150). Even Donald Pizer, who has done more than anyone to clarify our understanding of naturalism, occasionally misreads the place of melodrama in naturalism. In one article, Pizer argues that "the melodramatic sensationalism and moral 'confusion' which are often attacked in the naturalistic novel should really be

incorporated into a normative definition of the mode and be recognized as its essential constituents" ("Late Nineteenth-Century" 12). Yet elsewhere, under the category
of "inept narrative devices," he claims that "several of the stories of *Main-Travelled
Roads* are marred by melodramatic and sentimental touches" (Introduction xiii).

The New Critical perspective has so shaped our understanding of the narrative
strategies of naturalism that, occasionally, some critics have even resorted to *ad
hominem* attacks when encountering fictions that work upon a reader's sensibility in
order to promote acceptance of a certain vision of the world. After outlining the "dark
chain of necessity" evoked in Garland's "A Branch Road," Charles C. Walcutt notes
the optimistic close in which Garland sketches the promise of a better world awaiting
Will and Aggie, and then chides Garland for violating the unity of his conception: "It
is scarcely necessary to say that we expect some degree of wisdom, rather than day-
dreams, from a serious artist; we expect that he will pursue the logic of his situations
to the bitter end" (56). Walcutt concludes his discussion of Garland's "rather pathetic
failures" by claiming that Garland was too "unsophisticated and therefore completely
at the mercy of the literary techniques which [he] absorbed from [his] Victorian
world" to know how to "integrate the new ideas into a fictional structure" (62).

Rather than condemn Garland's fictions by insulting the intelligence of their
author, it is perhaps more useful to question whether our own interpretive assumptions prevent us from recognizing and appreciating the utility of melodramatic
sentiment and sensationalism in naturalistic works. Restoring melodrama's place in
naturalism—that is, understanding why the naturalists employed such narrative
strategies in their fiction despite their frequent condemnation of romantic and sentimental fiction—will enable us to recognize what Jane Tompkins calls the "cultural
work" of fiction. Like the sentimental novelists about whom Tompkins writes,
Garland, Norris, Dreiser, and London had "designs upon their audiences, in the
sense of wanting to make people think and act in a particular way" (xi). Because
these writers were attempting to elicit particular responses in their readers, they
employed narrative devices that worked upon their readers' sympathies—to motivate them to outrage, in the case of Garland; to recognize the dominance of sexual
instincts, in the case of Norris; to push them to pity, in the case of Dreiser; and to
persuade them to identify with primordial figures of strength, in the case of London.

To recognize the function of melodrama in their fictions is not, of course, to
explain why these particular writers were attracted to melodrama. We might arrive at
such an understanding first by recognizing that melodrama is not only a specific genre
(like tragedy and comedy), with defining plot movements and stylistic strategies, but
also that the melodramatist sees the world differently than does the tragedian or the
comedian (or the realist or satirist). As James L. Rosenberg notes, "Melodrama, like
tragedy, is a way of seeing, not a trick of writing. You write a melodrama—a *good*
melodrama—because you see the world that way, not because you think: 'Today I
think I'll write a melodrama'" (235). What distinguishes the imaginations of Garland,
Norris, Dreiser, and London from that of such an arch-realist as Howells is that the
former persisted in seeing the world melodramatically, despite their advocacy of
realism. The realists were chiefly committed to exploding romantic stereotypes and

reforming sentimental expression. They believed that romance had degenerated into works that "merely tickle our prejudices and lull our judgment, or that coddle our sensibilities or pamper our gross appetite for the marvellous" (Howells 95–96).

The naturalists, while sharing the realists' distaste for sentimentality, additionally were immensely attracted to Herbert Spencer's evolutionary synthesis, which encouraged a melodramatic perception of the world. Spencer's paradigm tends to polarize the subjects of inquiry—into the Knowable and the Unknowable, stability and instability, homogeneity and heterogeneity, evolution and dissolution, reflecting the late nineteenth century's preoccupation with either/or abstractions: the rich and the poor, supply and demand, science and faith, progress and poverty. Just as melodrama insists upon the ultimate defeat of misfortune, Spencer's evolutionary synthesis assured people that the conflict of forces tended toward a harmonious equilibrium in which conflicting forces achieved a balance that benefited society. Garland announced this faith in the peroration to *Crumbling Idols* (1894), his manifesto of a new American literary nationalism: "In evolution there are always two vast fundamental forces: one, the inner, which propels; the other, the outer, which adapts and checks. One forever thrusts toward new forms, the other forever moulds, conserves, adapts, reproduces. Progress is the resultant of these forces" (191). Spencer's system reaffirmed the ultimate benevolence of the universe and humanity's ability to comprehend the operations of that universe, for his "synthetic philosophy" documented, in exhaustive detail, exactly how the extant social inequities inescapably worked toward a better society. His evolutionary optimism thus reassured the naturalists that science would facilitate humanity's ascendancy through discovery of and adherence to nature's laws.

What prompted the naturalists to adopt Spencer so readily was the melodramatic determinism inherent in his system that explained so smoothly the interconnections among events. As Dreiser wrote in a meditation on Spencer for an 1897 issue of *Ev'ry Month*:

> All life has been comprehended best by him. He has explained the value of things that are, and the purposes for which they are intended. Rain, sunlight, the seasons; charity, generosity, virtue,—all these are set down in their true order, and having established the empire of the mind, he invites you, as subjects, to acquaint yourselves with its laws. They are unalterable laws. ("Reflections" 107)

In their desire to express Spencer's "unalterable laws," the naturalists gravitated toward the melodrama of deterministic plots, which pushed characters to inevitable conclusions. In a 1911 essay defining melodrama, Clayton Hamilton, a prolific playwright, critic, and drama editor for the *Bookman*, recognized the determinism of events as central to the genre. "By *melodrama*," he stipulated, "is signified a serious play in which the incidents determine and control the characters. . . . A train of incidents is foreordained and the characters are subsequently woven into the tiny pattern of destiny that has been predetermined for them" (310).

The naturalists seem to have recognized the congruence of the melodramatic and the Spencerian vision, for in their fictions and in their autobiographies they record again and again the moment when Spencerian thought shattered their faith in a Christian hierarchy of clear moral imperatives, only to replace that disruption with a new faith in evolutionary thought. That these writers should be led to accept Spencer's distortions and simplifications of evolution is not surprising, for, as Wylie Sypher suggests, melodrama is the characteristic modality of the nineteenth-century imagination, for which "[t]he world becomes a theatre of tensions between abstractions" (262). Following Spencer, the naturalists envisioned a world in which conflicting abstract forces both motivated and circumscribed humanity's actions. Such a view, Sypher observes,

> encourages not only a melodramatic ethics (the strong and the weak, the hard and the soft, the good and the bad) but also emotive history and emotive science, which, as Huxley confidently assumed, can satisfy the spiritual longings of man. Having done with a personal God, the 19th Century could now displace the drama in its mind into the universe itself by means of the laws of geology, biology, energy, and, more immediately, economics. (261)

Responding to the melodrama of Spencerianism, the naturalists adopted melodramatic plots and narrative strategies to affect their readers' emotions the better to convey the drama of the impingement of science upon human activity.

The Melodramatic Vision

Melodrama is particularly well suited as a form for the exposition of ideas because of its clarity of outline and coherence of vision. It is, Michael Booth observes,

> a dream world inhabited by dream people and dream justice, offering audiences the fulfillment and satisfaction found only in dreams. An idealization and simplification of the world of reality, it is in fact the world its audiences want but cannot get. . . . One of the great appeals of this world is clarity: character, conduct, ethics, and situations are perfectly simple, and one always knows what the end will be, although the means may be temporarily obscure. (14)[2]

Recognizing the naturalistic novel as a melodramatic "dream world" accounts for its simplicity of characterization, its reliance upon one or two motivating forces to propel its plots, the repeated employment of coincidence in and the polarized arrangement of its action, and the frequency of romantic subplots and stilted dialogue—all of which have been disparaged as "flaws" by critics who see naturalism as a variation of realism. If one approaches the naturalistic novel as an extension of realism—as realism intensified or as realism that focuses on environmental determinism—then of course all of the above "excesses" diminish the realism of the fictional portrayal. But to understand naturalistic art as a projection of the melodramatic vision is to account for these characteristics and to explain their place in this fictional world. The naturalistic imagination does not intend to offer an "objective" depiction of the world but an interpretation or recreation of the forces that control that world. As Frank Norris recognized in "The Novel with a 'Purpose,'" the naturalistic novel is not a novel that shows us something; it is a novel that "proves something, draws conclusions from a whole congeries of forces, social tendencies, race impulses, devotes itself not to a study of men but of man" (90).

This desire to "prove," to show how the world and its universal laws operate, is the motive of the melodramatist, not of the realist. As most scholars of melodrama have recognized, melodrama is a didactic genre that reaffirms social and family order. Melodramatists stereotype their characters to demonstrate the universality or "justice" of social norms. David Grimsted, in his exhaustive survey of American melodrama up to 1850, describes the conceptual paradigm of melodrama as being "the victory of the forces of morality, social restraint and domesticity over what was dark, passionate, and anti-social" (220). Thus the inevitable triumph of the hero, the fall of the villain, the preservation of chastity. Departures from the formula rarely occurred, and if they did, plots were arranged to explain the anomaly and to reaffirm the social norm. If, for example, the heroine's purity was sullied, she *had* to die by the play's end in order to maintain melodrama's insistence upon clear moral values. As playwright Bronson Howard blithely announced, "The wife who has once taken the step from purity to impurity can never reinstate herself in the world of art on this side of the grave; and so an audience looks with complacent tears on the death of an erring woman" ("The Autobiography of a Play," qtd. in Quinn 45).

While the naturalists seldom depicted plots that end happily and reaffirm the "social and family order," the didactic conceptual paradigm underlying melodrama—the belief that nature's laws are comprehendible and inevitable—also extends to the naturalistic novel. One of the distinctions between realism and naturalism is that the former typically "observes" life, depicting the details of the commonplace without overt moralizing or authorial commentary, while the latter frequently moralizes or sets out to demonstrate a particular thesis. Naturalism, like melodrama, is therefore a literature of propaganda. As a literature with a purpose, to adapt Norris's phrase, naturalism often employs the dichotomies and dramatic techniques of melodrama to articulate its thesis. Thus the prevalence of the sensational in plots, the emotional excesses in dialogue and characterization, the gothic portrayals of character, and the overt pronouncement of doctrine. In *Sister Carrie* (1900), for example, Dreiser frequently halts his narrative to explain why events are unfolding as they are. A well-known instance occurs at the beginning of chapter 8, where Dreiser argues for the random quality of life, its essential purposelessness, in the polarities of melodrama:

> Among the forces which sweep and play throughout the universe, untutored man is but a wisp in the wind. Our civilisation is still in a middle stage, scarcely beast, in that it is no longer wholly guided by instinct; scarcely human, in that it is not yet wholly guided by reason. . . . We have the consolation of knowing that evolution is ever in action, that the ideal is a light that cannot fail. He will not forever balance thus between good and evil. . . .

> In Carrie—as in how many of our worldlings do they not?—instinct and
> reason, desire and understanding, were at war for the mastery. She followed
> whither her craving led. She was as yet more drawn than she drew. (56–57)

Such overt expression of Spencerian doctrine shows little difference as a narrative
device from the melodramatic soliloquy; in both naturalism and melodrama, the
authorial intrusion clarifies the values the work is promoting by making explicit the
issues involved.

Recognizing the melodramatic quality of naturalism also enables us to account
for other rhetorical strategies of naturalism usually dismissed as lapses in aesthetic
judgment or as inconsistencies in conception. For example, few critics can resist
disparaging the melodramatic ending of *McTeague* where Marcus Schouler handcuffs himself to McTeague moments before the dentist kills him. Comments range
from that of Charles C. Walcutt, who reads the novel as ending "in outlandish melodrama rather than a controlled demonstration of inevitable consequences" (132), to
Carvel Collins, who terms the increase of melodramatic elements of the final chapters "excessive" (xviii), to Richard Chase, who sees the essentially melodramatic
form of the novel but tends to deride it as "forced" and "meretricious" (192).

The ending of *McTeague* borrows from melodrama the device of the *tableau*, a
climactic silent arrangement of actors that offers a symbolic picture of the preceding
conflict. In such scenes of stasis, Peter Brooks observes, "we grasp melodrama's primordial concern to make its signs clear, unambiguous, and impressive" (48). The
advantage of the tableau is that it impresses on the audience the didactic point of the
drama; a form of dramatic resolution, it is as essential to the melodrama as is
the expositional soliloquy that expresses the thematic values of the play. In the
closing paragraphs of *McTeague*, Norris sketches the final confrontation between
Marcus and McTeague in the fictional equivalent of the tableau:

> As McTeague rose to his feet, he felt a pull at his right wrist; something held it
> fast. Looking down, he saw that Marcus in that last struggle had found strength to
> handcuff their wrists together. Marcus was dead now; McTeague was locked to
> the body. All about him, vast, interminable, stretched the measureless leagues of
> Death Valley.
>   McTeague remained stupidly looking around him, now at the distant
> horizon, now at the ground, now at the half-dead canary chittering feebly in its
> little gilt prison. (243)

The scene is not an instance of mere "melodramatic excess" because the "signs" in
this scene—the handcuffs, the two men, one live, one dead, the wasteland of Death
Valley, and especially the canary imprisoned in its imitation gold cage—depict the
normative values of the story in a final stasis. We readers recognize the efficacy of
the signs, for they portray the abstractions of greed, jealousy, moral imprisonment,
and fate in a final resolution, a symbolic image denoting the ironic futility of
attempts to escape one's elemental nature and environmental influences. The scene
is certainly melodramatic, but it effectively conveys the values and imaginative
framework within which this fiction exists.

The naturalists' adaptation of melodrama also extends to their portrayal of character. The melodramatic hero is an essentially unified character, undivided by the complexities of conflicting motives or values. Indeed, characters typically lack psychological complexity—the villain is merely the personification of lust, avarice, or cruelty, an integer to set off the hero's honesty, fortitude, and bravery and the heroine's purity, dutifulness, and charity. "In this quasi-wholeness," Robert B. Heilman observes, the melodramatic character "is freed from the anguish of choice, and from the pain of struggling with counterimpulses that inhibit or distort his single direct 'action'" (84–85). This is not, however, to say that the "monopathic" character's motivation may not be complex, or that he or she may not vacillate between conflicting obligations, or that there are no alternatives presented. The typical dilemma in much melodrama, for example, is the heroine's choice between duty and passion—whether to obey her parents' (usually her father's) wishes or to follow her own desire to marry her lover. But the conflict is imposed from without; the heroine is never torn between an ethical determination to remain virginal and a conscious desire to experience sex. She is simply faced with some external obstruction that momentarily frustrates her ability to choose the correct course of action. Similarly, the melodramatic villain does not ponder the moral or ethical choice between altruism and self-interest. He is aware of but one desire, though circumstances may frustrate his acting on it. For the melodramatic character, there is no mixture of contradictory motives, no true moral or ethical dilemma of which he or she is conscious. And to maintain the character's singleness of purpose, the melodramatist usually orchestrates any conflict of motive so as to invalidate the dilemma by letting the choice occur through chance or unexpected revelation. As a result, there is no true anxiety attached to the choice, no incapacitating anguish, no psychological self-betrayal.

Rather than simply accept, as the melodramatist does, the moral nature of people as an ethical given—as a "moral abstraction," to use David Grimsted's phrase (222)—the naturalists focus much of their narrative on the causal forces that determine behavior. Yet the naturalist rarely attempts to portray a complex mental psychology that we would recognize as "modern"—a psychology that attempts to depict the conditional, to register the density of motive and its complex interrelations, and above all to render the uncertainty reflective of modern consciousness. For the naturalists, casual explanations for human motivation are typically reductive. Their portrayals of behavior concentrate on such externals as socioeconomic forces or elemental emotions of greed, lust, or ambition rather than indecision and reflective consciousness.

Even such works as *Martin Eden*, *McTeague*, and *Vandover and the Brute*, while locating scenes of conflict within the protagonist's mind, do not really vary the basic melodramatic ascription of behavior to a set of basic causes, nor do they attempt to render the complexity of character. The oft-noted scene in *McTeague*, where the dentist battles the brute within while Trina lies unconscious in his dental chair, illustrates the naturalist tendency to depict mental conflict in terms of the clash of elemental forces rather than through reasoned choices:

> Suddenly the animal in the man stirred and woke; the evil instincts that in him
> were so close to the surface leaped to life, shouting and clamoring.
>
>   It was a crisis—a crisis that had arisen all in an instant; a crisis for which he
> was totally unprepared. Blindly, and without knowing why, McTeague fought
> against it, moved by an unreasoned instinct of resistance. Within him, a certain
> second self, another better McTeague rose with the brute; both were strong, with
> the huge crude strength of the man himself. The two were at grapples. There in
> that cheap and shabby "Dental Parlor" a dreaded struggle began. It was the old
> battle, old as the world, wide as the world—the sudden panther leap of the
> animal, lips drawn, fangs aflash, hideous, monstrous, not to be resisted, and the
> simultaneous arousing of the other man, the better self that cries, "Down, down,"
> without knowing why; that grips the monster; that fights to strangle it, to thrust it
> down and back. (21)

While Norris does depict conflicting motives—the brute versus the better self—
McTeague is passive; he has little agency; and while he cries, " 'No, by God! No, by
God!' " the elemental force of sexual desire obviates choice: "Suddenly he leaned
over and kissed her, grossly, full on the mouth." McTeague lacks the capacity to
comprehend moral choice, just as he is powerless to resist the force of instinct: "its
significance was not for him," Norris writes. "To reason with it was beyond him. He
could only oppose to it an instinctive stubborn resistance, blind, inert" (22).
Heilman's distinction between the tragic and the melodramatic hero is helpful in
understanding the aim of the naturalist. The distinguishing characteristic of the
tragic character, Heilman suggests, is his divided mind:

> he is caught between different imperatives each of which has its own validity,
> or . . . he is split between different forces or motives or values. In other words, his
> nature is dual or multifold, and the different competing elements are present at
> the same time, are operative in the dramatic situation, and are known to us as
> realities that have to be reckoned with. (89)

By "competing elements," Heilman means that a character's motives or values present
him or her with irreconcilable alternatives. Macbeth is prompted to murder by his
avaricious desire to attain the crown, yet he hesitates to act because he knows that such
an act undermines what that crown represents. Macbeth is a divided character; his
motives are in conflict, and no single motive or value explains or accounts for his behavior. Moreover, he is always conscious of his alternatives and vacillates between them.

     In the naturalistic novel, as in the melodrama, characters are essentially whole.
McTeague does not experience any meaningful self-awareness; he is only dimly
conscious of conflicting desires; he is propelled by a single force, a latent atavism
that manifests itself in instinctive, physical desires. Norris, it is true, details the operations of this atavism, but McTeague remains unchanged at the novel's conclusion, essentially the same as when the novel began. Similarly, Martin Eden's strength
of will never wavers—he never exhibits any real self-doubt of his intellectual abilities;
the obstacles he faces are imposed by others, not by inner vacillation. Vandover is
perhaps naturalism's best claim to a fully developed character in the modern sense
in that at times he approaches self-awareness:

> And with the eyes of this better self he saw again, little by little, the course of his whole life, and witnessed again the eternal struggle between good and evil that had been going on within him since his very earliest years. He was sure that at first the good had been the strongest. Little by little the brute had grown, and he, pleasure-loving, adapting himself to every change of environment, luxurious, self-indulgent, shrinking with the shrinking of a sensuous artist-nature from all that was irksome and disagreeable, had shut his ears to the voices that shouted warnings of the danger, and had allowed the brute to thrive and to grow. (215)

But even here, Norris has depicted Vandover's marginal consciousness in melodra-matic dualities; Norris has merely shifted the usual external battle between forces of good and forces of evil to Vandover's mind. Vandover does have some conscious-ness of the brute within and of his "artist-nature," but Norris paints him as the pas-sive observer of his own degradation into the brute. Vandover is completely helpless to make an effective choice between his two natures; he is not free to act upon his self-awareness.

Although Norris prolongs the decline of his protagonist and allows him to be aware of his own decline, Vandover's behavior reveals Norris's essentially melodra-matic conception of the world and of his characters' place in it. In the naturalistic novel, as in the melodrama, characters are polarized both in their depiction and in their actions. Garland's farmers are on the side of right, the land speculators on the side of wrong; the former are motivated by the dream of success and the work ethic, the latter by greed. McTeague is an ignorant and unconscious but sympathetic everyman; he is blocked from achieving happiness by his own brute nature and by Trina's greed and by Marcus Schouler's jealousy.

Instead of portraying psychological complexity, the naturalist exteriorizes con-flict, as does the melodramatist, in what Peter Brooks terms "a drama of pure psy-chic signs—called Father, Daughter, Protector, Persecutor, Judge, Duty, Obedience, Justice" (35). Multiple motivations, in the sense of causal determinants, may be ascribed to the characters, but the causal forces are seldom in conflict with them-selves and, more important, the characters are seldom aware of the existence of potential conflict. In short, while the naturalistic imagination often seeks to explain human behavior by attributing actions to several causes (such as Trina's greed and her masochism; McTeague's hereditary sexual drive, his stupid passivity, and his fierce irritability; Schouler's jealousy and his vengefulness), the characters lack the ability to alter their course of action. To be a "monopathic" character—that is, to enjoy a "singleness of feeling that gives one the sense of wholeness" (Heilman 85)— is not necessarily to be unaware of choice or not to choose. Lee Clark Mitchell points out that while naturalist characters do have choices and do choose, they can never refrain from acting as their desires compel them to act, even if they have resolved to act otherwise (8–9). Vandover, for example, many times resolves not to give in to the brute, but time and again his self-indulgence and his "pliable nature" compel him to ignore his own resolve. Carrie Meeber knows that social morality proscribes living with a man without marriage, but her pliable and comfort-loving nature causes her to "drift" passively while stronger natures choose for her.

If the naturalist shares with the melodramatist a tendency to see the world in terms of a Manichaean struggle between opposing forces, the naturalist also tends to depict this struggle in allegorical terms. In melodrama, characters function as types representing abstractions: the hero typifies virtue, fidelity, fortitude, patience, and so forth; the villain represents greed, lust, heartlessness; the heroine, chastity, purity, domesticity, obedience. The naturalist tends to borrow from melodrama this allegorical typing to depict people and their conflicts as concrete manifestations of abstractions. The naturalists were likely attracted to melodrama because of its ability to depict what Peter Brooks terms "the moral occult." In tracing the melodramatic nature of much of Balzac's and James's fiction, Brooks argues that their "deep subjects, the locus of their true drama," is "the domain of spiritual forces and imperatives that is not clearly visible within reality, but which they believe to be operative there, and which demands to be uncovered, registered, articulated" (20–21). This interest in making the unseen visible, in exposing the hidden forces that motivate human interaction, thus leads the naturalists to adopt the methods of melodrama, with its clear visual enactments of right and wrong, justice and injustice, duty and passion, charity and exploitation.

Melodrama therefore becomes an ideal vehicle for the exposition of ideas— the naturalist can embody the idea in a character or in a conflict to reveal, dramatically and emphatically, the meaning of the idea as it impinges upon human lives. In Garland's "Under the Lion's Paw," written to advocate Henry George's doctrine of the single-tax as an equitable solution to the injustice of land speculation, the melodramatic conflict between landholder and tenant is only the concrete embodiment of the clash of two ideas. The farmers are heroic toilers of the soil, the principle of labor exerted to increase the value of property; the landholder, Jim Butler, is the heartless villain, the exploitation of labor to yield unearned increment of profit. The characters are types, representing honest labor and dishonest gain. To increase our sympathy with the farmer, Garland even adopts the language of melodrama, explicitly identifying the farmers with the forces of good: "There are people in this world who are good enough t' be angels, an' only haff t' die to be angels," Haskins says of the charitable Stephen Council (225).

The "distinct value" of melodrama, Peter Brooks observes, is that it is "about recognition and clarification, about how to be clear what the stakes are and what their representative signs mean, and how to face them" (206). Naturalism, then, at its core expresses a melodramatic vision of human beings at the mercy of forces over which they have little control but whose purpose is ultimately intelligible. The predominant characteristic of the melodramatic vision, I have suggested, is a tendency to see the world in terms of a polarized conflict between representatives of some simplified set of ideas. Such a cosmic melodrama occurs not only in the various allegories of "good" versus "evil" so characteristic of traditional stage melodrama, but also in the novels of naturalists such as Garland, Norris, London, and Dreiser.

NOTES

1. Others have noted the inclusion of elements from popular literature in naturalistic works, although without addressing the utility of these strategies for promoting a necessitarian vision. See Howard 142–82 for a discussion of popular narrative strategies applied to naturalism in general. Davidson and Davidson and Jurnak examine Dreiser's adaptation of popular literary conventions in *Sister Carrie*. Solomon discusses Stephen Crane's parody of popular literature; see especially his discussion of *Maggie* as a parody of contemporary melodrama (23–44).

2. For a dissenting view, see Sharratt 277–81. While Booth suggests that melodrama's appeal lies in its escapist nature, Sharratt questions the nature of that escape by arguing that audiences may enjoy the experience of fear itself, not as something to escape into, but as something to escape from. Melodrama reassures its audience that, in comparison to the violence and terror of the play, their lives are not so bad: "after coming out of a melodrama, it is the *normal* world which is made to seem more attractive" (280).

WORKS CITED

Booth, Michael R. *English Melodrama*. London: Herbert Jenkins, 1965.

Brooks, Peter. *The Melodramatic Imagination: Balzac, Henry James, Melodrama and the Mode of Excess*. 1976. New York: Columbia University Press, 1984.

Chase, Richard. *The American Novel and Its Tradition*. New York: Doubleday, 1957.

Collins, Carvel. Introduction. *McTeague*. By Frank Norris. New York: Holt, Rinehart, 1950. vii–xviii.

Cowley, Malcolm. "A Natural History of American Naturalism." 1947. *Documents of Modern Literary Realism*. Ed. George J. Becker. Princeton: Princeton University Press, 1963. 429–51.

Davidson, Cathy N., and Arnold E. Davidson. "Carrie's Sisters: The Popular Prototypes for Dreiser's Heroine." *Modern Fiction Studies* 23 (1977): 395–407.

Dreiser, Theodore. "Reflections." *Ev'ry Month* 3 (Feb. 1897): 2–4. Rpt. as "[Herbert Spencer]." *Theodore Dreiser: A Selection of Uncollected Prose*. Ed. Donald Pizer. Detroit: Wayne State University Press, 1977. 106–11.

———. *Sister Carrie*. Ed. Donald Pizer. New York: Norton, 1970.

Garland, Hamlin. *Crumbling Idols: Twelve Essays on Art and Literature*. 1894. Intro. Robert Spiller. Gainsville, Fla.: Scholars' Facsimiles & Reprints, 1952.

———. "Under the Lion's Paw." *Main-Travelled Roads*. Intro. Donald Pizer. Facsimile rpt. of 1st ed. Columbus: Merrill, 1970. 217–40.

Grimsted, David. *Melodrama Unveiled: American Theater and Culture, 1800–1850*. 1968. Berkeley and Los Angeles: University of California Press, 1987.

Hamilton, Clayton. "Melodrama, Old and New." *Bookman* 33 (1911): 309–14.

Heilman, Robert B. *Tragedy and Melodrama: Versions of Experience*. Seattle and London: University of Washington Press, 1968.

Howard, June. *Form and History in American Literary Naturalism*. Chapel Hill: University of North Carolina Press, 1985.

Howells, William Dean. *Criticism and Fiction*. New York: Harper, 1891.

Jurnak, Sheila Hope. "Popular Art Forms in *Sister Carrie.*" *Texas Studies in Language and Literature* 13 (1971): 313–20.

Martin, Ronald E. *American Literature and the Universe of Force.* Durham: Duke University Press, 1981.

Mitchell, Lee Clark. *Determined Fictions: American Literary Naturalism.* New York: Columbia University Press, 1989.

Norris, Frank. *McTeague.* Ed. Donald Pizer. 2nd ed. New York: Norton, 1997.

———. "The Novel With a 'Purpose.'" *The Literary Criticism of Frank Norris.* Ed. Donald Pizer. Austin: University of Texas Press, 1964. 90–93.

———. *Vandover and the Brute.* Intro. Warren French. Lincoln: University of Nebraska Press, 1978.

Pizer, Donald. Introduction. Garland, *Main-Travelled Roads* v–xvii.

———. "Late Nineteenth-Century American Naturalism." *Realism and Naturalism in Nineteenth-Century American Literature.* Rev. ed. Carbondale: Southern Illinois University Press, 1984. 9–30.

———. *Realism and Naturalism in Nineteenth-Century American Literature.* 1966. Rev. ed. Carbondale: Southern Illinois University Press, 1984.

———. *Twentieth-Century American Naturalism: An Interpretation.* Carbondale: Southern Illinois University Press, 1982.

Quinn, Arthur Hobson. *A History of American Drama from the Civil War to the Present Day.* Rev. ed. Vol. 1. New York: Appleton, 1936.

Rosenberg, James L. "Melodrama." *Tragedy: Vision and Form.* Ed. Robert W. Corrigan. San Francisco: Chandler, 1965. 232–44.

Sharratt, Bernard. "The Politics of the Popular?—From Melodrama to Television." *Performance and Politics in Popular Drama.* Ed. David Bradby, Louis James, and Bernard Sharratt. London: Cambridge University Press, 1980. 275–95.

Solomon, Eric. *Stephen Crane: From Parody to Realism.* Cambridge: Harvard University Press, 1966.

Sypher, Wylie. "Aesthetic of Revolution: The Marxist Melodrama." *Tragedy: Vision and Form.* Ed. Robert W. Corrigan. San Francisco: Chandler, 1965. 258–67.

Tompkins, Jane. *Sensational Designs: The Cultural Work of American Fiction, 1790–1860.* New York: Oxford University Press, 1985.

Walcutt, Charles Child. *American Literary Naturalism: A Divided Stream.* Minneapolis: University of Minnesota Press, 1956.

PART I

CONTEXTS

CHAPTER 1

ROMANCING THE MACHINE: AMERICAN NATURALISM IN TRANSATLANTIC CONTEXT

ZENA MEADOWSONG

FRENCH ORIGINS: THE PROBLEM OF THE "EXPERIMENTAL NOVEL"

Traditionally, critics of American naturalism have distanced the movement from its French antecedents. Founded and theorized by Émile Zola, European naturalism seems relevant to the American tradition to the extent that direct influence can be demonstrated, and though a writer like Frank Norris, signing himself the "Boy-Zola" (qtd. in McElrath and Crisler 380), obviously owes a debt to the French tradition, a similar allegiance cannot be shown for authors like Dreiser, Crane, Wharton, and others. Moreover, the fate of naturalism seems even more doubtful elsewhere in the English-speaking world. Smuggled across the Channel by George Moore in *A Modern Lover* (1883), naturalism in Britain is generally thought to be a short-lived tradition at best. In 1887, Zola was denounced in the French press for the ostensible indecency of *La Terre*, and the appearance of an English translation of the same novel induced, despite expurgation, a fierce reaction against the corrupting influence of French fiction. Zola's English translator was prosecuted and imprisoned, and even Moore—the self-proclaimed "Zola ricochet"—beat a retreat. In America, Zola enjoyed a more moderate reputation for obscenity, but the available translations were arguably mutilated beyond recognition. Thus, though French naturalism can be shown to have been "imported" by specific writers, the foundational French tradition is often acknowledged as a precedent only to be discarded as an inadequate explanation of naturalism in England and America.

The problem of defining French influence is further complicated by the fact that Zola was the only truly successful and persistent naturalist in France. In 1880, he and five younger writers—Paul Alexis, Henri Céard, Léon Hennique, Joris-Karl Huysmans, and Guy de Maupassant—collaborated on a joint volume of naturalist short stories, *Les Soirées de Médan*. Most of the "Medan group," however, strayed from the naturalist fold in the mid-1880s, and when the French journalist Jules Huret asked in 1891 whether the movement was dead, the prognosis was unfavorable. Maupassant refused to discuss the matter; Céard asserted that it could not die because it had never existed; and Zola's own response—"perhaps"—was not particularly life-affirming. Only Alexis, in a famous telegram—"Naturalism not dead. Letter follows."—defended the movement (407). Pointing to the seventy editions of Zola's most recent novel, and echoing Zola's theoretical pronouncements in *The Experimental Novel* (1880), Alexis described naturalism as the literature of the future—a "scientific" form of fiction, "a branching-out into the domain of literature of the broad general current which carries our age toward more science, more truth" (410). Naturalism would be the "literature of the twentieth century" (408), and if there was as yet no perfect naturalism—no literature of pure science—this was because "romanticism, whence we all came is still there, too near at hand. None of us has yet succeeded in purging his blood completely of the hereditary romantic virus" (410).

Posing romanticism as a "hereditary virus," Alexis broached one of the most problematic elements of the genre—its persistent association with a romanticism it claims to eschew—in the naturalistic language of experimental medicine. In *The Experimental Novel*, Zola had aligned the naturalist novel with the experimental physiology of Claude Bernard, arguing that the naturalists do for literature what Bernard had done for medical science. By following a "scientific" or "experimental" method, Zola argued, the naturalist denounces imagination for "analysis," produces a body of work free from "irrational and supernatural explanations" (54), and furnishes a literature capable of providing "human data" for the sciences themselves (53). In theory, then, the naturalist improves in documentary validity upon nineteenth-century realism, incorporates the scientific advancements of the day into the novel form, and purges what Alexis calls the "hereditary romantic virus." In practice, however, Zola's inoculation against the "romantic virus" has been disputed since the appearance of *The Experimental Novel*. With the exception of Alexis and (less durably) Céard, little theoretical support was expressed even among French naturalists for the idea of the "experimental novel" (Baguley 45), and Maupassant—voicing a common objection—contended that Zola, "son of the romantics, [is] a romantic himself in the way he deals with everything" (qtd. in Hemmings 88). Abroad, the verdict was similar: Frank Norris judged it a "strange perversion" that "Zola should be quoted as a realist, and as a realist of realists" ("Zola as a Romantic Writer" 168), and Thomas Hardy remarked that an insistence upon a "science of fiction" was, for "such a romancer as M. Zola, . . . singular indeed" ("Science of Fiction" 107). Even George Moore, the "Zola ricochet," embraced naturalist theory only to moderate his endorsement upon reflection. Receiving Zola's ideas—"*Naturalisme, la vérité, la science*"—like a "violent blow on the head" (*Confessions* 72), he did not immediately recognize that "the very qualities which set [his] admiration a blaze wilder than wildfire [were] precisely those that had won the victory for the romantic school forty years before" (77). Only gradually did he realize that he was chiefly impressed by the aesthetic design of texts like *L'Assommoir*—"its pyramid size, strength, height, . . . decorative grandeur, and . . . the immense harmonic development of the idea" (*Confessions* 77).

Zola's works are often described as feats of literary architecture, and the massive symmetries of novels like *L'Assommoir* (1877) disclose an overdetermined sense of narrative order that would seem, as numerous critics have remarked, "to make of *The Experimental Novel*'s more extreme denials of novelistic arrangement a grotesquely misleading account of [Zola's] own practice" (Lethbridge, Introduction 7). "Pyramidal" in shape, *L'Assommoir* devotes six chapters to its heroine's rise, one to her saint's day, and six to her fall. The "arching narrative line" reinforces the tragic plot (Walker 35), just as the total number of chapters (thirteen) "exactly figures misfortune" (Pierre-Gnassounou 93). Yet the care with which Zola constructed the text is not necessarily incompatible with the "experimental" objectives of the novel. A story of congenital alcoholism among the Parisian working classes, the work shows Zola's "scientific" preoccupation with the joint effects of physiology and environment and his obsession with documentary detail. Gervaise Coupeau, the heroine, is a laundress, and the operations of her trade are all minutely described. Likewise, her husband's precarious work as a roofer is detailed methodically, and though his fall from the Parisian rooftops ultimately seems to take on the inevitability of predestination, the accident is not implausible in itself.

The narrative of Coupeau's fall—"His body made a shallow arc . . . , turning over twice, crashing on to the middle of the road with the dull thud of a bundle of linen flung from high up above" (115)—is given with a kind of documentary precision that coexists in strange harmony with its symbolic dimension. Tumbling like a "bundle of linen" (115), Coupeau becomes, both literally and figuratively, a burden for his laundress wife, and his fall precipitates a physiological decline that is at once a logical consequence of his accident and a capitulation of biblical magnitude. Coupeau's father, also a roofer, died in a drunken fall, and Coupeau's deterioration (he takes to drink during his convalescence) appears to affirm a hereditary or "original" sin. That this weakness will eventually extend to his wife is prefigured in the brandied plum (the bite of alcoholic fruit) over which Coupeau courts Gervaise in the Assommoir, and the influence of demon drink—realized in the figure of the Assommoir's monstrous distilling apparatus—looms ominously from the earliest chapters. The big machine, in its "endless coils of piping," "weirdly-shaped containers," and "big copper belly" (42), is itself rendered in a detail that shifts curiously between the factual and the mythological. The "subterranean rumbling [of the still], coming from deep within" (42), is both sufficiently documentary and suggestively symbolic.

The process of distillation literally makes a rumbling noise, but it also figures the latent physiological weakness of the alcoholic, or—more mythically—the diabolical source of an inevitable capitulation. The "coils" of the still's piping suggest the serpent, and its "lackluster copper surface" gradually bodies forth an alcoholic hell. By the end of the novel, "the shadow cast by the apparatus . . . conjure[s] up obscene shapes, figures with tails, monsters opening wide their jaws as if to devour the world" (344).

In *L'Assommoir*, the enormous still gradually takes on the proportions of a demonic beast capable of transforming working-class Paris into an alcoholic underworld. As Peter Brooks puts it, the machine "is quite literally the energy source for the novel, and for the destructive dynamic of its characters' lives" (*Body Work* 149). Yet the monster apparatus unleashes a force that is not only destructive for the characters of *L'Assommoir* but potentially disruptive to the narrative itself. The "scientific" objectives of the novel falter in the mythic rendering of the machine. In *The Experimental Novel*, Zola repeatedly asserts that the naturalist novel does away with the "irrational and supernatural explanations" (54) of imaginative literature, and though his mythic monster seems to emerge from the documentary language of his descriptions, that monster—embodying the "irrational" and "supernatural"—also conflicts with the declared objectives of the naturalist narrative. Indeed, the documentary mechanics of Zola's narrative seem to collapse in the act of documentation: under the pressure of representing a specific reality—the force of an alcoholic proclivity—the still takes on demonic proportions, and the "trickle of crystal-clear alcohol" builds into a biblical flood, "a relentless spring which would eventually flood the bar-room, spill over the outer boulevards and inundate the vast pit that was Paris" (42). The mythic figure thus both describes and enacts a loss of control. Zola's documentary impulse appears to succumb to its own mythological deluge, bursting under the pressure of documenting an uncontrollable force. In the representation of the diabolical still, the documentary yields to the imaginary, the rational gives way to the irrational, and the machine—agent and emblem of the "scientific" narrative itself—produces all the "irrational and supernatural" effects the "experimental" novel theoretically denounces.

Zola and the Monster Machine

Though the "scientific" objectives of the experimental novel appear to break down in the figure of *L'Assommoir*'s monstrous still, the problem is not unique to this novel. The distilling apparatus is only one of the earliest and simplest of Zola's monster machines. As Peter Brooks has pointed out, Zola's novels are typically "centered on a piece of social or industrial machinery, which almost always provides the energetic source of the narrative" (*Body Work* 149)—and almost always bursts out of control. In *Germinal* (1885), the central machine is the mine, le Voreux, a "squatting god" feeding on the miners it is supposed to support. In *La Bête humaine* (1890), it is the railroad engine, a giant beast—its headlamp like "the living eye of a cyclops" (195)—that runs wild at the end of the novel. In *Au Bonheur des Dames* (1883), it is the department store, a "machine working at high pressure" (16), a monstrous "system for consuming [the] women" (76) to whom it ostensibly ministers. The list goes on; in novel after novel, the machine runs rampant, destructive, out of control.

The out-of-control machines of Zola's fiction appear to contradict, with stunning inconsistency, the objectives expressed in *The Experimental Novel*. In theory, Zola looks forward to "a century in which [humankind], grown more powerful," will exploit its scientific knowledge "to penetrate the wherefore of things, to become superior to these things, and to reduce them to a condition of subservient machinery" (24). In the novels, however, Zola follows the science to a darker conclusion: there are no "subservient" machines. Rather, intended to subjugate the forces of nature, the machine masters its maker. The engine of *La Bête humaine*, built to ease human travel, stalls, crashes, and runs wild, finally grinding its own engineer to death under its wheels. The monstrous still of *L'Assommoir*, intended to moderate the hardships of working-class life, exploits the weaknesses it is supposed to relieve. The department store of *Au Bonheur* feeds on its consumers, exploiting the desires it is supposed to serve. The mine of *Germinal* swallows its starving miners, subjugating those it is meant to support. Humanity's subjection to material circumstances is recreated, by science, as subjection to its own machines. The figure of the monster—the "irrational" and "supernatural" rendering of the emblem of the "experimental" method—turns out to be a perfectly rational expression of a modern reality. Zola's mythic monsters are not the antithesis but the consequence of scientific development.

There is always some debate concerning the extent to which Zola, persistently affirming in theory the scientific developments he critiques in practice, was conscious of his own effects. Yet the monster machine, appearing in novel after novel, could hardly have been an accident of execution in every case. Rather, the solution— the reason for the apparent contradiction between Zola's theory and practice— seems to lie in the circumstances the monster represents. Just as the mythic quality of the machine seems to emerge naturally from the documentary language in which the apparatus is described, the mythic monsters of the *Rougon-Macquart* novels are natural, as it were, to Zola's documentation of a specific historical reality. The whole *Rougon-Macquart* sequence is devoted, as the subtitle of the series reminds us, to the "natural and social history" of a family under the Second Empire in France; yet the "nature" of life under Napoleon III was curiously artificial. The Second Empire saw a period of unprecedented industrial and urban development: in Paris, Baron Haussmann demolished the medieval city, cutting new boulevards straight through the old streets with huge engines; and in the provinces, canals and railways were expanded, making mechanized France "the center of Europe with six great railroad lines converging on the capital" (Lehan, *Realism* 20). Thus, in *Au*

Bonheur des Dames and *L'Assommoir*, steam engines knock great holes in Paris, and in *La Bête humaine*, Zola envisions France as a huge body organized by the railway—a "giant creature laid out on the ground with its head in Paris, its vertebrae the length of the track, its limbs stretching out with every branch-line, and its hands and feet in Le Havre and other destinations" (44). This body is not organic but mechanical, and the "great circulation of the railway line" (163) becomes the new lifeblood of the nation as the "natural" world is reorganized by the machine.

The result of the Second Empire in France was a shift from an agrarian to an industrial society—the advent of a man-made, mechanical order. This man-made world is fast and orderly; in *La Bête humaine*, "precision [is] allied to power" (146) in the engines that drive it. Yet such developments need not end in a ringing endorsement of technological progress: the threatening force of the natural world, ostensibly mastered by the machine, is inevitably reproduced by it in Zola's novels. The world of the *Rougon-Macquart* is a world in which human beings are terrorized by mythic monsters and giant beasts, fatally vulnerable to brute forces—but a world in which these forces (demonic stills, cyclopean engines, god-like mines) are all man-made. Zola's "scientific" novels confront a situation that science itself has created—a world in which machines, magnificent in their power, inevitably overwhelm their creators.

Critical opinion is divided on the value of such representations. On the one hand, Irving Howe recognizes in the monster machine a powerful rendering of a real historical problem: for Howe, the monster—a "force bursting out of the control of its creators"—is merely a "physical emblem of the impersonality of commodity production" ("Zola" 287). Liberation lies in the demystification of the machine, in the recognition that "not in mines or factories lie the sources of [human] troubles but in the historically determined relations between contending classes" (287). On the other hand, Georg Lukács criticizes Zola for the pessimistic determinism of his vision: naturalism, he argues, implies the impossibility of contending with historical conditions that humanity itself has created.

On Lukács' side, Zola's monster machines do appear to dramatize the futility of human opposition to man-made circumstances; even Zola himself seems unable to contain the force he has unleashed. In *Germinal*, "it is as if the novel itself collapses into the abyss along with the Voreux mine" (Mitterand 118), and in *La Bête humaine*, both the railway engine and the novel seem to "[go] off the rails" (Lethbridge, "Zola" 140). Succumbing to internal contradictions in their representation of the very technological developments on which they are modeled, Zola's novels dramatize the failure of their own "scientific" objectives. Yet these "failures" may themselves finally serve a critical function. Yves Chevrel argues that Zola's texts internalize social problems as narrative problems in order to expose and critique the very systems on which they are built, and Jennifer Fleissner contends that such narrative complicity is the necessary condition of a social critique: "It is only by witnessing our failure to imagine a way out of a system that we are ever able to recognize that system as system, as that which places boundaries around what can presently be achieved" (49). Zola's novels, built on and powered by machines they represent as monstrous, expose a system from which they cannot themselves escape.

MAN-MADE MONSTERS IN ENGLAND
AND AMERICA

Zola's historical vision—a vision of the world as man-made and mechanical in its operation—is, together with the formal consequences of that vision, the unifying feature of naturalism in France, England, and America. In late nineteenth-century America, as in Second Empire France, a period of rapid industrialization marked a shift from a predominantly agrarian to a highly mechanized and urban culture. As Richard Lehan has observed, "the aftermath of the Civil War in America paralleled the kind of historical change taking place in France between 1848 and 1870, as both economies moved from a landed to a commercial/industrial world" ("European Background" 62). Between the Civil War and the turn of the century, the U.S. population nearly tripled; cities grew rapidly; agriculture was mechanized; manufacturing accelerated; and national production octupled (Howard 31). At the same time, the railroad and communications technologies expanded swiftly, transforming the American continent. In 1883, clock time was standardized by the railways, which established the time zones we use today, and in 1890 the U.S. Census declared the American frontier closed (Howard 32–33; Marx 340). A rural, agrarian nation—a continent that still seemed partly wild at the end of the Civil War—was transformed into a predominantly urban, industrial one.

As in France, industrialization and urbanization in America resulted in a tradition of literary naturalism—a series of fictions which, whether or not directly influenced by Zola, share with him a specific historical vision. Though Theodore Dreiser insisted that he never read Zola, and Stephen Crane claimed to find his works "tiresome" (qtd. in Link 6), Zola's outlook is mirrored in the "superhuman" allure of the city in Dreiser's *Sister Carrie* (1900), the oppressive industrial slums of Stephen Crane's New York novellas, and the monster machines—runaway engines, "mammoth" harvesters, "insatiable" mines—of Frank Norris's California novels. The American naturalists share with Zola a vision of the world as man-made—an urban, industrial world where human beings are subjected to mechanisms they themselves have created. In Crane's *Maggie, A Girl of the Streets* (1893), "[w]ithered persons" sit smoking in the corners of a hellish tenement, "in curious submission" (7) to a slum that, made by human beings, is inescapable for its inhabitants. In Dreiser's *Sister Carrie*, the city is gorgeous in its artifice, magnifying in its "cunning wiles" the myriad temptations of "the infinitely smaller and more human tempter" (1) who composes but does not control it. And in Norris, the monster machine reproduces the threat of the natural world it is intended to conquer or contain: in *The Octopus* (1901), the railroad engine takes on the proportions of a natural monster—it is "the leviathan, with tentacles of steel clutching into the soil, the soulless Force, the iron-hearted Power, the monster, the Colossus, the Octopus" (51).

In England, a similar apprehension is distinguishable among the writers most frequently classed as naturalist. Commemorating the plight of the Victorian writer in *New Grub Street* (1891), George Gissing represents the literary world as a vast machine—a man-made mechanism impervious to the hardships of the individual creator. George Moore's provincial heroine in *A Mummer's Wife* (1885) seeks (unsuccessfully) to escape a life that works "like a colliery, every wheel . . . turning, no respite day or night" (52). And Thomas Hardy, looking back to the period that gave rise to Gissing's urban machinery and Moore's industrial provinces, sets his novels in the causal moment—we might say the naturalist moment—in English history. Leading the Industrial Revolution, Britain was the first to produce the conditions hospitable for naturalist fiction, and though it is often said to have no tradition of literary naturalism—the prosecution of Zola's English translator made writing naturalist novels "a risky business" (Brooks, *Realist Vision* 12)—the historical vision that unites the French and American naturalists was by no means lost upon the English. Indeed, though Hardy criticized Zola's "science of fiction," we see in his works the belated realization of the genre England itself produced: in the backward-looking "Wessex" novels, we encounter the historical genesis of the monster machine.

The odd archaism of Hardy's novels—the name "Wessex" is derived from that of an ancient Saxon kingdom—looks back to the moment of England's transformation from a traditional, agrarian society into a modern, mechanized one. In *Tess of the d'Urbervilles* (1891), the "steam feeler" (251) of Norris's Octopus is just advancing into the preindustrial world it will inevitably destroy, and in the *Mayor of Casterbridge* (1886), the market town of Casterbridge—teetering on the edge of industrial modernity—is astonished by the sudden advent of a mechanical monster:

> It was the new-fashioned agricultural implement called a horse-drill, till then unknown . . . in this part of the country. . . . The machine was painted in bright hues of green, yellow, red, and it resembled as a whole a compound of hornet, grasshopper, and shrimp, magnified enormously. (127)

Though merely a horse-drawn mechanism, the machine creates "about as much sensation in the cornmarket as a flying machine would create at Charing Cross" (127), and—in its Frankensteinian combination of "hornet, grasshopper, and shrimp, magnified enormously"—a violation of the natural order. Arguably, Hardy's contraption pales in comparison to the monster machines of Norris and Zola—and yet, with an over-determination to rival Zola's, it represents a force of modernization that organizes the tragic course of the entire novel.

The title character of *The Mayor of Casterbridge*—a prosperous, old-fashioned grain merchant named Henchard—is obliquely responsible for the introduction of the "new-fashioned" (127) seeding machine. The seeder is imported by his manager, the modernizing Farfrae, and though both Farfrae and the machine promise to contribute to Henchard's prosperity, they initiate his inevitable decline. Henchard and

Farfrae fall out, Farfrae sets up in business as his competitor, and soon—by dint of modern methods and new-fashioned machines—edges him out of economic prosperity and social position. Further, at the moment of Henchard's economic downfall, news of an old sin is publicly revealed. The news seals his fate, and though critics typically complain that Hardy "overplots" the novel at this point—that he "rel[ies] too heavily upon mechanical devices" (Howe, *Thomas Hardy* 90)—the "machinery" of the plot has a curiously literal dimension. The mechanical plot is, after all, inextricably linked to the operation of real machines. Like Zola's monstrous contraptions, the monster seeder in Casterbridge market is both the emblem and agent of Henchard's decline. Like the old agrarian industry he represents, Henchard is doomed to inevitable destruction by the mechanisms he himself has introduced. Where the novel seems contrived, the contrivances point to the overwhelming force of mechanization; the narrative "devices" are attuned to the mechanical operation of the new, man-made world.

Like Zola's novels, formally determined by the mechanical forces they represent, Hardy's *Mayor of Casterbridge* expresses the historical problem of mechanization as a narrative problem. Ironically, his "mechanical" determinism often leads critics to exclude him from the company of other naturalists. Richard Lehan, for example, observes a "cosmic" force at work against Hardy's characters—a force in excess of more plausible (environmental or hereditary) forms of naturalist determinism (*Realism* 168). However, Hardy not only fits the naturalist mold but illuminates the critical features of the genre. Tracing the problem of mechanization back to its original moment in English history, *The Mayor of Casterbridge* links the shift from an agrarian to an industrial world to the production of a monster machine—and this machine, organizing the course of the novel as inexorably as it organized the course of history itself, exposes the monstrosity of the historical process of mechanization. In a sense, Hardy sacrifices his novel to indict the operations of the machine. His realism, becoming as "mechanical" as the machines it represents, appears to break down in its depiction of the operations of the monster. Yet such, it appears, is the price of the naturalist vision: like Zola's narratives, Hardy's novel is both defined and deformed by its submission to the mechanisms it indicts.

FRANK NORRIS AND THE MONSTER MACHINE

The formal problems associated with French and English naturalism crop up in the American tradition also. As Eric Link puts it, "For many years, a theme running through accounts of late-nineteenth-century American literature has been that [the naturalists] wrote 'flawed' narratives—fiction that is often labeled 'powerful' though less than masterful, if not downright inartistic" (22). It remains to determine whether the "flaws" of the American naturalists devolve, as in France and England, from the representation of the mechanized, man-made world—but the indications seem to affirm it. Significantly, the American writer most influenced by Zola, and most faithful to Zola's vision, is also usually considered the least "masterful." Frank Norris, more than any other American naturalist, has attracted critical attention for aesthetic imperfection—but this reputation appears to derive, like Zola's and Hardy's, from the representation of a monster machine.

Like Zola's, Norris's narratives are typically organized around a monster machine and appear to run wild in the rendering of a mechanism that has itself burst out of control. Most famously, in *The Octopus*, a railroad engine plows through a helpless flock of sheep, and the only witness—horrified by the "all but human distress" of the slaughtered animals, and the "brute agony he could not relieve" (50)—apprehends the man-made engine as a mythic monster:

> Faint and prolonged, across the levels of the ranch, [Presley] heard the engine whistling for Bonneville. Again and again, at rapid intervals in its flying course, it whistled for road crossings, for sharp curves, for trestles; ominous notes, hoarse, bellowing, ringing with the accents of menace and defiance; and abruptly Presley saw again, in his imagination, the galloping monster, the terror of steel and steam, with its single eye, cyclopean, red, shooting from horizon to horizon, but saw it now as the symbol of a vast power, huge, terrible, flinging the echo of its thunder over all the reaches of the valley, leaving blood and destruction in its path; the leviathan, with tentacles of steel clutching into the soil, the soulless Force, the iron-hearted Power, the monster, the Colossus, the Octopus. (51)

Here, simple referential language (whistles, road crossings, curves, and trestles) is transformed by a series of progressive substitutions; the machine is swiftly magnified into a superhuman force. Taking on the "hoarse" and "bellowing" tones of an enormous beast, the "ominous" whistle acquires the volitional note of "menace and defiance," until Presley "abruptly" apprehends the machine as a mythic monster. "Scientific" language gives way to the "imaginary" as Presley "sees again . . . the galloping monster, . . . leaving blood and destruction in its path." Exceeding documentary figuration, the engine becomes a "symbol" of overwhelming power, and the mythic terms pile up in a way that captures Presley's acute horror at the cost of expressive focus. The engine is not just the Cyclops, but the Leviathan, Colossus, Octopus—Presley's rhetorical precision collapses in the face of a power that, built by human beings, is beyond human control.

In Norris's novels, as in Zola's, the mythic magnification of the machine captures, with figurative authenticity, the horror of the man-made world. Yet it also tends to "naturalize" a set of man-made circumstances—to represent as natural, and thus potentially inalterable, the systems it figures as monstrous. In *The Octopus*, Presley is bestirred to acts of socialism and anarchism in opposition to the Railroad but is inevitably defeated by circumstances beyond his control. His socialistic poem, "The Toilers," is wildly successful, appropriated by the market forces it was intended to expose; his attempt to blow up the railroad agent, S. Behrman, is wildly unsuccessful, demolishing everything but the target himself; and his confrontation with the railroad boss, Shelgrim, ends in a discussion of a corrupt economic logic that appears, to Presley, irrefutable. Shelgrim denies responsibility for the depredations of the Railroad on the grounds that it is a fact of life, a force of nature: asserting that "Railroads build themselves" and "Wheat grows itself" in obedience to a "natural" force of supply and demand, Shelgrim insists that Presley "Blame conditions, not men" (576). Shelgrim's speech is an obvious mystification—a willful occlusion of the human source of the "conditions" he describes. Yet it strikes Presley "with the clear reverberation of truth" (576), and appears to be confirmed by his subsequent experience. Unable to intervene in the operations of the Railroad, Presley is ultimately consoled by the powers that have crushed him:

> But the WHEAT *remained.* Untouched, unassailable, undefiled, that mighty world-force, that nourisher of nations, . . . indifferent to the human swarm, gigantic, resistless, moved onward in its appointed groove. . . . The individual suffers, but the race goes on. . . . The larger view always and through all shams, all wickedness, discovers the Truth that will, in the end, prevail, and all things, surely, inevitably, resistlessly work together for good. (651–52; emphasis in original)

Exhausted by his contest with the Railroad, prostrated by the futility of his fight and grief for his friends, Presley ends up singing the praises of the forces that have crushed him.

The conclusion to *The Octopus* is oddly dissonant; the ending of the novel appears to extol the very mechanisms the narrative indicts in the figure of the monster machine. Yet that powerful, critical image of the man-made world—the monstrous Octopus—also produces the logic to which the narrative adheres. At once horrifying and resistless—a destructive force against which individuals are powerless—the machine necessarily determines the triumph of the Railroad and futility of Presley's opposition. This is not to say, however, that the "truth" Presley appears to discover in the final passages is any more reliable than the self-justifying "conditions" Shelgrim points to in the offices of the Railroad. Though the death of S. Behrman (swallowed by his own wheat in the hold of the ship that will carry Presley to India) appears to dole out appropriate comeuppances, the "force" that overwhelms him is morally neutral at best, and Behrman's own manipulation of that force ensures that it is not, as Presley thinks, "untouched, unassailable, undefiled." (The "undefiled" wheat is necessarily sullied by the corpse it has produced.) Further, though the optimism with which *The Octopus* ends appears to be Presley's, the closing passage is inflected by the tone and sentiments of a far less reliable character. Shortly before boarding the wheat ship, Presley takes leave of Vanamee, the mystical shepherd who insists that "Evil is short-lived. . . . The whole is, in the end, perfect" (636). Thus, it is Vanamee's perspective that is echoed in Presley's closing reflection—and the echo casts doubt upon the narrative's apparent endorsements. At the beginning of the novel, it is Vanamee's carelessness that sets the Railroad plot in motion (the sheep the railroad engine runs down are Vanamee's sheep, allowed to stray across the tracks), and the soundness of his perspective is emphatically called into question by the subplot he dominates in *The Octopus*.

The "allegorical side of the wheat subject" (qtd. in McElrath and Crisler 352), the Vanamee subplot involves the shepherd's successful attempt to summon his dead love, Angéle, from the obscurity of a seed ranch. As we know from Norris's notes for the novel, "Angéle is the wheat" (qtd. in Seltzer 33), and her resurrection—coincident with the sprouting of the crop—is apparently intended to align her "corruption" (the victim of rape, she died in childbirth) with the natural cycle whereby the death of one body nourishes the life of another. Yet Angéle, like the wheat, obeys "natural" forces that are emphatically unnatural, and man-made. Emerging from the "seed" ranch, she not only appears to be the product of asexual, masculine reproduction but embodies a kind of parody of the "natural" law of supply and demand: just as the wheat in *The Octopus* ostensibly moves—sprouts, grows, harvests, ships—in "resistless" obedience to this natural law, Angéle responds (unconsciously—asleep) to Vanamee's need. Supply, in other words, answers demand; Vanamee wishes, and Angéle appears. Thus, while Angéle ostensibly dem-onstrates that life comes out of death and good comes out of evil, this endorsement exposes its own perversity. Angéle is not miraculously summoned from Vanamee's desire, but is rather—quite horribly—the product of her mother's rape. Her restitu-tion depends upon her mother's violation, and this violation is repeated in the conditions of Vanamee's newfound happiness: "Angéle or Angéle's daughter, it was all one with him" (392). Like the wheat she stands for, Angéle is essentially a com-modity—an object subservient, like her mother, to the brute force of (masculine) demand. The whole Vanamee "romance" is based upon an appalling corruption, and though there appears to be no one to blame for it (Angéle's rapist, the myste-rious "Other," is never located), the horror is nonetheless man-made—produced and perpetuated by the men it benefits. The entire subplot thus exposes the fatuity of the economic "truths" it appears to endorse: good comes out of evil; Railroads build themselves; wheat grows itself; "blame conditions, not men."

UNROMANTIC MACHINES

In Norris's *Octopus*, the figure of the monster machine—a powerful rendering of a man-made force that exceeds human control—seems to "naturalize" the artificial systems it seeks to critique, involving the novel in a form of social and economic determinism that ultimately appears to endorse the operations of the monster. Yet the narrative's formal dissonances draw attention to the human source of its mon-strous operations, tracing the impersonal action of its "natural" laws to their origin in human corruption. Like Zola's and Hardy's novels, Norris's *Octopus* reproduces—and thus indicts—the mechanical operations of the man-made system it appre-hends as monstrous. Not all naturalist novels, however, internalize the problem in this way. Although the figure of the monster machine connects Norris, Hardy, and Zola, one might sketch a more "respectable," less "faulty" tradition of literary natu-ralism in the works of such writers as Gissing, Dreiser, Wharton, and Crane. Like Norris and Hardy, these writers confront a man-made world—a world in which social and economic systems operate with the impervious tenacity of a machine. Their machines, however, are merely machines, unmiraculous in their brutality.

While *The Octopus* dramatizes the perversity of man-made systems through a Vanamee-style celebration of female objectification, Dreiser's *Sister Carrie*, Crane's *Maggie, A Girl of the Streets*, Wharton's *The House of Mirth* (1905), and Gissing's *New Grub Street* demonstrate the economics of objectification quite directly: Carrie, in the Chicago shoe factory, is subjected to the "humdrum, mechanical movement of [a] machine" (28) that is totally devoid—apart from its "eternal" imposition of a single mechanical task (29)—of mystical qualities. Maggie looks upon the older women in the collar and cuff factory as "mere mechanical contrivances sewing seams" (35), finding nothing romantic or miraculous in their exploitation or her own. Wharton's Lily Bart confronts the material conditions of her own social refinement in the milliner's shop, her "creation of ever-varied settings for the face of fortunate womanhood" (219) demystifying the glamour to which she ostensibly ministers. And Gissing's Marian Yule considers herself "not a woman, but a mere machine for reading and writing" (137). The only mythic machine in the novel is a phantom of her desire for release from literary manufacture:

> [H]er startled eye had caught an advertisement in the newspaper, headed
> "Literary Machine"; had it then been invented at last, some automaton to supply
> the place of such poor creatures as herself, to turn out books and articles? Alas!
> the machine was only one for holding volumes conveniently, that the work of
> literary manufacture might be physically lightened. (138)

Marian's miraculous machine is merely a ruse, a device to aid in the perpetuation of her labors. There is no escape from the mechanism she serves.

In *The Octopus*, Angéle's sexual objectification—her status as an interchangeable love object—represents the invidious operations of man-made social and economic forces. In the less "romantic" naturalist novels, objectification is traced more methodically to its causes: it is both the alternative and the result of factory work. Maggie "beg[in]s to see the bloom upon her cheeks as valuable" (35), trading on her looks instead of her labors. Carrie nominally escapes the machine when she accepts Drouet's "two soft, green, handsome ten-dollar bills" (47), turning herself into a salable object to elude a harder subjection in the factory. Lily, unfitted for the physical hardship of millinery, and unwilling to sell herself into a profitable marriage, resolves the problem in an overdose of chloral. And Marian, aware that she is only purchasing an escape from her labors in her engagement to Jasper Milvain, loses both when her inheritance falls through. The women in these novels never escape the tyranny of the machine; rather, their physical subjection is both reproduced and reinforced by the conditions of their supposed liberation. There are no mechanical monsters; instead, monstrosity is a quality of their social condition—a quality of the man-made environment—which operates with the unrelenting tenacity of the machine.

In naturalist novels without monster machines, the mythic tyranny of the man-made world is generalized, attaching to the social mechanism that controls individual fates. Crane's Maggie escapes from the monotonous life of the factory only to be trapped in an industrial hell; she dies in a "gloomy distric[t]" where the "tall black factories shut in the street" (77). Dreiser's Carrie, selling herself from the shoe factory to the stage, is irresistibly attracted to the vast glitter of a "super-human" city impervious to the individuals it ensnares. Wharton's Lily, "chain[ed] to her fate" by the links of her bracelet (8), is fatally constrained by the organization of her own genteel society. And Gissing's Marian—like Lily, a "victim of the civilization which had produced her" (8)—is trapped in the British Library, a Dantescan hell where readers sit immobilized by the "great circle of the Catalogue," or wander "in an eternity of vain research along endless shelves" (138).

In these novels, the monstrosity of the man-made world is not—especially in comparison to the apparent excesses of Norris, Hardy, or Zola—noticeably ugly or narratively infelicitous. There is something grimly impressive in Crane's description of Maggie's fate, and Dreiser's city is simultaneously a monstrous threat and a gorgeous spectacle. The "sense of [Carrie's] helplessness amid so much evidence of power and force" coexists with an impression of urban magnificence, "all wonderful, all vast" (13). Yet aesthetic beauty, in these works, is itself relentlessly exposed as a mechanical production. In Carrie's shoe factory, Maggie's collar-and-cuff factory, and Lily's millinery, the narrative calls attention to the mechanical conditions of the aesthetic object—and to the mechanical conditions of the narrative (as aesthetic object) itself. *Sister Carrie* depends for some of its most powerful aesthetic effects on the system of exploitation it exposes; *New Grub Street* represents, in a work of literary manufacture, literature itself as an industrial product; and *Maggie*, following its heroine's fate from the factory to the industrial swamp, connects storytelling to the man-made mechanism it condemns. Like the women in the collar-and-cuff factory, "grinding out . . . tales of imagined or real girl-hood happiness" (35) together with their manufactures, the narrative grinds out a tragic story, obedient to the inexorable logic of the machine. These novels, no less than the more "faulty" works of Norris, Hardy, and Zola, are formally determined by the machines they condemn.

Transfixed by the horror—or the terrible beauty—of the man-made world, the naturalist novel reproduces the operations of a mechanism it cannot both escape and expose. The result is a form of narrative monstrosity—a form of collusion with the brutal machine. Often, this monstrosity is expressed as a "defect": In Zola's novels, the narrative appears to collapse under the pressure of representing a force that is itself beyond human control; in Hardy, the whole novel creaks under the pressure of inflexible "devices"; and in Norris, the text appears to endorse a system it simultaneously exposes as corrupt and perverse. Yet these "defects" are themselves representative and constitute a unique critical integrity: the failures of narrative mastery reproduce the failure of rational mastery—the failure to control a force humanity itself has created—embodied in the figure of the monster machine. In the less "faulty" fictions, the machines are comparatively unmiraculous. Yet these narratives also reproduce, with ruthless plausibility, a world organized and driven by mechanical forces. Determined by the very machines they condemn, and exposing their own aesthetics as machine-made, these novels draw attention to their inevitable complicity in the man-made mechanisms they deplore.

WORKS CITED

Alexis, Paul. "Naturalism Is Not Dead." *Documents of Modern Literary Realism*. Ed. George J. Becker. Princeton: Princeton University Press, 1963. 407–11.

Baguley, David. *Naturalist Fiction: The Entropic Vision*. Cambridge: Cambridge University Press, 1990.

Brooks, Peter. *Body Work: Objects of Desire in Modern Narrative*. Cambridge: Harvard University Press, 1993.

———. *Realist Vision*. New Haven: Yale University Press, 2005.

Chevrel, Yves. "Toward an Aesthetic of the Naturalist Novel." *Naturalism in the European Novel: New Critical Perspectives*. Ed. Brian Nelson. New York: Berg, 1992. 46–65.

Crane, Stephen. *Maggie, A Girl of the Streets and Other Tales of New York*. New York: Penguin, 2000.

Dreiser, Theodore. *Sister Carrie*. Ed. Donald Pizer. 2nd ed. New York: Norton, 1991.

Fleissner, Jennifer L. *Women, Compulsion, Modernity: The Moment of American Naturalism*. Chicago: University of Chicago Press, 2004.

Gissing, George. *New Grub Street*. New York: Penguin, 1968.

Hardy, Thomas. *The Mayor of Casterbridge*. New York: Norton, 2001.

———. "The Science of Fiction." *Thomas Hardy's Public Voice: The Essays, Speeches, and Miscellaneous Prose*. Ed. Michael Millgate. Oxford: Clarendon, 2001. 106–10.

———. *Tess of the d'Urbervilles*. New York: Penguin, 1978.

Hemmings, F. W. J. *Émile Zola*. 2nd ed. Oxford: Clarendon Press, 1966.

Howard, June. *Form and History in American Literary Naturalism*. Chapel Hill: University of North Carolina Press, 1985.

Howe, Irving. *Thomas Hardy*. New York: Macmillan, 1967.

———. "Zola: The Poetry of Naturalism." *Selected Writings 1950–1990*. San Diego: Harcourt Brace Jovanovich, 1990. 283–95.

Lehan, Richard. "The European Background." *The Cambridge Companion to American Realism and Naturalism: Howells to London*. Ed. Donald Pizer. Cambridge: Cambridge University Press, 1999. 47–73.

———. *Realism and Naturalism*. Madison: University of Wisconsin Press, 2005.

Lethbridge, Robert. Introduction. Lethbridge and Keefe 1–14.

———. "Zola and the Limits of Craft." Lethbridge and Keefe 133–49.

Lethbridge, Robert, and Terry Keefe, eds. *Zola and the Craft of Fiction*. New York: Leicester University Press, 1990.

Link, Eric Carl. *The Vast and Terrible Drama: American Literary Naturalism in the Late Nineteenth Century*. Tuscaloosa: University of Alabama Press, 2004.

Lukács, Georg. "Narrate or Describe." *Writer and Critic and Other Essays*. Trans. Arthur Kahn. London: Merlin, 1970. 110–48.

McElrath, Joseph R., Jr., and Jesse S. Crisler. *Frank Norris: A Life*. Chicago: University of Illinois Press, 2006.

Marx, Leo. *The Machine in the Garden: Technology and the Pastoral Ideal in America*. New York: Oxford University Press, 2000.

Mitterand, Henri. "The Great Hurricane Wind of *Germinal.*" *Émile Zola: Fiction and Modernity.* Trans. and ed. Monica Lebron and David Baguley. London: Émile Zola Society, 2000. 117–21.

Moore, George. *Confessions of a Young Man.* New York: Boni and Liveright, n.d.

———. *A Mummer's Wife.* Whitefish, Mont.: Kessinger, n.d.

Norris, Frank. *The Octopus.* New York: Penguin, 1986.

———. "Zola as a Romantic Writer." *Documents of American Realism and Naturalism.* Ed. Donald Pizer. Carbondale: Southern Illinois University Press, 1998. 168–69.

Pierre-Gnassounou, Chantal. "Zola and the Art of Fiction." *The Cambridge Companion to Émile Zola.* Ed. Brian Nelson. Cambridge: Cambridge University Press, 2007. 86–104.

Seltzer, Mark. *Bodies and Machines.* New York: Routledge, 1992.

Walker, Philip. "Zola and the Art of Containing the Uncontainable." Lethbridge and Keefe 28–43.

Wharton, Edith. *The House of Mirth.* New York: Norton, 1990.

Zola, Émile. *L'Assommoir.* Trans. Margaret Mauldon. New York: Oxford University Press, 1995.

———. *La Bête humaine.* Trans. Roger Pearson. New York: Oxford University Press, 1996.

———. *Au Bonheur des Dames.* Trans. Robin Buss. New York: Penguin, 2001.

———. *The Experimental Novel and Other Essays.* Trans. Belle M. Sherman. New York: Haskell, 1964.

———. *Germinal.* Trans. Peter Collier. Oxford: Oxford University Press, 1993.

....

CHAPTER 2

THE RESPONSE TO POWER IN AMERICAN LITERARY NATURALISM: VISIONS AND REVISIONS THAT TRANSFORMED A NARRATIVE MODE

....

RICHARD LEHAN

I begin with a series of assumptions involving literary naturalism as a literary movement, assumptions as to the nature of a literary text and as to naturalism as a narrative vision of life in America from about 1890 to the end of World War II. But the main assumption of this essay is that literary movements, in this instance literary naturalism, exist in textual forms that get transformed first by their major practitioners, then by a succeeding generation of authors, and finally by the rise of critical theories that involve transformations in the text itself and the way the text is read. There is thus no Literary Naturalism—but rather literary naturalisms—and the task of the literary critic is to describe how the core text works and to tabulate the variations in its being and evolution.

We will always have transformations that involve seeing older visions through the new: the revisions displace status quo authority and open up the text for new ways of discussing it. But despite the authority of the revisionary moment, there is an obligation to review from time to time the originary view, an obligation to see how newer interpretations are extrapolations of older ones, and the need to make clear how a revised naturalism changes the meaning of an originary view. We need, that is, to return from time to time to what Wallace Stevens calls the First Idea—the painting with the subsequent paint removed.

Second, I believe that a study of American literary naturalism gives us only half the picture of naturalism as a narrative movement. Naturalism had it origins in France and was accommodated in America because the narrative experience it depicted had an American equivalent. The aftermath of the Civil War in America corresponded to the social and political changes taking place in France between 1848 and 1870. In both countries, we move from a landed/agrarian economy to a commercial/industrial society. Thus it is not surprising that Frank Norris shared a historical moment with Émile Zola, and Theodore Dreiser with Honoré de Balzac. This does not mean that there was one naturalistic novel that kept getting written. Rather, there was a core naturalistic novel (what I have elsewhere called the "pre-text"), variations of which kept getting written ("re-presented"). One can think of such coalescing tendencies in terms of the synoptic meaning we give to the New Testament in which there is a core Gospel narrative albeit with variations (see Lehan, "Biological Model" 69).

Finally, in order to think of literary naturalism as a movement, we must think of a literary work as part of a narrative mode rather than as a product of literary form. Theories of literary form and of narrative mode are products of conjectured or paradigmatic thinking, each creating its own distinct reality. A theory of form puts emphasis on the work as an organic whole subject to the meaning of its individual parts, autotelic in nature, and distinct in meaning. A modal study, on the other hand, puts the emphasis on the work as part of an unfolding genre, evolutionary in content, intertextual in the way it plays off of related texts, creating an accretive history in its relationships to other works and to its own inevitable transformation. A formal work stands by itself; a modal work takes its meaning from both literary content and historical context—factors that distinguish it from other literary modes.

The move from context to content involves coming to terms with a number of historical factors. The main factor in such a composite picture involves naturalism as the product of forces shaping character and determining behavior. These forces are sometimes the product of the natural world and express themselves as Darwinian assumptions involving the problems of human adaptation and theories of heredity and environment (for a full-length study of the workings of natural forces, see Martin). They can also be the product of culture and express themselves in the form of legal or educational institutions. They can at other times be the product of technology and express themselves as a mechanical reality in the form, for example, of the steam engine that can move industry from the rural surrounding where power is derived from a river to the slum environment of urban factories; such forces can move us beyond human or animal capacities and power locomotives, conquering space by diminishing landscape. A theory of force might draw upon the idea of chance, perhaps cosmic chance, in which the powers at work seem connected to a whimsy that drives life before it.

Along with a theory of force, as the above commentary suggests, naturalism was the product of the radical shift in cultural meaning that came with the transition from an agrarian to an industrial society. The naturalistic novel examined in detail the fate of the farm worker (the peasant in France) who was now being displaced from the land, moving to the city to find work in the new factory system. This double focus—on the land and on the city—takes us from agrarian to urban concerns, from the working of the coal mines and the exploitation of labor, to the way money works in a commodity society, be it in the salon or the slums.

Naturalism as a modal reality was part of a deterministic system in which fate was a product of extrinsic influences. The situation here involves a predictable and fixed relationship between the reader of a naturalistic novel and the characters that compose it. While the reader anticipates the fate of naturalistic characters, the characters themselves are generally unaware of what awaits them; most naturalistic novels are written in this ironic mode, the reader anticipating a fate to which the characters are oblivious.

Most literary movements take their being from a vision of life, often the product of philosophical commentary. The most important influence of such commentary involving literary naturalism came from Charles Darwin as modified by Gregor Mendel and by Herbert Spencer, who revised Darwin's main ideas. The new science postulated a universe of at least ten billion years in which modern man evolved out of the primate species 160,000 years ago, 230,000 years if Neanderthals can be classified as human. Darwin brought forth his theory in two world-changing books: *On the Origin of Species by Means of Natural Selection* (1859) and *The Descent of Man* (1871). Darwin insisted that the human species evolved out of primate life. The residue of such connections are very much with us today: we know, for example, that chimpanzees share ninety-five percent of human genetic material, have similar blood types and brain structures, and are similar in behavior in the first three years of life and up to six years of life, at which time their animality becomes more pronounced. The animal-human connection supported the idea of atavistic influence, the rise of behavioral or genetic instincts that were dormant in the human past. These transformations challenged the belief that God was the source of all creation, that each species was unchanging, and that the Great Chain of Being was static.

In his journey around the world aboard the *Beagle*, Darwin observed that life in different environments was directly connected to its capacity to adapt to its surroundings. Once Mendel's understanding of how genetic transitions facilitated organic change, the evolutionary picture was complete. Darwin did not argue that such changes were in the form of progress; evolution did not make a species better, only different. But there were theorists who argued that evolution improved the species, and the most important of these Darwinian commentators was Herbert Spencer.

Spencer was important because he probably had more direct influence on the literary naturalists, especially Dreiser, than did Darwin himself. In *First Principles* (the introductory volume to *The Synthetic Philosophy* [1862–96]), Spencer argued that human society evolved from the communal hordes of primitive society and that we were moving from authoritarian forms of society to more liberal forms. The major concern of the modern was thus how to strike a balance between individualism and altruism, self-preservation and community welfare. He believed two forces were at work: military (based on authority) and industrial (based on cooperation), and he anticipated how modern politics would be a battle between forms of authority (totalitarianism) and forms of more liberal behavior (democracy).

The key to Spenser's philosophy was his belief that we lived in a material world subject to physical laws that explained the workings of natural forces. Spencer believed that physical force was part of an equilibrium that took its initial being in the form of a balance: life was a struggle between conflicting forces, between opposites: order and chaos, wealth and poverty, sickness and health, the beautiful and the ugly. Dreiser's characters are often caught between these extreme alternatives as well as moral dilemmas: Hurstwood is torn between looting or locking the safe; Clyde Griffiths is torn between turning back to Sondra or running away from the sheriff. When the alternatives are equal—that is, when they balance each other—the characters become morally paralyzed and are subject to an unresolved stasis.

Action engenders reaction; force is constant; and matter is in constant motion. If matter in motion involves chemical force, and human beings are a product of matter, then humans are also subject to chemical force. Dreiser extrapolated slightly from Spencer's paradigm: he believed that people were in pursuit of ideals, but at the same time subject to the limits of a material existence. This conflict between the pursuit of an ideal that is subject to physical limits explains why Eliseo Vivas has called Dreiser an "inconsistent mechanist" (498–508), and I have discussed him as subject to "the romantic dilemma": a contradictory principle inheres in his thinking leading to displacement. People are born to be one step behind themselves: they yearn for ideals in a material world that cancels out the ideal (Lehan, *Theodore Dreiser* 45–47).

Each individual will experience a cycle of both rise and fall, although the focus is usually on one cycle or the other. Dreiser depicted Carrie's rise and Hurstwood's fall; Norris depicted the fall of both McTeague and Vandover; Dreiser depicted both the rise and fall of Cowperwood. The cycle takes its being from a moment of stasis, which creates a reversal in the flow of matter upward or downward: dissolution is evolution in reverse.

Spencer believed that on the level of the individual, the process is regressive; on the level of the species, the process is progressive: the individual is subject to death, even as humankind in general was advancing. So long as the cycle kept repeating itself, Spencer believed that all matter was passing from homogeneity to heterogeneity—from the simple to the more complex. While the race can look ahead for progress, the individual spends half a life advancing and the other half in decline. Rise and fall, advance and decline—the force that controls each impulse was built into nature, which is why this process is called naturalism.

Spencer's ideas were in the air that both Theodore Dreiser and Frank Norris breathed. In his *Post-Historic Man* (1950), Roderick Seidenberg comes to terms with one of Spencer's main concerns: the difference between the individual and the community. His premise is that with the transformations brought on by capitalism we lost a sense of community to the rise of individualism and forms of narcissism. His thesis was consistent with the theories of the most respected sociologists at the turn of the twentieth century. Ferdinand Tonnies makes the same argument in his distinction between *Gemeinschaft* (community, beyond self-interest, common beliefs, family, division of labor, organic) and *Gesellschaft* (society at large, individual self-interest, mechanistic, motivated by money rather than cooperation and marked by class/social conflict); Georg Simmel in his theory of how money works in a capitalistic society; Émile Durkheim in his explanation of how a sense of individual helplessness led to the rise of suicide; Max Weber in his belief that a Protestant individualism was the basis for the inception of capitalism; and Thorstein Veblen in his belief that behind capitalism are forms of individual display or conspicuous consumption.

Seidenberg's thesis is also consistent with the assumptions of both literary naturalism and modernism. A novel like Frank Norris's *The Octopus* (1901), for example, depicts the breakdown of the community spirit as the railroad inflates its rates and prevents the wheat farmers from selling their product at a reasonable profit. If the railroad and the farmers could have functioned as a community, they both would have profited. In acting only in terms of self-interest and looking only for the largest profit, the railroad violated a sense of community and fragmented the farmers as a group, encouraging them to act individually, often in reckless ways.

Forces function differently, depending upon whether they are acting on the individual or the community. Norris's McTeague becomes subject to a series of forces as they might be defined by Herbert Spencer and redefined by Joseph LeConte, the biologist with whom Norris took courses at the University of California at Berkeley. Practicing dentistry in San Francisco and married to Trina, McTeague's world is conventional enough (Spencer would call it "balanced"). But under the calm is turbulence, the work of atavist sources that upset the balance. This force is brought into play when McTeague loses his license to practice dentistry and when he takes Trina away from Marcus Schouler, who develops a hatred of McTeague so powerful that it destroys all the principal characters in the novel.

The destructive elements that interrupt the balance are purely naturalistic. The calm brings with it a sense of peace before the storm. Then chance events interrupt that peace and initiate degenerative forces that lie buried in McTeague, forces of greed that dominate Trina, and forces of hostility that bring Schouler to a point of murderous rage. Once McTeague loses his sense of balance, his descent is swift, especially when coupled with an alcoholism that has long been in his family and that McTeague seems to have inherited from his father. McTeague's situation produces the degenerative condition that Norris took from the works of Caesar Lombroso, whom he knew through his reading of Max Nordau.

The evolutionary pull of animality, the destructive nature of a compulsive temperament (the physical possession of money becomes more important to Trina than its utility value, and gold for Zerkow becomes an end in itself), the workings of greed and jealousy—all of these elements create a sequence of events so powerful that they lead to multiple deaths. The move in the novel from a civilized realm to the locus of death is reinforced symbolically as we move from San Francisco to Death Valley. Once the forces of life create their own imbalance, it is only a matter of time before we have the violent unfolding that concludes the novel.

Dreiser's *Sister Carrie* (1900) is his retelling of a *McTeague*-like story, complete with Spencerian elements. As we have seen, Spencer's philosophy was a combination of nineteenth century mechanistic belief superimposed on romantic assumptions—assumptions that became a fundamental contradiction (imbalance) to Dreiser. As a mechanist, he believed matter was in motion, in constant change from a center, a balance, or equilibrium. As a romantic, he believed that it was only human to yearn for a more idealized being. Material desire in search of an ideal reality—built into Dreiser's view of life was a fundamental contradiction that his characters were fated to play out, often destructively.

Both Spencer and Dreiser were products of the new capitalism in which the individual was a product of desire in a world of limited capacity. Spencer's principle of balance (of a desired equilibrium to one's existence) was impossible to sustain. It is humanly impossible to reconcile romantic possibilities and mechanistic limits: each desire pulls the character in opposed directions, leading to the displaced character who is urged on by appetite and yet restrained by physical limits and diminished intelligence. Spencer had clearly seen that capitalism was based on an unending desire for more and more in a zero-sum world—that is, a world of physical limits.

Given both Norris's and Dreiser's use of Spencer's philosophy, it is not surprising that their characters are not at one with themselves but are frustrated by constant desire, for a constant wish for more and more, in a world of imbalance that will not be able to accommodate them. Dreiser made use of many elements that Norris had brought to *McTeague*. Carrie comes from a Wisconsin farm town to Chicago, which is alive with energy, with human, technological, and commercial forces. The city is ablaze with lights at night, awash with crowds, resplendent with consumer goods. Dreiser's novel is reworking the young man/woman from the provinces theme of Balzac: the journey from provincial town to urban center is a journey in pursuit of new opportunity, motivated by the longing for an expanded realm of being, in search of the heightened self.

At the center of each story is an irretrievable act that works persistently to shape the future. Norris based *McTeague* on an actual murder case. Dreiser based his novel on the story of his sister Emma who, while living in Chicago in 1885, met L. A. Hopkins, fifteen years her senior, the manager of Chapin and Gore, a successful tavern, from which he stole $3,500, absconding with Emma by way of Montreal to New York. Like the story of McTeague, Hurstwood's act turns him into a social outcast, a state of being that works against his equilibrium, the incapacity to fulfill desire.

Both Carrie and Hurstwood are out to fulfill themselves, and Dreiser gives us his version of the narcissistic self as abstracted from Spencer and personified by a transformed individual who takes the city as a field of force, energized by new opportunities (Carrie) or the victim of unseen limits (Hurstwood). As a member of a burlesque chorus line and later as an actress, Carrie goes in pursuit of greater desires, while Hurstwood fails at a number of opportunities that diminish his desire for fulfillment. What he succeeds in doing in Chicago, he fails to do in New York, which he finds less welcoming, more hostile, and more intimidating now that he is older and less energetic.

Spencer believed that along with natural forces are human-made forces, and in America the most persistent of these involve capitalism. Almost everything in Dreiser's novel turns on money. Drouet gives Carrie twenty dollars (equivalent to about $800.00 in today's money) to buy clothes; Carrie leaves twenty dollars for Hurstwood when she moves out. Carrie finds financial success on the Broadway stage; Hurstwood takes his saloon into foreclosure and invokes violence when he works against the streetcar strikers. Carrie pushes ahead and creates new possibilities for herself, although we are warned that these possibilities have limits. Hurstwood begins to experience those limits when he leaves his safe harbor (his realm of balance and equilibrium) and reverses the cycle that Carrie initiates.

Both Dreiser and Norris saw how conflict was built into life. We live in worlds of force: our very being is a product of biological forces; social meaning is built into environment. But even more telling are the forces that work on us within the capitalistic system: the American illusion of limitless freedom eventually confronts the limits of age and energy with varied results. Carrie is eighteen when the novel begins and twenty-six at the end; Hurstwood is twenty years older, thirty-eight at the beginning and forty-six at the end. It is hard to think of Hurstwood as old, until one remembers that life expectancy at this time was around fifty. Carrie's fortune is a matter of youth; Hurstwood's decline a matter of age—but age within the capitalistic system. Carrie dances on the stage with other beautiful women and resides at the Waldorf Astoria, while Hurstwood waits for a handout in breadlines and sleeps in a shelter. The economic (capitalistic) system works within the energy available at human extremes, takes us in two very different directions, and explains the variations that are built into literary naturalism and the transformations that come with its depiction.

The novel keeps coming back to the flux, the imbalances of life, the pursuit of a mirage. The metaphor of the rocking chair suggests that life is continued flux, perpetual change that keeps the principal characters at odds with themselves and others. Both Carrie and Hurstwood are confronted with options that pull them away from a social center: Carrie when she agrees to live with Drouet, Hurstwood when he takes the money from the safe. These actions are not really choices: both Carrie and Hurstwood are drawn latently toward material pursuits. They do not choose because their options are weighted: they are pulled in a Spencerian way more in one direction than in another. Their behavior stems from the imbalance of their options. Given Hurstwood's unhappy marriage, the desire for a new beginning with a beautiful woman is more compelling than social respectability. Given Carrie's hopeless living arrangements with her sister and her reluctance to return home, Drouet offers her the means to remain in Chicago with its boundless sense of opportunity, as opposed to the restricted opportunities of the small town. One side of a moral equation outweighs the other.

While they seem to have different options confronting them, both Carrie and Hurstwood share a social context; they must function in a society becoming more secular, more the product of a compelling narcissism than that of a community. Unappreciated at home, weary of his routine, the victim of middle-age crisis, Hurstwood welcomes a change, no matter the consequences. Aware of her sexual appeal, no longer inhibited by codes of sexual restraint, and aware that she can use her sexuality to command the abundant consumer goods that she sees in the windows of the new department store, which along with advertising creates a constant, unfulfilled desire, Carrie is the product of a radically transformed America. Carrie Meeber-Drouet-Hurstwood-Wheeler-Madena (the many names reveal her adaptive, far-seeking, chameleon nature) embodies a new secular state of mind in America. Both Carrie and Hurstwood have lost a sense of community. Their "me-first" attitude marks an end to the old Puritan restraint—an end to the old innocence.

Literary naturalism keeps coming back to one or another version of force, whether it be a life (vitalistic) force like that of the wheat that pushes life ahead of it, or the mechanistic (physical) force like the railroad that has its origins in human invention. In Frank Norris's *The Octopus* the two forces work antagonistically, and the characters define themselves by the way they align themselves to one force or another. On the side of the wheat are the wealthy farmers (Derrick Magnus and Annixter); on the side of the railroad are its executives and agents (S. Behrman); a mediating link between these force is the poet (Presley) whose understanding of the situation leads to an epic vision of conflict out of which comes his poetic warning to both the farmers and the railroad. As the forces of wheat and rail become stronger, the main characters become less self-reliant, diminished in their ability to change the situation. Derrick Magnus resorts to bribery; Annixter to self-destructive violence; Presley to bombing.

Vanamee is the character most in tune with the forces that move through nature. He is the Hebraic shepherd, mystic prophet, biblical visionary, whose mission is an errand in the wilderness. He incarnates the spirit of the land, can hold his flock of sheep in place or call to others by the power of mind. He mourns the death of Angéle, whose rape led to her death in childbirth, even as he believes her spirit lives on in nature and is as alive as the wheat that bursts from the land each spring. This spirit is the force that drives the novel, is the corrective to the injustices the novel depicts. When Presley returns for the last time to the ranch, Vanamee tells him that evil has no permanent status and is only a transitory phenomenon, ultimately subject to counter-forces that "work together for good" (448).

Norris thus concludes his novel on a note of Progress, the belief that a spirit that permeates the future will perpetuate good. Norris believed that civilization was moving west, jumping the Atlantic after the Crusades, progressing across the American continent, and then jumping to the Pacific: Dewey's exploits in Manila and the marines' invasion of China during the Boxer Rebellion in 1900 were concrete forms of testimony to this power, perhaps cosmic in nature ("Frontier" 71, 74, 77). In a latent way, this force is a synthesis; it works on the side of life as a corrective to greed, as the death of Behrman suggests. But while the novel ends on an optimistic note, there is nothing in it that suggests this germinal force is a corrective power or that some abstracted good is an end product in the unfolding of history. In fact, in Norris's other novels, the opposite conclusion is more readily plausible.

Despite the ending of *The Octopus*, Norris takes us to the end of innocence. Although his sympathy was with the ranchers, they were equally corrupted by money. In *The Pit* (1903), Norris indicted the speculative economy because it substituted a market economy for a natural one. The value of wheat was measured by abstract concerns that were matters of speculation; it all turned on whether the price would rise or fall and had nothing to do with working the land to produce the wheat. Moreover, such markets could be manipulated if one had the means to buy up future wheat in abundance and then hold it off the market, depleting the supply and inflating the eventual cost. Like the naturalists in general, Norris showed how the elements of life worked in terms of self-interest. Supposedly the larger forces at work in the universe would be a corrective to such self-interest, but Norris was more convincing in depicting greed at work than in demonstrating the existence of corrective forces.

Dreiser takes us more deeply into the new commercial world in *The Financier* (1912) and *The Titan* (1914). While Norris pondered a financial system that took its being from speculation, Dreiser was more sympathetic to the gamesmanship that underscored playing the market. Out of the speculative process came new realities such as a national railroad line, and out of that line "would spring up great cities and prosperous towns" (*Financier* 526). Dreiser's Cowperwood, modeled on Charles Yerkes, gave primary concern to his own interest, but at the same time his investments help build a new nation. Both Norris and Dreiser saw how America necessarily depended on a market economy, but Dreiser seemed more in awe of the process and more willing to engage the play that went along with speculation. Dreiser's stock market is a vast machine that creates its own power, is a force unto itself, and is true to its own laws that are as inexorable as the law of gravity. Capital markets circle the world and are responsive to historical events large and small (the Franco-Prussian War brought down Jay Cooke, the Chicago Fire of 1871 Yerkes). Dreiser believed we live in a world of equilibrium, and even the strong man like Cooke and Yerkes were subject to its working. The individual could manipulate economic events (like the gold standard) to some extent, but at some point in the process the system takes over with results indifferent to human desire. Like historicism, the prevalent theory of history at this time, the naturalist believed that laws were built into history (i.e., time) and that people were subject to forces that they barely understood and could not control.

The product of poverty most of his early life, Dreiser was fascinated by the difference in income within the classes. After the publication of *An American Tragedy* (1925) when he was financially independent, Dreiser carried on a systematic study involving the nature of the universe and the mechanics of capitalism. Dreiser became especially interested in the theory of one economist, Howard Scott, and his revision of capitalism into a theory he called Technocracy. Scott pondered the fact that employment in America reached its highest peak in 1918, while production reached its highest peak in 1929—at a time when the employment rate was declining. Scott believed that we had this inverse ratio between employment and production because the machine reduced the need for labor and yet produced more goods than could be turned out by hand. But machines cost money and depended upon banks and credit; by the time the machine was paid for, it was outdated and needed to be replaced, involving another round of more money/credit. When the debt increased faster than the sale of goods, the market collapsed, which, according to Scott, explained the Depression of 1929 (which supplies a parallel for the economic meltdown of 2007–9). The system depended on negotiations between commercial investors and industrial producers with the worker left out of the process, except as its victim when large-scale unemployment led to foreclosures and bankruptcy. Scott wanted to do away with all debt instruments (bonds, stocks, debentures), and he planned to replace owners and trustees with an engineer overseer who controlled the machine in the name of the state. The engineer could calculate the amount of goods the machine could produce within a fixed period of time, estimate the number that could be used by the prevailing population, and then distribute the goods on a pro rata basis, the total demand not to exceed the goods produced. If done successfully, this practice would better estimate the cost of producing the good, make better use of the machine, better distribute the goods to the general public, and include the worker within the system.

Scott's Technocracy plan had been more or less anticipated by Edward Bellamy in *Looking Backward* (1888), a futuristic projection of Scott's system at work. Both Scott and Bellamy saw that capitalism worked to keep prices high and, because surplus profit was added to the final cost, many goods were priced beyond the means of the worker who had brought the goods into existence. In making better use of the acquisition and deployment of the machine, the overseer could do away with this flawed system. But Bellamy's enthusiasm for Scott's ideas was not universally shared. Mark Twain attacked the idea in *A Connecticut Yankee in King Arthur's Court* (1889) on the grounds that the engineer overseer was a dictator, and it was politically dangerous to put that much power in one individual's hands. Ignatius Donnelly in *Caesar's Column* (1891) creates another futuristic city, but in this case the city is torn between two factions: a wealthy oligarchy and an exploited proletariat, who, once in control, would abuse the power that had long been used against them. Scott and Bellamy had given more thought to the workings of a machine society than to the use of power such a society would generate.

Another novel that treats what amounts to naturalistic economics is Jack London's *The Iron Heel* (1908), which picks up where Donnelly leaves off. London also begins with a capitalistic oligarchy and a discontented labor force, each at odds with the other. Unlike Bellamy, London believed any transfer of power between these two social entities would involve confrontation and class violence. London spent more time analyzing the specifics of Marxist theory than did Bellamy and Donnelly. He also considers the nature of modern power and the way it works—on the move from nation-state to imperialism and its effects on world markets, on the rise of national powers and the coming of World Wars I and II, on the rise of Japan as an Eastern empire, on the buildup of the military and global confrontations, and on the use of government subsidies along with the elimination of surplus goods. Many commentators have charged that the naturalists overstated the workings of force on our lives, but a look at works like *The Iron Heel* reveal an era edging toward global war and powerless to do anything about it.

Force in the naturalistic novel takes on a reality of its own. Zola wrote twenty novels depicting the effect of heredity and environment on two Parisian families. McTeague and Vandover become subject to a process of deterioration. The power of the railroad in Norris's *Octopus* is as tangible as the wheat that bursts from the land each spring. Stephen Crane's use of force seems especially noxious because it works so comfortably with the commonplace and the everyday. Rather than seeing force as the malignant workings of nature, Crane depicts it as an element of nature to be defined usually by a suffering humanity. In a novel like *Maggie* (1893), Crane depicted two elements at work: the hostile environment of the slums and a state of mind that plays off that hostility. Maggie is confronted by contradictory demands— the desire of her mother and her brother for respectability and that she remain a virgin versus the desire of Pete that she give herself to him. That Pete seems to offer her the means of escaping a life of poverty makes her belief in him all the more insidious. Maggie is as much a victim of a state of mind as she is a victim of the force of the ghetto.

In *The Red Badge of Courage* (1895), Crane sets out to prove that cowardice or heroism in battle stems from a state of mind, and like the forces that play in Maggie's mind, the stronger force wins. Henry Fleming runs when first attacked but holds his position during a second attack. The difference between courageous and cowardly behavior is a weighted state of mind: it becomes more important than life itself for Henry to win the approval of his comrades.

The same state of mind seems to be at work in Crane's short stories. In "The Open Boat" (1897), four men struggle in a lifeboat, a ten-foot dinghy, for two days and nights to reach the shore. During this time, their state of mind changes. At first they think of themselves as ants, helpless against the forces of an antagonistic nature that is indifferent to their condition. A sense of camaraderie sustains a sense of hope until the boat is swamped, and each man is thrown on his own into the raging sea. As the men get closer to shore, their situation becomes both more tenuous and ironic. It is ironic, for example, that the strongest man of the four, the oiler, is the one who drowns.

Crane depicts men in confrontation with the forces of nature. These forces are indifferent to the suffering of the men who humanize the force, seeing it first as indifferent and later as hostile. On final analysis there are two forces at work— human and nature, agent and state of mind, with man's state of mind intensifying the workings of nature as well as the vulnerability of the human condition.

A major element in the transformation of literary naturalism into modernism occurred when naturalism morphed into neo-realism. Neo-realism involves literary naturalism without the naturalistic documentation. Dos Passos's *USA* (1937) trilogy, for example, depicted characters caught in the realm of force, but the source of force now was primarily historical, the product of the ups and downs of the capitalistic system, culminating in a novel devoid of hereditary and environmental commentary. Another example of this kind of transformation would be James M. Cain's *The Postman Always Rings Twice* (1934), which also moved away from naturalistic theory, presenting a naturalistic story without the racial or inherited background—without, that is, the documentation that previously made it naturalistic.

Cain's transformation of the naturalist novel made it suitable for the philosophical uses to which Albert Camus put it. In writing *L'étranger* (1942), Camus needed an "elemental" character, someone who lived on the level of his senses, but not naturalistic reality. Camus found such a character in Cain's Frank Chambers. Camus worked other similarities: the climax of each novel is a murder, followed by a court hearing; the novels conclude in a murder cell with the principal characters waiting to be executed, talking or writing to a priest. The most obvious parallel between the two novels is that both Frank Chambers and Meursault are misfits, passive heroes who respond to immediate stimuli. Described in terms of their external behavior, they react rather than act, qualities of behavior they share with naturalistic characters.

Even earlier, other novelists such as Ernest Hemingway kept their characters in contact with nature. They did this not to demonstrate theories of evolution or degeneration, but to test them against natural events such as the big-game hunt, deep-sea fishing, or the bullfight. Hemingway created a natural aristocracy outside of society, which allowed more individual will and self-determination than one would find in naturalistic fiction. Hemingway's narrative aim was to get the protagonist outside of modern history, especially outside a mechanical urban order, on a boat or on an island, where a code of primitive values ruled. Such a narrative maneuver allowed Hemingway to contrast elemental and civilized individuals. Another device involved locating a story in a moment of transition, like that of the Spanish civil war, in which two ways of life—primitive and modern—were in conflict. And lastly, Hemingway set up geographical opposites, as he did in *The Sun Also Rises* (1926), when he contrasted Jake Barnes in Paris and Jake in Burguete. Hemingway struggled to locate his pre-urban vision in idealized action and rituals that partake of the land and the sea, until finally he displaced urban reality with the extended arena.

Hemingway not only contrasted the primitive and civilized, but he depicted this world impressionistically. Impressionism accompanied the move from naturalism to modernism, from an objective to a subjective reality. The distinction between descriptive detail (in which the detail controls the mind) and impressionistic detail (in which the mind controls the detail) is objectivity on the way to becoming subjectivity. Walter Pater first came to terms with this process, a lesson learned by Joseph Conrad, who influenced Stephen Crane, who in turn influenced Hemingway. Hemingway's is a naturalistic world seen through a Paterian prism, the emphasis upon a recording consciousness rather than biology, heredity, or environment.

Another falling away from the "pre-text" (i.e., core or synoptic text) of literary naturalism involved the rise of noir. Literary noir also owes much to Hemingway. In the traditional novel, good and evil are demarcated with the protagonist on the side of "good," the antagonist on the side of "evil." In noir fiction, these terms are reversed: the noir character, whose perspective dominates what and how we see, works outside the realm of good—that is, the noir character is transformed into the antihero, like Hemingway's Harry Morgan; instead of embodying the values of society, he lives outside the law, on the edge of community. The women in noir literature and film are femme fatales, like Margot Macomber: they have no desire to settle down or raise a family. Their presence is destructive: when not out to destroy a man, they demand the dominant role.

With noir comes the end of innocence: everyone is degraded; good and evil blur and become ambivalent moral choices; redemption and betrayal are one and the same. The noir novel with its antihero takes us to the edge of a democratic society, to marginal men and women living by their wits. Once they are further socially removed, they will become the drifters in the novels of James M. Cain, the seekers in Jack Kerouac, the homeless derelicts in Nelson Algren and William Kennedy, and the family outcasts in Joyce Carol Oates. Hemingway supplied the model; popular culture did the rest. Once we have a novel like *To Have and Have Not* (1937), we have the basis for the "tough guy" novel of Raymond Chandler and Dashiell Hammett. Hemingway's code hero owes much to the western, the subgenre whose values Hemingway brought to his depiction of Africa and the Spanish civil war. But central to both Hemingway and noir fiction is the protagonist caught in a world of forces that, unlike the naturalistic protagonist, he wills to resist.

The most radical transformation of literary naturalism came when critical consent was given to structuralism. We have been discussing literary naturalism as a system of forces that manifest themselves physically in an external world. But under the influence of Ferdinand de Saussure's theory of language and Roland Barthes's derivative theory of lexies, the idea of the mimetic has been seriously questioned, challenging the whole idea of what we mean by realism and text. Barthes contends that a realistic story like Balzac's "Sarrasine" drew no more on "life" than any other kind of writing. Barthes divided the text into what he called "lexies" (codes involving action, hermeneutics, fashions, symbols, and tropes) and then read the story in terms of their meaning, producing over two hundred pages of commentary on a thirty-page story. This method empties literary realism, including naturalism, of its primary meaning by cutting it off from physical reality. The same is true when Saussure's structuralism is applied, and we proceed through a constructed reality based upon substituting critical paradigms for physical reality (see Engler). Both Marxist structuralism and the new historicism create an idealized system to read an empirical text, robbing the text of its linear history and its causality—that is, robbing it of its ontological being, of its very origins and primary meaning.

American literary naturalism is a product of its era. While it reaches all the way to the Second World War, the origins and its foundation date from about 1890 to

1910. Theodore Roosevelt was president for half this time, and his fame stemmed from a willingness to take on the trusts (at least to a point), to engage in imperial pursuits, and to keep alive the spirit of the West with the ideals that that spirit incarnated. Roosevelt was sympathetic to the rise of America as an imperial nation and to the acquisitions of the Philippines and Cuba. The census of 1890 marked the end of the American frontier, at least as it was famously defined by Frederick Jackson Turner, who saw this as the moment that America changed historical course and looked out to the world rather than inward toward its western frontier. The rise of industrial America after the Civil War, along with the corresponding rise of corporate fortunes, brought with it the corruption that became the corrective task of the progressive movement with its investigating journalists like David Graham Phillips, who paid for the exposure of corruption with his life, assassinated by a distraught anti-crusader. These movements swept up a nation, including the naturalists, who participated in the transformation of an older world into something new: literary naturalism depicted what was at the end of the yellow brick road, what was going on behind the curtain, why an idealized nation had come to the end of its innocence.

This essay has been an exercise in variations on these themes. We have examined the idea of force as the major naturalistic writers in America have depicted it, and we have cataloged the various responses to the forms of force: combative in Norris, conciliatory in Dreiser, politically driven in London, stoical in Crane. We have moved from a sense of inevitability (Dreiser), to a willingness to combat the universe of force (Crane), to assigning thematic significance to the idea of force as it is played out in war and in the big-game hunt and deep-sea fishing and other forms of the arena (Hemingway). Naturalism has a center and takes its meaning from the variation of responses to that center.

Naturalism has been attacked for presenting a deterministic view of life, but that view has been more reinforced than contested by recent genetic and DNA theories. Naturalism found a complementary philosophical system in historicism—the belief that each age or culture has a controlling Geist or spirit, a central documentable meaning. Recent movements like Ludwig von Bertalanffy's system theory has challenged the naturalists' order, and the novels of Don DeLillo work a very different order of literary assumption. That we can today read the early naturalists with appreciation proves that such cultural paradigms (that is, systems of reality) are more a state of mind than a physical barrier to a sense of truth. Naturalism still awakens a sense of experience, and while we move through different realities as we move from naturalism to modernism to postmodernism, we can still find in its best expressions moments of conflict and resolution that apply to our own sense of life. (This is why a novel like *Sister Carrie* is by definition a "masterpiece": it goes beyond its own generation and tells a story for the ages.) For close to a full century—1870 to 1945 in France and America combined—literary naturalism was an availing when not prevailing literary mode. And while it has been long displaced, it still speaks to us—which is to say that when seen in its proper historical context, it still lives.

WORKS CITED

Barthes, Roland. S/Z. Trans. Richard Miller. New York: Hill and Wang, 1974.

Bertalanffy, Ludwig von. *General Systems Theory*. New York: G. Braziller, 1968.

Dreiser, Theodore. *The Financier*. 1912. New York: Dell, 1961.

Durkheim, Émile. *On Suicide*. Intro. Richard Sennett. Trans. Robin Buss. New York: Penguin, 2006.

Engler, Rudolf. "The Making of the *Cours de linguistic générale*." *The Cambridge Companion to Saussure*. Ed. Carol Sanders. Cambridge: Cambridge University Press, 2004. 47–58.

Lehan, Richard. "The Biological Model." *American Realism*. San Diego: Greenhaven, 2000. 69–78.

———. *Theodore Dreiser: His World and His Novels*. Carbondale: Southern Illinois University Press, 1969.

Martin, Ronald E. *American Literature and the Universe of Force*. Durham: Duke University Press, 1981.

Norris, Frank. "The Frontier Gone at Last." *The Responsibilities of the Novelist*. New York: Doubleday, Doran, 1901. 69–81.

———. *The Octopus*. 1901. Boston: Houghton Mifflin, 1958.

Scott, Howard. *Introduction to Technocracy*. New York: John Day, 1933.

Seidenberg, Robert. *Post-Historic Man*. Chapel Hill: University of North Carolina Press, 1950

Simmel, Georg. *Philosophy of Money*. Marburg: Metropolis-Verlag, 2000.

Tonnies, Ferdinand. *Community and Society*. Trans. Charles P. Loomis. East Lansing: Michigan State University Press, 1957.

Veblen, Thorstein. *The Theory of the Leisure Class*. New York: Penguin, 2006.

Vivas, Eliseo. "Dreiser: An Inconsistent Mechanist." *Ethics* 47 (1938): 498–508.

Weber, Max. *The Protestant Ethic and the "Spirit" of Capitalism*. Trans. Peter Baehr. New York: Penguin, 2002.

CHAPTER 3

....

NATURE IN NATURALISM

....

BERT BENDER

FIRST-TIME readers of American naturalists such as Stephen Crane, Jack London, Frank Norris, and Theodore Dreiser might justifiably wonder what naturalism has to do with nature. It's easy to see how London's famous stories of the north feature landscapes from those latitudes, but what about the other naturalists? Expecting to find scenes from the green, or at least the white world, one finds instead the squalor of Crane's Bowery, Norris's San Francisco, or Dreiser's Chicago. Aren't these naturalists supposed to be nature writers? And those who might want to approach this question from another angle will find little help in such recent volumes as *Literature and Nature: Four Centuries of Nature Writing* (2001), where the editors avoid any mention of naturalism and include only two famous stories from that movement, Crane's "The Open Boat" and London's "To Build a Fire." Worse, the editors' only comment about these two pieces is that they describe the "struggle for survival" and serve mainly to "question American self-confidence and technological prowess" (Keegan and McKusick 771). If, having gone this far in their efforts to understand what naturalism has to do with nature, students can take comfort in knowing that even Henry James shared their confusion. Grappling with the meaning of naturalism in his 1880 review of Zola's *Nana*, James wrote testily that "the only business of naturalism is to be—natural" ("Nana" 91). He felt that the novel contained only "filth" and he wondered how Zola could "call that vision of things . . . *nature*" (92). James went on to suggest that "The mighty mother, in her blooming richness" would "blush" at Zola's presentation of herself, and he demanded to know "on what authority does M. Zola represent nature to us" in this way (92)?

The best way to clear up this confusion is to underscore the point that American literary realism (including the later and more pessimistic variety we think of as naturalism) arose largely in response to the scientific revolution that began in the 1830s with the discovery of geological time. As Lyell's *Principles of Geology* (1830–33) helped clear Darwin's way in formulating his theory of evolution by means of natural selection, the *Origin of Species* contributed to Lyell's own new work in *The Geological Evidences of the Antiquity of Man, with Remarks on Theories of the Origin of Species by Variation* (1863), and, more importantly, to the book published that same year by Thomas Henry Huxley, *Evidence as to Man's Place in Nature*. The idea of studying the human's place in nature—that is, to study human nature as a branch of Darwinian natural history—absolutely displaced the work of earlier writers such as Emerson or Thoreau, who believed that the soul transcends nature.

Darwinian evolution transformed the face of "nature," shattering the idea that nature exists in a state of grand repose and projecting instead a reality of struggle, competition, and violent change—not only among plants and animals, but in human society and even within the individual chaotic mind. During the first decades of the Darwinian revolution, the young, self-described realists such as W. D. Howells and Henry James showed little interest in the supposed beauty and simplicity of rural life and were inclined instead to present scenes of city life, wherein the nature of civilized humanity could be studied with ease. They echoed new work in anthropology and sociology that reflected evolutionary change and emphasized the origins of marriage in the capture of brides. Like most writers of their generation, they took comfort in the idea that Anglo-Saxon and, especially, American civilization had evolved to such a high state that we scarcely resembled the "savage" or "barbaric" humans who still occupied the lower fringes of society. These unfortunates (particularly Native Americans and African Americans) were usually to be found only at a safe distance from the civilized town square and seemed doomed to evolutionary extinction. Of course, even civilized whites were descended from the lower primates, but writers could smile at their characters' faintly vestigial animality and take heart in the idea that evolution was constantly lifting us to ever higher planes.

But as the Darwinian revolution developed, affecting every field of thought, realist narratives began to shift from comic to more tragic presentations of people's place in nature. The most disturbing problem had arisen from Darwin's prediction in the *Origin of Species* that "psychology will be based on a new foundation, that of the necessary acquirement of each mental power and capacity by gradation" (488). Within a decade after Darwin had driven that point home with startling force in *The Descent of Man, and Selection in Relation to Sex* (1871) and *The Expression of the Emotions in Man and Animal* (1872), William James began formulating the first evolutionary psychology, *The Principles of Psychology* (1890), and young novelists were exploring the Darwinian unconscious. By the mid-1890s, naturalist novelists such as Harold Frederic and Stephen Crane would begin dramatizing what they called the "chaos" of their characters' minds.

Although the realists/naturalists agreed that human nature was their essential subject, they sharply disagreed on how to define that nature. It is important to realize that, while the evolutionary view of life was reshaping virtually every discipline, even biologists, including Darwin and Wallace themselves, disagreed on just exactly how evolution by means of natural selection proceeds. Similarly, while the realists/naturalists all assumed an evolutionary reality of some kind, they differed in their interpretations of evolution and human nature. Sharp disagreements often arose even among writers who considered themselves Darwinists, especially when writers from different social points of view sought to represent the evolution of sexual difference and racial difference. Moreover, such disagreements became even more complicated during the decades surrounding 1900, when a number of anti-Darwinian theories arose to challenge the theory of natural selection. Known in the history of science as "the eclipse of Darwinism," this movement ended only in 1942, with what Julian Huxley called "The Modern Synthesis" of Mendelian genetics and natural selection. During the "eclipse," writers could project the evolutionary "reality" in various ways, some embracing theories that best supported their own views in the social disagreements over sexual or racial difference, or over questions concerning eugenics or the possibility of evolutionary progress. Some writers aligned themselves with particular anti-Darwinian theories that would support narratives wherein some higher power such as "love" (as in Joseph LeConte's *Evolution*, 1888) or "creative evolution" (as in Henri Bergson's *Creative Evolution*, 1911) promises to lift us beyond the gross workings of natural selection.

Although the realists/naturalists produced narratives that interpreted human nature and evolution in a variety of ways, they agreed in general that the human's place is *in* nature; and they continued in this way well beyond the period of time that was long delineated in the title of the leading journal, *American Literary Realism, 1865–1910* (the dates were recently dropped from the title). Just as many novels from the years surrounding the Scopes Trial (1925) reflected our culture's intense interest in the controversies over Darwinism, many literary works of the present time share the assumption that the human being exists in nature, particularly those works that examine the human's place in the ecological web. And to help clarify this context in the study of American literary realism and naturalism, it is worth noting that the contemporary scholars (mostly in philosophy and psychology, and none in literature) associated with The Center for Naturalism underscore the point that their guiding philosophy is "that human beings are fully included in nature" (*Center*); that is, without absolute free will or recourse to any "sky hooks" to lift the mind above the biological fray.

The realists/naturalists construed human nature in a variety of ways, depending in large part on the particular writer's point of view as the stream of evolutionary thought developed over time—that is, as a number of theorists sought to reinforce or redefine Darwinian evolution. To illustrate this point it is useful to note the example of Henry James, even though few would describe him as a naturalist. By considering James's keen interest in Darwinian evolution in the 1870s and '80s, we can better understand how the first currents of evolutionary thought developed over time to inform not only works by naturalists such as Jack London, but a wide range of other narratives by writers such as Charles W. Chesnutt and F. Scott Fitzgerald.

Only four years after James expressed confusion and distaste for Zola's form of naturalism, he was referring to himself as "quite the Naturalist"—after having visited Millbank Prison to take notes for scenes in his 1886 novel *The Princess Casamassima* (Edel 315). But he had long since become a kind of naturalist. He had met both

Darwin and Huxley and was well aware that the struggle for survival includes what Darwin called "the sexual struggle," for no organism can evolve without achieving reproductive success. Thus both he and his colleague in founding American realism, Howells, fixed their attention on Darwin's theory of sexual selection. This was the underlying subject of the famous story he gave us in his mid-thirties, "Daisy Miller: A Study." The subject of his "study" is not the title character, Daisy, but his main character, John Winterbourne, and how he came to miss the opportunity James presented him when the "pretty American girl" (Daisy) came to stand before him "in a garden" (309). Though this would be one of countless courtship narratives that explored Darwin's theory of sexual selection during those years, its tragic conclusion is often misunderstood. In James's study, the courtship fails not because of Daisy's melodramatic death or because she selected another male, but because Winterbourne "had lost his instinct in this matter, and his reason could not help him" (314). And the consequences for him are graver than most realize: in the "garden" of life, from the evolutionary point of view, the prize goes only to those who obey the first law and achieve reproductive success. There will be no evolutionary future for Winterbourne. The story is replete with Darwinian imagery of the courting male, but even though Winterbourne possesses one of the male's important secondary sexual characters for attracting a female, a moustache (James shows him "smiling and curling his moustache" [319]), he cannot compete in the sexual struggle as do successful Darwinian males, by either dancing or singing, or by battling with his competitors. He falters at a crucial moment in his courtship when the thought that Daisy "was surrounded by half-a-dozen moustaches" in Rome "checked [his] impulse to go straightway to see her" (333).

James explains that his hero lost his "instinctive certitude" (356) by having lived so long in Geneva, the "metropolis of Calvinism" (306), where he "had become dishabituated to the American tone" (314). Now, if at this point we could ask of James the same question he asked of Zola—"on what authority does [he] represent [human] nature to us" in this way?—the obvious first answer is that James was relying on Darwin's analysis of the male's role in the sexual struggle. But James was also relying on the authority of contemporary theorists of his own time, such as his brother William. In his *Atlantic Monthly* essay of 1880, "Great Men, Great Thoughts, and the Environment," William James not only championed Darwin's work but extended it by explaining "the function of the environment in *mental* evolution" (455). Praising Darwin's "triumphant originality" in showing how spontaneous variations are subjected to the environmental forces of natural selection and sexual selection, James begins his study of mental evolution by citing "the facts . . . drawn from the lower strata of the mind . . . from the region of intelligence which man possesses in common with the brutes," and by emphasizing how "excessively instable" the "human brain" is (443, 456). But James goes on to explain how mental variations—such as those that tilt an individual "towards masculinity or femininity, towards strength or weakness, towards health or disease, and towards divergence from the parent type"—are acted upon by the individual's *social* environment (444). Just as the geographical environment "selects" certain variations above others, the "habits and associations" one gains from one's social environment are crucial to that person's evolutionary fate (455). This is not to say that William would have agreed with Henry's fictional exploration of mental evolution in his portrait of Winterbourne; only that, by considering this kind of scientific background during the 1870s and 1880s, readers can better appreciate the unexpectedly powerful role that nature plays in narratives such as "Daisy Miller."

Assuredly, it can be discouraging to know that critical readings of naturalist fiction should be informed by a knowledge of relevant developments in the stream of evolutionary thought. But readers who are willing to follow up on this point will not only achieve a clearer understanding of literary history, but gain respect for, and insight into, particular works by the authors whom they most admire. It is a great disservice to writers such as Stephen Crane, Kate Chopin, or Edith Wharton, for example, to ignore both the extent to which they were inspired by Darwinian thought and their ingenuity in testing and interpreting it in their own studies of human nature. Also, it would be a mistake to imagine that it is either impossible or not worth our while to track this line of thought among the naturalists.

THE COURTSHIP PLOT AND SEXUAL SELECTION

At the risk of oversimplifying the issues in question, it helps to realize how much of the evolutionary puzzle in literature can be traced back to the theory of sexual selection. Yet this should be no surprise, for Darwinian evolution depends on reproduction. As Darwin wrote in the *Origin of Species*, there is "one general law leading to the advancement of all organic beings—namely, multiply, vary, let the strongest live and the weakest die" (208). Taking this into account, novelists realized that Darwin had re-invigorated the age-old courtship plot and that his theory of sexual selection was the key to their own further explorations of human reality.

Many pre-Darwinian writers from Shakespeare to Jane Austen had observed features of human courtship that were faintly animalistic—such as the male's passion and combativeness in his pursuit of the female and her coyness in judging her suitors' strength or beauty. But none had anticipated the way that Darwin's theory of evolution would establish the human's common descent with the so-called lower animals, much less the way that his theory of sexual selection would define courtship as part of the general struggle for existence, the evolutionary prize going to those who best succeed in propagating the species. According to Darwin's theory, then, "the sexual struggle" involves mainly (1) the male's efforts to "drive away or kill [his] rivals" in order that he may possess the female; (2) the male's effort "to excite or charm" the female, in hopes that she will select him; and (3) the female's power to select the male who most pleases her, usually based on the criteria of his strength and beauty (*Descent* 2: 398). As Darwin repeatedly noted, one should not be misled by the seeming simplicity of these main features, for sexual selection is "an extremely complex affair" (*Descent* 1: 296). This is certainly the case in the realm of fiction, where naturalist courtship plots often reflect not only a particular writer's social point of view, but his or her interest in certain aspects of Darwinian thought that were being developed in his or her own time, perhaps in the work of a favored theorist such as Joseph LeConte, Ernst Haeckel, Henri Bergson, or Havelock Ellis.

Realist and naturalist writers agreed in general with Darwin's assertion that "the season of love is that of battle" and that the "law of battle" pertains within the human community (*Descent* 2: 48, 325–26). In *The Portrait of a Lady* (1881), for example, James names one of Isabel's suitors Lord Warburton but suggests that his nature as a warring male is now scarcely evident in his highly civilized state, as when James notices his "large, white, well-shaped fist" (196). A decade later, though, Stephen Crane focuses on Maggie's favorable response to her lover Pete's stories of his fights: "It appeared that he was invincible in fights" and that he "disdained the strength of a world full of fists" (*Maggie* 27). Later still, Frank Norris created a melodramatic "law of battle" scene in which McTeague breaks Marcus Schouler's arm, and he noted that when the "bestial fury" subsided, one of the female observers giggled "hysterically" (*McTeague* 430). And in *The Sun Also Rises* (1926), the boxer Cohn's appeal as a competitor for Brett Ashley is exceeded only by that of the bullfighter Romero. Generally speaking, as writers began to take Darwin's theory of common descent more seriously, the male's combativeness gradually emerged as the most difficult problem to be overcome in social evolution.

Similarly, many realist/naturalist narratives from the 1870s well into the twentieth century feature courtship scenes of music and dance (or "love-antics," to use Darwin's term), wherein characters of either sex seek to excite or charm their prospective mates. Working with Darwin's analysis of biological beauty as an adaptive strategy in the struggle for existence, especially his theory that birdsong and music evolved by means of sexual selection, Edmund Gurney produced his revolutionary aesthetics of music in *The Power of Music* (1880), and nearly every novelist produced scenes of musical courtship. But here, too, there is a discernible development over the decades in the authors' views of human nature. In Howells's *The Lady of the Aroostook* (1879) the heroine's church-singing is both "like a mermaid's" and "like an angel's," and it causes "the long red neck" of one man to perspire (113, 258). In the late 1890s, both Harold Frederic (in *The Damnation of Theron Ware*) and Kate Chopin (in *The Awakening*) would feature powerfully erotic scenes in which music by Frederic Chopin arouses the characters' sexual emotions in explicitly Darwinian terms. But only a few years later, Frank Norris dramatized the power of music in quite other terms, linking it to the kind of evolutionary evil that his mentor Joseph LeConte traced back to the lower stages of existence (LeConte 365). In describing the character Laura's response to a musical performance in *The Pit* (1903), Norris relies on key passages from *The Descent of Man* and *The Expression of the Emotions in Man and Animals*, but he names the male musician Corthell and arranges for his melodramatic performance of Liszt's *Mephisto Walzer*. In the following decades, however, spurred by both popular Freudianism and the first strains of the jazz age, many naturalist narratives affirmed the expression of erotic emotions that Norris had sought to repress. Both Sherwood Anderson and F. Scott Fitzgerald, for example, give us many such scenes, often drawing on Darwinian theory through Havelock Ellis's *Studies in the Psychology of Sex* (1897–1928) and *The Dance of Life* (1923). In *Dark Laughter* (1925), for example, Anderson celebrates "The dance of life!" and seeks to heal his characters' sexual repression by advising, "Dance the dance out to the end. Listen, do you hear the music?" (92).

An especially interesting development concerning courtship scenes of music and dance in naturalist fiction occurs during the Harlem Renaissance. But the back-drop to this involves literary history's failure to appreciate why many African Americans were not just interested in, but felt liberated by, Darwin's theory of racial evolution. He maintained that the "so-called races of men" are not "constant" or fixed by design, like the leopard's spots, as many southerners maintained. Arguing that racial differences have merely evolved, Darwin explained why marked differences in skin color would have been produced more by sexual selection than by different climates (*Descent* 1: 248–50). Pointing out that there is no "universal standard of beauty with respect to the human body" and that "each race . . . possesses its own innate ideal standard of beauty," Darwin argued that marked differences in skin color were established in the remote past, when humanity was in a state of "savagery" and when the most powerful males in particular tribes left the largest numbers of offspring (*Descent* 2: 353–54). Because "people of each tribe admire their own characteristics," the dominant males would have mated with the "most strongly characterized" females, and through this process the particular characteristic (e.g., darkness of skin color) would have "been slowly and gradually exaggerated" (*Descent* 2: 384). Charles W. Chesnutt was the first African American novelist to embrace Darwin's theory of racial evolution, believing that nature's "laws" of natural selection and sexual selection were more just than American law and southern traditions. Chesnutt (who was so light-skinned that he sometimes passed for white) wrote of light-skinned blacks who passed for white and whose biological attributes made them attractive mates for whites. Perhaps because of his own social position along "the color line," Chesnutt imagined that the race problem in America would be resolved only through further evolution and complete racial amalgamation. For this reason, Chesnutt sometimes presented his own prejudicial portraits of darker people as being outcast or left behind by evolution itself, and this theme—the conflict within the African American community between those of lighter and darker skin—would be hotly debated among novelists of the Harlem Renaissance.

While most of the Harlem novelists affirmed Darwinian theory, they were further conflicted over the question that W. E. B. Du Bois posed in a symposium published in the influential journal *Crisis*, titled "The Negro in Art: How Shall He Be Portrayed?" The underlying issue in Du Bois' question involved the added complication that popular Freudianism had brought to the discussion of the race problem. Some white and African American novelists (e.g., Carl Van Vechten or Claude McKay) sought to affirm the race's so-called "sexual primitivism," as an indication of its good mental health—that is, its freedom from white America's neurosis of sexual repression. But Du Bois and others hoped to portray a more elevated, spiritual love among African Americans. Thus, while some writers affirmed the blues as the

truest expression of African American nature, Du Bois maintained that the soul
song, sorrow song, or spiritual best expressed the African American reality.

Two Harlem writers, Claude McKay and Rudolph Fisher, were especially attuned
to the evolutionary biology of their time, particularly as it pertained to the evolution
of race. Fisher, a physician who had taught embryology at Howard University and coauthored articles in scientific journals, believed that evolution was the "savior" of
modern science (McCluskey xiv), and McKay recalled having discovered "suddenly
like a comet . . . the romance of science in Huxley's *Man's Place in Nature* and Haeckel's
The Riddle of the Universe," key elements in what he called the "emotional-realist
thread" that defined his work (*Long Way* 12, 250). But Fisher and McKay disagreed
with W. E. B. Du Bois, whose own credentials in modern science were impeccable.

The difference between these writers' views on music and human nature is evident in their scenes set in Harlem cabarets. In *Dark Princess* (1928), Du Bois developed the theme that he had presented in *The Souls of Black Folk* (1903), that the soul
song or sorrow song is the essential black music. Thus, his brief cabaret scene features a degraded woman who sings "her vulgar 'blues'" with writhing movements
and an unnatural "harsh shrill voice" (66) that appeals mostly to the whites and bores
the blacks. Du Bois' hero is only momentarily affected by this kind of music, which
the novel finally overwhelms with spontaneous outbursts of "Go down, Moses!" and
"I am seekin' for a City" (310). McKay, on the other hand, celebrated the blues and
even the African drum beat because they best expressed the unrepressed racial life.
Thus, in *Home to Harlem* (1928), McKay describes the blues rhythm as "simple-clear
and quivering . . . like a primitive dance of war or love" suggesting the "sacred frenzy
of phallic celebrations" (196–97). And in a chapter called "Spring in Harlem," he
reunites his hero and heroine in a cabaret scene wherein, at the first notes of the
music, the dancers showed "all their teeth" and "started shivering for their partners
to come." Soon, they all "picked up the refrain and jazzed and shouted with delirious
joy" (296–97). Similarly, though not quite as boldly as McKay, Fisher (a jazz musician
in his own right) produced cabaret scenes that celebrated so-called primitive music
and dance in a number of short stories, such as "Common Meter" (1930); and, in *The
Walls of Jericho* (1928), he playfully suggested that "a rising tide of rhythm" in the
music of that era might be America's best hope for allaying racial fears (82). Orches-
trating this scene at the racial improvement society's annual ball, Fisher remarks that
on the dance floor, people of all varieties of skin color "rubbed joyous elbows, laughing, mingling, forgetting differences"—until the music stopped (82, 74).

Darwin's theory of sexual selection gives the female a powerful role in influencing evolutionary development—her power to select her mate and thus produce
such physical attributes as the increasingly intricate designs on the peacock's plumes
or, among humans, relative hairlessness. But biologists and novelists alike have long
disagreed about the female's freedom to choose, and about the particular male
attributes that most impress her. Darwin contributed to these disagreements by
writing that among human beings, males had gained much of the power to select in
primitive times, when marriage originated in the capture of brides. Thus novelists
from the 1870s on have presented this aspect of human nature in a variety of ways.

For example, wanting to project evolutionary progress that led to a genteel society, Howells gave us many heroines who select strong but gentle males who scarcely exhibit the kind of passion that drives the Darwinian male, and he suggests that behind the female's unconscious choice is a higher evolutionary power somewhat like manifest destiny, promising evolutionary progress if not utopia. At the same time, Henry James gave us a number of heroines like Isabel Archer (*Portrait of a Lady*) or Verena Tarrant (*The Bostonians*) who naively believe in their freedom to select or even not to select a male. But, revealing both his belief in the violent origins of marriage and his own views on women's rights, James's narratives end when such women are captured by men of exceptional mental strength.

Perhaps the most impressive exploration of female choice in naturalist fiction is Kate Chopin's study of her heroine Edna Pontellier in *The Awakening* (1899). Anyone with a serious interest in Chopin should read what was certainly her favorite chapter in *The Descent of Man*, chapter 14 of volume 2, which she mined in creating Edna Pontellier and other women such as Mrs. Mallard (in "The Story of an Hour"). Although Darwin takes up the question of "Choice exerted by the female" in this chapter on birds, Chopin followed his assertion that "the mental powers of birds . . . do not fundamentally differ from ours" (*Descent* 2: 124). Thus, working with Darwin's point that "every male of the same species" does not "equally excite or attract the female" (2: 99), Chopin first establishes that Edna's sexual antipathy toward her husband was only natural, and she then supports that analysis by drawing on Darwin's discussion of female pigeons who refuse to mate with males selected for them by breeders. One of Edna's ways of asserting her independence from Mr. Pontellier is to arrange to have her own "pigeon house." Also, building on Darwin's point that the female pheasant not only selects her mates, but sometimes actively courts the male, Chopin describes Edna's active role in pursuing her affairs with two other males. Described by the Darwin-like Dr. Mandelet as "some beautiful, sleek animal waking up in the sun" (952), Edna first awakens to the sexual power of music in a memorable scene that closely echoes Darwin's description of such emotions. Moreover, Chopin arranges for Edna to defend her choice of a lover. Denying that women "select" for the typical qualities that Darwin imagined civilized women found most attractive—social position and wealth—Edna explains that she is drawn to her lover, Robert, because of his eyes, nose, lips, and so forth: that is, apparently, because she finds him beautiful and because she herself is "happy to be alive" (965). Chopin was only one of many writers to feel liberated by Darwin's theory of human nature.

Among the innumerable versions of women exerting their power to select in naturalist narratives is Edith Wharton's well-titled story, "The Choice" (1916). Here another married woman feels antipathy for her husband and selects a lover with the appeal that he is somewhat androgynous (as is Edna's lover, Robert) compared with her hyper-masculine husband. But in the final crisis, when the two males are joined in battle, she cries out for her husband, unconsciously revealing her desire for a powerful, even somewhat brutal mate. Similarly, the character Edith in Harold Frederic's *The Market-Place* (1899) frankly acknowledges her desire for the ruthless financier Thorpe, an "exceptionally strong and masterful character" who can reduce her "brain to a sort of porridge" (160–62). But in another narrative, Wharton gave us a woman (in *The Custom of the Country*, 1913) who elevates her social position by choosing a series of ever-more wealthy mates, even abandoning her own child along the way. In *Sister Carrie* (1900), Dreiser presents Carrie's power to select more sympathetically. After Carrie is more or less caught by her first mate, a "rudimentary" man named Drouet, she leaves him for Hurstwood, who "she instinctively felt . . . was stronger and higher"—until she meets Ames (58, 82). Now, with "an ideal to contrast men by" (239), Carrie refuses to sleep with Hurstwood, but because Ames is beyond her reach, Dreiser last pictures Carrie in a state of wistful loneliness.

Still, in the early decades of the twentieth century a number of novelists continued to place their faith in the female's power to select as the key to possible evolutionary progress. In *The Valley of the Moon* (1913), for example, Jack London produces a promising marriage by emphasizing his heroine's care in selecting her mate. Repeatedly asking herself, "*Is this the man?*" she rejects a number of suitors, one, for example, who was too brutal in his battle with other suitors, and one who was too soft and ineffectual (13). She selects a man, Billy, who has the requisite biological features of strength (he is a champion boxer) and beauty (in his physical features and in his grace as a dancer). London's key points are that Billy is a gentle man who fights only when fighting is necessary, and that, in touching the heroine, Saxon Brown, Billy exhibits the kind of sensitivity that Havelock Ellis was advocating at the time (in *Sexual Selection in Man*) as an essential part of the psychology of sex. Thus, having found a man who does not arouse "the old sex antagonism" that Saxon had felt with other men, she solved what London calls "the pre-nuptial problem of selecting a husband" (78, 117). Then, after Saxon solves "the post-nuptial problem of retaining a husband's love" (117; here again London draws on Havelock Ellis), London's ideal couple can proceed on their quest to find a way of life best suited to deal with the larger evolutionary problem that London addresses, the world's population explosion, including the social ills that then plagued Oakland, California.

Some final examples of naturalist fiction that centered on the female's power to select are to be found in several novels of the Harlem Renaissance. After a half century of realist/naturalist narratives that had focused on courtship as the essential pathway to the evolutionary future, and on the civilized female's power to select, novelists of the Harlem Renaissance generally agreed that any further racial evolution would depend largely on the female's choice of mates. While other realists and naturalists had looked ahead to possible "new" men and women, the Harlem novelists' more immediate sense of a brutal past propelled their interest in racial "betterment," "uplift," and "the Younger Generation" to whom Alain Locke dedicated his landmark anthology, *The New Negro* (1925). Nella Larsen, for example, was greatly affected by the novelist T. S. Stribling's belief that "no people can become civilized until the woman has the power of choice among males" (Davis 153). But Larsen's own narratives on racial evolution were tragically complicated by her own position along the color line as a woman of mixed race and by her intensely introspective Freudianism. The heroine of *Quicksand* (1928), Helga Crane, is first drawn to a black man, largely for the Darwinian reason that his "deep voice" was "particularly pleasing" and that it produced in her "a mystifying yearning which sang and throbbed in her"; but these emotions simultaneously produce in her "something very like hysteria," the classic Freudian symptom of sexual repression (19–20). Thus Helga flees from this opportunity to select a mate and then, in Denmark, selects against a white suitor because of "some impulse of racial antagonism" (84). She has a "curious feeling of repugnance" both for his physical features (his, hair, his voice, the shape of his nose) and for what he brings to mind regarding American history: she tells him, "I'm not for sale . . . to any white man" (86–87). Finally, back in America, she is drawn by strains of church music into an encounter with the black "Reverend Mr. Pleasant Green." After a quick marriage they return to his "primitive flock" in Alabama, where she sinks into the quicksand of primitive religion and sexuality. Her "palpitating, amorous" emotions sprang up in her "like rank weeds . . . with a vitality so strong that it devoured all shoots of reason," leaving her not only with the several children she had contributed to her "despised race" but an overpowering sexual "aversion" to Green and his belief that his persistent love-making is "a natural thing, an act of God" (125, 127).

Other Harlem novelists, however, were committed to the idea of evolutionary progress and saw great promise in the female's power to select. In Du Bois' *Dark Princess*, the promising couple (Matthew Towns, a black man from Virginia, and Kautilya, a woman from India) meet at an international conference, "The Great Council of the Darker Peoples." In an incident there, Matthew stands out as a beautiful and combative—that is, Darwinian—male, when he drives away a white man who made a pass at Kautilya. As Kautilya later recalls, "you knocked him down quite beautifully," and "I had a curious sense of some great inner meaning to your act" (17). Eventually, the two consummate their love and produce a son whom Kautilya's countrymen view as a "Messenger and Messiah to all the Darker Worlds!" (311). Projecting an evolutionary future that was attuned to the music of "Go down, Moses!" and definitely not the blues, *Dark Princess* is something between "outright propaganda" and "quaint romance," as Arnold Rampersad remarks (204); but it is scarcely more of a romance than Frank Norris's narrative of Anglo-Saxon supremacy in *The Octopus*, which Du Bois had in mind.

In a much more inventive variation on the theme of female choice in the Harlem Renaissance, in *The Walls of Jericho* Rudolph Fisher introduces a "young Titan" of a male, noting that "an acknowledged master of men is usually attractive to women" (13, 80). Indeed, the heroine Linda quickly selects the hero Shine at the "General Improvement Association's Annual Costume Ball," after he had rescued her from an offensive male: she "flung herself impulsively toward him" (132). Fisher eventually sends his ideal couple "into another land," toward a scene overspread with "sunrise like a promise . . . straight into the kindling sky," but not until he has subjected both lovers, especially the titanic male, to his own kind of "general improvement." Linda initiates this improvement in Shine by taking him to church, where they hear a sermon counseling that a man's tendency to "boast that he is evil and merciless and hard" is only a shield to hide his true spirit of compassion and gentleness. Developing this point, in part by having Linda frequently advise Shine that mere muscle isn't everything, and that he isn't as hard as he pretends he is, Fisher suggests that much of Shine's violence stems from his sexual repression, a neurosis that is most evident when Shine turns into "a gigantic madman" in a battle with his sexual rival. Thus, writing during the years when popular Freudianism was at its height, Fisher the physician suggests again and again that Linda and, especially, Shine will enter the evolutionary future only if they overcome the sexual repression that each exhibits along the way when they block impulses to reach out to the other. Fittingly, a key moment in Fisher's effort to improve these two lovers comes in a hospital, where Shine is a patient. When, "not fully aware of his gesture," Shine reaches out to Linda, she responds, creating a spark that Fisher describes as "the closing of a switch, the making of a circuit through which leaped new, strange, shattering impulses" (260–61).

RELATED ELEMENTS IN THE
PUZZLE OF HUMAN NATURE

While we can learn a great deal about the naturalists' views of human nature by focusing on the courtship plot and the theory of sexual selection, it is important to note that some naturalist novels and many short stories are not structured around the courtship plot (e.g., *The Red Badge of Courage* and "To Build a Fire") and that the naturalists were also quite interested in several related pieces of the evolutionary puzzle, such as heredity, the environment, and other elements of evolutionary psychology not directly related to courtship. The naturalists' views on these issues vary, but, in general, their increasing pessimism about biological determinism follows certain key developments in evolutionary thought over the decades. One very important example came in 1889, when August Weissman was credited for disproving the Lamarckian principle that traits acquired through training or education could be passed on to one's offspring. This diminishment of the Lamarckian possibility gave renewed emphasis to the power of heredity in determining one's fate—a power that grew even more oppressive with Ernst Haeckel's studies in embryology over the next decade, and finally with the rediscovery of Mendelian genetics shortly after the turn of the century.

One of the unfortunate effects of the growing emphasis on heredity was to reinforce the already virulent strain of racism that promoted the idea of Anglo-Saxon supremacy. Virtually every naturalist was affected by this malaise, whether in portraits of African Americans, Native Americans, Mexican Americans, Asian Americans, Jews, Irish, or Southern Europeans. Though it is hard to imagine any uglier examples of Anglo-Saxonism in American writing than those to be found in the novels of Thomas Dixon Jr., Frank Norris comes close in his portraits of Maria Macapa, Zerkow (the red-headed Polish Jew), and their child in *McTeague*. Relying in part on his mentor Joseph LeConte's writings on mixed races, Norris describes the sickly, short-lived child as "a strange, hybrid little being . . . combining in its puny little body the blood of the Hebrew, the Pole, and the Spaniard" (431). Even with her much more impressive scientific credentials, Gertrude Stein's studies of characters such as the black woman Malanctha and the German women Anna and Lena (in *Three Lives*), as well as Julia Dehning (in *The Making of Americans*), suggest that such people's hereditary makeup leaves them in a nearly sub-human state. And writing only a short time later, F. Scott Fitzgerald combined the Darwinian elements of sexual selection with those of modern genetics to explain the tragic fate of Jay Gatsby. Fitzgerald was only one of many writers (such as Edith Wharton and Jack London) to have been influenced by Ernst Haeckel's *The Riddle of the Universe*. He was especially impressed by Haeckel's study of embryology and the idea that one's identity is determined at the moment of conception, leaving the individual locked by accident within "the chain of generations" (Haeckel 143); and his sense of hereditary determinism was powerfully reinforced by the widespread interest in eugenics that was fostered by E. G. Conklin at Princeton University. Partly from these elements, he produced demeaning portraits of blacks and Jews while constructing a character (Gatsby) whose life and death are subject to a number of accidents. The first and most important of these is the accident of his lowly birth, which his wealth and social glitter cannot hide from Daisy's selective eye, but his fate is further sealed by the famous automobile accident and finally by the "accidental" circumstances that Fitzgerald emphasizes in his description of the dead Gatsby afloat in his pool.

The environment as another shaping force in human nature did not engage the naturalists' interest to the extent that sexual selection did, perhaps because it was not so easily fitted to the courtship plot. Still, writers such as Stephen Crane, Jack London, and Eugene O'Neill depicted the environment created by American industry as a crushing influence on workers' lives and quite possibly their evolutionary fates. "The air in the collar and cuff establishment strangled" Maggie, causing her to realize that she was "surely shriveling in the hot, stuffy room" where other women bent over their machines like "mere mechanical contrivances." Thus, she began to worry about her "youth" and "to see the bloom upon her cheeks as valuable" (Crane 34). London, too, presents his heroine Saxon Brown as "an entrapped animal" in the laundry where she works. Before Saxon can find her way into the evolutionary future that London has in mind for her, she must escape the crushing conditions that are "enough to kill a dog" (4). In London's analysis, attuned to the emerging Freudian interest in female hysteria, Saxon's workplace posed an explicit threat to her reproductive health because the women's restricted and mechanically repetitive movements created an atmosphere of sexual repression that brought on occasional outbursts of hysteria. And even more melodramatically, the working environment of the steamship's low-ceilinged stokehole in Eugene O'Neill's *The Hairy Ape* (1921) caused the character Yank and his fellow firemen to walk with the stooped posture of apes.

Occasionally, naturalists such as Norris also drew on scientific theories that were only very tenuously connected to Darwinian evolution, such as Cesare Lombroso's *Criminal Man* (1876) and Max Nordau's *Degeneration* (1892), but there is a far more important, though unrecognized, trend in naturalist writing that gradually drew on Darwinian and related theories to explain and justify not the abnormal or monstrous, but the range of normality in human nature. That is, in our efforts to understand nature in naturalism, or the ways in which the realist/naturalist movement has explored human nature, it helps to remind ourselves how that approach to understanding humankind's place in nature was initiated by "the biological blow" that Darwinian evolution dealt "to human narcissism," according to Freud's famous remark (Freud 17: 141). Looking at the realist/naturalist movement in this way, it is clear that the first realists, such as Howells or James, were far less troubled by the blow than were older writers such as Melville or Tennyson, who received it as a great spiritual wound. Though the young Howells and James were no doubt troubled by the biological blow, they could both welcome it as the new world view that helped them shoulder their older rivals aside (as in James's critique of Hawthorne), and fend it off by imagining that, as highly civilized citizens of the new world, they were relatively untouched by the evolutionary past. They were encouraged by the evolutionary hierarchy that modern anthropology had erected, wherein the animals, certainly, and then the "savages" and "barbarians" served to define their difference as almost a new species of highly civilized Americans whose main worry was that, like Winterbourne, they might have become overcivilized.

Only later in Howells's career did he, and then naturalists such as Crane, London, Norris, and Chopin, begin bolder explorations of their characters' place within the community of common descent. Howells referred to his character Dylks (in *The Leatherwood God*, 1916) as a stallion, because of his sexual passion, and London suggests the animal nature in his character's name, Wolf Larsen (in *The Sea-Wolf*, 1904). In the heat of battle, Crane's soldiers in *The Red Badge of Courage* express many of the emotions that Darwin had described in *The Expression of the Emotions in Man and Animals*; and Norris described McTeague's "hereditary evil" (285) and the degenerate beast that lurked in and finally came to life in Vandover (in *Vandover and the Brute*, 1914). All these characters embody aberrations, to be overcome, in London's case, when the female selects against the brutal captain to signal his evolutionary extinction. Unlike these explorations of human nature, however, Kate Chopin's study of Edna Pontellier is a landmark in our culture's gradual awakening to, and acceptance of, the human's place within the community of common descent. Edna's awakening sexuality is certainly problematic in its threat to her marriage and because it leads to her own emotional instability, but Chopin gives her liberated character a certain dignity and beauty, as when Dr. Mandelet sees Edna "palpitant with the forces of life," with "no repression in her glance or gesture," like a "beautiful, sleek animal waking up in the sun" (952).

Chopin's prescient reference to Edna's freedom from repression echoes Darwin's pre-Freudian use of the term (in *The Expression of the Emotions in Man and Animals*), but it occurs in the history of naturalism at precisely the time when Freud was building on Darwin's analysis of sex and the emotions to construct his own theory of hysteria and related neuroses as arising from sexual repression. Inspired by Darwin, Chopin celebrated the daring idea that a woman's sexual emotions were natural and normal. Also, during the first decades of the twentieth century a number of other naturalists had begun to deal with the biological blow in similar ways. Whereas Howells had presented Bartley Hubbard's mere flirting as a kind of evolutionary weakness in *A Modern Instance* (1882), Dreiser would somewhat confessionally analyze the male's polygamous sexual appetite as normal though socially disruptive. Moreover, building on Darwin's analysis of the bisexual embryo (and subsequent studies of the same phenomenon by Havelock Ellis and Freud), a range of novelists such as London, Anderson, Stein, Fitzgerald, and Hemingway explored the normality of their own androgynous sensibilities. And many African American writers embraced Darwin's theory of race as justifying their claims to equal footing within the natural community of mankind, rather than outcasts by Biblical design. As T. S. Stribling wrote in *Birthright* (1922), a novel which created a great stir within the Harlem Renaissance, "what Christ did for theology, Darwin did for biology,—he democratized it" (219).

Such developments in naturalist thought certainly met with powerful resistance. Chopin's *The Awakening*, for example, was highly offensive even to readers such as Willa Cather. And a good many newly uncovered facts or supposed facts about evolutionary biology were so disturbing that only the most courageous writers could include them in their explorations of human nature. Some wondered, for example, whether the frog's sexual impulse, persistent even in males whose heads had been cut off, was related to that in human beings; whether cannibalism as a reproductive strategy among certain organisms reflected in any way on human "love"; what we can make of the startling sexual impulse among human infants; or to what extent the connection between sexual pleasure and pain might be considered within the range of human normality. In short, contemplating such questions about human nature, many naturalists grew increasingly introspective and shared what Gertrude Stein specified as her character's "deepest interest": in exploring "the varieties of human experience" and desiring "to partake of all human relations" (*Fernhurst* 19). By the time Stein wrote this (sometime between 1903 and 1905), naturalists had explored many new and troubling questions about the human being and his/her place in nature, but it would be a mistake to claim that the naturalist movement as a whole produced anything like a clear, general advance toward ultimate "truths." In her later work, Stein, for example, came under the sway of Bergson's *Creative Evolution*.

HUMAN NATURE AND THE ECOLOGICAL WEB

By 1913 at least one naturalist, Jack London, had extended his study of human nature to the point that he was prepared to write the first novel in American literature to explore what, from our point of view in the early twenty-first century, seems the most urgent question involving people's place in nature: how we can accept our place in the ecological web and devise sustainable economies. In *The Valley of the Moon*, London built on his impressive studies of Darwinian evolution to imagine a couple who overcome the personal and social troubles that his earlier characters had encountered regarding sexual selection and marriage and who then proceed to find a new way of life in small-scale farming. In this way, they save themselves from the industrial pollution and labor strife then troubling the San Francisco Bay area, help bring an end to large-scale farming's rape of the soil, suggest ways to deal with the world's exploding population, and also insure their own survival by preserving their marriage and achieving reproductive success. London's ambitious novel was certainly not the last word in literary naturalism. By the 1940s, Aldo Leopold and John Steinbeck were exploring ecological questions in their non-fictional works *A Sand County Almanac* (1949) and *The Log from the Sea of Cortez* (1941). And in *The Old Man and the Sea* (1952) Ernest Hemingway probed an essential feature of human nature that London and other naturalists before Steinbeck left untouched— Santiago's struggle to accept and deal not with his reproductive needs (as many other Hemingway characters must do), but with his need to kill and eat (i.e., the second of the two forces that move the world, as Freud put it, love and hunger).

Whatever questions involving humankind's place in nature might arise to shape naturalist fiction in years to come, it seems inevitable that the chief motive in generating such work will endure in our culture's general resistance to the idea that there *is* any human nature. Similarly, organizations like the Center for Naturalism will no doubt redouble their efforts to counter our culture's reluctance to embrace Darwinian evolution—its devotion to the ideas that human beings enjoy complete free will and that *super*natural forces define humanity. Still addressing the old question that Steinbeck posed in 1941 in *The Log from the Sea of Cortez*, why do we "so dread to think of our species as a species?" (266), the Center for Naturalism believes that, "by acknowledging our origins in evolution, the naturalist perspective" can enhance "our feeling of kinship with the other species with which we share this planet, and our desire to sustain and nurture the planet itself" (*Center*). Regarding recent American fiction, it is clear that the evolutionary view of humanity's place in nature is still a vibrant theme in a number of works such as T. C. Boyle's *Drop City* (2003). There, quite in the tradition of Jack London (including a reference to "To Build a Fire," 390–91), Boyle portrays a community of hippies in California who talk about "getting back to the earth" (16) and believe in free love; but as that experiment collapses of its own weight, he ends the book in celebrating an Alaskan couple's survival in the Alaskan wilderness. Like London, Boyle constructs this elemental social unit largely from the heroine's painstaking selection of her mate, whom we see at last looking around to appreciate "the natural order" while "heading home, . . . a man clothed in fur at the head of a team of dogs in a hard wild place, going home to his wife" (444).

WORKS CITED

Anderson, Sherwood. *Dark Laughter*. 1925. Mattituck, N.Y.: Aeonian, n.d.

Boyle, T. C. *Drop City*. London: Bloomsbury, 2003.

The Center for Naturalism. 9 Dec. 2008. http://centerfornaturalism.org.

Chopin, Kate. *The Awakening. The Complete Works of Kate Chopin*. Ed. Per Seyersted. Baton Rouge: Louisiana State University Press, 1969. 881–1000.

Crane, Stephen. *Maggie: A Girl of the Streets. Prose and Poetry*. New York: Library of America, 1984.

Darwin, Charles. *The Descent of Man, and Selection in Relation to Sex*. 1871. Princeton, N.J.: Princeton University Press, 1981. 2 vols. in 1.

———. *On the Origin of Species by Means of Natural Selection Or the Preservation of Favored Races in the Struggle for Life, and The Descent of Man and Selection in Relation to Sex*. 1859. New York: Modern Library, n.d.

Davis, Thadious M. *Nella Larsen: Novelist of the Harlem Renaissance, a Woman's Life Unveiled*. Baton Rouge: Louisiana State University Press, 1994.

Dreiser, Theodore. *Sister Carrie*. 1900. Ed. Donald Pizer. New York: Norton, 1970.

Du Bois, W. E. B. *Dark Princess: A Romance*. 1928. Millwood, N.Y.: Kraus-Thomson, 1974.

Edel, Leon. *Henry James: A Life*. New York: Harper and Row, 1985.

Fisher, Rudolph. *The Walls of Jericho*. 1928. New York: Arno, 1969.

Frederic, Harold. *The Market-Place*. 1899. Fort Worth: Texas Christian University Press, 1981.

Freud, Sigmund. *The Standard Edition of the Complete Psychological Works of Sigmund Freud*. Ed. James Strachey. London: Hogarth Press and the Institute of Psycho-Analysis, 1953–74. 24 vols.

Haeckel, Ernst. *The Riddle of the Universe at the Close of the Nineteenth Century*. New York: Harper, 1900.

Howells, William Dean. *The Lady of the Aroostook*. Boston: Houghton, Osgood, 1879.

James, Henry. "Daisy Miller: A Study." *Collected Stories*. Ed. John Bayley. Vol. 1. New York: Everyman's Library, 1999. 2 vols. 305–64.

———. "Nana." *The Future of the Novel: Essays on the Art of Fiction*. Ed. Leon Edel. New York: Vintage, 1956. 89–96.

———. *The Portrait of a Lady. Novels, 1881–1886*. Ed. William T. Stafford. New York: Library of America, 1985. 191–800.

James, William. "Great Men, Great Thoughts, and the Environment." *Atlantic Monthly* 46 (Oct. 1880): 441–59.

Keegan, Bridget, and James C. McKusick, eds. *Literature and Nature: Four Centuries of Nature Writing*. Upper Saddle River, N.J.: Prentice Hall, 2001.

Larsen, Nella. *Quicksand and Passing*. New Brunswick, N.J.: Rutgers University Press, 1986.

LeConte, Joseph. *Evolution: Its Nature, Its Evidences, and Its Relation to Religious Thought*. 2nd ed. New York: Appleton, 1897.

London, Jack. *The Valley of the Moon*. 1913. Berkeley and Los Angeles: University of California Press, 1999.

McCluskey, John Jr., ed. *The City of Refuge: The Collected Stories of Rudolph Fisher*. Columbia: University of Missouri Press, 1987.

McKay, Claude. *Home to Harlem*. New York: Harper, 1928.

———. *A Long Way from Home*. 1937. New York: Arno, 1969.

Norris, Frank. *McTeague. Novels and Essays*. Ed. Donald Pizer. New York: Library of America, 1986. 261–572.

Rampersad, Arnold. *The Art and Imagination of W. E. B. Du Bois*. Cambridge: Harvard University Press, 1976.

Stein, Gertrude. *Fernhurst, Q. E. D., and Other Early Writings*. New York: Liveright, 1971.

Steinbeck, John. *The Log from the Sea of Cortez: The Narrative Portion of the Book, Sea of Cortez, by John Steinbeck and E. F. Ricketts, 1941, Here Reissued with a Profile "About Ed Ricketts."* New York: Penguin, 1982.

Stribling, T. S. *Birthright: A Novel*. New York: Century, 1922.

PART II

NATURALISM AND GENRE

CHAPTER 4

DEFINING AMERICAN LITERARY NATURALISM

ERIC CARL LINK

IN 1895, high school English teacher George Merriam Hyde wrote a brief essay for the *Dial* in which he lamented the fact that the terms "realism," "romanticism," and "naturalism" have not had stable definitions during the nineteenth century. "We suspect," noted Hyde, that if these "terms were clearly defined, all argument would, as in matters political and religious, be either needless or useless" (232). Hyde's lament cannot but elicit a sympathetic sigh from any modern literary historian who has tackled the problem of defining a literary movement, be it naturalism, realism, romanticism, modernism, or some other "ism" *de jour*. In fact, it has become a convention of such exercises in definition to offer up, in the spirit of Hyde, the observation that any attempt to fix the definition of a literary movement is fraught with peril, for the "ism" in question—whatever it happens to be—inevitably raises unique challenges for the literary historian. Let us break this tradition—or, in the very least, let us allow the lament of Hyde to perform surrogate duty in this case.

AMERICAN LITERARY NATURALISM: A DEFINITION

"American literary naturalism" is the phrase used to describe the thematic exploration, in American literature, of concepts arising out of post-Enlightenment developments in science and philosophy. Or, put another way, it is the literature born out of the tension between older, traditional belief systems and the new science of the post-Darwinian nineteenth century. Specifically, the American literary naturalists are those authors who engage, at the thematic level, post-Darwinian reconsiderations of the relationship between humans and nature. This engagement manifests itself in explorations of natural law, evolution, atavism, and degeneration, as well as in the philosophical, sociological, and psychological implications of such engagement. As a result, the issues pursued by the American literary naturalists are wide ranging but include, to cite just a few examples, questions concerning the deterministic pressures of heredity and environmental forces, the theologically challenging implications of materialism and biological reductionism, the emergent issues in race and gender theory invoked by aspects of evolutionary theory, and the ethical complications of social Darwinism.

WHO ARE THE AMERICAN LITERARY NATURALISTS?

There are authors who are more or less explicit in their attempts to chart the thematic implications of naturalist theory—which is to say, the amorphous collection of post-Enlightenment scientific and philosophical theories that revised our understanding of human development and expanded our understanding of nature and natural law. These authors—including Stephen Crane, Jack London, Theodore Dreiser, and Frank Norris—have tended to be the focal points of much scholarship on American literary naturalism. But there is no one set of conventions, styles, forms, or even philosophical positions that defines American literary naturalism. Just as naturalist theory itself is a scientific and philosophical sprawl radiating outward from a Darwinian core, so too American literary naturalism as an aesthetic movement is one with an identifiable core, in effect, but whose edges are not clearly defined and whose influence extends far and wide. Thus, rather than treat American literary naturalism as a closed and clearly defined set of authors and texts sharing a particular philosophical perspective or having a certain conventional commonality, it is of more merit to borrow, at least as a metaphor, Wittgenstein's concept of family resemblances in order to allow for the diversity of perspectives, forms, and aesthetic conventions exhibited by those texts that thematically engage naturalist theory.

Thus, to speak of a "school" of American literary naturalists is to refer to that loose confederation of authors whose texts are profitably discussed within the context of the above definition and whose works bear some family resemblance—for instance, through their portrayal of human nature as circumscribed by external forces, or their use of extreme, typically urban, landscapes, or their sometimes bleak challenge to any theory that posits the uniqueness of human nature and human endeavor—even if they do not share a particular set of formal conventions.

Although the first texts to participate in the "school" emerged in the 1860s with such works as Rebecca Harding Davis's "Life in the Iron-Mills" (1861) and Oliver Wendell Holmes's *Elsie Venner* (1861)—and pre-Darwinian heralds of the school can be traced back at least to the early 1850s in the work of Herman Melville—American literary naturalism was, at its height of influence and popularity in the 1890s and early 1900s, bookended by Stephen Crane's *Maggie, a Girl of the Streets* (1893) and Jack London's *Star Rover* (1915). After World War I, American literary naturalism would remain a key feature of the American literary landscape through the later productions of Theodore Dreiser and the mid-twentieth-century works of James Farrell, among others. Recently, Cormac McCarthy has been profitably discussed as a writer whose works bear some family resemblance to the American literary naturalists of the 1890s.[1] Despite the seeming decline in popularity and influence of American literary naturalism during the modernist and postmodernist movements of the twentieth century, the intellectual energy that fueled American literary naturalism in the late nineteenth century did not dissipate into the cultural atmosphere. Instead, much of the energy of American literary naturalism in the twentieth century was channeled into the rise of science fiction as a dominant cultural force. It is, indeed, difficult to read far into science fiction without confronting numerous treatments of the biological, social, and philosophical implications of evolutionary theory, and many science fiction authors—such as Philip K. Dick and Alfred Bester—raise questions in their works about the nature of free will, the efficacy of human endeavor, the brute nature of the human animal, and the coercive pressures of heredity and environment.

One of the nineteenth-century precursors to twentieth-century science fiction is the utopian novel, and, not surprisingly, the rise of literary naturalism in post-Darwinian American literature runs parallel to the rise in popularity of the utopian novel, of which Edward Bellamy's *Looking Backward* (1888) is the best known example, but which includes such novels as Howells's *A Traveler from Altruria* (1894) and Charlotte Perkins Gilman's *Herland* (1915). Traditionally, the utopian novel is viewed as distinct from literary naturalism—so distinct, in fact, that one rarely sees the two mentioned in the same analysis.[2] What is worth noting, however, is that many utopian novels in the late nineteenth century—including the three mentioned above—owe as much to the influence of naturalist theory as to the works of the traditional literary naturalists. Acknowledging this influence, suddenly American literary naturalism, as defined above, is a far larger and influential literary movement than many scholars initially believed.

Despite the early efforts of Holmes and Davis in the 1860s, the curious phenomenon of the utopian novel, and the pervasive use of naturalist theory in twentieth-century science fiction, most debates over the shape and size of the school of literary naturalists tend to come to, first, arguments over literary figures and texts that fall between *Maggie* and *The Star Rover*; and, second, to a kind of literary scavenger hunt for post–World War I figures (beyond Dreiser and Farrell) and texts that fall within the province of literary naturalism and carry its flag forward into the potentially hostile territory of modernism and postmodernism. Debates over who is and is not a literary naturalist are of necessity connected to definitional debates, and more than one scholar has been compelled to conclude that there were, in fact, no literary naturalists.[3] Such extreme positions as this one are not common: there is a general acceptance among American literary historians that, regardless of whatever else they may be, Crane, Norris, London, and Dreiser are certainly literary naturalists. Beyond this group, treatments of literary naturalism often include Kate Chopin, Hamlin Garland, Harold Frederic, David Graham Phillips, Ellen Glasgow, Henry Blake Fuller, Robert Herrick, as well as certain texts by Mark Twain, William Dean Howells, Charles Chesnutt, Upton Sinclair, Edith Wharton, and perhaps even some Henry James. A trend in recent scholarship has been to examine the relationship between literary naturalism and both women and minority authors of the late nineteenth century, and, in a parallel set of investigations, to look at the gendered aspects of literary naturalism. The end result of these and related studies has been to broaden our understanding of the cultural influence of literary naturalism in America at the turn of the twentieth century, and this broader vision has resulted in extending the discussion to include such figures as Zitkala-Ša, James Weldon Johnson, Pauline Hopkins, Paul Dunbar, Charlotte Perkins Gilman, Abraham Cahan, and Sui Sin Far. Pushing beyond World War I, there is no consensus regarding who is or is not a literary naturalist. In a sense, particularly with the advent of quantum mechanics and the greater acceptance of evolutionary theory, as well as the influence of modernism, postmodernism, and avant-garde aesthetic movements, the cultural forces that gave rise to American literary naturalism evolved. It would indeed be quaint if a modern author were to write *McTeague* today. Nevertheless, even setting aside science fiction, there are numerous twentieth-century authors who have written one or more works linked to literary naturalism in one way or another, including John Steinbeck, James Farrell, Ernest Hemingway, John Dos Passos, Sinclair Lewis, Richard Wright, Don DeLillo, Joyce Carol Oates, Cormac McCarthy, and others, including the occasional poet such as Edgar Lee Masters in his *Spoon River Anthology* (1916) and Edwin Arlington Robinson in *Children of the Night* (1897). Whether or not one of these twentieth-century novelists or poets is best labeled a literary naturalist (as opposed to something else) is grounds for continued debate, and the debate will certainly hinge on whatever a given critic accepts as the definition of literary naturalism. What can be said, however, is that many of the works by these authors bear strong family resemblances to the body of American naturalistic narrative.

    In the end, two things are clear: the canon of American literary naturalism is far from settled, and literary naturalism in America is no minor aesthetic movement but spans at least a full half-century, from the 1860s to the 1910s, and then spins off into several different directions in the remainder of the twentieth century, expanding its influence as it evolves in response to twentieth-century science and culture.

Naturalism in the Late Nineteenth Century

The problem with determining who is a literary naturalist and who is not is primarily a definitional problem, and as definitions of literary naturalism have changed over the years, so too have the boundaries of the school. The definition of American literary naturalism offered at the outset of this chapter is an exercise in critical hindsight. One may search the literature of the nineteenth century, but one will not find this particular definition anywhere. There are a couple of authors whose thinking about naturalism, and about nineteenth-century American literature in general, anticipates this definition in significant ways—Frank Norris for one; James Oscar Pierce for another—but for the most part the term "naturalism" was used in very different ways in the nineteenth century. In the 1870s and 1880s, the "scientific spirit of the age" (a phrase encountered throughout the literary criticism of the day) pushed literature in two directions, both deemed "naturalistic." One path was aesthetic, metaphorically linking the detailed study of nature—in terms of accurate representation and documentation of one's physical and social environment—to the efforts of the literary realists. Another path was toward philosophical speculation about the position of humankind within nature. It is this second path that resulted in American literary naturalism as an aesthetic movement, but it is the first path that shaped how the term "naturalism" was often—perhaps even primarily—used among literary critics of the late nineteenth century.

One thing many critics agreed upon was that the late nineteenth century was a scientific age.[4] Literature simply could not remain the same after Darwin: the rules had changed. As might be expected, there is a natural connection in the eyes of most critics of the time between this scientific spirit of the age and the emergence of realism and naturalism. In 1890, James Sully noted that the scientific reverence for accuracy in detail and for a factual rendering of observed data was a direct influence on the shift toward realism in literary art (650). Thus, to write novels of social realism, with a fidelity to the accurate representation of the commonplace manners and activities of the characters, is to write under the influence of this general cultural shift toward the methods of scientific investigation and the general post-Enlightenment appreciation for empirical data. It is within this context that Zola's theories of the "experimental novel" emerged, and it should come as no surprise to find critics in the late nineteenth century associating Zola's concept of the experimental novel with literary realism in general, and with the novels of social realism produced by Howells and James specifically. For instance, in 1890 Edmund Gosse noted that in 1877 Henry James "inaugurated the experimental novel in the English language" with *The American* (392), and James Sully made the sweeping observation that the novel "flatters science by imitating her experimental activity" (654). Certainly, not all critics accepted the theory that the novel form could mimic the methodologies of science. William Thayer, for just one example, argued in 1894 that the "scientific method" when applied to the craft of novel writing is incapable of capturing accurately the depth and range of human nature (477).

The picture gets a bit more complicated when the terms "realism" and "naturalism" are introduced. Sometimes critics in the late nineteenth century will use the terms interchangeably or as relatively synonymous when the critical situation does not call for a particularly nuanced use of the terms. But, when a more nuanced use of the terms is needed, critics generally take one of two paths: either they view naturalism as the larger term, positioning realism as a type or subset of naturalism, or they make a valiant attempt to distinguish in some manner between realism and naturalism, and there was no consensus about how to do so.

One witnesses the first of these paths in numerous essays from the period. For instance, Edmund Gosse in 1890 wrote that "the realistic novel, or at all events the naturalistic school, out of which it proceeded" was coming to the forefront of literary culture in the early 1880s (392). The implication is clear: for Gosse, the novel of social realism is a by-product of the larger developments of the naturalistic school of art and literature, which rose up as a reaction to the fancies of romanticism. Indeed, several authors of the period view the key dichotomy in literary art of the nineteenth century to be between the naturalistic novel and the romance, as opposed to the realistic novel and the romance. For example, in 1903 H. B. Marriott Watson observed that the antagonism between "romance and naturalism" has existed from "time immemorial" and will likely continue forever (430). In like manner, Israel Zangwill noted in 1896 that every "novel that deals truly with life is 'naturalistic'—in fact, the word 'novel' should mean the 'naturalistic novel'—any other kind of story should be classified as romance" (292). The novel, Zangwill went on to say, is a "picture of life and manners" regardless of whether the life or manners depicted are wholesome or morbid (292). To critics of similar convictions, it is possible, as one anonymous reviewer demonstrated in 1885, to view Howells as a practitioner of "unvarnished naturalism" whose naturalism is of a "healthy, sensible, wholesome kind" ("Current Criticism" 190). As these critics bear witness, there was among a certain group of authors no clear distinction between realism and naturalism; if anything, naturalism was the broader term, used to identify the general tendency in art to render the elements of nature truthfully, and realism is the more specialized term for the contemporary novel of manners, in a sense, in which the social landscape of the novel is portrayed with detailed accuracy.

Some critics, however, did not adopt this strategy. Instead, they either defined naturalism outright (without regard for realism), or they offered a variety of nuanced distinctions between realism and naturalism. Occasionally critics of the time would offer colorful commentary, such as Edgar Saltus's view of naturalism in 1889 as a "silk stocking filled with mud" (584), but what such metaphors suggest is the attitude among many critics of the time that naturalism as an aesthetic movement was tied—whether directly or indirectly—to immorality, obscenity, atheism, pessimism, and/or philosophical materialism. Richard Burton, for example, claimed in 1895 that the "morbid, the cynical, the naturalistic, and the decadent" in late nineteenth-century literature emanates from "the lack of faith and courage following on the loss (or at least change) of definite and canonical religious conviction" (251). A similar sentiment had been expressed by W. S. Lilly in 1885 who, in an essay titled "The New Naturalism," distinguished between the "old naturalism" steeped in philosophical idealism and the "new naturalism"—of which Zola is the chief proponent—which "claims to be scientific" and is "strictly materialistic and frankly professes atheism" (244). Both the old and new naturalism propose "conformity to nature" as the great law, but they diverge widely in their perceptions of the relationship between humans and their environment. By removing the spiritual dimension of life, the "New Naturalism," claims Lilly, "eliminates from man all but the ape and tiger," and it "banishes from human life "all that gives it glory and honour" (252).

It would be difficult to overstate the impact Zola had on the nineteenth century's understanding of literary naturalism, and his theory of the experimental novel was cause for all manner of debate (pro and con) in Anglo-American periodicals. One critic in 1886 noted that the traditional understanding of the term naturalism as "fidelity to nature" had been redefined in recent years as "fidelity to nature after the manner of Emile Zola" (Francis 146). For critics of a more delicate mindset, what this meant was fidelity to nature, so long as one focuses on the unseemly side of life and catalogs all manner of vice and crime along the way. "Naked naturalism," as one critic would write in 1894, is the "attempt to set forth the hideously abnormal, as the general average of humanity." In fact, according to this critic, the entire "method of Zola" is "loaded with pollution" ("Bourget and Zola" 105). Theodore Osborne in 1897 would second this criticism in his brief article "The Misleadings of Naturalism." Osborne warned that readers can be led down paths of immorality by exposing themselves to the catalog of vices in the typical naturalistic novel. By dwelling upon such things, evil passions grow and the human imagination becomes perverted (481). As with most things in life, however, what is worthy of condemnation by one is often worthy of praise by another, and there were occasional critics who interpreted Zola's—and naturalism's—descent into the world of vice as an essentially moral gesture: by exposing the ruin that comes to those who veer from the path of morality and healthy living, Zola and others wrote novels that serve as object lessons for their readers. In this way, the works of literary naturalism exhibit a type of reformist impulse born out of an essentially moral—or moralistic—position.[5]

To be sure, no theorist of literary naturalism looms larger than Zola, and his essays in Le Roman expérimental (1880) are the centerpiece of many discussions of literary naturalism, both in America and in Europe. Zola affirmed a materialistic, positivistic worldview and advocated the direct, non-ironic application of the scientific method to the drafting of a novel, so that the novel can in a real sense be used as a scientific tool for the study of human documents. Divested of supernaturalism, human nature becomes a matter of biochemical interactions controlled by the coercive forces of heredity and environment. Thus, for the experimental novelist, characters can be created and inserted into a carefully designed, realistic narrative environment modeled after direct observation of contemporary reality. If the experiment is carried off by a true craftsperson with a keen eye for detail and an unwavering commitment to scientific accuracy and methodology, the novel will represent a kind of scientific case study and will produce data about human nature that will be observable and verifiable in the real world. Zola's theory was influential, and it is no surprise that many twentieth-century critical treatments of American literary naturalism look to Zola as the godfather of the movement. There are three problems with this critical trend, however. The first is that Zola was not the only theorist of literary naturalism. Even in Europe, where Zola had the most influence, of course, he had detractors. Spanish critic and author Leopoldo Alas, for instance, directly challenged Zola's definition of literary naturalism, rejecting Zola's application of the methodologies and metaphysics of Claude Bernard and pointing out that literary naturalism is not necessarily pessimistic, positivistic, or deterministic. The second problem—a problem pointed out repeatedly by nineteenth-century critics of naturalism and commentators on Zola's theories—is that there is a disjunction between Zola's theory and the actual works whose creation was allegedly governed by these same theories. What critics repeatedly pointed out was that naturalistic novels—including Zola's own works—violate the principles established by Zola for the "experimental" novel. They are not objective. They are not realistic. They are moralistic. They do not produce data that would withstand the scrutiny of any "scientific" test.[6]

The third problem, and the one with the most consequence for any attempt to define American literary naturalism (as distinct from French or English or Russian literary naturalism), is that there is simply no clear evidence that any of the principal literary naturalists in the American literary tradition read—or if read, paid any heed to—Zola's theories. There is no question that Zola's novels were widely read and were highly influential among American authors in the late nineteenth century, but there is no evidence to suggest that any of the American literary naturalists themselves ever read *Le Roman expérimental*, let alone attempted to put his narrative theories into practice. Notably, the American author most directly influenced by Zola was Frank Norris, and Norris's own theories of literary naturalism are radically different from those of Zola. Norris was not unaware of the common association of realism and naturalism in the late nineteenth century, but he took a contrary position, finding naturalism to be distinct from realism in measurable ways. Norris wrote in his 1896 essay "Zola as a Romantic Writer": "It is curious to notice how persistently M. Zola is misunderstood. . . . For most people Naturalism has a vague meaning. It is a sort of inner circle of realism—a kind of diametric opposite of romanticism, a theory of fiction wherein things are represented 'as they really are,' inexorably, with the truthfulness of a camera. This idea can be shown to be far from right, that Naturalism, as understood by Zola, is but a form of romanticism after all" (71). Indeed, noted Norris, "that Zola should be quoted as a realist, and as a realist of realists, is a strange perversion" (71). Naturalism, Norris concluded, is a "form of romanticism, not an inner circle of realism" (72). What distinguishes literary naturalism from realism, according to Norris, is that it finds its material not in the probable and ordinary course of human activity, but in vast and terrible dramas that resemble Hugo more than Howells.

Norris would expand on these ideas in two other essays. In his "Weekly Letter" of 3 August 1901, Norris suggested that literary naturalism takes the realistic pursuit of accuracy in detail and blends it with the romantic quest for Truth, thus producing a hybrid form that borrows from both the antebellum romance tradition and the post-bellum novel of social realism. A few months later, in December 1901, in an essay titled "A Plea for Romantic Fiction," Norris would repeat his basic premises of the previous two essays, noting, again, that Zola is a romantic writer, not a realistic novelist, and would expand on his claim that the romance allows the author an opportunity to pursue Truths that lie far beneath the empirically confined realm of the realistic novel. Norris called for the creation of a "romantic literature" that would explore "the unplumbed depths of the human heart, and the mystery of sex, and the problems of life, and the black, unsearched penetralia of the soul of man" (78).[7]

Norris's definition of literary naturalism has provoked a wide range of response. His essays have been overlooked, dismissed, treated as the self-serving statements of an insecure author, taken as the naïve speculations of a young author, and even, on rare occasions, taken seriously. But there is a minor chord ringing throughout criticism of the past hundred years that takes note, to one degree or another, of the connections between American literary naturalism and the tradition of American romance. When placed in the full context of nineteenth-century aesthetic theory, Norris's claims are certainly of a piece with theories of the romance in American letters.[8] Moreover, several of Norris's contemporaries sought to describe the texts of American literary naturalism in terms similar to Norris's, even if they did not invoke the term "naturalism" in the process. For instance, in his 1899 essay "New Phases of the Romance," James Pierce wrote, "We have still another school, who aim to show us the romantic features of the everyday life around us; who find the romantic in the midst of the real; in a word, who transmute the Novel into the Romance." In these new romances, the "marvels of the present day in science, in the arts, in psychology, and in occult learning and the dreams of the mystic, the ambitions of the philosopher, and the schemes of the social reformer,—all these are proved to have their romantic phases" (71). Notably, as an example of this emergent romance tradition, Pierce cites Holmes's *Elsie Venner*, one of the earliest works of literary naturalism in American literature.

NATURALISM IN THE TWENTIETH AND TWENTY-FIRST CENTURIES

As the survey above demonstrates, there was no fixed definition within the literary community in the late nineteenth century over the meaning of naturalism as it applied to literary productions. There was not definitional chaos, however, and certain trends and premises are readily identifiable:

A. There is a general consensus that both naturalism and realism are intricately linked to the general post-Enlightenment interest in scientific developments. Evolutionary theory is the leading influence at this time.

B. For some critics, naturalism is synonymous in a general sense with realism and refers to the same basic set of literary works, a list that for most critics includes Howells, James, Zola, Balzac, Flaubert, and Tolstoy.

C. For other critics, naturalism is the broad term for the truthful representation of nature in art. Literary realism is a particular type of naturalism that came into the forefront of literary endeavor in the mid-to-late nineteenth century in Europe and America.

D. For still other critics, naturalism is the term for those primarily realistic narratives that take as their subject matter vice-driven characters from lower socioeconomic strata.

E. Finally, for a few critics, such as Norris and Pierce, literary naturalism diverged sharply from the realism typical of the 1870s and 1880s. For these critics, literary naturalism had clear affinities with the romance tradition, and the naturalistic novel was one that responded to the scientific spirit of the age by paving new pathways to truth about human nature that swerved aside from the commonplace activities of real men and women.

In the twentieth century—particularly in the first half of the century—critics have tended to accept A, reject or ignore C, and build definitions of American literary naturalism out of some combination of elements either explicit or implicit within B, D, and, to a lesser extent, E. Because of the association of naturalism with the sordid—Zola is the model in most critics' eyes—discussions of literary naturalism in America soon became discussions of authors such as Stephen Crane, Jack London, Theodore Dreiser, and Frank Norris. Howells and James are generally held up as archetypal literary realists, but not literary naturalists, despite the claims of certain critics in the late nineteenth century. There is also a tendency in the twentieth century to bring into the equation the materialistic implications of naturalism as a philosophical position, which leads to a heightened emphasis on the eradication of supernatural phenomena and the acceptance of various deterministic theories of human nature.

As a result of these trends, one finds that the earliest critical treatments of American literary naturalism define it as a type of literary realism that is steeped in a pessimistic view of human nature and is philosophically committed to a deterministic interpretation of human endeavor. Although retrospective treatments of European literary naturalism (centered inevitably on Zola and his circle) had appeared in American periodicals as early as Martin Schütze's 1903 essay "The Services of Naturalism to Life and Literature" (in which Schütze generally sees literary naturalism as literature that is born out of philosophical materialism in the late nineteenth century), retrospective treatments of American literary naturalism generally date from the third volume of Vernon Louis Parrington's intellectual history of America published in 1930. In his influential volume, Parrington summed up

American literary naturalism as a type of "pessimistic realism" that situates the individual within "a mechanical world and conceives of him as victimized by the world" (325).

"Pessimistic, deterministic realism" as a kind of intellectual shorthand definition of American literary naturalism became the gold standard among many subsequent critics, including Oscar Cargill (1941), Malcolm Cowley (1947), Philip Rahv (1949), Lars Åhnebrink (1950), and Alfred Kazin (1950). At its least nuanced, literary naturalism has been defined by George Becker, in 1963, as "no more than an emphatic and explicit philosophical position taken by some realists, showing man caught in a net from which there can be no escape and degenerating under those circumstance; that is, it is pessimistic materialistic determinism" (35). The focus in the Parrington/Becker definitions on the deterministic convictions of the authors involved would result in such studies as John J. Conder's 1984 analysis, which defines American literary naturalism as the outgrowth of a coherent philosophical position rooted in a deterministic philosophy informed and shaped by Thomas Hobbes and reconceived and corrected by Henri Bergson. Understood in this way, according to Conder, American literary naturalism is not a jumble of tensions or contradictions but is unified by a recognizable and coherent philosophical position. This conclusion, it might be pointed out in passing, is not a common one among critics of American literary naturalism. Indeed, it would be fair to say that what sets treatments of American literary naturalism apart from treatments of European literary naturalism is the presence of competing philosophical visions and narrative forms one finds in the American naturalists. And, to take it a step further, Conder's reduction of American literary naturalism to a tradition of pseudo-philosophical discourse certainly diminishes appreciation of the aesthetic achievements of the naturalists.

And yet, despite the assuredness of Becker, Conder, and a few others—even in some of the earliest accounts of American literary naturalism—critics often place an asterisk after what we might call the Parrington definition of literary naturalism and proceed to qualify the definition by suggesting ways in which it does not quite fit the American literary naturalists as well as it perhaps should. For instance, in his excellent 1947 overview of the movement, Cowley writes, "Naturalism has been defined in two words as pessimistic determinism, and the definition is true so far as it goes. The Naturalistic writers were all determinists in that they believed in the omnipotence of abstract forces. They were all pessimists so far as they believed that men and women were absolutely incapable of shaping their own destinies" (414). Yet, Cowley explains, there is an undercurrent of optimism about the potential progress of human development and human society in many naturalistic works that serves as a counterpoint to the pessimism of the texts, and, in addition, there are ties between the naturalists and the antebellum romance tradition that separate literary naturalism from literary realism as it is manifested in the novels of Howells and James.

On occasion, the degree to which critics find themselves having to qualify their acceptance of the Parrington definition is so extreme one can only wonder why they did not simply abandon the Parrington definition at the outset and start from scratch. For instance, Everett Carter in 1954 began with the Parrington definition, then proceeded to dismantle it piece by piece, eventually concluding that American literary naturalism is little more than a "deepening and broadening of the realistic and critically realistic techniques and attitudes extended to larger areas of society" (237). Carter immediately followed this summation with a paragraph pointing out how Norris, Crane, and Frederic began to break down the methods and approaches typically associated with literary realism. In his 1971 study of realism in American fiction, Edwin Cady found himself having to adopt an even more extreme position than Carter's. Starting with the notion that American literary naturalism is a type of realism that expresses a philosophically naturalistic worldview (one, therefore, which might easily tilt toward pessimism and a deterministic and materialistic interpretation of human endeavor), Cady ultimately concluded that there "really are no naturalists in American literature" and those authors who attempt to embody a naturalist philosophy in their works wind up looking like "new romancers" rather than novelists of social realism (45, 49).

In the 1950s and 1960s, several critics began to rethink American literary naturalism. One thing that separates this line of thinking from the Parrington line is that these critics began to disassociate literary realism from literary naturalism, and to examine literary naturalism on its own terms, rather than taking as axiomatic the belief that literary naturalism is a type or subset of literary realism. The first major study to do so was Charles Child Walcutt's *American Literary Naturalism: A Divided Stream* in 1956. Walcutt argues that American literary naturalism is the "offspring of transcendentalism" (vii). What Walcutt suggests is that in the late nineteenth century, the transcendentalist position that the bond between humans and nature can be affirmed both through science and intuition divides into two streams of thought. One, the approach through intuition, spins off into a philosophical idealism and a political progressivism that feeds the development of utopian fiction and the emergence of radical social reform efforts. The approach through science, however, mutates into a dark and pessimistic view of human nature characterized by a "mechanistic determinism" (viii). American literary naturalism, Walcutt believes, emerges from the tension inherent in this divided stream of American transcendentalist thought. This was a productive tension whose by-products occur in the work of the literary naturalists in the form of questions about the ways in which human endeavor is shaped by natural forces, a reevaluation of orthodox versions of metaphysical dualism, and a vigorous exploration of natural processes (20). For Walcutt, naturalism is a philosophical position, whereas realism is a set of literary conventions—a style (23). Thus, one need not, in Walcutt's view, treat naturalism and realism as competing or overlapping narrative methodologies. They belong to different categories altogether. Thus, although the works of the American literary naturalists are often aligned with the techniques of literary realism, they need not be, at least in theory. In Walcutt's final estimation, American literary naturalism fails repeatedly in its attempts to integrate idea and form (a position that several important later studies would reject). But, by separating American literary naturalism from a particular literary methodology or set of aesthetic techniques, he demonstrated that it was possible to discuss literary naturalism separately from literary realism, and to do so in productive ways.

In his 1964 essay "Naturalism as a Literary Form," Robert Figg argued that treatments of literary naturalism in the twentieth century have fallen into two categories: those in the Parrington tradition, which view naturalism identical in kind with literary realism but different in degree, and those in what we might call the Walcutt tradition, which view naturalism as different in kind from realism (and thus are able, as Walcutt does, to treat naturalism on its own terms, rather than as a subset of literary realism). Figg places Parrington, Kazin, Chase, and Rahv in the first camp, and Norris, Walcutt, Stuart P. Sherman, and himself in the other. Figg's central argument is that when the literary naturalists consciously integrated a specific philosophical position characterized by a materialistic determinism into their narratives, they were compelled to manipulate their material, thus violating the main principle of literary realism, which calls for the objective and accurate portrayal of human nature and environmental conditions. Figg writes, "Since in the novel meaning is a function of form, the deterministic idea, seriously entertained, prescribes a particular structural pattern, a certain type of characterization, and a definite amoral orientation. In addition, the idea also implies the presence of a certain type of imagery. We cannot imagine adding the impress of so powerful a governing idea to a novel we have hitherto called 'realistic' without admitting that the main fictional elements of that novel would have to be radically and essentially redisposed" (310). Figg, thus, holds on to the notion that literary naturalism is rooted in a certain materialistic and deterministic view of human nature and endeavor, but he discards the idea that the texts that embody this world are within the traditions of the novel of social realism, particularly in regard to the use of commonplace characters exhibiting typical and probable behavioral patterns.

There is little debate that the most influential critic of American literary naturalism for the past half century has been Donald Pizer. Given the vast body of scholarship Pizer has contributed to the field, it would be unfair to claim that there is one distinct definition of literary naturalism developed and advocated by Pizer, for his thoughts on the matter have developed over the course of his career. However, his principal essay on the definition of literary naturalism first appeared in the *Bucknell Review* in 1965 under the title "Late Nineteenth-Century American Naturalism." In this influential essay, Pizer provides a kind of bridge between the Parrington tradition and the Walcutt tradition, acknowledging both that there is a certain historical inevitability in the critical connection between realism and naturalism and that the deterministic implications of post-Enlightenment science and philosophy have a distinct shaping influence on the thematic structure of naturalistic narratives, but also recognizing that the narratives written by authors such as Norris, Dreiser, Crane, and London have aesthetic value beyond the expression (flawed or not) of a certain philosophical vision and that the literary styles and techniques employed in these narratives do not reflect those of the literary realists. As a result of these observations, Pizer suggests that "the naturalistic novel usually contains two tensions or contradictions, and that the two in conjunction comprise both an interpretation of experience and a particular aesthetic recreation of experience. In other words, the two constitute the theme and form of the naturalistic novel" (10). The first of these tensions is between the "subject matter of the naturalistic novel and the concept of man which emerges from this subject matter" (10). In other words, what one finds in the naturalistic novel are characters drawn from the everyday round of common human experience; yet, unlike the literary realist, the naturalist finds in these characters illustrations of the "extraordinary and excessive in human nature" (11). The second tension is thematic, for against the background of a worldview predicated on deterministic ideologies, the naturalist author "suggests a compensating humanistic value" which "affirms the significance of the individual" (11). The naturalistic narrative emerges out of the creative alembic of these two tensions. In defining literary naturalism in this manner, Pizer provided a means to approach the works largely on their own terms, and to view them as works of literary art, rather than as flawed philosophical treatises or unrealistic works of literary realism. Much of Pizer's subsequent work on the defining characteristics of literary naturalism has been to test, refine, and add context to this early definition. And, indeed, whether directly or indirectly, many critics since the 1960s who have tackled the definitional problems of literary naturalism have grappled with the same tensions in theme and form identified by Pizer.

In the evolution of thinking on the topic from Parrington to Walcutt to Pizer, most of the terms of the debate over the proper definition of literary naturalism had been set. And, to an extent the majority of critics that would follow either accepted (in whole or in part) some variation of the Parrington or Pizer thesis or turned their attention away from definitional debates altogether and pursued questions not directly tied to matters of definition and genre characteristics. The period from the mid-1980s to the present has featured numerous major studies of American literary naturalism, and they cannot be discussed individually here. Nevertheless, speaking in general terms, the resurgence of scholarship on literary naturalism that occurred in the 1980s and continues to the present has reflected the shift in literary theory away from old historicism, formalism, and New Criticism and toward structuralist (and post-structuralist) language theory, new historicism, neo-Marxism, and sociologically and culturally oriented approaches. During this period, major studies of American literary naturalism have tended to focus not so much on defining the phrase "American literary naturalism" or on delineating its formal features, but on a variety of other concerns, such as the relationship between the texts commonly associated with literary naturalism and the sociological circumstances surrounding their creation, as in studies by Walter Benn Michaels (1987), Mark Seltzer (1992), and, more recently, in the studies of John Dudley (2004) and Jennifer Fleissner (2004). Meanwhile, June Howard's 1985 study begins to question the validity of prior ways of thinking about literary genre itself, and Lee Clark Mitchell's 1989 examination takes a fresh approach to the study of determinism as a defining theme of literary naturalism by looking at the ways in which deterministic ideologies are embedded in complex ways into the linguistic structure of the narratives themselves. There are exceptions to these trends in the 1980s and 1990s, such as Paul Civello (1994), who returns to an approach rooted in a type of intellectual history characteristic of earlier studies, and both Donna M. Campbell (1997) and Richard Lehan (2005), who position literary naturalism against a larger picture of late nineteenth-century literary culture. These important studies, where they concern definitional matters, often work in general terms within the set of genre-related questions raised by Parrington, Walcutt, Pizer and others when it comes to defining terms. In addition, however, they broaden in productive ways our understanding of the significance of literary naturalism as an aesthetic movement and as a by-product of cultural forces and popular ideologies of the late nineteenth century. They serve, collectively, as a strong endorsement of the proposition that a full understanding of American literary naturalism must stretch beyond formalistic and aesthetic concerns into the realm of the cultural, the historical, the sociological, and the economic. These were not new revelations in the 1980s, but the attention these matters have received in the past thirty years is a clear by-product of various shifts in theoretical perspective, a broader understanding of the literary canon, and new approaches to literary analysis.[9]

THE TYRANNY OF CUSTOM

Given these surveys of both nineteenth- and twentieth-century attempts to define and describe American literary naturalism as an aesthetic movement, a school of literature, and a literary methodology, how does one arrive at the definition presented at the outset of this essay? In the spirit of Rene Wellek's answer to Arthur Lovejoy in the controversy over the definition of romanticism, the answer to this question requires a return to the literature of American literary naturalism itself. Much of the confusion regarding the definition of American literary naturalism stems from the disjunction evident between the conventional critical alliance of realism and naturalism, the parallel disjunction between the philosophical ideas that the narratives are predicted by critics to embody, and the actual ways (ironic, subversive, contradictory, and otherwise) that the ideas themselves actually do manifest within a given text. These two disjunctions have been the foci of numerous debates over the definition of American literary naturalism ever since they were first discussed, in other terms, by Pizer in 1965. To define American literary naturalism in a manner that does not provide some answer to the questions posed by these disjunctions is to create an interpretive dynamic in which either the definition, the texts, the authors involved, or all three, are subject to charges of failure and dismissal.[10]

For example, if literary naturalism is defined as a narrative mode in which authors work out the implications of a deterministic philosophy, then the definition errs on two counts. First, it confuses literary and philosophical discourses, which certainly overlap at times but are not co-equal. Second, it does not describe the literature commonly associated with literary naturalism in America. Does *The Octopus, The Pit, The Red Badge of Courage*, or *The Sea-Wolf* serve as a mere vehicle for promoting a deterministic philosophy of human nature? To be sure, human agency is called into question in each of those works, but these novels can hardly be said to embody a clear philosophical position of one sort or another. They certainly are not philosophically didactic. They do what much good art does: they pose questions in provocative ways. To expect them to serve as surrogate philosophical treatises intended to express a coherent philosophical dogma is to confuse modes of discourse and to set up a situation where these works will be subject to potentially unjust criticism as fundamentally flawed narratives.

The same kind of problem emerges if one takes the connection between realism and naturalism as a defining characteristic. The works typically associated with American literary naturalism did at times employ what can generally be called a realist aesthetic. But they just as often veered from that aesthetic. They make use of the gothic, the grotesque, the symbolic, the improbable, the melodramatic, and the sensationalistic. In terms of aesthetic conventions, the literary naturalists were as likely to draw upon the romance tradition—a point Norris shouted with a barbaric yawp—as upon the tradition of the novel of social realism in the manner of Howells or James. Thus, any definition of literary naturalism that prescribes a certain set of aesthetic principles or narrative techniques is more likely to provoke controversy than anything else. In similar fashion, although it is evident that many of the texts associated with literary naturalism share a variety of conventions—such as the creation of a non-Aristotelian tragedies built on the back of a plot of decline, or the use of animal imagery in the depiction of human characters, or the creation of bleak and violent urban landscapes, or the portrayal of humans as brutes—these are not defining characteristics, per se. They are, instead, motifs, image patterns, and structural devices that that proved useful for integrating certain themes into a narrative.

Custom is a tyrant. Unless one wishes to rewrite a century of American literary history, a definition of American literary naturalism should be descriptive of at least a good portion of the texts and authors that have been labeled as naturalist. We could strike bravely at tradition—we could define American literary naturalism as some critics in the late nineteenth century did, as a type of literature that retains a certain realistic fidelity to the representation of the natural world. Then we may speak of Howells and James (again following the lead of some nineteenth-century critics) as leading American literary naturalists and the rest be damned. We would then have the exciting opportunity of trying to decide what to call Norris, who is the one major author in American literary history (or, at least during the period between *Maggie* and *The Star Rover*) who actually tried to define literary naturalism. We would, of course, have to overlook those essays by Norris where he actually defined literary naturalism: they would only get in the way. And, in fact, that has been the strategy of a number of critics of literary naturalism who take as axiomatic naturalism's link with realism.

An important first step in establishing a working definition of literary naturalism is to make crucial distinctions among philosophical naturalism, scientific naturalism, and literary naturalism. To confuse philosophical naturalism with literary naturalism is, as noted above, to confuse separate modes of discourse and to ascribe to authors philosophical opinions they may not have held. And, although we need not wave the banner of New Criticism in order to admit it, even if an author did hold a certain philosophical position, that does not mean he or she intended to use a particular novel as a vehicle for dogmatic expression. The novels, to some extent, should speak for themselves. Not always, and never entirely, but sometimes. Meanwhile, even though Zola advocated for transforming the novel into an instrument for scientific investigation, his theories bear only oblique resemblance to his own novels, let alone the novels of American literary naturalists who likely knew little if anything about Zola's theoretical writings. Or, if they did, it clearly had little effect on their own writings. Norris may have signed a letter as "The Boy Zola," but what Norris admired was Zola's novels rather than theories. He admired Zola's fearless portrayal of material that would constitute a veritable campaign of shock and awe on Western culture in the 1870s and 1880s.

The main point here is that if one reviews attempts by scholars from Parrington forward to define literary naturalism, what one finds is that if the critic too closely associates the ideology or methodology of philosophical or scientific naturalism with literary naturalism, then inevitably the definition of literary naturalism that results does not accurately describe the works customarily associated with the aesthetic movement.[11] This has led to countless charges by critics that even the greatest achievements of American literary naturalism (Crane's *The Red Badge of Courage*, Norris's *McTeague* and *The Octopus*, Dreiser's *Sister Carrie*, Frederic's *The Damnation of Theron Ware*, among others) are flawed texts. They fail to properly illustrate a prescribed and coherent philosophical position (typically identified as materialistic in its theory of nature and deterministic in its theory of human nature), or they fail to adhere to the expectations of literary realism (they are sensationalistic, melodramatic, symbolic).

The American literary naturalists are different from their European counterparts, despite whatever admirations they had for each other or however they may have influenced each other. The American literary naturalists are not united under a common aesthetic banner: they are not all realists by trade. They are sometimes realists, sometimes symbolists, sometimes romantics. They are impressionists at times; they are meticulous documenters of the social landscape at other times. They distance themselves from their material, and then they turn around and yearn for reform. They dissect their characters with the cold insensitivities of a scalpel and then they drown between the Scylla and Charybdis of melodrama and sentiment.

The American literary naturalists do not share a common worldview, and their works are not philosophical treatises. They grow and evolve. They ask questions. They contradict themselves. They are atheists; they are theists. They are the rebellious sons of Methodist preachers; they are quiet Episcopalians. God lies dead in heaven and Angèle comes walking out of the wheat field. Determinism is a question not a statement. Evolution is a religion that offers salvation and damnation. Human nature is both knowable and clouded in mystery. Old Grannis and Miss Baker fall out of a Norman Rockwell print, while down at the park Marcus and McTeague make Mike Tyson and Evander Holyfield look like fine-tooled, ascot-wearing gentlemen.

In 1889, Maurice Thompson—Midwesterner, acquaintance of Howells, and vocal critic of realism—offered this prophecy: "In the far future," he claimed, "the most valuable significance of the theory of evolution will attach to the fertilizing effect it had upon the imagination of its age" (332). This proved a rather poor bit of prophecy, as any casual perusal of a biology textbook will reveal. Still, to be fair to Thompson, evolutionary theory in the late nineteenth century did spill out of the laboratory and profoundly affect Western cultural and intellectual life. What the American literary naturalists share is not a set of aesthetic techniques or a desire to use their narratives as linguistic laboratories for the collection of scientific data: instead, they share a common desire to try to make sense of human nature in the wake of the scientific and philosophical revelations and revolutions of the nineteenth century. They are writers whose works are best understood within the context of what their contemporaries called the "scientific spirit of the age." Their texts take up as themes the ideas—philosophical, sociological, biological—that shook Western intellectual culture to its core and reshaped our most basic understandings of human nature.

NOTES

1. For treatments of Cormac McCarthy, see Frye and Giles.

2. See, however, Link 68–93 and Lehan 175–76.

3. See Gendin; see also Cady 45.

4. For a few examples of critics who note that the late nineteenth century is a "scientific" age, see Thompson, Moore, Harding, and Morse.

5. For examples of this kind of criticism, see "Modern Naturalism" 215 and Wilker 124. See also Pizer, "True Art Speaks Plainly."

6. See Alas 266–70. For further discussion of Alas's response to Zola, see Link 3–10.

7. For more on the theories of Norris and their nineteenth-century critical context, see Link 45–54.

8. For a full discussion of these claims, see Link 21–67 as well as Thompson and Link ch. 3–5.

9. The most recent work that engages the definitional debate head-on is my *The Vast and Terrible Drama: American Literary Naturalism in the Late Nineteenth Century*. Because there is a close connection between the conclusions drawn in this essay and that 2004 study, I will forego summary of that work here and will merely direct readers to that work for a fuller treatment of some of the issues raised in this particular chapter. For two other useful introductions to some of the issues associated with attempts to define American literary naturalism, see Pizer, Introduction and Den Tandt.

10. For a good introduction to the ways in which naturalistic novels have been viewed as "flawed," see Pizer, "Problem" 1–3.

11. For a much fuller treatment of this idea, and for an extended discussion of the differences between philosophical, scientific, and literary naturalism, see Link 10–20.

WORKS CITED

Åhnebrink, Lars. *The Beginnings of Naturalism in American Fiction*. Cambridge: Harvard University Press, 1950.

Alas, Leopoldo. "What Naturalism Is Not." 1891. Becker 266–73.

Becker, George, ed. *Documents of Modern Literary Realism*. Princeton: Princeton University Press, 1963.

"Bourget and Zola, Candidates for Immortality." *Current Literature* 16 (Aug. 1894): 105.

Burton, Richard. "The Healthful Tone for American Literature." *Forum* 14 (Apr. 1895): 249–56.

Cady, Edwin H. *The Light of Common Day: Realism in American Fiction*. Bloomington: Indiana University Press, 1971.

Campbell, Donna M. *Resisting Regionalism: Gender and Naturalism in American Fiction, 1885–1915*. Athens: Ohio University Press, 1997.

Cargill, Oscar. *Intellectual America*. New York: Macmillan, 1941.

Carter, Everett. *Howells and the Age of Realism*. Philadelphia: Lippincott, 1954.

Chase, Richard. *The American Novel and Its Tradition*. Baltimore: Johns Hopkins University Press, 1957.

Civello, Paul. *American Literary Naturalism and Its Twentieth-Century Transformations*. Athens: University of Georgia Press, 1994.

Conder, John J. *Naturalism in American Fiction: The Classic Phase*. Lexington: University Press of Kentucky, 1984.

Cowley, Malcolm. "'Not Men': A Natural History of American Naturalism." *Kenyon Review* 9 (1947): 414–35.

"Current Criticism." *The Critic* 17 Oct. 1885: 190.

Den Tandt, Christophe. "American Literary Naturalism." *A Companion to American Fiction, 1865–1914*. Ed. Robert Paul Lamb and G. R. Thompson. Malden: Blackwell, 2005. 96–118.

Dudley, John. *A Man's Game: Masculinity and the Anti-Aesthetics of American Literary Naturalism*. Tuscaloosa: University of Alabama Press, 2004.

Figg, Robert M., III. "Naturalism as a Literary Form." *Georgia Review* 18 (1964): 308–16.

Fleissner, Jennifer L. *Women, Compulsion, Modernity: The Moment of American Naturalism*. Chicago: University of Chicago Press, 2004.

Francis, Averic Standish. "A Talk About Novels." *Unitarian Review and Religious Magazine* 26 (Aug. 1886): 140–50.

Frye, Steven. "Cormac McCarthy's 'world in its making': Romantic Naturalism in *The Crossing*." *Studies in American Naturalism* 2 (2007): 46–65.

Gendin, Sidney. "Was Stephen Crane (or Anybody Else) a Naturalist?" *Cambridge Quarterly* 24 (1995): 89–101.

Giles, James R. "Teaching the Contemporary Naturalism of Cormac McCarthy." *ALN: The American Literary Naturalism Newsletter* 1.1 (2006): 2–7.

Gosse, Edmund. "The Limits of Realism in Fiction." *Forum* 9 (June 1890): 391–400.

Harding, Edward J. "Cutting Adrift." *The Critic and Good Literature* 20 (17 May 1884): 229–30.

Howard, June. *Form and History in American Literary Naturalism.* Chapel Hill: University of North Carolina Press, 1985.

Hyde, George Merriam. "The Allotropy of Realism." *Dial* 18 (16 Apr. 1895): 231–32.

Kazin, Alfred. "American Naturalism: Reflections from Another era." *The American Writer and the European Tradition.* Ed. Margaret Denny and William H. Gilman. Minneapolis: University of Minnesota Press, 1950.

Lehan, Richard. *Realism and Naturalism: The Novel in an Age of Transition.* Madison: University of Wisconsin Press, 2005.

Lilly, W. S. "The New Naturalism." *Fortnightly Review* 38 (1885): 240–56.

Link, Eric Carl. *The Vast and Terrible Drama: American Literary Naturalism in the Late Nineteenth Century.* Tuscaloosa: University of Alabama Press, 2004.

Michaels, Walter Benn. *The Gold Standard and the Logic of Naturalism: American Literature at the Turn of the Century.* Berkeley and Los Angeles: University of California Press, 1987.

Mitchell, Lee Clark. *Determined Fictions: American Literary Naturalism.* New York: Columbia University Press, 1989.

"Modern Naturalism—As Seen in the Works of Giovanni Verga." *Nassau Literary Magazine* 45 (Nov. 1889): 209–17.

Moore, Charles Leonard. "Feeling a Direction." *Dial* 25 (16 Nov. 1898): 335–37.

Morse, James Herbert. "The Native Element in American Fiction: Since the War." *Century* 26 (June 1883): 362–75.

Norris, Frank. "A Plea for Romantic Fiction." 1901. Norris, *Literary Criticism* 75–78.

———. "Frank Norris' Weekly Letter." 1901. Norris, *Literary Criticism* 73–75.

———. *The Literary Criticism of Frank Norris.* Ed. Donald Pizer. Austin: University of Texas Press, 1964.

———. "Zola as a Romantic Writer." 1896. Norris, *Literary Criticism* 71–72.

Osborne, Theodore M. "The Misleadings of Naturalism." *Current Literature* 21 (June 1897): 481.

Parrington, Vernon Louis. *Main Currents in American Thought.* Vol. 3. New York: Harcourt, 1930.

Pierce, James Oscar. "New Phases of the Romance." *Dial* 26 (1 Feb. 1899): 69–72.

Pizer, Donald. Introduction: The Problem of Definition. *The Cambridge Companion to American Realism and Naturalism: Howells to London.* Ed. Donald Pizer. Cambridge: Cambridge University Press, 1995. 1–18.

———. "Late Nineteenth-Century American Naturalism." *Realism and Naturalism in Nineteenth-Century American Literature.* 1966. Rev. ed. Carbondale: Southern Illinois University Press, 1984. 9–30.

———. "The Problem of American Literary Naturalism and Theodore Dreiser's *Sister Carrie.*" *American Literary Realism* 32 (1999): 1–11.

———. "'True Art Speaks Plainly': Theodore Dreiser and the Late Nineteenth-Century American Debate over Realism and Naturalism." *American Literary Naturalism: Recent and Uncollected Essays.* Bethesda: Academica Press, 2002. 143–65

Rahv, Philip. "Notes on the Decline of Naturalism." *Image and Idea.* Norfolk: New Directions, 1949.

Saltus, Edgar. "The Future of Fiction." *North American Review* 149 (Nov. 1889): 580–85.

Schütze, Martin. "The Services of Naturalism to Life and Literature." *Sewanee Review* 11 (1903): 425–43.

Seltzer, Mark. *Bodies and Machines*. New York: Routledge, 1992.

Sherman, Stuart P. "The Naturalism of Mr. Dreiser." *Nation* 2 Dec. 1915: 648–50.

Sully, James. "The Future of Fiction." *Forum* 9 (Aug. 1890): 644–57.

Thayer, William R. "The New Story-Tellers and the Doom of Realism." *Forum* 18 (Dec. 1894): 470–80.

Thompson, G. R., and Eric Carl Link. *Neutral Ground: New Traditionalism and the American Romance Tradition*. Baton Rouge: Louisiana State University Press, 1999.

Thompson, Maurice. "The Domain of Romance." *Forum* 8 (Nov. 1889): 326–36.

Walcutt, Charles Child. *American Literary Naturalism, A Divided Stream*. Minneapolis: University of Minnesota Press, 1956.

Watson, H. B. Marriott. "The Old Controversy." *Living Age* 239 (14 Nov. 1903): 430–39.

Wilker, Victor. "Zola as an Apostle of Temperance." *Lippincott's* (July 1898): 122–24.

Zangwill, Israel. "The Test of the Naturalistic Novel." *Critic* (14 Nov. 1896): 292–93.

....

CHAPTER 5

SAND IN YOUR MOUTH: NATURALISM AND OTHER GENRES

....

JUNE HOWARD

DISCUSSIONS of literary naturalism always seem to involve other genres. Naturalism is said to be a gritty version of realism—or perhaps its opposite, similar yet falsifying. Key critical works characterize it as responding to regionalism or as recurring to romance. Particular naturalist novels are described as (or accused of) being sentimental or melodramatic.

In fact, it is so difficult to establish a stable boundary between naturalism and other genres that the category itself often seems in danger of collapsing. Eric Carl Link confronts this prospect more directly than most scholars, beginning his 2004 definitional study with the sentence, "Naturalism is dead," and immediately citing the possibility that it "never lived" at all. More commonly—as Lisa Long points out in a recent review essay treating Link's book and two other studies published the same year (by Jennifer Fleissner and John Dudley)—naturalism is treated as an a priori category even as its meaning is contested to the point of bewilderment. In the end, Link argues not only for the viability but also for the importance of the category. Long, on the other hand, finds it implicated in the unfortunately taxonomic and even evolutionary tendencies of American literary history and argues that naturalism limits and hampers us both conceptually and in our efforts to tell an inclusive story that does not relegate the works of women and African American authors to the margins. She suggests that we consider taking another approach—although she does not explicitly say that we should discard the category of naturalism, she clearly implies that American literary history would be better off without it.

Scholars who write about American literary naturalism, including myself, have a professional investment in the category. Indeed, anyone who picks up this *Handbook* has provisionally consented to believe that the phrase refers to something that is—let us call it—real. We are accustomed to encountering gritty, uncompromising actualities in fiction, but Long's critique may make us feel as if we have sand in our mouths. Let us, however, live up to our object of study and chew on the possibility. For the space of this essay, let us question the coherence and stability of "naturalism." Given current challenges to the national model of literary history, we should ask as well what it means to call it "American." These are radical questions—radical, in the word's root sense of going to the root. But they are necessary ones, if we are to be sure that naturalism can be rigorously distinguished from other literary genres, or—what is, in complicated ways, a separate question—that it is good judgment to continue to talk and write about it.

The first question to be asked is if naturalism is especially porous and fluid, or if any form we consider would be just as difficult to define. This is my challenge squared: does the problem I'm raising apply distinctively to this generic category, or is it more general? My answer is, both. To take up the second possibility first—part of the difficulty is a general lack of consensus about what constitutes a genre. Whatever role post-structuralism might have played (or not played) in our intellectual formation, we inhabit an intellectual universe that is sophisticated, and skeptical, about classification. My own work has been profoundly shaped by the recognition that entities are defined by contrast and inextricably involve each other (as Derrida vividly educes in "The Law of Genre"). Furthermore, with all prose fiction in the modern era, we are dealing with commercially circulating forms in which elements of all sorts are constantly appropriated and reappropriated. The novel itself is characterized by generic discontinuity, so that the conventions and themes linked to naturalism—or realism, or modernism—circulate through a variety of works rather than constituting a category that contains them.

These are not new ideas. They have been powerfully articulated for several decades, and their power should be reinforced by the sophisticated treatment of genre as a social arrangement that has now emerged in the scholarship of rhetoric and composition. On these views—and my own—it does not make sense to assert a definition of a form, or to ask of any modern fiction, "does this belong to that genre? or not?" as if the literary system were a series of pigeonholes and the problem was to find and properly label the right one. Rather, we need to ask, "what is the intellectual history of this term, and what is usage doing with it now? how is its value assigned through differentiation (within literary forms, and between literature and other discourses)?" Or, in other words, "what is its place in cultural history?"

These perspectives have not, however, been fully incorporated into standard practice in American literary studies. I think that is why genre criticism seems to suffer from an especially acute version of the legitimation crisis that afflicts literary studies in general. So far, these problems are not unique to naturalism. Similarly, in the mid-1990s, Michael Anesko complained that critics working on naturalism no longer seemed to feel that they must refer to others' work on closely related topics, but that observation could surely be made about many, or even most, topics in literary studies. I do not want to exaggerate the coherence of earlier eras, and all specialized discourses of interpretation probably have an inherently centrifugal tendency. Also, this erosion of disciplinary coherence is linked to intellectual movements that I appreciate and support: challenges to literary canons, interdisciplinarity, and critiques of objectivity and abstraction that lead to skepticism about formal reason itself. None of that should stop us from recognizing that such sprawl impairs the professional credentials of literary scholarship and undermines our ability to do intellectual work. Thus Lisa Long (independently, or in any case without reference to Anesko) compares those three books about naturalism published in the same year and reaches the devastating conclusion that they produce an account of naturalism so broad that it can account for "nearly any book written during an 80-year span" (173).

The generic difficulty of writing about genre, and the difficulty of creating consensus given the enormously expanded horizons of literary scholarship, are necessary but surely not sufficient conditions for the confusion Long describes. It is hard to escape the impression that the fog rises more quickly with this than with other forms. The next logical question, then, is, "what might be distinctively difficult about distinguishing naturalism from other genres?" We should note, as we move forward, that Long's mention of a specific eighty-year time frame—presumably the later nineteenth through the mid-twentieth century—implies periodization and thus invokes another classificatory scheme, one with an ambiguous relation to genre. I will argue below that the distinctive, emerging complexity of the literary system in that span of time means that it is not a simple matter to decide how many of the "books written" then count in this discussion. But whether we yield to the suspicion that the status of naturalism is unusually precarious, or focus on its historical moment, what we need to understand is not an entity but a configuration of categories.

It is uncontroversial to begin that analysis by considering the asymmetrical twinning of realism and naturalism. That is not a balanced pair, because critics find it quite possible to discuss realism without reference to naturalism—in fact, it's constantly done—but the reverse is not so. That does not mean that realism is a more stable category, or that it is more easily defined than naturalism. Inevitably, characterizations of realism as a genre in theory raise the same problems I have been reviewing—and in practice they are facing similar critical challenges. Recently, in *Questionable Charity* (2004), William Morgan has argued persuasively that realism incorporates, rather than opposes itself to, didactic and domestic themes; in fact, he writes (implicating a genre with each word): "realism modernizes sentimentality" (2). Just as my own book about naturalism shows that both determinism and reformism are foundational to the form, he demonstrates an integral relation between realism and humanitarianism. Gregory Jackson, in *The Word and Its Witness* (2009), makes the case that Protestant homiletics—that is, the art of preaching—and literary realism were mutually constitutive and that evangelical culture has had a powerful role in shaping the American media; he subtitles his book *The Spiritualization of*

American Realism. Again, in these books we see that a genre includes that which it has been defined against: realism may be rational and secular, but it is also emotional and moral.

Understandings of realism necessarily refer to what we think is "real." As I have argued in my work on sentimentality, we tend to underestimate the interpenetration of expert and everyday vocabularies. Eric Carl Link draws careful distinctions and connections among philosophical, scientific, and literary naturalisms; in parallel, we need to consider how aesthetic ideologies implicitly depend on popular discourse. Observing vernacular usage in the contemporary United States quickly demonstrates that people often invoke the real, that the stakes of such claims are sometimes high, and that they tend to slip from one epistemological ground to another. Every day, injunctions to "be realistic" or "get real" vaguely suggest shared, comprehensive accounts of how the world works; they imply that the speaker's clear-eyed assessment of possibility will assuredly supplant whatever naïve view has previously been articulated. References to "the real thing" rely on positioning something else as inauthentic, whether the topic is courage or regional food. Here, too, the appeal is usually to intuition, based on common sense or (alternatively) insider experience—either of which trumps expert knowledge. But most strongly in each case, explicit reference to the real involves competition between different accounts.

Literary realism, similarly, relies on gestures of refutation. In American writing, both artistic manifestos and the narratives themselves disparage the conventions of other genres as too idealistic, too emotional, too literary. One of the most familiar examples is the discussion of the social impact of novel reading at the Bromfield Coreys' dinner party in *The Rise of Silas Lapham* (1885), by the realist standard-bearer William Dean Howells; it's proposed, for example, that a (fictional) popular novel, titled *Tears, Idle Tears,* ought to be called *Slop, Silly Slop.* We can look back to the origins of the novel and find the same gesture: *Don Quixote* clears room for its formal innovations and social implications by critiquing the romance. Or we can look forward to cinema—for example, in *E.T.,* this exchange takes place as children discuss how to help the stranded alien: "'Can't he just beam up?' 'This is reality, Greg.'" In each case the appeal is both to immediate experience and, somewhat paradoxically, to an educated sophistication about representation. Thus the term "reality television" both refers to an unscripted form and carries an ironic overtone (we all know it is not unedited). This complexity probably contributes to how rapidly the phrase "keepin' it real" has opened itself to parody (although its link to the especially fraught and contested immediacy of African American experience also contributes). From the seventeenth century to the present, both immediacy and skepticism serve as warrants for cognitive advantage.

We have many analyses of the conventions that produce verisimilitude across this long period. From Erich Auerbach's *Mimesis* (1946) and Ian Watt's *Rise of the Novel* (1957) to current publications, discussions of realism have been foundational to the study of the novel. And the novel has anchored our arguments for the social importance of literature: as a pedagogy of subjectivity, as an index of ideology, as a support of nationality. What has not been attended to in this discussion is the category of "fiction."

Indeed, the distinction between fiction and nonfiction has been so thoroughly naturalized that it has become difficult to see. As inhabitants of the modern world, we find it obvious; so while the novel has been a privileged, constant object of study, scholars have treated fiction—as Catherine Gallagher has shown—as a transhistorical constant. Yet, she argues, until the second quarter of the eighteenth century, English literature lacked both the *concept* of fiction and a body of "believable stories that did not solicit belief" (340). Romances, allegories, fables, and fairy tales are manifestly incredible stories; no one supposes that they are literally true. They may be retrospectively classified as fiction, but in the earlier period their form is defined rather by contrast with narratives that are understood to refer to actual events. Note that Gallagher is not suggesting that the gesture contained in fiction has never been made before, in England and elsewhere (*Don Quixote* alone could falsify that claim). The issue is, rather, the development of a consistent, continuing practice of writing and reading—we might say, the emergence of a genre. Thus, in 1720 Defoe "insisted that Robinson Crusoe was a real individual"; in 1742, when *The History of the Adventures of Joseph Andrews* was published, Henry Fielding "urged just as strenuously that his characters were not representations of actual specific people" (Gallagher 344). The novel-writer was no longer in danger of being thought to disseminate scandal by telling true stories about real people under false names or of being considered a liar. From Jane Austen through William Dean Howells to the present day, we take it for granted that fiction tells believable stories—that people simply agree not to believe.

Gallagher and Mary Poovey (in her *Genres of the Credit Economy*) link this literary history to a broad range of social transformations, and especially to economic innovations. In Gallagher's words, "Modernity is fiction-friendly because it encourages disbelief, speculation, and credit" (345). Ironically, but similarly, the modern phenomenon of humanitarianism has been linked to this kind of epistemological innovation: to an ability to foresee consequences that also enables entrepreneurship (see Haskell). Just as it's possible to make money by successfully imagining what people might want, constructing long chains of causal connection lets us see that we are responsible for suffering that occurs many miles away, perhaps on a different continent. Money itself is a fundamentally modern fiction, depending on a social contract in which we agree that it is valuable—even though neither coins nor paper money are of any use if people decide not to believe in them. We are reminded of this in moments of philosophical reflection; I have found that when I am teaching about the power of representations and an undergraduate student says "but it's just fiction!" it works well to say "yes—but *just* fiction? How is it different from, say, our bank accounts?" And, of course, we are also firmly reminded that money and credit are based on trust in moments of financial crisis.

The notion that novels create the modern world of the credit economy (*and* the deep interior self, *and* the nation) may offend our own subsequent vision of causality. The clash leads historians, and historically oriented literary scholars like myself, to think skeptical thoughts—or even to make cautionary remarks—that can veer uncomfortably close to "but it's just fiction." I would never advocate retreat from the mission of the humanities, which recognizes the power of representation and the extraordinary ability of expressive culture to reach across time and space. But arguably critics of realism and naturalism should be immersed in problems of causation and should be equally wary of the dangers of determinism and idealism— and especially careful to specify and limit our claims. Think of the parallel argument that the medieval cathedral is, in its era, a uniquely multimodal and immersive spectacle embodying a specific, historical world order; the suggestion is immensely illuminating, as we moderns view those structures through the very different, lim- iting lenses of tourism and secular historicism (see Griffiths). We can recognize the power of these innovations in architecture without claiming that they create Chris- tianity. It misrecognizes literature to see it as a cause—although imagination may well be a limiting factor. It works better to think of the novel as a kind of leading indicator, contributing to and indexing transformations.

Looking at naturalism through this long history (what is often called the *longue durée*) directs our attention to the way genres mobilize different kinds of truth. As Gallagher puts it, the "founding claim" of fiction was "*a nonreferentiality that could be seen as a greater referentiality*" (342). This reframes the contest between versions of realism, or between realism and naturalism, as a more general phenomenon; but maneuvering between competing knowledge regimes also remains utterly crucial to this particular generic system. In this context we can see clearly the importance, for example, of the connection that Gregory Jackson makes between homiletics and realism. He shows us the similarities between scrutinizing the world for providen- tial signs—that is, for markers of a spiritual reality—and focusing on "facts," or "typ- ical" characters, that point toward a social whole. Indeed, it seems to me that the connection that Georg Lukács makes between dialectics and realism, in his classic essays, has a similar structure.

The novels we call naturalist have tended to foreground aggressively secular, assertively—if not actually—rigorous understandings of causality. Often they appeal to specifically scientific systems. Of course, science arrives at all kinds of improbable truths by scrutinizing the immediate with extraordinary precision and detail, or directing our gaze beyond the human to the vastness of geological time and cosmic space. The quotidian is partly a matter of scale; look closely enough, or far enough, and the world becomes incredible. Thus naturalism invokes science to warrant its counterintuitive claims—which helps to explain its relationship to romance. Authors—most conspicuously Frank Norris—and critics alike declare that natu- ralism has affinities with the romance, indeed that is more closely aligned with romance than with realism. Characters and events must be "twisted from the ordi- nary" (as Norris wrote, commenting on Zola)—because to represent the extraordi- nary is to discard a lesser for a greater referentiality. Novels may appeal to systems that imbue reality with coded spiritual meaning (thus homiletics), with signs of his- torical teleology (thus dialectics), and with an immanent natural order (thus deter- minism). In each case, the gesture is: this story is even truer than the truth.

It was Émile Zola who originated both the term "naturalism" and the appeal to science. In *Le Roman expérimental* (1880), he parallels the methods of the novelist and the biologist; both study life. *Les Rougon-Macquart* was conceived (not, as with Balzac's *Comédie humaine*, retrospectively assembled) as an immense thought experiment. And the model was, in its moment, immensely successful. It is difficult to imagine that we would still be engaged with the category of naturalism if Zola had not cleared such a space for it and if so many other European writers had not found the opening attractive. In *The World Republic of Letters*, Pascale Casanova calls French naturalism "a genuine literary revolution" (101) and traces its impact in Germany, Spain, and Scandinavia. There is much to argue with in Casanova's work—its paradoxical Eurocentrism often gets American literature wrong (although it is better on the romance-language-speaking South than on the North), and it only skimpily reckons with Africa and Asia (a problem virtually predicted within her own argument). But it is illuminating to think of naturalism through her account of how value is negotiated in global literary space.

For Casanova, what naturalism does is to allow "writers in all parts of the world . . . to free themselves from the yoke of academicism and conservatism (which is to say, the literary past) to obtain access to modernity" (103). That effectively describes how the term worked both for Emilia Pardo Bazán and for Frank Norris. We need to attend to Casanova's world of rivalry, which constantly inclines discussion toward questions I have resisted: whether a particular novel is or is not naturalist, and whether that is a good thing or not. But in more distanced and analytical modes of reading, we can learn something from thinking about novels in terms of naturalism even when authors have not so described their work, and even when critics have not yet so characterized it. (The latter is especially to the point in the United States, where academics have been more interested in the genre than authors.) Casanova valuably directs our attention to the global nature of struggles over aesthetic ideology and how they shape writing and reading; but the project of literary scholarship asks and enables us to reckon with what is not said, directing us to the dimly but deeply recognized significance of form itself.

Authors' and critics' polemics alike position realism and naturalism as separate—but as scholars we cannot expect to disentangle them. First, prose fictions in the modern era are fundamentally characterized by generic discontinuity. They are traversed by rather than contained in specific forms (the phrase is originally Fredric Jameson's). Print is their medium, which enables them to expand to incorporate the conventions of multiple discourses as they voraciously seek readers (that is, both markets and understanding). More specifically, writers whose pronouncements volunteer, or whose work provokes, one or the other category inhabit the same terrain of asserted referentiality and puzzling causality. I now think that the concern with the spectator emphasized in my earlier work on naturalism is equally characteristic of realism, and that this web of issues always has the potential to put agency into question. As spectatorship shades toward paralysis, from Zola's *Thérèse Raquin* (1867) through Elwood Reid's *If I Don't Six* (1998), we may sense a shift toward the darker register of naturalism, but it is very difficult to make any systematic distinction on this basis.

On the other hand, it still seems to me that when novels concerned with causality and haunted by the problems of agency also mobilize the topos of the brute, foregrounding the category of naturalism becomes productive. Such images—in Reid's novel, for example—entail a difficult confrontation with human insensitivity and unfreedom, producing that characteristic sensation of sand in the mouth. Here the tendency to classify writers into a single genre hampers our work (to this extent I agree with Long). For example, Ernest Hebert's six-volume Darby series is usually—and appropriately—read in the context of regionalism. Its New Hampshire setting is crucial to all aspects of this work—which is also pervaded by a commitment to give voice to characters who appear brutal, who are disconnected and even disabled from public expression. The first novel, *The Dogs of March* (1979), asks us to enter into the perspective of the illiterate (until the end of the novel) Howard Elman and recognize his full humanity and inarticulate insight: "He lit a cigarette and watched the smoke drift aimlessly, like the fog. His mind went blank for a time, and that look came across his face that made nice people think, Oh, what a stupid brute. Thanks be to God I'm not like him. Then he heard a bird call. 'Whooo-eee, whooeee,' the bird said, but Howard thought he heard something else; he thought he heard the bird call his name, not the name he carried in his wallet but the name that was lost" (230). The same work introduces the "Shack People"—"the most despised and least understood of Americans" who provide the protagonists of two subsequent novels ("People" 6). Meanwhile, his novels without embarrassment embed small essays on social class and other topics into their narratives. Recognizing generic discontinuity can both illuminate Hebert's fiction and engage us in productive thinking about the related resources of realism, regionalism, and naturalism.

Naturalism mingles with more recently invented forms as well, and it is striking how useful it remains to seek connections to Zola as we look world-wide for the genre's continuation and connections with other genres. Elif Shafak's *The Flea Palace* (2005), for example (a best-seller in Turkey), uses the same device as *Pot-Bouille* (1882): the stories of the diverse residents of an apartment building serve as an index to life in the modern city—in Istanbul and Paris, respectively. Yet Shafak's story is profoundly "twisted from the ordinary," in the interests of greater referentiality. So is Tim Winton's *Cloudstreet* (1991), which also focuses the gritty, often unpleasant details of life in a specific building in Perth and also includes fantastic elements as it aspires to an account of a specifically Australian actuality. Neither of these authors discusses naturalism or Zola (so far as I have been able to find), but magical realism, global regionalism, and naturalism are all useful frameworks to bring to bear on these novels—not in order to figure out which category fits, but to help us think about both the works and the forms.

Acknowledging generic discontinuity can also help us recognize connections to naturalism in more radically experimental works. In B. S. Johnson's novel *The Unfortunates* (1969), the author's experience reporting a routine soccer match in Nottingham, and his memories of a friend who died a "tragic and pointless" early death from cancer in the same city, mingle without chronology. Its ordering of quotidian detail and chaotic mental life is—literally—random, because the novel is printed in twenty-seven separate sections of varied lengths and sold in a box; twenty-five of them may be read in any order. Johnson objected to the label "experimental," because it seemed to him that reviewers used it to mean unsuccessful: "Certainly I make experiments, but the unsuccessful ones are quietly hidden away" (*Aren't You* 19). Like Shafak and Winton, Johnson does not invoke Zola and Zola's version of the experimental novel—his affinities are, rather, with Beckett and Brooke-Rose. But he does push hard on questions of form and fiction. Like Gallagher, he notes the usually elided distinction between novels and fiction—and objects not only to being called experimental but also to having his work characterized as fiction because literature "teaches one something true about life; and how can you convey truth in a vehicle of fiction? The two terms, truth and fiction, are opposites. . . . I choose to write truth in the form of a novel" (*Aren't You* 14).

These persistent questions of referentiality foreground the relation of literature to knowledge. For most people, that connection is a crucial element of their reading. This is not only true of realism and naturalism; think for example of Janice Radway's *Reading the Romance* (1984), in which the women she interviews say forcefully that they value the instruction that they get from fiction. They believe that romance-novel authors research the places and periods in which their novels are set and that they are gaining reliable information when they read. This is one of the less-attended-to findings of Radway's classic study; we still think of romance readers as seeking pleasure and not knowledge. Yet every undergraduate teacher must grapple with students' conviction that the correspondence, or lack of correspondence, between fiction and their own experience matters. And it took me less than a minute to go to the Amazon website and find this comment on Khaled Hosseini's *The Kite Runner* (2003) (admittedly, a novel I selected quite purposefully): "What I liked most about this book was how it showed what life was like in Afghanistan before and after the fall of the Monarchy. It is interesting to know what a different culture is like and what their traditions are like."

Recently, Rita Felski has written eloquently about the gap that has opened up between professional readers and other users of literature. We need to reckon with the fact that people invest their time in novels at least partly for the sake of knowledge. Indeed, despite academic critics' commitment to more "literary" values, if we are honest with ourselves we will recognize that we have spent so many hours reading that much of our information about the world comes from fiction. There has been more exploration of the relation of literature and knowledge than Felski acknowledges—in, for example, Michael Wood's *Literature and the Taste of Knowledge* (2005). And, indeed, the constitutive relation between late nineteenth-century realism (and affiliated genres) and the emerging social sciences (especially ethnography) has been a frequent theme in recent critical studies (see Elliott and Evans, among others). The association continues in the contemporary period; Hebert, for example, writes about his study of the Shack People as "a sort of anthropological project in my backyard" ("People" 6). The ethical problems of this kind of Othering remain alive in today's fiction. And they remain inextricably entangled with the epistemological problems of knowledge claims that are made from within the zone of literature—so their value is understood as non-instrumental—and through the device of fiction—so their referentiality is non-referential. This constitutive paradox seems no less fascinating and powerful today than when naturalism was new.

When we enlarge the topic "naturalism and other genres" to include non-literary forms, we should include not only learned academic and professional discourses but also the mass media. Janice Radway follows many other scholars in noting that "Virtually every writer in the pantheon now associated with naturalism apprenticed with essays in the columns of fast-multiplying newspapers and then went on to write for the monthlies" ("Learned" 215). Indeed, more than twenty years ago Amy Kaplan pointed out that realism is shaped by, and partly against, the enormous expansion of mass culture; she writes that it is "a debate, within the novel form, with competing modes of representation" (13). Christopher Wilson's work comes to mind as well, of course. More recently, in *Narrating the News* (2005), Karen Roggencamp gives a detailed account of the intricate and important mutual influence of journalism and literary fiction. Here, too, the problems posed for us by naturalism seem changed in intensity rather than substance, as the penetration of the media into everyday life, and their interpenetration, keeps increasing. As Lisa Gitelman puts it, "Media and their publics co-evolve" (13)—and those publics themselves overlap and distinguish themselves as a complex open system. Thus—again in Gitelman's words—"media history and literary history share the same groundwater" although neither "drives or determines the other" (153). There is much to be learned as we study naturalism and other literary forms on this broader landscape.

"Naturalism and other genres" has proved to be a consequential topic, pointing us not only to fundamental questions about the practice of genre criticism but also to central problems in literary and cultural history. My investigation has not resulted in any strikingly new observations about the form, but it has—I hope—assembled known points into a frame of reference that makes a somewhat different kind of sense. While I certainly have not shown that the genre is stable or coherent, let alone drawn a firm boundary around it, I believe I have demonstrated that it can be useful both as an historical and as an interpretive category. Any sand remaining in our mouths is a resistance necessary to the form. The terms of literary studies are constantly transformed—but "naturalism" remains a valuable resource in our thinking about modern genres.

WORKS CITED

Anesko, Michael. "Recent Critical Approaches." *The Cambridge Companion to Realism and Naturalism: Howells to London.* Ed. Donald Pizer. New York: Cambridge University Press, 1995. 77–94.

Casanova, Pascale. *The World Republic of Letters.* 1999. Trans. M. B. DeBevoise. Cambridge: Harvard University Press, 2004.

Derrida, Jacques. "The Law of Genre." Trans. Avitall Ronell. *Critical Inquiry* 7 (1980): 55–81.

Dudley, John. *A Man's Game: Masculinity and the Anti-Aesthetics of American Literary Naturalism.* Tuscaloosa: University of Alabama Press, 2004.

Elliott, Michael A. *The Culture Concept: Writing and Difference in the Age of Realism.* Minneapolis: University of Minnesota Press, 2002.

Evans, Brad. *Before Cultures: The Ethnographic Imagination in American Literature, 1865–1920.* Chicago: University of Chicago Press, 2005.

Felski, Rita. *Uses of Literature.* Malden, Mass.: Blackwell, 2008.

Fleissner, Jennifer. *Women, Compulsion, Modernity: The Moment of American Naturalism.* Chicago: University of Chicago Press, 2004.

Gallagher, Catherine. "The Rise of Fictionality." *The Novel.* Vol. 1: *History, Geography, and Culture.* Ed. Franco Moretti. Princeton: Princeton University Press, 2006. 336–63.

Gitelman, Lisa. *Always Already New: Media, History, and the Data of Culture.* Cambridge: MIT Press, 2008.

Griffiths, Alison. *Shivers Down Your Spine: Cinema, Museums, & the Immersive View.* New York: Columbia University Press, 2008.

Haskell, Thomas L. "Capitalism and the Origins of the Humanitarian Sensibility." Pts. I and II. *American Historical Review* 90 (1985): 339–61, 547–66.

Hebert, Ernest. *The Dogs of March.* 1979. Hanover, N.H.: University Press of New England, 1993.

———. "People of the Kinship." *The Kinship: Two Novels from the Darby Series.* [*A Little More Than Kin,* 1982; *The Passion of Estelle Jordan,* 1987.] Hanover, N.H.: University Press of New England, 1993.

Howard, June. *Form and History in American Literary Naturalism.* Chapel Hill: University of North Carolina Press, 1985.

Jackson, Gregory S. *The Word and Its Witness: The Spiritualization of American Realism.* Chicago: University of Chicago Press, 2009.

Jameson, Fredric. "Generic Discontinuities in SF: Brian Aldiss' *Starship*." 1973. *Archaeologies of the Future: The Desire Called Utopia and Other Science Fictions.* New York: Verso, 2005. 254–56.

Johnson, B. S. *Aren't You Rather Young to be Writing Your Memoirs?* London: Hutchinson, 1973.

Kaplan, Amy. *The Social Construction of American Realism.* Chicago: University of Chicago Press, 1988.

Link, Eric Carl. *The Vast and Terrible Drama: American Literary Naturalism in the Late Nineteenth Century.* Tuscaloosa: University of Alabama Press, 2004.

Long, Lisa. "Genre Matters: Embodying American Literary Naturalism." *American Literary History* 19 (2007): 160–73.

Lukács, Georg. *Studies in European Realism.* Introd. Alfred Kazin. New York: Grosset & Dunlap, 1964.

———. *Writer & Critic and Other Essays.* Ed. and trans. Arthur D. Kahn. New York: Grosset & Dunlap, 1970.

Morgan, William H. *Questionable Charity: Gender, Humanitarianism, and Complicity in U.S. Literary Realism.* Lebanon: University of New Hampshire Press, 2004.

Poovey, Mary. *Genres of the Credit Economy: Mediating Value in Eighteenth- and Nineteenth-Century Britain.* Chicago: University of Chicago Press, 2008.

Radway, Janice A. "Learned and Literary Print Cultures in an Age of Professionalization and Diversification." *A History of the Book in America.* Vol. 4: *Print in Motion—The Expansion of Publishing and Reading in the United States, 1880–1940.* Chapel Hill:

University of North Carolina Press, in association with the American Antiquarian Society, 2009. 197–233.

———. *Reading the Romance: Women, Patriarchy, and Popular Literature*. 1984. Chapel Hill: University of North Carolina Press, 1991.

Roggencamp, Karen. *Narrating the News: New Journalism and Literary Genre in Late Nineteenth-Century American Newspapers and Fiction*. Kent, Ohio: Kent State University Press, 2005.

Wilson, Christopher P. *The Labor of Words: Literary Professionalism in the Progressive Era*. Athens: University of Georgia Press, 1985.

Wood, Michael. *Literature and the Taste of Knowledge*. New York: Cambridge University Press, 2005.

CHAPTER 6

....

THE DOCUMENTARY
STRATEGIES
OF NATURALISM

....

KEITH NEWLIN

WHAT do we mean when we say that naturalism is characterized by its use of documentary detail? It's common in studies of naturalism to refer to its "documentary strategies," its "documentary detail," or simply its "documentation." But with the exception of the concluding chapter in June Howard's *Form and History in American Literary Naturalism*, one looks in vain for any significant scholarship that discusses the narrative strategies of naturalism. In part, this is because scholarship tends to focus on the ideas in naturalism, not its style or aesthetic methods. Or it may be that the question itself seems simplistic, as if everyone already knows. As William Stott pointed out forty years ago in *Documentary Expression and Thirties America*, a book examining documentary nonfiction, we commonly use "document" in two ways: one, the common or dictionary meaning, refers to that which "gives information to the intellect" (12)—the material of fact, verifiable and quantifiable, tangible and impersonal—typically comprised of historical records, objective observations, and other sorts of specific evidence. "Document" in this case "assumes that intellectual verification of some sort is possible. It asks for concrete examples, for documentation"; it relies on an appeal to some sort of objective authority. But we also use "document" to refer to that which "informs the emotions" (12)—the representative case, the illustrative anecdote, the pathetic or inspiring story, the human document. Stott's example is a news story in which a pack of dogs killed two small boys while their father helplessly tried to drive the animals away. The story contains verifiable facts, or documentation in the first sense; but it also "defies comment; it imposes its meaning. It confronts us, the audience, with empirical evidence of such nature as to render dispute impossible and interpretation superfluous" (14). It is a human document that offers "a lesson in living . . . an event that shows one what life is like; an epiphany that strips reality bare" (16).

The American literary naturalists were drawn to both sorts of document in their fiction, but they were especially attracted to the human document, the illustrative human example that pointed to a larger truth, one that offered a "lesson in living." Many of the most prominent naturalists—Stephen Crane, Frank Norris, Jack London, Theodore Dreiser—began their craft as journalists, and the conventions of late nineteenth-century reporting not only directed them to their subjects but also shaped the narrative strategies that inform their writing. What follows is an effort of typology, an attempt to describe what naturalists do when they write.

A Typology of the Documentary

Documentary description, based on observation, is probably the hallmark of naturalistic writing. Detailed description is common to both realism and naturalism, and for both genres, description functions as an effort to depict the truth of a scene, to show readers how it was. Scholars have found Georg Lukács's distinction between narration and description to be a useful means of discriminating between the two genres. In his discussion of the narrative distinctions between Tolstoy and Zola, Lukács observes that in conveying the details of scene Tolstoy tends to narrate events from the perspective of a participant, whereas Zola describes them from the perspective of an observer. In describing the differences in the portrayal of a horse race in Tolstoy's *Anna Karenina* and Zola's *Nana*, Lukács comments that "Vronsky's ride is thoroughly integrated into the total action of the novel. . . . [It is] an event of essential significance in Vronsky's life." Tolstoy describes the race twice: first relating "with precision and sophistication everything of significance in the preparations and in the race itself" (111); and then through the perspective of Anna, as an "inner drama" that forms the "climax of the entire day" (112). For Zola, however, "Every possible detail at a race is described precisely, colourfully and with sensuous vitality. . . . However, for all its virtuosity the description is mere filler in the novel. The events are loosely related to the plot and could easily be eliminated" (110). For realists, Lukács concludes, description serves as an integral part of the plot and characterization; it is more than mere incident; description is interwoven into the narrative of plot and characterization so that readers are thereby encouraged to experience the events through the characters' perception. For naturalists, however, whose typically excessive description of events often serves as background for sensational plots and eccentric characters, "characters are merely spectators, more or less interested in the events.... We are merely observers" (116). What separates the realist and the naturalist is not the tendency toward description but the choice of what to describe and the purpose of that description. Naturalists are more concerned with the symbolic or emotional potential presented by the "human document," and their descriptions tend to reflect their interest in showing the emotional resonance of a scene, which they then present to the reader as a spectacle for amusement or instruction. This emphasis on spectacle is also the reason most naturalist fictions adopt an objective third-person narrative point of view.

We can see this spectatorial description operating in the opening paragraph of Frank Norris's *McTeague* (1899):

> It was Sunday, and, according to his custom on that day, McTeague took his dinner at two in the afternoon at the car conductors' coffee-joint on Polk Street. He had a thick gray soup; heavy, underdone meat, very hot, on a cold plate; two kinds of vegetables; and a sort of suet pudding, full of strong butter and sugar. On his way back to his office, one block above, he stopped at Joe Frenna's saloon and bought a pitcher of steam beer. It was his habit to leave the pitcher there on his way to dinner. (5)

Its specificity stands out: we know the day of the week, the time, the place, the specific items of McTeague's meal, even the incongruity of very hot meat served on a cold plate as well as the dentist's habit of leaving his pitcher to be filled with cheap, gassy beer while at dinner. We are invited to be spectators at McTeague's Sunday meal. While we often encounter detailed description in the work of realists—see Bartley Hubbard's sketch of Silas Lapham's physical features in the opening of William Dean Howells's *The Rise of Silas Lapham* (1884)—such description usually functions to provide texture, to provide verisimilitude for the scene; in the case of Lapham, Hubbard's comic description of Lapham's personal appearance reveals him to be a representative type of self-made man, which accords with Howells's belief that realists should write about the typical rather than the extraordinary. But in the *McTeague* example, the detail also exists to show that the dentist is a creature of habit; Norris's opening gambit is to demonstrate the thesis that will control his narrative. A principal function of documentary description, then, is to pile up detail to prove the existence, as well as the accuracy, of the subject being depicted. But it also serves to lead readers to draw conclusions, to make connections, and, sometimes, to more direct action. In *The Jungle* (1906), Upton Sinclair's notorious documentary descriptions of unsanitary processes in Chicago's packinghouses, conveyed in a painstaking tour-guide narrative, led outraged readers to clamor for the passage of the Pure Food and Drug Act of 1906. While Sinclair had intended to rouse sympathy for exploited and mistreated workers, the effect of his piling up of detail instead focused attention on the practices of meatpackers. As Sinclair famously remarked, "I aimed at the public's heart, and by accident I hit it in the stomach" ("What Life" 351).

Naturalists also take pains to sketch the details of the milieu of their plots. In the second chapter of *Sister Carrie* (1900), before he sends Carrie out to look for a job,

Dreiser painstakingly describes the city environment that confronts his little country traveler:

> In 1889 Chicago had the peculiar qualifications of growth which made such adventuresome pilgrimages even on the part of young girls plausible. Its many and growing commercial opportunities gave it widespread fame, which made of it a giant magnet, drawing to itself, from all quarters, the hopeful and the hopeless—those who had their fortune yet to make and those whose fortunes and affairs had reached a disastrous climax elsewhere. It was a city of over 500,000, with the ambition, the daring, the activity of a metropolis of a million. Its streets and houses were already scattered over an area of seventy-five square miles. (11)

For three dense paragraphs, Dreiser continues his sketch of the growing city. We learn of the growth of industry, the spread of street-car lines, of its streets and sewer systems, the establishment of gas lamps, the rise of the shopping district whose buildings include "large plates of window glass, now so common, [but which] were then rapidly coming into use." We peer through these windows to observe "clerks hard at work, and genteel businessmen"—and even take note of their clothing: the men wear "'nobby' suits and clean linen" (12). Indeed, the distinctive feature of naturalistic prose, Howard argues, is this emphasis on looking, where the writer invites readers to assume the role of spectator of the unfamiliar, which the writer will then describe in painstaking detail (148–52).

This effort to depict the fictional world accurately and completely for the eyes of a spectator stems from the revolution in journalism in which so many naturalists served their apprenticeship. The growth of cities and their immigrant populations hungry for stories about celebrities and sensational treatments of news events, coupled with a journalistic ethos that demanded accuracy of treatment and a reliance upon verifiable facts, led newspapers and magazines to compete with each other through accurate reporting and detailed human-interest stories, often based on interviews that carefully described the subject's appearance and words. A popular genre of story was the "Human Document"—as *McClure's* explicitly titled a series appearing in the first issue of the magazine in 1893—at first a set of photographs of famous men, but soon morphing into a "Real Conversations" series of extended and lavishly illustrated profiles of such public figures as Howells, Bret Harte, James Whitcomb Riley, and Robert Louis Stevenson, among others, that combined close description of the subject, often witty dialogue, and high-toned gossip. The naturalists cut their teeth in this sort of feature writing, with Dreiser, for example, contributing dozens of profiles of famous men to the leading magazines. In their writing for newspapers, Crane, Norris, and London were careful observers of events and people and took pains to convey their observations accurately, for editors realized that in competing for circulation, readers were drawn to accurate, vivid depictions of unusual events that revealed the human drama underlying the episode. As a placard on the walls of the *New York World* reminded Dreiser when he worked for that paper, "The Facts—The Color—The Facts" were what readers wanted (Fishkin 97). The emphasis on accuracy in reporting occurred, the historian Michael Schudson observes, because "[r]eporters in the 1890s saw themselves in part, as scientists uncovering the economic and political facts of industrial life more boldly, clearly and realistically that anyone before" (qtd. in Fishkin 98). As the naturalists learned from their stint as journalists, to describe events accurately is to understand them, and they therefore tend to saturate their fiction with details, to pile fact upon fact, as a way of documenting the accuracy of their fictional representation.

The attempt to describe accurately often led writers to investigate the causes of the behavior and events they depicted in their fictions, and another hallmark of the documentary method is research to provide the "facts" underlying the fictions. One celebrated example of research employed to explain behavior is Dreiser's depiction of Hurstwood's decline into near-catatonic depression. Dreiser was deeply impressed by the physiological experiments of Elmer Gates that led the scientist to assert that there was a biochemical cause for changes of mood, and he therefore attributed the onset of Hurstwood's depression to changes in biochemistry: "Now, it has been shown experimentally," Dreiser writes,

> that a constantly subdued frame of mind produces certain poisons in the blood, called katastates, just as virtuous feelings of pleasure and delight produce helpful chemicals called anastates. The poisons generated by remorse inveigh against the system, and eventually produce marked physical deterioration. To these Hurstwood was subject.
>
> In the course of time it told upon his temper. His eye no longer possessed that buoyant, searching shrewdness which had characterised it in Adams Street. His step was not as sharp and firm. He was given to thinking, thinking, thinking.

The effect of these "poisons," Dreiser explains, is that "slowly, exceedingly slowly, [Hurstwood's] desire to greet, conciliate, and make at home these people who visited the Warren Street place passed from him" (240). What is notable about this example is not its particular content—the specific physiological cause of mood changes—but rather Dreiser's desire to explain character psychology in scientific terms. As John Berger observes, a characteristic of the late nineteenth-century mind is a "belief that observable quantifiable facts, recorded by scientists and experts, would one day offer man such total knowledge about nature and society that he would be able to order them both" (qtd. in Howard 147). Dreiser's lifelong habit of dipping into scientific and pseudo-scientific explanations for human action and then incorporating them into his fiction reveals his desire to achieve this "total knowledge" and therefore make sense of his world.

Like Dreiser, Norris also drew on scientific or technical explanations when he needed to develop the texture of a character's life. For example, to make more plausible the preposterousness of McTeague's profession—the character, after all, is so inherently stupid he has difficulty following conversations—Norris drew upon the details of Thomas Fillebrown's A Text-book of Operative Dentistry for the technical particulars of McTeague's professional activity, and he sketches his dentist periodically consulting the textbook to learn how best to fix Trina's broken teeth. At some point in the composition of the novel, and in a bit of sophomoric playfulness, Norris hit upon the idea of connecting McTeague's youthful occupation as miner to dentistry, as the narrative voice later acknowledges in the novel, with the correspondence between the Burley drill and dental engine serving to establish a link to the atavistic forces driving McTeague. Of McTeague's escape into mining near the novel's close, Norris writes: "It was the same work he had so often performed in his 'Parlors,' only magnified, made monstrous, distorted, and grotesqued, the caricature of dentistry" (217). He therefore sought out the technical details to make this bit of whimsy more credible. Thematically, the reason for the occupational resemblance is to establish the primacy of McTeague's instinctual drive, which led him from mining to dentistry and then back to mining, but it also functions to set up the atavistic, instinctive sixth sense that propels McTeague onward, one step ahead of Marcus and the law.

This tendency to move from concrete, scientific, or technical detail to larger force—biochemical causation, in the case of Dreiser; latent atavism, for Norris—is characteristic of the naturalists' use of research based on interviews, study of official records, and delving into newspapers with an eye open for the illustrative "human document." Consider, for example, Upton Sinclair's research into the workings of the Chicago stockyards to establish the details of the meatpacking industry as a springboard for commentary on labor practices and the ultimate salvation of socialism, Dreiser's poring over newspapers in search of representative murder cases to provide the impetus for *An American Tragedy* (1925) and to reveal the pattern of murder for social gain, or Jack London's research into the minutia of sled-dog activity for *The Call of the Wild* (1903), largely culled from Egerton Young's *My Dogs in the Northland* (1902), with the aim of illustrating the workings of evolution. What distinguishes naturalist from realist prose is the naturalist's tendency to move toward a thesis: the desire to prove a position, usually the workings of a natural or environmental law. Documentary research provides evidence, proof of the inevitability of the law.

Writers are often inspired by real events; naturalists are particularly drawn to headlines and sensational news stories and illustrations for the plots and themes of their fictions, which brings us to a third type of documentation: the naturalists' tendency to base their fictions on actual events and at times incorporate portions of other writers' prose into their own work, and often verbatim. Frank Norris picks up his newspaper one day in 1893 and reads the headline, "Twenty-Nine Fatal Wounds. Sarah Collins Slaughtered by Her Husband Because She Would Not Give Him Money"—and the idea for *McTeague* is planted. Patrick Collins, he reads, is a "brute" and "whenever he got drunk he beat [his wife], and if she did not give him money he knocked her down" (249, 250). Four days later he reads the sensational follow-up story, headlined "He Was Born for the Rope," and learns that "Patrick Collins, the Savage of Civilization," was a "Human Beast," a "Mixture of Moral Idiocy, Egotism, and Shallow Cunning" (253). In the sensationalist copy of the time, Collins is depicted as a savage, a brute, a type of primitive man, subject to hereditary drunkenness that inflames his brutality and leads him to "slaughter" his wife with multiple stab wounds, "every one of them good and hearty and satisfying" (256). At its core, the sensational event is unusual, not the commonplace event typical of realism. Naturalists thus seem drawn to sensational news stories for their fictions because they see in them examples of the operations of natural law or scientific principles or, as in the Collins case, an example that illustrates and confirms Cesare Lombroso's theories of criminal behavior, which Norris had encountered through his reading of Max Nordau. Their fictions thus become in part an effort to explain why unusual events occur. As Shelly Fisher Fishkin explains in comparing *An American Tragedy* to its sources, Dreiser remained close to his sources because he had a thesis to prove, that "fact was fate": "In all of the clippings Dreiser collected, the young murderer sought to eradicate the fact of his initial sexual transgression and the need for any responsibility for its consequences. But, repeatedly, fact would prove to be destiny; the young man's deeds and words would follow him regardless of the cleverness of his attempts to evade them" (120). Dreiser's saturation of detail in the novel stems from his desire to challenge "his readers' most unquestioned assumptions" to reveal Clyde's story as a story of class ambition and to explore "the normality underlying the criminal" as well as the "criminality underlying the normal" (125).

But the naturalists did not merely slavishly copy the events that inspired their fictions and dress them with detail and causal explanations; they often were selective in what they chose to incorporate—or leave out—with the idea of pointing their readers to a particular didactic conclusion. Stephen Crane's "The Open Boat" is a case study in the naturalists' art of writing fiction based on sources. In 1897, Crane embarked on the filibustering steamer *Commodore*, bound for Cuba to supply arms and other cargo to the Cuban insurrectionists. The ship struck a sandbar near the mouth of the St. Johns River and sprung a leak; a few hours later, the *Commodore* sank. Crane spent thirty hours at sea in a ten-foot lifeboat, accompanied by Captain Edward Murphy, Steward C. W. Montgomery, and Oiler William Higgins. Soon after reaching shore, Crane published "Stephen Crane's Own Story," a nonfiction account of the events leading to the wreck that concludes, "The history of life in an open boat for thirty hours would no doubt be instructive for the young, but none is to be told here and now" (475). Six months later, in June 1897, Crane published a fictional account of his hours on the lifeboat as "The Open Boat: A Tale Intended to Be after the Fact" in *Scribners' Magazine*. Several critics have argued that "The Open Boat" is in reality creative nonfiction, rather than fiction, because Crane's narrative so closely follows the facts of the aftermath of the ship's sinking. But Crane is selective in his use of details: while most of the memorable events of the story did occur—the incessant rowing, the captain's injured shoulder, the overcoat sail, the Mosquito Inlet lighthouse that appears as a pinpoint on shore, the fact that only the cook and Crane had lifebelts, and so on—Crane also changes or omits details that, if reported, would substantially alter his theme. Some news reports mention that five men were in the lifeboat, that Crane was the first (not the last) man to enter the lifeboat, that Crane saved a sailor from drowning in the surf (this is from the account of Montgomery, the steward), that the captain fired his pistol to attract attention when one-half mile from shore (see documents collected in "A Tale of the Sea"). Had Crane included these details, he would have overpopulated his representative crew and undermined his theme of the insignificance of human beings because the correspondent would emerge as heroic—the term two news reports ascribe to Crane. In short, while their fictions are typically solidly informed by documentary fact, Crane and the other naturalists often select from their sources those details that enable them to demonstrate the thesis that so often characterizes their work.

DOCUMENTARY AND THE PROBLEM OF PLAGIARISM: THE CASE OF JACK LONDON

At times, however, naturalists include passages from their sources with little alteration. A well-known example is Dreiser's incorporation of lines from the play *Under the Gaslight* in *Sister Carrie*; he does so, of course, because his characters speak the lines when they perform the play. But what of his verbatim repetitions of Nathan Swartz's notes and trial transcripts in his play *The Hand of the Potter* (1918), his use of Grace Brown's love letters and portions of the Gillette trial transcript in *An American Tragedy*; and of Richard Wright's similar repetition of trial transcript language in *Native Son* (1940)? These latter instances appear to be examples of sheer sloth and laziness, for Dreiser and Wright could have created new language rather than reprinting the source. Here, the influence of the source seems to have so dominated their imagination that they have, in effect, fetishized the source—and it seems no accident that the trial scenes in all three works are the most tedious portions of the narratives. Here also, in Dreiser's case at least, his training in journalism seems to have led to a reverence for fact and quotation for its own sake.

Sometimes, however, a writer's fetishism of source materials is so pronounced that an incredulous public levies the charge of plagiarism. The pattern of response of those accused of plagiarism is usually the same: first denial, then excuses—typically of unconscious borrowing, then of sloppy note-taking, and then often a rationalization to the effect that all writers borrow and imitate—with Shakespeare being the most prominent example. But few accused plagiarists have been as brazen as Jack London, who repeatedly denied the charge and instead justified his "borrowings" as simply part of the normal writing methods of all creative writers: that is, writers often base their fictions upon sources, upon facts, whether observed from life or gleaned from the headlines. As we have seen, writers often do base their fictions upon words others have inscribed, and fiction, plays, movies, and television shows afford ample examples of such borrowing. An examination of Jack London's plagiarism, and especially his defense, is of considerable interest for understanding the documentary strategies of naturalism, and particularly for distinguishing influence and documentation from imitation and theft.

On 25 March 1906, the *New York World* headlined a story, "Singular Similarity of a Story Written by Jack London and One Printed Four Years Before a Literary Puzzle," provided eighteen examples of similar passages in parallel columns, and proceeded to imply that London plagiarized his story "Love of Life" from Augustus Bridle and J. K. Macdonald's "Lost in the Land of the Midnight Sun," though the columnist was careful not to use the term "plagiarism" and instead tactfully described London's method as his "uncredited obligation to the earlier narrative." And indeed there are striking similarities. "Lost in the Land of the Midnight Sun" is about the wanderings of Archie Bunn, a Canadian geological surveyor who, carrying a sack of ore samples, becomes lost in the Coppermine River valley at Dease Bay on the Arctic Sea. Ill-clothed, with worn-out moccasins, no compass, no provisions, and an empty rifle, Bunn slips and sprains his ankle during the second day. His companion disappears. Alone, Bunn struggles to survive as he makes his way toward the bay shore, repairs his moccasins with strips torn from a blanket, and encounters a ravenous wolf, until he is fortuitously rescued by a band of Yellow Knife Indians. Those who know "Love of Life" will immediately recognize the key elements common to both narratives: the setting, the lost traveler, the sack of rock (gold in London's story), the sprained ankle, the disappearing companion, the tattered moccasins, the empty rifle, the wolf, the fortunate rescue, and especially the long, arduous struggle to survive in a hostile environment.

Coincidently, both article and story had appeared in *McClure's* magazine. When Samuel S. McClure wrote to London for an explanation, London replied,

> It is a common practice of authors to draw material for their stories, from the newspapers. Here are facts of life reported in journalistic style, waiting to be made into literature. . . . So common is this practice of authors, that it is recommended by all the instructors in the art of the short story, to read the newspapers and magazines in order to get material. . . . Now to the "Love of Life," which the New York *World* so generously paralleled with "Lost in the Land of the Midnight Sun." "Lost in the Land of the Midnight Sun" is not a story. It is a narrative of fact. It was published in *McClure's Magazine*. It tells the actual sufferings of a man with a sprained ankle in the country of the Coppermine River. It is not fiction, and it is not literature. I took the facts of life contained in it, added to them many other facts of life gained from other sources, and made, or attempted to make, a piece of literature out of them. (10 April 1906; *Letters* 568–69)

Less than a year later, the *Independent* repeated the charge under the title "Is Jack London a Plagiarist?" this time in regard to *The Call of the Wild*, which "shows certain startling resemblances" to Egerton Young's *My Dogs in the Northland*, especially "marked similarities in the personnel of the leading dog characters, and in circumstances and situations" (Bosworth 373). In columns of deadly parallel, the magazine made its case. After making himself snug in his nest, for example, Young's dog Rover "curled round and round . . . and rested until the . . . call to supper brought him . . . his allowance of two well thawed fish"; when he returned to his "resting place in the snow [he] almost invariably found it occupied." London's Buck similarly makes a "nest," eats thawed fish, and "when Buck finished his ration and returned, he found his nest occupied." One of Young's dogs "resented being silently approached on his blind side"—as does London's Sol-Leks, who "did not like to be approached on his blind side" (Bosworth 374) The examples spread over three pages.

As he had to McClure, London wrote to the editor of the *Independent* to explain that his novel reflected the usual practice of creative writers—that is, to write convincing, realistic narratives, writers often base their fictions on documents, observation, experience, and an eye for the telling anecdote—the "human document."

> Fiction-writers have always considered actual experiences of life to be a lawful
> field for exploitation—in fact, every historical novel is a sample of fictional
> exploitation of published narratives of fact.
>
> Take an instance from the article accusing me of plagiarism, now in your
> hands—that of the dog that lay down on its back with its paws in the air and
> begged for moccasins. This happened to one of Mr. Young's dogs and I exploited
> it in my story. But suppose that I am in the Klondike. Suppose this incident
> occurs with one of my dogs. I can utilize this material in a story, can I not?
> Agreed. Now suppose it doesn't happen with my dog, but with some one else's
> dog, but that I happen to see the incident. May I use it? Agreed again. Now,
> however, I do not see the incident, but the man with whose dog it occurred tells
> me about it. May I use it? Again agreed. A step further, instead of telling me about
> it, a man writes the incident, not in a story, but in a plain narrative of incidents.
> May I use it in my story? And if not, why not? (? Jan. 1907; *Letters* 667)

Is London's defense that he is simply gathering up "facts" and "incidents" and turning them into literature persuasive? As we have seen, naturalists are commonly inspired by journalistic accounts of sensational or puzzling events, and some of the most important naturalistic novels are drawn from the headlines. Frank Norris was inspired by newspaper accounts of a brutal murder for some of the sensational scenes and characterization in *McTeague*. Theodore Dreiser based *An American Tragedy* on the Chester Gillette-Grace Brown murder case, closely paraphrasing some of Grace Brown's letters and even quoting verbatim from newspaper accounts of the trial. Richard Wright similarly drew upon the Leopold and Loeb case for many of the incidents in *Native Son*, and, like Dreiser, closely paraphrased some of the trial language while also quoting some phrases verbatim. And more recently, Joyce Carol Oates drew upon many of the particulars in a *Life* magazine article about an Arizona serial killer for her widely anthologized story "Where Are You Going, Where Have You Been?" (1966), including some of the most memorable details of her story—the cowboy boots stuffed with cans and rags, the killer who used makeup to appear younger—as well as the theme of teenagers who find solace in music while their parents are oblivious to the reality of their children's lives (see Moser). Yet no one has accused these writers of plagiarism for their use of "facts" in their works.

In both letters, London justifies his methods by distinguishing between "facts" and "fiction": it is legitimate for creative writers to use the facts of others, he argues, even if in written form, because the fictionist has combined them in a new way to create a work of art. An analogy in the art world would be the artist who combines found materials into a collage. Here the premium is on creation, the writer as originator, which is a relatively recent development, for until the romantics conceived of authorship as organic origination, the prevailing conception of the author was one who either wrote out of divine inspiration or one who was a craftsman who arranged materials for some prescribed effect. After the romantics, the author came to be seen as a creator of new things, one "who is solely responsible—and therefore exclusively deserving of credit—for the production of a unique work" (Woodmansee 426).

So when London explained to McClure that he "took the facts of life contained in ["Lost in the Land of the Midnight Sun"], added to them many other facts of life gained from other sources, and made, or attempted to make, a piece of literature out of them," he is describing the legitimate work of a creative author who originates new literature from nonliterary sources—that is, source materials that are fair game for creative work. As Justice Oliver Wendell Holmes opined in a famous copyright case about the distinction between reproducing a copy of a painting and creating a new painting from the same original, "Others are free to copy the original. They are not free to copy the copy" (qtd. in Gaines 2). In both letters, London is careful to distinguish his source material as nonfiction, as "facts"—that is, as the "original" material that others can later arrange into new creative works. Both "Lost in the Land of the Midnight Sun" and *My Dogs in the Northland* are, London explains, "a narrative of fact" and a "narrative of incidents"; neither is a creative work of the imagination. Creative works are not fair game for use in fiction because copying creative work mocks the idea of origination. But if part of origination means combining ideas and facts in new ways, as a collage artist does, then authors may legitimately copy the ideas and facts reported by others. Plagiarism is therefore odious because it is a pretense at originality. If authors invent, create the new, plagiarists are not authors.

What lies behind London's justifications is the notion that no one has property rights in the facts and incidents of life. One writer's use of them does not preclude another writer's. But London's justifications extend to creative work as well. In his view, if the original expression is an inferior work of art, that lesser narrative practically demands to be appropriated and transformed by the better artist. When a *New York Times* reporter wrote to sound out London's reaction to being accused of plagiarizing yet another writer, Stanley Waterloo, whose *The Story of Ab* (1897) seemed to anticipate the scenes and characters of London's *Before Adam* (1907), London countered with a hypothetical argument that makes plain his belief that in literature, like the natural world, the fittest creation survives. "Suppose, however, the plagiarism is so eminently great that it outshines the original?" he wrote to B. W. Babcock on 3 December 1906. "Who has any complaint coming? The world is better off for the bigger creation. The original creation stands where it was, and it's ridiculous for the original creator to yowl because somebody else has made a bigger mudpie. . . . The real question of plagiarism is not Did he do it the way I did it?—but is, Did he do it better than I did it? And if he did it better, why take off your hat to him" (*Letters* 645).

The issue of justifying plagiarism on the grounds that it transforms a poor original into a greater work of art has often been echoed by other writers. T. S. Eliot once remarked that

> One of the surest tests [of an artist] is the way in which a poet borrows. Immature poets imitate; mature poets steal; bad poets deface what they take, and good poets

make it into something better, or at least something different. The good poet
welds his theft into a whole of feeling which is unique, utterly different from that
from which it was torn; the bad poet throws it into something which has no
cohesion. (qtd. in Mallon 26)

We have only to look to Eliot's "The Wasteland" (1922), with its pastiche of allusions
and borrowings, to see Eliot's contention in practice.

In his letter to Babcock, London justified his use of Waterloo's story on the
grounds that he was making it better, a "bigger creation": "I wrote *Before Adam* as a
reply to the *Story of Ab* because I considered the latter unscientific. Mr. Waterloo
crowded the social evolution of a thousand generations into one generation. . . .
Also, I tried to reproduce the primitive world in an artistic form, which same
Mr. Waterloo did not do. . . . Mr. Waterloo failed to create the convincing illusion
that is proper to any work of fiction" (*Letters* 644). In London's evolutionary aesthetic, it was thus quite proper to appropriate portions of the *Story of Ab*.

Or so London argues. And this is what Dreiser, Wright, and Oates do in their
fictions—that is, copy the letters, trial transcripts, and pivotal incidents reported by
others and transmute them into new creative works of the imagination. But let's
look at what London actually copies for his. In "Lost in the Land of the Midnight
Sun," "The white partridges began to whirr and wheel over the ledges and muskegs
as far as the eye could see. Bunn lost half an hour throwing stones at them. . . .
'Ker-ker-ker' went the cry of the white partridges as they rose . . ." (155, 156). In "Love
of Life" London's traveler "came upon a valley where rock ptarmigan rose on whir-
ring wings from the ledges and muskegs. 'Ker-ker-ker' was the cry they made. He
threw stones at them, but could not hit them" (423). In the former story Bunn
"hunched his pack a little over his left shoulder"; in London's story his traveler
"hitched his pack farther over on his left shoulder." The examples of similarity in
phrasing go on and on.

What London copies here are not just the "facts"—the partridges/ptarmigans,
their cry, the setting among ledges and muskegs, the throwing of stones, the pack,
the left shoulder—but the plot, the setting, the sequence of events, the characters: he
copies the *narrative* that makes sense of the facts. London's appropriation in many
ways is analogous to the student who copies another's explanation. In both cases,
the real sin is the pretense of origination, the claim of ownership of the narrative
that makes sense of "facts."

At one point in his letter to the editor of the *Independent*, London wrote that he
wished his accuser would include "a definition of what constitutes plagiarism."
What London never properly understood is that plagiarism means more than
merely copying the facts related by others. Even though he has alchemized that
narrative into a "bigger creation," "Love of Life" and portions of *The Call of the Wild*
follow the originals so closely that his authorship, his originality, is called into question—that's his real sin, one he is disingenuous about. "Love of Life" and *The Call of
the Wild* are indeed better works of art, but they are inevitably tarnished because
part of the reason we value these stories is the presumption of London's creative

originality. Knowing that London is not wholly responsible for much of the narrative inevitably cheapens the value of the work as "art."

The naturalists revered the "human document"—the story that pointed to human foibles, perplexing events, astonishing coincidences, behaviors that tested credulity—and in their effort to explain that story, they drew upon their training as journalists, an education that taught them to pay attention to the unusual event and to describe it accurately, with the aim of producing a narrative to enable readers to see, not just the event itself, but also the underlying reasons or causes of that event. In constructing their fictions, they often incorporated the "facts" as they found them in newspapers and other documents, sometimes altering them but more often reproducing them accurately, knowing that the texture of detail convinces. Some, like Dreiser and London, were so enthralled with the fact itself that they lost sight of the necessity of selection, and so their fictions sometimes incorporate documents wholesale, piling on detail upon detail to demonstrate the accuracy of scene, behavior, or character as a means of illustrating the causes of behavior. Unlike realism, naturalism is an essentially didactic literature with a thesis to prove, whether it be economic determinism, the latent atavism of man, or the inescapable force of heredity. To entertain readers while also convincing them of the plausibility of the thesis that controls their fictions, the naturalists therefore adapted the narrative strategies of documentary reporting to their larger fictional aim.

WORKS CITED

Bosworth, L. A. M. "Is Jack London a Plagiarist?" *Independent* 62 (1906): 373–75.

Bridle, Augustus, and J. K. Macdonald. "Lost in the Land of the Midnight Sun." *McClure's* 18 (Dec. 1901): 477–92.

Crane, Stephen. "Stephen Crane's Own Story." *Stephen Crane: An Omnibus*. Ed. Robert Wooster Stallman. New York: Knopf, 1952. 465–76.

Dreiser, Theodore. *Sister Carrie*. Ed. Donald Pizer. 2nd ed. New York: Norton, 1991.

Fishkin, Shelly Fisher. *From Fact to Fiction: Journalism and Imaginative Writing in America*. New York: Oxford University Press, 1985.

Gaines, Jane M. *Contested Culture: The Image, the Voice, and the Law*. Chapel Hill: University of North Carolina Press, 1991.

"He Was Born for the Rope." *San Francisco Examiner* 14 Oct. 1893: 8; rpt. in Norris, *McTeague* 253–57.

Howard, June. *Form and History in American Literary Naturalism*. Chapel Hill: University of North Carolina Press, 1985.

London, Jack. *The Letters of Jack London*. Ed. Earle Labor, Robert C. Leitz III, and I. Milo Shepard. Vol. 2. Stanford: Stanford University Press, 1988.

———. "Love of Life." *Novels & Stories*. Ed. Donald Pizer. New York: Library of America, 1982. 418–37.

Lukács, Georg. "Narrate or Describe?" *Writer and Critic and Other Essays*. Trans. and ed. Arthur D. Kahn. New York: Grosset and Dunlap, 1970. 110–48.

Mallon, Thomas. *Stolen Words: Forays into the Origins and Ravages of Plagiarism.*
New York: Ticknor & Fields, 1989.

Moser, Don. "The Pied Piper of Tuscon." *Life* 4 (Mar. 1966): 18–24, 80c.

Norris, Frank. *McTeague.* Ed. Donald Pizer. 2nd ed. New York: Norton, 1997.

Sinclair, Upton. "What Life Means to Me." *The Jungle.* Ed. Clare Virginia Eby. New York:
Norton, 2003. 348–53.

"Singular Similarity of a Story Written by Jack London and One Printed Four Years Before
a New Literary Puzzle." *New York World* 19 Apr. 1906: 1E

Stott, William. *Documentary Expression and Thirties America.* New York: Oxford University
Press, 1973.

"A Tale of the Sea." *Stephen Crane: An Omnibus.* Ed. Robert Wooster Stallman. New York:
Knopf, 1952. 415–76.

"Twenty-Nine Fatal Wounds." *San Francisco Examiner* 10 Oct. 1893: 12; rpt. in Norris,
McTeague 249–53.

Woodmansee, Martha. "The Genius and the Copyright: Economic and Legal Conditions of
the Emergence of the 'Author.'" *Eighteenth-Century Studies* 37 (1984): 425–48.

PART III

THE SCIENTIFIC AND PHILOSOPHIC BACKGROUND

DETERMINISM, FREE WILL, AND MORAL RESPONSIBILITY IN AMERICAN LITERARY NATURALISM

IAN F. ROBERTS

For Liam

LITERATURE AND PHILOSOPHY

What more can possibly be said about the issue of determinism in literary naturalism? Writes Eric Carl Link, "For a century, virtually every study of naturalistic fiction in America has had something to say about determinism" (103). And Donald Pizer has lamented that discussions of literary naturalism centering on its determinism typically degenerate into little more than complaints about individual works' logical inconsistency ("Study" 2–3, 9–10). As Pizer puts it, "an entire generation of critics has argued . . . that naturalists have been hopelessly confused because they introduce elements of free will and moral responsibility into accounts of a supposedly necessitarian world" ("Three" 14). Consequently, Pizer has sought "to break the hold of the criterion of an absolute determinism in the definition of American naturalism" ("Study" 9). Such is Pizer's stature as a critic, and such is his success at redirecting analysis away from the topic of determinism, that further discussion of the subject now calls for justification. Pizer has downplayed the place of determinism by viewing naturalistic philosophy metaphorically, by regarding philosophical passages as interpretively unreliable, by blurring the distinctions between naturalism and humanism, and by insisting on a broad separation of art and ideas. While Pizer's desire to avoid the confusions and complaints characterizing previous criticism is certainly understandable, none of these strategies are ultimately successful at budging determinism from its central place in naturalistic fiction or at obviating the need to yet again consider determinism's meaning and implications.

In "The Problem of Philosophy in the Naturalistic Novel," Pizer argues that ideas in naturalistic fiction play a "primarily" or "principally" (113, 114) metaphorical role and that these ideas "are often inadequate guides to the interpretation of the novel in which they appear" (114). However, while ideas may function metaphorically, Pizer gives no compelling justification for considering them "primarily" so. Writes Pizer:

> *Vandover and the Brute* . . . is only indirectly or secondarily a novel about the
> struggle for existence. It is primarily a novel about the choices open to the artist
> in late nineteenth century America. . . . The struggle-for-existence idea in
> *Vandover*, in other words, is principally an image of fear. Norris does indeed
> subscribe to the idea as idea, but the major function of this idea in the novel is not
> to state the idea but to dramatize the emotion. (113)

Yet it is just as reasonable to consider Vandover's artistic devolution as primarily serving to express the idea of the struggle for existence and as only secondarily reflecting the situation of artists. Even if Pizer is right that the idea's major function is here metaphorical, its ideational content is not so easily dismissed. Pizer's view that "the philosophy of the struggle for existence in *Vandover* should be viewed as a modern critic might view the pastoralism of a Renaissance poet" (114) seems motivated principally by his desire to "bypass the hazards which result from considering naturalism primarily as a movement closely allied to its contemporary intellectual and social background" ("Nineteenth-Century" 104). Besides which, naturalists' beliefs in materialistic determinism and natural selection are most unimpressively like the conventions of pastoralism. Pizer goes so far as to claim that the philosophical beliefs held throughout the course of civilization are "less absolute commentaries upon human nature and experience than metaphors in a huge and endless historical poem" ("American Literary" 37). One is left to wonder what ideas, in literature or elsewhere, are to be taken seriously rather than regarded as merely dramatizing some emotion.

"The Problem of Philosophy" also overemphasizes that "the history of literature abounds in examples of writers who are both great artists and inadequate critics of their own work" (115). While this is true enough, Pizer conflates the comments of a novel's narrator with those of its author, thereby attempting to justify disregarding what he chooses to view as "blatantly intrusive" passages of "quasi-philosophical discourse" (110) as little more than an author's "false or superficial discursive grasp" (114) of their own work. However, what Pizer here assumes to be self-evidently superfluous and misguided passages are first and foremost narrative parts of the work under consideration, not extraneous appendages to be thematically dismissed. To reduce a novel's intellectual contents to little more than emotional stimulants, and to presume that relatively discursive passages and narrators' comments are essentially disposable, opens the door to an anti-intellectual aestheticism that could justify any number of interpretations in the name of simply avoiding discussions of ideas that are inconvenient to a critic's thesis or personal beliefs.

Pizer further attempts to domesticate naturalism and muzzle its philosophical bite by leashing it to comparatively milquetoast humanism. In "American Literary Naturalism and the Humanistic Tradition," Pizer argues that "American naturalism can be considered part of the humanistic tradition" (40). Unfortunately, Pizer's implicit conception of humanism is so vague and capacious as to be meaningless. Pizer emphasizes that Zola shared what is a supposed "cornerstone of the humanistic tradition," which is "the belief that men can benefit from the truth" and that "the truth is worth pursuing for this reason" (39). Yet this overlooks the fact that the deterministic truth that Zola and other naturalists believe beneficial is at odds with that professed by humanists. Pizer asserts that for naturalism "a primary goal is the dramatization of the value and uniqueness of man's felt inner life" (36). However, to claim that naturalism "affirms a humanistic center to experience" is to miss the point. Naturalism does not deny that human experience is central and uniquely valuable to human beings, but dramatizing its value or centrality in any cosmic sense is far from being "a primary goal." Rather, naturalism flatly denies humanism's arrogant privileging of humanity with a unique freedom or special status. To echo Laplace's famous reply to Napoleon when asked about the place of God in his philosophical system, naturalists have no need of that hypothesis.

Indeed, what is most central, unique, and valuable about naturalism, its characteristically objective and scientific perspective, stands in stark opposition to humanistic thought. It was with good reason that Robinson Jeffers referred to his naturalistic outlook, with its "shifting of emphasis and significance from man to not-man," as Inhumanism (vii), and that Dreiser described humanism as naturalism's "arch enemy" ("New Humanism" 259). Pizer implies that the only alternative to humanism is "a simple and single deterministic creed" and the production of "an emotionally sterile portrait of 'forces at work'" ("American Literary" 40). However, humanism is but one of many viable worldviews, and there is nothing at all about acceptance of philosophical naturalism that requires crassness, uniformity, or stolidity. Nor does responsibly engaging with a novel's philosophy necessitate ignoring the work's form or artistic subtlety. Intellectually acknowledging the ideas in a novel does not entail simply equating the work with a set of philosophical doctrines; it means not dismissing the ideas before they have been understood. This is the real problem of philosophy in the naturalistic novel.

Finally, Pizer endeavors not just to render naturalistic philosophy primarily metaphorical, expendably unreliable, or essentially humanistic, but to sever philosophy and the history of ideas from art generally. In his review of John J. Conder's *Naturalism in American Fiction*, Pizer states that for both Charles C. Walcutt and himself, "the key to a meaningful reading of a naturalistic novel was the need to stress that it is a novel and not an oblique form of philosophical argumentation" ("John J. Conder" 201). Pizer also states that "harm is done both to the novel and to the movement of which it is a part by the reduction of the work to an act of pseudo-philosophical discourse" (202). Yet a novel is at least in part "an oblique form of philosophical argumentation," or else it is as intellectually vacuous as it is socially irrelevant. And while Pizer seeks to avoid the type of criticism in which "the examination of the fiction itself is subordinate to a constant reference to philosophical and cultural ideas" (Preface xiii), there is arguably no such thing as "fiction itself" apart from its philosophical content and cultural commentary. Moreover, knowledge of philosophical naturalism is more than a helpful supplement to critical analysis, for misunderstanding of its ideas has seriously undermined literary study. Thus, good intentions notwithstanding, discussion of determinism cannot be justifiably ignored or avoided without leaving intact the misunderstandings that lead to claims of naturalism's inconsistency.

COMPATIBILISM AND ETHICS

Despite critics' best attempts to either address or avert the issue of determinism and its relationship to free will and moral responsibility, it remains inseparable from a reflective analysis of American literary naturalism. Definitions of naturalism as a movement, perceptions of naturalism's optimism or pessimism, estimations of naturalism's success or failure as art, evaluations of naturalism's moral and social significance, and specific interpretations of individual works all rest squarely on beliefs and assumptions about determinism and free will. Unfortunately, this aspect of naturalistic philosophy remains the most superficially understood, despite having been so frequently discussed. Until critics' misunderstandings of determinism are squarely addressed, complaints about naturalism's logical inconsistency will persist. And, as Donald Pizer has opined, "the study of naturalism often is still bedeviled by the incubus of determinism" ("Study" 9). His choice of metaphor is apt, as myth has it that sexual union with an incubus results in the birth of monstrous offspring, and criticism about literary naturalism is indeed malformed. As John Stuart Mill long ago demonstrated, however, determinism (or what was once called necessitarianism) is not the incubus Pizer imagines, as free will need not be seen as incompatible with determinism.

In his *Autobiography* (1873), John Stuart Mill writes that "the doctrine of what is called Philosophical Necessity weighed on my existence like an incubus." He continues:

I felt as if I was scientifically proved to be the helpless slave of antecedent circumstances: as if my character and that of all others had been formed for us by agencies beyond our control, and was wholly out of our own power. . . . I pondered painfully on the subject, till gradually I saw light through it. . . . I saw that though our character is formed by circumstances, our own desires can do much to shape those circumstances; and that what is really inspiriting and ennobling in the doctrine of free will, is the conviction that we have real power over the formation of our own character; that our will, by influencing some of our circumstances, can modify our future habits or capabilities of willing. All this was entirely consistent with the doctrine of circumstances, or rather, was that doctrine itself, properly understood. (110–11)

Mill espoused what is known as a compatibilist position, or the view that free will is compatible with determinism, because free will is most logically and meaningfully defined as the ability to act as one wishes, without denying the fact that one's wishes are themselves determined by one's upbringing, genetics, and circumstances. Hence, a free act is not one that is undetermined, but simply one which is not constrained by certain types of coercion or psychological compulsion. In other words, to exercise free will is just to behave in a way that is amenable to reason and in accordance with one's character and desires. Indeed, for an act to be free it must be determined by one's own personality and preferences, or else it is not one's own action. Hence, rather than being incompatible with determinism, free will actually requires it (See also Mill's *A System of Logic*, Book 6, Ch. 2).

In contrast to Mill's position is the incompatibilist or libertarian view, in which free will is held to be inconsistent with determinism. According to a libertarian position, free will requires that there be no causal chain leading inevitably to every choice and action. Rather, for the libertarian, freedom requires the genuine existence of alternative possibilities, not merely the compatibilists' hypothetical alternatives. Or, if accepting of determinism in the physical world, a libertarian might conceive of human free will in spiritual or supernatural terms, making it somehow immune to the physical laws observed elsewhere in the universe. Problematically for this outlook, science has increasingly shown that the natural world obeys deterministic laws and that the human brain and consciousness offer no exceptions. Moreover, even should random or non-deterministic events occur, they would hardly seem of any logical use for establishing a meaningful conception of free will. The same is also true for mysterious, supernatural events or entities. It is unclear whether any coherent notion of indeterministic free will can even be given. Certainly, literary critics have yet to make intelligible the sort of libertarian free will implicit in their unsympathetic analyses of naturalistic texts.

Mill argues that ethics, like free will, is also compatible with determinism. In *An Examination of Sir William Hamilton's Philosophy* (1865), the relationship between determinism and ethics is reflected in Mill's discussion of punishment. Mill explains that

[p]unishment proceeds on the assumption that the will is governed by motives. If punishment had no power of acting on the will, it would be illegitimate, however

> natural might be the inclination to inflict it. Just so far as the will is supposed to
> be free, that is, capable of acting *against* motives, punishment is disappointed of
> its object, and deprived of its justification. (291)

Hence, contrary to the assumptions of literary critics, the efficacy and legitimacy of
praise and punishment actually require determinism.

Mill, as is well known, advocated a utilitarian or consequentialist form of ethics,
according to which actions should be judged good or bad on the basis of their consequences. People are to be held legally responsible for their actions and are to be
praised or blamed according to the effects of their behavior and the practical utility
of reward and punishment for increasing or decreasing the occurrence of similar
behavior in the future. On a strictly consequentialist account, ultimate or absolute
responsibility is an illusory metaphysical concept that is irrelevant to questions of
praise or blame. In contrast to consequentialist ethics, duty-based or deontological
ethics views actions as inherently right or wrong and regards people as responsible
in some ultimate or metaphysical sense that transcends consequentialist concerns.
In other words, on this account praise and blame are justified even if they have no
pragmatic justification whatsoever. Indeed, most strikingly, deontological ethics
holds that certain actions are right regardless of their practical consequences and
emphasize notions of moral deserts and retribution of the kind that would justify
eternal salvation or damnation. The potentially radical and violent implications of
such an outlook remain all too evident in the world today.

As the philosopher Robert Kane explains, the compatibilist position has been
around "since Thomas Hobbes in the seventeenth century," and "[t]he idea that
free will and determinism are compatible continues to be a majority view among
philosophers and scientists" (10). One wonders why a philosophy that has been
successfully defended by many of the most brilliant and influential philosophers
of the Western world for the past 350 years, and which continues to be a dominant philosophical outlook, is so alien to literary critics. Given that Mill was the
most influential English-language philosopher of the nineteenth century, appreciation of his relevance to the understanding literary naturalism is long overdue.
Despite the *Norton Anthology of English Literature*'s claim that "a knowledge of
Mill's writings is essential to our understanding of Victorian literature," and that
his thought "was to have a profound influence on writers" (1043), its selections
emphasize the influence of Wordsworth on Mill more than any specific influence
of Mill on literature.

FATALISM AND CHANCE

More than the supposed incubus of determinism, the study of naturalism has been
bedeviled by the succubus of fatalism. Mill stressed that it is wrong to consider "that
the doctrine of the causation of human actions is fatalism at all, or resembles

fatalism in any of its moral or intellectual effects" (*Autobiography* 298). Yet literary scholars have persistently confused the two philosophically distinct concepts. Critics' confusion about this point is especially disturbing, given that Émile Zola explicitly discusses the distinction in his manifesto "The Experimental Novel." Quoting Claude Bernard, Zola emphasizes that "fatalism assumes the appearance of any phenomenon is necessary apart from its conditions, while determinism is just the conditions, essential for the appearance of any phenomenon . . ." (653). Put another way, determinism is the view that all events are caused by preceding events such that, given a complete knowledge of conditions in the universe at any given time, it would be theoretically possible to predict any and all future events. However, this view does not entail that human beings have no causal influence on the future. Whereas determinism asserts that human actions can and do determine the future, fatalism implies that humans have effectively no control over their lives and suggests a defeatist submission to some divinely predestined outcome. Fatalism, then, is the view that future events are unavoidable regardless of deterministic causality.

In 1942, the critic George W. Meyer correctly diagnosed the confusion between determinism and fatalism, which had already become a tiresome critical misunderstanding. Meyer quotes Zola at length and shows again that the belief in determinism does not condemn one to a pessimistic outlook. For his trouble, Meyer was subsequently accused by Charles Child Walcutt of having committed "the extreme of left-wing error" of "accepting Zola's desperate distinction between 'determinism' and 'fatalism'" (172). Having offhandedly dismissed Meyer's "unhappy attempt to free determinism of 'fatalism'" (173), Walcutt proceeded to plunge naturalism and its critics into fatalistic darkness once again. Even earlier, in 1940, Willard O. Eddy discussed Zola's philosophy in some detail and made clear that "the individual is at once an effect and a cause in the process of determinism" ("Quintessence" 523):

> The assumption that man is able to make a choice, to combine factors so as to produce one thing in preference to another, does not imply a break in the principle of determinism. The choice, like any other phenomenon, is predetermined. It is determined partly by the desires of the individual, which in turn are determined by other things. Nevertheless, man is able, within limits, to satisfy those desires. And to that extent, determinism is a philosophy of optimism. ("Quintessence" 528)

Yet in a second article written fourteen years later, Eddy flip-flops and writes that if one "interprets the principle of physical causation as applying to choice itself, the result is determinism in the realm of human action, man being subordinated to nature in such a way as to leave no intelligible grounds for effecting reform, and the result is a thorough-going pessimism" ("Scientific Bases" 219–20). Such confusions persist to this day.

In addition to confusing determinism with fatalism, literary critics have sometimes appealed to quantum mechanics or chaos theory to support claims that the naturalistic worldview is false or scientifically obsolete (Civello 112–24). Such appeals have been at best strained and superficial. A knowledge of physics, and the history of quantum theory in particular, makes clear that interpretations of quantum mechanics that are non-deterministic, and that attribute uncertainty to nature itself, gained influence as much for ideological as for empirical reasons. Not only have non-deterministic interpretations of quantum mechanics been sharply criticized by those who study the philosophy of science, but there are a number of competing interpretations that are thoroughly deterministic. Physicists are largely agnostic about the ontological implications of the mathematical formalism of quantum mechanics, and contemporary physics offers little of value to critics of literary naturalism.

Likewise, chaos theory only demonstrates that the evolution of a complex system is highly sensitive to initial conditions. The behavior of complex systems may deviate exponentially from expectations due to incomplete knowledge or slight perturbations, thus appearing random; nonetheless, chaotic systems are entirely deterministic, their evolution being a product of earlier states with no randomness or chance involved. A determinist's reference to "chance" should therefore be understood epistemically as indicating a subjective lack of knowledge about a given event's causes or probability, rather than ontologically as indicating the objective existence of events that are truly random or uncaused. No determinist argues that it is possible in practice to accurately predict, for example, the behavior of human beings. As weather forecasts demonstrate, our predictions of complex systems must remain imperfect instances of a theoretical ideal. Nonetheless, it is a mistake to assume that even if the universe were indeterministic at the subatomic level, that this would be relevant to the macroscopic world in which we live, and humanistic critics overlook what the destructive implications of macroscopic indeterminism or chance would be for ethics.

Rather than being undetermined, however, the picture of human behavior painted by contemporary neuroscience is more materialistic and deterministic than ever. Of course, psychologists long ago demonstrated that "we humans exaggerate the extent to which our actions are voluntary and rationally chosen" (Zimbardo B7), but behavioral genetics has increasingly demonstrated the powerful influence of genes on the biology and functioning of the brain. Meanwhile, fears about the purported political and sociological dangers of so-called "genetic determinism" have been shown to be overblown. Vastly improved brain-imaging techniques have led to revealing discoveries about moral decision-making and have changed attitudes toward free will in ways with potentially profound implications for the law and social policy. Moreover, in philosophy, scientific advances have stimulated and informed debate about free will and evolutionary ethics. Far beyond simply equating the mind with a physically determined brain, much research has demonstrated that our thoughts and behavior rest upon unconscious neuronal processes. Recently, researchers have shown that it is possible to predict someone's actions as much as ten seconds prior to the person's own awareness of making a decision (Soon 543–45). Hence, we become aware of thoughts and behaviors only after they have already been generated unconsciously, and the left hemisphere of the brain rationalizes justifications for actions after the fact, thus giving rise to the subjective illusion that our conscious volitions were the cause of our behavior (Gazzaniga). It is now unclear when our conscious will might actually direct our actions. What is clear is that we incorrectly believe any number of events to be caused by our willing them; equally clear is that our conscious will and behavior are driven by everything from differences in brain structure and neurochemicals to priming effects, smells, disorderly environments, and common microbes.

Despite the overwhelming wealth of available research, the only critics to mention relevant scientific studies are Karen F. Jacobson and Donald Pizer. In "Who's the Boss? *McTeague*, Naturalism, and Obsessive-Compulsive Disorder," Jacobson observes "that Norris uses this novel as a laboratory for examining the relationship between determinism and responsibility" (28). But Jacobson fails to use her scientific knowledge meaningfully for any interpretive purpose and simply reiterates the assumption that "if humans are governed by outside forces, then they cannot be held responsible for their actions" (30). If, as is undoubtedly true, the novel "has much to say to us today" (40), then what exactly does *McTeague*'s reflection of obsessive-compulsive disorder signify? How should we construe the complex results of Norris's "experiment" on determinism and responsibility? What of naturalism's depiction of all human beings, not just abnormal or pathological cases, "as determined by forces beyond their control" (30)? What of Norris's singular handling of these materials as an artist and intellectual? These and other issues remain to be explored.

Ironically, given his resistance to discussions of determinism, Donald Pizer is the only critic of literary naturalism to refer to evolutionary psychology or scientific studies concerning the hereditary influences on alcoholism, crime, and sexuality. In "The Biological Determinism of *McTeague* in Our Time," Pizer provisionally acknowledges that "research in the biological and social sciences in our day tends toward at least a partial confirmation of the biological determinism dramatized in the novel" (27). Pizer then mildly and tentatively concludes that *McTeague* is "a suggestive anticipation of several strains in the biological conditioning of experience that are again attracting great attention" (31). However, like Jacobson, Pizer fails to find any interpretive significance in this fact, commenting only on the alleged "ethical awkwardness in Norris's depiction of the theme of biological determinism" (31). Pizer also rejects as unscientific the "now discredited Lamarckian version of evolutionary change, in which behavior could affect genetic material" (28). Even this aspect of Norris's naturalism, though, is supported by epigenetics, which shows that the behavior of ourselves and those around us does indeed affect the expression of genetic material, even across generations, in a Lamarckian manner. Consequently, Pizer's outright rejection of this thesis now seems overly simplistic. Focusing on the relative weights historically given to heredity and environment in determining our actions, Pizer refrains from directly commenting on the most significant fact of all, which is that regardless of what emphasis one may place on "nature or nurture," contemporary science and philosophy have largely concluded that some combination of both determines our actions entirely.

PESSIMISM AND THE BURDEN OF PROOF

James T. Farrell observed in 1954 that "a number of the literary critics of 'naturalism' who base their criticisms on free will do so on grounds of temperament" (148), to which he added that "[t]hose who dispute over literary naturalism in terms of free will versus determinism are generally opposing the scientific spirit" (149). It is difficult to deny that literary criticism has tended to remain in the realm of a priori beliefs, dismissing appeals to physical science as "scientism." However, professional philosophy and contemporary science are not without bearing on, and have implications for, the interpretation and appreciation of naturalistic literature. Specifically, scholars without at least a basic knowledge of standard philosophical arguments and empirical scientific research are in a poor position to make pronouncements about free will and moral responsibility, and considerations of literary naturalism's meaning and significance that lack such a foundation are correspondingly impoverished and suspect. That critics of naturalism have not felt the need to seriously evaluate or defend their own inescapably present philosophical perspective further suggests a paucity of intellectual diversity and theoretical introspection. And the comments of scholars themselves also indicate a lack of open-mindedness and self-criticism.

Writes Lee Clark Mitchell: "As products of pasts, we rightly suppose that behavior is partly explained through historical causes. . . . At the same time, we assume that the force of such pasts can somehow be transcended" (*Determined* 13). This transcendence is nowhere explained, and one is forced to wonder how critics can in good conscience condemn naturalists for not reconciling determinism with free will, ethics, and reform while their criticism espouses a terminally obscure notion of free will that itself bears no logical relationship to any of these concepts. Mitchell merely offers that "[w]e seem in fact to live in the alternation of two conflicting views, neither of which is capable of dislodging the other" (*Determined* 14). Thus, when literary scholars subscribe to beliefs that are mutually irreconcilable, they are merely exhibiting a worldly and sophisticated "alternation" of views. Literary naturalists, who in the course of creating a work of art do not overtly explicate their entire philosophy to the unreceptive critic's satisfaction, however, are perforce "puerile" (Pizer, "Problem" 110), "simpleminded," "superficial" (114), and "intellectually disreputable" ("Nineteenth" 102). Finally, Mitchell confides that "we find it just as difficult to allow that characters are determined by forces beyond their control as we do in imagining ourselves or our friends somehow similarly constituted" ("Naturalism" 540–41). Yet Mitchell's presumed possession of a will that is independent of biological and environmental, hence all causal, influences is an example of wishful, not to say magical, thinking. More recently, Mary E. Papke flatly states that "we simply cannot accept that we live in a purely naturalist world" (xi). Critics need not pitch their personal beliefs out the window, but the ability to at least imaginatively, if not sympathetically, inhabit a work's worldview is surely a requisite of sensitive literary analysis.

Rejecting the ideas that the course of events genuinely contains alternate possibilities and that actions are right or wrong independent of their consequences is moderately to highly revisionist with regard to popular assumptions, beliefs, and attitudes. But so were heliocentrism, evolution, germ theory, relativity, continental drift, and any number of other discoveries. Accepting the truth of determinism does not mean that feelings of shame and regret are meaningless or that we cannot take a certain pride in our accomplishments and enjoy the rewards of success, for both the experience of regret and the fear of its future recurrence can shape our behavior in ways that are beneficial. We are in a very real sense the originators and owners of our actions, since without our unique contribution to the chain of events our accomplishments could never have been achieved and the universe as a whole would be ineluctably altered. Likewise, to the extent that we shape our behavior to achieve beneficial consequences, actions have practical justification, in addition to being enjoyable in their own right. Neither does determinism commit one to pessimism, as one can successfully use encouragement and discouragement to effect personal and social reform. While retributivism may not be compatible with a consequentialist ethic, since no one truly "deserves" blame in an ultimate, metaphysical, or deontological sense, this is not obviously a bad thing. Rather, such a recognition might well have a salutary influence on the treatment of criminals.

Belief in libertarian free will and acceptance of deontological ethics are no doubt common because they seem a natural outgrowth of our daily, subjective impressions and our reflexive, reactive attitudes to others' behavior. However, among philosophically knowledgeable and scientifically literate intellectuals, their justification is less obvious. In fact, upon reflection, considerable philosophical sophistication is required to counter the serious objections that have been made to both. This is not to say that compatibilism does not have its opponents. However, given the current state of argument and evidence, the burden of proof now clearly lies with believers in indeterministic free will and absolute moral responsibility. This is especially true given that it is unclear whether a libertarian or incompatibilist concept of free will is the intuitive or default position of people generally, contrary to the invariable assumption of such an outlook among critics. Thus, literary scholars cannot legitimately assume that naturalistic authors express a hopelessly contradictory and depressingly fatalistic philosophy that automatically dooms their works to moral confusion and artistic inferiority.

DETERMINISM AND NATURALISTIC AUTHORS

Outlooks like Mill's compatibilist and consequentialist position were hardly unknown or uncommon during the nineteenth century. Charles Darwin, for example, privately expressed in his notebooks an outlook like that of Mill's:

The general delusion about free will obvious. . . . One must view a wrecked man, like a sickly one—We cannot help loathing a diseased offensive object, so we view wickedness.—it would however be more proper to pity than to hate & be disgusted. [*sic*] with them. Yet it is right to punish criminals; but solely to *deter* others. . . . This view should teach one profound humility, one deserves no credit for anything. (yet one takes it for beauty & good temper), nor ought one to [deontologically] blame others. (608)

Herbert Spencer, too, seems to have denied the existence of libertarian free will and defended a consequentialist ethics. And T. H. Huxley wrote an entire book on the compatibilist philosophy of David Hume. Of Hume's compatibilist definition of liberty in *An Inquiry Concerning Human Understanding*, Huxley comments, "Half the controversies about freedom of the will would have no existence, if this pithy paragraph had been well pondered by those who oppose the doctrine of necessity" (*Hume* 191). Huxley echoes Hume's arguments that "the very idea of responsibility implies the belief in a necessary connexion [*sic*] of certain actions with certain states of the mind" (192) and concludes, "So far, therefore, from necessity destroying moral responsibility, it is the [consequentialist] foundation of all praise and blame" (193). In his essay "On the Hypothesis that Animals are Automata, and Its History," Huxley writes that "the feeling we call volition is not the cause of a voluntary act, but the symbol of that state in the brain which is the immediate cause of the act" (244). He then reiterates that "We are conscious automata, endowed with free will in the only intelligible sense of that much-abused term—inasmuch as in many respects we are able to do as we like—but none the less parts of the great series of causes and effects . . ." (244). A familiarity with Huxley's writings alone would therefore have sufficed to familiarize nineteenth-century readers with compatibilist ethics.

Not only was such a naturalistic philosophy accepted among prominent philosophers and scientists of the nineteenth century, as it still is today, but it was promptly understood and adopted by literary intellectuals like Mark Twain, Jack London, Frank Norris, Stephen Crane, and Theodore Dreiser. It was no doubt resistance to naturalistic thought among a predominantly Christian and humanist audience with a belief in libertarian free will that led Mark Twain to publish his philosophical work *What Is Man?* anonymously. Developing at length ideas that would be more obliquely and humorously utilized in "The Man That Corrupted Hadleyburg" (1899) and "The Turning Point of My Life" (1910), *What Is Man?* (1906) expresses a consistent, naturalistic outlook which is in keeping with contemporary science and philosophy. However, as early as 1912, Twain's own friend Albert Bigelow Paine complained that the admonition in *What Is Man?* was in "conflict with that other theory—the inevitable sequence of cause and effect" (744). Virtually without exception, every other critic has followed suit. Alexander Jones writes that "[a] man's will is not free because he must choose that which will most satisfy his inner master; but since that inner master can be trained to desire those things which will 'confer benefits upon . . . [his] neighbor and the community,' the end result will still be worthwhile" (15). However, it becomes clear from a footnote that Jones, too, confuses determinism and fatalism, when he claims that Twain lost "faith in the power of training" once he came to see "each event in a man's life as absolutely determined by those preceding it" (15).

Similarly, in his discussion of "The Man That Corrupted Hadleyburg," which offers a fictional embodiment of the ideas in *What Is Man?* Clinton S. Burhans states that the story is "neither as inconsistent nor as pessimistic as it is usually considered" (384). But he does not explain how Twain's "moralism functions here in terms of his determinism" (376), and he still considers Twain's ethical philosophy to be "generally inconsistent" (383). The most knowing comments on the philosophy of *What Is Man?* are those of Howard G. Baetzhold, who at least seems to grasp that "Clemens conceived of the 'Admonition' as a procedure by which the moralists could assist in the improvement of mankind, and not an appeal to individuals to train *themselves*" (223). Hence, concludes Baetzhold, "Clemens' argument is by no means so contradictory as has been charged" (223). Again, however, Baetzhold fails to elucidate the logical relationship between determinism and moralism in any meaningful detail. Sadly, then, even the most sympathetic critics of Twain have proved unable to properly appreciate the logical coherence of his beliefs. Worse, the overwhelming majority of critics writing on Twain and other American literary naturalists have not advanced beyond the complaint voiced by Paine a century ago.

In addition to his reading of Spencer and Huxley, among the works known to have been read by Jack London that explicitly argue for a compatibilist philosophy and consequentialist view of ethics are M. H. Fitch's *The Physical Basis of Mind and Morals* (Hamilton 32), Paul Carus's *Primer of Philosophy* (Hamilton 13), and Enrico Ferri's *Criminal Sociology* (Hamilton 117–18). In a 1902 letter to Cloudesley Johns, Jack London wrote that "Man is not a free agent, and [libertarian] free will is a fallacy exploded by science long ago" (*Letters* 270). London clearly saw that determinism made nonsense of the traditional, libertarian notion of free will. At the same time, he understood that it was not incompatible with holding people accountable for their actions. On the endpapers of his copy of Ferri's book, London recorded his reactions by writing, "Question raised—is he, or is he not, a free agent. Is he a born criminal, or is he a criminal by contracted habits? A criminal he must be, for responsibility to society enters in. He is guilty of crimes against society, and society must protect itself" (qtd. in Hamilton 117). Thanks therefore in part to his reading of science and philosophy, London understood the bearing of determinism on beliefs concerning free will and responsibility better than his latter-day critics.

Frank Norris's deterministic thought has also been subject to philosophically questionable interpretations. For example, in his haste to "rescue" Frank Norris from the supposed logical inconsistencies of a materialistic determinism concerned with morals, Pizer makes him into an "evolutionary ethical dualist" merely because one of Norris's Berkeley professors, Joseph LeConte, held such a view ("Evolutionary" 552–54). Yet, as Joseph McElrath has pointed out, "LeConte's name does not appear once in a canon of approximately 300 writings mentioning many a less distinguished contemporary" (58). Moreover, as McElrath has also made clear,

Norris's philosophical work "The Puppets and the Puppy" suggests that Norris rejected such any dualistic outlook. Failing to discuss this work, Pizer merely asserts that "LeConte's system appears to have struck an answering chord in Norris's intellectual and emotional make-up" ("Evolutionary" 554). On the strength of Pizer's simple assertion and his well-established reputation as a critic, LeConte's "influence" has become, to use McElrath's phrase, an *idée fixe* (59). In order to save Norris from a naturalistic philosophy that would "undermine the validity of . . . works as artistic wholes and the stature of Norris as a serious artist . . . drawing on a coherent system of ideas" ("Evolutionary" 552), Pizer seems to think it sufficient to recruit Norris into the ranks of dualism—which as a philosophy is, at best, deeply problematic. It would appear that, for literary critics, some inconsistent worldviews strike more of a political and temperamental chord than others. In any case, neither Pizer's ascription of dualism to Norris nor Pizer's obvious preference for dualism as a basis for art seems well justified.

Among those who have written on the naturalism of Stephen Crane is the professional philosopher Sidney Gendin. Given his knowledge of philosophy, Gendin might be expected to give a deeper analysis of Crane's determinism than prior critics. Gendin points out that, according to one theory, "determinism and free will are compatible" (96), and he goes on to say that, given a certain understanding of terms, "free will is actually dependent upon determinism and inconceivable without it" (97). Gendin also remarks that such a compatibilist view "has been one of the dominant views in Anglo-American philosophy since David Hume" (96). However, Gendin unaccountably claims that "[e]laboration of the theory would derail us," and he proceeds to demonstrate a debilitating lack of familiarity with literature and literary theory. Having apparently never read any works of literary naturalism other than Crane's, and based on only a second-hand account of Zola's ideas, Gendin expostulates, "The unvarnished truth is that nothing ever occurs in any novel that has the slightest implication for or against the existence of free will" (98). Conversely, "Determinism has nothing to say concerning how novels should be written" (99). Gendin then answers his titlular question "Was Stephen Crane (or Anybody Else) a Naturalist?" by saying, "No one ever has been" (101). And, as if denying the existence of an entire literary movement were not enough, Gendin also presumes to posthumously read Crane's mind, proclaiming that "[h]e held no view whatever about freedom of the will" (100). Clearly, even a professional knowledge of philosophy, in the absence of a basic understanding of literature, is inadequate for critical purposes. However, the body of analysis on literary naturalism shows that the reverse is equally true.

While no professional philosopher, Theodore Dreiser "read voraciously, and reread" the works of Jacques Loeb (Moers 240), who argued that while humans like to imagine themselves unique in possessing free will, this is but a product of ignorance concerning the operative forces involved in premeditated acts (Loeb, *Forced* 171–72). Moral behavior is no less automatic or "tropistic" than other behavior, though this does not mean that ethical concepts are without foundation. Loeb argued that "[n]ot only is the mechanistic conception of life compatible with ethics:

it seems the only conception of life which can lead to an understanding of the source of ethics" (*Mechanistic* 33). Of his own similar ethical outlook, Dreiser explains:

> The myth of responsibility for any actions or deeds other than those we have been trained or conditioned to perform is obvious. Consider the education or training of animals. Do we, in their relations with us consider them responsible for anything other than what we have trained or taught or conditioned them to do? Of course not, for we know that by a proper application of rewards and punishments they may be taught any course of action within their powers—even those most contrary to their natural instincts and propensities. . . . So has nature done—and still does with you. Its evolutionary instruments—the state, the tribe, the social group—threaten you with law, ostracism, poverty, hate, pain, and reward you with salary, respect, applause, social favor and what not. And like the dog you respond. But only for reasons of these. And with these removed neither you nor the dog would have the faintest trace of responsibility. (*Notes* 133)

This perspective is logically consistent both internally and with external scientific evidence, but opinions on Dreiser are well reflected in the title of Eliseo Vivas's article, "Dreiser, an Inconsistent Mechanist." Though Dreiser may have had conflicting beliefs and interests, his attitude toward free will and determinism appears to have been well thought out. The critic Shawn St. Jean is an exception in arguing that Dreiser's works "may not be, as has been charged over and over, wildly inconsistent" (256), and even St. Jean unconvincingly supports his position by attempting to fit the square, naturalistic peg of Dreiser's thought into the round hole of classical dramatic conventions.

Space prevents discussion of other authors, such as Oliver Wendell Holmes, Ambrose Bierce, Henry James, Kate Chopin, Harold Frederic, Edith Wharton, Paul Lawrence Dunbar, James M. Cain, Dashiell Hammett, John Steinbeck, James T. Farrell, Richard Wright, Thomas Pynchon, and others. Likewise, close readings of texts is beyond the scope of the present essay. Clearly, however, there is more to be said about the issue of determinism in American literary naturalism. Despite the boastful tone of Pizer's claim that "[t]he late nineteenth-century phase of American naturalism has been fully studied by a number of critics, including myself" (Preface xii), critics have yet to fully comprehend, let alone fully study, the real intellectual, moral, and emotional significance of literary naturalism. A majority of Americans still do not accept the theory of evolution (Miller 765–66). What, then, of the naturalists' further de-centering of humanity by their belief that our metaphysical, deontological, retributivist notions of ultimate moral responsibility and our categorical, subjectivist, and incompatibilist notions of libertarian free will are illusions? What are or should be the psychological, sociological, and ecological consequences of this realization? What varieties and combinations of rejection, accommodation, acceptance, and even celebration might naturalism prompt when fully grasped? How does naturalistic literature artistically relate scientific knowledge, in Matthew Arnold's phrase, "to our sense for conduct" and "to our sense for beauty" (1421)? What it is it like to live with the knowledge of our blindly evolved, purely physical, and thoroughly conditioned nature? To answer these questions will require of critics a greater philosophical sophistication, scientific awareness, and willing imagination.

WORKS CITED

Arnold, Matthew. "Literature and Science." *The Norton Anthology of English Literature: The Victorian Age*. Vol. E. 8th ed. New York: Norton, 2006. 1415–27.

Baetzhold, Howard G. *Mark Twain and John Bull: The British Connection*. Bloomington: Indiana University Press, 1970.

Burhans, Clinton S., Jr. "The Sober Affirmation of Mark Twain's Hadleyburg." *American Literature* 34 (1962): 375–84.

Civello, Paul. *American Literary Naturalism and its Twentieth-Century Transformations: Frank Norris, Ernest Hemingway, Don DeLillo*. Athens: University of Georgia Press, 1994.

Darwin, Charles. *Charles Darwin's Notebooks, 1836–1844: Geology, Transmutation of Species, Metaphysical Enquiries*. Ed. Paul H. Barrett, Peter J. Gautrey, Sandra Herbert, David Kohn, and Sydney Smith. Ithaca: Cornell University Press, 1987.

Dreiser, Theodore. "The New Humanism." 1930. *Theodore Dreiser: A Selection of Uncollected Prose*. Ed. Donald Pizer. Detroit: Wayne State University Press, 1977. 259–62.

———. *Notes On Life*. Ed. Marguerite Tjader and John J. McAleer. Tuscaloosa: University of Alabama Press, 1974.

Eddy, Willard O. "The Quintessence of Naturalism." *Studies in English Literature* [Tokyo Imperial University] 20 (1940): 520–35.

———. "The Scientific Bases of Naturalism in Literature." *Western Humanities Review* 8 (1954): 219–29.

Farrell, James T. "Some Observations on Naturalism, So Called, in Fiction." *Reflections at Fifty and Other Essays*. New York: Vanguard, 1954. 142–55.

Gazzaniga, Michael S. "Spheres of Influence." *Scientific American Mind* June/July 2008: 33–39.

Gendin, Sidney. "Was Stephen Crane (or Anybody Else) a Naturalist?" *Cambridge Quarterly* 24 (1995): 89–101.

Hamilton, David Mike. *The Tools of My Trade: The Annotated Books in Jack London's Library*. Seattle: University of Washington Press, 1986.

Huxley, Thomas Henry. *Hume*. London: Macmillan, 1879.

———. "On the Hypothesis That Animals Are Automata." *Collected Essays*. Vol 1. New York: Greenwood, 1968. 199–250.

Jacobson, Karen F. "Who's the Boss? *McTeague*, Naturalism, and Obsessive-Compulsive Disorder." *Mosaic* 32.2 (1999): 27–41.

Jeffers, Robinson. Preface. *The Double Axe and Other Poems*. New York: Random, 1948. vii–viii.

Jones, Alexander E. "Mark Twain and the Determinism of *What Is Man?*" *American Literature* 29 (1957): 1–17.

Kane, Robert. Introduction: The Contours of Contemporary Free Will Debates. *The Oxford Handbook of Free Will*. Ed. Robert Kane. Oxford: Oxford University Press, 2002. 3–41.

Link, Eric Carl. *The Vast and Terrible Drama: American Literary Naturalism in the Late Nineteenth Century*. Tuscaloosa: University of Alabama Press, 2004.

Loeb, Jacques. *Forced Movements, Tropisms, and Animal Conduct*. 1918. New York: Dover, 1973.

———. *The Mechanistic Conception of Life*. 1912. Ed. Donald Fleming. Cambridge, Mass.: Belknap, 1964.

London, Jack. *The Letters of Jack London*. Ed. Earle Labor, Robert C. Leitz III, and I. Milo Shepard. Vol. 1: *1896–1905*. Stanford: Stanford University Press, 1988.

McElrath, Joseph. "Frank Norris' 'The Puppets and the Puppy': LeContean Idealism or Naturalistic Skepticism?" *American Literary Realism* 26 (1993): 50–59.

Meyer, George W. "The Original Social Purpose of the Naturalistic Novel." *Sewanee Review* 50 (1942): 563–70.

Mill, John Stuart. *Autobiography*. 1873. *The Harvard Classics*. Ed. Charles W. Eliot. New York: Collier, 1909. 51 vols.

———. *An Examination of Sir William Hamilton's Philosophy*. 1865. Boston: William V. Spencer, 1866.

———. *A System of Logic*. 1843. London: Longman, 1979.

Miller, Jon D., Eugenie C. Scott, and Shinji Okamoto. "Public Acceptance of Evolution." *Science* 313 (Aug. 2006): 765–66.

Mitchell, Lee Clark. *Determined Fictions: American Literary Naturalism*. New York: Columbia University Press, 1989.

———. "Naturalism and the Languages of Determinism." *Columbia Literary History of the United States*. Ed. Emory Hill. New York: Columbia University Press, 1988. 525–45.

Moers, Ellen. *Two Dreisers*. New York: Viking, 1969.

The Norton Anthology of English Literature: The Victorian Age. Vol. E. 8th ed. New York: Norton, 2006.

Paine, Albert Bigelow. *Mark Twain: A Biography*. New York: Harper and Brothers, 1912.

Papke, Mary E. Preface. *Twisted from the Ordinary: Essays on American Literary Naturalism*. Ed. Mary E. Papke. Knoxville: University of Tennessee Press, 2003. vii–xiv.

Pizer, Donald. "American Literary Naturalism and the Humanistic Tradition." Pizer, *Theory* 36–53.

———. "The Biological Determinism of *McTeague* in Our Time." *American Literary Realism* 29.2 (1997): 27–32.

———. "Evolutionary Ethical Dualism in Frank Norris' *Vandover and the Brute* and *McTeague*." *PMLA* 76 (1961): 552–60.

———. "John J. Conder, *Naturalism in American Fiction*." Pizer, *Theory* 200–02.

———. "Nineteenth-Century American Literary Naturalism: An Approach Through Form." Pizer, *Theory* 102–9.

———. Preface. *Twentieth-Century American Literary Naturalism: An Interpretation*. Carbondale: Southern Illinois University Press, 1982. ix–xiii.

———. "The Problem of Philosophy in the Naturalistic Novel." Pizer, *Theory* 110–19.

———. "The Study of American Literary Naturalism: A Retrospective Overview." Pizer, *Theory* 1–10.

———. *The Theory and Practice of American Literary Naturalism: Essays and Reviews*. Carbondale: Southern Illinois University Press, 1993.

———. "The Three Phases of American Literary Naturalism." Pizer, *Theory* 13–35.

Soon, Chun Siong, Marcel Brass, Hans-Jochen Heinze, and John-Dylan Haynes. "Unconscious Determinants of Free Decisions in the Human Brain." *Nature Neuroscience* 11 (13 Apr. 2008): 543–45.

St. Jean, Shawn. "'Aye, Chance, Free Will, and Necessity': *Sister Carrie*'s Literary Interweavings." *Midwest Quarterly* 42 (2001): 240–56.

Twain, Mark. *Collected Tales, Sketches, Speeches, and Essays 1891–1910*. New York: Library of
    America, 1992.

———. "The Man That Corrupted Hadleyburg." Twain, *Collected* 390–438.

———. "The Turning Point of My Life." Twain, *Collected* 929–38.

———. *What Is Man?* Twain, *Collected* 731–804.

Vivas, Eliso. "Dreiser, an Inconsistent Mechanist." *Ethics* 48 (1938): 498–508.

Walcutt, Charles Child. "From Scientific Theory to Aesthetic Fact: The 'Naturalistic' Novel."
    Quarterly Review of Literature 3 (1946–47): 167–79.

Zimbardo, Philip. "Revisiting the Stanford Prison Experiment: A Lesson in the Power of
    Situation." *Chronicle of Higher Education* 30 Mar. 2007: B6–7.

Zola, Émile. "The Experimental Novel." Trans. Belle M. Sherman. *The Naturalist Novel*. Ed.
    Maxwell Geismar. Montreal: Harvest, 1964. 1–32.

CHAPTER 8

"FIRST PRINCIPLES OF MORALS": EVOLUTIONARY MORALITY AND AMERICAN NATURALISM

RICK ARMSTRONG

In his autobiography *Newspaper Days*, Theodore Dreiser recalls that when he first read Herbert Spencer's *First Principles* in 1894, the book "quite blew me to bits intellectually" (610). Like many thinkers of his time, Dreiser was overwhelmed by the evolutionary worldview that Spencer depicted. While he had rebelled from the stringent Catholicism of his father, Dreiser still believed in "the existence of Christ" along with "the soundness of His moral and sociologic deductions" (610). Reading Spencer served to eliminate the last vestiges of Dreiser's religious identification. Beginning in 1859 with the American publication of Charles Darwin's *On the Origin of Species*, the rise of evolutionary theory had a similar effect on many other American writers. Upon the book's publication, the *New York Times* correctly predicted that Darwin's thesis would bring "a radical reconstruction of the fundamental doctrines of natural history" ("Origin" 3). While Darwin meticulously explained the biological details of evolutionary theory, Darwin's English colleague Herbert Spencer articulated a cosmic evolutionary determinism that the general public could easily understand. As Richard Hofstadter notes, Spencer was widely read by people "who were partly or largely self-educated" (34).

Although evolution changed the scientific landscape, one issue that it could not resolve was the origin of ethical behavior. And while Darwin and Spencer could explain the many struggles that a species endured to survive, their explanations for the development of moral behavior were flawed. Aggression, ruthlessness, and violence were beneficial attributes for survival, and Spencer coined the phrase "survival of the fittest" to refer to those who successfully adapted to changing conditions (*Principles of Biology* 580). However, this does not necessarily mean the morally fittest. Biologist Alfred Russel Wallace asserted that a refined moral disposition might actually harm those possessing it, while evolutionist George Lyell maintained that the disjunction between the animal and human minds was too large to find evolved moral behavior in the animal world (Richards 213). The evolutionists' task in defining an evolutionary morality was a formidable one given that many biological functions are mechanical and can be objectively measured. However, morality is a more qualitative issue that involves questions of context, judgment, and motivation.

While much evidence supports the scientific validity of evolution, the amoral element was a significant obstacle to its popular acceptance as a theory of human and social development; this is one reason for the religious objection to evolution. The moral quandary galvanized many American novelists who were especially fascinated and disturbed by the implications of human evolution. Henry James, Theodore Dreiser, Edith Wharton, Frank Norris, and Jack London wrote pessimistic stories of the consequences of human and social development. James and Wharton appropriated evolutionary ideas in order to reveal the way group dynamics force certain individuals to conform or perish, while Dreiser, Norris, and London examined directly the ethical limitations of human evolution. These narratives inevitably criticized the evolutionary worldview as too deterministic, reductive, and aggressive.

The Debate over Evolutionary Morality

Spencer believed that free-market economics is one of the universal life forces, and so he merged evolutionary science and laissez-faire economics to indicate that society was evolving progressively. Despite the novelists' pessimistic take on the evolutionary worldview, Spencer became quite popular in the United States after the Civil War because his theories appealed to many Americans who were looking for an evolutionary philosophy that could reinforce their sense that the nation was improving despite the economic crises that wracked the last thirty years of the nineteenth century. Spencer was influenced by zoologist Jean Baptiste de Lamarck, who believed in the validity of the inheritance of physically acquired characteristics, as well as by the nebular hypothesis as propounded by Marquis de Laplace and William Herschel, which posits that the solar system is moving from an undifferentiated chaos to an organized complexity (Brush 255). Spencer appropriated the Lamarckian concept of inherited adaptations to prove that the fittest passes its adapted traits directly to its offspring, thus improving the species physically and morally. Using the nebular hypothesis, Spencer in fact argued that existence was moving from an undifferentiated, simple, and uniform chaos to a heterogeneous, complex, and coherent stability, using the specialization represented in market society as a metaphorical model (*First Principles* 327).

In his first book, *Social Statics* (1851), Spencer explains human moral evolution through the moral sense, which—like the senses of taste, touch, and smell—exist in all people "to dictate rectitude in our transactions with each other" while "receiv[ing] gratification from honest and fair dealing, and . . . giv[ing] birth to the sentiment of justice" (20). Spencer asserts that this sense will adapt to new external conditions, much like any physical attribute, with the result being the improvement of the human species; he concludes that "evil results from the non-adaptation for constitution to conditions" (63, 59). After defining the moral sense in *Social Statics*, Spencer returned to the issue of morality in the second edition of *Principles of Psychology*, published in 1867, where he focuses more on the evolution of this supposed instinct, which he now labeled altruism, leading him to emphasize the influence of the environment over the development of the moral sense. Sociality is the condition in which individuals feel a kinship with other individuals within their social group; this leads to altruistic feelings for others within the community (610). In both texts, Spencer regards the individual as a passive entity in the formation of his or her own ethical values. In *Social Statics*, Spencer defines ethics as a biological entity, ignoring the specifics of individual judgment. In the *Principles of Psychology*, Spencer assumes that the individual is a passive recipient of group values.

Darwin also emphasized group values as guiding moral evolution. However, his reasoning falls into a quandary that he cannot reconcile, explaining in *The Descent of Man* (1871) that a person's actions "are in a higher degree determined by the expressed wishes and judgment of his fellow-men, and unfortunately very often by his own strong selfish desires" (109–10). Here, Darwin acknowledges that the individual's desires are often in conflict with the values of the community, thus questioning the effect of group values on the individual. Both Spencer and Darwin have trouble accounting for the complicated interaction between an individual's ethics and those of the group.

In his Romanes Lecture of 1893, "Evolution and Ethics," Thomas Huxley cautions against people "apply[ing] the analogy of cosmic nature to society," contradicting Spencer's and Darwin's view of evolutionary ethics (82). He points out that survival depends on the conditions in which the organism must survive, pointedly saying "the practice of that which is ethically best . . . involves a course of conduct which, in all respects, is opposed to that which leads to success in the cosmic struggle for existence." Huxley believes that humans need to exercise their intellectual and moral judgments for the improvement of humanity. He states that point quite clearly: "the ethical progress of society depends, not on imitating the cosmic process, . . . but in combating it" (81–82).

Moreover, in "The Dilemma of Determinism" (1884) William James pointed out that evolutionary ethics left no space for individual judgment. He defined the dilemma as consisting not merely in the insignificance of human action but more importantly in the irrelevancy of human judgment because a determinist passively accepts all that happens as right no matter the individual or social consequences.

Instead, James argues that the world should not be viewed as a determinist machine but rather "as a contrivance for deepening the theoretic consciousness of what goodness and evil in their intrinsic natures are" (581). James believes that individuals are compelled to exercise their abilities to make ethical distinctions, connecting individual will to a more ethical world and asserting that determinism left a void of moral passivity.

EVOLUTIONARY ETHICS IN NATURALIST FICTION

The novelists of the era responded to the debate over ethical evolution by crafting narratives that reveal the suffering and death that such a theory implies. One type of narrative approach was to create protagonists who are fated to die because of their deviant birth and subsequent inability to adapt to their environment. In *The Princess Casamassima* (1886), Henry James appropriates evolutionary determinism to heighten the tragic existence of Hyacinth Robinson, the child of a homicidal working-class woman and the French aristocrat whom she killed. James reveals the consequences of a reductive model of existence based on biology. Because of his inter-class birth, Hyacinth is an outsider who cannot adapt either to the working-class world in which he was raised by his adoptive mother or to the aristocracy of the titled character. Notably, James specifically refers to both Darwin and Spencer as philosophical revolutionaries in the narrative (215), illustrating the insurrectionist import of evolutionary theory in late nineteenth-century London.

Hyacinth joins an underground radical organization and is instructed to assassinate a prominent leader (527). However, he is unable to replicate his mother's act of murder due to his identification with the elite. During his sojourn in Paris, Hyacinth admits to himself that "he had become conscious of a transfer of his sympathies . . . now he pitied the rich, those who were regarded as happy" (339). His identification with the upper class along with his rejection by both the aristocratic princess and the working-class Millicent Henning lead him to realize that "he had become vague, he was extinct" (528). The two female characters are emblematic of their class positions, to which Hyacinth does not belong. James explicitly evokes the language of evolution in order to heighten Hyacinth's tragedy of inherited defects that brands his alienated status. Hyacinth literally enacts his dissolution by killing himself, thereby extinguishing his tainted inheritance. He is caught by his biology, attempting to assert his own will against his determined fate by refusing to carry out his assignment. However, since his fate is determined by his biology, Hyacinth cannot survive. James appropriates Spencerian and Lamarckian concepts of inheritance to tell a tragic story of someone who did not fit into his environment. In the process, James reveals the problems with defining people purely by their biology and, in the process, leaving Hyacinth and characters like him to perish.

As Michael Davitt Bell indicates, Hyacinth's death represents the tragic inability of the people around him to appreciate his unique characteristics (104). Even though James was not particularly concerned with the actual details of evolutionary theory, his narrative involves the ethics of natural selection. Bell compares James's novel with Nathaniel Hawthorne's *The House of the Seven Gables*, which features a conventionally masculine character triumphing at the expense of a sensitive artist figure much like Hyacinth (103). In this schema of adaptation, brute aggression wins the battle for survival and reproduction while a more refined sensibility disappears. Thus, James indirectly reveals the moral quandary provided by a survival-of-the-fittest model: if brute masculine figures always survive, then society is left with the amoral consequence that Thomas Huxley criticized.

While James appropriated Spencerian determinism to demonstrate the ethical dilemma posed by evolutionary theory, Theodore Dreiser was more overtly influenced by Spencer's attack on a worldview that assumed people direct their own destiny. "All that I had deemed substantial," Dreiser reflected in *Newspaper Days*, "man's place in nature, his importance in the universe and on this too too solid earth . . . was questioned and dissolved. . . . I was completely thrown down in my conceptions or non-conceptions of life and made very gloomy" (610).

He would take this concern into his first novel, *Sister Carrie* (1900), written not long after he had read *First Principles*. Dreiser wondered where individual people would fit into Spencer's deterministic system; this in large part explains his depressed reaction to Spencer's ideas. Michael Davit Bell points out that *Sister Carrie* is split between an "'immediate' voice whose style mimics the thoughts, feelings, and values of these characters, and an 'omniscient' voice whose interest is less in these characters than in the historical facts and general ideas they exemplify" (156). In articulating the desires, fears, and hopes, the "immediate voice" functions as a type of corrective to Spencer's deductive analysis. Dreiser uses the "immediate voice" to communicate Carrie's conflict between her desire for an affluent urban life and her awareness that social mores restrict her ability to act upon that desire. After Carrie first sleeps with Drouet, the narrator, in an "omniscient voice," asserts that morality cannot be reduced to a scientific law because a rigidly empirical explanation of ethics cannot consider beauty, desire, and emotion:

> For all the liberal analysis of Spencer and our modern naturalistic philosophers,
> we have but an infantile perception of morals. There is more in the subject than
> mere conformity to a law of evolution. It is yet deeper than conformity to things
> of earth alone. It is more involved than we, as yet, perceive. Answer, first, why the
> heart thrills; explain wherefore some plaintive note goes wandering about the
> world, undying; make clear the rose's subtle alchemy evolving its ruddy lamp in
> light and rain. In the essence of these facts lie the first principles of morals. (*Sister
> Carrie* 65)

The narrator specifically contradicts Spencer's materialist conception of desire, the implication being that people are more complicated than being mere products of their natural environment. Thrilling hearts and "plaintive" notes exemplify this complexity because they cannot be explained through evolutionary theory. Bell observes that the narrator's reference to Spencer represents "an assertion of science's inadequacy" (158).

Within the novel, the passage explains Carrie's inability to adhere to conventional morality. The narrator anticipates the moral judgment that the reader may pronounce on her and proceeds to explain that ethical behavior is not so simply defined, given its complex role in living human experience. Hence Carrie can (and will) become morally worse, but materially better, and in the process a celebrity. While this reading is valid, the passage better applies to Hurstwood, because he experiences the harshest consequences of an evolutionary morality. John Fiske articulated the most coherent view of this perspective. In countering religious criticism of his and Spencer's brand of evolutionary theory, he combined a religious sense of morality with a rather harsh evolutionary ethics. In the fourth volume of his *Outlines of Cosmic Philosophy* (1874), Fiske argues that moral unfitness and physical unfitness are indistinguishable and that moral unfitness will be punished by physical extinction (308).

Dreiser enacts Fiske's conception of an uncompromising evolutionary ethics. Hurstwood suffers the type of fate Fiske mentions above: he cheats on his wife; steals money, albeit reluctantly, from his bosses; and kidnaps his reluctant lover and takes her to New York, where he begins a slow and painful physical and financial decline until he commits suicide. Thus, Hurstwood suffers his appropriate evolutionary fate. However, given Hurstwood's central role within the narrative, the tragedy of his demise, and the narrator's comment on evolutionary ethics, Hurstwood's story is not so easily categorized.

In his nonfiction, Dreiser expressed contradictory views about Spencer's ideas. In "Equation Inevitable," published twenty years after *Sister Carrie*, Dreiser's argument parallels Spencer's belief that life evolves from the simple to the complex, creating a balance in the universe (166). From this supposition, he asserts that any attempt by humans to alter this pattern of evolution is futile, quoting a suitably humbled "humanitarian" who concludes that "'the law of the survival of the strongest cannot be set aside'" (164). Dreiser wrote this essay to debunk the idea that God is ordering the universe, turning to Spencer's positivist form of evolution to support his point. *Sister Carrie* could then be read in terms of Carrie's evolution and Hurstwood's demise, indicating that Hurstwood's death is part of the natural evolutionary process.

However, Dreiser did not fully embrace all aspects of Spencer's evolution. In his editorials for *Ev'ry Month*, Dreiser expressed skepticism of the result of a survival of the fittest paradigm and thus of Spencer's benign form of evolution and devolution. In an August 1896 column, Dreiser points out, "the failures in this world are not to blame for their condition. They did not make the environment in which they were born; they could not regulate the early influences that prevailed over them. Poverty: it was not of their making" ("Reflections" 144). Hurstwood is an example of the failures who should not be blamed for their condition. Lawrence Hussman Jr. argues that Dreiser's novels "record his characters' attempts to resolve profound conflicts that he deeply felt himself" (17). Dreiser portrays Hurstwood's specific psychological conflicts, revealing a person suffering rather than a biological construct. Similarly, Richard Lehan claims that Dreiser's conflict between his "romantic aspirations" and "his belief in a world of physical limits led in his fiction to the displaced hero—the man whose desire for essential self-fulfillment is in conflict with his environment" (47). Lehan's point explains Hurstwood's decline: Dreiser shows the destructive reality of Spencer's uncompromising evolutionary ethics.

The writers of this period often wrote about characters who are alienated from their environments. Hyacinth Robinson mistakenly defines himself as a revolutionary, leaving him unable to fulfill his responsibility to kill someone, while George Hurstwood thinks that he can liberate himself from his stable though sterile middle-class life. Both commit suicide as a result of their inability to adapt to their surroundings, leading these narratives to question Spencer's and Darwin's faith in group dynamics instilling moral values. In her writings, Edith Wharton also depicts larger group values hindering individuals from expressing their true beliefs or attaining their desires. The biologist Linyard, in "The Descent of Man" (1904), is forced to compromise his values to succeed; similarly, Lily Bart, in *The House of Mirth* (1905), strives futilely to find a stable financial position within the elite of New York, leading her to commit suicide, as do Hyacinth Robinson and George Hurstwood. In recalling her first introduction to evolutionary theory in the 1880s, Wharton asserts, "it is hopeless to convey to a younger generation the first overwhelming sense of cosmic vastness which such 'magic casements' let into our little geocentric universe" (*A Backward Glance* 94). Wharton expresses a sense of both wonder and distress at the immensity of evolutionary development, and her fiction reveals trepidation at the way evolutionary materialism negates the dynamics of the specific mind.

In "The Descent of Man," Wharton describes the life of an academic who researches beetles and engages in the battle over the validity of the "transmission of acquired characteristics" (348). The Lamarckian reference indicates that Wharton was aware of the debates among evolutionists as well as of Herbert Spencer's popularizing of evolutionary theory. As Wharton's protagonist, Professor Linyard, laments, "Everyone now read scientific books and expressed an opinion on them. The ladies and the clergy had taken them up first; now they had passed to the schoolroom and the kindergarten" (349). Linyard proceeds to call this mass science "a pseudo-science masquerading in the garb of the real divinity" (350). The story thus becomes an indirect critique of the type of popularized evolutionary science practiced by Spencer, whose "ringing optimism of faith in man's destiny and the supremacy of good" (357) exemplifies the elements of Spencer's brand of progressive evolution that became fashionable in Wharton's time.

To combat this "pseudo-science," Linyard decides to write a book that satirizes popular science by parodying the language and ideas embedded in it. However, his publisher mistakes the book as a serious "apologia" from a scientist (352). After some brief personal debate between his integrity as a scientist and the financial benefits of a bestseller, Linyard assents to his publisher's will, and the book becomes a big success, leading Linyard to become a major celebrity, an irony that results in his "leading a double life" to allow his scientific standing to remain reputable (360). Marysue Schriber connects Linyard's dilemma to Darwin's concept of the moral sense inculcated by group values. She asserts that "if 'service to fellow-men,' as Darwin calls it, is for the scientist the discovery and dissemination of truth, then Linyard ignores his social instincts and chooses instead the reward of praise and money" (33).

In her analysis, Schriber defines Linyard's social responsibility as rejecting the publisher's offer and instead continuing to live his penurious life in the disinterested pursuit of scientific truth. However, the group values within the story are not so easily defined. As a husband and father, Linyard has the responsibility to provide for his family. Also, the majority-group values within the story praise his book as an important statement on the faith in progressive development. Schriber is probably right in the purest sense to define Linyard's altruistic obligation as pursuing scientific knowledge. Nevertheless, she does not consider that Linyard's conflict reveals the contradictory definitions of altruistic behavior in a heterogeneous society.

Linyard exists in diverse group structures: his family, his fellow researchers, and the readers of his book—all have their conflicting ethical demands. Marketing the book as serious does not necessarily gratify Linyard's selfish desire so much as it satisfies his family's needs for money or the public's desire for pleasure. Wharton's narrative reflects the complicated relationship between the individual and the group, undermining a scientific definition of morality. In Linyard's case, acting against the majority of society would have been the moral act because the values of the group lead him to compromise his personal integrity.

Like Linyard, Lily Bart's machinations are frustrated by her environment, making *The House of Mirth* a determinist narrative. In crafting the novel, Wharton recalled, she created Lily Bart because "a frivolous society can acquire dramatic significance only through what its frivolity destroys. Its tragic implication lies in its power of debasing people and ideals" (*Looking Backward* 207). Toward the end of the novel, Lily realizes that she cannot change her life from one of leisure to one of work because she was not made that way. She realizes, "Inherited tendencies had combined with early training to make her the highly specialized product she was: an organism as helpless out of its narrow range as the sea-anemone torn from the rock" (406). Wharton invokes Lamarckian concepts of inherited behavior to explain Lily's behavior. Because of the way her environment conditioned her, Lily is unable to overcome her reluctance to marry for money and cannot adapt to changing circumstances, so she becomes subject to the machinations of others, especially Bertha Dorsett, who ruins Lily's reputation among the wealthy (300–1).

Sharon Kim points out that the narrative functions on a Lamarckian paradigm because Lily cannot "keep herself intact within [the exchange] culture" in which she exists (189). Lamarck maintains that the organism survives based on its inheritance of characteristics that are successful in the struggle for life. These characteristics are developed through the organism's interaction with its environment, leading to changed habits (Eisley 55). Lily is unable to survive, as Kim indicates, because she does not adopt new habits through interacting with her environment.

Spencer argued that this interaction with the environment could lead to the gradual development of certain traits, including moral ones. Because of Lily's internalizing the values of her set, she cannot live outside of "the gilt cage" as Lawrence Selden does (71). Despite their differences, both *The House of Mirth* and "The Descent of Man" reveal the conflict between the individual and her environment, undermining Darwin's and Spencer's emphasis on group values. Lily fails to bridge her own needs and desires with those of her group, and her failure causes her death; Linyard is able to negotiate the conflicting demands that differing groups make on him, but his project of satirizing popular science fails.

Unlike Wharton, who was skeptical of an evolutionary materialism and believed that it destroyed individual uniqueness, Frank Norris believed in a progressive evolutionary development in which the unfit disappear and the fittest survive. While Wharton consciously examined the ways people adapt or do not adapt to the dominant ethics of their environments, Norris wrote novels in which he attempted to replicate Spencer's version of cosmic evolution; however, in replicating it, he often undermined Spencer's ideas, though unlike Dreiser, Norris did not refer directly to either Darwin or Spencer in his fiction. In his criticism, Norris often mocked the genteel realism of Wharton and James, deriding it as "the tragedy of the broken teacup" ("Plea" 1166). He envisioned a more melodramatic and catastrophic tragedy that would explore the motivations at the root of human behavior, "the mystery of sex, and the problems of life, and the black, unsearched penetralia of the soul of man" ("Plea" 1168–69). In his essay "'The Novel with a 'Purpose,'" Norris argues that "[t]he elemental forces, then, contribute to the novel with a purpose to provide it with vigorous action" (1197).

Joseph LeConte, from whom Norris took classes in geology and zoology while he attended the University of California at Berkeley, exerted a strong influence on the young writer (Pizer 12–16). LeConte was concerned about the amoral character of evolutionary development and thus articulated an optimistic evolutionary theory that assumed divine providence guided species development (Pizer 14). In *Evolution: Its Nature, Its Evidences, and Its Relation to Religious Thought*, first published in 1888, LeConte asserted, "In organic evolution, when the struggle for life is fierce and pitiless as it is now among the higher animals, natural selection is undoubtedly by far the most potent factor" (97). However, LeConte wants human evolution to be more than mere random brutality. He defines evolution as "continuous *progressive change, according to certain laws*, and by means of *resident forces*" (8). He believes that natural selection is neither progressive nor a very certain law. Like Spencer, he asserts that the inheritance of functionally acquired characteristics leads to the general improvement of humanity, and he emphasizes Spencer's concept of evolution as a force that underlies all existence: "The process pervades the whole universe, and the doctrine concerns alike every department of science—yea, every department of human thought" (3). In *First Principles*, Spencer asserts, "We come down, then, finally to Force as the ultimate of ultimates" (146).

Norris received a variety of ideas from LeConte, including the existence of "unknowable" forces that regulate organic and human development, a partiality to the Lamarckian mechanism of development as one of these forces, and a belief in progressive evolution in which humanity is perpetually improving. All of these ideas play a crucial role in *McTeague* (1899), where Norris invokes general concepts of heredity to explain the protagonist's predetermined fate: "Below the fine fabric of all that was good in him ran the foul strain of hereditary evil, like a sewer. The vices and sins of his father and his father's father, to the third and fourth and five hundredth, generation tainted him" (285). This passage refers to Lamarckian ideas of inherited behavior to define McTeague's lack of moral development as he acquires his ancestors' lascivious inclinations. In the novel, Norris implies that a Lamarckian form of adaptation performs useful moral action by leading to McTeague's extinction due to his inherited pathologies.

Norris continued his belief in a benign Lamarckian materialism in his later novel *The Octopus* (1901), which he wrote as the first book of his planned "Epic of Wheat" trilogy and which was based on a true story of farmers resisting the Southern Pacific Railroad in Tulare County, California, a battle which resulted in death on both sides. In writing his novel, Norris knew that he was engaging in the conflict between laissez-faire capitalism and reform. In a letter to a friend, Norris acknowledged that he was "in a beautiful 'political muddle' . . . in *The Octopus*" (qtd. in Walker 251). In addition to suggesting the influence of Spencer's concepts of force and evolution, the novel evokes the ethics of survival and extinction through the conflict between Spencer's idea of evolutionary development through unregulated capitalism and reformers' belief in the destructive elements of laissez-faire.

These conflicts are evident at the conclusion of the novel. After a violent confrontation that leaves most of the ranchers dead, the poet Presley confronts the railroad's owner, Shelgrim, with the fatal consequences of his business practices. However, Shelgrim manages to silence Presley by invoking Spencer's concept of laissez-faire as an elemental life force:

> *Railroads build themselves.* Where there is a demand sooner or later there will be
> a supply. . . . You are dealing with forces, young man, when you speak of Wheat
> and the Railroads not with men. . . . The Wheat is one force, the Railroad,
> another, and there is the law that governs them—supply and demand. (1036–37)

Shelgrim asserts that no individual moral responsibility exists in elemental forces. Therefore, individual suffering is a necessary outcome of development because society will keep evolving through those forces.

Norris appears to share Shelgrim's view, given Presley's final realization that "[t]he larger view always and through all shams, all wickednesses, discovers the Truth that will, in the end, prevail, and all things, surely, inevitably, resistlessly work together for good" (1098). Presley invokes Spencerian optimism to support Shelgrim's ideas of Spencerian force. However, the melodrama of Norris's own narrative undermines such optimism of progressive hope. Families are destroyed in the clash with the railroad. After the German immigrant farmer Hooven is killed by the railroad, his wife and their daughter Hilda starve in the streets of San Francisco, which Norris juxtaposes with a fancy dinner at the home of a railroad baron (1065–67).

Norris uses this contrast for maximum dramatic effect. Still, it, along with other depictions of suffering, clash with Presley's hopeful assertion at the conclusion of the novel.

Given that Norris wanted to write novels of horrible tragedy in opposition to the refined and contemplative bourgeois stories of Wharton and James, *The Octopus* becomes a work split between Norris's apparent belief in a benign evolution and his melodramatic style; this conflict serves to disrupt a sense of a unified evolutionary ethics. Ronald Martin asserts that Norris "feel[s] the social injustice keenly . . . but he seems to believe the Spencerianism too, and the two perspectives are irreconcilable" (174). As Martin points out, Norris's novel appears as an affirmation of Spencer's optimism in confronting Joseph LeConte's concerns about the amorality of natural selection. However, such hope is unconvincing given the personal suffering that occurs at the end of the novel. Norris wanted to write "the vast and terrible dramas" of life that led him to show the destruction of the unfit ("Zola" 1107). These depictions cause Norris to reveal unwittingly the consequences of social evolution, reinforcing Le Conte's fear of the amoral nature of species development.

Norris's West Coast colleague Jack London was more aware of his inner conflicts over Spencerian evolution because they were so acute. For most of his life, London searched for systems to help him understand the world around him, not all of them consistent with each other. In a letter dated 15 March 1900 to Cloudesley Johns, London asserts that "to be well fitted for the tragedy of existence (intellectual existence), one must have a working philosophy, a synthesis of things" (*Letters* 1: 170). As Earle Labor and Jeanne Campbell Reesman point out, London "could unblinkingly accommodate to his weltanschauung the disparate philosophical attitudes of Friedrich Nietzsche, Karl Marx, Ernst Haeckel, Herbert Spencer, and Benjamin Kidd" (3). Because of these conflicting influences and because his own experience was dynamic and varied, London's fiction often undermines the notion that one philosophy can guide someone in life's pursuit. Ronald Martin asserts that "as an artist [London] showed in his best works an intuitive awareness that there was more to life than any single paradigm could express" (185).

At a young age, London discovered Karl Marx and became a believer in socialism (Kershaw 39–40). When he entered the University of California, he discovered Spencer and became a believer in evolutionary materialism (Kershaw 49). While Marxism and Spencerian evolution both focus on change, these two philosophies contradict each other because Spencer believes in an inexorable social development through laissez-faire economics while Marx believes laissez-faire leads to exploitation and social degradation. Because of this contradiction, London embraced Spencerian evolution as a philosophy to help him understand the way the biological world worked, though he was never quite certain of its validity (Martin 185).

Although London admired Spencer's ability to create a comprehensive and empirical philosophy, he intuitively knew that Spencer's explanation was not complete since his experience growing up poor taught him that the lower class was not necessarily the unfit. Thus, London also sought socialism as an empirical explanation for human suffering. Still, he had an intuitive sense of social injustice at an early age before he even discovered Marx (Kershaw 31). Because of his experience, London also had a contradictory relationship to Nietzschean individualism. Much as does his character Martin Eden in the novel of the same name, London rose from being a poor uneducated youth to being a major writer. He saw himself as an individualist who mastered whatever skills were necessary to survive, and Eden, like London, becomes first a sailor, then a journalist, and then a novelist. Still, London was also troubled by the type of "fanatical individualism" justified by both Nietzsche and Spencer.

Spencer and Nietzsche differ in their forms of individualism. Spencer believes in the salutatory elements of competitive commerce, arguing that commerce is a fitting way for the human race to channel its aggressive urges and that commerce would inevitably transcend those urges (*Principles of Psychology* 2: 609). In London's novel *Martin Eden* (1909), the title character, a working-class striver who has educated himself, criticizes Spencer's form of evolution from a Nietzschean perspective when he tells the bourgeois Mr. Morse and Judge Blount, who espouse a belief in Republican economic regulation, that "Nietzsche was right. I won't take the time to tell you who Nietzsche was, but he was right. The world belongs to the strong—to the strong who are noble as well and who do not wallow in the swine-trough of trade and exchange" (848–49). Despite this criticism, London portrays Eden as an acolyte of Spencer's, depicting Eden's initial reading of *First Principles* as a type of discovery: "And here was the man Spencer, organizing all knowledge for him, reducing everything to unity, elaborating ultimate realities" (653). Spencer's brand of social evolution strongly influences Eden, although he yearns for a Nietzschean superman who will rescue society from the banalities of commerce. Therefore, Eden is split between his beliefs in Nietzschean romanticism and in Spencerian evolution.

In both *Martin Eden* and *The Sea-Wolf* (1904), London criticizes individualism, though his own individualist bent complicates the power of his message. In a 5 November 1915 letter to Mary Austin, London describes his novel as an "attack on the super-man idea, namely, my *Martin Eden*. Nobody discovered that this was such an attack" (*Letters* 3: 1513). *The Sea-Wolf*, published five years earlier than *Martin Eden*, is a clearer criticism of individualism, though it too reflects London's conflicted acceptance of Spencer's thought. Wolf Larsen is the embodiment of the ideal masculine organism. When the narrator Humphrey Van Weyden finds Larsen shirtless, he states, "But Wolf Larsen was the man-type, the masculine, and almost a god in his perfectness" (593). Larsen is emblematic of the Nietzschean superman, reflecting London's fascination with male Anglo-Saxon power. Moreover, Larsen is a self-taught sailor who pursues learning in spite of his anti-intellectual surroundings. Van Weyden is impressed when he discovers that Larsen has read Spencer and can talk with some authority about him (544).

His god-like features are not paired with a refined demeanor, however, as Larsen believes in unprincipled power. He tells Van Weyden, "Might is right and that is all there is to it. Weakness is wrong. Which is a very poor way of saying that it is good for oneself to be strong and evil for oneself to be weak" (543). As their conversation proceeds, Larsen admits that he has read Spencer's *Data of Ethics*, but that he does not believe in altruism, proudly assenting that he is "a man utterly without . . . morals" (543–45). Larsen's materialism leads him to reject altruism as a viable belief, instead seeing life as an evolutionary struggle for survival in which primal strength endures. Believing this, Larsen spends much of the novel inflicting sadistic punishment on his crew. However, the narrative rejects Larsen's evolutionary materialism. At the conclusion, the formerly effete writer Van Weyden has learned to be an exemplary sailor and survivor while Larsen is slowly dying from a paralyzing brain tumor.

Jonathan Berliner attempts to synthesize London's Spencerian evolutionary beliefs with his socialism. He argues that "[t]he conception of nature at the heart of London's socialism is violent in character. From naturalistic, muckraking scenes of immersion in the abyss of the slums of London, to his recurrent praise of primordial supermen, London presents nature as a brutal force but crucially one that could be harnessed for socialistic purposes" (56). Berliner focuses most of his analysis on *The People of the Abyss* (1903), London's investigation into poverty in London. However, his analysis could be applied to *The Sea-Wolf* as well, for Larsen's antisocial aggression can be seen as a force to be harnessed for more socially oriented purposes. The novel ends with the competent Van Weyden uniting with Maud Brewster to liberate themselves from Larsen's ship. Such a union relates more to gender issues than political issues; nevertheless, Berliner offers a way to reconcile London's seemingly paradoxical beliefs in Spencerian evolution, Nietzschean individualism, and socialism.

In a different reading, Bert Bender points out that in London's system of sexual selection, the poet Maud Brewster "selects against the merely brutal but beautiful Wolf, and for Van Weyden, whose superiority inheres in his moral sense, the highest evolutionary development according to the *Descent of Man*" (76). The connection to Darwin is valid because Van Weyden is both a good sailor and a literary gentleman; still, his latter sensibility draws Maud to him. Van Weyden maintains his refined personality and does not become as hardened as the sailors, thus resisting their aggressive values. Therefore, Maud and Van Weyden's connection is over their shared sensibility as thoughtful people stuck in a pitiless world.

London ends his novel by "sending the *Ghost* into the evolutionary future with the vigorous and highly developed lovers, Maud and Van Weyden," as Bender asserts (76). Unlike the other writers in this study, London appears to endorse an evolutionary ethics grounded in a physically and morally developed unified self. Still, London presents an individual in conflict with his environment. In order for Van Weyden and Maud to be completely developed, they have to hold onto their moral values. A few years later, London depicted Martin Eden as a highly evolved individual who is able to transcend his working-class roots only to find himself alienated from both those roots and the elite world to which he rose, leading, like Hyacinth Robinson, George Hurstwood, and Lily Bart, to suicide. While some have seen Eden as an affirmation of individualism, his isolation and death reveal a version of individualism with no benefits.

In *The Sea-Wolf*, London offers a more optimistic vision of human evolution than other writers of his time. However, as *Martin Eden* shows, London is not entirely convinced that evolutionary processes lead to the improvement of human ethics. Like William James, many of the novelists of the period reveal the problems with a determinist model that makes people pure products of their own biology and of supposedly primary forces. The novelists in this study sought to dramatize people's inability to adapt to their environments, utilizing certain elements of evolutionary discourse to heighten the impact of their stories. In appropriating evolutionary discourse, they all reveal the complicated nature of an evolutionary ethics, thus questioning the validity of that discourse.

WORKS CITED

Bell, Michael Davitt. *The Problem of American Realism: Studies in the Cultural History of a Literary Idea*. Chicago: University of Chicago Press, 1993.

Bender, Burt. *Evolution and "the Sex Problem": American Narratives during the Eclipse of Darwinism*. Kent: Kent State University Press, 2004.

Berliner, Jonathan. "Jack London's Socialistic Social Darwinism." *American Literary Realism* 41 (2008): 52–78.

Brush, Stephen G. "The Nebular Hypothesis and the Evolutionary Worldview." *History of Science* 25 (1987): 245–78.

Darwin, Charles. *The Descent of Man and Selection in Relation to Sex*. The Works of Charles Darwin. Vol. 9. New York: AMS, 1972.

Dreiser, Theodore. "Equation Inevitable." *Hey Rub-A-Dub-Dub: A Book of the Mystery and Wonder and Terror of Life*. New York: Boni & Liveright, 1920. 157–81.

———. *Newspaper Days*. Ed. T. D. Nostwich. Philadelphia: University of Pennsylvania Press, 1991.

———. "Reflections." *Theodore Dreiser's Ev'ry Month*. Ed. Nancy Warner Barrineau. Athens: University of Georgia Press, 1996. 134–45.

———. *Sister Carrie*. New York: Norton, 2006.

Eisley, Loren. *Darwin's Century*. New York: Doubleday, 1958.

Fiske, John. *Outlines of Cosmic Philosophy*. Vol. 4. 1874. Boston: Houghton Mifflin, 1902.

Hofstadter, Richard. *Social Darwinism in American Thought: 1860–1915*. Philadelphia: University of Pennsylvania Press, 1945.

Hussman, Lawrence, Jr. *Dreiser and His Fiction: A Twentieth Century Quest*. Philadelphia: University of Pennsylvania Press, 1983.

Huxley, Thomas H. "Evolution and Ethics." Romanes Lecture. 1893. T. H. Huxley and Julian Huxley, *Evolution and Ethics 1893–1943*. New York: Kraus, 1969.

James, Henry. *The Princess Casamassima*. New York: Penguin, 1978.

James, William. "The Dilemma of Determinism." *The Will to Believe and Other Essays in Popular Philosophy. William James: Writings 1878–1899*. Ed. Gerald E. Myers. New York: Library of America, 1992. 566–94.

Kershaw, Alex. *Jack London: A Life*. New York: St Martin's, 1997.

Kim, Sharon. "Lamarckism and the Construction of Transcendence in *The House of Mirth*." *Studies in the Novel* 38 (2006): 187–210.

Labor, Earle, and Jeanne Campbell Reesman. *Jack London*. 2nd ed. New York: Twayne, 1994.

LeConte, Joseph. *Evolution: Its Nature, Its Evidences, and Its Relation to Religious Thought*. New York: Appleton, 1891.

Lehan, Richard. *Theodore Dreiser: His World and His Novels*. Carbondale: Southern Illinois University Press, 1969.

London, Jack. *The Letters of Jack London*. Ed. Earle Labor, Robert C. Leitz III, and Milo Shepard. Stanford: Stanford University Press, 1988. 3 vols.

———. *Martin Eden. Novels and Social Writings*. Ed. Donald Pizer. New York: Library of America, 1982. 555–931.

———. *The Sea-Wolf. Novels and Stories*. New York: Library of America, 1982. 449–771.

Martin, Ronald. *American Literature and the Universe of Force*. Durham: Duke University Press, 1981.

Norris, Frank. *McTeague*. Norris, *Novels and Essays* 261–572.

———. "The Novel with a 'Purpose.'" Norris, *Novels and Essays* 1196–1200.

———. *Novels and Essays*. Ed. Donald Pizer. New York: Library of America, 1986.

———. *The Octopus*. Norris, *Novels and Essays* 573–1098.

———. "A Plea for Romantic Fiction." Norris, *Novels and Essays* 1165–69.

———. "Zola as a Romantic Writer." Norris, *Novels and Essays* 1106–8.

"The Origin of Species." *New York Times* 28 March 1860: 3.

Pizer, Donald. *The Novels of Frank Norris*. Bloomington: Indiana University Press, 1966.

Richards, Robert J. *Darwin and the Emergence of Evolutionary Theories of Mind and Behavior*. Chicago: University of Chicago Press, 1987.

Schriber, Marysue. "Darwin, Wharton, and 'The Descent of Man': Blueprints of American Society." *Studies in Short Fiction* 17 (1980): 31–38.

Spencer, Herbert. *First Principles*. 6th ed. Westport, Conn.: Greenwood, 1976.

———. *Principles of Biology*. Vol. 1. Osnabruck, Germany: Otto Zeller, 1966.

———. *Principles of Psychology*. 3rd ed. New York: Appleton, 1906. 2 vols.

———. *Social Statics*. New York: Augustus M. Kelley, 1969.

Walker, Franklin. *Frank Norris: A Biography*. New York: Russell & Russell, 1963.

Wharton, Edith. *A Backward Glance*. New York: Touchstone, 1998.

———. "The Descent of Man." *The Collected Short Stories of Edith Wharton*. Vol. 1. Ed. R. W. B. Lewis. New York: Scribner, 1968. 347–63.

———. *The House of Mirth*. New York: Macmillan, 1987.

CHAPTER 9

··

NATURALISM AND RELIGION

··

STEVEN FRYE

As the late Victorian Age brought with it a rapidly changing intellectual culture, an inevitable tension among dominant worldviews emerged as a focal point for intellectual interchange, cross-fertilization, and contention. The relationship between the new science and the monotheistic faith traditions of Europe and America, primarily Western Christianity in its varied post-Reformation forms, is tremendously complex. In the popular mind and even among many in the academic community, this complexity has not always been recognized. Partly as a result of questionable studies charting the history of science written in the late nineteenth and early twentieth centuries, a common assumption has emerged, one that asserts an essential conflict between science and religion. This notion has conditioned how we understand the relationship between scientific naturalism as a worldview and religion both as an intellectual sensibility and a social practice. A perceived conflict revolving around modes of conceptualization has further influenced the critical perception of the major writers of American literary naturalism, specifically with respect to religion in all its forms. But recent historiography of science has served to enrich our understanding of this relationship. Certainly, the major naturalists of the American tradition, specifically Stephen Crane, Jack London, Frank Norris, and Theodore Dreiser, engaged with differing degrees of sympathy the dominant scientific ideas that defined their age. But their manner of engagement often reflects the various ways in which scientific ideas and theories were influenced by a two-thousand-year theological and religious tradition. This density and thematic texture is commonly missed, since their works are often read through interpretive frameworks that assume a simple dissonance between the claims of modern science and traditional religion. Under this assumption, scientific naturalism, particularly in the wake of the natural philosophy of Jean Baptiste Lamarck, Herbert Spencer, and Charles Darwin, stands in stark opposition to antiquated premodern theological traditions. Further, as naturalists the authors who engage scientific epistemologies provide an artistic rendering of compelling modern scientific theories, specifically evolution in its multiple varieties. A close scrutiny of the works themselves, however, as well as the historical contexts out of which they emerge, presents a more textured portrait of varied colors and hues, multiple shades and blendings, in which stark descriptions of naturalistic scenes, characters, and situations are integrated with religious and quasi-religious conceptions in addition to evocative intimations of a potentially divine mystery. The works of Crane, Norris, London, and Dreiser, among others, are deeply ensconced in the science of their times. Their works incorporate scientific naturalism in explicit terms. But in all cases, religion and the humanist tradition it embodies remains a resonating force and an important thematic strand.

The fact that these authors have often been seen as single-minded literary avatars of the scientific age owes itself in part to the so-called "conflict" thesis or "warfare" thesis. Interestingly, this historiographic assumption emerged out of a Victorian and, by extension, an American naturalist context. In America, this strand of thinking continues in two histories of science written in the late nineteenth century that exerted an incalculable influence on the public understanding of science and religion. They are John William Draper's *History of the Conflict between Religion and Science* (1874) and Andrew Dickson White's *A History of the Warfare of Science with Theology in Christendom* (1896). These studies were followed in the early twentieth century by J. Y. Simpson's *Landmarks in the Struggle between Science and Religion* (1925). Motivated by concerns both personal and intellectual, these works posit a progressivist conception of historical change, as science contends with religion in an epic battle between secular reason and the politically embedded forces of traditional religion and theology. At the heart of this historical chronicle are the well-known cases of Copernicus, Galileo Galilei, Charles Darwin, and in an American popular context, John Thomas Scopes. However, more recent studies in the historiography of science reveal a rather complex relationship between science and religion. James Turner's *Without God, Without Creed: The Origins of Unbelief in America* (1985), charts the rise of agnosticism and atheism as viable intellectual options in the late nineteenth century, seeing them emerge, not as a result of definitive conclusions that mandated a purely secular orientation, but as a shift in intellectual sensibility and practice that came to dominate university culture. More specifically, Gary B. Ferngren edited a collection entitled *The History of Science and Religion in the Western Tradition: An Encyclopedia* (2000), which contains essays later included in a smaller volume, *Science and Religion: A Historical Introduction* (2002), and Ronald L. Numbers and David C. Lindberg edited a volume of articles entitled *God and Nature: Historical Essays on the Encounter between Christianity and Science* (1986). In the various essays in these collections, a "complexity" thesis emerges, describing the relationship of science and religion as a complicated series of interchanges involving conflict, cooperation, and interchange. The conflicts that emerge were sometimes purely intellectual but not always so, many being political and social, with the contention revolving around Galileo arising as much from the insecurity of the Catholic Church under the threat of the Reformation as from anything inherent in his post-Copernican advances in cosmology (see Wilson). Cooperation is revealed as Christianity appears as a central force in fostering the ideas of Johannes Kepler (1571–1630), Robert Boyle (1627–91), Isaac Newton (1642–1727), and René Descartes (1596–1650). Even in a nineteenth-century British context, when the notion of conflict is most commonly assumed, major efforts among scientists to effectively blend scientific and religious understanding were supported by both secular and sectarian factions. These include the works of Michael Faraday (1791–1867), James Joule (1818–89), James Clarke Maxwell (1831–79), William Thomson (Lord Kelvin [1824–1907]), and George Gabriel Stokes (1819–1903). These revisionary historical perspectives are motivated, not primarily or exclusively by sympathy for religion, but by skepticism of Enlightenment-based progressive historiography, as well as by utopian ideals that assume the inevitability of human improvement over time, which in many histories written during the late nineteenth century influenced the interpretation of historical data (see White).

In fact, the relationship between science and religion involves this intricate blend of interaction, cooperation, and conflict, which took place over hundreds of years in Europe and America. The most essential feature of conflict revolved around distinctions between religious and scientific conceptions of reality. These contentions were not so much based on truth or fact but over the nature of legitimate thought in the intellectual realm. What can be classed as "fact" was rather simple, and for centuries in an academic context had been defined by evolving empirical methodologies. What can be classed as "truth" was more difficult. Even today, the most strident scientific naturalist worldview would define "fact" and "truth" as roughly synonymous, arguing that both emerge from rigorous scientific inquiries into material phenomena and verifiable natural law. The religious worldview broadly construed (factoring out extremist perspectives) distinguishes between "objective" truth, which is derived from empirical methodology and the observation of nature, and "subjective" truths involving personal experiences that in the end may be collectively shared, through faith traditions and figuratively interpreted mythologies and theologies. These subjective truths emerge from more mysterious affective modes of experience and might conventionally be associated with "divine revelation." But they may also be linked to aesthetics, with the apprehension and deep appreciation of art, which arguably involves a blended emotional and epistemic content. Thus from a scientific naturalist perspective, a poem might be seen as a linguistic construct, with an identifiable phonology, morphology, and syntax. It might further be seen as an aesthetic artifact that may be productively scrutinized for its intricate formal textures—rhythm and rhyme scheme, the use of symbol, complex metaphor, imagery, and tone. All of these broadly rationalist modes of inquiry form the basis of much modern literary criticism as currently practiced and taught. But from the religious, aesthetic, and subjectivist point of view, that same poem is also an art object that lives in the singular consciousness of the individual perceiver, who may be personally transformed by the interaction in a manner inexpressible in words, except perhaps in the allusive language of poetry itself. This latter experience is central to the religious sensibility, but it is highly circumspect, at least with respect to truth value and epistemology, to the scientific naturalist world-view. Thus in the complex relationship between science and religion, which intensifies in a naturalist context in the late nineteenth century, conflict exists not so much over known facts but over contending worldviews, which in some quarters and on both extremes are held as mutually exclusive. However, the writers of American literary naturalism challenge this partitioning, principally because they are artists sympathetic to science rather than scientists exclusively, and in their works they blend various facts, truths, and modes of epistemic perception in fiction that charts the intricate and complicated relationship between naturalism and religion.

Naturalism in Science and Theology

The scientific naturalism of the late nineteenth century, defined primarily by the evolutionary theories of Lamarck, Spencer, and Darwin, has a long antecedent in the seventeenth- and eighteenth-century Enlightenment and before, specifically in the inquiries of natural philosophy, mechanical philosophy, and natural theology, all of which assume in various forms an argument from design. (The term "argument from design" is the common parlance in scientific, philosophical, and religious circles, but it is in essence a modern rearticulation of St. Thomas Aquinas's cosmological argument.) Literary naturalism in its relation to religion cannot be properly understood without a general apprehension of this complicated history. These accounts of natural law and physical phenomena emerge from their foundation in Aristotle and Epicurus and in the thirteenth-century synthesis of theology and Aristotelian philosophy articulated by St. Thomas Aquinas. Broadly construed, natural philosophy is a branch of intellectual inquiry that deals with the objective observation of physical nature and is roughly understood as the precursor to modern science, though its empirical methodologies had yet to be fully defined. As academic disciplines evolved in the context of universities, natural philosophy derives its name from its historical relationship to philosophy and theology as it emerges from various classical and Judeo-Christian sources including Plato, Aristotle, Epicurus, Augustine, Moses Maimonides, St. Thomas Aquinas, and St. Anselm, among others. In the sixteenth century, the term "natural philosophy" was current, most obviously when Jacopo Zabarella was appointed as the first Professor of Natural Philosophy at the University of Padua. Religion worked at the center of natural philosophy, which in various ways assumed the divine origin of matter and natural law and sought to understand its conditions and operative principles. This tradition of blending religion and scientific inquiry exerted a tremendous influence on the two most important figures in a refinement of natural philosophy called "mechanical philosophy." The first was Pierre Gassendi (1592–1655), a Catholic priest whose work involved an integration of Epicurean "atomism" (a conception of nature in which particles collide in an empty space) with Christian notions of spiritual incarnation in matter. The second was René Descartes (1596–1650), who in *Principia philoso-phiae* (*Principles of Philosophy* [1644]) asserted a rigorously constituted mechanical philosophy, insofar as he sought to explain natural phenomena in terms of discern-able material causation but departed from Epicureanism in his rejection of the atomic view. He drew a firm distinction between Matter and Mind, thus dividing the material world, which is subject to observation and inquiry, from the Mind of the observer, which is itself a fully realized if mysterious emanation of the divine. Knowledge of the world is dependent upon a reasoning capacity separate from that world. For Descartes, God was the warrant for empirical inquiry (see Osler).

Thus, while the personal beliefs of many of these natural and mechanical phi-losophers remain devoutly if variously religious, and while the motives driving their inquiries were often explicitly oriented to support the argument from design, their patterns of thought encouraged a firm division between subjective and objective modes of epistemic conception. Though many such as Gassendi and Descartes were rooted in a religious tradition that acknowledged the value of subjective truth, their intellectual practice firmly privileged an evolving scientific methodology. Empirical processes and mind-sets began to coalesce in the assumption that notions of the divine can and must be subject to rational and even empirical investigation. This epistemic partitioning was rarely overt or openly asserted. But the time spent in objective inquiry into natural phenomena suggests a slow but inexorable shift in worldview and intellectual orientation, from the religious and philosophical to the secular and scientific. Yet as conceptions changed in European intellectual culture, religion remained, not just as a privately held assumption and practice, but as a motive that governed many inquiries. The mind and intention of the Prime Mover was often the fundamental issue at hand. Where genuine conflict existed between science and religion, then, it often centered on habits of mind rather than the essen-tials of belief, and these intellectual practices came over time to dominate an intel-ligentsia increasingly governed by the scientific sensibility. Thus in public discourse outside the confines of the church, the "objective" truths emerging from empirical methodologies held sway over the "subjective" claims of faith and communal reli-gious tradition, even among those scientists who professed a personal faith. In equal terms, the more subjective experiences in the aesthetic realm, the study and appre-ciation of art in all its forms, was increasingly marginalized, especially later in the nineteenth century, by an institutionalized academic culture increasingly driven by empiricism. This dynamic, especially with respect to theology and science, was no more evident than in the life and work of the most important scientist of the Enlightenment, Sir Isaac Newton (1642–1726), who devoted himself both to science and theology and arrived ultimately at an unorthodox religious perspective derived from the early Arian controversy that perhaps anticipates Unitarianism. This "Ari-anism" was derived originally from Arius (ca. AD 250–336), an early Christian priest whose teachings challenged the emerging doctrine of the Holy Trinity, which was firmly accepted as a theological precept under Emperor Constantine at the First

Council of Nicaea in AD 321. Newton and other Enlightenment figures, most of whom remained variously devout, began to question paradoxical conceptions such as the Trinity, which seemed to confound rational apprehension and mathematical and physical categorization.

The division of sensibility that forms the basis of a conflict between science and religion is most evident in the practice of natural theology, which runs parallel with the scientific inquiries emerging in the Renaissance and Enlightenment periods and which is a defining force and a complex site of contention in the physical sciences of the nineteenth century. Natural theology is at the center of the argument from design historically considered and is a form of theological reflection that seeks the attributes of the deity through the use of human reason rather than divine revelation (see Brooke, "Natural Theology"). Natural theology was a formative substructure in the scientific inquiries that emerged in the nineteenth century among many natural philosophers, perhaps most notably Thomas Malthus (1798), William Paley (1743–1805), Jean Baptiste Lamarck (1744–1829), Charles Darwin (1809–82), and Herbert Spencer (1820–1903), all of whom present varied affirmations and challenges to the assumptions of natural theology.

This period in intellectual history marks a transformative and revolutionary shift in understanding and is characterized by manifold discoveries in the natural world, specifically with regard to the biological sciences and geology, many of which presented firm challenges to biblical accounts of creation and popular conceptions of the divine. Since this new knowledge either contradicts literalist interpretations of biblical stories or offers new scientific accounts of human origins and evolution, the complex relationship between naturalism and religion intensifies dramatically, and this tension and dynamic interaction might find its metaphorical bookends in the French naturalist Georges Louis Leclerc, Comte de Buffon's *Epoques de la nature* (1778) and Charles Darwin's *Origin of Species* (1859). Perhaps the most influential work that dealt simultaneously with theology and science was conducted by the Cambridge theologian William Paley, who in his dual role as natural philosopher and theologian grounded his inquiries in an argument from design. In his *Natural Theology; Evidences of the Existence and Attributes of the Deity* (1802), his notion of design placed humankind at the apex of creation and was firmly teleological, as he articulated a concept of earth's history running parallel with a biblical account of creation that was both directional and rife with divine purpose. Paley's emphasis was anatomy, with the apparent intricacy of the human form providing the most compelling evidence of design, but he also explored the structure and function of various plants and animals. As a part of his formal schooling, Charles Darwin read Paley's works and was initially convinced by them, though as his own experiences and ideas came into focus, he departed from Paley's claim that design was necessary and unavoidably apparent in the natural world. This work in natural theology attained its height in the 1830s with *The Bridgewater Treatises*, commissioned by the eighth Earl of Bridgewater, which were ostensibly scientific works motivated by the design argument, most notably William Buckland's *Geology and Mineralogy Considered with Reference to Natural Theology* (1836).

These various studies in natural philosophy and natural theology were a central current in the intellectual culture of the time, and as such became essential reading for the scientists who followed later in the century. As with the various inquiries and treatises that preceded them, they were often sympathetic to religion, and in many cases were principally works of theology. But their methodology, though comparatively primitive, was empirical in orientation and emphasis, conceding the epistemological ground to primarily scientific modes of understanding. Certainly, a tertiary respect for divine revelation remained but was slowly and increasingly pressed to the margins of public discourse in the academic realm. Running parallel with this intellectual trajectory, however, was a revolution in aesthetics under romanticism in its various permutations. It is virtually impossible to measure the impact of romantic conceptions of innovation, imagination, mystery, and the sublime in the arts, but it can safely be assumed that few writers in the nineteenth century escaped its mark. Although few romantics were opposed to scientific inquiry broadly construed, many claimed it had epistemic limitations. In "Sonnet: To Science" (1829), Edgar Allan Poe laments the "peering eyes" of a science that "prayest . . . upon the poet's heart," resolving material reality into a systematic understanding that disallows the enchantment of myth, which by its nature inspires an affective appreciation for Supernal Beauty and mystery. In "When I Heard the Learn'd Astronomer" (1865), Walt Whitman echoes similar themes, as the persona becomes "tired and sick" at the scientist's "charts" and "diagrams," which "divide" and "measure," in the end seeking solace in the simple appreciation of the stars in the night sky. A more nuanced treatment of this perspective appears in the "Cetology" chapter of Herman Melville's *Moby-Dick* (1851), in which he ostensibly composes a work of natural philosophy only to abandon it, concluding that inquiries of this sort are valuable but limiting. For Melville, the whale is an embodied symbol of mystery and the sublime, and there are important, more subjective, and quasi-religious ways of knowing that must be preserved and acknowledged. All of these considerations emerged alongside the rapid development of the physical sciences.

Anticipating modern theories in the late eighteenth and early nineteenth centuries, Jean Baptiste Lamarck presents a model of evolutionary speciation grounded in eighteenth-century materialism but centered on the notion of progressive development. Of course, on this point Charles Darwin is distinct not only from Lamarck but also from his contemporary Herbert Spencer. In *First Principles of a New System of Philosophy* (1862), Spencer builds upon Lamarckian notions of use inheritance, the idea that traits perpetuate over time based upon functional utility. Like Lamarck, Spencer argued that evolutionary development was purposeful, productive, and directed, reflecting Enlightenment notions of progressive development, with the evolutionary process arriving at an end point in a kind of physical equilibrium. These ideas stand in measured contrast to Darwin's principle of natural selection, which is predicated on the notion of random variation. In this sense, Darwin both participates in and departs from the tradition of natural theology. In his introduction to an essay collection entitled *Darwinism and Divinity: Essays on Evolution and Religious Belief*, John Durant claims that the *Origin of Species* might be considered the last great work of Victorian natural theology. Understanding the striking nature of this association, he qualifies his statement by adding that it might also be considered the greatest, though not the first, work of Victorian evolutionary naturalism. Durant's purpose in pairing these broadly disciplinary categories is to emphasize the intellectual roots of Darwin's work.

Rightfully considered the most important and foundational work in the biological sciences, *Origin of Species* was written by a man trained in the tradition of English natural theology. The essential framework of scientific and philosophical concerns addressed in the book emerged from questions explored by Malthus and Paley, among many others. Its primary audience was a broad but identifiable group of English natural theologians. Virtually all of Darwin's training in natural history and scientific investigation occurred as he was studying for the Anglican ministry at Christ's College, Cambridge, where he worked with Paley as well as the natural theologians John Stephens Henslow and Adam Sedgwick. This initial association with the tradition of natural theology should highlight the theological subtexts inherent in Darwin's ideas. *Origin of Species* fits firmly within the conventions of this discipline, which is made clear in Darwin's own words in his final chapter: "to my mind it accords better with what we know of the laws impressed on matter by the Creator, that the production and extinction of the past and present inhabitants of the world should have been due to secondary causes, like those determining the birth and death of the individual (757–58; see Durant, "Darwinism" 17). One might reasonably speculate that this comment is meant to calm the fears of those threatened by a model of evolution that eliminates the necessity of divine intervention, but Darwin's use of the term "secondary cause" is drawn straight from theology, and he uses the concept precisely and logically. His subsequent separation from religion is a complex matter and is certainly due in part to the materialist possibilities inherent in the principle of natural selection. Whereas the tradition of natural theology assumed the existence of the Designer as a foundation for inquiries into natural phenomena and natural law, Darwin's theory of natural selection relegates the divine to the realm of the "possible" rather than the "necessary." He understood this from the beginning, as did his teacher Adam Sedgwick, who after reading *Origin* wrote Darwin a letter on Christmas Eve 1859, saying that he read parts of the book "with absolute sorrow, because I think them utterly false and grievously mischievous" (qtd. in Durant, "Darwinism" 18). Sedgwick noted immediately the theological implications inherent in Darwin's ideas, and other natural theologians did as well, but they were less anxious about them, and the controversy revolving around the *Origin of Species* was vociferous in some circles but relatively mild elsewhere. Charles Kingsley, another Anglican clergyman, received a complimentary copy, and in a letter of thanks responded quite differently than Sedgwick. Acknowledging that he would now be forced to reconsider some of his most essential assumptions, he wrote, "I have gradually learnt to see that it is just as noble a conception of Deity, to believe that He created primal forms capable of self-development into all forms needful *pro tempore* and *pro loco*, as to believe that He required a fresh act of intervention to supply the *lacunas* which he himself had made. I question whether the former be not the loftier thought" (qtd. in Durant, "Darwinism" 19).

Darwin's slow but inexorable movement out of the frameworks of the Christian faith is a matter of some debate but is certainly complex, owing at least in part to his growing frustration with the Church of England and the doctrine of eternal punishment, the death of his beloved daughter, and the profound theological challenges his scientific inquiries introduced. This led him finally to a noble doubt. In his autobiography written shortly before his death, he commented, "In my most extreme fluctuations . . . I have never been an Atheist is the sense of denying the existence of God" (qtd. in Brooke, "Relations" 42). He goes on to speak of his contentment with his agnosticism but in doing so defines the term unconventionally, writing of his "inward conviction" that the universe itself could not be the product of chance. With forthright honesty, he ponders the validity of this subjective experience, but this man of science trained in the tradition of natural theology and known ultimately as the founder of modern biological science finishes his life's work with a thought that speaks to the epistemic relevance of the subjective. The power of "inward conviction," which in his case blends with empirical inquiry, settles in a measured uncertainty with regard to ultimate questions, which themselves are often seen as the particular though not the exclusive province of religion, philosophy, and the arts.

In this sense the relationship of science and religion framed in the context of literary expression becomes problematic and fascinating. In modern and contemporary discourse, the term "humanism" is often used in concert with the term "secular," and it is associated with agnosticism or even atheism. This usage makes sense insofar as it encourages a focus on human behavior and human reason in contrast to metaphysical and religious considerations. But extreme versions of scientific naturalism systematically deny the traditional distinction between human beings and the rest of the animal world, preserving it only by acknowledging human reason as a distinctive but random outcome of evolutionary process. In fact, the term "humanism" has a long history in the Classical Period, the European Renaissance, and the Enlightenment. In this context, it is necessarily linked to Christian conceptions of human distinctiveness both intellectual and spiritual. This former conception of humanism, which was so formative in the realm of aesthetics, often blends with scientific naturalism in the works of naturalist authors.

RELIGION AND THE AMERICAN LITERARY NATURALISTS

American writers of the late nineteenth and early twentieth century lived in a society defined in part by tremendous religious diversity, made more complex by a changing intellectual culture and a social transformation fueled by the Industrial Revolution and the inexorable shift from rural to urban life. Before the major works of the literary naturalists began engaging religious issues in social context, a number of authors explored the physically and spiritually debilitating effects of industrialization. This concern appears in the "Try-Works" chapter of Melville's *Moby-Dick*, a work of intensely religious concern, as well as in his "The Paradise of Bachelors and the Tartarus of Maids." In "Life in the Iron-Mills" (1861) Rebecca Harding Davis is motivated by active religious reform movements such as the American Temperance Union as she deals with the tragic consequences of factory life on the immigrant Welshman Hugh Wolfe, a man of artistic temperament destroyed by conditions in the factory. Central to the novella's themes is a blend of romantic and Christian religiosity, conveyed as a Quaker woman and social reformer works in the interest of Wolfe's cousin Deborah, under the assumption that religious transcendence is integral to social salvation. Internal religious conflict is more directly portrayed in Harold Frederic's *The Damnation of Theron Ware* (1896). The novel charts the process by which a Methodist minister descends into spiritual crisis as he learns of the intellectual limits inherent in his religious training and education. Frederic inverts the situation typical of sentimental religious novels, which often involved the conversion of the skeptic by the evangelical skills of a beautiful woman, using the same device to initiate Theron Ware's eventual disenchantment with his Methodist faith. After meeting Father Forbes, a Catholic priest, and a beautiful Catholic girl, Celia Madden, Ware is attracted by their learning and culture, and he is crestfallen at discovering his own provincialism. In a gradual process of counter-conversion, driven by his increasing love for Celia and a series of events that distance him from his congregation and his wife, he concludes that he is unsuited for the Methodist ministry. The novel is filled with caricatures of late nineteenth-century Evangelical Protestantism, and though the Catholic characters appear flawed, the church itself is rich in aesthetic and intellectual content. Theron Ware becomes a semitragic product of a diverse and contradictory intellectual culture, full of a rich array of secular and religious strands of thought and practice. On the one hand, the novel can be read as critical, not so much of religion or belief writ large, but of the particular brands of denominational Christianity active on the American religious scene. But this diversification of faith, though rooted in the Reformation, accelerates in a post-Enlightenment and nineteenth-century context, and Theron Ware's movement away from his Methodism must be seen as a response to the broader intellectual diversity he encounters as he is exposed to other worldviews. His spiritual demise lies in his inability to fully maintain his faith in the context of intellectual currents he finds compelling. Thus the novel portrays the essential trauma as worldviews collide, a dynamic central to the works the four central practitioners of American literary naturalism: Stephen Crane, Frank Norris, Jack London, and Theodore Dreiser.

Stephen Crane's relationship to religion is fascinating and complex. His novels, short stories, and poems often express a programmatic naturalism, and *The Red Badge of Courage* (1895) is perhaps the most widely read naturalist "classic." But he was raised in a devoutly religious household. His father, who died when he was nine years old, was a Methodist minister, and his mother was intensely religious and served as a member of the Woman's Christian Temperance Union. He rejected institutional orthodoxies in adulthood, but his work is often preoccupied with questions of divinity. Not unlike Charles Darwin, he is firmly critical of an institutional Christianity that emphasizes the punitive nature of God. But in many works, he ponders the potential of God's existence and the nature of the divine encounter, all in the context of a naturalist frame of reference. Crane is most known for his fiction, which involves varied expressions of deterministic philosophy and scientific naturalism. Often regarded as the first work of American literary naturalism, *Maggie: A Girl of the Streets* (1893) is commonly read as a novella that directly foregrounds social determinism in the context of American city life. The female protagonist is a product of environmental conditioning and is driven into prostitution by environmental and biological forces that narrowly circumscribe her capacity to choose. All of this occurs in the Bowery of New York, and the story reflects concern with the human implications of urbanization and industrialization in America. Firmly naturalist in its deterministic framework and plot of decline, the novel embodies little in terms of religious affirmation, though there is a sacrificial quality to Maggie's character that lends credence to the reformist impulses common among Christian movements active at the time. In this sense it is similar in theme to Davis's "Life in the Iron-Mills." But it is in his poetry that Crane becomes noticeably obsessed with God.

Many of these "God poems" appear first in *Black Riders* (1895), published two years after *Maggie* and in the same year as *The Red Badge of Courage*. Perhaps his most commonly anthologized poem, "A Man Said to the Universe" is a concise and pithy expression of naturalist indifference unambiguously rendered, with God either absent or abstracted in the figure of the universe itself. "God Lay Dead in Heaven" conveys a similar theme, as the bestial forces of the natural world consume creation after the death of God. The poem laments this prospect, ironically in the powerful image drawn from a Christian iconography reminiscent of Michelangelo's *Pieta*, in which a man lies in the arms of a woman who tries to protect him from the jaws of "the final beast." Many of his other poems deal with the figure of God directly, with varying degrees of sympathy and tension. There is an ironic tone in many of these brief poems, and institutional Christianity is associated with a divine wrath the persona renders absurd. In "Blustering God," the speaker rails against the swagger of the deity and pronounces himself fearless. In "A God in Wrath," a wicked man is beaten by a "redoubtable" God, as onlookers observe in horror and reverence. His most overt criticism of institutional religion appears in "You Tell Me This is God," the persona pondering a "printed list" of laws and a candle, asserting God's absence from conventional religious practice. However, the image of the divine is by no means uniformly critical or dismissive. "In Heaven" is a simple allegory about a beneficent God who listens to blades of grass as they speak of their actions in life, in the end acknowledging the value of humility and self-sacrifice. "God Fashioned the Shape of the World Carefully" imagines a designer God who creates the world but allows for freedom of choice. Though Crane expresses no firm metaphysical position, these poems seem preoccupied not so much with the existence of God but with the nature of the divine and its manifestation in traditional forms and practice. Competing conceptions of a wrathful and a benevolent creator are paired in "A Man Went Before a Strange God." In this brief lyric, a man appears before a "God of many," presumably the deity of institutional Christianity and Judaism, who coldly demands worship and homage. Turning from this fearful image of divine retribution, he finds "the God of his inner thoughts" who looks to him with "soft eyes" and treats him kindly. This poem might be read as a rejection of the transcendent and an elevation of the immanent self, but the religious content of the poem is heightened when considering the subjective "inner being" that is made divine, separate and distinct from the rest of nature, capable of "infinite comprehension" and kindness. In many of these poems, human entities and human consciousness stand out markedly from their surroundings as they wrestle in isolation with the absolute.

This tension between scientific naturalism and a quasi-religious humanism also appears in many of Crane's stories and novels, perhaps most notably in *The Red Badge of Courage* and "The Open Boat" (1897). Both works convey naturalistic determinism and indifference in programmatic terms but pair these expressions with portrayals of human brotherhood, which are not explained in terms of naturalist self-interest, thus distinguishing human behavior from the rest of the material world. In the case of *The Red Badge of Courage*, Crane's religious imagery, specifically the image of the chapel and the sun described as the wafer of Eucharistic ritual, suggests an intricate blend of naturalism narrowly construed with traces of Christian humanism that heightens distinctive features of human nature. Incidents of self-sacrifice and brotherhood, appearing in *The Red Badge of Courage* and particularly in "The Open Boat," pair a natural world defined by brutality and indifference with a pure altruism that finds no firm explanation in natural law.

As an author, Frank Norris represents perhaps the most obvious expression of the confluence of science and religion in the tradition of natural theology. His many short stories and novels involve the plot of decline and describe natural conditions involving protagonists driven by brutish instinct. But they also involve a form of idealism and seeking that reflect his modest but expressed religious faith. Norris was raised in relative privilege, and he attended art school in France and studied at Berkeley and Harvard. At Berkeley, he worked with the celebrated geologist Joseph LeConte, who taught a renewed form of natural theology to reconcile more or less traditional Christian theology with evolutionary biology. Central to this conception was amelioration, the notion that all brutality and evil are mitigated by a natural process that serves an ultimate good. Divine intent informs the natural world and the laws that define it in a teleological process that is directed and meaningful. Novels such as *McTeague* (1899) and *Vandover and the Brute* (1914) seem less interested in the question of religion and more preoccupied with the animal nature of the human species, which becomes more dominant under the stress of survival. But Norris was a practicing Episcopalian and a member of St. George's Episcopal Church, which he joined in 1899. He published two short stories in 1897 and 1898 under the same title, "Miracle Joyeux," which involve images of Jesus and expressions of religious sympathy. Though there is some debate as to the sincerity of his

religious faith and his commitment to the practice of church tradition, his association with the Episcopal community must be understood in context. The mainline
Episcopal church was typically less strident and its parishioners devout but less
overtly expressive. The influence of the church on Norris and his work can be seen
more clearly when considering the leadership and writing of his rector, Reverend
William S. Rainsford, who in *The Reasonableness of Faith* (1902) emphasized the
importance of social work and, like many natural theologians that preceded him,
made a claim for the intellectual veracity of religious belief. Though the effort is
inconsistent throughout Norris's novels and short stories, many involve this same
attempt to reconcile the findings of modern science and the assumptions of scientific naturalism with an ameliorative and idealistic model of the natural world.

This effort is most notable in *The Octopus* (1901), the first volume in the proposed but never completed "Epic of Wheat" trilogy. The novel is a fictionalized
account of the conflict between railroad and farming interests in the Central Valley
of California that culminated in the Mussel Slough Tragedy. With social Darwinism
forming the backdrop, the sweeping narrative recounts the process by which the
railroad managed to take control of the land and wealth of the farming interests.
Reflecting a measured sympathy for the farmers, which echoes the social gospel of
Rainsford and the Episcopal Church, the novel nevertheless reveals the greed and
material aspirations of all involved, expressed in part by a penultimate pronouncement of naturalism given by the railroad administrator Shelgrim. A more intricate
blend of religious and naturalist concerns appear in the subplot, in which the mystic
Vanamee, after having lost his beloved, comes to see her spirit revived in the wheat
harvest itself. As the novel concludes, he experiences a religious apotheosis which
he recounts to the narrator Presley, reflecting the reconciliation of naturalist determinism and ameliorative faith expressed by Joseph LeConte. Some critics have
argued that this conclusion strikes a false note, standing in stark contrast to the
brute reality of struggle that has defined the novel to this point. Others claim that
this seeming falsity is deliberate, involving an intentional irony that challenges the
notion of amelioration. But given the influence of LeConte, Norris's apparent commitment to the Episcopal Church, and the social gospel of Rainsford, together with
the omnipresence of evolutionary naturalism, it is best to read the novel as a fictionalized expression of a long tradition of natural theology, rife with the tension typical
of the period, that attempts to find transcendent meaning amid a tragedy config-
ured in overtly naturalist terms. Whether that reconciliation is successful remains
open to question, but the novel's purpose in part is to engage questions of nature
and the divine in a manner similar to that of natural philosophers and theologians
from the seventeenth century forward. More particularly, Norris pairs the worldviews of scientific naturalism with religion and aesthetics, as the artist Presley is
enraptured when he recounts the subjective experience of the mystic Vanamee.

Jack London's works are perhaps as varied thematically as they are numerous,
and his commitment to naturalist conceptions is notable from beginning to end.
Whether his fiction is set on the sea, in the city, or in the Klondike, he embodies
Darwinian principles of natural selection and more particularly the Spencerian

notion of "survival of the fittest." But as an author committed to "living" rather than "existing," he embraced a host of political, scientific, and philosophical perspectives, including socialism, an eclectic blend of evolutionary naturalisms, and even the radical materialism of Friedrich Nietzsche. In all of these interests, there is a latent religious resonance as well as a quasi-religious humanism that appears in some of his fiction, which he often places in direct tension with scientific materialism. His widely known classic *White Fang* (1906) asserts a theory of environmental determinism in which the wild dog becomes domesticated and tamed, brought to civilized behavior and response through human benevolence. In an early account of London's life and work entitled "A Study of Jack London in His Prime," George Wharton James recalls a conversation in which London describes his motive for the novel. He commits himself firmly to an "optimistic" model of evolution predicated on the "divine possibilities" inherent in human beings, which might be realized through the complexity and variability, the "plasticity" of human identity (382). A number of works display this tendency, including his short stories "The Apostate" (1906) and "The White Silence" (1899) as well as his novels *The Iron Heel* (1908) and *The Sea-Wolf* (1904).

Considered perhaps the first modern dystopian novel, *The Iron Heel* charts the rise of an American oligarchy in the twentieth century. Socialist and political in orientation, it is nevertheless structured in the form of a quasi-religious fable and is infused with biblical phraseology and symbolism, emphasizing in a social context the Christian themes of deliverance through sacrifice and martyrdom. However, religion in the novel is employed primarily as metaphor. Theistic considerations become more explicit in his early story "The White Silence," in which a group of three people—a man, his Native American wife, and his comrade—travel across Northern Alaska in the bitter cold, confronting disaster when the man is mortally wounded in an accident. Thematically, the story works firmly within the conventions of literary naturalism. The term "natural selection" is explicitly evoked and nature's brutality and force are made painfully evident. But as the story reaches its climax, nature's "white silence" becomes more than purely material and is personified as a malevolent force that "sneers" in "pitiless" indifference. The man's comrade is portrayed with deep sympathy as he recalls the bond that has defined them, and the woman's love for her dying husband is expressed with tremendous pathos. Standing against the story's unvarnished naturalism is the comrade's tenuous sense of the divine, made evident as he contemplates how the white silence draws him toward God, since "in the hope of the Resurrection and the Life, the yearning for immortality, the vain striving of the imprisoned essence—it is then, if ever, man walks alone with God" (144). By no means can this be counted as religious affirmation, and in the end the "yearning" may be "vain," but neither is it an ironic rejection of divinity, since it confirms the mysterious "essence" that strives, hopes, and in the end may initiate a connection with God. All this takes place in the context of a human encounter with a brutal world, together with the sustaining reality of brotherhood and connection disassociated from materialist explanations of benevolence based in self-interest.

This theme is more fully explored in *The Sea-Wolf*. Though compelling in his presentation of naturalist conceptions, Wolf Larsen by no means presents a triumphalist view of science. In his character, the Nietzschean "Superman" blends with scientific materialism in a figure that stands forth as a challenge to both perspectives. London affirms the ideas Wolf Larsen articulates, but he also presents the alternative views of Humphrey Van Weyden and Maud Brewster. These characters express patterns of human relations that are implicitly theistic and firmly humanistic in a Judeo-Christian sense because they affirm the human soul, which becomes incarnate in acts of benevolence, self-sacrifice, and love. These affirmations contrast with Larsen's compelling claims, which assert that all animal species, including human beings, are mere material creatures driven by brutish instinct rather than by a transcendental ethics derived from a potentially divine source. His death by no means eradicates the force and potential validity of these assertions. Thus, many of London's works display a tension between the theistic and naturalistic perspectives dominant from the late nineteenth century until today. In all of this, any religious sentiments are divorced from formal commitment and are certainly removed from traditional orthodoxies. But late in London's career, these naturalist and religio-humanist ideas coalesce in an interest with Jungian psychology. London's wife Charmian's biography describes his preoccupation as recorded in his annotated copy of Jung's *Psychology of the Unconscious* (1912): "Throughout Dr. Jung's chapter on 'Symbolism of Mother and Rebirth,' there are penciled indications of Jack's grasp of the meaning of folk-lore and recorded time and also a comprehension of how to raise lower desires to higher expression. He has underscored Jesus's challenge to Nicodemus, cited by Jung: 'Think not carnally or thou art carnal, but think symbolically and then thou art spirit'" (2: 354). This should not be read as an assent to the value of religion in a conventional sense, especially considering the eclectic nature of London's artistic and intellectual journey. But the author's fascination with Jung suggests the complexity of his naturalism as he explores the new science of psychoanalysis, which by its very nature blends subjective and objective modes of epistemic perception, competing worldviews that typify the age.

The varied and expansive works of Theodore Dreiser represent some of the most direct expressions of scientific naturalism, and in many cases his religious characters are caricatures. It is certainly true that Dreiser was in the broadest sense a "philosophical" writer, and his novels often reflect his reading at the time of their composition. After having read Herbert Spencer's *First Principles* in 1894, novels such as *Sister Carrie* (1900) and *An American Tragedy* (1925) are rooted in Darwinian and Spencerian evolution, and *The Financier* (1912) embodies the Nietzschean *ubermensch* (Superman). He often inveighs against organized religion, particularly Catholicism. Critics who have tended to see a programmatic naturalism as the subsuming worldview of his work often point to his 1928 "Statement of Belief" in *Bookman*, in which he writes: "I catch no meaning from all that I have seen, and pass quite as I came, confused and dismayed" (25). Intellectually, Dreiser was perhaps more than any writer a man of his time, which is to say that he absorbed the dominant ideas current in his intellectual culture and struggled with question of

God, meaning, purpose, and value. Rejecting the traditional division between mind and experience, his focus remained consistently on lived reality and the laws that govern the material world. But his treatment of religion varies throughout his work, and through different characters he addresses the subject directly, sometimes in the context of institutional denominations, exploring a spectrum of potential systems and forms of religious understanding: Lutheranism in *Jennie Gerhardt* (1911); Evangelical Protestantism in *An American Tragedy*; Quakerism in *The Bulwark* (1946); Christian Science in *The "Genius"*(1915), among others. With regard to naturalism and religion, Dreiser remains secular in the broadest sense, often critical of religious orthodoxy. But considering his work in total, he functions outside any one particular intellectual system, religious, scientific, or philosophical.

Dreiser's mother was initially a Mennonite but left her family to marry his Catholic father. He was raised as a Catholic, though it appears that his mother acquiesced only to avoid conflict. She was of an expressive and artistic temperament and exerted a tremendous influence on her children. His father was initially successful in the wool business in Terra Haute, Indiana, but after a series of tragic setbacks he became increasingly doctrinaire in his Catholicism. In his autobiography, *Dawn* (1931), Dreiser describes his father's behavior and the harsh and punitive discipline he used to force his children to conform. This led Dreiser and his siblings to flee the household and the faith, and in his autobiography Dreiser is particularly perplexed by his father's focus on the afterlife and his limited regard for the present. From this experience, it appears that Dreiser became disenchanted with organized religion but, like Matthew Arnold, sought a form of religious consolation in art. This becomes clear in the character of Carrie Meeber in *Sister Carrie*, who faces the prototypical naturalist scenario as she attempts to survive and adapt in the cities of Chicago and New York. The novel is perhaps one of the most firmly naturalist works of the period, as the third-person narrator intersperses description with expository commentary that emphasizes instinct, survival response, and both biological and environmental determinism. But as Carrie works to survive, she unwittingly discovers her artistic talents as an actress. The conventional plot of decline in the naturalist novel remains in place for Hurstwood, but for Carrie it is oddly reconfigured. She survives and even thrives, but in the act of self-discovery in part initiated by Ames, she apprehends an elusive and subjective reality in the realm of aesthetics, a reality that remains beyond her reach. Artistic beauty then, its apprehension and expression, takes on qualities of the transcendent, and Dreiser's naturalism stands in tension with a brand of humanism that secularizes the divine through art, simultaneously elevating Carrie beyond her instinctual nature and ironically leaving her in the realm of a vague, shadowy, even subjective apprehension of something more.

A certain antipathy to the effects of social and biological determinism appears in other works associated with Dreiser's naturalism. *Jennie Gerhardt* involves the same deterministic forces, but as the Lutheran protagonist, after being abandoned by her lover, commits herself to raising a pair of adopted children, Dreiser places a premium on the transformative quality of emotion and benevolence, indirectly associated with Judeo-Christian ethics and commitment. In some of his later works he becomes overtly preoccupied with religion, but in all of this, his emphasis on the indifference of the natural world remains. Like the other principal writers of American literary naturalism, Theodore Dreiser engages questions of naturalism and religion in various and complex ways, using the fluid and expressive quality of language to embody the "objectivist" worldviews of modern science, together with the mysterious "subjective" considerations of religion and art. In this way, he embodies the "complexity" thesis of modern historians of science and religion, rather than the "warfare" thesis of previous historians. At times, his works display a high regard for scientific materialism and a hostility to an institutional religion that appears to deny the reality of the living present. But at other times, especially in the various encounters of religion, art, and life, religion is integrated in various ways in the minds of characters as they struggle under challenging social and personal conditions.

The late nineteenth and early twentieth centuries, then, involve an intricate and fascinating confluence of ideas, philosophical conceptions, and new discoveries both theoretical and factual. The works of many American literary naturalists are varied in their response to a changing intellectual culture and increasing religious diversity. To be properly understood, the scientific culture of the nineteenth century must be considered in the context of its history, as it emerges from natural philosophy, mechanical philosophy, and natural theology, a context revealing the complexity inherent in the evolving relationship of science and religion. At the forefront of any inquiry into the scientific concerns of literary naturalism must be a fundamental assumption: the works under consideration are principally works of art. As such, they embody an impressive array of historically conditioned cultural currents, but they do so through the singular but indefinable consciousness of the artist and the artistic process. These artists may admire scientific methodology, but they are by no means governed by it, and the works they create rarely involve singular or coherent conclusions about the nature of the material world. Especially in a narrative art, numerous historical tensions, many involving sectarian and secular concerns and sensibilities, are put in play as characters encounter a complex, compelling, and rapidly changing world.

WORKS CITED

Brooke, John Hedley. "Natural Theology." Ferngren 163–75.
———. "The Relations Between Darwin's Science and his Religion." Durant, *Darwinism* 40–75.
Crane, Stephen. *The Black Riders and Other Lines*. Boston: Copeland and Day, 1895.
Darwin, C. R. *The Origin of Species . . . A Variorum Text*. 1859. Ed. Morse Peckham. Philadelphia: University of Pennsylvania Press, 1959.
Dreiser, Theodore. "Statement of Belief." *Bookman* Sept. 1928: 25.
Durant, John. "Darwinism and Divinity: A Century of Debate." Durant, *Darwinism* 9–39.
———, ed. *Darwinism and Divinity: Essays on Evolution and Religious Belief*. Oxford: Basil Blackwell, 1985

Ferngren, Gary B., ed. *Science and Religion: A Historical Introduction*. Baltimore: Johns Hopkins University Press, 2002.

James, George Wharton. "A Study of Jack London in His Prime." *Overland Monthly* May 1917: 361–99.

London, Charmian Kittredge. *The Book of Jack London*. London: Mills and Boon, 1921. 2 vols.

London, Jack. "The White Silence." *The Complete Short Stories of Jack London*. Ed. Earle Labor, Robert C. Leitz III, and I. Milo Shepard. Vol. 1. Stanford: Stanford University Press, 1993. 141–55.

Osler, Margaret J. "Mechanical Philosophy." Ferngren 143–52.

White, Hayden. *Metahistory: The Historical Imagination in Nineteenth-Century Europe*. Baltimore: Johns Hopkins University Press, 1973.

Wilson, David B. "The Historiography of Science and Religion." Ferngren 13–29.

CHAPTER 10

THINGS FALL APART: DEGENERATION AND ATAVISM IN AMERICAN LITERARY NATURALISM

GINA M. ROSSETTI

A review of the texts that comprise the American naturalist canon suggests a preoccupation with a culture in retrograde. So much of this concern manifests itself in the era, where anxieties about increased numbers of immigrants would signal an end to a "unified" American identity. In this greater cultural context, the era's sociologists offer warnings about the "alien's" ability to assimilate. For William Graham Sumner, Franklin Giddings, and Edward Ross, so much of their work becomes examples of efforts to find and use biological evidence of an inherent inferiority among the lower classes as justification for perpetuating Anglo-American dominance in the culture's social organization. This essay will chart, then, not only the cultural context for writers' interest in degeneration and atavism but also the extent to which literary texts register and engage with this preoccupation, thus signaling how this sub-genre becomes a site onto which these fears and concerns are projected.

In his *What the Social Classes Owe to Each Other* (1883), William Graham Sumner argues that the impoverished inhabitants of cities, many of whom are immigrants, represent dangerous atavisms, reminiscent of our barbarian, pre-civilized past. Such persons threaten American identity because unmediated contact with them will spell a return to a pre-civilized order. Part of Sumner's solution to this social and cultural "problem" is for social Darwinism to take effect: the vices that consume such persons will be the seeds of their demise, thus saving civilized, American culture from such contagion. Such a scientific solution is threatened, Sumner believes, by a push for social uplift, and in doing so, this legislative act threatens not only American culture but also nature itself. Writing about the "degenerate," Sumner argues that "nature has set upon him the process of decline and dissolution by which she removes things which have survived their usefulness" (113–14). By attempting to uplift such persons, Sumner reasons, the era's moralists defile nature and American cultural identity by attempting to absorb that which cannot survive, thus imperiling the broader culture.

Echoing some of Sumner's concerns, Franklin Giddings also posits two seemingly contradictory theories: first, biology is a race's destiny insofar as its longevity is contingent upon its ability to "naturally" remain in existence, and second, a race survives based upon its proximity to a "higher" race. In terms of the first point, Giddings's conclusion differs little from Sumner's theories because both are predicated upon an application of social Darwinism. Where Giddings parts from Sumner is in his claim that mere exposure to an elite race is enough to reverse the biological predisposition to fail. Illustrating his point, Giddings examines the contrasting "histories" of Native Americans and African Americans. In his analysis, Giddings speculates that Native American culture failed because it was unable to adapt. Without adaptation, Giddings reasons, no race survives. Unlike the Native American, African Americans possess the potential to survive because of their proximity to white culture. By interacting with white culture, according to Giddings, African Americans gain a vicarious access to civilized manners. Such proximity becomes the formula for adaptation that Giddings posits is essential to survival. While Giddings provides some space for other races to exist, his theory still relies upon a stratification of higher and lower races, which informs Sumner's approach.

Departing from Giddings with respect to African Americans, Edward Ross extends Sumner's conclusions about cultural atavism and suggests that immigrants and African Americans threaten Anglo-Americans because their inferior compositions will impede American cultural progress. The very presence of such low-born persons, Ross reasons, is the trigger for "race suicide." This term suggests that evolutionary progress will be destroyed because the well-born, who are surrounded by "degenerate" persons, will become frightened by the sheer number of inferior persons, thus preventing them from reproducing. The low-born persons, who are ruled by their passions, will continue to reproduce, thus putting into the American cultural "gene pool" persons of inferior stock, which will destroy American identity.

What gives Ross's theory added virulence is the extent to which some of the literary texts from the era use his theory as a foundation for their narratives. Thomas Dixon's Trilogy of Reconstruction, for example, uses and invokes such propositions in his novels *The Leopard's Spots* (1902), *The Clansman* (1904), and *The Traitor* (1907). The first novel of the trilogy, *The Leopard's Spots*, foregrounds the threat of miscegenation as the formula for the destruction of American culture. In doing so, the text raises the question, "shall the future American be an Anglo-American or a Mulatto?" (159). Time and again in the novel, African Americans are represented as possessing biological traits that are inferior and menacing. The only protection from such racial amalgamation is the emergence of the Ku Klux Klan as the racial standard-bearers of American cultural identity. In Dixon's second novel, *The Clansman*, the feared racially mixed American culture has not only come into existence, but it has been sanctioned into law with the adoption of miscegenation practices. The text chronicles, then, an interesting invocation of atavism: here, because the "inferior" race has assumed control of government and culture, the "throwback" is the Anglo-American heritage that has been sullied and replaced. The novel posits, then, that a positive return to the past is necessary because the present is morally and racially destructive. The Klan re-emerges by the novel's end as the guardian that restores Anglo-American supremacy. At the novel's conclusion, the Klan's leader asserts, "we are great because of the genius of the race of pioneer white freemen who settled this continent, dared the might of kings, and made a wilderness the home of Freedom. Our future depends on the future of this racial stock" (291). By the last novel of the trilogy, *The Traitor*, one notes that the profile of the Klan goes "underground," and while the organization is still necessary for the protection of Anglo-American identity and security, what makes the group stronger is the extent to which its members are tied by blood. In other words, the reification of Anglo-American identity becomes entrenched in notions of familial bonds, thus suggesting that anyone outside of the organization is both external to the family and outside of the construct known as the "American."

What is most striking in an analysis of the era's literary and sociological texts is that no one notion of the atavistic return is rendered as quintessentially positive or negative. In other words, what the texts hold in common is a preoccupation with what is atavistic at the end of the nineteenth century. Where the texts depart is over the question of whether such a return is emblematic of a culture in decline or whether it becomes an attempt to purify an industrialized society of its deadening forces. In some cases, texts within an author's canon may register contradictory reactions to this preoccupation, leaving as the only constant a focus on this return to the past. The remainder of this essay will chronicle, then, the shifting and contradictory literary responses and the extent to which they register with, as well as depart from, their sociological contexts.

Nowhere is the link between atavistic degeneration and the decline of Anglo-American identity stronger than in the connection between Cesare Lombroso's theories of criminality and the fiction by Frank Norris. Lombroso concluded in his 1912 text *Crime: Its Causes and Remedies* that criminal behavior is the manifestation of atavistic impulses: "the criminal is an atavistic being . . . in whom hunger, syphilis, trauma, and still more frequently, morbid conditions inherited from insane, criminal, or diseased progenitors, is a return to the characteristics peculiar to primitive savages" (136). For Lombroso, much of his conclusions rest, then, on tracing the current manifestations of criminal acts to a biologically determined cause. Criminality, he reasons, becomes an entire culture's return to an atavistic past, and such a reversion can be predicted based upon the connections he envisions between a race's features and its predilection toward crime. In other words, when he compared the features of darker-skinned, southern Europeans to those of the lighter-featured Anglo-Americans, Lombroso concluded that the darker-featured persons' differences were attributable to their proclivity toward crime, as their features were indicative of this long-buried, ancestral connection to deviance.

Relying on Lombrosian theories, Frank Norris's story "A Case for Lombroso" (1897) documents—in fictional terms—the dangers that a latent potential toward degeneration and criminality poses to the dominant culture. In the text, we have two pure-blood characters from two entirely different cultural backgrounds. Stayne is the Anglo-American who falls for the mysterious and alluring Spanish woman Cresencia. The text notes that "had they never met, Miss Hromada and young Stayne would yet have been fine specimens of womanhood and manhood as you could wish to know. Once having met, they ruined each other" (132). According to the text's logic, by (inter)marrying, the couple degenerates because Cresencia's latent and base impulses destroy Stayne, thus illustrating the threat that such persons pose to Anglo-American identity.

Norris's novels *McTeague* (1899) and *Vandover and the Brute* (1914) underscore the perils that atavism and degeneration pose in the complete devolution of the title characters in ways that move beyond the crisis depicted in "A Case for Lombroso." For McTeague, his complete collapse is figured throughout the text as he is described as one in whom "the evil of an entire race flowed in his veins" (285). His struggles in the novel become, then, ones where he must wrestle against the impulses of his "inner brute" that chafe against his exterior persona. This persona is complicated, however, by the fact that his "profession" is that of a charlatan dentist, and his ethics of care come to be compromised by his lack of actual educational training, his ignorance, and his inability to stave off his baser impulses.

McTeague's debasement is emblematic of the city's mixture of ethnic and working-class persons, whose attempts at middle-class respectability fail because of their biological predisposition to destructive acts. Such defilement is rendered most startling in the depiction of Trina. While at the beginning of the text she is represented as the embodiment of Victorian womanhood, her marriage to McTeague brings to the fore the fact that "a good deal of peasant blood ran undiluted in her veins, she had all the instinct of a hardy and penurious mountain race" (358). While such a description would seemingly coincide with a Protestant thriftiness, such is not the case with Trina, as her hoarding of gold coins transforms her into a female Zerkow. As a result, Trina, "who had once been of cat-like neatness, now slovened all day about the room in a dirty flannel wrapper" (497). This decline is exacerbated by her relocation to Zerkow's abandoned home, and it is at this point that her miserliness and manipulation of McTeague intensifies. Her destruction at the novel's conclusion, along with McTeague's all-too-certain death in the desert, suggest the extent to which neither character is fit to reproduce themselves in the culture. Their demise merely reinforces the notion that their circulation in the community contained the potential to destroy it.

If *McTeague* rationalizes the destruction of the lower classes based on their inherent contagion, *Vandover and the Brute* moves this argument one step further by noting the extent to which an upper-class character's unmediated contact with the low-born is enough to spell his degeneration. Vandover's visits to the Imperial, which is a club frequented by prostitutes, leads him to unsafe sexual dalliances that become the source of his untreated syphilis. In turn, this untreated sexually transmitted disease destroys Vandover's lucidity by manifesting itself as a case of lyconthropy-pathesis, or the act of becoming a werewolf. For the remainder of the text, not only is Vandover a resident of the flop-house known as Lick House, but Norris continually depicts him as "down on all fours" as "he fancied that he was in some manner changing . . . that he was no longer human, that he was sinking, all in a moment, to the level of some dreadful beast" (203–4). His submission to both poverty and madness at the text's conclusion becomes a startling point for middle-class readers as they discover the dangers of a porous social boundary line among the classes.

This indebtedness to Lombrosian theories of depravity and criminality manifest themselves, not only in these selected texts by Frank Norris, but also in Theodore Dreiser's atypical play *The Hand of the Potter* (1918). Described as "one who is so strangely composed mentally and physically he is bizarre" (27), Isadore Berchansky is a Jewish immigrant, an epileptic, and a pedophile, whose depravity becomes a dramatization of Lombroso's theories. For Lombroso, "the criminal is only a diseased person, an epileptic. . . . A return to the early brutal egotism natural to the primitive races, which manifests itself in homicide, theft, and other crimes" (73). If the criminal is a throwback to an earlier time, along with the fact that epilepsy becomes the link that establishes that such behavior is inborn, then Isadore accentuates Lombroso's conclusions because each time he encounters a young girl, "a strange, fierce, animal light comes into his eyes. He breathes heavily and clenches his hands" (34). Isadore's wild and animalistic movements become harbingers of his natural proclivity toward crime, which is then pathologized in a Lombrosian vocabulary. While the concluding act attempts to understand Isadore within a Freudian context, such an analysis never materializes—nor does it counter the text's dominant focus on a biological explanation for Isadore's actions.

If *The Hand of the Potter* spotlights the link between immigrants, disease, and crime, Eugene O'Neill's *The Hairy Ape* (1922) offers the ultimate reverse evolutionary tale in Yank's reversion to his seemingly simian roots. Time and again in the text, Yank is coded as one who is evolutionarily and socially inferior, as embodied in the constant reference to him as resembling "*a brainless ape*" (302). It is not Yank alone who receives this pre-human label. Rather, the play's opening description casts all of the sailors in terms of this simian language: "*they cannot stand upright.* . . . *The men themselves should resemble those pictures in which the appearance of Neanderthal Man is guessed at. All are hairy-chested, with long arms of tremendous power, and low, receding brows above their fierce, resentful eyes*" (251). Here, their economic deprivation plays itself out in the physical description of the men, thus legitimizing them as pre-human. Among these men, Yank is said to be "*broader, fiercer, more truculent, more powerful, more sure of himself than the rest*" (252). At the same time, Yank is out of place in the modern city and finds himself displaced on the ship and on shore. His estrangement is rendered all the more powerful in the repeated instances where he attempts to mimic the pose of Rodin's sculpture *The Thinker*, and frequently he admonishes those who interrupt him when he is "tryin' to t'ink" (254). Adrift from both career and others, he finds his way to the gorilla house at the zoo, where he attempts to find kinship with his fellow simians. And much like Yank, one of the gorillas also assumes *The Thinker*'s posture. Of course, it is here that Yank is crushed by the gorilla with whom he imagined kinship, and as his lifeless body lies in the cage, the stage directions note, "*and, perhaps, the Hairy Ape at last belongs*" (308). For Yank, to belong as a deceased member of the gorilla house renders, once again, the extent to which he is unfit to dwell in any community.

Complicating a neat trajectory of the era's depiction of atavism are those moments where the text brings readers back to primitive roots in a manner that is not critical of the past. Rather, the point of emphasis becomes a re-articulation of the noble savage theory, where the pre-human is represented as possessing a truer sense of the human that has been lost in what was becoming an industrialized society. No two texts better capture these impulses than Jack London's *Before Adam* (1907) and *The Call of the Wild* (1903). In *Before Adam*, the unnamed protagonist lives in the twentieth century but his dreams take him back to a prehistoric and pre-civilized Pleistocene Africa where he is his own ancestor, Big-Tooth. Recalling this past, the narrator recognizes "I, the modern, am incontestably a man; yet I, Big-Tooth, the primitive, am not a man." Further, he recognizes that "Big-Tooth did stamp into the cerebral constitution of one of his progeny all the impressions of his life, and stamped them in so indelibly that the hosts of intervening generations have failed to obliterate them" (241). The text's logic seemingly argues that atavism must be a controlled act for the sole purpose of reconnecting modern man to a virile past that will enable him to reject modern culture's deadening forces.

While *Before Adam* romanticizes modern people's ability to call up their ata-vistic past, *The Call of the Wild* fully embraces the lore of a natural world untouched by the vestiges of civilization. Much like the unnamed narrator in *Before Adam*, Buck in *The Call of the Wild* also experiences dreams where he enjoys the freedom of a younger world, populated by wild dogs, and uninhibited by his work-beast function in a capitalist, modern society. Each time Buck has one of these dreams, "the claims of mankind slipped farther from him" (62). As Buck acclimates to the Northland, he not only embraces his atavistic return to a wild-dog heritage, but he also rejects the forced labor that marked his existence in the "civilized" landscape. His return to a premodern existence reverses other literary depictions that atavistic impulses spelled the destruction of the character and the culture itself.

If London's two novels seemingly complicate a neat trajectory that charts lit-erary responses to atavism and degeneration, his own literary canon offers a contra-dictory depiction of these complex issues. On the surface, Jack London's *White Fang* (1906), for instance, seems almost atypical of his other Yukon-based fiction because the title character leaves behind all of the vestiges of the wild for the safe harbor that civilization or, more precisely, domestication provides. While this initial approach registers the seeming disparity between this novel and others, it does not fully address the extent to which the text uses the logic of naturalism to argue for an assimilationist conclusion. From his early aversion to "associating with his own kind" to his recognition of the superiority of the white "man-gods," White Fang undertakes a journey that not only removes him from his homeland, but he also embarks upon a change that legitimizes the era's theories about civilization, assimilation, and the boundaries of culture. By directly confronting and/or symbolically rejecting the lesser man-gods (e.g., Grey Beaver, Beauty Smith, Jim Hall) and by eschewing the company of his fellow wolves (e.g., his mother and the other pack animals), White Fang proves himself as an instrument for a white majority culture. By working in service for the white "man-gods," White Fang commits two acts simultaneously: he rejects his old-world wolf culture for new-world domestication, and at the same time, his eventual assimilation is not only inevitable but is absolutely natural. Indeed, "in this new orientation, it was the thumb of circumstance that pressed and prodded him, softening that which had become hard and remo[l]ding it into fairer form. Weedon Scott was in truth this thumb. He had gone to the roots of White Fang's nature, and with kindness touched life potencies that had languished and well-nigh perished. . . . Weedon Scott had set himself the task of redeeming White Fang" (242–43). Consequently, White Fang's redemption becomes his avenue to avoid degeneration, thus rejecting the possibility of becoming a relic of his past—to avoid, in other words, a story that warns about atavistic dangers. Indeed, the novel concludes with the litter of puppies he has fathered, and he takes the uncharacteristic steps of lovingly embracing them, despite the fact that "in neither his father nor mother was there any weakness, or in the generations before them. A constitution of iron and the vitality of the Wild were White Fang's inheritance" (282).

If *White Fang* underscores the possibilities of reversing the threat of inherited wildness, and in doing so, keeping at bay the threat posed by atavistic tendencies, London's short story "Bâtard" (1902) shows the dangers of what occurs when such a propensity toward destruction is not reversed. Introduced as "hell's spawn" (387), Bâtard inherited "much of evil and much of strength" from his "progenitors, and, bone and flesh of their bone and flesh, he had inherited it all" (388). This proclivity to depravity is not limited to canines. His owner, Black Leclère, "was also a devil" (387), and he becomes for Bâtard another uncivilized influence. As the narrator comments, "with a proper master Bâtard might have made an ordinary, fairly efficient sled-dog. He never got the chance: Leclère but confirmed him in his congenital iniquity" (388). If White Fang reverses the influence of inherited wildness through the introduction of a good master, Bâtard's lack of such positive influence leaves him defenseless against his own ancestry: "the thousands of Bâtard's ancestors had clung at the throats of unnumbered moose and caribou and dragged them down, and the wisdom of those ancestors was his" (301). To minimize the threat that Bâtard and Leclère pose to civilization, both are removed by the story's conclusion in a fight with each other that takes their lives. As a result, the story seemingly argues that neither is fit for the present, as their brutality is reminiscent of an older order, thus rationalizing the depiction of the dangers of atavistic manifestations.

If these initial London texts offer serious representations of atavism, his short story "South of the Slot" (1909) burlesques this preoccupation with its comic representation of the inner split between Freddie Drummond and Bill Totts. From the beginning of the story, the cleavage between upper and lower classes, and more precisely, the desire to maintain the separateness of these spheres, is represented in the description of the iron cable-car slot that divides respectable business enterprises from the slums. The narrator comments, "the slot was the metaphor that expressed the class cleavage of society" (817). In order to add realistic detail to his sociological studies, ones that actually demonize the factory worker, Freddie Drummond immerses himself south of the slot as the working-class character Bill Totts. But such success comes with consequences, and "he was too successful at living in both worlds. This strange dualism he had developed was after all very unstable, and, as he sat in his study and meditated, he saw that it could not endure. . . . He would inevitably have to drop one world or the other. He could not continue in both" (823). While these lines suggest a dispassionate choice, the story that unfolds is one where Freddie/Bill's attraction to the working-class life is an inner siren call because "all seemed well with him, but Freddie Drummond could not quite shake off the call of the underworld, the lure of the free and open, of the unhampered, irresponsible life south of the slot" (826–27). With his final emergence as Bill Totts, the story concludes that the work he now accomplishes is that of a labor organizer who brings together seemingly disparate groups, thus ironically commenting about the wisdom of his "call to the wild."

London's "South of the Slot" is not the only wry commentary about the impact of atavistic impulses. In his short story "Told in the Drooling Ward" (1914), London seemingly offers a rationalization of Lombrosian theories regarding epileptics, who are committed because their interaction with society, and more precisely, their ability to reproduce themselves, become a threat to the society at large. This story offers a first-person narrator, Tom, who is one of the patients in the "drooling ward," and who adamantly contends that he is actually the most developed of the patients: "I don't look like a drooler. . . . I'm a high-grade feeb" (945). Each time Tom asserts his relative superiority, the story's disjointed narrative undermines the lucidity he believes he possesses. When he vows to stage another escape, he backpedals and notes, "the drooling ward's a better snap than gold mines, and I hear there's a new nurse coming" (954). When he has the "opportunity" to enter organized society, his congenital "unfitness" stops him from entering an organization that is threatened by his very presence.

If these selected London texts comment about atavism, his short stories "The Law of Life" (1901) and "To Build a Fire" (1908) focus on issues pertaining to degeneration. In both stories, readers recognize the demise of Old Koskoosh and the unnamed protagonist of "To Build a Fire" as inevitable, thus rationalizing their deaths as simply the natural order because both have ceased to be productive persons to the larger unit. Such a deterministic quality is best represented in the depiction of nature and Old Koskoosh's recognition of his own irrelevance. Musing about his impending death, he recognizes that "nature's interest lay in the species." Further, the story indicates that this recognition is something the tribe has long understood, and that "they did not count; they were episodes. They had passed away like clouds from a summer sky. [Old Koskoosh] was also an episode, and would pass away. Nature did not care. To life she set one task, gave one law. To perpetuate was the task of life, its law was death" (367). His death at the end of the text by an encircling group of wolves posits two conclusions: Koskoosh contributes nothing to the tribe and so his degeneration and death become necessary steps, and second, his death foreshadows what will eventually befall all members of the tribe, suggesting the unfitness of the entire tribe to survive into the future.

With London's short story "To Build a Fire," the protagonist's death is not only rendered as inevitable because of his inexperience in the Yukon, but what becomes most striking is that the one who recognizes that the man has lost touch with his inner instinct is his work dog. By valorizing the dog's reliance on instinct, the story seemingly endorses a conclusion whereby this modern man degenerates because he is unable to access an older and less civilized version of himself. Curiously, the man's degeneration and the dog's escape from his ignorance comes to be rendered in the language of heredity: "this man did not know cold. Possibly all the generations of his ancestry had been ignorant of cold, of real cold. . . . But the dog knew; all his ancestry knew, and it had inherited the knowledge" (468). Here, degeneration occurs because the man lacks immediate access to an atavistic past, which the dog possesses. His removal at the end of the story legitimizes the ultimate form of degeneration, which is death, as the penalty for his neophyte manner.

While London's selected texts offer inconsistent treatments of atavism and degeneration, their focus on these issues do resonate with the era, one which served as a call to arms against those who seemingly represented a threat to the majority culture. The era's sociological discussions foreground such persons as the embodiment of a reverse evolutionary impulse that will plunder the American legacy. By recognizing the influence of this ideology on American literary naturalism, one gains an understanding of the impact of such values on these writers.

WORKS CITED

Dixon, Thomas. *The Clansman*. 1904. Gretna: Firebird, 2001.
———. *The Leopard's Spots*. 1902. Gretna: Firebird, 2001.
———. *The Traitor*. 1907. Gretna: Firebird, 2001.
Dreiser, Theodore. *The Hand of the Potter*. New York: Boni & Liveright, 1918.
Giddings, Franklin. *The Principles of Sociology*. New York: Macmillan, 1896.
Lombroso, Cesare. *Crime: Its Causes and Remedies*. Boston: Little, Brown, 1912.
London, Jack. "Bâtard." 1902. London, *Novels and Stories* 387–401.
———. *Before Adam*. 1907. Lincoln: University of Nebraska Press, 2000.
———. *Call of the Wild*. 1903. London, *Novels and Stories* 1–86.
———. "The Law of Life." 1901. London, *Novels and Stories* 365–71.
———. *Novels and Stories*. Ed. Donald Pizer. New York: Library of America, 1982.
———. "South of the Slot." 1909. London, *Novels and Stories* 817–33.

———. "To Build a Fire." 1908. London, *Novels and Stories* 462–78.

———. "Told in the Drooling Ward." 1914. London, *Novels and Stories* 945–54.

———. *White Fang.* 1906. London, *Novels and Stories* 87–284.

Norris, Frank. "A Case for Lombroso." *Wave* 11 Sept. 1897: 6; rpt. in *The Apprenticeship Writings of Frank Norris, 1896–1898.* Ed. Joseph R. McElrath, Jr. and Douglas K. Burgess. Vol. 2: *1897–1898.* Philadelphia: American Philosophical Society, 1996. 127–32.

———. *McTeague.* 1899. Norris, *Novels and Essays* 261–572.

———. *Novels and Essays.* Ed. Donald Pizer. New York: Library of America, 1986.

———. *Vandover and the Brute.* 1914. Norris, *Novels and Essays* 1–260.

O'Neill, Eugene. *The Hairy Ape.* 1922. New York: Penguin, 1998.

Ross, Edward. *The Foundations of Sociology.* New York: Macmillan, 1905.

Sumner, William Graham. *What the Social Classes Owe to Each Other.* 1883. Caldwell: Caxton, 1966.

CHAPTER 11

AMERICAN LITERARY NATURALISM AND PSYCHOLOGY

STEPHEN C. BRENNAN

By the time naturalism emerged as an important literary mode in 1890s America, Jay Martin writes, "Americans had committed themselves to science and were ready to follow where it led" (8). All novels embody assumptions about how the mind works, and American literary naturalists, who embraced the Darwinian belief that human beings are products of heredity and environment, were naturally led to descriptions of mind congenial with that deterministic world view. Although scholars today downplay Émile Zola's influence in America, those naturalists who did read "The Experimental Novel" (1880) would have been struck by Zola's contention that "[o]ne and the same determinism must govern the stone in the road and the brain of man" (171). "To a certain extent," Zola writes of naturalist authors, "we are doing scientific psychology, as a complement to scientific physiology" (172).

All the psychologists considered below questioned the existence of free will. In the late nineteenth century, Herbert Spencer and William James promoted a species of "scientific physiology" that defined human action in terms of impulses flowing though neural pathways fixed by evolution or by the experience of the individual. As James put it, habit, another name for reflex action, is "the enormous fly-wheel of society" that "dooms us all to fight out the battle of life upon the lines of our nurture or our early choice" (*Psychology* 145). Both Sigmund Freud and his early disciple Alfred Adler began their careers in traditional medicine at the end of the nineteenth century, and Freud turned from neurology to the formulation of his "dynamic" and largely metaphorical theory of conflicting psychic forces only after recognizing that the current state of scientific knowledge was inadequate for a purely physiological explanation of human behavior. When psychoanalysis entered the American consciousness in the 1910s, it did so as a challenge to American optimism about human nature. Those who think "purposive ideas" control our actions, Freud insisted, "ignore the vast realms of determinism in our mental life. Here, as in still other spheres, determinism reaches farther than we suppose" (*Psychopathology* 150).

Though important studies by Tom Lutz and Jennifer L. Fleissner have dealt with mental disorders such as neurasthenia (Lutz) and compulsion (Fleissner) as concerns of American literary naturalists of the late nineteenth and early twentieth centuries, close psychological readings of individual works are rare. As Donald Pizer observes in a discussion of Theodore Dreiser's increasingly sophisticated depictions of internal conflict, American literary naturalism "has generally been judged to be either inadequate or inept in its portrayal of the inner life" ("Dreiser" 69) owing to the common perception that naturalists were concerned primarily with dim-witted characters struggling against hostile environments.

A consideration of five important naturalistic works published between 1895 and 1925 may help modify this perception. The works have been selected to reveal the diversity of psychological themes during naturalism's classical age—Stephen Crane's *The Red Badge of Courage* (1895) and Theodore Dreiser's *Sister Carrie* (1900) for the pre-Freudian period and Sherwood Anderson's *Winesburg, Ohio* (1919), Ellen Glasgow's *Barren Ground* (1925), and Dreiser's *An American Tragedy* (1925) for the early Freudian period. If there is an implicit thesis in the discussions that follow, it is that America's naturalists read psychology not to depict mindless puppets in the hands of implacable forces or animals snared in the trap of circumstances but to portray convincingly the often undecided struggle for dignity at that intersection of inner and outer reality, the human consciousness.

Literary Naturalism and Pre-Freudian Psychology

Psychology in the late nineteenth century was characterized by the "somatic style," the effort to discover the relationship between the nervous system and mental processes.[1] Early American psychologists were medical doctors, often neurologists, who generally believed that mental disorders were attributable either to heredity or to "lesions," "weakness," or "degeneration" in the nervous system. Then as now, descriptions of insanity, split personalities, and perversions titillated the popular imagination. Frank Norris, one naturalist attracted to the bizarre in human nature, may well have encountered current ideas about mental pathology in 1894–95 while studying creative writing at Harvard, where William James was teaching a popular undergraduate course on the subject. Donna M. Campbell has speculated that Norris may have heard James lecture or heard his ideas discussed (198 n39), and it is not a stretch to think that Norris picked up ideas from Henry Maudesly's widely read *The Pathology of Mind*, which came out in a revised third edition in 1895 and which James would use the next year in a graduate course in abnormal psychology (Taylor 3).

Whatever his actual source, Norris found in psychology material for melodramatic narratives about characters he described as "twisted from the ordinary, wrenched out from the quiet, uneventful round of every-day life, and flung into the throes of a vast and terrible drama that works itself out in unleashed passions, in blood, and in sudden death" (72). In *McTeague* (1899), which evolved from his Harvard themes, Norris portrayed men and women whose hereditary greed, alcoholism, and sexuality erupt from the unplumbed depths in obsession, mania, hysteria, sexual perversion, and murder.

Not all naturalists, however, were as concerned as Norris about insanity and perversion. James's most important psychological works, like those of his predecessor Herbert Spencer, dealt primarily with the structure and function of the normal human mind. Stephen Crane found in James, as did Theodore Dreiser in Spencer, the basis for depicting the way the mind finds or creates a sense of worth and purpose in a world in which the concept of an autonomous will operating in a moral universe was losing its meaning.

"A WORLD FOR HIM": WILLIAM JAMES AND *THE RED BADGE OF COURAGE*

William James was not only America's foremost academic psychologist but also the one most widely read by the public. He frequently lectured to audiences in and out of academia and published many of his lectures aimed at the educated reader in such popular magazines as *Scribner's* and *Popular Science Monthly*. His two-volume *Principles of Psychology* (1890) and its abbreviated version, *Psychology: Briefer Course* (1892), were the most widely used textbooks in university psychology courses, and by 1902 the first had sold 8,144 copies and the second 51,658 (Richardson 425). There is no direct evidence that Crane read James, though he left very little information about any of his reading. In *The Pluralistic Philosophy of Stephen Crane* (1993), however, Patrick K. Dooley argues that Crane was "philosophically astute and aware of the intellectual developments of the late-nineteenth century" (25) and demonstrates strong similarities between James's and Crane's epistemology, metaphysics, ethics, and religious beliefs. Following Dooley's lead opens the possibility for a better understanding of why Henry Fleming, at the end of *The Red Badge of Courage*, is not quite the deluded, unheroic egotist he is often taken to be.

Crane's own commentary on the novel has a Jamesian cast. English reviews praised the book, he wrote in a letter from about 1897,

> for just what I intended it to be, a psychological portrayal of fear. . . . I know what the psychologists say, that a fellow can't comprehend a condition that he has never experienced, and I argued that many times with the Professor. Of course, I have never been in a battle, but I believe that I got my sense of the rage of conflict on the football field, or else fighting is a hereditary instinct, and I wrote intuitively. (*Correspondence* 1: 322)

Crane does not name his opponent in what are probably imaginary arguments, but he may well have had Professor William James in mind. James did devote considerable space to fear in his psychological works, and a reading of *Red Badge* in light of these passages reveals suggestive parallels. For example, James writes that "We both fear, and wish to kill, anything that may kill us," the response depending on "collateral circumstances of the particular case" (*Psychology* 380). Here, perhaps, is the germ for the novel's structure: on the first day Fleming reacts with fear to the rebels who want to kill him; on the second, with murderous rage under altered circumstances. No transformation of his nature occurs or is necessary.

Despite his denial, Crane actually comes very close to agreeing with James about the necessary link between experience and action. Like other psychologists of the day, James considered that virtually all action is reducible to "involuntary responses we know as 'reflex' acts" (*Psychology* 98), another name for habits. Habits can become so strong as to modify instincts, which also "conform to the general reflex type" (366). When a complex sequence of acts becomes habitual, "a single instantaneous 'cue'" will trigger the first act and the rest of the "chain" will follow automatically: "The marksman sees the bird, and, before he knows it, he has aimed the gun and shot" (141). In the moments before his first engagement, Fleming is wondering whether he has loaded his rifle when, like James's marksman at the sight of a bird, he receives the visual cue that sets off the chain of habitual reflex acts: "He got the one glance at the foe-swarming field in front of him. . . . Before he was ready to begin . . . he threw the obedient, well-balanced rifle into position and fired a first wild shot. Directly he was working at his weapon like an automatic affair" (112).

Fleming, in fact, has been in a "battle sleep" (114) during the engagement, and from the opening chapter, when he falls into "a little trance of astonishment" (83) at hearing a rumor of impending battle, he frequently lapses into various unconscious and semi-conscious states, the kind of dissociation of a portion of consciousness James and other psychologists found in hysteria and hypnotic trances. Telling in this regard is Fleming's response to the mortally wounded Jim Conklin's fear of falling under the wheels of "them damned artillery wagons": "The youth cried out to him *hysterically*: 'I'll take care of yeh, Jim! I'll take care of yeh! I swear t'Gawd I will!'" (134; emphasis added). In his discussion of hysteria in the *Principles of Psychology*, James notes that "hysterics are apt to possess a very narrow field of attention, and to be unable to think of more than one thing at a time" (1: 203). The hysteric thus possesses by nature the focused attention that the hero achieves by an act of will, as James defines it:

> *The essential achievement of the will, in short, when it is most "voluntary," is to attend to a difficult object and hold it fast before the mind . . .* and it is a mere physiological incident that when the object is thus attended to, immediate motor consequences should ensue.
>   *Effort of attention is thus the essential phenomenon of will. (Psychology* 417–18)

One may, of course, make value judgments about the object of attention, but according to this theory a base object and a noble object can require the same amount of willed attention to produce their motor effects.

In one common reading of *Red Badge*, Fleming's ferocity on the second day of the battle is "never consciously willed" and is "as mindless as his first day's flight" (Horsford 110), when he runs like "a proverbial chicken" (Crane, *Red Badge* 119). In a real sense, though, his battle-fury is the opposite of mindless and unconscious, for only consciously willed attention to a single idea filling his mind enables him to perform in the chaos of battle. No conventional hero could do more.

The second day's second engagement, a charge in which Fleming first wins a reputation for heroism, will illustrate the point. In this moment of extreme danger, he does not, as his mother has urged him to, think of "what's right" (85), but he nevertheless thinks of what works under the circumstances:

> He fixed his eye upon a distant and prominent clump of trees where he had concluded the enemy were to be met, and he ran toward it as toward a goal. . . . His face was drawn hard and tight with the stress of his endeavor. His eyes were fixed in a lurid glare. . . .
>   The youth, light footed, was unconsciously in advance. His eyes still kept note of the clump of trees. (182)

Fleming is *un*conscious only of his place at the head of the regiment; he is fully conscious of his "goal," a word reminiscent of Crane's contention that football was the closest thing to war in his experience. The point is that Fleming does not need the experience of an infantry charge to lead one; he needs only to have created the neural pathways required for running toward a goal, something a country boy like him would have done countless times. As James explains the utility of habits, "The idea of the end, then, tends more and more to make itself all-sufficient. . . . Keep your *eye* on the place aimed at, and your hand will fetch it" (*Psychology* 392). If James had used "legs" instead of "hand," he could have been advising soldiers like Fleming in their first combat.

The most controversial willed act in the novel occurs during the defeated army's retreat on the second day, when Fleming suppresses images of his previous day's shameful behavior and glories in his "quiet manhood" (212). A general review of James's notion of the self can help us understand the mental process at work here. For James, the self is "duplex, partly known and partly knower" (*Psychology* 174), the knower being the "I," the known the "me," or "empirical" self. The empirical self known to another is a "social" self (176): "Properly speaking, *a man has as many social selves as there are individuals who recognize him* and carry an image of him in their mind" (177). Our sense of self-worth depends largely on how others judge our social selves, and the "most fiendish punishment" imaginable is to be treated by others as "non-existing things" (176). After running from battle on the first day, Fleming is terrified of what others will think of him, but after he displays courage on the second day, he knows that his comrades and officers carry an image of him in their minds as a "good un'" and a "jimhickey" (198). Fleming's problem is to decide which of his empirical selves to embrace as his own.

From the beginning, Crane has treated the self as a matter of empirical evidence. Before the battle Fleming has been an "unknown quantity" (88) and decides that he must follow the method of the "chemist" by becoming, as James would put it, an "I" observing the "me": "the only way to prove himself was to go into the blaze, and then figuratively to watch his legs to discover their merits and faults" (91). After two days of battle, however, the evidence is mixed, and Fleming faces precisely the situation James says we all do:

> I am often confronted by the necessity of standing by one of my empirical selves and relinquishing the rest. . . . The seeker of his truest, strongest, deepest self must review the list carefully, and pick out the one on which to stake his salvation. All other selves thereupon become unreal, but the fortunes of this one are real. Its failures are real failures, its triumphs real triumphs, carrying shame and gladness with them. (*Psychology* 182–83)

This passage accurately renders Fleming's thought processes as his "brain emerged from the clogged clouds" of battle and "he struggled to marshal all his acts." Fleming does not "review the list," exactly, but he does assume the role of a commander reviewing his troops: "Regarding his procession of memory he felt gleeful and un-regretting, for in it his public deeds were paraded in great and shining prominence" (210). At this point there is obviously no "necessity" of choosing between empirical selves of different orders of value. But when he recalls his two betrayals of the previous day—deserting his regiment under fire and leaving the "tattered soldier" to die alone in the woods—he is filled with shame and faces that difficult kind of decision that James says requires a "creative contribution" from the "slow dead heave of the will" (*Psychology* 402). At this point, Fleming slowly wills the effort to suppress the shameful empirical self and keep in mind the one approved by his comrades and officers: "Yet gradually he mustered force to put the sin at a distance. And at last his eyes seemed to open to some new ways." From James's perspective, Fleming's sinless chosen self—a "quiet manhood, nonassertive but of sturdy and strong blood"—is "real" enough to stake his salvation on: "the youth smiled, for he saw that the world was a world for him" and his future one of "soft and eternal peace" (212).

There is certainly much irony in a self-satisfaction that blinds Fleming to the horrific fighting that must lie ahead, and that readers know does lie ahead, in places like Gettysburg, Spotsylvania, and Cold Harbor. Still, Crane makes of his protagonist a recognizable version of our capacity to make a world that holds as long as we have the will to believe in it. James, we should remember, says only that we *seek* our "truest, strongest, deepest self," not that we actually find it.

THE POWER OF SYMPATHY: HERBERT SPENCER AND *SISTER CARRIE*

Herbert Spencer was much more influential in America than Charles Darwin, who emphasized random variation as the driving force in an evolutionary process going nowhere. Spencer's massive *Synthetic Philosophy* traced the development from simplicity to complexity in the formation of the cosmos, the evolution of life, and the development of all facets of society and culture; it appealed to American optimism by offering a seemingly plausible reconciliation of science and religion and by treating evolution as a progressive movement towards perfection. "In the three decades after the Civil War," Richard Hofstadter asserts, "it was impossible to be active in any field of intellectual work without mastering Spencer" (33). In an extended paean to the philosopher in an 1897 "Reflections" column in *Ev'ry Month*, Dreiser calls Spencer "a great father of knowledge" (240) who has connected the human mind with the underlying order of the cosmos: "Our minds belong to the universe which Spencer has united; our thoughts upon its meaning are subject to the laws which he has laid down" (241). Spencer's theory of mind informs such diverse works as *Social Statics* (1850) and *The Data of Ethics* (1879), a heavily marked copy of which is in Dreiser's library at the University of Pennsylvania. It finds its fullest expression in the *Principles of Psychology* (1855), the text James assigned in 1876, no doubt in the expanded edition of 1870, when he began teaching Physiological Psychology at Harvard (Richardson 178). It also structures Carrie Meeber's evolution from a girl possessing "a mind rudimentary in its power of observation and analysis" (2) to a celebrated actress potentially at the forefront of social evolution.

Dreiser structures Carrie's development in terms of the single principle governing all mental development defined in *The Principles of Psychology*: "From the most complex and most abstract inferences down to the most rudimentary intuitions, all intelligence proceeds by the establishment of relations of *likeness* and *unlikeness*" (2: 281). But since even consciousness of likeness requires some change in mental state, "the relation of unlikeness is the primordial one" (2: 285). Like all hearts, Carrie's "understands when it is confronted with contrasts" (230). When she meets Drouet on the train to Chicago in chapter 1, she quickly notices "an inequality" between her shabby clothes and his spiffy garb (4). When she meets Hurstwood, she "almost unconsciously" recognizes "a distinction" in favor of his "elegance" of dress compared to Drouet's flashiness (69); she eventually leaves Drouet because "[i]n contrast, Hurstwood appeared strong and sincere" (96). Contrast creates desire, and desire drives her on to higher and higher levels of intellectual and moral development until "[n]o longer the lightest word of a man made her head dizzy. . . . It required . . . the superiority of a genius like Ames" (303), the handsome inventor from the Midwest who becomes Carrie's ideal in the novel's last third largely because she compares him to Drouet and Hurstwood and finds that "the difference was painful" (237).

Carrie's famously insatiable desire for beauty, ease, and pleasure also conforms well with Spencer's hedonistic psychology, which holds that "the good is universally the pleasurable" (*Data* 30). While it has been argued that *Sister Carrie* represents Spencer's belief that social evolution means the triumph of reason over emotion and altruism over egoism (Zanine 43), Spencer actually argues that altruism develops only to the degree that it supplies egoistic pleasure and that there is "scarcely any connection . . . between morality and . . . culture of the intellect" (*Social* 382). The vital function exercised in altruism is sympathy, the capacity to experience an emotion by witnessing its expression in others. Those who can not only experience their own pleasure but also "sympathetically participate in the pleasurable emotions of all others" will greatly increase "the sum-total of happiness" (84). Carrie certainly likes the pretty things men buy her, but what most makes her happy is sympathy. For example, when Drouet picks her up on the cold Chicago streets, he is able to overcome her scruples not because he buys her a hot meal but because "his admiration" is "powerfully backed by his liberality and good humor," altruistic feelings grounded in "genuine sympathy" (44). "In his presence," Dreiser informs us, "she was of his own hopeful, easy-way-out mood" (45).

Sympathy depends on the power of expression, what in his *Principles of Psychology* Spencer calls the "language of the emotions." Besides the signs and words human beings use to communicate conscious intentions, "there are the effects, much deeper in origin, much more powerful, and in a sense more important, which they unconsciously produce on one another's feelings by the physical manifestations that accompany feelings" (2: 539).[2] In his first chapter, Dreiser declares that "words are but vague shadows of the volumes we mean" (6), and he is throughout the novel unusually attentive to revealing how strong emotion is represented in bodily responses—gestures, facial expressions, tones of voice, and the like. When Drouet accuses Carrie of cheating on him with Hurstwood, he is stunned by the sight of her body "alive with feeling, her eyes snapping, her lips quivering, her whole body sensible of the injury she felt, and partaking of her wrath" (157). This expressive power is perhaps what Dreiser means in claiming that Carrie possesses an "emotional greatness" (261) that the moody Hurstwood does not recognize.

Dreiser also follows Spencer in connecting sympathy and art. For Spencer, the evolution of "sociality" depends on the expansion of sympathy, and "the degree and range of sympathy depend on the clearness and extent of representation" (*Principles* 2: 565). The artist plays an important role in such progress: "The joys and sorrows of human beings form a chief element in the subject matter of art; and evidently the pleasures which art gives increase as the fellow-feeling with these joys and sorrows strengthens" (*Data* 214–15). During Carrie's several meetings with Robert Ames after she has become a Broadway celebrity, Ames offers a Spencerian explanation for her potential for success as a more serious artist. "I should judge you were rather sympathetic in your nature," he tells her during their brief initial encounter (340). But it is in their third and final meeting that he makes his point most clearly by telling her, "there is something about your eyes and mouth which fits you" for serious drama. He sees in her "pain-touched" curve of lip and "depth" of eyes a "natural expression" of the world's "longing" (341).

This emphasis on the depth of Carrie's eyes may explain what Ames means a moment later when he tells her that her face is "representative of all desire" (342). Spencer asserts that "a great part of what we commonly call emotions" are feelings "*deeper* than individual experience" because they "result from inherited experience—vague feelings which we may call organic representations" (*Principles* 2: 514; emphasis added). Spencer means that the feelings are organic representations in the brain, but Dreiser places the locus of representation in Carrie's face, where, by virtue of an accidental variation that fits her for a niche in the arts, she continuously expresses "all desire" from time immemorial and increases the power of sympathy in all who see her perform. Since in Spencer's view social evolution is intimately bound with the increase of representativeness and sympathy, Carry does indeed, as Ames says, have "a burden of duty" (342). Carrie, however, never trusts her own power of representation. Having mistaken Drouet and Hurstwood for "personal representatives of a state most blessed to attain," she continues to seek an Other to arouse her emotions, the "show of soul in some passing eye" that "the heart knows" and to which it "makes answer" (354).

LITERARY NATURALISM IN THE EARLY FREUDIAN AGE

William James brought the emerging "depth" psychology to the attention of the American scientific community in an 1894 review of a paper on hysteria by Sigmund Freud and Josef Breuer (Richardson 336), but it was only in the aftermath of Freud's lectures at Clark University in 1909 that enthusiasm for psychoanalysis began to spread among the American public and literary community. In a misreading of Freud as a proponent of sexual liberation, American naturalists joined with their contemporary modernists in embracing psychoanalysis as a weapon against a repressive "Puritan" society. To many, the so-called "cathartic" method, or "talking cure," of psychoanalysis seemed almost magical. Theodore Dreiser proclaimed that Freud's "brilliantly revealing researches" had unlocked the "grisly prison doors," dragging the "old sorrows . . . from the depths of the repressed subconscious" and allowing them to "come forth into the light" ("Neurotic" 133), yet "neurotic" America with its continued "sex oppression" remained in the dark.

Naturalists also found in Freud a determinism supporting their worldview and an inherently conflict-ridden, "dynamic" psychic process suitable for fictional treatment and dramatic representation. In the 1910s and 1920s, they began to portray victims of repressive childhoods and sexual traumas and to assign their violent and often self-destructive actions to unconscious, irresistible impulses that made their moral responsibility problematic. After celebrating Spencer as a psychologist in the autobiographical novel *Martin Eden* (1909), Jack London explored the fictional potential of psychoanalysis in *The Little Lady of the Big House* (1915), perhaps the first Freudian novel written by an American, and in his last short stories of 1916, which were influenced by the myth-oriented theories in Carl G. Jung's *Psychology of the Unconscious* (1916).[3] In the 1920s, especially in New York, writers committed to "terrible honesty" discovered that "people *are* . . . their instincts. . . . Indeed, all the writing of the urban 1920s is a gloss on . . . what Freud called 'the primitive mind'" (Douglas 44). In the naturalistic tragedy *Desire Under the Elms* (1924), Eugene O'Neill dramatized the destruction of a nineteenth-century New England farm family by the primitive lust and violence inherent in the Oedipus Complex. At the same time, Sherwood Anderson, Ellen Glasgow, and Theodore Dreiser were offering sympathetic depictions of men and women whose lives were deformed or destroyed by a world offering few outlets for overpowering instinctive drives.

THE "MASCULINE PROTEST" IN *WINESBURG, OHIO*

Sherwood Anderson learned about psychoanalysis in 1913 from Floyd Dell (Rideout 1: 193), and by the middle of the 1920s critics were calling him the "American Freudian" (Hoffman 229). But Anderson denied that he ever read Freud, and in recent decades critics have tended to downplay a significant Freudian influence on his work, including his best book, *Winesburg, Ohio*. Moreover, no one seems ever to have pointed out the close resemblance between Anderson's psychological studies in that book and the theories of Freud's one-time disciple Alfred Adler.[4] Although Adler's most important book, *The Neurotic Constitution*, was not published in an English translation in America until 1917, after Anderson had composed the stories published in 1919 as *Winesburg, Ohio*, Adler's ideas had been absorbed into the popular conception of psychoanalysis and were not often distinguished from Freud's and Jung's (Makari 324). Adler had broken with Freud in 1911 because he disagreed with Freud's emphasis on the sexual basis of neurosis, offering in its place a gendered theory reflecting the hyper-masculine culture that had emerged in the West under industrial capitalism. If Anderson never read Adler he would have encountered Adler's rather simple theory in conversation and in the larger culture's widespread discussions of the new depth psychology. *Winesburg, Ohio*, can be read, in fact, as a set of variations on that most-scoffed-at-of-all psychoanalytical constructs—Adler's "inferiority complex."

Drawing upon Hans Vaihinger's *Philosophy of "As If"* (1911), which argued for the centrality of fictional constructs in all aspects of human life, as well as on Friedrich Nietzsche's "Will to power" and "Will to seem," Adler asserted that all neurosis "is to be recognized in an exaggerated 'masculine protest'" (ix) that results when a child, with its innate "psychic hermaphroditism," discovers "the superiority of the manly principle in our society" (51). The neurotic finds an "expedient" in a fictional goal, which becomes "a fixed picture in the vicissitudes of life" and eventually leads to being "suspended in the meshes of a fiction" (7). The "final object" of the masculine protest is always "domination," which is often sought by "the depreciation and emasculation of all other persons" (22). While Adler devotes most of his attention to men and boys, he makes clear that the cultural denigration of the feminine produces a masculine protest in all women.

The destructive consequences of the masculine protest lie near the thematic center of *Winesburg, Ohio*. That "manhood" is not an ideal in the novel's world is indicated in the introductory "The Book of the Grotesque." Here the narrator describes approvingly an old writer in androgynous terms: "He was like a pregnant woman, only the thing inside him was not a baby but a youth. No, it wasn't a youth, it was a woman, young, and wearing a coat of mail like a knight" (5). The writer is at work on a book with "one central thought"—that when "people" came into the world, each "snatched up" an originally "beautiful" truth and "called it his truth, and tried to live his life by it"; as a consequence "he became a grotesque and the truth he embraced became a falsehood" (6). This myth of the fragmentation of an original youthful androgyny into grasping individuals deformed by a "falsehood" corresponds closely to Adler's account of the child's psychic hermaphroditism destroyed by the rigid fiction of the masculine protest.

The most bizarre masculine protest in *Winesburg, Ohio*, is found in "Respectability," the tale of Wash Williams, a man so hideously ugly, fat, and dirty that he reminds the narrator of "a huge, grotesque kind of monkey" (64). Wash had been a "comely youth" and had married after having retained his virginity with "a kind of religious fervor." But in transposing this religious fervor to his wife, he tells George Willard, he had demeaned himself: "There in the dusk in the spring evening I crawled along the black ground to her feet and groveled before her. I kissed her shoes and the ankles above her shoes." When he discovered that his wife had been regularly entertaining three lovers while he was at work, he sent her home with all his money and "cried like a silly boy" (67). Still he "ached to forgive and forget" and responded eagerly to a summons from her "respectable" mother. All seemed well until the woman pushed his naked wife into the room in hopes that his sexual desire would effect a reconciliation. In a fit of rage, he bludgeoned the mother nearly to death with a chair.

Having experienced his own sexual desire as a threat to his manhood, Wash has turned himself into a hideous creature as protection against the threat of sexual relations. He has also become "enmeshed" in a fiction that demeans all women below the contempt of men: "I would like to see men a little begin to understand women. They are sent to prevent men making the world worth while. . . . They are creeping, crawling, squirming things, they with their soft hands and their blue eyes. The sight of a woman sickens me. Why I don't kill every woman I see I don't know" (66). Wash hates with the "abandon of a poet" (65) and weaves a spell that leaves George feeling "ill and weak" and dangerously identified with Wash's grotesque misogyny: "In imagination, he also became old and shapeless" (68).

George Willard appears in the center or periphery of many of the book's stories, and he thus provides much of the book's thematic and structural coherence. In "An Awakening," he suffers a deep humiliation in his effort to seduce Belle Carpenter, one of the many women in the novel who feel impelled to the masculine protest: "She was tall and strong. When black thoughts visited her she grew angry and wished she were a man and could fight someone with her fists" (98). In small-town Ohio, a woman cannot express her aggression openly, and so, as Adler would put it, she must overcompensate for a "feeling of inferiority" in "insidious ways" (102). She goes off with George, who is "half drunk with the sense of masculine power," only to make the man she really wants "suffer" (103). At the moment of George's expected conquest, the rival appears, repeatedly tosses him aside, and leaves him filled with the sense of impotence and rage typical of the Adlerian neurotic: "As he crept down the hillside his heart was sick within him. He hated himself and he hated the fate that had brought about his humiliation" (104), a humiliation that makes him want to escape Winesburg more than ever.

In the book's last two stories, Anderson offers some hope that George may one day free himself from his neurotic, grotesque need to triumph over the feminine. "Sophistication" depicts George, confident in his "new sense of maturity" (130), achieving a moment of intimacy with Helen White, the girl he once tried to impress by boasting, "I'm going to be a big man" (132). After a few desultory kisses, they pull apart and experience a "mutual respect" that grows "big in them" and restores the androgyny of childhood: "In some way chastened and purified by the mood they had been in they became, not man and woman, not boy and girl, but excited little animals. . . . In the darkness they played like two splendid young things in a young world" (136). This capacity to return to a pre-lapsarian, pre-grotesque state, the narrator proclaims in the story's last sentence, is "the thing that makes the mature life of men and women in the modern world possible" (136).

However, the concluding story, "Departure," leaves us uncertain whether George will retain this capacity for play. In the book's last paragraph, George dozes off while the train is still at the station and awakens to discover that "the town of Winesburg had disappeared and his life there had become but a background on which to paint the dreams of his manhood" (138). Whether fulfilling dreams of "manhood" will permit a return to that innocent animalism necessary for mature life in the modern world is left in doubt.

RETURN OF THE REPRESSED IN *BARREN GROUND*

In her memoir *The Woman Within* (1954), Ellen Glasgow is ambivalent about psychoanalysis, at one point saying that she "deliberately avoided the current patter of Freudian theory" (227) but later asserting that "the novel, as a living force, if not as a work of art, owes an incalculable debt to what we call, mistakenly, the new psychology, to Freud, in his earlier interpretations, and more truly, I think, to Jung" (269). While *Barren Ground* (1925) contains mythic elements suggestive of Jung (Raper 157) and while the narrator places its opening events in rural Virginia of the 1890s, "that pre-Freudian age" when people "knew not psychoanalysis" (13), Glasgow certainly knew psychoanalysis and drew heavily on it in writing what she, like many readers, considered her best novel. In the view of her biographer Susan Goodman, Glasgow found in writing fiction a means of coping with her own emotional conflicts: "she read extensively in psychology and came to think of her writing as a version of the 'talking cure'" (158–59). It is the misfortune of her protagonist in *Barren Ground* to have no such outlet.

The novel recounts Dorinda Oakley's difficulty in undergoing the normal development described most succinctly in Freud's "Formulations on the Two Principles of Mental Functioning" (1911): "transformation from a *pleasure-ego* into a *reality-ego*" (305). The pleasure-ego, characteristic of infancy, is governed by an instinctive "pleasure principle" and "can do nothing but *wish*, work for a yield of pleasure, and avoid unpleasure." The reality-ego, which gradually assumes dominance in the course of development, is governed by the "reality principle" and "need do nothing but strive for what is *useful* and guard against damage." As the child develops, instinctive desires, or wishes, undergo repression into the unconscious, though the sexual instincts are especially recalcitrant and find indirect paths to satisfaction in dreams, slips of the tongue, jokes, and neurotic symptoms. In fact, Freud writes, "[a]n essential part of the psychical disposition to neurosis . . . lies in the delay in educating the sexual instincts to pay regard to reality" (304). Whether Dorinda is finally able to educate those instincts is the central, and finally unanswered, question in *Barren Ground*.

Growing up on a meager Virginia farm under an emotionally distant and "ineffectual" father and a neurotic Presbyterian mother suffering from "suppressed religious mania" (9), Dorinda Oakley is the victim of sexual repression that causes her libido to seek "escape in the fabrication of dreams . . . enkindled by the ardour that makes a woman fall in love with a religion or an idea" (12). At twenty she falls in love with a romantic idea of Jason Greylock, a young doctor who has returned home from the North in order to care for his ailing father. Until he jilts her, Dorinda experiences Jason more as a figure in a dream than as a real person, indicating that she is largely ruled by the pleasure principle characteristic of infancy and early childhood.

On the day she discovers she is pregnant with his child, Dorinda learns that Jason has been cowed into marrying another woman, and this traumatic assault from reality drives her to hysteria and a psychotic compulsion to kill the man who has wounded her. Fortunately, the gun goes off prematurely in what is clearly the sort of unconsciously motivated "mistake" Freud described in *Psychopathology of Everyday Life*. As a consequence of this psychic trauma, Dorinda determines to live her life under the reality principle: "She had finished with romance, as she had finished with Jason, for ever" (187). "If experience had taught her nothing else," the narrator comments later, "it had at least made her a realist" (257).

Under the sway of the reality principle, Dorinda devotes the next thirty years of her life to a neurotic effort to, in Freud's words, "guard against damage" to her ego. The defense mechanisms she employs are "sublimation" and "reaction formation," concepts that Freud links closely in his widely read *Three Contributions to the Theory of Sex* (1916). Sublimation is the "deflection of sexual motive powers from sexual aims to new aims" (262); reaction-formations are "psychic counter-forces (feelings of reaction), which build up [against unacceptable sexual impulses] the . . . psychical dams of disgust, shame and morality" (262). In *The Ego and the Id* (1923), Freud asserts that while "love-impulses" can "transform themselves into impulses of aggression against the object," the ego often manages to isolate these impulses in the id, the unconscious reservoir of instinctive and repressed impulses, by means of "reaction-formations" (55).

Dorinda flees to New York, where her pregnancy is aborted following a traffic accident, but after two years in the North, she feels the impulse to return to the family farm and to sublimate her sexual desire for Jason into working the land. Sublimation, however, is usually associated with directing libido to "higher" aims; Dorinda's sublimation takes on an ominous cast when she decides the reason she is not respected in the community for her success with the farm is "that she had drilled her energy down into the soil instead of training it upward" (356). Her decades of hard work in truth represent a sublimation of the vengeance that motivated her attempted murder of Jason as well as the sexual desire that prevented her from completing the act, an inference supported by her eventually buying the Greystock farm to demonstrate her superiority to and independence from a Jason sinking into alcoholism and destitution.

Dorinda also has a strong Presbyterian conscience that contributes to the dams of morality and disgust she sets up as a reaction-formation against the pain of desire: "the thought of love, the faintest reminder of its potency, filled her with aversion, with an inexpressible weariness. She simply could not bear, she told herself bluntly, to be touched" (250). After a decade of devoting herself to work on the farm, she marries Nathan Pedlar only as "an available refuge from loneliness" (373), and never in their decade of married life does she get beyond liking him for his "moral integrity" and willingness to love her while "refrain[ing] from the demands of love" (424).

Dorinda's neurotic defenses, however, cannot keep the erotic and aggressive components of her id under complete repression, for over the three decades after the jilting they periodically break through, sometimes in painfully vivid waking memories, sometimes in erotic and aggressive dreams of barely disguised wish-fulfillment, so it is hard to accept her sense of "triumph" over Jason and her belief that she "had outlived every emotion toward him except disgust" (466). In fact, when he dies, memories of Jason in the "radiance" of their first love return in "delusive mockery" (523) and lead to the realization that "[l]ove was the only thing that made life desirable, and love was irrevocably lost to her" (524). Her ambivalent feelings for Jason, it turns out, have been the buried wellspring of her emotional life.

The ending, however, takes a puzzling optimistic turn that lacks the obvious irony of Fleming's optimism at the end of *Red Badge*. When Dorinda wakes from a night of "hag-ridden dreams" she is suddenly filled with an Emersonian sense of spiritual union with the land that constitutes her "permanent self" and experiences a "serenity of mind . . . above the conflict of frustrated desires" (524). The novel closes with her response to her stepson's assertion that she can marry again if she will: "Dorinda smiled, and her smile was pensive, ironic, and infinitely wise. 'Oh, I've finished with all that,' she rejoined. 'I am thankful to have finished with all that'" (526). While it is possible to see Dorinda's peace of mind as a "reward" for a "life of affirmation and deprivation" (Wagner 76), it may well be a reaction formation against the trauma of Jason's death. She has sworn off love before, and she has understood in the past that her "kinship with the land" is a "transfigured instinct . . . blended of pity, memory, and passion" (306). There is irony in her smile, so chances are she knows she may not be "finished with all that" any time soon.

LOVE AND DEATH IN *AN AMERICAN TRAGEDY*

Theodore Dreiser encountered psychoanalysis no later than 1914, when he moved to Greenwich Village to find the place abuzz with Freud and what seemed to be Freud's condemnation of Puritan repression and celebration of sexual freedom. In 1915, he asked Floyd Dell, a leading figure among the Village's leftist intelligentsia who was then undergoing psychoanalysis, to explain the new theory (Swanberg 197), and three years later he became friends with A. A. Brill, America's most prominent psychoanalyst and translator of Freud's works. He began reading works by Freud and others on the subject, including Brill's own *Psychanalysis* (1912), which affected him deeply. Soon Freudian ideas began appearing in his creative work, most notably his psychological murder tragedy *The Hand of the Potter* (1918). Around 1923, while working on *An American Tragedy* in New York, he began consulting about the novel with Brill, "his informal technical adviser on matters criminological" (Lingeman 223). Although it has sometimes been dismissed as marginal to the horror and pathos of Clyde Griffiths's doomed quest for beauty and pleasure,[5] the novel's Freudian language points to the underlying motive of his perverse sexuality, the universal death instinct.

Like Dorinda Oakley, Clyde Griffiths has lingered too long under the sway of the pleasure principle. He has a "soul," Dreiser tells us early in Book Two, "that was not destined to grow up" (193). By the time he reaches adolescence, he has been "so starved" for pleasure that "he listened with all too eager ears to any account of anything that spelled adventure or pleasure" (58). At the heart of his fantasy life is the delusion that to be rich means "you went how, where and when you pleased" (49). At his trial for the murder of his pregnant lover Roberta Alden, Clyde is still hoping somehow for freedom when the testimony of a girl who witnessed him with Roberta on the death journey confronts him with knowledge "of the unbreakable chain of facts that could thus be built up by witnesses from such varying and unconnected and unexpected places" (756). Even in the death house, however, Clyde is "naturally more drawn to romance than reality" and prefers to read "the light romantic novel that pictured some such world as he would have liked to share, to anything that even approximated the hard reality of the world without, let alone this" (891). Only when he enters the death chamber in a scene of almost unbearable pathos is he forced to recognize that "the chair he had so often seen in his dreams" (930) is real, perhaps the first and last reality he will ever know for sure.

A more complicated matter is the sadomasochism underlying the novel's important sexual relationships. Dreiser introduces the topic most explicitly in Book One in describing how Hortense Briggs enjoys withholding sex from Clyde: "And she liked to think that he was suffering from repressed desire for her all of the time; that she tortured him, and that the power to allay his suffering lay wholly in her—a sadistic trait which had for its soil Clyde's own masochistic yearning for her" (120). Neurotics have what Freud in *Beyond the Pleasure Principle* (1920) calls a "compulsion to repeat" (19–20), and in Book Two, Clyde compulsively repeats his first sadomasochistic relationship by pursuing the heiress Sondra Finchley, a "less savage, although scarcely less self-centered, Hortense Briggs" (368).

Clyde's masochism does not by itself explain why some critics think Clyde unconsciously intends his murder plot to fail (Gogol 107; Cassuto 121). When we meet Clyde, he is already subject to "a kind of mental depression or melancholia which promised not so well for his future. It served to make him rebellious and hence lethargic at times" (17). This description of aggression turned outward in rebellion and then inward in self-defeating passivity invites a reading in terms of Freud's "Mourning and Melancholia" (1917). Here Freud argues that while melancholia and mourning both concern a lost love object, the melancholic "vilifies himself and expects to be cast out and punished" (584). The real object of vilification is not, however, the self but the lost object. Either because of the ambivalence in all love relationships or because of actual wounds inflicted by the lost object, the melancholic first internalizes and then takes "revenge" on the object "by the circuitous path of self-punishment" (588). In a brief digression near the end of his essay, Freud notes "one particular striking feature of melancholia" that has much relevance for understanding the Clyde fleeing the demeaning poverty of his youth—"the prominence of the fear of becoming poor" (589).

Freud concludes that the sadism in melancholia "solves the riddle of the tendency to suicide which makes melancholia so interesting—and so dangerous" (588). Largely unnoticed is Clyde's suicidal impulse following his reading a newspaper story about an accidental double drowning:

> he was struck by the thought (what devil's whisper?—what evil hint of an evil spirit?)—supposing that he and Roberta—*no, say he and Sondra*—(no, Sondra could swim so well, and so could he)—he and Roberta were in a small boat somewhere and it should capsize at the very time, say, of this dreadful complication which was so harassing him? (506; emphasis added)

This "devil's whisper" will soon become the hallucinated voice of his unconscious pleasure-ego: "the very substance of some leering and diabolic wish or wisdom concealed in his own nature" (532). But why would the pleasure principle produce a fantasy not simply of Roberta's death but of a *liebestod* involving Clyde and his beloved ("no, say he and Sondra"), the latter fantasy abandoned only with the thought that he and Sondra can swim?

One reason is that Sondra is just as much a source of pain as Roberta is, and not simply because of her sadistic teasing. At the first sight of her at his uncle's mansion, Clyde experiences "a curiously stinging sense of what it was to want and not to have. . . . It tortured and flustered him" (251). Shortly after learning of Roberta's pregnancy, Clyde rejects the impulse to repeat his flight from Kansas City after the automobile accident that killed a girl, for "then he would lose Sondra, his connections here, and his uncle—this world. The loss! The loss!" (495). Thoughts of Sondra are repeatedly connected with the torturing thought that he does not have her. To his unconscious, killing her and himself would make for as good a revenge as killing Roberta and would mean an even more successful escape from his intolerable conflict since he wouldn't be around to feel guilty.

A second reason is perhaps to be found in Freud's *Beyond the Pleasure Principle*, an English translation of which was published in 1924 by Boni and Liveright, Dreiser's own publisher. That fact and his intimacy with Brill suggest Dreiser's familiarity with the most striking aspect of the work—Freud's contention that the "organic compulsion to repeat" (44) reveals that "*the aim of all life is death*" (46), that "the most universal endeavour of all living substance" is "to return to the quiescence of the inorganic world" (76). Sadism, Freud posits, "is in fact a death instinct" (65) directed away from the self and toward an object, an idea that leads him to posit a "primary" masochism (66). In this perspective, the evolution of complex life forms and life cycles produces only "circuitous paths to death" (46).

Clyde's "primary" masochism, diverted into sadism, leads him on a circuitous path to death and release from the tormenting excitations of his desires. Most obviously, he experiences a death wish when he gazes into Big Bittern Lake moments before Roberta's drowning and thinks of "Death! Death! . . . a still, quiet, unprotesting type of death into which one, by reason of choice or hypnosis or unutterable weariness, might joyfully and gratefully sink. So quiet—so shaded—so serene" (560). He does not yet surrender to the death instinct, and when events precipitate the boat's capsizing and his life instinct, speaking in the voice of the "efrit," persuades him to let Roberta drown, he resumes his circuitous path.

That death has been his unconscious destination all along is suggested during the death trip when he asks a local guide a question that he immediately recognizes as incriminating: "'Many people over there [at Big Bittern] to-day?' a question which the moment he had propounded it, seemed almost insane. Why, why, of all questions, should he ask that? Oh, God, would his silly, self-destructive mistakes never cease?" (552). As Freud asserts in the concluding sentence of *The Psychopathology of Everyday Life*, mistakes are often eruptions from the unconscious of "*unwelcome, repressed, psychic material*" (178). Clyde's mistakes express a disguised wish of the pleasure-ego to achieve the peace of death paid for in the coin of suffering for the reality-ego. Even as Clyde, on death row, tries to explain himself to the

Reverend Duncan McMillan, the minister feels the narrative to be "an evil and cruel self-torturing and destroying story" (912), and Clyde's illusion that he has found "peace" (927) in Jesus is but the last effort of the life instinct to escape into the "quiescence of the inorganic world."

"The ego," Freud says, "can kill itself only if . . . it can treat itself as an object" ("Mourning" 588). Clyde does not technically kill himself, but in his last moments as a dead man walking to the electric chair, he says his "Good-by, all" in a voice "strange and weak," a voice seeming to issue not from his own impoverished ego but from "another being walking along beside him, and not from himself." Only by experiencing himself as object can Clyde go quietly to occupy the chair "to which he was now compelled to go" (930)—compelled, of course, by the inhuman penal system that tortures its victims to madness but also by the deepest need of his being.

As these readings indicate, American literary naturalists were from the start committed to a truthful account of the human mind in conflict with itself and its environment. At their best, they produced novels of power and complexity, not reductive illustrations of reflex action or neurosis. Each of the novels examined here ends on a note of ambiguity, not the snapping shut of a trap, and indicates the need for broadening our understanding of the mode. In a recent essay exposing the ahistorical nature of much recent criticism, Richard Lehan calls for a return to understanding American literary naturalism in terms of "a system of philosophical and social assumptions" expressed in fiction "infused with historical reality" (Lehan 17). I would add "psychological" to the list. Historical reality includes the way people think their minds work, and we should expect naturalists in the future, as their predecessors always have, to express their own assumptions about that working.

NOTES

1. For the best account of American psychology before Freud, see Hale 3–177. The phrase "somatic style" is in Hale 47.

2. Darwin would draw upon Spencer's account of the language of the emotions in writing *The Expression of the Emotions in Man and Animals* (1872). For the fullest account of Darwin's, and to a lesser extent Spencer's, influence on American realists and naturalists, see the two studies by Bender.

3. No one to my knowledge has explored Spencerian psychology in the highly autobiographical *Martin Eden*, though Martin embraces it. The first work he reads of Spencer's is the *Principles of Psychology* (651); initially he finds it hard going, but after becoming an enthusiastic Spencerian, he engages in a heated defense of the philosopher's "genius" in which he proclaims Spencer "the father of psychology" (851). For the fullest account of London's use of Jung, see McClintock 151–74. According to Labor and Reesman, London read Freud as early as 1912 (107). For a Freudian reading of *The Little Lady of the Big House*, see Auerbach 236–37.

4. Critics have, however, dealt with aspects of *Winesburg* that parallel Adler's ideas. For a discussion of the ideal of androgyny in the book and the evils of male aggression, see

Bidney. For an extended account of how fiction and narrative govern the psyches of the book's characters, see Lindsay. For an account of Anderson's response to Freud, see Sutton 305–6 and Hoffman 229–50.

    5. For an argument that "Dreiser's overexplicit reliance" on Freud weakens the novel, see Pizer, *Novels* 211–14. For an argument that Poe's influence is more important than Freud's for the terror Dreiser evokes, see Riggio.

WORKS CITED

Adler, Alfred. *The Neurotic Constitution: Outlines of a Comparative Individualistic Psychology and Psychotherapy*. Trans. Bernard Glueck and John E. Lind. 1917. New York: Moffat, Yard, 1921.

Anderson, Sherwood. *Winesburg, Ohio*. Ed. Charles E. Modlin and Ray Lewis White. New York: Norton, 1996.

Auerbach, Jonathan. *Male Call: Becoming Jack London*. Durham: Duke University Press, 1996.

Bender, Bert. *Evolution and "the Sex Problem": American Narratives during the Eclipse of Darwinism*. Kent: Kent State University Press, 2004.

———. *The Descent of Love: Darwin and the Theory of Sexual Selection in American Fiction, 1871–1926*. Philadelphia: University of Pennsylvania Press, 1996.

Bidney, Martin. "Anderson and the Androgyne: 'Something More than Man or Woman.'" *Studies in Short Fiction* 25 (1988): 261–73.

Campbell, Donna M. *Resisting Regionalism: Gender and Naturalism in American Fiction, 1885–1915*. Athens: Ohio University Press, 1997.

Cassuto, Leonard. "Lacanian Equivocation in *Sister Carrie, The 'Genius,'* and *An American Tragedy*." *Theodore Dreiser: Beyond Naturalism*. Ed. Miriam Gogol. New York: New York University Press, 1995. 112–33.

Crane, Stephen. *The Correspondence of Stephen Crane*. Ed. Stanley Wertheim and Paul Sorrentino. New York: Columbia University Press, 1988. 2 vols.

———. *The Red Badge of Courage. Prose and Poetry*. Comp. J. C. Levenson. New York: Library of America College Edition, 1996. 79–212.

Dooley, Patrick K. *The Pluralistic Philosophy of Stephen Crane*. Urbana: University of Illinois Press, 1993.

Douglas, Ann. *Terrible Honesty: Mongrel Manhattan in the 1920s*. New York: Farrar, Straus and Giroux, 1995.

Dreiser, Theodore. *An American Tragedy*. Ed. Thomas P. Riggio. New York: Library of America, 2003.

———. "Neurotic America and the Sex Impulse." *Hey Rub-A-Dub-Dub: A Book of the Mystery and Wonder and Terror of Life*. New York: Boni and Liveright, 1920. 126–41.

———. "Reflections." *Ev'ry Month* Feb. 1897: 2–7; rpt. in *Theodore Dreiser's Ev'ry Month*. Ed. Nancy Warner Barrineau. Athens: University of Georgia Press, 1996. 240–42.

———. *Sister Carrie*. Ed. Donald Pizer. 3rd ed. New York: Norton, 2006.

Fleissner, Jennifer L. *Women, Compulsion, Modernity: The Moment of American Naturalism*. Chicago: University of Chicago Press, 2004.

Freud, Sigmund. *Beyond the Pleasure Principle*. Trans. and ed. James Strachey. New York: Norton, 1961.

————. *The Ego and the Id*. Trans. Joan Riviere. Rev. and ed. James Strachey. New York: Norton, 1960.

————. "Formulations on the Two Principles of Mental Functioning." *The Freud Reader*. Ed. Peter Gay. New York: Norton, 1989. 301–6.

————. "Mourning and Melancholia." *The Freud Reader*. Ed. Peter Gay. New York: Norton, 1989. 584–89.

————. *Psychopathology of Everyday Life*. *The Basic Writings of Sigmund Freud*. Trans., ed., and intro. A. A. Brill. New York: Modern Library, 1938. 33–178.

————. *Three Contributions to the Theory of Sex*. *The Basic Writings of Sigmund Freud*. Trans., ed., and intro. A. A. Brill. New York: Modern Library, 1938. 553–629.

Glasgow, Ellen. *Barren Ground*. San Diego: Harcourt Brace, 1985.

————. *The Woman Within: An Autobiography*. Ed. and intro. Pamela R. Matthews. Charlottesville: University Press of Virginia, 1994.

Gogol, Miriam. "'That oldest boy don't wanna be here': Fathers and Sons and the Dynamics of Shame in Theodore Dreiser's Novels." *Theodore Dreiser: Beyond Naturalism*. Ed. Miriam Gogol. New York: New York University Press, 1995. 95–111.

Goodman, Susan. *Ellen Glasgow: A Biography*. Baltimore: Johns Hopkins University Press, 1998.

Hale, Nathan G., Jr. *Freud and the Americans: The Beginnings of Psychoanalysis in the United States, 1876–1917*. New York: Oxford University Press, 1995.

Hoffman, Frederick J. *Freudianism and the Literary Mind*. 2nd ed. Baton Rouge: Louisiana State University Press, 1957.

Hofstadter, Richard. *Social Darwinism in American Thought*. Rev. ed. Boston: Beacon Press, 1955.

Horsford, Howard. "He Was a Man." *New Essays on* The Red Badge of Courage. Ed. Lee Clark Mitchell. Cambridge: Cambridge University Press, 1986. 109–27.

James, William. *Principles of Psychology*. New York: Dover, 1950. 2 vols.

————. *Psychology: The Briefer Course*. *William James: Writings 1878–1899*. Comp. Gerald E. Myers. New York: Library of America, 1992. 1–443.

Labor, Earle, and Jeanne Campbell Reesman. *Jack London*. Rev. ed. New York: Twayne, 1994.

Lehan, Richard. "Naturalism and the Realms of the Text: The Problem Restated." *Studies in American Naturalism* 1 (2006): 15–29.

Lindsay, Clarence. *Such a Rare Thing: The Art of Sherwood Anderson's* Winesburg, Ohio. Kent: Kent State University Press, 2009.

Lingeman, Richard. *Theodore Dreiser: An American Journey 1908–1945*. New York: Putnam, 1990.

London, Jack. *Martin Eden*. *Novels and Social Writings*. Ed. Donald Pizer. New York: Library of America, 1982. 555–931.

Lutz, Tom. *American Nervousness, 1903: An Anecdotal History*. Ithaca: Cornell University Press, 1991.

Makari, George. *Revolution in Mind: The Creation of Psychoanalysis*. New York: Harper, 2008.

Martin, Jay. *Harvests of Change: American Literature 1865–1914*. Englewood Cliffs, N.J.: Prentice Hall, 1967.

McClintock, James I. *White Logic: Jack London's Short Stories*. Cedar Springs, Mich.: Wolf House, 1976.

Norris, Frank. "Zola as a Romantic Writer." *The Literary Criticism of Frank Norris*. Ed. Donald Pizer. Austin: University of Texas Press, 1964. 71–72.

Pizer, Donald. "Dreiser and the Naturalistic Drama of Consciousness." *The Theory and Practice of American Literary Naturalism: Selected Essays and Reviews*. By Donald Pizer. Carbondale: Southern Illinois University Press, 1993. 69–82.

——. *The Novels of Theodore Dreiser*. Minneapolis: University of Minnesota Press, 1976.

Raper, Julius Rowan. "*Barren Ground* and the Transition to Southern Modernism." *Ellen Glasgow: New Perspectives*. Ed. Dorothy M. Scura. Knoxville: University of Tennessee Press, 1995. 146–61.

Richardson, Robert D. *William James in the Maelstrom of American Modernism: A Biography*. Boston: Houghton Mifflin, 2006.

Rideout, Walter B. *Sherwood Anderson: A Writer in America*. Madison: University of Wisconsin Press, 2006. 2 vols.

Riggio, Thomas P. "American Gothic: Poe and *An American Tragedy*." *American Literature* 49 (1978): 515–32.

Spencer, Herbert. *The Data of Ethics*. New York: Appleton, 1879.

——. *The Principles of Psychology*. 3rd ed. 2 vols. New York: Appleton, 1897.

——. *Social Statics; or, The Conditions Essential to Human Happiness Specified, and the First of Them Developed*. New York: Appleton, 1886.

Sutton, William A. *The Road to Winesburg: A Mosaic of the Imaginative Life of Sherwood Anderson*. Metuchen, N.J.: Scarecrow, 1972.

Swanberg, W. A. *Dreiser*. New York: Scribner, 1965

Taylor, Eugene, ed. *William James on Exceptional Mental States: The 1896 Lowell Lectures*. By William James. New York: Scribner, 1982.

Wagner, Linda W. *Ellen Glasgow: Beyond Convention*. Austin: University of Texas Press, 1982.

Zanine, Louis J. *Mechanism and Mysticism: The Influence of Science on the Thought and Work of Theodore Dreiser*. Philadelphia: University of Pennsylvania Press, 1993.

Zola, Émile. "The Experimental Novel." *Documents of Modern Literary Realism*. Ed. George J. Becker. Princeton: Princeton University Press, 1963. 162–96.

CHAPTER 12

AMERICAN NATURALISM AND MODERN EVOLUTIONARY PSYCHOLOGY

JEFF P. TURPIN

ONE of the main attractions of modern evolutionary psychology (EP) is its ability to efficiently explain those aspects of human behavior that seem to be counterproductive, like xenophobia, jealousy, greed, overeating, road rage, and various addictions. By examining their evolutionary roots, evolutionary psychologists offer us insights about the causes of human behavior and the ability to explain (and, for some writers, justify) otherwise inscrutable actions. For the most part, naturalist writers already had questions in mind about human behavior and were attracted to Darwin, Spencer, Huxley, and others because they seemed to offer sensible answers. Writers are (usually) keen observers, particularly of human behavior, and they develop causal claims, or questions about causality, from their observations of life. In this sense, writers are amateur psychologists. In the same sense, the naturalist writers were amateur evolutionary psychologists, combining observation with theory to come up with evolution-based causal equations and conclusions. The deep-time history of adaptation and selection gave them efficient, scientifically justified answers to questions that they and many other people were already asking.

Modern evolutionary theorists have not uncovered radical errors in Darwin's original description of evolutionary theory and its implications, but they have modified old ideas and come up with new explanations to extend Darwin's theories into more complex aspects of human behavior. We would expect some mistakes to be visible in the early naturalist equations, and there are errors—for example, Spencerian evolution, the foundation for the progressivist tone taken by Jack London and other naturalists, has fallen into disrepute. But more remarkable than these predictable errors are the places where writers seemed to anticipate developments that science would not "discover" for another half-century (see Gottschall). Modern studies of sexual selection and reciprocal altruism, when applied to works like Edith Wharton's "Roman Fever" (1934) and John Steinbeck's *Of Mice and Men* (1937) and *The Grapes of Wrath* (1939), reveal some surprising, prescient aspects of the works. These authors were not just dramatizing the theories handed to them by evolutionary science, but they were extending the evolutionary hypotheses well beyond the reach of their contemporaries. In Wharton's case, retrospective evolutionary analysis shows that, contrary to traditional criticism, some of her more famous female characters were radically empowered, subtle, and competent survivors; and in Steinbeck's case, that the author cut directly across contemporary ideas about altruism to both complicate theories of human morality and advocate for true morality and true selflessness.

THE "SEXY SON" HYPOTHESIS
AND EDITH WHARTON

There is disagreement in EP camps between those who feel we are best adapted to the common elements of the hunter-gatherer environment that our ancestors occupied for the first hundred thousand years or so since our species' inception, and those who question whether our adaptations are more flexible and more in-sync with present needs. This debate is complicated by the fact that while humans have adapted physically to a set of known conditions, generally present in the Pleistocene era, we have also adapted to a social milieu that is not fixed and evolves in pace with us as we adapt to it so that environment and adaptation are constantly in flux, in a feedback cycle that began with the species' inception and has increased in intensity since.

We are evolving with and against our social environment, changing it as we evolve, and competing within it daily for status, resources, and reproductive opportunities, and our successes and failures are immediately reflected in the number and quality of our children, who in turn move on to compete against this fluctuating environment and then pass on their successes and failures. It is this sociocultural environment that plays such a large role in Wharton's "Roman Fever." This story, with roots found in Wharton's earlier writings, dramatizes the ultimate concerns and outcomes of sexual selection, competition, and reproduction—the basis of all biological life.

The Sexy Son hypothesis asserts that females can benefit by mating with males who are judged to be attractive by other females because they are likely to produce similarly attractive sons, who in turn can be more productive breeders, passing on the female's genes more successfully than a less attractive male might. The theory was generated from one of the basic facts of biology—in most animals, males can be more prolific reproductively than females can because females produce fewer gametes than men, and the gestation and nurturance phases of typical maternity take up more time and energy than the minimum effort typically required of males to contribute to a pregnancy (see Weatherhead and Robertson). The mathematics of reproduction are correct in this case: an individual man can, at least in theory, contribute to a lot more babies than an individual woman can, simply because there are a billion sperm to every egg, and men have to contribute only a minute or two to their future children, while women generally have to contribute at least nine months. Thus, while on the surface the Sexy Son hypothesis seems, well, sexist, the reproductive math adds up.

There are of course different definitions of "sexy." What evolutionary psychologists usually mean when they are discussing male "sexiness" is high status within a given community. Current studies in EP make the point that people in general quickly recognize high status in men and pay more attention to men to whom they assign high status. It is important to keep in mind that women ultimately decide which male is "sexy" by choosing whether to mate with men with a specific set of characteristics. Nathan C. DeWall and John K. Maner point out that physical attractiveness is an important signal of reproductive fitness for both men and women but that multiple studies have shown that an attractive appearance weighs more heavily in assessment of female suitability, while status counts more heavily in assessment of male suitability (329). So a Sexy Son can be physically attractive or physically average, as long as he has high status or seems likely to gain high status in a given community.

One offshoot of the Sexy Son hypothesis has been the claim that some women are selectively, adaptively promiscuous, choosing to sleep with "sexy" men when they are most likely to get pregnant, yet pair-bonding with men less likely to benefit from wanderlust when they need familial support for child-rearing ("facultative polyandry," in the jargon). In biology, these sorts of dalliances are called extra-pair copulations, or EPCs (see Buss 348–60, 362–63, 375–76), and they are also common in various other species. Another study of human mate choices complicates this claim in ways even more relevant to Wharton's story: according to the study, women who rate themselves as attractive expect more from potential mates, while women who do not think as highly of themselves expect less (Buss and Shackelford 134).

The Sexy Son theory has been critiqued on a variety of levels, chauvinism and binary generalization not the least among them. But what the title of the theory elides, and what is suggested by the above study of attractive women, is the amount of sexual/reproductive power that resides solely in the female of the species. Again, no man is "sexy" unless and until a majority of women decides he is. Beyond this, women are always certain who the mother of their child is, but men must always be less certain of their paternity. If successful reproduction—the passing on of one's genes—is the brass ring in biological life (and it is), then knowing that the child you are raising is yours is and should be extremely important to men. But women never have to wonder, and this certainty is power in the most basic biological sense. Clearly, the ability to control your wife's exposure to other men has reproductive valence—but what about the ability to control your husband's exposure to other women?

History has also amply demonstrated that attractive women have more repro-ductive agency than their less-attractive peers, both in direct competition with those peers and in indirect competition with males for resources and familial attention. This is one reason they are called "attractive." Evolutionary science has begun to pay more attention to this part of the reproductive equation, with several articles being published in the last decade on female attractiveness and agency. Yet even these more egalitarian approaches are not likely to salve modern gender sensitivities, concentrating as they do on female physical attributes. However, Wharton's story clears this hurdle by taking female power well beyond simple physical attractiveness.

Evolutionary Feminism in "Roman Fever"

In "Roman Fever," Alida Slade accidentally instigates the act which produces rival Grace Ansley's illegitimate daughter Babs by sending a fake letter to Grace, purport-edly written by Alida's fiancé Delphin, asking Grace to meet him at night in the Colosseum. Alida is jealous of Grace's "quiet ways [and] sweetness" (841) and writes the letter to tempt Grace out into the potentially infectious airs of the Roman night. The duplicitous act is copied from a similar action by Grace Ansley's own great aunt, who, competing with her younger sister for the same man, sent the sister out for flowers one night, whence she caught fever and actually died. Unfortunately for Alida, Grace replies to the letter, and, since good Sexy Sons recognize reproductive opportunities, Delphin shows up, meeting her in the Colosseum for an EPC (he was engaged to Alida at the time, but Grace was apparently unattached). The liaison goes undetected, Grace "takes ill" after her night out (apparently satisfying Alida's desire to remove her from the scene), leaves Rome, and quickly marries good old Horace Ansley, while Alida marries Delphin. Twenty-five years later, we learn that dynamic, good-looking daughter Babs Ansley is the result of the tryst.

Assessments of the story have frequently been negative about the behavior of the protagonists. Critic Barbara White reiterates a common opinion of "Roman Fever" as a "bleak story about the fallen condition of women in patriarchal culture" (qtd. in Donovan 82). Susan Sweeney views the story as "an account of the curse of patriarchy, which turns women against each other and themselves" (328); for Barbara White, the main characters are "women . . . wracked by the disease of jealousy and competition" (11); and for Dale M. Bauer, the characters "represent . . . the repressions of patriarchal culture that has infected them" (689).

An evolutionary psychologist might see the story a bit differently. The interpretation of jealousy and competition as unnatural diseases, and these women as hapless victims of patriarchy, misses the facts that (1) jealousy and competition are normal, universal parts of the human (animal) condition; (2) patriarchy has been the rule in human and hominid groups for millions of years (see Bamberger; Brown; and Eller); and (3) one of these women is the loser, and the other the indubitable victor, in the eternal competition for genetic perpetuation. Since survival and reproduction are evolution's sine qua non, Mrs. Ansley's snaring of attractive genes from one mate and support from a second is a victory of the highest order.

David Buss and other evolutionary psychologists have pointed out that women who pursue a "mixed-mating strategy" generally have lower appraisals as potential mates than women who do not pursue polyandry—that they are more likely to seek good genes from one man and support from another (Buss and Shackelford 134). By the fifth paragraph of "Roman Fever," Wharton has begun to grade her protagonists' agency, status, and attractiveness: Grace Ansley is "the smaller and paler one" (833), while Alida Slade is "fuller, and higher in color, with a small, determined nose supported by vigorous black eyebrows" (833). This introduction establishes who is dominant in the pair. A few paragraphs later we are reminded that Mrs. Slade is "the lady of the high color and energetic brows" who describes Mrs. Ansley as "old-fashioned," after which the narrator adds, "[Mrs. Ansley] was evidently far less sure than her companion of herself and her rights in the world." Alida agrees that Grace is the less attractive of the pair, ironically comparing Grace to her daughter Babs, who is less "pretty" but who has more "edge," a characteristic absent, in Alida's mind, from both of Babs's parents (835). Since many of Alida's qualities are related to us by Alida herself, it is clear that she regards herself as, in EP's criteria, a "high mate value" woman. And for Alida, her successful marriage to a high-ranking man is part and parcel of her own self-worth (see Bauer 687).

Grace Ansley, her beauty aside, is not quite as high on herself. Modern psychological studies on the correlation between perceived self-worth and mate requirements make the point that a woman's self-rating of her own attractiveness strongly influences her mating decisions (Buss and Shackelford 137). While beautiful enough to attract sufficient male attention and unsettle Alida, Grace, "far less sure than her companion of herself and her rights in the world," clearly has a lower self-rating and, by the evidence presented by these multiple studies, might be expected to pursue "facultative polyandry," obtaining support from a marriage partner and good genes from an EPC.

This is, of course, exactly what she does.

Alida's husband Delphin, the "famous corporation lawyer" and "*the* Slade" (836), is his generation's version of a Sexy Son. A quotation from another EP study adds piquancy to this description: "Based on all available ethnographic data, the most reproductively successful men historically and cross-culturally were those who married young, secured multiple wives, and opportunistically engaged in sex with other men's wives when the risks were low." Further, "[m]en who were successful at having extra-pair copulations were precisely the same men who were successful at acquiring wives—those who were high in status, good hunters, successful warriors, headmen, and successful intrasexual competitors" (Buss and Shackelford 136). Wharton's narrator asserts Delphin's status in his own community by reminding the reader of his "big *coup* in Wall Street" and the Slades' consequent new home on Park Avenue (835). Readers familiar with Wharton's work are aware that this same community would inhibit this Sexy Son from marrying subsequent wives after Alida, and his relatively early death assures that he can't divorce and acquire a trophy wife later in life. If he is a true Sexy Son, his best chances for extra-pair copulation come early in life, before New York society requires him to settle down.

MACHIAVELLIAN INTELLIGENCE AND COMPETITION FOR MATES

But these emphases on "sexiness," self-esteem, and status seem too unilateral and sexist to explain the outcome of both life in general and "Roman Fever" in particular. Given the posited more-than-100,000-year history of the human species, the high heritability of stable traits like attractiveness and assertiveness, and the predicted success of Sexy Sons and high-self-esteem women, we might expect to look out on a world populated by dominant, attractive women and men, all descended in direct line from a prehistoric set of successful Slades. Empirical observation suggests that this is not quite the case.

   In the last thirty years, evolutionary and cognitive psychologists have begun to hypothesize that the development of "Machiavellian intelligence" in human beings (and other primates) is a direct result of intense social competition during prehistory. Their point is that our minds have evolved to navigate the extremely complex straits of our social environments, and that this evolution, as in all evolution, tends toward the adaptive—the survival-and-reproductive—benefit of the organism:

> According to this hypothesis, most of human psychological adaptation was driven
> by the human social environment, not by our physical environment. For the
> compelling problems whose solutions required true intelligence were those
> involved in social life: competing with others of the same sex for mates,
> competing with others for resources, recognizing and responding appropriately to
> deception and hostility, . . . and so on. (Buller 99)

Most readers realize that "Roman Fever" is not a tale about Pretty Women and Sexy Sons (although such stories have a large audience). Its nuances and complications concern the overt hostility of Alida and the covert hostility of Grace; the deception of Horace by Grace and of Alida by Delphin; the competition for mates, for resources, and for status in a battle that takes a quarter century to complete and in which the victor is the woman who, at least on the surface, seems born—biologically determined—to lose.

It doesn't hurt that Grace *was*, in Mrs. Slade's words, "exquisitely lovely . . . charming, distinguished" (835). But this physical attractiveness by itself cannot accomplish the competitive coup. With nerve and Machiavellian connivance, Mrs. Ansley takes advantage of the opportunity that accident, Delphin's lax morals, and Mrs. Slade's letter provide her: to produce an attractive, agentive daughter with a fair amount of control over her own reproductive options. Mrs. Slade, using the same reproductive object (Mr. Slade), has failed twice—once in keeping her attractive mate away from Mrs. Ansley, and again where her own genes could not combine with Mr. Slade's to produce equally viable offspring (a barely mentioned Sexy Son of the Slades died in infancy, with no cause given). This competition thus takes place in both the biological and cultural spheres, and in both arenas Mrs. Slade is the loser, Mrs. Ansley the victor.

In animals in general, high status and overt assertiveness are not the exclusive path to reproductive success. Blue-gilled perch are one famous example of a species where males occupy both passive and aggressive social niches, where a stable percentage of "cheater" males imitate females to gain access to spawning grounds, feign sex with dominant males, and deposit their own sperm over eggs deposited by various females, germinating the eggs and cuckolding the "normal" males into raising them (see Gross and Charnov). Examples of similar behavior are abundant in biology for fish, sea mammals, and birds. Similar role plasticity is found in orangutans and other primates (Maestripieri 467–68). In animals, these deceptive mating strategies are considered to be evolutionarily stable adaptations—the behavior perpetuates in the species because it is successful. As Wharton shows, in "Roman Fever," as in nature, status is not the sole key to success.

From an evolutionary standpoint, Wharton's story thus complicates gender criticism on a variety of levels. While female physical attractiveness clearly plays a role, it is the Machiavellian guile of the two protagonists that provides the real drama. In a story sometimes categorized as a depressing illustration of the ills of patriarchy, we see men reduced to one-dimensional relationship objects who, contributions (genetic or social) exhausted, simply die before the story even begins. Here the agentive women experience the angst of paternal uncertainty traditionally reserved for anxious males: "who is the father?" becomes a different question, heavily loaded, but not because the men in question care—they are dead. And a Dominant Daughter, not a Sexy Son, is the brass ring. By these standards, "Roman Fever" is a feminist triumph.

This Machiavellian feminine subtlety has roots in Wharton's other works. In her short novel *Ethan Frome* (1911), Ethan is the male protagonist, his cousin Mattie is the attractive potential reproductive winner, and Ethan's wife Zeena is the ultimate Machiavellian victor. Mattie is essentially the hapless victim (a later version of *The House of Mirth*'s Lily Bart, "an organism as helpless out of its narrow range as the sea-anemone torn from the rock," 487), but the reader watches Ethan's struggles to escape his sterile life and marriage, and the almost-supernatural interdictions of Zeena that prevent that escape, with fascination and horror. Fate makes the final move in this story, but the table is set before that move by Zeena, who checks Ethan's every attempt to escape. The ultimate sterile ménage—frozen in the stark New England winter—is Wharton's commentary on the outcome of this sexual competition.

A similar tableau unfolds in her novel *The Age of Innocence* (1920), where a tense love triangle exists between Newland Archer, his supposedly naive wife May, and her provocative cousin Ellen Olenska. Ellen's seductiveness affects Newland, and his clumsy, two-steps-forward-one-step-back attempts to consummate the affair provide the novel's dramatic tension. May is initially shown by Wharton to be oblivious to Newland's struggles and machinations, and the reader sees her as the ignorant, soon-to-be-betrayed wife for most of the novel. But when push comes to shove and Newland decides to leave May, we discover that she and her "tribe" have anticipated and blocked this move with shocking political adeptness, and the adroitness of the check renders Newland impotent (342–43). Later, after Newland has, despite all, decided to follow Ellen to Europe, May confesses the pregnancy that checkmates that move, and "her blue eyes [are] wet with victory" (346; see also Ohler 149). Here, as in the case of Grace Ansley in "Roman Fever," the apparent dupe is revealed to be the master of her social environment: the subtly agentive woman gains reproductive victory while the nearest representative of the patriarchy lies pinned to the page in abject impotence.

In "Roman Fever," Grace stares down from the lunchtime terrace at "the outspread glories of the Palatine and Forum" of Rome, the birthplace of Western culture, the "great accumulated wreckage of passion and splendor," with approval— she is above it all (833, 838). Wharton's characters in these texts run the gamut, from the anti-hero Zeena who, despite being in the moral catbird's seat, is usually viewed unsympathetically by readers; to May Archer, a similarly morally positioned character who is a bit more sympathetic; to Grace Ansley, morally debauched (she sleeps with her girlfriend's fiancé and deceitfully raises the resulting baby with another man) yet somehow the most sympathetic of the three. In these three works, there are three dramas of sexual selection with different outcomes, but in each case women are in control while men are pawns in the game and clearly suffer, either immediately or in the biological future, from the conflict.

The claim that these women compete in an arena built and ordered by patriarchy suffers from anthropocentrism: success in survival and reproduction is not assigned value from a human, male perspective but is the same for all organic life, from amoeba to redwood to blue whale to wily American socialite. The benefits of rank are no different for women than for men and generally hold true across species. As Denise Cummins observes,

> Status (or rank) is most frequently defined as *priority of access to resources in competitive situations*. . . . There is a direct relationship between social status and reproductive success, with higher status individuals being less likely to die of predation or starvation and more likely to leave living offspring. . . . Your status is directly tied to your ability to survive, reproduce, and take care of yourself, your offspring, and your kin. (677–78)

Female intrasexual competition for status and reproductive opportunities is found in many animals and has been documented in lions, sea lions, lizards, langurs, and multiple primate species (Cheney and Seyfarth; Cummins 685). Such competition may be even more common in species in which females have higher status than males—in female-dominant species like the primate bonobo, for instance, where alpha females frequently interfere with mating attempts by subordinate females while males exercise little intra- or inter-sexual choice (see Vervaecke and Van Elsacker).

Again, many critics refer to Wharton as a victim of patriarchy who writes about victims of patriarchy. But viewed in the light of modern evolutionary psychology, Wharton has turned patriarchy on its head, with Grace Ansley (or May Archer or Zeena Frome) as a sort of modern Odysseus or Cleopatra, outwitting her competition for the evolutionary spoils of battle. Modern studies in sexual selection strongly validate this thematic subtext of Machiavellian women who outwit rivals of both sexes to get what they want and demonstrate that competitive behavior is a common response to the reproductive inequities across species.

Charles Darwin in his "Summary and Conclusion" to *The Descent of Man* describes women's (and men's) roles in sexual selection:

> The sexual struggle is of two kinds; in the one it is between the individuals of the same sex, generally the male sex, in order to drive away or kill their rivals, the females remaining passive; whilst in the other, the struggle is likewise between the individuals of the same sex, in order to excite or charm those of the opposite sex, generally the females, which no longer remain passive, but select the more agreeable partners. (qtd. in Bender 347)

The words "passive" and "select" in the passage sound like they are taken from a description of a mushroom hunt. But the female characters in Wharton's *Ethan Frome*, *The Age of Innocence*, and "Roman Fever" dictate the behavior of the men in their lives and control the reproductive success of the characters around them (see Salmon 247). It seems likely in this case that both Darwin and many of Wharton's critics were observing selectively when they described women as passive or victimized. Modern studies in evolutionary psychology support the claim that Wharton's women compete, naturally and instinctively, in their own way and on their own terms, and are often victorious over both men and other women, in the most important of all battles.

ALTRUISM AND RECIPROCITY IN *OF MICE* AND *MEN* AND *THE GRAPES OF WRATH*

Charles Darwin saw that altruism posed a problem for his simple model of natural selection—how could an individual contribute to his or her own adaptive fitness by giving resources away to a potential competitor? At the same time, Darwin realized that altruism was fundamental to moral behavior and that it could contribute to the adaptive fitness of a group: "No tribe could hold together if murder, robbery, or treachery were common. [A tribe] superior in patriotism, fidelity, obedience, courage, sympathy, *mutual aid, and readiness to sacrifice for the common good* [will be naturally selected over a tribe lacking in these faculties]" (106; emphasis added).

On the other hand, Herbert Spencer saw altruism as less a problem than a solution. He thought that altruism and selfishness ("egoism") were interdependent, and that altruistic acts were likely to produce the most pleasure for the greatest number (227–28). He expressed a concern with motive, "distinguishing between the altruism which is pursued with a foresight of the pleasurable feeling to be achieved through it, and the altruism which, though it achieves this pleasurable feeling, does not make pursuit of it a motive" (214). Finally, he concluded that "pure" altruism was suicidal, and that humans would evolve to a point where altruism would no longer be necessary (229, 230; see also Wilson 155–75).

Altruism and its costs animate two of John Steinbeck's most popular works, *Of Mice and Men* and *The Grapes of Wrath*. According to Brian Railsback, there is no evidence that Steinbeck ever read Spencer (7), but both Railsback (19–22) and Bender (313) note the probable influence of biologists and evolutionary theorists Jan Christian Smuts, John Elof Boodin, and W. C. Allee. Steinbeck had clearly read Darwin, and both Darwinian and Spencerian evolution had insinuated themselves into the turn-of-the-century zeitgeist, providing studies and theories for naturalist authors to expand and continue through a variety of routes to reach second-generation naturalists like Steinbeck. Steinbeck's works were prescient, for he explored the implications of altruism well beyond the levels of his contemporaries and predecessors. In particular, he realized that reciprocity could require us to act against traditional morality and that true altruism should not be thought of as reciprocal.

It's Not All In The Family

Early in the 1970s Robert Trivers, basing his analysis on earlier seminal work in population genetics by W. D. Hamilton, proposed the idea that reciprocal altruism could have evolutionary benefits, particularly when a family member or frequent associate was the beneficiary. Research in and development of altruism theory has continued since, with recent books by Richard Dawkins (*The Selfish Gene*) and Robert Wright (*The Moral Animal, Nonzero*) exploring the further ramifications of Trivers's and Hamilton's work.

Some definitions are in order. Evolutionary psychologists are so inured to the phrase "reciprocal altruism" that the oxymoron has become invisible. "Altruism" is traditionally defined as giving with no expectation of repayment. "Reciprocity" is the exchange of goods, favors, and services—the Golden Rule, an eye for an eye, or quid pro quo, depending on the context. One is selfless, the other consciously self-serving, and the two should not normally be combined in one phrase unless by accident. "Reciprocal altruism" is thus an action that appears selfless but that is part of a system in which payback of some kind is obligatory. According to Trivers, Hamilton, and others, this reciprocity is what makes putative altruism adaptive.

There are three forms of altruism that are relevant to this discussion. Kin-selection altruism (sometimes called "nepotistic altruism"; see Pinker 242–43) is simply "altruistic" behavior between close relatives (Hamilton; Trivers). The adaptive function of this behavior is explained by the simple fact that when we help relatives we are helping portions of our own DNA survive and reproduce. Reciprocal altruism is the ongoing exchange of goods and services between people in general (Wright, *Nonzero* 23), and is a bit harder to justify, a difficulty which is dramatized by Steinbeck. The third form is a subset of the second: non-zero-sum altruism is the exchange of goods or services where the giver loses very little value and the receiver receives great value (Wright, *Nonzero* 5). This third form is also dramatized by John Steinbeck.

Reciprocity in *Of Mice and Men*

In their 2005 book *Madame Bovary's Ovaries: A Darwinian Look at Literature*, David and Nanelle Barash discuss reciprocity and altruism in various works of John Steinbeck and describe *Of Mice and Men* as "the finest buddy novel in modern times" (236). In this novel, Steinbeck directly explores the uncomfortable obligations that come with reciprocal relationships. That George and Lennie have such a relationship is made clear early on, when George is telling the oft-repeated story of why he and Lennie are different from the solitary men who ride the rails and work the ranches, and Lennie breaks in, "But not us! An' why? Because I got you to look after me, and you got me to look after you, and that's why!" (13).

We find out quickly that Lennie needs George, that if he were not in jail or dead by lynching, he would probably starve without him. But George's motive for traveling with Lennie is less clear: "We kinda look after each other. . . . I've knew him for a long time. . . . It's a lot nicer to go around with a guy you know" (32–33). George later elaborates his motives in a discussion with Slim, yet the extra details still don't quite explain the ongoing partnership:

> "Him and me was both born in Auburn. . . . When his Aunt Clara died, Lennie just come along with me out workin'. Got kinda used to each other after a while. . . . I ain't got no people," George said. "I seen the guys that go around on the ranches alone. That ain't no good. . . . But you get used to goin' around with a guy an' you can't get rid of him." (37–39)

Slim has been Steinbeck's (and the reader's) interrogator for several pages, and his questions reveal that there is no rational explanation for George and Lennie's relationship. Yet readers do not question the pairing because human beings are social animals, and such relationships are instinctive to us.

And yet we know that the relationship is dysfunctional. Crooks the stable hand speaks for the reader: "You travel 'round with George, don't ya? . . . Sometimes he talks, and you don't know what the hell he's talkin' about? . . . George knows what he's about. Jus' talks, an' you don't understand nothing" (66–67). The relationship is not exactly reciprocal. George gives more than Lennie. Yet when Crooks hints maliciously to Lennie that George might not come back one night and might leave him, Lennie expresses his obligations to and dependency on George:

> "S'pose George don't come back no more? . . . What'll you do then? . . . S'pose he gets killed or hurt so he can't come back? . . . Want me to tell you what'll happen? They'll take ya to the booby hatch. They'll tie ya up with a collar, like a dog."
> Suddenly Lennie's eyes centered and grew quiet, and mad. He stood up and walked dangerously toward Crooks. "Who hurt George?" he demanded. (67–68)

Lennie is willing to attack anyone who has hurt or might hurt George and is even willing to attack Crooks for fashioning the idea. Such is the depth of his need and obligation. Later in this same section, Crooks will drive home Steinbeck's message about "buddies":

> "Maybe you can see now. You got George. You know he's goin' to come back. S'pose you didn't have nobody. . . . A guy needs somebody—to be near him." [Crooks] whined, "A guy goes nuts if he ain't got nobody. Don't make no difference who the guy is, as long's he's with you. I tell ya," he cried, "I tell ya a guy gets too lonely an' he gets sick." (69)

George's benefit is clarified. With Lennie he is not alone.

Yet when Curley's wife enters the stable to express similar sentiments a few pages later, she is ostracized by the men. Crooks, Lennie, and Candy are bonding in what is supposed to become a reciprocal relationship. But Curley's wife will not be allowed to join and benefit from group membership. She will be alone. When she is rejected, she will punish them, each in his own specific manner. She will attempt to connect again with Lennie later, in the barn, beginning the events that bring the story to its tragic end.

After Lennie kills the puppy, and then Curley's wife, the dark obligations of the reciprocal relationship slowly become apparent to George. The surreal final act is a frenetic recitation of the tenets of reciprocity. Lennie's Aunt Clara comes back to him by the banks of the Salinas River and lectures him:

> "Min' George, because he's such a nice fella an' good to you. . . . You never give a thought to George. . . . He's been doin' nice things for you alla time. When he got a piece of pie you always got half or more'n half. And if they was any ketchup, why he'd give it all to you. . . . All the time he coulda had such a good time if it wasn't for you. . . . But he got to take care of you." (96–97)

Aunt Clara is replaced in Lennie's mind by the giant rabbit, who continues, "Christ knows George done ever'thing he could to jack you outta the sewer, but it don't do no good." Lennie's only defense in his madness is to reaffirm the reciprocal relationship: "I know George. Me an' him travels together" (98), at which point George appears, as if summoned by Lennie's need. Lennie begs him to repeat the story of their communal difference from the story's beginning, and he does:

> "Guys like us got no fambly. They make a little stake an' then they blow it. They ain't got nobody in the worl' that gives a hoot in hell 'bout em. . . .
>   "But not us," Lennie cried happily. "Tell about us now."
>   George was quiet for a moment. "But not us," he said.
>   "Because—"
>   "Because I got you an'—"
>   "An' I got you. We got each other, that's what, that gives a hoot in hell about us," Lennie cried in triumph. (99–100)

With the reciprocal relationship reaffirmed, George has no choice but to fulfill his obligation, and he does so by shooting Lennie in the head, keeping him from a lynching or the madhouse and leaving him with a last vision of their dream ranch. When Slim arrives, he validates George's action, and reconfirms his responsibility to Lennie: "You hadda, George. I swear you hadda." (102)

This conclusion is dystopic, regressive, and anti-humanist. Evolutionary psychologist Robert Wright offered the opinion that reciprocal altruism and non-zero-sum exchanges would lead to better lives for us all (*Nonzero* 318–34). Herbert Spencer said something similar a century earlier. But here our finest instincts, the roots of our morality, lead us to conclude that George is right to kill—murder—his best friend. Reciprocal altruism is the root of human moral behavior. But is George's choice moral? And who benefits? Steinbeck is asking questions here, and providing answers, that are different than those of either contemporary or modern evolutionists. Yet, again, the reader seems to understand. The author's assertion of this highest level of reciprocal obligation makes sense to us.

SOUR GRAPES AND THE WINE OF BROTHERHOOD

The responsibilities of reciprocity are ultimately tragic in *Of Mice and Men*, but in *The Grapes of Wrath* they receive more nuanced consideration. As Barash and Barash observe, the novel begins with Tom Joad's reluctant confession that he has just been released from prison—an effort to repay a reciprocal obligation to the truck driver who gives him a ride (240). Steinbeck spends most of the novel establishing and exploring the Machiavellian aspects of reciprocal systems—the fact that, as evolutionary psychologists from Trivers to the present assert, we give in order to receive later. But the variation in *Grapes* has to do with non-zero-sum exchanges. In a zero-sum equation, items of equal value are exchanged: one dollar purchases one dollar's worth of goods. In non-zero-sum equations, however, the exchange is for items of different value. The difference in value can be extreme and important. If I am a billionaire and you are a migrant laborer with a sick child, I can pay for a doctor for the child and save his life without denting my own assets. The cost to me is negligible, while the gain to you is immense. This is "non-zero-sum altruism." According to Robert Wright, such exchanges can become more common as human populations increase and can evolutionarily select for true altruism (contra Spencer's claim that "pure" altruism is suicidal).

Modern game theorists test a social strategy commonly referred to as "tit-for-tat," in which an organism initially offers cooperative action to a stranger organism and then offers further action based on the stranger's response—if the stranger reciprocates, they form a reciprocal relationship; if the stranger is hostile or "cheats," the initial actor responds in kind. Multiple simulations and competitions have shown tit-for-tat to be a stable survival strategy, one that in most social environments will insure the success of the initial actor and subsequent reciprocators (see Dawkins 210–20).

Early in *Grapes*, Tom offers a drink of whisky to Jim Casy (26), imparting a reciprocal obligation to Casy that the latter will repay multiple times throughout the novel. This simple first act establishes a "tit-for-tat" exchange that determines the novel's outcome and leads to Steinbeck's radical conclusion. Many other instances of reciprocal and kin-related altruism are found in the first half of the book, establishing tit-for-tat systems and creating unity in the group that will travel to California together. Steinbeck explains the power of these unified systems in chapter 14 of the book, where solitary groups of Okies meet to share resources and stories on the road west:

> Here is the node, you who hate change and fear and revolution. Keep these two
> squatting men apart; make them hate, fear, suspect each other. Here is the anlage
> of the thing you fear. This is the zygote. For here "I lost my land" is changed; a cell
> is split and from its splitting grows the thing you hate—"We lost *our* land." *The
> danger is here, for two men are not as lonely and perplexed as one.* And from this
> first "we" there grows a still more dangerous thing: "I have a little food" plus "I
> have none." If from this problem the sum is "We have a little food," the thing is on
> its way, the movement has direction. . . . This is the thing to bomb. *This is the
> beginning—from "I" to "we."* (194; emphasis added)

Later we are told, "And a kind of insurance developed in these nights. A man with food fed a hungry man, and thus insured himself against hunger" (251). Tit-for-tat combines here with non-zero-sum altruism, showing why and how such reciprocal strategies can become adaptive.

While enforcing and reinforcing these instinctively driven behaviors among his Okie "in-group," Steinbeck shows the same rules being violated by out-group members—the banks that drive the Joads off the land, the police that move them from camp to camp, and the California farmers who dump or burn their excess crops rather than giving them to the starving Okies. Tit-for-tat and the rule of reciprocity are not in place everywhere. The Okies and the Californians are competitors, not reciprocators.

Casy's reappearance later in the book and his stories about people who are giving their lives—the ultimate altruistic act, since repayment is unlikely—ratchet up the level of obligation and repayment (493). Anthropologist Robert Ardrey relates a story from Eugene Marais's *Soul of the Ape*, about a baboon troop that is cut off from its nesting place by a hungry leopard. While the leopard eyes his prey, two male baboons sneak off from the pack and quietly climb a cliff above the leopard. As a pair they jump on the leopard, attacking his vulnerable areas. The leopard kills both in an instant, but the last baboon has managed to bite through the leopard's jugular vein, and the leopard dies on top of its assassins. The troop is saved as a result of the sacrifice (Ardrey 80–81).

Anthropomorphism is unavoidable. The giving of one's life for one's group is the literal definition of altruism—of selflessness. Casy first describes this giving, citing George Washington and Abraham Lincoln as examples, then gives his own life fighting for the cause (493–95). Reciprocity demands that Tom make a similar sacrifice.

Tom's departure speech reinforces sentiments expressed earlier in the novel and even earlier in *Of Mice and Men*:

> Two are better than one, because they have a good reward for their labor. For if they fall, the one will lift up his fellow, but woe to him that is alone when he falleth, for he hath not another to help him up. . . . Again, if two lie together, then they have heat: but how can one be warm alone? (535–36)

But Tom's reciprocal sacrifice is only the preamble to Steinbeck's conclusion. The closing act of the story, where Rose of Sharon gives her breast milk to a man who would otherwise die, drives home the point of tit-for-tat and non-zero exchanges. The breast milk is useless to her and her dead baby, but it saves the life of the stranger and allows him to continue to care for his own son. This is Steinbeck's ultimate point. He made this clear in a letter to his editors:

> I'm sorry but I cannot change that ending. . . . If there is a symbol, it must be an accident, it must be a stranger, and it must be quick. To build this stranger into the structure of the book would be to warp the whole meaning of the book. The fact that the Joads don't know him, don't care about him, have no ties to him— that is the emphasis. (Steinbeck and Wallsten 178)

Bender cites this same correspondence and other post-*Grapes* commentary by the author to emphasize Steinbeck's claim that he was emphatically avoiding a symbolic, feel-good conclusion and was simply portraying the drama and possible outcome of social competition (313–14). My claim is that Steinbeck was, as Bender notes, intentionally writing about human conflict but that the author's intellectual honesty demanded the sort of insight that is represented by this final tableau—that non-zero-sum exchanges and tit-for-tat responses, if managed by good will and reason, can move human conditions in a positive direction. While it is possible to read this evolution of altruism as inevitable, it is worth remembering that the Joads and Okies do not in the end seem to improve their odds of surviving and reproducing, nor to adapt well to their new environment. Altruism here is not linked directly to the success of the altruists, nor to the social movement and ideology with which they are affiliated. It is not "adaptive."

Steinbeck is clearly arguing for a world like that hypothesized by Robert Wright in which the haves share with the have-nots—in which "pure" altruism is a requisite virtue, rather than an act of suicide. He thus addresses one of Darwin's problems while countering one of Spencer's conclusions. His conclusion in *Of Mice and Men* asks us to question the obligations of reciprocity and further question what is and is not a moral act. His conclusion in *The Grapes of Wrath* asserts that irrational, suicidal "pure" altruism is the highest moral act we can perform. Together these works dramatize what esteemed modern sociobiologist E. O. Wilson once wrote:

> Generosity without hope of reciprocation is the rarest and most cherished of human behaviors, subtle and difficult to define. . . . We sanctify true altruism in order to reward it and thus to make it less than true, and by that means to promote its recurrence in others. Human altruism, in short, is riddled to its foundations with . . . ambivalence. (155)

Literary Darwinism is the application of evolutionary theory to the production and consumption of stories. Story-telling is a human universal, present in every human culture ever encountered, and this universality suggests quite strongly that storytelling is an adaptive response to our environment. The idea that stories help us to survive and reproduce allows discussion of stories as "good" or "bad" in the adaptive sense. It is implicit in literary Darwinism that stories which are categorized as good, which stand the test of time, and which continue to provoke critical interest, must have some superior adaptive benefit. In this analysis, Edith Wharton's story "Roman Fever" appears to lay the foundation for an approach to feminism that is much broader and deeper than the traditional feminist criticism of the last half-century—to represent women as agentive, potent, and competent in an era when, in popular and critical thought, the reverse was true. By the same token, John Steinbeck seems to have had insights into altruism and reciprocity that complicate these supposed sources of human morality. In *Consilience*, sociobiologist Wilson argues for a new approach to thinking about art and science: in this new "consilience" there will no longer be a gap between the two. Insights from the one will inform the other, and vice-versa. Naturalist writers made their own attempts to close the gap at the beginning of the twentieth century. Now, at the dawn of the twenty-first century, new science is once again helping to bridge the gap, and giving new energy to literary criticism.

WORKS CITED

Ardrey, Robert. *The Territorial Imperative*. New York: Atheneum, 1966.

Bamberger, Joan. "The Myth of Matriarchy." *Woman, Culture, and Society*. Ed. Michelle Zimbalist Rosaldo and Louise Lamphere. Stanford: Stanford University Press, 1974. 263–80.

Barash, David, and Nanelle Barash. *Madame Bovary's Ovaries: A Darwinian Look at Literature*. New York: Bantam, 2005.

Bauer, Dale M. "Edith Wharton's 'Roman Fever': A Rune of History." *College English* 50 (1988): 681–92.

Bender, Bert. *Evolution and "the Sex Problem": American Narratives during the Eclipse of Darwinism*. Kent: Kent State University Press, 2004.

Brown, Donald. *Human Universals*. Philadelphia: Temple University Press, 1991.

Buller, David J. *Adapting Minds: Evolutionary Psychology and the Persistent Quest for Human Nature*. Cambridge: MIT Press, 2005.

Buss, David M. *The Handbook of Evolutionary Psychology*. Hoboken: Wiley, 2005.

Buss, David M., and Todd K. Shackelford. "Attractive Women Want It All: Good Genes, Economic Investment, Parenting Proclivities, and Emotional Commitment." *Evolutionary Psychology* 6 (2008): 134–46.

Cheney, D. L., and R. M. Seyfarth. "The Representation of Social Relations by Monkeys." *Cognition* 37 (1990): 167–96.

Cummins, Denise. "Dominance, Status, and Social Hierarchies." Buss 676–97.

Darwin, Charles. *The Descent of Man, and Selection in Relation to Sex*. Intro. John Tyler Bonner and Robert M. May. Princeton: Princeton University Press, 1981.

Dawkins, Richard. *The Selfish Gene*. Oxford: Oxford University Press, 1976.

DeWall, C. Nathan, and John K. Maner. "High Status Men (But Not Women) Capture the Eye of the Beholder." *Evolutionary Psychology* 6 (2008): 328–41.

Donovan, Josephine. *After the Fall: The Demeter-Persephone Myth in Wharton, Cather and Glasgow*. University Park: Penn State University Press, 1989.

Eller, Cynthia. *The Myth of Matriarchal Prehistory: Why an Invented Past Will Not Give Women a Future*. Boston: Beacon, 2000.

Gottschall, Jonathan. "Sexual Selection and the American Novel." [Rev. of Bender, *Evolution and the Sex Problem*.] *Evolutionary Psychology* 3 (2005): 56–58.

Gross, Mart R., and Eric L. Charnov. "Alternative Male Life Histories in Blue-Gill Sunfish." *Proceedings of the National Academy of Sciences of the United States of America* 77 (1980): 6937–40.

Hamilton, W. D. "The Genetical Evolution of Social Behaviour I and II." *Journal of Theoretical Biology* 7 (1964): 1–52.

Maestripieri, Dario. *Primate Psychology*. Cambridge: Harvard University Press, 2005.

Ohler, Paul J. *Edith Wharton's "Evolutionary Conception": Darwinian Allegory in Her Major Novels*. New York: Routledge, 2006.

Pinker, Stephen. *The Language Instinct*. New York: Harper, 2000.

Railsback, Brian E. *Parallel Expeditions: Charles Darwin and the Art of John Steinbeck*. Moscow: University of Idaho Press, 1995.

Salmon, Catherine. "Crossing the Abyss: Erotica and the Intersection of Evolutionary Psychology and Literary Studies." *The Literary Animal: Evolution and the Nature of Narrative*. Ed. Jonathan Gottschall and D. S. Wilson. Evanston: Northwestern University Press, 2005. 244–57.

Spencer, Herbert. *The Data of Ethics*. London: Williams and Norgate, 1879.

Steinbeck, Elaine, and Robert Wallsten, eds. *Steinbeck: A Life in Letters*. New York: Viking, 1975.

Steinbeck, John. *The Grapes of Wrath*. New York: Penguin, 1976.

———. *Of Mice and Men*. New York: Penguin, 2002.

Sweeney, Susan Elizabeth. "Edith Wharton's Case of Roman Fever." *Wretched Exotic: Essays on Edith Wharton in Europe*. New York: Peter Lang, 1993. 313–31.

Trivers, Robert. "The Evolution of Reciprocal Altruism." *Quarterly Review of Biology* 46 (1971): 35–37.

Vervaecke, Hilde, and Linda Van Elsacker. "Sexual Competition in a Group of Captive Bonobos (*pan paniscus*)." *Primates* 41 (2007): 109–15.

Weatherhead, P. J., and R. J. Robertson. "Offspring Quality and the Polygyny Threshold: 'The Sexy Son Hypothesis.'" *American Naturalist* 113 (1979): 201–8.

Wharton, Edith. *The Age of Innocence.* New York: Random, 1920.

———. *Ethan Frome.* New York: Scribner, 1911.

———. *The House of Mirth.* New York: Scribner, 1905.

———. "Roman Fever." *The Collected Short Stories of Edith Wharton.* Ed. R. W. B. Lewis. Vol. 2. New York: Scribner, 1968. 833–43.

White, Barbara A. *Edith Wharton: A Study of the Short Fiction.* New York: Twayne, 1991.

Wilson, E. O. *Consilience: The Unity of Knowledge.* New York: Vintage, 1999.

———. *On Human Nature.* Cambridge: Harvard University Press/Bantam, 1978.

Wright, Robert. *The Moral Animal.* New York: Vintage, 1998.

———. *Nonzero: The Logic of Human Destiny.* New York: Pantheon, 2000.

PART IV

NATURALIST TENSIONS

CHAPTER 13

....

WOMEN WRITERS AND NATURALISM

....

DONNA M. CAMPBELL

IN the middle to late 1890s, a new generation of Americans born in the 1860s and 1870s began writing fiction that questioned Victorian orthodoxies and challenged the by-then prevailing realism of the day, a realism that seemed too genteel to confront the difficult social realities of a nation undergoing constant change from industrialization, immigration, urbanization, and monopoly capitalism. Armed with the biological theories of Herbert Spencer, Charles Darwin, and Ernst Haeckel, these writers sought to expose the biological underpinnings of social behavior and to chronicle the forces and drives that affected human beings. Their subjects were often people who lived near the edge of poverty and starvation, in harsh wilderness environments, or in social groups that ostracized individuals for differences from the norm. The conflicts in their fiction featured confrontations between the forces of heredity and environment and the struggles of individuals to assert free will in a deterministic universe. Their novels featured plots of decline and a frank treatment of sexuality. When their fiction began appearing in the late 1890s, critical responses ranged from praise for the writers' innovations to shock and disgust at their subject matter.

In the critical assessments of twentieth-century literary history, however, these writers were divided into two groups. Writers in the first group, consisting of Stephen Crane, Theodore Dreiser, Jack London, and Frank Norris, were called "naturalists." Writers in the second group, consisting of Edith Wharton, Kate Chopin, Willa Cather, and Ellen Glasgow, were called "women writers." This essay is an attempt to question that literary history and that division, not so much to discover its causes, which have to do with the ways in which canons are shaped and nurtured, as to consider the implications of treating the two groups together. It investigates the relationship between women writers and naturalism, or, more specifically, the ways in which late nineteenth- and early twentieth-century American women writers wrote naturalistic fiction. In so doing, it may complicate if not erase the exclusionary boundaries that have separated the two groups—one defined by philosophical and literary outlook, and the other by gender—in ways that provide a clearer sense of naturalism as a whole. In addressing the issue of literary classification, this essay focuses broadly on three questions. First, it analyzes the ways in which Chopin, Wharton, Glasgow, and Cather—the four women writers of this generation most frequently identified as naturalists—were writing within or against the conventions of classic naturalism. Second, it explores the ways in which the inclusion of women writers and certain features of their work, such as the relationships of female characters to the land and the trope of the female body as spectacle, might serve to stretch definitional boundaries of naturalism itself. Finally, it concludes by addressing briefly the importance of discussing women writers as part of a naturalistic tradition.

KATE CHOPIN, EDITH WHARTON, ELLEN GLASGOW, AND WILLA CATHER

Chopin, Wharton, Glasgow, and Cather make exemplary test cases for American naturalism. Despite their differing approaches and subjects during the major portions of their careers, in the 1890s all four published fiction that exhibited the hallmarks of naturalism: their novels and stories were influenced by evolutionary theory, employed a scientific perspective, and transgressed the conventional boundaries of literary subjects. These authors did not know one another, nor were they seeking to ally themselves with any school of naturalism. All took care to distance themselves from schools and factions, especially those composed solely of other women writers. In this they resembled Dreiser, Crane, and London, who likewise scorned identification with movements and schools in order to forge their own brand of fiction; even in reviews, as Nancy Glazener observes, "naturalism barely surfaced in influential journals except with reference to Zola, and . . . the authors we associate with naturalism were not grouped together by contemporary reviewers" (6). With the exception of Norris, who claimed a literary kinship with Zola, and Crane, who claimed to have followed no literary creed at all, several of the female and male naturalists identified evolutionary as well as literary theorists as influences. For example, Kate Chopin credited her reading in Darwin, Spencer, and Huxley, her "daily companions" in "the study of the human species," as central to her work, although she "quarreled" with Darwin's theory of female passivity in the matter of sexual selection (qtd. in Toth 89).[1] In the stories of Guy de Maupassant, which she translated for publication, she found "life, not fiction" ("Confidences"

700), and she studied his techniques closely. Yet although Chopin kept a notebook and took notes until she felt as though she were "wearing Zola's coat" ("Emile Zola's 'Lourdes'" 704), Zola's methodically detailed naturalism was antithetical to her own. In fact, she attacked Zola's *Lourdes* because the reader can never "lose sight of the author and his note-book" (697) and criticized Zola's clumsy editorializing through characters whose words express "what the author himself thinks of those things" (698). In *A Backward Glance* (1934), Edith Wharton paid tribute to her intellectual awakening through a family friend who "directed and systematized my reading" in Darwin, "Huxley, Herbert Spencer, Romanes, Haeckel, Westermarck, and the various popular exponents of the great evolutionary movement" (856), a measure of influence reflected in the Darwin-inspired title of her third story collection, *The Descent of Man* (1904). Wharton's extensive reading in philosophy, history, and anthropology also informed her study of human beings within social systems, especially that of "Old New York." In *The Woman Within* (1954), Ellen Glasgow recalled that she "could have passed successfully an examination on every page" of *The Origin of Species* (88), to the distress of her pious family, including a sister who quietly offered her a gold piece to "exchange Lecky's *History of Rationalism in Europe* for some 'nicer book like *The Lives of the Poets*'" (93). As a journalist for the Lincoln *Courier*, the *Nebraska State Journal*, and the Pittsburgh *Leader*, Willa Cather participated in the growing critical discourse on naturalism; for example, although she believed that Zola would not "last," she "thought well of Norris's *McTeague* and *Blix*" (Lawlor 169) and by her own admission admired Stephen Crane to the point of hero worship. Despite their differences in setting and subject matter, all four clearly saw their fiction as being informed by evolutionary theories central to naturalism.

Although most of Kate Chopin's stories fit within the regionalist or local color tradition, her novels *At Fault* (1890) and *The Awakening* (1899) demonstrate characteristics of naturalism. As Winfried Fluck contends, *At Fault* is a novel caught between genres, among them local-color fiction, the sentimental novel, and the social-problem novel, an insight borne out in the language of the text. Early in the novel, its heroine, Thérèse Lafirme, remarks, "It's an ungrateful task, this one of reform" (*At Fault* 745), yet she forges ahead, using the strategies of renunciation and self-sacrifice common to the sentimental novel to manage the love and work issues of the social-problem novel—in this case, her love for a divorced man, David Hosmer, and the transformation of her plantation and its African American workers from an agricultural to an industrial economic base through her establishment of a sawmill. Neither plan succeeds without a significant cost: the deaths of Fanny, Hosmer's alcoholic ex-wife, and of Joçint, a displaced African American and Native American worker who sets fire to the mill and is killed by Thérèse's cousin. Thérèse's failure to effect change signifies Chopin's rejection of the power of sentiment as a means of social reform, a central principle of sentimental and benevolence fiction. Instead, the language and plot of the book affirm the power of naturalistic forces, including environment, addiction, and race, to trump the best-laid schemes of social regulation.

In contrast to *At Fault, The Awakening* has long been treated as a work of naturalism, but Chopin modified naturalism, as she did all genres, as part of her "long-standing opposition to the constraints of literary tradition" (Nolan 118). In one sense, the plot of *The Awakening* echoes the familiar naturalistic plot of the awakening of the "human beast" beneath a veneer of civilization, a process that may mean the making or the breaking of a character—the restoration of masculinity, in London's *The Sea-Wolf* (1904), or the devolution of the human being, in Norris's *Vandover and the Brute* (1914). In her awakening to sexual desire, Edna Pontellier finds rather than loses her sense of self; she emerges from the role of wife and mother to cast off the trappings that she comes to see as inessential for happiness, elements that Chopin symbolizes in Edna's shedding her restrictive clothing. Although she ignores social rules, Edna cannot ignore the laws of biology; her response to the "sensuous touch of the waters of the Gulf" (Nolan 125) suggests the all-or-nothing quality of her immersion in sexuality, just as Edna's children compel her recognition that maternity follows sexual expression.[2] Edna's recognition of the consequences of her actions and her decision to choose the end that she can control—suicide by drowning—rather than the one she believes she cannot control—repeated love affairs and possibly more children—has been read by feminist critics as a triumphant liberation from the constraints of patriarchy, but it also marks her determination not to be a standard naturalistic heroine such as Jeanne in Maupassant's *Une Vie*. Like Edna, Jeanne has a vividly sensual relationship to nature. She recalls the scents of flowers, as Edna recalls the "musky odor of pinks" (1000), and awakens to sensual pleasure and sexual desire, as Edna does, when she learns to swim far out to sea.[3] Despite this awakening, Jeanne's life dwindles to a series of disappointments and dull, repetitive days, a fate that Edna forestalls through her suicide. Edna's self-willed death is incidental and secondary to her primary desire: to stop time and arrest the cycle of meaningless repetitions that her life is in the process of reenacting—a form of repetition that Jennifer Fleissner identifies as the "stuckness in place" (9) central to naturalism.

In her naturalistic fiction, Edith Wharton concentrates less on the physical laws of a deterministic universe than on the ways in which those laws are transmuted into the rules of a rigid, multilayered social world in which each positive action toward change ironically leads to disproportionately negative consequences. As Nancy Bentley explains, Wharton did not focus on "the extinction of the social" being in favor of the physical, animal self, as Norris did; rather, she made the "social self" the focus of her scientific and anthropological investigations (50). Wharton pursued this idea in her fiction from her early stories through *The House of Mirth* (1905), *Ethan Frome* (1911), and *The Age of Innocence* (1920). Indeed, all her novels convey a sense of desperation as circumstances tighten around the protagonists largely as a result of their attempts to free themselves from an intolerable future. In *The House of Mirth*, Lily Bart meets her death when she refuses to align her inner self with her social self. A gambler at the bridge table and in the marriage market, Lily accepts at one level that she is a beautiful object, "a moment's ornament" with a variable value in a culture of acquisition and speculation exemplified by Percy Gryce's collecting of Americana and Gus Trenor's speculation in stocks.[4] Yet Lily protests this "ethics of exchange" and disrupts it, both by refusing to accept its valuation of her and by paying her debts "within a system in which nonpayment is the norm" (Dimock 383). At odds with her culture, Lily sees herself in Darwinian terms as "rootless and ephemeral, [a] mere spin-drift of the whirling surface of existence, without anything to which the poor little tentacles of self could cling before the awful flood submerged them" (515), when in fact she is not simply an individual but a type, an icon of racial perfection at the moment of "Anglo-Saxon extinction" (Kassanoff 56). She becomes a naturalistic heroine not only by reason of her entrapment but also because she embodies the fetishization of the Anglo-Saxon "race" common to Norris's and London's fiction.

The desperation in *Ethan Frome* and *The Age of Innocence* arises from a similarly naturalistic tightening of the rings of a plot in which both characters find that their choices diminish with each action that they take. Ethan's most decisive action is his sled ride with Mattie, which he imagines will kill them both and free them from the tortures of living without one another. But at the last moment, "his wife's face, with twisted monstrous lineaments, thrust itself between him and his goal" (150), causing him to miss the tree and consign Mattie to a life of invalidism from her injuries. On a symbolic level, Zeena has blocked him in his quest for death as in his quest for life, but her grotesque woman's face with its "twisted lineaments," a consistent trope in naturalistic fiction, suggests both the face of the Medusa-like Mrs. Johnson that turns the children's "blood to salt" (18) in Stephen Crane's *Maggie* (1893), and the Furies, the monstrous forces of fate and retribution, that haunt Lily Bart in *The House of Mirth*. Newland Archer of *The Age of Innocence* repeats Ethan's pattern of inevitable entrapment because he cannot admit the truth of his feelings for Ellen Olenska to himself, to his fiancée May Welland, or to the New York social world that he simultaneously criticizes for its hypocritical morality and takes care not to offend. Each instance of attraction to Ellen leads Archer to take steps that actually make their relationship impossible, such as urging May to hasten the date of the wedding or advising Ellen not to divorce her husband. Archer orders the latest books, thinks of himself as a modern man, and laments the metaphorical "bandage" (52) that blinds innocent young women like May to life's realities, yet he is himself one of the least-informed members of a primitive culture, as Wharton's use of anthropological language implies. This language also emphasizes the beauty and the uselessness of the sacrifice demanded by old New York, as when, in meeting at the Metropolitan Museum, Ellen and Archer ponder the "small broken objects" of dead civilizations, now labeled 'Use unknown'" (186). The novel's action hinges on the interplay among three language registers: the language of society, which conceals truth and stifles any attempt at conveying information; the absence of language in the characters' silent pauses, which reveal truths that they can never speak; and the language of anthropology adopted by the impersonal narrator, who interprets the events in terms of tribal norms but neither judges nor affects the characters' actions. Only when the guests at the final dinner for Ellen expertly deflect Archer's attempts to announce his departure for Europe can Archer interpret all three levels of meaning; in a flash of illumination, he understands that "the whole tribe" "by means as yet unknown to him" had conveyed without speaking their support of

May and their belief that he was Ellen's lover (201). The "veneer of civilization" may seem at first to be an unusually thick layer in Wharton's fiction, but the primitive emotions that lie underneath it erupt as easily as they do in more traditionally naturalistic settings.

Professing a desire to infuse "blood and irony" into the "elegiac tone" of Southern literature (*Woman Within* 104), Ellen Glasgow uses the naturalistic principle of environmental determinism to challenge the adage that "blood will tell." According to Nancy Walker, Glasgow is the "woman writer of the 1890s whose work is most obviously and consistently the product . . . of naturalism" (124), as is evident in her first novel, *The Descendant* (1897). *The Descendant* tests the deterministic hypotheses of heredity and environment in the character of Michael Akershem, the prototype of the self-made entrepreneur that later appears in Dreiser's *The Financier* (1912) and *The Titan* (1914), David Graham Phillips's *The Cost* (1904), and Robert Herrick's *The Memoirs of an American Citizen* (1905). Akershem is the illegitimate child of a woman with a "bulging brow" (7) signifying native intelligence, for, like Norris, Glasgow endows her characters with Darwin-inspired physical traits. With an amoral ferocity and a Darwinian approach to life that makes him a precursor to Dreiser's Frank Cowperwood, Akershem achieves a brilliant success with his publication *The Iconoclast* and converts Rachel Gavin, an artist, to his disdain for conventions such as marriage. As if to proclaim that Akershem is as much type as individual, Glasgow divides the book into four sections, each bearing a title from Darwin: "Variation from Type," "The Individual," "Domestication," and "Reversion." Varying from the "type," or the Southern stereotype, of his poor white family, Akershem reverts to type when he becomes enraged, kills a man, and is sent to prison for manslaughter.[5] Although other Progressive Era "self-made man" novels feature a protagonist who understands too late the cost of his success, Akershem completes only part of the journey toward self-awareness: released from prison and stricken with tuberculosis, he returns to Rachel, whom he had earlier abandoned, but he is incapable of insight into his behavior. As the "blood-red seal" (276) of his fatal condition stains his lips, he recognizes neither his own mortality nor the self-defeating quality of his quest; instead, he renews his vow of revenge against humanity, never realizing that he is driven by naturalistic forces beyond his control.

Less schematic in structure but equally naturalistic in its testing of environmental determinism is Glasgow's *Barren Ground* (1925), in which Dorinda Oakley confronts not only the conditions of near-poverty on her family's farm but also the biological imperatives of sexual passion and potential motherhood. Glasgow employs naturalistic and Darwinian images to characterize Dorinda's struggle: she is "caught like a mouse in the trap of life . . . held fast by circumstances as by invisible wires of steel" (44) and responds with an ecstasy that "quiver[s] over her" (185) when hearing music—music being, in Darwin's terms, an essential part of animal courtship and mating rituals. But unlike Edna Pontellier, whose passionate response to Mlle. Reisz's performance of Chopin prefigures her affair with Alcée Arobin, Dorinda's "ecstasy" leads her to recall the landscape of her youth, suggesting her displacement of energy and desire from men to the land. Dorinda redeems her land from a constantly encroaching and hostile natural environment, here embodied in the wild broomsedge that threatens to take over the cultivated acres of the farm. Like Akershem and other naturalistic characters, she is part of the environment she transcends, yet she triumphs over it by treating her body as a machine, not for the production of passion and children, a possibility she deliberately denies herself, but for the successful production of crops on her land. As Tanya Ann Kennedy concludes, the "double displacement of female reproduction—the suppression of the female body and the extraction of the labor" (58) are necessary elements of her success. The very tools of stoicism and detachment that she has needed to rise above the uncontrollable naturalistic circumstances of her youth have replaced her sense of "romantic glamour" with an "integrity of vision" (*Barren Ground* 408), a veiled commentary on the process of detached vision, and of the primacy of the material world, in naturalism.

Willa Cather made region a primary component of her naturalistic vision, and, like Glasgow, she mingles an elegiac sense of the land's beauty with a bitter knowledge of the hard work that farming demands.[6] *O Pioneers!* (1913) parallels *Barren Ground* in its depiction of a woman, Alexandra Bergson, who wrests a living from the unforgiving earth through her farsighted adoption of better farming methods such as crop rotation and the scientifically hygienic care of animals, a topic that the novel shares with Jack London's *Valley of the Moon* (1913) and *Little Lady of the Big House* (1915). But *O Pioneers!* is not a simple tale of a farm woman's triumph over adversity: in contrast to the happy families of such novels, Alexandra's brothers, with the exception of Emil, are greedy and suspicious; the tight-knit immigrant communities celebrate their religious heritage with colorful festivals but have no tolerance for an outsider like the elderly mystic Ivar; and of the two love stories, that of Emil and Marie Shabata ends in their murder by Marie's jealous husband and that of Alexandra and Carl Linstrum is deferred for twenty years until Emil's death reunites them. As Alexandra and Carl walk to the top of a hill to contemplate their future together, Alexandra reflects that "[w]e come and go, but the land is always here" (289), a convergence of romance and philosophical acceptance that suggests a subdued happy ending. Yet even this consolation cannot erase her memory of her brother's murder and the greed, passion, and violence that characterize the events of the novel—events that with a less elegiac tone would suggest a naturalistic novel.

CHARACTERISTICS OF NATURALISM
IN WOMEN'S WRITING

Chopin, Wharton, Glasgow, and Cather adapted standard characteristics of naturalism in their fiction, including a frank treatment of sexuality, the primacy of heredity, including race, as a motivating factor in characters' actions, and the power of natural and mechanical forces to determine the course of human lives. Less obvious but equally significant are naturalistic features such as Chopin's use of the plot of decline, Wharton's techniques of ironic plotting, Glasgow's critique of the South's obsession with heredity, and Cather's transformation of the naturalistic romance. Within the past ten years, critics have also proposed other features that can be considered constitutive of naturalism, such as Barbara Hochman's analysis of the signifying function of readership, Jennifer Fleissner's assertion that naturalistic novels are structured by "ongoing, nonlinear, repetitive motion" (9), Monika Elbert's reading of the naturalistic fetishism and consumerism of Mary E. Wilkins Freeman's stories, and Bill Brown's analysis of habit, repetition, addiction, and the role of "object matter" in Norris's fiction.[7] Other recent studies of naturalism that include women writers are Mary E. Papke's edited collection *Twisted from the Ordinary* and books by Bert Bender, Gina Rossetti, Eric Carl Link, Richard Lehan, Donald Pizer, and John Dudley. To these may be added the significant surface features that signal a naturalistic text, such as the familiar landscapes of littered urban streets culminating in a lovingly detailed description of a disgusting collection of objects, a "catalogue of refuse," as in Norris's *Vandover and the Brute*, Wharton's "Bunner Sisters" (1916), or Ann Petry's *The Street* (1946); or the extensive use of animals, either as vicious predators or as dumb brutes, as a symbolic commentary on the characters' position as human beasts. Two strands of criticism are especially pertinent when considering women as writers of naturalism. The first is the issue of place, or the way in which female characters are represented within landscapes not typically identified with naturalism, such as the frontier or borderlands regions of the West, small factory towns, or the farms of the rural South. The second issue is that of women's bodies functioning as spectacles within the larger culture.

The place of women in rural or wilderness landscapes broadens the perspective of naturalism by extending its settings beyond either the poverty-ridden streets of large cities or the open spaces of wilderness environments; instead, the rural Midwest and frontier West serve as settings for such writers as Mary Austin, Mary Hallock Foote, and Elia Peattie. Nicolas Witschi has characterized Mary Austin's Southwestern writings as "post-Howellsian realism" rather than naturalism, since she practices the "Howellsian model of morally inflected critical discernment" in her fiction and nonfiction (113), but Anne Raine finds Austin's *The Ford* (1917) drawing upon "the imagery of American naturalism to conflate nature and capital" (253). According to Laura Gruber, the Western writer Mary Hallock Foote, like Austin, represents gender and location as factors that are naturalistic in their determinism, especially given the hostile natural landscapes Foote represents in "The Fate of a Voice" (1886) and "Maverick" (1894). Elia Peattie's "After the Storm: A Story of the Prairie" (1897) features the cruel farmers and downtrodden women common to the regional stories of Rose Terry Cooke and Mary E. Wilkins Freeman, but Peattie renders the characters and events in terms of naturalism: a dying woman worn out in service to the farm; her drunken, abusive husband, Sharpneck, who tries to recapture their daughter, Kitty, from her job in town so that she can slave for him on the farm for the rest of her days; and an English observer, Tennant, who, like the Easterner Steavens in Cather's equally grim "The Sculptor's Funeral" (1895), watches in horror as the reality behind the pastoral dream of American prairie myth unfolds before him. Sharpneck's Nebraska cattle ranch lacks even the transitory beauty of the debt-ridden farms in Hamlin Garland's *Main-Travelled Roads* (1891): the farmhouse is filled with "voracious" cats whose "eyes shone with evil phosphorescence" as they circle the dead body in "grim carnivorous atavism" (Peattie 395). With a show of piety, Sharpneck pretends to bury his wife in an elaborate coffin, which he returns to the undertaker for cash after selling her corpse to the town doctor for dissection. Because Kitty refuses to return to the farm or stay in town, Tennant helps Kitty to escape with him to Council Bluffs, where the two are married. Yet this happy ending, to which Peattie devotes several pages of domestic details, seems almost to belong to a different story, so different is it in tone and perspective from the rest.

The happy endings, however improbably rendered, of the rural stories of Foote, Cather, and Peattie raise another issue central to naturalism, that of the sentimentalism that naturalism officially eschews. Francesca Sawaya and Jennifer Fleissner have argued that sentimentalism is not antithetical to naturalism but is integrated into its plots. In her reading of *The Octopus* (1901), for example, Sawaya contends that "naturalist sentimentalism" (56) allows the reader to sympathize with the feminized artist, Presley; and Fleissner sees the "begging man," such as Hurstwood in *Sister Carrie*, as a central figure in a naturalism that exemplifies its rewriting of the sentimental novel's seduction plot (163). In *O Pioneers!* Alexandra's position as the strong, self-sufficient farmer to Carl Linstrum's failed, sensitive graphic artist fits the pattern of "naturalist sentimentalism" that Sawaya identifies, and the novel arguably includes a "begging old man" in the person of Ivar, the mystic, who lives on the bounty that Alexandra provides. Moreover, the ballad-like tenor of the murder scene in Cather's novel, with its symbolic white butterflies fluttering above the murdered lovers Emil and Marie, is no more surreal than the mystical return of Angèle, who "was realised in the wheat" (1087) in Norris's *The Octopus*. In thinking about the wheat, Presley concludes that it is "untouched, unassailable, undefiled, that mighty world-force" that "moved onward in its appointed grooves" (1097) as smoothly and inexorably as the railroad engine. But wheat also becomes an irresistible force: embodied in Angèle, the wheat is the figure of the organic, eternal feminine called forth by men's fantasies, just as the force of the railroad signifies the manufactured product of men's visions. Cather, Glasgow, Edith Summers Kelley, and other women writers of naturalism dismantle this dichotomy between female embodiment and male production. Characters such as Alexandra Bergson, Dorinda Oakley, and Judith Blackford work the land, but they are neither earth mothers nor the land's symbolic representatives. Unlike the poet and dreamer Presley, they have learned that the "resistless" wheat cannot "move on" or, in fact, be produced at all without the practical intervention of human bodies—especially the bodies and minds of women who know how to farm.

A second significant trope in naturalistic works by male and female writers is that of the woman's body as spectacle.[8] Female protagonists function as spectacles of desire in Theodore Dreiser's *Sister Carrie* (1900), Stephen Crane's *Maggie: A Girl of the Streets* (1893), David Graham Phillips's *Susan Lenox: Her Fall and Rise* (1917), and Edith Wharton's *The House of Mirth* (1905). Within each novel, the protagonist performs for an audience of male spectators, speaking someone else's words or remaining mute, a stance that permits her to serve as a focal point of the male gaze without disrupting the audience's fantasies by the expression of her own personality. *Sister Carrie* and its eponymous heroine are driven by unsatisfied desire as epito-mized in Carrie's ability to express "the world's longing" in a "face representative of all desire" (356), an ability that she capitalizes upon by her performances before admiring men. Maggie Johnson's nearly wordless performance as "a girl of the painted cohorts of the city" (70) likewise depends on the spectator's interpretation, as does Susan Lenox's stage appearance after the playwright Brent has drilled her in a natural, understated style of acting devoid of the usual tricks. In addition to its suggestions of the slave market—and, for Progressive Era novels, of the traffic in white slaves—displaying a woman's body without permitting her to speak allows the audience to dictate not only their fantasies but her price. In naturalism, the display of a woman's body as a spectacle of desire always involves the exchange of money, thus implicating the body in the processes of capitalism along a continuum that in these novels ranges from acting to prostitution. Carrie, Maggie, and Susan have all learned their value on this continuum by testing their performances before an audience of men: Ames explains to Carrie the source of her appeal, much as Pete reassures Maggie by saying that he is "stuck on yer shape" (27); even Susan Lenox, the most self-aware of the three, must divest herself of her natural stage behaviors and learn an entirely new set of gestures based on Brent's theories of performance. In contrast, Wharton does not elide the process of establishing exchange value but emphasizes the uncertainties of doing so in a market dominated by men. Lily Bart relies on no male mentor when posing as Joshua Reynolds's *Mrs. Lloyd* in the *tab-leaux vivants* scene; her overconfidence in her own powers of logic means that she lacks a stable value, or a stable story to be interpreted. She falls prey to Gus Trenor's interpretation that her appearance on one end of the continuum—posing—allows him to place her at the other end—prostitution.

Considered as a characteristic theme in naturalism, the woman's body as a spectacle of desire enlarges the category of works that could be considered as natu-ralistic. For example, the entire plot of Cather's *A Lost Lady* (1923) hinges on Niel Herbert's alternating visions of Marian, the wife of the elderly pioneer Captain Forrester. The novel is filled with scenes of Niel gazing admiringly at Marian; he reveres her for the air of graciousness she gives to life in their small town but also for the "white lilacs" (62) of her complexion and the long earrings that swing by her cheeks. The surface illusion of her personality is pierced twice: once when Niel stands outside her door and hears the voices of Marian and her lover, Frank Ellinger, and again when Niel glances through the frame of an open door and sees the ethically and physically repulsive Ivy Peters embracing her. Preferring the illusion of her performance, which embodies his longing for a broader, more gracious world, to the sexual being that she is in reality, Niel refuses to see her again. The elegiac tone of the narration obscures what in other hands would be a fully naturalistic story of a woman's decline and fear of aging as she loses one lover, begins to drink excessively, and then sells herself another lover who supports her financially, all with a dark undercurrent of "festering" sexuality beneath the surface of her charm. With its imagery of surfaces and depths, its incidental cruelties (such as Ivy Peters's slashing the eyes of a bird), and its exploration of female sexuality and male disillusionment, *A Lost Lady* is, in effect, a naturalistic story concluded by a happy ending that calls attention to itself by its very unreality: Niel hears that Marion has married a man rich enough to take care of her at last. The ending of *A Lost Lady* shares with many works of naturalism the odd flash of sentimental consolation in a tale of otherwise unrelieved bleakness, such as Vanamee's discovery of Angèle in Norris's *The Octopus* or the intervention of the Quaker woman in Rebecca Harding Davis's "Life in the Iron-Mills" (1861).

The concept of the spectacle of desire also provides an additional means of examining race as a factor in naturalism: conflating sexuality and race as signifiers of value in Nella Larsen's *Passing* (1929), for example, renders both race and sexuality more visible as socially constructed rather than genetically or physically determined factors. In *Passing*, Clare Kendry functions as an object of desire for Irene Redfield, not only because, like Marian Forrester, she creates a sense of spectacle and excitement but also because Irene conflates her same-sex attraction for Clare with the daring performances of whiteness with which Clare fools her racist husband.[9] Like *A Lost Lady*, *Passing* is structured on a series of encounters in which the point-of-view character, Irene, observes the object of desire, Clare, often through a proscenium-like frame such as a window or doorway. Irene's last sight of Clare occurs as she "stood at the window, as composed as if everyone were not staring at her in curiosity and wonder" (238) after her husband discovers that she is African American. But as she has done repeatedly by entering the spaces that Irene inhabits comfortably and disrupting them, Clare refuses to stay in this or any other frame. She falls—or is pushed by Irene—from the window. Despite the modernist indeterminacy of its ending, *Passing* evokes naturalism in its representation of desire, its interrogation of consumer capitalism, and its emphasis on performance.

The opposing image, the spectacle of the body that inspires revulsion or fear rather than desire, also pervades naturalist novels. The grotesque body in naturalism often signifies a threat to the social order, typically less because of its actual power to harm than because of its uncanny and disturbing nature. Crane's "fat man" in *Maggie*; Henry Johnson, the African American hostler disfigured by fire in "The Monster" (1898); and Maggie's mother, Mary Johnson, all exemplify some of the forms that the grotesque body takes in naturalism.[10] These include the body of unusual size, such as those marked by obesity or dwarfism, as in Mary E. Wilkins Freeman's *By the Light of the Soul* (1907); the disabled body, often marked as a character also disadvantaged by class, race, or gender; and the body laboring in and transformed by childbirth. Obese characters such as Glasgow's Edmonia Breadalbane of *The Romantic Comedians* (1926), Marie Louise of Chopin's *At Fault*, and Mrs. Manson Mingott of Wharton's *Age of Innocence* gain power by maintaining a body weight that exceeds the norm and places them beyond the power of social criticism; in a repressive culture, they become its truth-tellers, the only figures as unconstrained by social conventions as they are by corsets. Ann Petry's *The Street* (1946) includes both figures: Lutie Johnson as a spectacle of desire, and Mrs. Hedges, the scarred and hairless madam, as its truth-telling figure of repulsion.[11] Lutie Johnson cannot escape being a spectacle of desire for the other characters, not only for the madam, Mrs. Hedges, and Jones, the building's superintendent, but also for Boots Smith, her would-be lover, and Junto, the white man who controls the club where she sings. Their framing of her in largely physical terms completes the imprisonment imposed by her surroundings, even though the narrative logic of the text shows that Lutie resists these forms of objectification and subjugation.[12]

A second version of the trope of the body as disturbing spectacle is that of disabled characters. Naturalism is a genre that celebrates physical strength in its characters because in a Darwinian, or, more accurately, Spencerian universe, as the naturalists understood it, the survival of the fittest depends upon the ability not only to outwit but to outfight one's enemies. But strength is at best on one end of a continuum with age, disability, and death at the other, a fact that some naturalistic novels keep firmly in focus either through the insights of major characters or through the presence of a person with disabilities. If a major feature of classic naturalist novels by male authors is an obsession with physical strength, a curious minor note in naturalistic fiction by women is the figure of the disabled body, often used as a means of critiquing forms of social injustice as in the works of Elizabeth Stuart Phelps and Rebecca Harding Davis. As Rosemary Garland-Thomson has argued, in the works of Phelps and Davis the "benevolent maternalism" (556) shown toward characters injured "by capitalism's laissez-faire morality" (557) enables a movement "from sympathetic identification with the disabled figures to a distancing repudiation of them" (556). Wharton and Cather employ this form of critique but focus on the oppressors rather than the oppressed: Bessy Westmore Amherst, in Wharton's socially conscious novel *The Fruit of the Tree* (1907), breaks her back and becomes paralyzed in a riding accident; and Cather's *Sapphira and the Slave Girl* (1940) explores the abuses of slavery through the character of the wheelchair-bound Sapphira Colbert. Both female characters occupy positions of power within the social systems they inhabit, yet they are rendered powerless by disabilities, a critique of their deformation under the social systems of industrialism and slavery that ostensibly serve to empower them.

The figure of the disabled body also evokes issues of social justice and thus enables the chronological extension of naturalism from the industrial novel of the mid-nineteenth century to the Progressive Era social-problem novel early in the twentieth century. As Donald Pizer has argued in "Late Nineteenth-Century American Literary Naturalism," studies of naturalism must recognize its strain of social protest and resurrect its roots in the exposure of social injustice and protests against the workings of capitalism, with which Walter Benn Michaels and others see naturalism as complicit. In reinstating naturalism within the realm of history rather than pure theory, Pizer and by Richard Lehan locate naturalism's beginnings in the historical fact of late nineteenth-century economic instability and social uncertainty; despite naturalism's official position of scientific objectivity, the journalistic experiences of writers such as Stephen Crane and Theodore Dreiser inevitably influenced their perspective on "the failings of the nation's industrial system" (Pizer, "Late Nineteenth-Century" 201). If social critique does not disqualify works from being considered as naturalistic, the timeline of naturalism can be extended to include social-protest works such as Rebecca Harding Davis's "Life in the Iron-Mills," which Sharon Harris has characterized as "one of the earliest renderings of naturalism in American literature" (29), and Elizabeth Stuart Phelps's *The Silent Partner* (1871), which Sara Britton Goodling reads as naturalistic in its indictment of industrialism. Reconsidering the prohibition against overt social critique would also allow a reevaluation of novelists such as David Graham Phillips and Upton Sinclair, who have sometimes been classed as naturalists; Paul Laurence Dunbar, whose strongly naturalistic *The Sport of the Gods* (1902) contains passages of authorial moralizing similar to Dreiser's; and writers such as Mary Wilkins Freeman, whose *The Portion of Labor* (1901) focuses on industrial conditions and a labor dispute.

Crane's Mary Johnson provides a key to a third form of the grotesque female body: her red-faced, writhing, and uncontrollable presence suggests the laboring woman's body in the throes of childbirth. Scenes of childbirth occur with more than usual frequency in naturalistic fiction by women, and the process is often represented as an act of violence, a bodily deformation equivalent to the destruction of the laboring body under capitalism that informs Jack London's fiction. For example, in *The Awakening*, Edna, called to the childbed of Adéle Ratignolle, watches the "sweat gather in beads on [Adéle's] white forehead" as she bites her lower lip through a contraction at the "scene of torture" (994). The spectacle of a woman's body in pain additionally signifies the naturalist concept of an involuntary human struggle against the processes of nature, a struggle that, like childbirth, must take its inevitable course. As depicted in these novels, the process of labor renders the body an inhuman machine driven by forces that the mind cannot control. In Edith Summers Kelley's *Weeds* (1923), Judith Pippinger Blackford labors like a machine to give birth to her son, "her body driving, driving, driving with the force and regularity of some great steel and iron monster" (345).[13] Winnie, the heroine of Evelyn Scott's *The Narrow House* (1921), cannot feel her feet and is floating far from the bed until "the child emerged from the blackness in which she was still caught" (174) shortly before Winnie dies. Larsen's Helga Crane of *Quicksand* (1928) also descends into "that appalling blackness of pain" where she "hover[s] for a long time somewhere in that delightful borderland on the edge of consciousness" before returning to earth (128). Scenes of childbirth incorporate a common metaphor in naturalism: the connection between industrial production and human reproduction, an association that analogizes the production of human beings to the assembly-line creation of consumer goods, rendering consumers as no more unique than that which they consume. Combining the naturalistic characteristics of violence and primitivism, scenes of childbirth render in graphic terms the struggles of the individual against an indifferent nature, a struggle no less significant because it is waged within the four walls of a house rather than in an urban streetscape or on a Yukon trail.

WOMEN AS NATURALIST WRITERS

The question, then, is not so much whether women writers wrote in a naturalistic tradition; ample evidence from the texts of novels by Wharton, Chopin, Petry, Glasgow, and Cather, among others, and numerous critical studies suggest that they did. Instead, we need to ask what is gained by considering naturalism as a tradition within which women writers should be situated, not only as individual writers in a group of six or seven male writers, the current methodology in most scholarly monographs, but as integral figures with distinctive contributions to make. Two possibilities suggestive of further directions for research may help to address this question. First, considering women writers of naturalism as a group, separately or with male naturalists, allows the discussion of parallels among their works and helps to determine the ways in which they were using naturalistic techniques. It challenges the categories to which they have been assigned— women writers, regionalists, novelists of manners—and asks other questions about naturalism as well. For example, one feature of classic naturalism is its use of lower-class protagonists, which would seem to exclude Edith Wharton, yet Norris's *The Pit* (1903) deals with a similar social world. In the same manner, naturalism is supposed to lack overt moralizing or sentimentality, yet Dreiser's *Jennie Gerhardt* (1911) and *Sister Carrie* feature philosophical passages laced with both. If these variations from the hypothetical rules of classic naturalism are permissible in texts by male naturalists, the same latitude can govern the treatment of work by women writers. Second, according to Donald Pizer, two common misconceptions about naturalism are that "it failed to survive its high point in the 1890s" and that it is a "young man's game" ("American Naturalism" 127, 128). Investigating the naturalistic elements in women's writing helps to reveal the ways in which naturalistic elements continued throughout the twentieth century and in the fiction of those who were neither young nor men, such as in women's regionalist farm novels of the 1910s and 1920s, the urban fiction of Alice Dunbar-Nelson's *The Annals of 'Steenth Street* stories and Ann Petry's *The Street*, and even the stylistically modernist but conceptually naturalistic novels of Evelyn Scott and Nella Larsen. Canons built on exclusion rather than inclusion become static as they fall prey to the kinds of narrow misconceptions that Pizer describes. Treating women writers as part of an integrative canon of naturalism, on the other hand, promises to yield not only new information on women writers but fresh ways of approaching the classic works that have defined the movement for generations of readers.

NOTES

1. For an account of Chopin's quarrel with Darwin, see Bender.

2. See Pizer, "Note"; and Margraf.

3. Several critics have argued that *The Awakening* is naturalistic, among them Per Seyersted, Nancy Walker, Peggy Skaggs, Bert Bender, Donald Pizer ("Note"), Erik Margraf, and Jean Witherow. Bender focuses on the novel's echoes of Darwin whereas Pizer and Seyersted emphasize the elements of biological determinism in Edna's position as mother; Walker finds the novel's naturalism incompatible with its feminism, but Margraf argues for "naturalism as feminism" (93). Pizer reads Edna's recognition that she cannot overcome the processes of the natural world as proof of the novel's naturalism, and Fleissner reads the characters' repetitive actions within the novel as a set of natural rhythms that Edna tries to, but ultimately cannot, resist.

4. "A Moment's Ornament" was one of Wharton's projected titles for *The House of Mirth*.

5. In analyzing Glasgow's complex scheme of heredity in the novel, Julius Rowan Raper describes Akershem as morally deficient, which causes his "reversion in crisis" (81).

6. Although Donald Pizer notes that Cather is seldom considered as a naturalist author (*American Naturalism and the Jews* x), Pizer, Rossetti, Lawlor, Lehan, and Ahearn are among those listing Cather with the naturalists.

7. For discussion of this issue specifically, see Campbell.

8. See Howard, Gandal, and Seltzer on the female body as spectacle.

9. Deborah McDowell makes the case for reading Irene's response to Clare's passing as same-sex desire in her introduction to *Quicksand and Passing*.

10. See Giles's analysis of the "fat man" figure.

11. Clare Virginia Eby reads *The Street* as a critique of naturalism.

12. See William Scott for a discussion of Lutie Johnson's sense of agency within her environment.

13. As Janet Galligiani Casey explains, the chapter was cut before publication. See Casey's introduction to *Weeds*.

WORKS CITED

Ahearn, Amy. "Full-Blooded Writing and Journalistic Fictions: Naturalism, the Female Artist and Willa Cather's the *Song of the Lark*." *American Literary Realism* 33 (2001): 143–56.

Bender, Bert. *The Descent of Love: Darwin and the Theory of Sexual Selection in American Fiction, 1871–1926*. Philadelphia: University of Pennsylvania Press, 1996.

Bentley, Nancy. "'Hunting for the Real': Wharton and the Science of Manners." *The Cambridge Companion to Edith Wharton*. Ed. Millicent Bell. New York: Cambridge University Press, 1995. 47–67.

Brown, Bill. *A Sense of Things: The Object Matter of American Literature*. Chicago: University of Chicago Press, 2003.

Campbell, Donna. "'Where Are the Ladies?' Wharton, Glasgow, and American Women Naturalists." *Studies in American Naturalism* 1 (2006): 152–69.

Cather, Willa. *A Lost Lady. Willa Cather: Later Novels.* Ed. Sharon O'Brien. New York: Library of America, 1990. 1–98.

———. *O Pioneers! Willa Cather: Early Novels and Stories.* Ed. Sharon O'Brien. New York: Library of America, 1987. 133–290.

Chopin, Kate. *At Fault.* 1890. Chopin, *Complete Works* 741–880.

———. *The Awakening.* 1899. Chopin, *Complete Works* 881–1000.

———. *The Complete Works of Kate Chopin.* Ed. Per Seyersted. Baton Rouge: Louisiana State University Press, 1997.

———. "Confidences." 1896. Chopin, *Complete Works* 700–2.

———. "Emile Zola's 'Lourdes.'" 1894. Chopin, *Complete Works* 697–99.

Crane, Stephen. *Maggie: A Girl of the Streets. Stephen Crane: Prose and Poetry.* Ed. J.C. Levenson. New York: Library of America, 1984. 1–78.

Dimock, Wai Chee. "Debasing Exchange: Edith Wharton's *The House of Mirth.*" *The House of Mirth: Case Studies in Contemporary Criticism* Ed. Shari Benstock. New York: St. Martin's, 1993. 375–90.

Dreiser, Theodore. *Sister Carrie.* Ed. Donald Pizer. 2nd ed. New York: Norton, 1991.

Dudley, John. *A Man's Game: Masculinity and the Anti-Aesthetics of American Literary Naturalism.* Tuscaloosa: University of Alabama Press, 2004.

Eby, Clare Virginia. "Beyond Protest: *The Street* as Humanitarian Narrative." *MELUS* 33 (2008): 33–53.

Elbert, Monika M. "The Displacement of Desire: Consumerism and Fetishism in Mary Wilkins Freeman's Fiction." *Legacy* 19 (2002): 192–215.

Fleissner, Jennifer L. *Women, Compulsion, Modernity: The Moment of American Naturalism.* Chicago: University of Chicago Press, 2004.

Fluck, Winfried. "Kate Chopin's *At Fault*: The Usefulness of Louisiana French for the Imagination." *Creoles and Cajuns: French Louisiana-La Louisiane Française.* Ed. Wolfgang Binder. Frankfurt: Peter Lang, 1998. 247–66.

Gandal, Keith. *The Virtues of the Vicious: Jacob Riis, Stephen Crane, and the Spectacle of the Slum.* Oxford: Oxford University Press, 1997.

Garland-Thomson, Rosemarie. "Extraordinary Bodies: Figuring Physical Disability in American Culture and Literature." *Kaleidoscope: Exploring the Experience of Disability through Literature and the Fine Arts* 42 (2000): 18–26.

Giles, James Richard. *The Naturalistic Inner-City Novel in America: Encounters with the Fat Man.* Columbia: University of South Carolina Press, 1995.

Glasgow, Ellen. *Barren Ground.* 1925. New York: Hill and Wang, 1957.

———. *The Descendant.* New York: Harper and Brothers, 1897.

———. *The Woman Within.* 1954. New York: Hill and Wang, 1980.

Glazener, Nancy. *Reading for Realism: The History of a U.S. Literary Institution, 1850–1910.* Durham: Duke University Press, 1997.

Goodling, Sara Britton. "The Silent Partnership: Naturalism and Sentimentalism in the Novels of Rebecca Harding Davis and Elizabeth Stuart Phelps." Papke 1–22.

Gruber, Laura Katherine. "'The Naturalistic Impulse': Limitations of Gender and Landscape in Mary Hallock Foote's Idaho Stories." *Western American Literature* 38 (2004): 353–73.

Harris, Sharon. *Rebecca Harding Davis and American Realism.* Philadelphia: University of Pennsylvania Press, 1991.

Hochman, Barbara. "Highbrow/Lowbrow: Naturalist Writers and the 'Reading Habit.'" Papke 217–36.

Howard, June. *Form and History in American Literary Naturalism.* Chapel Hill: University of North Carolina Press, 1985.

Kassanoff, Jennie Ann. *Edith Wharton and the Politics of Race*. New York: Cambridge University Press, 2004.

Kelley, Edith Summers. *Weeds*. Ed. and intro. Janet Galligiani Casey. New York: Feminist Press, 1996.

Kennedy, Tanya Ann. "The Secret Properties of Southern Regionalism: Gender and Agrarianism in Glasgow's *Barren Ground*." *Southern Literary Journal* 38 (2006): 40–63.

Lawlor, Mary. *Recalling the Wild: Naturalism and the Closing of the American West*. New Brunswick: Rutgers University Press, 2000.

Larsen, Nella. *Quicksand and Passing*. Ed. and intro. Deborah McDowell. New Brunswick: Rutgers University Press, 1986.

Lehan, Richard. *Realism and Naturalism: The Novel in an Age of Transition*. Madison: University of Wisconsin Press, 2005.

Link, Eric Carl. *The Vast and Terrible Drama: American Literary Naturalism in the Late Nineteenth Century*. Tuscaloosa: University of Alabama Press, 2004.

Margraf, Erik. "Kate Chopin's *The Awakening* as a Naturalistic Novel." *American Literary Realism* 37 (2005): 93–116.

Michaels, Walter Benn. *The Gold Standard and the Logic of Naturalism: American Literature at the Turn of the Century*. Berkeley and Los Angeles: University of California Press, 1987.

Nolan, Elizabeth. " *The Awakening* as Literary Innovation: Chopin, Maupassant, and the Evolution of Genre." *The Cambridge Companion to Kate Chopin*. Ed. Janet Beer. Cambridge, U.K.: Cambridge University Press, 2008. 118–31.

Norris, Frank. *The Octopus. Novels and Essays*. Ed. Donald Pizer. New York: Library of America, 1986. 573–1098.

Papke, Mary E., ed. *Twisted from the Ordinary: Essays on American Literary Naturalism*. Knoxville: University of Tennessee Press, 2003.

Peattie, Elia. "After the Storm: A Story of the Prairie." *Atlantic Monthly* Sept. 1897: 393–405.

Pizer, Donald. *American Naturalism and the Jews: Garland, Norris, Dreiser, Wharton, and Cather*. Urbana: University of Illinois Press, 2008.

——. "American Naturalism in Its 'Perfected' State: *The Age of Innocence* and *An American Tragedy*." *Edith Wharton: New Critical Essays*. Ed. Alfred Bendixen and Annette Zilversmit. New York: Garland, 1992. 127–41.

——. "Late Nineteenth-Century American Literary Naturalism: A Re-Introduction." *American Literary Realism* 38 (2006): 189–202.

——. "A Note on Kate Chopin's *The Awakening* as Naturalistic Fiction." *Southern Literary Journal* 33.2 (2001): 5–13.

Raine, Anne. "'The Man at the Sources': Gender, Capital, and the Conservationist Landscape in Mary Austin's *The Ford*." *Exploring Lost Borders: Critical Essays on Mary Austin*. Ed. Melody Graulich and Elizabeth Klimasmith. Reno: University of Nevada Press, 1999. 243–66.

Raper, Julius Rowan. *Without Shelter: the Early Career of Ellen Glasgow*. Baton Rouge: Louisiana State University Press, 1971.

Rossetti, Gina M. *Imagining the Primitive in Naturalist and Modernist Literature*. Columbia: University of Missouri Press, 2006.

Sawaya, Francesca. *Modern Women, Modern Work: Domesticity, Professionalism, and American Writing, 1890–1950*. Philadelphia: University of Pennsylvania Press, 2004.

Scott, Evelyn. *The Narrow House*. 1921. New York: Shoreline, 1986.

Scott, William. "Material Resistance and the Agency of the Body in Ann Petry's *The Street*." *American Literature* 78 (2006): 89–116.

Seltzer, Mark. *Bodies and Machines*. New York: Routledge, 1992.

Seyersted, Per. Kate Chopin. *A Critical Biography*. Baton Rouge: Louisiana State University Press, 1969.

Skaggs, Peggy. *Kate Chopin*. Boston: Twayne, 1985.

Toth, Emily. *Unveiling Kate Chopin*. Jackson: University Press of Mississippi, 1999.

Walker, Nancy. "Women Writers and Literary Naturalism: The Case of Ellen Glasgow." *American Literary Realism* 18 (1985): 133–46.

Wharton, Edith. *The Age of Innocence*. 1920. Ed. Candace Waid. New York: Norton, 2003.

———. *A Backward Glance*. 1934. *Novellas* 771–1068.

———. *Ethan Frome*. 1911. *Novellas* 61–156.

———. *The House of Mirth*. New York, Scribner, 1905.

———. *Novellas and Other Writings*. Ed. Cynthia Griffin Wolff. New York: Library of America, 1990.

Witherow, Jean. "Flaubert's Vision and Chopin's Naturalistic Revision: A Comparison of *Madame Bovary* and *The Awakening*." *Southern Studies* 8.1–2 (1997): 27–36.

Witschi, Nicolas S. *Traces of Gold: California's Natural Resources and the Claim to Realism in Western American Literature*. Tuscaloosa: University of Alabama Press, 2002.

CHAPTER 14

....

AMERICAN LITERARY NATURALISM AND SEXUALITY

....

LINDA KORNASKY

By the close of the 1890s, American literary naturalism had established itself decisively as the first American genre committed to the direct representation of heterosexuality and its discontents, or, in Kate Chopin's phrasing, "the disturbing fruit of the tree of knowledge" ("Western" 691). Defying conventions governing the depiction of sexuality in public discourse, naturalist writers emphasized the power of sexual desire to shape human experience. In their fiction, sexuality becomes, as Donald Pizer posits, "the great theme of modern art—the dynamic center of man's tragic nature as well as the subterranean living stream of his daily life" (Introduction 6). The initial group of 1890s naturalist writers—Charlotte Perkins Gilman, Stephen Crane, Harold Frederic, Ellen Glasgow, Frank Norris, Edith Wharton, and Kate Chopin—were joined in the first third of the twentieth century by Theodore Dreiser, Jack London, Evelyn Scott, Nella Larsen, Edith Summers Kelley, Dorothy Scarborough, James T. Farrell, Marjorie Kinnan Rawlings, Richard Wright, and Ann Petry, all of whom would contribute one or more sexually oriented novels to a growing American naturalist tradition. Collectively rejecting the religiously oriented sexual guilt and repression employed by dominant social conservatives of the era as well as the gratuitous sexual titillation employed by 1890s decadent fiction writers, the naturalists committed themselves to the shared project of depicting the vagaries of heterosexual behavior and psychology, both reproductive and non-reproductive.

The complexity of naturalism's engagement with sexual issues during the late nineteenth and early twentieth-century period derives from the heated debate over the social meanings of sexuality between feminist and masculinist factions taking place then in the American progressive movement. Entering this polemical fray, naturalist writers produced works of fiction emphatically inflected toward either masculinist *or* feminist sexual politics and thereby created a genre divided along its authors' gender lines.

In late nineteenth-century America, public debate about heterosexuality hinged on claims to authority by two conflicting arbiters—Judeo-Christian religious doctrine and empirical science. Along with a substantial faction of like-minded intellectuals in the social and biological sciences, naturalist writers collectively advocated for science rather than religion as the primary authority in this debate and objected to the repressive attitude toward sexuality of conventional Judeo-Christianity. For instance, Chopin argues in an 1894 review essay of Hamlin Garland's *Crumbling Idols* that literature should focus on organic, specifically heterosexual, "human impulses" that "do not change and can not so long as men and women continue to stand in the relation to one another which they have occupied since our knowledge of their existence began" ("Crumbling" 693), countering Garland's de-emphasis of sexuality as a subject for fiction. She claims authority over sexuality for science, positing a secularized revision of Edenic origin to refute religion's authority to assign sexual guilt via the punitive myth of the Fall and humankind's expulsion from a paradisiacal nature.

Dreiser makes much the same point in his 1903 essay, "True Art Speaks Plainly," in which he claims ethical authority for fiction that empirically seeks "to express . . . what we see honestly and without subterfuge" and to reveal "the wretched results of modern social conditions" (155). According to Dreiser, ignorance about sexuality— an ignorance promoted by people who either are indifferent to or benefit from sexual forms of "social injustice," notwithstanding their professed solicitude for "the mental virtue of the reader" (156)—causes avoidable human suffering.[1] In these critical essays and in their fiction, Chopin and Dreiser thus critique the sexually repressive rhetoric popular in late nineteenth-century journalism written by right-wing Christian conservatives, suggesting, along with other naturalists, that seemingly prohibitive or puritanical conservative sexual discourse had produced, as Michel Foucault has characterized the nineteenth-century middle class, "a society of blatant and fragmented sexual perversion" (47).[2]

Much of this conservative rhetoric was associated with the anti-science spiritualism of the New Thought Movement and some followed the pseudo-scientism of popular "social Darwinism," embracing its expedient use of evolutionary thought to justify traditional Judeo-Christian class, race, and gender hierarchies.[3] Aligned with right-wing conservatives were moderate conservatives, who advocated a more tolerant approach to indirect depictions of sexual subject matter but drew the line at frank depictions of heterosexuality and entirely excluded both homosexuality and bisexuality from fictional representation. Both moderate and right-wing sexual conservatives linked social evolution—embodied for them primarily in white, Anglo-Saxon, Protestant culture—to a future reduction of humankind's allegedly excessive sexual activity and other sexual pathologies. Alongside a large group of newspaper journalists, the moderates included many of the popular fiction and nonfiction writers in the Social Purity Movement, such as renowned feminist health reformer, novelist, and Social Purity advocate Alice Stockham, M.D., and literary realists William Dean Howells and Garland. The sunny-minded literary moderates in this faction conjectured that the objectivity of realism necessitates a diminishment of sexual subject matter to match the allegedly de-emphasized place in Anglo-American high- and middle-brow culture that sexuality occupied.

Opposing the conservatives were the progressive proponents of what one might call sex-centrism, a pervasive, radically reformist movement that spanned across late nineteenth-century American culture. Sex-centric intellectuals and artists, including naturalist writers, believed, as Dreiser articulates, that sexual desire constitutes "an all but dominant force in life," propelling "the seeker in every field of endeavor" ("Neurotic America" 132, 134), but when unwisely repressed becoming a source of harm. At first glance, it seems logical to categorize this literary sex-centric camp as liberal feminist, as opposed to the patriarchal conservatism of the opposing camp, but though the feminist designation would fit the above-mentioned women naturalists, it would be problematic in reference to Norris, Crane, Dreiser, and London, all of whom tended to maintain a liberal, yet masculinist, line of thinking about heterosexuality.[4]

This gendered, political division in late nineteenth-century American sex-centric thought is pervasive, originating and proliferating outside of the literary world but becoming particularly marked in 1890s and later naturalist fiction.[5] While these gendered approaches share a liberal, reformist commitment to de-stigmatizing a range of sexual attitudes and behaviors and to approaching sexuality empirically rather than religiously, they differ markedly on the question of whether heterosexual women are, by nature, passive in the process of sexual selection or are, by nature, mutually proactive with men in this process. Feminist sex-centrists argue for the naturalness of female and male mutual proactivity in sexual selection, its social benefits, and the need for social reforms to be implemented that would allow women to follow sexual inclinations freely. In contrast, masculinist sex-centrists argue for the naturalness of exclusively male sexual proactivity in sexual selection and thus accept conventional sexual double standards within traditional social conventions, though they, like feminist sex-centrists, disagree whether a virtuous and healthy woman is—and should be—sexually passionless. Masculinist sex-centrists instead hold that a woman is—and should be—sexually responsive when a suitable male partner selects her as a lover and initiates feminine sexual desire, that is, the desire to be seduced. Memorable examples of female characters who demonstrate this conception of sexual desire in masculinist naturalist novels are Norris's Turner Ravis in *Vandover and the Brute* (1914), Frederic's Alice Ware in *The Damnation of Theron Ware* (1896), and Dreiser's Aileen Cowperwood in *The Financier* (1912).

The most vocal of the feminist sex-centrists was Charlotte Perkins Gilman, who authored optimistic sociological nonfiction texts, including *Women and Economics: A Study of the Economic Relation between Men and Women as a Factor in Social*

Evolution (1898), *The Home: Its Work and Influence* (1903), and *The Man-Made World or, Our Androcentric Culture* (1909), that predict a social utopia arising out of evolutionary forces that will strongly favor women's sexual autonomy and proactivity. She fictionalizes this vision in her evolutionarily utopian novel *Herland* (1915). However, today Gilman is better known for her pessimistic naturalist story "The Yellow Wall-Paper" (1892), which implicitly challenges the optimistic perspective of her social reform writings. This autobiographical story of an intellectual young mother's descent into insanity (via postpartum depression) raises troubling questions about the inevitability of evolutionary advantage going to sexually autonomous, independent-minded women, considering how men, represented by the narrator's husband, manipulate women by drawing upon the behavioral adaptability of human beings. Gilman's dark story suggests that a social environment that punishes the very traits that evolution would favor if they were free to develop will ironically cause some of the most competent and promising women to destroy themselves, rather than, as Gilman conversely contends in her optimist writings, bringing about an inevitable, progressive revolution in gender roles for succeeding generations of increasingly more intelligent and physically vigorous women.

Gilman has ample company in both her optimistic efforts to reconceive female sexual identity as proactive and autonomous in sexual selection, and her darker thinking about the ways that female instincts toward sexual autonomy are destructively subverted by conservative sexual ideology. Paving the way in the feminist faction of sex-centrism's proponents for Gilman are many less well-known writers and social scientists who advocate reforms of the conventionally non-agentic roles of daughter, wife, and mother during the second half of the nineteenth century. They include free-love proponent Mary Gove Nichols, anti-marriage activist and first woman presidential candidate Victoria Woodhull, novelist and pacifist Lois Waisbrooker, and reformer and sociologist Lester F. Ward (the dedicatee of Gilman's *The Man-Made World or, Our Androcentric Culture*), as well as many others.[6]

The most vocal of the masculinist sex-centrists in the social scientific community was Havelock Ellis, a British physician and self-styled "sexologist," whose copious volumes, including the six-volume *Studies in the Psychology of Sex*, were widely read in America and elsewhere. Ellis posits that women's sexual drive is "less energetic in its manifestations" than men's: "In men the sexual instinct is a restless source of energy which overflows into all sorts of channels" (*Man and Woman* 441). While in men this sexual drive arises spontaneously, Ellis argues, "[i]n a very large number of women the sexual impulse remains latent until aroused by a lover's caresses. The youth spontaneously becomes a man; but the maiden—as it has been said—'must be kissed into a woman'" (*Studies* 187). For Ellis, the female passive sexual role (an allegedly instinctive performance of passivity which, he insists, is indispensable yet superficial) does not, however, indicate that sexual experience is not as psychobiologically necessary or physically pleasurable to a woman as it is to a man. He maintains, nevertheless, the conventional idea that a woman's sexual fulfillment depends entirely on her male partner's sexual proactivity and skills, as well as on her passive receptiveness to his sexual advances.

Like his counterpart Gilman, Ellis is not alone in promoting his faction's position. Speaking for the masculinist sex-centric position with Ellis are geologist and natural historian Joseph LeConte (whose writings on evolution in general as well as on sexual selection influenced his student Frank Norris); psychologist G. Stanley Hall; lawyer and public intellectual Clarence Darrow; prose writer, poet, and critic James Lane Allen; economist and sociologist William Graham Sumner; and the canonical, male naturalist fiction writers of the genre's early phase.[7] All of these thinkers build their ideas about sexual selection, of course, on Darwin's conclusion about male sexual agency in *The Descent of Man and Selection in Relation to Sex*:

> Man is more powerful in body and mind than woman, and in the savage state he keeps her in a far more abject state of bondage than does the male of any other animal; therefore it is not surprising that he should have gained the power of selection. . . . As women have long been selected for beauty, it is not surprising that some of their successive variations should have been transmitted exclusively to the same sex. (584)

Following Darwin, masculinist naturalist fiction thus depicts an active male/passive female opposition, as Mark Seltzer and John Dudley have argued. Male naturalists employ this sexual metaphor in non-sexual contexts, displaying a generally dominant and aggressive stance toward a conventionally "feminized Nature" (Dudley 71) and advocating its supposedly civilizing control by (upper-class Anglo-Saxon) masculinity. Feminist naturalism, in contrast, as Jennifer Fleissner argues, challenges this opposition, emphasizing actual reproduction, depicted as a natural process that shapes human understanding of nature in the abstract, rather than converting reproduction into political figurative language. A long-standing touchstone for feminist activism and philosophy, reproduction constitutes, as Fleissner argues, one of the central "living concerns" for women that, feminism contends, are "adduced but not exhausted when they are examined within this particular [late-nineteenth-century] historical frame" (100).

Naturalist women writers therefore focus their narratives on the conception, bearing, and rearing of children and the institutions of marriage and the family that motivate and shape this behavior. These feminist naturalists contrast markedly with their masculinist peers, who are more focused on heterosexually coupled characters who are childless by chance, or because of implied physical defects, or become childless via infant mortality caused by environmental conditions or congenital disease. Most of the women writers of naturalism instead explore conflicts that arise in the reproductive mating system that biologists call social monogamy, the operative human mating system. Social monogamy involves long-term pair bonding that provides beneficial stability in the conception and the care of young offspring but also often includes "extra-pair" reproductive mating behavior, which is evolutionarily advantageous for both men and women in creating genetic diversity that increases the survival chances of offspring. Late nineteenth-century social and religious conventions stigmatize this sexual instinct, inflicting such severe punishments on female transgressors that they may be physically or psychologically destroyed as a result.

The plots of novels by feminist naturalists often constitute revisionist variations on the marital infidelity plot of Gustave Flaubert's *Madame Bovary*. These include, of course, Chopin's *The Awakening* (1899), as well as Wharton's *The House of Mirth* (1905) and *The Custom of the Country* (1913), Kelley's *Weeds* (1923), Scarborough's *The Wind* (1925), Glasgow's *The Sheltered Life* (1932; in the subplot of the elderly General Archibald's remembered young manhood), and Rawlings's *South Moon Under* (1933). These novels' sexually unfaithful female protagonists are ultimately punished with literal and/or emotional death(s), including even Wharton's superficially triumphant social-climber Undine Spragg, who in the end shifts from keeping an emotional distance from the expedient of her own sexual exploitation in her climb up the social ladder to perversely enjoying the spectacle of her own sexual objectification. The case of Kezzie, the female protagonist of *South Moon Under*, differs from the other protagonists as well, since her would-be lover, Lant, kills her husband, Cleve, partially in self-defense, thus making their sexual relationship viable. But after the killing, Kezzie, with her two young sons, must live with Lant as fugitives in the dangerous panther- and rattlesnake-infested Big Scrub wilderness of central Florida because the sexual factor in their case would prevent Lant from receiving a fair trial for the killing of Cleve. The other female protagonists—Edna in *The Awakening*, Lettie in *The Wind*, Judy in *Weeds*, and the unnamed married lover (like Chopin's Edna and Rawlings's Kezzie, a mother with two young sons) of General Archibald in *The Sheltered Life*—all turn to suicide as a way out of the untenable conditions caused by sexual infidelities.

Further, in each of the above protagonists' cases, children and reproduction poignantly complicate the issue of women's entrapment within marital sexual relationships. In *The Awakening*, for instance, the children Etienne and Raoul alternately represent to Edna "antagonists" (999) and the only people in her life with a legitimate claim to limit her personal and sexual autonomy. Because such a separation from her husband Léonce would mean, according to latenineteenth-century divorce law, severing her maternal relationship with her sons, Edna becomes conflicted over her desire for a long-term sexual relationship with Robert Lebrun. She sublimates the psychological intensity of her dilemma by sending her sons to visit indefinitely with their grandmother in the country, but in doing so, her sanity disintegrates to the point that she believes suicide constitutes a third choice free of the painful sacrifice of self-determination inherent to the first choice—staying in her marriage—or the guilt following on the second choice—beginning a relationship with Robert without her sons. The irony is that suicide offers only a delusion of self-determination, because she destroys the physical body and mind fundamental to human identity, and a delusion of sparing her children from emotional pain, because her death will not only cruelly deprive them of her presence but will also present to them an image of their mother as impulsive and foolish, a false image confirming their father's unjust estimation of her. Her distress over the welfare of her children should she abandon them to begin a sexual relationship with Robert or another future lover on conventional terms is illustrated by her confused wavering between bitterness and solicitude toward her young sons in the novel's final pages.

Edna's emotions about her brief affair with Alcée Arobin figure less in her psychological breakdown, for these emotions are too muted and lacking in conventional guilt to become the deciding factor in bringing on her depression; Chopin thus rejects gendered sexual ethics that hold women to a different standard of sexual restraint. By paralleling Edna's merely sexual relationship with Alcée with Robert's merely sexual relationship with an unnamed woman in Mexico, Chopin suggests that both relationships are understandable, albeit misdirected, physical responses to Edna's and Robert's unsatisfied mutual sexual attraction.

Chopin does, however, imply that Robert's hypocritical intolerance of Edna's affair with Alcée, which he correctly intuits, would remain insurmountable and would prevent him from standing by Edna in what Adele unknowingly hints will be a struggle that hinges on Edna's children. He is not capable of imagining divorce and child-custody terms that would be based, not on the notion that Edna would be transferred from Léonce to himself as property, but on the notion that Edna is an autonomous person with a right to sexual agency and partial custody of her children. At the end of the novel, Edna realizes that Robert, the man of her choice and the only "human being whom she wanted near her" (999), is not able to flout conservative sexual conventions—he is not the possessor of the "grand espirit" (964) in regard to sexual politics that Mademoiselle Reisz cryptically recommends as worthy of a free woman's sexual commitment. Though he had seemed to be fond of the two boys during the past summer—indeed, he used his easy rapport with them to contrast himself favorably in Edna's eyes with their emotionally detached father— Robert does not, as Adele later states in her warning to Edna, "think of the children" in his naïve plan to take her as his wife, failing to mention them when he speaks of a future life with Edna.

In *Weeds*, Kelley addresses similar conflicts for another young mother who also becomes suicidal over the conflict between extramarital sexual desire and reproductive responsibilities. However, Kelley envisions an unwanted pregnancy resulting from a short-lived sexual relationship between Judy, the novel's protagonist who is a graphic artist like Edna, and a travelling evangelist, whose profession is just a front to facilitate serial seductions of unhappily married women and a pretext for ending sexual relationships, which suddenly become repulsive to his newly sensitive conscience when he tires of them. Judy attempts unsuccessfully to abort this pregnancy using dangerous folk methods and afterward terminates it inadvertently through a failed attempt at suicide by drowning. She lives only to face a death in life, initially vowing coldly to eschew all sexual activity with her husband or anyone else to avoid future pregnancies and then relenting to traditional marital sexuality and its reproductive consequences. She resigns herself to the sacrifice of art and bodily health to reproduce an indeterminate number of future children. In the end, the aesthetic deprivation, drudgery, confinement, and physical discomfort of her rural domestic life constitute a final figurative burial, particularly after the unexpected death by influenza of her only intellectual, artistic companion—an older bluegrass musician who, despite mutual erotic feelings, never became her lover because of their unfortunately wide difference in age.

Paralleling the death-in-life ending of *Weeds* is that of Nella Larsen's chilling, semi-autobiographical first novel *Quicksand* (1928) although, unlike the other feminist naturalist novels discussed above, it does not feature a marital-infidelity plot. Instead, it demonstrates the marriage of a similarly artistic young female protagonist, named Helga Crane, who, being a beautiful, racially mixed woman, becomes disillusioned with her sexual objectification by both white and black economically privileged, urban men. She impulsively marries a black Alabama evangelical preacher to live with him in rural poverty, mistakenly reasoning that the traditional Christian female gender role will offer a way out of sexual objectification and give her a permanently satisfying occupation: motherhood. Successive pregnancies undermine her weak health within a few years, and in the end, pregnant again, she seems likely to die soon in childbirth or from related complications shortly afterward.

Ann Petry, in *The Street* (1946), envisions a similar sexual/reproductive figurative suffocation of her protagonist, would-be nightclub singer Lutie Johnson, an attractive and intelligent young single mother of an eight-year-old son, but in Lutie's case, the existence of her one child, Bub, is the motivation for rejecting heterosexual relationships after her sexually unfaithful husband, Jim, abandons them. Jim's infidelity and departure occur after Lutie has taken live-in domestic work in another state, compelled by his inability to find any work that would provide enough money to feed and clothe the two-year-old Bub. Ironically, Lutie's employment includes caring for the emotionally neglected son of a rich white family, allowing his sexually dissatisfied mother time to pursue a series of extramarital sexual relationships, while Lutie's absence undermines her previously sexually satisfying marriage with Jim. When Jim leaves, Lutie gets a low-paying civil service position and moves to a cramped, filthy, and dangerous apartment in Harlem. To protect Bub, Lutie eschews all sexual desire, but several men who find her attractive nonetheless attempt to use her sense of responsibility to provide financially for her child as a means of exploiting her sexually. In the climatic final scene, she kills one of these exploiters when he tries to rape her, and she flees by train to Chicago, abandoning Bub.

In contrast, the sexual concerns in novels by male naturalist writers rarely focus on a struggle involving transgressive sexual desire and reproductive duty. Masculinist naturalism more often represents moments in courtship when male sexual importunity overcomes female reluctance. Yet masculinist naturalists simultaneously scrutinize those aspects of sexual selection embodying the ironic, deterministic paradox that sexually selective behavior—always undertaken by male characters in their works—may appear to an individual's mind to be motivated by his or her rational human will when it is actually most compelled by previously repressed sexual instinct.

Norris's *McTeague* (1899) and Crane's *Maggie: A Girl of the Streets* (1893), two model examples, represent clearly the near avoidance of reproductive issues in masculinist naturalism and its greater concern with the active male/passive female opposition of masculinist sexual ideology. Norris's narrator in *McTeague* articulates this ideology explicitly, defining it as "the changeless order of things—the man desiring the woman only for what she withholds; the woman worshipping the man for that which she yields up to him" (50). The sexual relationships of the two central couples in these novels, newlyweds Trina and McTeague and unmarried lovers Maggie and Pete, respectively, proceed similarly: pretty, very young, sexually inexperienced women meet by chance and become sexually involved with unworthy men—one being stupid, ugly, and brawny; the other sly, handsome, and pugnaciously dominant—who eventually abandon them. Neither woman conceives children. Eventually, both women are murdered as a result of the bad luck that brought these men into their lives during their early adulthood.

Trina's avoidance of pregnancy is never explained by Norris's narrator to be the result of contraception, and that prospect does not appear plausible in any case given Trina's family background and sexual innocence at the time of her marriage as well as McTeague's dim-wittedness and sexual inexperience. Yet Norris imagines many months pass in the affectionate early stage of their marriage without a resulting pregnancy. Further, when Trina's interconnected pathological miserliness and masochism sets in, she substitutes her four hundred gold coins, stolen by McTeague prior to his deserting her, for a baby, likening her now-empty chamois bag and match-box to reminders of a baby's death and weeping "over them as other women weep over a dead baby's shoe" (194). Prior to McTeague's leaving, his loss of sexual interest in her, as well as the physical stress she suffers because of physical abuse (beatings and bitten fingers), her poor diet, and incessant work making (ironically) children's toys with toxic paint might be assumed to have severely affected her fertility. Less likely to result in pregnancy, the sexual relationship of Maggie and Pete lasts for only a short time, and Crane's emphasis on Pete's considerable prior sexual experience covertly suggests that he uses contraception, which could not at the time of the novel's publication be explicitly mentioned.

Other characters in these two novels have children, such as Zerkow and Maria Macapa in *McTeague* and, in *Maggie*, Maggie's brother, Jimmie, and two unnamed lovers who "caused him considerable annoyance by breaking forth, simultaneously, at fateful intervals, into wailings about marriage and support and infants" (16). But these children and their care do not play crucial parts in these novels' plots. The unnamed, "wretched, sickly" baby born to Maria and Zerkow dies within ten days (134), becoming "a mere incident in their lives, a thing that had come undesired and had gone unregretted" (135). Norris briefly links the mixed ethnic heritage of the "strange, hybrid" baby to his or her ill health (135), but the child's main purpose is to be not merely a racist symbol but also an ironic catalyst for Maria's amnesia in regard to the story of her family's gold dishes, the precisely phrased repetition of which had become a sexual fetish for the pathologically miserly Zerkow. Maria's inability to remember her story of the lost gold dishes, and her denial of ever having told it, maddens Zerkow so much that, becoming psychotic, he eventually murders Maria and commits suicide by drowning (or drowns through an accident caused by his mental disorder). Trina's murder by the sadistic, alcoholic McTeague occurs soon after, with Maria and Trina serving as victims of a misdirected, allegedly essential female sexual instinct to submit that leads them, not to constructive reproduction, but to self-destructive masochism. This alleged female sexual passivity becomes dangerously pathological, in large part, because Maria and Trina become sexual confidants, perversely inciting masochistic sexual pleasure by recounting and comparing their husbands' violent physical abuse, finding in middle-class marriage's institutional convention of confidential sexually explicit discourse between two wives one of the "delineated areas of [perverse] sexual saturation" that Foucault has shown to have proliferated in late nineteenth-century middle-class society (46).

As *McTeague* illustrates, masculinist naturalist novels tend to be concerned with uncommon, troubling cases in which the course of sexual selection is redirected from eroticized nurturance to sexualized violence. They delve into the reasons, biological and socially constructed, for such sexual perversion, particularly focusing on the complications of alleged female sexual passivity, envisioned as biologically determined, and of instinctive male competition for sexual partners. Thus, their plots often feature triangular situations in which two men compete callously for the possession of one passive woman, such as McTeague, Marcus, and Trina in *McTeague*; Drouet, Hurstwood, and Carrie in Dreiser's *Sister Carrie*; and Van Weyden, Larsen, and Maude in London's *The Sea-Wolf* (1904). (Though not as pervasive, triangles of two women competing for one man are more typical in feminist naturalist novels, such as Wharton's *Ethan Frome* [1911] and Glasgow's *Virginia* [1913].)

Crane's *Maggie* seems to present a twist on this masculinist plot element because Maggie's desertion by Pete is caused by what seems on one level to be her failure to compete actively for Pete with Nellie, "the woman of brilliance and audacity" (43), who convinces him to disavow his relationship with Maggie. But Nellie brings about this result by dishonestly making Pete believe that he has entered into competition for her sexual affection with a young man who uses the pseudonym Freddie and is designated as "a mere boy" (43). However, Nellie does not actually desire Pete or Freddie, or any other man, as a lover, exploiting him and other men for money alone. And Maggie, in the scene of her displacement, remains passive, shocked at the adored Pete's manipulation by Nellie, but lacking any initiative to compete with her for Pete. Crane hereby imagines an ironic advantage for manipulative women of unusual attractiveness, an advantage inherent to their so-called biologically inferior position in sexual selection as passive objects of male choice and their chance development of physical beauty that men are compelled to pursue. Dreiser's Carrie, though less unethical or consciously manipulative than Nellie, has the same paradoxical power over men who admire her winsome performances as a chorus dancer and a comic actor, yet neither character is portrayed as wielding active sexual agency.

Crane's uncertain, disturbingly violent conclusion of *Maggie*, suggesting a sexual encounter by Maggie, now a prostitute, with a malevolent, drunken man and leading either to her murder by him or her suicide by drowning, exemplifies the concern with sexualized violence that characterizes masculinist 1920s–1940s naturalist fiction as well as much contemporary naturalist fiction. Further, these novels' focus on sexualized violence offers pointed critiques of the familial, psychological, and cultural influences that spur the most extreme forms of this violence. Dreiser's *American Tragedy* (1925) and Richard Wright's *Native Son* (1940), for example, illustrate the low value placed on individual women's bodies and lives as they are objectified to become expendable extensions of male identity. Moreover, James T. Farrell's *Studs Lonigan* trilogy (1932, 1934, and 1935) reveals, as does *Native Son*, how homophobia works in a variety of individual psychological and institutional forms to generate sexualized violence against women and gay men.

Contemporary naturalism retains this concern with sexualized violence, and, equally significantly, much of it until recently has continued to exhibit gendered polemical opposition in depicting female heterosexual agency. Male authors of naturalist fiction published in the past thirty to forty years, such as Cormac McCarthy (*Child of God* [1973], *Blood Meridian* [1985], and *The Road* [2006]), and William Kennedy (*An Albany Trio: Legs* [1975], *Billy Phelan's Greatest Game* [1978], and *Ironweed* [1983]), primarily follow masculinist ideology in the portrayal of female victims of sexual violence, emphasizing male characters' sexual control of women, while female writers, such as Joyce Carol Oates (in her trilogy, *A Garden of Earthly Delights* [1967], *Expensive People* [1967], and *them* [1969], as well as *You Must Remember This* [1987]) take up the feminist naturalist perspective, demonstrating destructive consequences to women characters when they attempt to exercise sexual agency and taking up reproductive issues in more direct terms.

For instance, comparing Oates's *them* and Kennedy's *Legs*, published just six years apart and both based on the lives of actual people, reveals the persistent gendered distinction among recent naturalist writers. Oates's *them*, winner of the National Book Award, devotes most of its narrative space to chronicling the sexually traumatic lives of a mother (Loretta) and daughter (Maureen). The novel begins with Loretta's first, consensual sexual experience. The incident prompts her controlling brother to shoot the young man lying with her, killing him and compelling her to allow the corrupt police officer who investigates the shooting to have sexual intercourse with her and to marry him. The middle of the novel recounts Maureen's decision to raise money from prostitution so that, ironically, she can escape from the threat of rape by her stepfather, as well as her slow recovery from her nearly fatal beating by him and its resulting coma. At the close of the novel, Maureen carries out a plan to seduce, marry, and have children with a junior college instructor, forcing him to abandon his wife and three children, not because she loves him or sexually desires him, but because she mistakenly believes he can supply permanent security and because she is instinctively motivated to compete for him against his wife. In the last chapter, seven months pregnant, she argues with her brother Jules's false masculinist prediction that, when she accepts that she is one of "them"—that is, like her sexually exploited and passive mother—men "will come back in your life . . . beat you up and force your knees apart" and that she will "really want it to happen" (507). But to protect her own instinct for sexual agency, she ironically renounces sexual desire altogether and imprisons herself sexually, metaphorically remaining in her earlier comatose state, "press[ing] her hands against her ears" in response to her brother's statement and picturing herself mentally only as an asexual expectant mother (508). Moreover, despite his masculinist rhetoric in this closing chapter, the sexually charismatic Jules, the novel's sole male protagonist, informs Maureen that he plans to marry a woman who, rather than passively accepting his sexual infidelities, attempted to kill him and nearly succeeded.

Kennedy's *Legs*, in contrast, evades reproductive sexual issues and represents female sexuality in conventionally masculinist terms. The story centers on the infamous 1920s–1930s New York gangster, Jack "Legs" Diamond and two women—his wife, Alice, and his showgirl mistress, Marion "Kiki" Roberts—whom he arranges to live with simultaneously, the two women accepting one another as friends. A consummate male gangster, Jack embodies sexual dynamism and brutal violence. As a librarian with whom Jack has a brief affair states, he "turns women into swine" (85). Yet they are drawn by apparent instinct to welcome his sexual advances, for as Kiki explains, "fucking is one thing, but fucking with Jack was another thing altogether" (150). The sexiest-man-alive and the most-fearsome-man-alive types merge in Jack's characterization.

This slippage between male sexual desire and violent aggression occurs as well in the less common, yet increasingly present, treatment of homosexuality by contemporary male naturalist writers. Both Don DeLillo (in *End Zone* [1972]) and Cormac McCarthy (particularly in *Blood Meridian* [1985] and *The Road* [2006]) deal with homoerotic violence ironically prompted by the homophobia inherent to militaristic patriarchy. DeLillo punctuates violent college football practices and games with repeated, anxious rumors that one of the players has been hiding his homosexual orientation and with sexually objectifying comments about women's genitalia. This caustic ideology is contextualized by the obsession with the consequences of prospective nuclear warfare of the narrator, Gary Harkness, a talented yet underachieving running back. More directly depicted is the exploitative, violent homosexual activity in *Blood Meridian* of McCarthy's legendarily menacing character, Judge Holden, who sodomizes and breaks the neck of a twelve-year-old boy and later sexually abuses a cognitively disabled man. Similarly graphically depicted is the sexual sadism in *The Road* of the blood cults who terrorize migrant refugees, keeping women, girls, and boys as sex slaves, during a future period of nuclear world devastation (much like that imagined by DeLillo in Gary's speculations).

Though less common, naturalist depictions of initially affirmative homoerotic emotions and/or homosexual orientation that gradually become destructively distorted by heterosexism stand out throughout naturalism's history. Chopin's *The Awakening* and Truman Capote's *In Cold Blood* (1966) are apt examples of this treatment of homoeroticism/homosexuality from, respectively, early and later naturalism. In Chopin's opening chapters, Edna and her beautiful pregnant friend Adele become homoerotically attracted to each other, and this incipient sexual emotion fires Edna's artistic creativity as she turns to her painting with more seriousness than in the past. But her inability to comprehend the depth and sensuality of her feelings for Adele also clouds her understanding of her sexual response to Robert. Capote's nonfiction naturalist novel, *In Cold Blood*, a narrative product of Capote's extensive interviews with Perry Smith, a co-perpetrator (with Richard Hickock) of a heinous quadruple murder of a Kansas family at their farm, similarly hints at homoerotic attraction between both Hickock and Smith and Capote (as narrator) and Smith. Following the lead of Chopin and Capote in employing homoeroticism and homosexual desire as aspects of naturalistic plots, future naturalist writers will have much new material to explore.

Moreover, in addition to the inclusion of previously excluded sexualities, the next stage of the history of naturalism will likely witness a more complete break from the genre's past polarized approaches in regard to its long-term principal focus on the vicissitudes of heterosexuality. In the first decade of the twenty-first century, the genre has begun to break with this polarizing tendency since masculinist sexual ideology has lost much of its popularity and credibility in the wake of Second Wave feminism and in light of research from the social and biological sciences that disprove masculinist claims about male dominance in heterosexuality.[8] For instance, while McCarthy's *Blood Meridian* has a more masculinist approach to male sexual aggression, *The Road* represents a departure from this ideology in McCarthy's emphasis on childbirth and childrearing and of the mother/wife's catastrophic dilemma. She, like Chopin's Edna and Wharton's Lily Bart in *The House of Mirth* among others in feminist naturalism, commits suicide because of an instinctive recoil, incontrovertibly valid in her horrific situation, from the consequences of masculinist sexual exploitation of vulnerable bodies, leaving "the man" (the child's father, who is also the novel's narrator) to become the traditionally maternal figure to his child. Seemingly, today's well-known evolutionary research advances in human sexuality have helped to draw the two distinct masculinist and feminist branches of the genre together in, at least, this 2006 novel.

However, while looking ahead, one should be fair to the past. Even in acknowledging the now-clear limitations of the masculinist naturalist conceptualization of sexuality, one should not forget the artistic and cultural achievement of naturalism—masculinist and feminist—in depicting heterosexuality overtly in fiction. The genre's defiance of the puritanical rebukes of social conservatives and, most significantly, their analyses of the sexually perverse results of prevailing conservative heterosexual ideology contributed to reforming sexual attitudes in America. Indeed, over the more than one-hundred-year period of naturalism's continuing presence in American fiction, naturalist writers have used their fiction to move intuitively toward new insights in their engagement with evolutionary theories of sexual selection, notwithstanding some missteps. Many decades before the recent breakthroughs of interdisciplinary theorists studying heterosexuality, naturalist writers explored this problematic topic to reach similarly complex conclusions.

NOTES

1. For a thorough discussion of this debate over the direct depiction of sexuality in American realist and naturalist fiction and the role played by the conflict between religious faith versus science in this fiction, see Pizer, "True Art Speaks Plainly."

2. A more conventional approach to sexuality in American naturalism would argue that its sexual subject matter itself constitutes an ostensibly "moralizing" type of discourse, albeit politically liberal, that in fact, as Foucault elaborates, creates the conditions that produce sexual perversion as "the real product[s] of the encroachment of a type of [social] power on bodies and their pleasures" (48). Conversely, I would argue that American naturalism is more directed at delineating and interrogating this "encroachment" than reproducing it, unlike, for example, popular late nineteenth-century decadent fiction.

3. Although Dreiser does not refer in "True Art Speaks Plainly" to "New Thought" directly, he describes social conservatives' "own little theories concerning life" as based on their complacent view that human life and sexuality consist of "a variety of interesting but immutable forms" (156), evoking popular totalizing religious and/or philosophical ideas about sexuality and spirituality emphasized by New Thought proponents. To them, as historian Beryl Satter has demonstrated, female sexuality was unselfish, temperately minimalist, and holy, while male sexuality was lustful, intemperate, and morally and racially degenerate (41–45).

4. Jennifer Fleissner has made this very argument, positing insightfully that there is an "association between feminism and a rationalized modernity" that the literary and historical period of naturalism initiates (8). As Fleissner demonstrates, mapping out feminist underpinnings of naturalism reveals the extent to which the genre has been boxed in conceptually as a one-dimensional masculinist genre by the most vocal of the early male practitioners (particularly Norris) and by its later critics. However, not surprisingly, Fleissner's analysis of male naturalists' anxious engagement with feminism and the New Woman's sexual prerogatives relies heavily on a limited selection of male-authored texts—*McTeague* and *Sister Carrie* principally.

5. American literary critics have been slow to take seriously the importance of Darwin's 1871 study of sexual selection on late nineteenth-century and early twentieth-century fiction, as Bert Bender has demonstrated in *The Descent of Love: Darwin and the Theory of Sexual Selection in American Fiction, 1871–1926* (1996). Bender has worked to remedy this critical gap, particularly in his 2004 study, *Evolution and the Sex Problem: American Narratives during the Eclipse of Darwinism*.

6. See Leach 19–37 for discussion of the ways this large and diverse group of thinkers and activists, many of them men, employed science rather than religion to redefine ideal human sexuality.

7. See LeConte 81–98; chapter 11, "The Education of Girls," in Hall; Darrow; Allen; and Sumner 342–94.

8. Since the 1970s, when the contemporary interdisciplinary field of sociobiology was established, both masculinist and feminist models of sexual selection have been forwarded, and new data have supported the feminist sex-centric position on mutual sexual selection rather than the masculinist position. For an overview of masculinist and feminist theories of sexual selection, see Zuk. And for an elegant pro-mutual-selection argument, see Miller.

WORKS CITED

Allen, James Lane. "Two Principles in Recent American Fiction." *Atlantic Monthly* Oct. 1897: 433–42.

Bender, Bert. *The Descent of Love: Darwin and the Theory of Sexual Selection in American Fiction, 1871–1926*. Philadelphia: University of Pennsylvania Press, 1996.

———. *Evolution and the "Sex Problem:" American Narratives during the Eclipse of Darwinism*. Kent, Ohio: Kent State University Press, 2004.

Capote, Truman. *In Cold Blood*. New York: Modern Library, 1966.

Chopin, Kate. *The Awakening*. Chopin, *Complete Works* 881–1002.

———. *The Complete Works of Kate Chopin*. Ed. Per Seyersted. Baton Rouge: Louisiana State University Press, 1969.

———. "'Crumbling Idols' by Hamlin Garland." Chopin, *Complete Works* 693–94.

———. "The Western Association of Writers." Chopin, *Complete Works* 691–92.

Crane, Stephen. *Maggie: A Girl of the Street*. 1893. Ed. Thomas A. Gullason. New York: Norton, 1979.

Darrow, Clarence. *Realism in Literature and Art*. Chicago: C. H. Kerr, 1899.

Darwin, Charles. *Darwin: The Origin of Species by Means of Natural Selection and The Descent of Man and Selection in Relation to Sex. 1859, 1871*. Chicago: University of Chicago Press, 1952.

DeLillo, Don. *End Zone*. 1973. New York: Penguin, 1986.

Dreiser, Theodore. "Neurotic America and the Sex Impulse." *Hey Rub-A-Dub-Dub: A Book of the Mystery and Terror and Wonder of Life*. New York: Boni & Liveright, 1920. 126–41.

———. "True Art Speaks Plainly." 1903. Ed. George J. Becker. *Documents of Modern Literary Realism*. Princeton: Princeton University Press, 1963. 155–56.

Dudley, John. *A Man's Game: Masculinity and the Anti-Aesthetics of American Literary Naturalism*. Tuscaloosa. University of Alabama Press, 2004.

Ellis, Havilock. *Man and Woman*. Boston: Houghton Mifflin, 1929.

———. *Studies in the Psychology of Sex*. Vol. 3. Philadelphia: F. A. Davis, 1927.

Fleissner, Jennifer. *Women, Compulsion, Modernity: The Moment of American Naturalism*. Chicago: University of Chicago Press, 2004.

Foucault. Michel. *The History of Sexuality. Volume I: An Introduction*. 1978. Trans. Robert Hurley. New York: Vintage, 1990.

Gilman, Charlotte Perkins. "The Yellow Wall-Paper." 1892. *The Charlotte Perkins Gilman Reader*. Ed. Ann J. Lane. New York: Pantheon, 1980. 3–20.

Glasgow, Ellen. *The Sheltered Life*. 1932. Charlottesville: University of Virginia Press, 1994.

Hall, G. Stanley. "The Education of Girls." *Youth: Its Education, Regimen, and Hygiene*. New York: D. Appleton, 1906.

Kelley, Edith Summers. *Weeds*. 1923. New York: Feminist Press, 1996.

Kennedy, William. *Legs*. New York: Coward, McCann, 1975.

Larsen, Nella. *Quicksand*. 1928. *Quicksand and Passing*. Ed. Deborah McDowell. New Brunswick: Rutgers University Press, 1986. 1–142.

Leach, William. *True Love and Perfect* Union: New York: Basic, 1980.

LeConte, Joseph. *Evolution: Its Nature, Its Evidences, and Its Relation to Religious Thought*. 1888. 2nd ed. New York: D. Appleton, 1898.

McCarthy, Cormac. *Blood Meridian, Or the Evening Redness in the West*. 1985. New York: Random, 2001.

———. *The Road*. New York: Vintage, 2006.

Miller, Geoffrey. *The Mating Mind: How Sexual Choice Shaped the Evolution of Human Nature*. New York: Anchor, 2000.

Norris, Frank. *McTeague*. 1899. Ed. Donald Pizer. 2nd ed. New York: Norton, 1997.

Oates, Joyce Carol. *them*. New York: Vanguard, 1969.

Petry, Ann. *The Street*. 1946. New York: Houghton Mifflin, 1991.

Pizer, Donald. Introduction: American Naturalism in the 1890s. *Twentieth-Century American Naturalism: An Interpretation*. Carbondale: Southern Illinois University Press, 1982. 3–10.

———. "'True Art Speaks Plainly': Theodore Dreiser and the Late Nineteenth-Century American Debate over Realism and Naturalism." *Nineteenth-Century Prose* 23 (1996): 76–89.

Rawlings, Marjorie Kinnan. *South Moon Under*. New York: Scribner, 1933.

Satter, Beryl. *Each Mind a Kingdom: American Women, Sexual Purity, and the New Thought Movement, 1875–1920*. Berkeley and Los Angeles: University of California Press, 1999.

Scarborough, Dorothy. *The Wind*. 1925. Austin: University of Texas Press, 1979.

Seltzer, Mark. *Bodies and Machines*. New York: Routledge, 1992.

Sumner, William Graham. *Folkways: A Study of Mores, Manners, Customs, and Morals*. Boston: Athenaeum, 1906.

Wharton, Edith. *The House of Mirth. 1905. Novels*. Ed. R. W. B. Lewis. New York: Library of America, 1985. 1–348.

Zuk, Marlene. *Sexual Selections: What We Can and Can't Learn about Sex from Animals*. Berkeley and Los Angeles: University of California Press, 2003.

CHAPTER 15

AFRICAN AMERICAN WRITERS AND NATURALISM

JOHN DUDLEY

FOR a number of institutional and theoretical reasons, critical work on the African American tradition has rarely intersected with that involving literary naturalism, despite the obvious connections between these fields. While critics have extended studies of literary naturalism to include African American writers, these writers are largely presented as appropriating or responding to an established literary movement rather than helping to construct the movement themselves. Conversely, extensive recent explorations of late nineteenth- and early twentieth-century African American writers who might well be classified as naturalists approach these writers and their works within a complex tradition that arises from the slave narratives of the nineteenth century and blossoms in the Harlem Renaissance of the 1920s. Although several recent studies of this period, including Eric Sundquist's *To Wake the Nations: Race in the Making of American Literature* (1993), Kenneth Warren's *Black and White Strangers: Race and American Literary Realism* (1993), Cathy Boeckmann's *A Question of Character: Scientific Racism and the Genres of American Fiction, 1892–1912* (2000), Jennifer Fleissner's *Women, Compulsion, Modernity: The Moment of American Naturalism* (2004), and Robert Dowling's *Slumming in New York: From the Waterfront to Mythic Harlem* (2007), have placed issues of race, as well as works by black authors, at the center of the discussion of realism and naturalism, there have been few attempts to define the particular characteristics of African American naturalism.

As a literary approach, naturalism attempts to represent and explore the themes, questions, and tensions associated with the explosive growth of science and social science in the late nineteenth century, as well as the limits and consequences of formal and philosophical determinism, and few writers or readers had more at stake regarding these issues than did African Americans. If naturalist fiction often chronicles the limitations and restrictions imposed on individual freedom, there can be no stronger example of the denial of free will than that imposed by the system of chattel slavery in the United States and the concurrent linkage of a slave's ontological status with legal subservience and inferiority. While the scientific discourse that gained currency during the nineteenth century, and which informed the emergence of literary naturalism, served as a powerful and oppressive tool for the perpetuation of slavery and the maintenance of racial segregation in its aftermath, this same discourse gave African American naturalists a forceful device with which to chronicle and critique the historical legacy of slavery and the effects of racism. Donald Pizer argues that naturalist writers, above all else, sought to create "a literature of the authentic" (194), a form of representation that could accurately depict and critique the inequities and shortcomings of a rapidly changing society. For African Americans, the question of authenticity is inextricably linked with the question of race and its complex straddling of the line between nature and culture. As Pizer claims, "Naturalism in its own day was often viewed as a threat to the established order because it boldly and vividly depicted the inadequacies of the industrial system which was the foundation of that order" (201), and African American naturalists took on the added responsibility of addressing the racial distinctions—legal, scientific, and otherwise—upon which the political, economic, and industrial systems affecting black Americans relied.

Beginning in the 1890s, the most prominent and influential African American intellectuals and artists, including W. E. B. Du Bois, Charles Chesnutt, Pauline Hopkins, Paul Laurence Dunbar, Sutton Griggs, and James Weldon Johnson, participated in the creation of seminal naturalist texts that responded to immanent social and political conditions and that together offer a more diverse and inclusive portrait of naturalism itself. Their commitment to documentary detail and focus on deterministic forces would be reflected most explicitly in later works by Richard Wright, James Baldwin, Ann Petry, and Chester Himes, but this interest in documentation and determinism resonates throughout the ongoing African American literary tradition. If, as Du Bois claims in *The Souls of Black Folk* (1903), "[t]he problem of the twentieth century is the problem of the color line" (3), naturalist fiction became the dominant mode through which to dissect this problem.

As is the case with literary naturalists in general, those African American writers most often connected to the naturalist tradition form, at best, a loosely-knit "school," lacking the philosophical or stylistic cohesion that defines many literary movements. Their literary naturalism is a diverse and fluid enterprise, marked by a broad concern with interrogating what is "natural" and inevitable about African American identity and experience, a problem underscored by the Jim Crow policies enacted in the wake of the 1896 Supreme Court ruling on *Plessy v. Ferguson*. In its accommodation of everything from sentimentalism to pseudo-science, African American naturalism might be understood as an unusually syncretic form, adopting and adapting a wide range of historical and aesthetic traditions.

In assessing the features of African American naturalism, therefore, it is essential to interrogate the paradigm of African American texts as primarily derivative of white prototypes. Certainly, W. E. B. Du Bois, a classically trained graduate of the American and German academic establishment, drew heavily upon the work of Émile Zola and Frank Norris in his 1911 novel *The Quest of the Silver Fleece*, but as an example of a distinctively African American literary naturalism, the book is marked by unique formal and thematic characteristics, drawing upon Du Bois's earlier work as a social scientist, his debates with Booker T. Washington over issues of citizenship and education, oral and written narratives of the agrarian South, both black and white, and the unique politics of class and skin color within the African American community. Such texts must be read as not only reflective, but constitutive, of an ongoing naturalist tradition, and, as such, works which actively incorporate African American vernacular culture, literary tropes, and aesthetic practices into the fabric of naturalist fiction.

With the diversity of these texts in mind, a rereading of the African American naturalist fiction of this period, therefore, suggests a narrative of convergence, rather than one solely of influence or appropriation. In these works, readers encounter several recurring thematic, cultural, and theoretical issues, including the connection between historical trauma and black subjectivity, the impact of a growing print culture upon the vernacular tradition, the challenges posed by urban migration and mob violence, and the overlapping discourses of eugenics and authenticity. Each of these characteristics reinforces the validity and value of naturalism as a category under which to consider these authors' works, both as unique artistic statements and as part of a complex literary movement.

The representation of the African American experience as the struggle of a solitary individual against monumental forces can be traced to the slave narrative tradition. Despite its investment in the romantic individuality representative of the New England intellectual milieu inhabited by the abolitionists who were his primary audience, Frederick Douglass's 1845 *Narrative* contains the author's unflinching characterization of his former self as something less than human: "My natural elasticity was crushed, my intellect languished, the disposition to read departed, the cheerful spark that lingered about my eye died; the dark night of slavery closed in upon me; and behold a man transformed into a brute!" (66). Such radical detachment from the self, seen as object, not subject, predicts Du Bois's celebrated identification of black subjectivity as "double-consciousness," "this sense of always looking at one's self through the eyes of others, of measuring one's soul by the tape of a world that looks on in amused contempt and pity" (*Souls* 5). Likewise, Harriet Jacobs's *Incidents in the Life of a Slave Girl* (1861) offers a similarly bifurcated depiction of the self, divided between a slave past and the narrator's liberated present. In her narrative, Jacobs confesses her relationship with "a white unmarried gentleman" who expressed sympathy for the cruelty and sexual predation of Jacobs's master: "I know I did wrong. No one can feel it more sensibly than I do. The painful and humiliating memory will haunt me to my dying day. Still, in looking back, calmly, on the events of my life, I feel that the slave woman ought not to be judged by the same standard as others" (56). While Jacobs's narrative consistently invokes the discourse of sentimentalism and domesticity, in contrast to Douglass's version of Emersonian "self-reliance," both texts establish the author's slave self as "Other"—a "painful and humiliating memory" which must nonetheless be kept alive by the narrative itself. In its central emphasis, the slave narrative—an objective record of the individual's struggle against larger historical forces—anticipates the aesthetic structure of literary naturalism.

The burden of history, as well as its connection with the female body, is powerfully represented in what is perhaps Charles Chesnutt's best-known short story, "The Wife of His Youth," which first appeared in the *Atlantic Monthly* in 1898. This overtly allegorical tale describes the ethical dilemma of Mr. Ryder, a light-skinned member of the "Blue Vein Society," whose members consisted of "individuals who were, generally speaking, more white than black" (58). Obsessed with the promise of marriage to the beautiful Molly Dixon, whose light skin and educated background will facilitate his ongoing "upward process of absorption" (60), Mr. Ryder instead finds himself confronted with an unwanted reminder of his own past when 'Liza Jane, his wife from a slave marriage, interrupts his postbellum life. With a calico dress, "bright and restless eyes," and hair like "a tuft of short gray wool, the woman is "very black,—so black that her toothless gums, revealed when she opened her mouth to speak, were not red, but blue." "She looked," Chesnutt continues, "like a bit of the old plantation life, summoned up from the past by the wave of a magician's wand" (63). In the story's climax, Ryder tells the assembled crowd at a dress ball the story of 'Liza Jane and her lost husband, and after confessing his true identity as this very husband, introduces her to the onlookers as "the wife of my youth" (70). The story conforms neatly to the conventions of literary realism at its most didactic, presenting the reader with a moral quandary, an epistemological puzzle, and a glimpse at the distinctive characteristics of a social milieu unfamiliar to the urbane, middle-class audience of the *Atlantic Monthly*. Within the confines of these realist conventions, however, Chesnutt's emphasis on physiognomy and visual markers of racial difference, as well as sexual selection, suggest the naturalistic concerns he would explore more explicitly in his later novels.

Certainly, the allegory of Mr. Ryder's choice between a light-skinned future and a darker past seems to offer an unambiguous statement regarding the obligation to acknowledge what Douglass refers to as "the dark night of slavery" despite the price to self-interest. Among the curious elements of the story, however, is the fact that Ryder and 'Liza Jane both offer no sign of recognition upon meeting. Indeed, Ryder seems unable to remember his own past: after studying a daguerreotype of his own youthful face and dismissing 'Liza Jane, Ryder looks at his image in the mirror, "gazing thoughtfully at the reflection of his own face" (66). The narrator provides no indication of the reason for Ryder's contemplation, yet the photographic representation of his former self reawakens in Ryder his sense of responsibility As Eric Sundquist notes, "'Liza Jane seems summoned up as though by conjure, a reminder of Ryder's as well as Chesnutt's obligation to confront and, as Ryder finally does, to embrace a painful past and the culture that is carried with it" (299). The story suggests that the unsophisticated, "primitive" 'Liza Jane, like Ryder's own forgotten slave name, is more authentic than the younger, more attractive, and lighter Mrs. Dixon or the new identity Ryder has created for himself. For Chesnutt, the older, darker woman's inarticulate, matronly presence and the physical fact of her blackness seem to represent the unwelcome truth about African American cultural identity. For Chesnutt and his contemporaries, African American subjectivity relies upon a painful recognition of one's self as "Other"—as the faded image in the daguerreotype—and the detachment and ironic distance provided by Chesnutt's prose reveals the consequence of this "double-consciousness" from within and without.

Of course, the painful truths about the African American experience extended beyond the abolition of slavery. Given the significance of the anti-lynching movement at the turn of the century, from the advocacy of newspapers such as the *Chicago Defender* and the *Indianapolis Freeman* to the early work of the National Association for the Advancement of Colored People (NAACP), it is hardly surprising that the historical reality of lynching figures so prominently within African American literature of this era. Moreover, the relationship between journalism and literary naturalism has been widely explored. In the late nineteenth century, as Christopher Wilson explains, "American audiences adopted the reporter not only as a social and political pathfinder but indeed as a symbol of a burgeoning cultural aesthetic" (17). While the young reporter in Theodore Dreiser's 1901 story "Nigger Jeff" vows to "get it all in" when he writes his account of a brutal lynching (165), it could hardly be said that the fictional representations of race constructed by white writers, including Dreiser, succeeded on this count. Nonetheless, in their own determination to "get it all in"—to document the violent reality behind the myth of Southern gentility and romance—African American writers turned to the unflinching journalistic methods Dreiser espouses.

The 1898 "race riot" in Wilmington, North Carolina, which provided the backdrop for Chesnutt's *The Marrow of Tradition* (1901), also inspired David Bryant Fulton's *Hanover; or, The Persecution of the Lowly: a Story of the Wilmington Massacre* (1900), and both novels graphically depict the appalling mob violence and explicitly critique the sexual politics underpinning the cultural logic of lynching. At the center of the Wilmington cataclysm, and represented in both fictional works, were the outspoken editorials of Alexander Manly, editor of the *Wilmington Daily Record*, in which Manly acknowledged both the existence of romantic relationships between black men and white women and the legacy of white male sexual violence against black women. The discursive tensions surrounding race and sexuality would serve as the focus of the most politically charged fiction and nonfiction of this period, and telling the truth about these issues would prove a costly enterprise for many writers.

Prominent among these writers, Ida B. Wells set a high standard for outspoken truth-telling in her newspaper editorials and pamphlets of the 1890s, which included *Southern Horrors: Lynch Law in All Its Phases* (1892), *A Red Record* (1895), and *Mob Rule in New Orleans* (1900). In May 1892, in a series of events that predicted the insurgency in Wilmington six years later, an anti-lynching editorial by Wells in the Memphis *Free Speech*, a weekly newspaper owned and published by Wells herself, triggered a violent uprising that included the burning and looting of the newspaper's offices. In her editorial, Wells challenges "the old threadbare lie that Negro men rape white women." "If Southern white men are not careful," Wells continues, "they will over-reach themselves and public sentiment will have a reaction; a conclusion will then be reached which will be very damaging to the moral reputation of their women" (79). Like many female members of the emerging black intelligentsia at the end of the nineteenth century, including Anna Julia Cooper, Mary Church Terrell, Frances E. W. Harper, and Pauline Hopkins, Wells walked a fine line between the domestic and public spheres, contributing to a redefinition of the role of African American womanhood and, at grave risk to her own life, expanding the limits of acceptable discourse for social critique.

In her anti-lynching pamphlets, Wells deploys frank and direct language in chronicling the abuses associated with lynch laws in the United States, and her descriptions of burning with hot irons, dismemberment, and other forms of torture remain shocking to modern readers. This steadfast commitment to full and accurate accounting of such violence is likewise reflected in fictional representations of lynching in key African American naturalist texts, including Du Bois's "Of the Coming of John" (a chapter from *The Souls of Black Folk*), Dunbar's "The Lynching of Jube Benson" (1904), and the climactic scenes in James Weldon Johnson's *The Autobiography of an Ex-Colored Man* (1912). Such depictions establish formal and thematic conventions, matching troubling themes with detailed language that documents the violence with cold precision.

If depictions of violence appear with increasing intensity within naturalistic writing, few are more striking than the lynching images in Sutton Griggs's *The Hindered Hand* (1905). In a scene that Trudier Harris aptly describes as "shockingly stomach-turning" (2), Bud Harper and his wife Foresta are lynched after killing a white man in self defense:

> The mob decided to torture their victims before killing them and began on
> Foresta first. A man with a pair of scissors stepped up and cut off her hair and
> threw it into the crowd. There was a great scramble for bits of hair for souvenirs of
> the occasion. One by one her fingers were cut off and tossed into the crowd to be
> scrambled for. A man with a cork screw came forward, ripped Foresta's clothing
> to her waist, bored into her breast with the corkscrew and pulled forth the live
> quivering flesh. Poor Bud her helpless husband closed his eyes and turned away
> his head to avoid the terrible sight. Men gathered about him and forced his
> eyelids open so that he could see all.
>   When it was thought that Foresta had been tortured sufficiently, attention
> was turned to Bud. His fingers were cut off one by one and the corkscrew was
> bored into his legs and arms. A man with a club struck him over the head,
> crushing his skull and forcing an eyeball to hang down from the socket by a
> thread. A rush was made toward Bud and a man who was a little ahead of his
> competitors snatched the eyeball as a souvenir. (133–34)

As Harris points out, the horrifyingly vivid details in Griggs's text, including the use of a corkscrew to extract "quivering flesh," closely match those from an account of a actual lynching published in a Vicksburg, Mississippi, newspaper. Moreover, these images correspond to those found in Wells's anti-lynching pamphlets, as well as in other accounts of these ritualized public spectacles. Bud's punishment includes being forced to watch the torture of Foresta, and the narrative does not allow the reader to "avoid the terrible sight." The level of violence in Griggs's writing indicates the degree to which naturalistic fiction facilitates a full accounting of the truth behind the mythology promulgated by such well-known apologists for lynching as novelist Thomas Dixon and South Carolina Senator Ben Tillman. Far from protecting the virtue of white womanhood, lynching is revealed as sadism and political terrorism that has nothing to do with a search for truth or justice. *The Hindered Hand* includes a "supplementary" chapter refuting the veracity of Dixon's *The Leopard's Spots* (1902), and in an explanatory note, Griggs claims, "We stand ready to furnish ample evidence of the absolute correctness of each and every portrayal to be found in 'The Hindered Hand'" (299). Although almost certainly not what Frank Norris had in mind when he described naturalism as "a vast and terrible drama that works itself out in unleashed passions, in blood, and in sudden death" (72), the lynching narratives of Griggs and his contemporaries pushed the boundaries of naturalistic fiction in pursuit of an explicitly political agenda, informed by the brutal honesty of the slave narrative tradition, as well as a sense of urgency about conditions in Jim Crow America.

Nowhere is the riveted gaze of the spectator more crucial to the dynamics of racial identity than in James Weldon Johnson's *The Autobiography of an Ex-Colored Man*. Johnson's novel occupies an important position, not only as a kind of rewriting of the autobiographical slave narrative, but as an early example of naturalist fiction that employs a distinctive first-person point-of-view in its exploration of the limited subjectivity of its protagonist. Johnson reveals the damaging psychological effects of racism on his mixed-race narrator, from his "dim recollection" of his early childhood to his final confession that "[s]ometimes it seems to me that I have never really been a Negro, that I have been only a privileged spectator of their inner life; at other times I feel that I have been a coward, a deserter, and I am possessed by a strange longing for my mother's people" (361). Throughout the novel, the narrator is, according to Robert Stepto, "not a guide, but a bystander—an observer in the most unambiguous sense" (116). June Howard has explored the complementary naturalistic tropes of brute and spectator, and within Johnson's novel, the narrator simultaneously occupies both positions, however precariously. In naturalism, Howard argues, "We encounter the brute in its far-flung manifestations as a creature perpetually outcast, yet perpetually to be cast out as it inevitably reappears within self and society" (95). The narrator of *The Autobiography*, confronted by the sight of a lynching while passing for white in the deep South, describes the victim as a grotesque brute: "There he stood, a man only in form and stature, every sign of degeneracy stamped upon his countenance. His eyes were dull and vacant, indicating not a single ray of thought" (351). While the narrator condemns the "brutality and savagery" of a civilization that permits lynching, his primary response, as an example of Howard's "immobilized observer" (115), is "[s]hame at being identified with a people that could with impunity be treated worse than animals" (353). These events precipitate the decision to become an "ex-colored man" and thereby renounce his racial allegiance with "his mother's people" (361). This renunciation and his subsequent success as a white businessman leave the narrator materially comfortable but spiritually empty, a soulless shell with hard-earned wisdom but no means to apply it. Christophe Den Tandt argues that "[b]y entrusting the novel's narration to a character that falls so radically in between ethnic and class lines, Johnson creates a text that switches with bewildering ease between different generic frameworks of reading" (231). As naturalism, proto-modernism, or first-person confessional, the novel serves to sum up the African American narrative tradition that preceded it and suggest the diverse directions that would follow.

Although, like many recent critics of Johnson's work, Jacqueline Goldsby avoids the generic term "naturalism," her application of Cathy Caruth's trauma theory to Johnson's work makes clear the ways in which the immanence of violence and the workings of chance conspire to limit the ex-colored man's perceptions and responses. As she notes, Johnson's own experience with a near-lynching as a young reporter in Jacksonville helped shape his comprehension of the role of experience in shaping narrative truth, and in this way, "it is the narrative form of *The Autobiography of an Ex-Colored Man* that captures Johnson's most sophisticated understanding of lynching's 'terribly real' power as both an historical act and literary trope" (168). Like Griggs in *The Hindered Hand*, Johnson forces the reader to share the trauma of witnessing the ghastly murder: "Before I could make myself believe that what I saw was really happening, I was looking at a scorched post, a moldering fire, blackened bones, charred fragments sifting down through coils of chain; and the smell of burnt flesh—human flesh—was in my nostrils" (352). The abjection of the narrator following this scene drives him to disappear just as thoroughly as the "charred fragments" that had once been a man: "I would change my name, raise a mustache, and let the world take me for what it would" (353). The narrator's unwillingness to identify with either the victim or his brutalizers leaves him with a self-negating identity: he remains an "ex-colored man." Johnson's novel reminds us of the role of systemic violence in perpetuating the radically circumscribed subject position that forms the legacy of slavery in the twentieth century, and, in the narrator's "unbearable shame" (353), it demonstrates the "double-consciousness" of simultaneously occupying the positions of spectator and brute.

Recent literary and cultural criticism has recognized the persistence of a "blues impulse" unique to African American culture. If, as Ronald Radano claims, the blues serves as a "general signifier for all African-American culture forms forged under oppression" (56), naturalist fiction likewise explores the limits of assimilation and uplift within the racial antagonisms endemic to modern American culture. The lyrical form of the blues expresses the outrage, regret, and injustice endured by African Americans, and its central concerns coincide with those explored by the literary naturalists: the impact of urbanization, poverty, and labor unrest, the violence lurking beneath an alarmingly thin social fabric, the influence of sexual drives and urges, and the uncertain boundaries between nature and culture that define human behavior.

While the blues form's influence on the poetry of Langston Hughes, Sterling Brown, and others has been long recognized, its connections to naturalist fiction are somewhat less widely acknowledged. Among the significant texts which critique what Amiri Baraka calls "the final fantasy" of middle-class assimilation for African Americans (56), Paul Laurence Dunbar's *The Sport of the Gods* (1902) illustrates the deployment of naturalist literary form in the context of a pivotal work which, according to Houston Baker, "gestures toward what I call 'a blues book most excellent'" (115). Exemplifying what Ralph Ellison describes as the "near-tragic, near-comic lyricism" of the blues, *The Sport of the Gods* offers an uncompromising critique of racial inequality, documents the perils of the black urban experience, and interrogates cultural assumptions about black identity. In the book, a loyal domestic servant, Berry Hamilton, is framed for theft, and his wife and two children flee their rural home in the South for New York City, where they each fall victim to the abundant pitfalls of the urban ghetto. Unjustly victimized by the hypocrisy of the Jim Crow South and ill-prepared for the temptations and deceptions of an apparently "free" North, the Hamiltons' collective fate provides an object lesson in the terrible inequality and injustice facing African Americans at the turn of the twentieth century.

What Baker defines as the "liminality" of the blues narrative is represented in the novel's central thematic tensions between urban and rural, North and South, free and limited, as well as the unresolved formal ambiguities in Dunbar's depiction of the ill-fated Hamilton family and their futile struggle to escape injustice and degradation. Alongside the novel's sober portrait of inequality and degradation runs a biting, darkly humorous tone, which not only parallels that of such canonical naturalist novels as Norris's *McTeague* or Crane's *Maggie*, but also corresponds to the predominant narrative strategy found in the blues lyric. In a typical blues performance, a bemused, world-weary outsider offers a sobering lesson in the hard truths of life, often delivered with acerbic wit and a distinctly unsentimental attitude. In Dunbar's novel, this blues perspective is most clearly represented by the character known as Sadness, who serves as a sort of underworld guide through Manhattan for Joe, Berry Hamilton's ill-fated son. Over drinks at the Banner Club, a "black-and-tan" saloon typical of New York's then-infamous Tenderloin neighborhood, Joe listens to Sadness tell the bitter story of his father's lynching, "done with a very good rope and by the best citizens of Texas" (385). Despite his descent into alcoholism and despair, Sadness displays a penchant for truth-telling and a hard-won cynicism which makes him, as Bernard Bell claims, "a living embodiment of the blues" (73). Sadness's biting irony, in fact, matches that of the narrator, who describes the Banner Club as "an institution for the lower education of negro youth" in which its "pupils" drank to excess and "talked of the eternal verities" (372). As Samuel Floyd suggests, "The words and music of blues songs express both the profundities and trivialities of the black experience in America" (77). Although conveying a studied detachment, these "objective" observations themselves offer a pointed critique of the social reality of Northern ghettoes in which African Americans like the Hamiltons have sought refuge.

After Sadness chronicles the misdeeds, moral lapses, and disappointments among the denizens of the Banner Club, Dunbar concludes, "There was not a lie in all that Sadness had said either as to their crime or their condition" (386). The narrative that Sadness reveals is, above all else, the truth about urban black life, and the naturalistic milieu of the novel matches both the audience and subject matter of the blues music that emerges from this period. Dunbar's aesthetic strategy mirrors that espoused in Theodore Dreiser's 1903 essay, "True Art Speaks Plainly": "It matters not how the tongues of the critics may wag, or the voices of a partially developed and highly conventionalized society may complain, the business of the author, as well as of other workers upon this earth, is to say what he knows to be true, and, having said as much, to abide the result with patience" (179). Along with other chroniclers of the city slums, including Crane, Dreiser, and Jack London, Dunbar adopts the perspective of a social scientist, albeit one whose attitude about the unsavory scene he describes is all too clear. Laced with caustic irony, moral indignation, and unflinching honesty, the novel, like Sadness himself, tells the unpleasant truths of "the great hulking, fashionably uniformed fraternity of indolence" that gathers in New York's saloons and clubs (386).

Like the increasingly "modern" blues music that emerged from the rural South, the development of literary naturalism in the United States chronicled the tensions between the rural past and the urban future. Describing the role of urbanization in the rise of naturalist fiction in the late nineteenth century, Richard Lehan claims, "Naturalism revealed the biological transformation involved in the move from country to city, away from the rhythms of the land, away from craft to factories, away from the farmhouse or the ranch and cottage to the townhouse and tenement" (22). For African Americans, however, any nostalgia for the agrarian past must be tempered with the shocking realities of segregation, lynching, and mob violence which would define the rural South following Reconstruction and which would fuel the Great Migration northward. For new arrivals in New York, like Dunbar's fictional Hamiltons, there were few good options, and their collective descent follows the pattern of the degeneration narrative so pervasive in naturalist fiction. The trope of the city as a dangerous trap plays a significant role in the moral and physiological degeneration of such protagonists as Vandover, in Norris's *Vandover and the Brute* (1914) or George Kelcey, in Crane's *George's Mother* (1896). For Dunbar, however, environmental forces dominate such factors as heritability or ethnicity. The "biological transformation" that Dunbar's characters undergo is triggered by the social realities of the modern city. As Thomas Morgan states, "Dunbar's *The Sport of the Gods* demonstrates his personal knowledge of the limited possibilities offered to African Americans in American social space" (219).

While the cities of the North promised freedom and self-determination for African Americans fleeing the poverty and racial violence of the South, they too often delivered an extension of the violence the newcomers sought to escape. In *The Sport of the Gods*, a "tragicomic vision of life" (Bell 74) allows Sadness to survive the Tenderloin, but the credulous Joe falls victim to its temptations, eventually murdering the seductive and deceitful Hattie Sterling, the woman whom he blames for his fall into vice and weakness. Hattie witnesses Joe's transformation into the very archetype of a violent and atavistic black male: "She gazed at him fascinated. She tried to scream and she could not. This was not Joe. This was not the boy that she had turned and twisted about her little finger. This was a terrible, terrible man or a monster" (412). Like Richard Wright's later depiction of Bigger Thomas, Dunbar's description of Joe's transformation into the archetypal naturalist brute serves to confirm society's worst fears about black manhood even as it critiques the circumstances that have given rise to this degeneration.

For quite different reasons, savagery and the primitive maintain a strong appeal within the white and black imaginations at the turn of the twentieth century. Despite the dangers of degeneration illustrated by Norris's *Vandover and the Brute* or Crane's *George's Mother*, for London, Theodore Roosevelt, and others, the primitive offers an ameliorative response to the perceived "over-civilization" of the middle classes. John W. Roberts, Roger Abrahams, and Lawrence Levine, among others, have chronicled the central role within African American folk expression of the "badman" or "bad nigger" figure—a sadistic outlaw whose violent rejection of laws and social norms seems largely unmotivated. This figure gains increasing prominence in the 1890s, at least partly in response to the restrictive legislation surrounding segregation and the rise of lynching. While the monstrous characteristics associated with black masculinity pose a challenge to those writers seeking to redefine African American identity during this period of intense racial division, there persists, within these texts, as within black culture at large, an attraction to the badman as a heroic counterforce to the stifling effects of white racism.

Perhaps the most striking example of badman as hero occurs with the figure of Josh Green in Charles Chesnutt's *The Marrow of Tradition*. The novel primarily focuses on the valiant, if unsuccessful, struggle of its protagonist, Dr. William Miller, to combat the campaign against "Negro domination" in "Wellington," Chesnutt's fictional version of Wilmington, North Carolina, and the gradual transformation of its white citizens into a pack of murderers. As the novel's riot gathers momentum, a small group of men including Josh Green, a physically imposing figure who displays fierce independence and a reckless disregard for the law, approach Dr. Miller, "lookin' fer a leader" (413) to help them stand up to the growing mob. While Miller urges patience and argues, "we would only be throwing our lives away" (414), Josh himself leads the men and eventually dies while in the act of killing the sadistic white leader of the crowd. To the end, Josh remains true to his claim, "I'd ruther be a dead nigger any day than a live dog" (415). Caught between the abject victim and the monstrous outlaw, Josh Green chooses the latter, in contrast to Miller's caution and equanimity.

The specter of the black man as an inhuman monster haunts the American popular imagination, and this image informs the depictions of African American masculinity during the Progressive era. To be sure, issues of racial injustice figure prominently in key works by white naturalist writers of this era. As its title suggests, Stephen Crane's "The Monster" (1899), in which a black hostler is horribly disfigured by fire while saving the life of his employer's young son, incorporates popular perceptions of racial difference into its exploration of human cruelty and ethical responsibility. Likewise, Dreiser's "Nigger Jeff" is among the rare works by white writers to confront the rise of lynching at the end of the nineteenth century. Despite portrayals of black characters that seem, to readers more than a century later, irredeemably limited to crude racial stereotypes, these stories stand in stark contrast to such immensely popular novels as Thomas Nelson Page's *Red Rock* (1898) and Thomas Dixon's Klan trilogy, *The Leopard's Spots* (1902), *The Clansman* (1905), and *The Traitor* (1907), which promote an idealized and romanticized image of the antebellum South, a paranoid revisionism regarding "Negro domination" during Reconstruction, and white supremacy as their goal for the twentieth century. Together with the racist populism of politicians like Ben Tillman and the neo-Darwinian racial doctrines that dominated scientific inquiry, Page's and Dixon's works relied upon the image of the hypersexualized, predatory black male for their emotional and ideological power.

In their naturalistic response to these popular and influential historical romances, Chesnutt's *The Marrow of Tradition*, Du Bois's *The Quest of the Silver Fleece* (1911), and the novels of Sutton Griggs and Pauline Hopkins sought to correct the record by transforming historical events into fictional epics featuring strong black male protagonists who functioned as alternatives to the "monsters" of the popular imagination. Figures such as Chesnutt's Dr. Miller, Du Bois's Bles Alwyn, Belton Piedmont, of Sutton Griggs's *Imperium in Imperio* (1899), and Will Smith, of Pauline Hopkins's *Contending Forces* (1900), epitomized the masculine ideal for Du Bois's "talented tenth": educated, dutiful, physically robust, driven by racial pride and loyalty, and willing to face death for their beliefs. The heroic status of these "race men," however, often belies their marginal status within the black community itself. Like Du Bois himself, these characters are often marked as outsiders by their skin tone, education, or geography and must prove themselves through interaction with more "authentic" counterparts.

If naturalism fundamentally concerns itself with the authentic, African American writers must contend with a particular set of questions involving authenticity. Specifically, who is black, and what is the basis for this distinction? Rather than a clear answer to these questions, however, what emerges from the literature of the early twentieth century is a notion of blackness that simultaneously, and paradoxically, relies upon tropes of performance and essence. The stylized appropriation of racist imagery, from Chesnutt's hypermasculine Josh Green to Hopkins's revisionist "tragic mulatta" Sappho Clark in *Contending Forces*, represents the interplay between ethnography and aesthetics that is both proto-modernist and fundamentally naturalist, as signaled in the early twentieth century by Lamarckian evolutionary discourse, the anthropological work of Franz Boas, and shifting definitions of "culture" itself. In exploring Dunbar's and Chesnutt's turn away from the restrictions of regionalism toward what he calls "a more unabated social realism" in the early twentieth century (213), Steven Belluscio argues that "late-nineteenth and early-twentieth-century African American literature exhibits a greater urgency to critique the premises of racialism than white ethnic literature of the same time period" (147). In considering the shift toward "culture" over "nature" in these works, however, the complex, and often paradoxical, interplay of these two forces should not be overlooked. While late nineteenth- and early twentieth-century African American writers critique the endemic racialism of their day, the category of race nonetheless functions as both a natural and cultural marker of difference within these texts. Moreover, while the pop- ular manifestations of Darwinism might seem antithetical to the social and political objectives of these writers, naturalist philosophy and evolutionary thought helped to transform both African American culture and an understanding of the ongoing resonance of literary naturalism within this tradition.

As Bert Bender has convincingly argued, African American authors in the early twentieth century looked to Darwinian ideas about sexual selection as potentially liberating in their effort to dismantle prevailing attitudes about racial inferiority. Of course, white fears about miscegenation, "race suicide," and "mongrelization," were reinforced by the neo-Darwinism of Herbert Spencer, Joseph LeConte, Ernst Haeckel, and others. Nonetheless, as Bender establishes in his reading of Chesnutt's *The House Behind the Cedars* (1900), "Realizing that his central problem would be to undercut the white supremacists' efforts to justify their cause with racial 'science,' Chesnutt was determined to defeat them on their own terms" (300). Chesnutt's willingness to address the issue is reflected in his three-part essay "The Future American," published in 1900 in the *Boston Evening Transcript*. In the essay, Ches- nutt bluntly states that "the future American ethnic type will be formed by a fusion of all the various races now peopling this continent" (131). Using the very words deployed by white supremacists—amalgamation, fusion, miscegenation—Chesnutt argues for the "absorption" of the black race into the new "ethnic type" through the selection of healthy, strong individuals of all races.

Thus, in Chesnutt's fiction, mixed-race figures such as Rena Walden in *The House Behind the Cedars* and Janet Miller in *The Marrow of Tradition*, like Hop- kins's Sappho Clark, are strong, beautiful, as well as physically and emotionally healthy—a rejoinder to the popular conception of the mulatto as genetically infe- rior. Likewise, the narrator of Johnson's *Autobiography of an Ex-Colored Man*, though tormented and deeply flawed, is introduced as an attractive and vigorous child, "a perfect little aristocrat" drawing the compliments of "a great many ladies" who would "tell my mother what a pretty boy I was" (275). Rather than a source of weakness, the mixture of races allows the narrator to pass freely between black and white society, and, as a successful businessman, to attract a beautiful white wife. As M. Giulia Fabi observes about twentieth-century rewritings of the "tragic mulatto" narrative, "[t]he trope of passing functions as an aggressive strategy to reinterpret race as a sociocultural construct, rather than a biological destiny, and to appropriate and deconstruct the oppressive, albeit elusive, notion of whiteness that served as the normative standard to identify and evaluate blackness (39).

While Johnson's novel, like Nella Larsen's later *Passing* (1929), highlights the social construction of race, the narrator's final words serve as a reminder of the role of nature. "I cannot repress the thought," he bemoans, "that, after all, I have chosen the lesser part, that I have sold my birthright for a mess of pottage" (362). Johnson associates the pursuit of wealth with the decision to pass for white, but the narrator's white father has never recognized his son's right to inherit name, property, or social status. The narrator's reference to the Biblical story of Esau refers not to a paternal birthright but to the ex-colored man's "strange longing for his mother's people" (361). The inheritance he has squandered includes his musical talent and his gift for improvisation, characteristics bestowed on him by his mother and her race.

The centrality of marriage and sexual selection within African American naturalism reinforces the importance of evolutionary science and philosophy in these works. In *Unnatural Selections: Eugenics in American Modernism and the Harlem Renaissance*, Daylanne English argues that eugenics, not race, emerges as the dominant American ideology in the early twentieth century, and that the attraction for African American intellectuals of explicitly Spencerian or Lamarckian ideas about breeding, class, and progress is reflected not only in the central texts of the 1920s Harlem Renaissance but emerges consistently in earlier works by Du Bois, Hopkins, and others, as Chesnutt's "The Future American" makes clear. Despite the prevailing racism manifested in the fashionable social Darwinism of the era, English points out that "not all eugenics sympathizers were white supremacists; nor were all white; nor did all advocate racial purity." Moreover, Hopkins's novels, English continues, "can be seen as constructing an early 'hybrid vigor' version of eugenics" (17). In her discussion of biological and cultural notions of race in Hopkins's *Hagar's Daughter* (1902), one of the novels serialized in the *Colored American*, Augusta Rohrbach notes that, for Hopkins, "one's past, as a way to confirm racial origin, cannot be dispensed with.... Yet, the present also plays an important part in assigning meaning to race. Together, as Hopkins makes palpably clear, the two determine and undermine identity" (485). The ideology of racial uplift advocated across the spectrum of African American publishing, from the popular fiction of Hopkins and Griggs to the highbrow essays of Du Bois and Johnson, incorporates this ambivalence about the extent to which nature explains racial difference.

A connection between ontology and epistemology in the construction of racial identity haunts Du Bois's work, and the utopian impulses of *The Quest of the Silver Fleece* reinforce a faith in evolutionary progress. In the novel, hope for the future resides in the eventual union of Bles and Zora, who each represent complementary elements of black culture—he, the educated member of the "talented tenth," "blessed," as his name suggests, with rhetorical and intellectual gifts; she, an earthy child of the swamp, "ethereal, splendid, like some tall, dark, and gorgeous flower of the storied East" (132). In selecting Zora over both Caroline Wynn, the light-skinned sophisticate from Washington, and "white and sandy-haired" Emma (364), Bles affirms Du Bois's agenda for racial unity and vitality. Within Zora, "[t]endencies merely had become manifest, some dominant. She would, unhindered, develop to a brilliant, sumptuous womanhood; proud, conquering, full-blooded and deep bosomed—a passionate mother of men" (104). In his 1897 essay, "The Conservation of Races," Du Bois, in stark disagreement with Chesnutt, argues firmly against "absorption by white Americans" (23), yet both Chesnutt and Du Bois deploy the discourse of sexual selection in their vision of racial justice and equality.

As in naturalist fiction in general, the utopian impulse in the work of these authors reflects both a progressive faith in humanity and the conviction that aesthetic representation can engender real change. Directly challenging the veracity of Thomas Dixon's fiction at the end of *The Hindered Hand*, Sutton Griggs claims that "[s]oberly the great world consciousness will deal with this enemy [Dixon] of the human race, and the universal finger of scorn that will surely in the end be pointed toward him will render it certain that no other like unto him shall ever rise" (332). Griggs's optimism and sense of purpose match those of Dreiser or London, and like his more widely recognized contemporaries, Griggs participated in defining literary naturalism in the United States. The variety of texts by African Americans that adopt naturalist themes, motifs, and strategies during the period often described as the nadir of American race relations demonstrates the value of a more inclusive definition of naturalism, as well as the power of literary naturalism as an experimental form that would have widespread effects throughout the subsequent century of African American literature.

WORKS CITED

Abrahams, Roger D. *Deep Down in the Jungle: Negro Narrative Folklore from the Streets of Philadelphia*. New York: Aldine de Gruyter, 1970.

Baker, Houston A., Jr. *Blues, Ideology, and Afro-American Literature: A Vernacular Theory*. Chicago: University of Chicago Press, 1984.

Baraka, Amiri. *The LeRoi Jones/Amiri Baraka Reader*. Ed. William J. Harris. New York: Thunder's Mouth, 1991.

Bell, Bernard. *The Afro-American Novel and Its Tradition*. Amherst: University of Massachusetts Press, 1987.

Belluscio, Steven J. *To Be Suddenly White: Literary Realism and Racial Passing*. Columbia: University of Missouri Press, 2006.

Bender, Bert. *The Descent of Love: Darwin and the Theory of Sexual Selection in American Fiction, 1871–1926*. Philadelphia: University of Pennsylvania Press, 1996.

Chesnutt, Charles. "The Future American." *Essays and Speeches*. Ed. Joseph R. McElrath Jr., Robert C. Leitz III, and Jesse S. Crisler. Palo Alto: Stanford University Press, 1999. 131–36.

———. *The Marrow of Tradition*. 1901. Chesnutt, *Portable* 209–448.

———. *The Portable Charles W. Chesnutt*. Ed. William L. Andrews. New York: Penguin, 2008.

———. "The Wife of His Youth." 1899. Chesnutt, *Portable* 58–70.

Den Tandt, Cristophe. *The Urban Sublime in American Literary Naturalism*. Urbana: University of Illinois Press, 1998.

Douglass, Frederick. *Narrative of the Life of Frederick Douglass, an American Slave.* Garden City, N.Y.: Doubleday, 1963.

Dreiser, Theodore. "Nigger Jeff." *The Best Short Stories of Theodore Dreiser.* 1918. New York: Fawcett, 1961. 142–65.

———. "True Art Speaks Plainly." 1903. *Documents of American Realism and Naturalism.* Ed. Donald Pizer. Carbondale: Southern Illinois University Press, 1998. 179–81.

Du Bois, W. E. B. "The Conservation of Races." 1897. *W. E. B. Du Bois: A Reader.* Ed. David Levering Lewis. New York: Henry Holt, 1995. 20–27.

———. *The Quest of the Silver Fleece.* 1911. New York: Harlem Moon, 2004.

———. *The Souls of Black Folk.* 1903. New York: Penguin, 1996.

Dunbar, Paul Laurence. *The Sport of the Gods and Other Essential Writings.* New York: Modern Library, 2005.

Ellison, Ralph. *Shadow and Act.* New York: Vintage, 1972.

English, Daylanne K. *Unnatural Selections: Eugenics in American Modernism and the Harlem Renaissance.* Chapel Hill: University of North Carolina Press, 2004.

Fabi, M. Giulia. "Reconstructing the Race: The Novel after Slavery." *The Cambridge Companion to the African American Novel.* Ed. Maryemma Graham. New York: Cambridge University Press, 2004. 34–49.

Floyd, Samuel A., Jr. *The Power of Black Music.* New York: Oxford University Press, 1995.

Goldsby, Jacqueline. *A Spectacular Secret: Lynching in American Life and Literature.* Chicago: University of Chicago Press, 2006.

Griggs, Sutton. *The Hindered Hand: or The Reign of the Repressionist.* 3rd ed. Nashville: Orion, 1905.

Harris, Trudier. *Exorcising Blackness: Historical and Literary Lynching and Burning Rituals.* Bloomington: Indiana University Press, 1984.

Howard, June. *Form and History in American Literary Naturalism.* Chapel Hill: University of North Carolina Press, 1985.

Jacobs, Harriet. (Linda Brent). *Incidents in the Life of a Slave Girl.* 1861. New York: Harcourt, Brace, Jovanovich, 1973.

Johnson, James Weldon. *The Autobiography of an Ex-Colored Man. The Selected Writings of James Weldon Johnson.* Ed. Sondra Kathryn Wilson. Vol. 2. New York: Oxford University Press, 1995. 273–362.

Levine, Lawrence W. *Black Culture and Black Consciousness: Afro-American Folk Thought from Slavery to Freedom.* New York: Oxford University Press, 1977.

Morgan, Thomas L. "The City as Refuge: Constructing Urban Blackness in Paul Laurence Dunbar's *The Sport of the Gods* and James Weldon Johnson's *The Autobiography of an Ex-Colored Man.*" *African American Review* 38 (2004): 213–37.

Pizer, Donald. "Late Nineteenth-Century American Literary Naturalism: A Re-Introduction." *American Literary Realism* 38 (2006): 189–202.

Radano, Ronald. *Lying up a Nation: Race and Black Music.* Chicago: University of Chicago Press, 2003.

Roberts, John W. *From Trickster to Badman: The Black Folk Hero in Slavery and Freedom.* Philadelphia: University of Pennsylvania Press, 1989.

Rohrbach, Augusta. "To Be Continued: Double Identity, Multiplicity and Antigenealogy as Narrative Strategies in Pauline Hopkins' Magazine Fiction." *Callaloo* 22 (1999): 483–98.

Stepto, Robert B. *From Behind the Veil: A Study of Afro-American Narrative.* 2nd ed. Urbana: University of Illinois Press, 1991.

Sundquist, Eric J. *To Wake the Nations: Race in the Making of American Literature.* Cambridge: Harvard University Press, 1993.

Warren, Kenneth W. *Black and White Strangers: Race and American Literary Realism.*
    Chicago: University of Chicago Press, 1993.
Wells, Ida B. *Southern Horrors and Other Writings: The Anti-Lynching Campaign of Ida B.
    Wells, 1892–1900.* Ed. Jacqueline Jones Royster. Boston: Bedford, 1997.
Wilson, Christopher. *The Labor of Words: Literary Professionalism in the Progressive Era.*
    Athens: University of Georgia Press, 1985.

....

CHAPTER 16

RACE AND NATURALISM IN THE SHORT FICTION OF NORRIS, CRANE, AND LONDON

....

JEANNE CAMPBELL REESMAN

AT the turn of the twentieth century, naturalism offered rich opportunities for writing about race because of its sources in biology, determinism, and Darwinism and because American readers were consumed by debates on race, immigration, nativism, imperialism, the effects of the latest economic panic, and the systemic and growing class inequalities of the era. The pseudo-scientific theories of racialism and eugenics permeated intellectual, artistic, and popular discourse, and fears of biological degeneracy dictated public policy on immigration, miscegenation, labor, and criminality. Naturalism was uniquely suited to address the racial debates of the era especially in terms of beliefs in inborn criminality. Unfortunately, instead of treating race or criminality objectively, most naturalists went along with popular beliefs in hereditary determinism that fueled both racism and racialism. However, Jack London, a white supremacist in some novels and nonfiction but the author of short fiction that powerfully attacked racism and racialism, questioned racial and cultural prejudices in a manner altogether foreign to other naturalists. Though beyond his story "Nigger Jeff" Theodore Dreiser did not seem particularly concerned with race, Frank Norris, Stephen Crane, and Jack London demonstrate in their fiction how racialism fundamentally interferes with the presumed goals of naturalism, especially if defined by Donald Pizer's widely accepted concept of "ethical" naturalism.

Pizer argues that the naturalist hero or heroine does not merely capitulate to social, economic, biological, and other naturalistic forces arrayed against him or her, but instead in the struggle against such forces evinces an admirable moral goal, and further that the struggle itself is predicated on ethical grounds. Ethics is seen by Pizer as that which opposes, if it does not overcome, naturalistic forces. He thus sees the naturalist hero or heroine as tragic, for he identifies "a compensating humanistic value . . . which affirms the significance of the individual." Although individuals may seem to be mere pawns in an amoral world, due to heredity, race, or class, "the imagination refuses to accept this formula as the total meaning of life" (11).

Some definitions are in order. The term "racialism" has a precise historical meaning that is often obscured when it is (incorrectly) used as a polite term for a person's taking note of racial differences, as one sometimes hears it from those eager to protect a favorite historical or literary figure. But Tzvetan Todorov has memorably argued that we must distinguish in the work of authors "between *racism*, which is a ubiquitous form of behavior, and *racialism*, or theories of race, whose heyday extended from the middle of the eighteenth through the middle of the twentieth centuries" (173). While "racist attitudes have always existed" in human history, "they have not always had the same amount of influence." Ironically, he notes, when societies approach democracy racism becomes "an increasingly influential social phenomenon" (172). In traditional, hierarchical societies, a common ideology makes physical differences of less importance, as "it is more important to know who are masters and who are slaves than whose skin is light and whose is dark" (172–73). But in democratic societies, although actual equality does not prevail, "the ideal of equality becomes a commonly shared value." In order to maintain power, those at the top turn to "apparently irrefutable and 'natural' physical differences." The abolition of slavery led to the rise of racialism in the United States: "we attribute to 'race' what we no longer have the right to attribute to social difference." He also reveals the surprising relationship between the development of the natural sciences and racialism: they are coevals. Documenting physical appearance and social behavior is a "typically scientific mode of reasoning, since science consists in the effort to replace chaos with order" (173). It is important to note that unlike racism, racialism has had a beginning, middle, and end, and though it was a widely respected "scientific" theory of its day, it is now utterly rejected by thinkers on the subject.

All three naturalists treat the theme of the racial "Other" as a criminal in works of short fiction. However, they adopted differing modes to convey their attitudes: Norris chose the narrative of descent; Crane, the fable; London, satire. As naturalist "muckrakers," they shared a sense of wanting to explore racism as an important social problem in their time, particularly in the aftermath of the Civil War, but if they shared similar concerns, they did not share the same goals. Norris and Crane employ stereotypes and conceal the narrator's point of view—and their own position as author—in stories that ask few questions about race or racism but instead indulge in self-questioning by the authors, framed in terms of an incongruous irony. Unlike London's, their results do not seem to clamor for social justice.

FRANK NORRIS: "A CASE FOR LOMBROSO"

Norris expressed interest throughout his career in genetic degenerates, eugenics, determinism, perverted sexuality, and racialism. In his essay "Among Cliff Dwellers" (1897), Norris describes the immigrant population of San Francisco: "The hill is swarming and boiling with the life of them. . . . A great milling is going on, and a fusing of peoples, and in a few more generations the Celt and the Italian, the Mexican and the Chinaman, the Negro and the Portuguese, and the Levantines and the 'scatter-mouches' will be merged into one type. And a curious type it will be" (264–65). According to John Dudley, "Like the aboriginal cliff-dwellers of the American West, to which Norris's title refers, these people represent an evolutionary dead end; their miscegenation is nothing less than a blueprint for extinction" (63). Criminality is thus seen by Norris as ingrained in immigrants and racial "Others." There is no sense of the crime of racism itself, and "A Case for Lombroso" (1897) closely follows the standard racialistic fears of the day. As Dudley observes, "Lombroso and his disciples believed in the identification, through empirical data, of 'born criminals' whose ancestry and physical traits foretell the proclivity toward violent or anti-social behavior," helping shape U.S. penal reform that discriminated between those deemed correctable (parole) and those deemed incorrigible (life in prison or death; 60–61).

As Stephanie Bower notes, in several stories "Norris racializes the language of disease and degeneration by locating the source of the 'decline' so characteristic of naturalism in contact between Anglo-Saxons and racial 'inferiors.'" She also notes that "[d]egeneracy, identified here with race, spreads through sexual liaisons to corrupt the manly virtues of the upper-echelon, turning well-bred gentlemen into the image of the other they both crave and despise" (43–44). "A Case for Lombroso" recounts the ill-fated attraction between Stayne, a Harvard-educated "torrowbred" [sic] whose "fine male strength and honesty and courage" represent the epitome of Anglo-Saxon manhood, and Cresencia, a woman whose beauty and intelligence is marred only by her racial heritage, the "red-hot, degenerate blood" of her Spanish ancestry (127, 129). The story was also based on a newspaper account Norris read about John M. Oakley, a millionaire who had led an upright life but who ended up drinking himself to death in the company of a prostitute at the Palace Hotel in San Francisco. Norris took this case and set out to tell a story, according to Joseph McElrath, that would show "that respectability and other appearances of civilization may prove either veneerlike or revelatory of only particular dimensions of multifaceted human nature." The story reveals "an anarchic second personality within the self conditioned to socially proper behavior—an amoral, barbaric, and perhaps bestial influence" (19–20). Norris (mis)interprets Darwinism and attributes the Anglo-Saxon protagonist's decline to be the result of "racial" mixing with a Spanish woman, even as he blames her but also warns of the criminal, atavistic self in the protagonist. Norris thus chooses to treat biological determinism and racialism as a narrative of descent, as in his later novel *McTeague* (1899), whose racial stereotypes include

Zerkow, Maria, and the Irish and Germans, and in *The Octopus* (1901), with its racial stereotypes of Mexicans. He complicates his narrative by depicting sexuality itself as a descent toward the bestial.

Quite the man-about-town, Stayne has "gone through the mill like any other city-bred man," engaging in many light-hearted flirtations; yet his dalliance with Cresencia proves dangerously beyond his ken, and he fatally underestimates the "veritable fury" of her passion (130). Soon the influence of Cresencia's "degenerate blood and jangled nerves and untamed passions" overwhelms him, and he sinks to her level, their sexual union symbolized by Aesop's fable of "two jars" that "when they . . . come together . . . break and fill and sink," the "finest clay" of Stayne's heritage and upbringing shattering upon contact with Cresencia's "coarser fiber" (130–31). All notions of honor and dignity thrown by the wayside, his name "erased from the rolls of his club," Stayne moves backward on the evolutionary ladder to become "a brute," living proof of the contagious atavism disseminated by degenerates like Cresencia (131–32). However, as we will see, Cresencia is far from being the "criminal," and Stayne goes beyond criminality to beastliness in his abuse of her. The story is further complicated by its own definitions of race: is Norris really saying that because Cresencia's Hromada bloodline is unmixed and untainted since the time of the Ostrogoths in Spain, she is degenerate? In "Cliff-Dwellers," it is miscegenation that is to be feared, not racial purity. Moreover, who says Spanish blood is another "race"? Norris's readers would likely have been more worried at the time by Mexicanness than Spanishness. The two were often conflated, but the story is so far-fetched it seems more a pathology of two persons' shared mental illness in a cycle of abuse than a serious comment on racialism. Perhaps it is a joke, an expression of Norris's sarcasm toward his characters' and readers' notions of racialism.

Racialism as a "science" made no sense at all, as is now universally accepted among scientists, and trying to force it to make sense in the story as a logical argument will not get us far. But one thing we must understand is that in the racialism of the period, a narrow definition prevailed as to exactly who was "white": in fact, for racialists before 1920 only Anglo-Saxons were truly considered white, not Germans, Italians, Jews, or Spaniards. Thus, what looks like a case of pure European blood is actually seen as inordinately dangerous to the Anglo-Saxon American. In his retelling of Aesop's fable, meant to teach a lesson, is Norris trying to warn other American men, or is he satirizing racialist beliefs? It is hard to know, but the fact that we don't know is to the detriment of the story. Is Norris advocating miscegenation or crossing diverse bloodlines to ensure adaptability, a Darwinistic model for future matings, or is he merely exposing the limitations of racialism? No matter what his intent, he shows no compassion for these characters nor a sense of why they behave as they do, beyond Cresencia's "degenerate" Spanish blood. The two characters are merely stereotypes out of melodrama. It is hard to know what Norris's readers made of the story, but perhaps the best way to read this story today is as camp—"pure" camp.

Cresensia's "race," interestingly, relates her to the artistic: she "was blessed or cursed (whichever you will) with a temperament as delicately poised and as sensitive as goldsmith's scales, nerves as tightly stretched and as responsive as the strings of a Stradivarius. The odours of certain flowers giddied her, she could see eight colours in the rainbow, a musical discord made her head ache upon the instant, and she could feel the spots on a playing card with her finger tips" (128). However, her sensitivity is tied to degeneracy instead of creativity:

> But at the end of a week Cresencia's passion for him had become a veritable fury. The red-hot, degenerate Spanish blood of her sang in her veins, and her high-strung nerves crisped and recoiled upon themselves like the ends of broken violin strings. She used to sit in her room—so a girl told me—at night, after a dance or dinner, rolling her head to and fro upon her folded arms, or biting at the bare flesh of them, in a very excess of passion. (129–30)

For her part, Cresencia mourns, "Why is it that I have got to love you whether I will or no? It isn't love—is it a disease? Is it a kind of insanity? Oh, what is it that has happened to me these last weeks?'" For his part, Stayne seems unable to resist her temperament, and furthermore her temperament calls up something of the bestial in him:

> Fancy the scene, if you can—both of them excited beyond all control, talking wildly into each other's faces, neither of them heeding what was said by the other, and all the while clasped in an embrace like that of wrestlers! There in the darkness of that drawing room, in the isolation of that country house, the two jars, floating helplessly in ungovernable currents, crashed together. That of the finest clay shivered and sank at once—the other, of coarser fibre, settled slower to its ruin. (130–31)

"The finest clay" would seem to refer to someone with an unmixed bloodline, but Norris means Stayne. So much for the sturdy Anglo Saxon.

Not only is "alien" blood dangerous, but so is sex itself. What this couple is confronting is a perverted love story comparable to McTeague and Trina's: because the depiction of sex was something so taboo at the time, what may really be going on is only a "crime" of sexual passion, with the idea that sex undoes rationality and human values; this is particularly striking in the image of Stayne and Cresencia embracing like "wrestlers." Inappropriate sexuality is shown in both but is blamed on Cresencia's "racial" origins. We are to understand that Stayne's sadism emerges because it has been "fired," so to speak, by Cresencia's Spanish blood:

> She had been degrading far more rapidly than he. Though she rolled upon her bed, hurting herself with the nails of her hands, in unspeakable humiliation, she could not let Stayne go. And this was the same girl whose pride and self-respect had hitherto been her strongest traits. She managed to see Stayne three and four times each week. She came to his office, contrived to meet him on his way to lunch, managed to be invited to the same places—even began to take strange, perverted pleasure in forcing herself upon his company and in submitting to his brutalities. (131)

The exploration of biological determinism (sex) morphs into something as pathological as sexuality in Émile Zola's *Thérèse Raquin*, Zola being Norris's naturalist hero. Stayne, like McTeague, immediately moves from sexuality to sadism:

> He suddenly discovered that nothing—literally and quite truly—nothing he could
> do would offend Cresencia. He realized that she would take anything from him—
> that she would not, or rather, that she could not, resent any insult, however gross.
> And the knowledge made the man a brute. . . . It became for him a pleasure—a
> morbid, unnatural, evil pleasure for him to hurt and humiliate her. He hurt her
> while he sickened at the thought of his own baseness, and she submitted to it
> while she loathed herself for her own degradation. They were a strange couple.
> (131–32)

Norris suggests that beneath the surface, every man wants to have complete power
over a woman, and having it brings out the atavism in men, as it does for McTeague.
This is a serious statement about the role of biological determinism in shaping
human behavior, but one also has to note the odd comic tone of the remark that
they "were a strange couple." Again, as suggested earlier, perhaps the entire story is
a sort of hoax and Norris, typically looking down on his characters, is writing a
comic tour de force, as in "Fantaisie Printanière." Norris raises the issue of his intentions when the narrator complains of how difficult the story is to narrate: "Had they
never met, Miss Hromada and young Stayne would yet have been as fine specimens
of womanhood and manhood as you could wish to know. Once having met, they
ruined each other. The effect of these different characters upon one another was
something well-nigh impossible to reduce to language" (132). Like Flannery
O'Connor, Norris is always aware of his distance from his characters and his disdain
for them, the spectatorship of his narrator-observers, and the narrative of descent.
It is important that he draws on his own memories of Harvard, including Deturs (an
underclassman honor awarded at Harvard), as well as the Hasty Pudding Society
and Porcellian, both exclusive Harvard clubs. Is he attacking the gentlemen of these
clubs, trying to warn them, or signaling his own lofty background? Whatever Norris
means to say about sexuality, masculinity, and racialism, the story remains unclear
in its effect.

STEPHEN CRANE: "THE MONSTER"

Crane is rather more complicated in his attitude toward race than Norris, and there
is no better example of Crane's treatment of race than "The Monster" (1899). In this
story, the narrator's spectatorship and use of stereotype are turned upside down
along with the narrative of descent; Crane deconstructs a broad social descent and
suggests a more problematic definition of criminality. Through the use of the fable
and the gothic—in the Aesopian sense of teaching a lesson—Crane's powerful
imagery is the strongest source of irony in "The Monster," making it one of his most
troubling stories, insofar as its intended lesson. It may be seen as a meditation
on the limitations of human nature, the aftermath of the Civil War, and racism in
the North. The failure of post–Civil War society to see blacks as human beings

demonstrates how society as a whole devolved. The story contains disturbing racial elements, complicated by a theme of appearance versus reality, between surfaces and interior reality. It is a fable not of wisdom, like Aesop's fables, but of the deep illogic and darkness of the human spirit, as symbolized by a "happy" town. Finally, the odd orientation of the narrator to the events he describes, and the way he describes them, raise questions about Crane's intent with regard to race.

Like "A Case for Lombroso," "The Monster" was based on fact, a lynching in Port Jervis, New York, Crane's hometown, of a Robert Lewis, witnessed by Crane's brother, Judge William Crane, who tried to stop it but was overcome by the mob. Ida B. Wells publicized the lynching widely. When Crane's story came out, Port Jervis residents were furious at how he had portrayed "Whilomville's" reaction to Johnson's disfigurement. "The Monster" was written and published during the all-time high of lynchings in the United States; indeed, Jacqueline Goldsby points out that the story's publication was bookended by notorious lynchings, including that of Sam Hose and those in the Wilmington, North Carolina, race riots (111).

But is "The Monster" an anti-lynching story? Critics describe it as one, if only figuratively, but is Crane's purpose to expose racial and social crimes? Crane's racial stereotypes along with his withering irony result in another confusion of purpose; Crane's multiple ironies pose challenges to most readers.

According to John Cleman, critics of "The Monster" have "tended either to ignore the evidence of Crane's racism, to dismiss it as a cultural influence irrelevant to his larger purposes, or to reconfigure it within his irony in such a way as to enable the story and its author to achieve an unintended racial insight" (121). But "The Monster" does not really allow for any of these single interpretations, but instead fills readers with uncertainty, especially in its violent imagery: the broken flower, the racist stereotypes the town holds against Johnson, the eerie description of the blue and red "lady" and "snake" of the chemicals in the fire, the faceless hero himself.

Because in other works Crane tends to treat blacks as minstrel figures—in *Maggie: A Girl of the Streets* (1893), "The King's Favor" (1891), "At the Pit Door" (1900), and "The Knife" (1900)—Lee Clark Mitchell inquires into Norris's intentions in "The Monster":

> Is "the monster" the disfigured black man or is it the town that comes to disfigure him? . . . The story's upturned faces may be symptomatic of authorial obsession; but from a rhetorical perspective, they figure forth a pattern more complex and less pathological, one that reveals paradoxical connections among the processes of acquiring language, having a voice, losing face, acting ethically, and generating a plot. (176, 178)

Johnson is "Othered" when he loses his face; he also becomes more and more inarticulate. Trescott similarly loses his voice and agency when he loses "face" (Mitchell 180–81). Cleman addresses the story's elements of horror but more importantly its "lack of clarity about . . . ethical meaning," especially of race (119). Though both Johnson and Dr. Trescott are heroes, their actions seem "to symbolize the unjust situation of African Americans generally in the 1890s" (120). When Johnson is blamed for the fire, Crane further establishes the town's racism. Yet elsewhere in the story, "Crane often appears blatantly racist, utilizing the sort of negative racial stereotyping common to minstrel shows and pro-slavery accounts of the Old South. Simply put, such depictions seem incongruous with the elevation of Johnson as self-sacrificing hero and with the story's overall attack on bigotry" (Cleman 120).

Cleman sees the rescue scene as especially stereotypical because Johnson panics and experiences apathy. When confronted with the "sapphire shape" that "doomed him," he haphazardly flings Jimmie toward the window (Crane 213). "Clearly this is not a case of calm, purposeful action under fire. In the final analysis, Jimmie's salvation, like that of the three survivors in 'The Open Boat' (1897) is due as much to chance as to concerted human efforts, including the vicissitudes of what is characterized as Johnson's instinctive racial behavior" (Cleman 128). Dr. Trescott thinks he represents the world of rational order, but as Cleman notes, in his self-satisfaction he resembles Dr. Frankenstein, "usurping nature's creative power ostensibly in the service to humanity" (128). Trescott seems to be a severe father to Jimmie, and a coldly logical one, as we see in the scene that opens the story when he is deeply displeased at Jimmie's having broken one of his peonies; Jimmie runs for solace to Henry Johnson, the hostler. Cleman wonders whether Trescott's desire to save Johnson is presented as a kind of instinct or as an obligation: "He will be what you like, judge," he says, and "He will be anything" (Crane 213), "suggesting his disregard for both the community, and, ultimately, for Johnson himself" (Cleman 130). Dr. Trescott's pledge undercuts Johnson's humanity by making him Dr. Trescott's creation. Perhaps it is motivated not by altruism but by "the hostler's service to him and the obligation it has created." As Cleman concludes, "[t]he images of slavery and battle in the fire scene, the themes of rescue and moral obligation, seem echoes of the Civil War and its aftermath," which Crane may see as "blunders of virtue," to use his own phrase. Thus Johnson remains "locked in the author's version of a black identity" (131–32). In the end, Crane has written a profoundly unsettling story revising racial stereotypes, but its intent is mixed up in the narrator and author's racial attitudes. Johnson violates his "racial" identity as a coward by acting heroically. However, Johnson's real identity, hidden behind layers at first of performance and later his depersonalization after the fire, remains unknown, but the question of identity is the core of the story. Again, the narrator questions his ability to tell the tale and seems at times to satirize the town, but at other times he hides behind racial stereotypes in his imagery.

Crane offers his readers both a humorous stereotype of Johnson when he describes Johnson dressing for the evening and a sense of his interior life, and these do not match. While the men gathered at the barbershop window laugh at him as he proceeds to call on his lady friend in Watermelon Alley, Crane also notes that the figure Johnson cuts in town "was not altogether a matter of the lavender trousers, nor yet the straw hat with its bright silk band. The change was somewhere far in the interior of Johnson. But there was no cake-walk hyperbole in it. He was simply a quiet, well-bred gentleman of position, wealth, and other necessary achievements out for an evening stroll, and he had never washed a wagon in his life" (194). The notion of Johnson's outer appearance not matching his interiority becomes increasingly central to the story. Though the "saffron Miss Bella Farragut" and her mother are portrayed as minstrel-show comic stereotypes, Johnson is all elegant manners: "After Johnson has gone, Bella, who encouraged herself in the appropriation of phrases, said, "Oh, ma, isn't he divine?" (197). Their hysterical reaction when he returns disfigured—the mother "hurled herself backward with a dreadful upheaval of the Earth's surface" and then goes over the back fence (228)—makes one wonder what Crane is doing with such buffoonery.

But even more contradictory to a presumed anti-racism, Crane's imagery of African Americans actually includes the image of monkeys. When the fire is starting,

> A wisp of smoke came from one of the windows at the end of the house and drifted quietly into the branches of a cherry-tree. Its companions followed it in slowly increasing numbers, and finally there was a current controlled by invisible banks which poured into the fruit-laden boughs of the cherry-tree. It was no more to be noted than if a troop of dim and silent gray monkeys had been climbing a grape-vine into the clouds. (201)

"Monkeys" contribute to the story's animal imagery, but the image of smoke as mischievous monkeys is also a direct negative allusion to blacks. Elsewhere in the story Crane depicts the characters through animal imagery: Jimmie as a "bawling calf," Huntington a bellowing "bull," Bella Farragut as a "horse," the Williams children to "ducklings," Jimmie's young friends as "roosters and lambs," and so on (Wilson-Jordan 53). Here the fire, with its smoke-monkeys, is tied to Johnson as a trapped "animal" whose instincts cause him to hesitate; the image points to the town's initial suspicion that Johnson actually caused the fire through (racially determined) carelessness.

But Crane adds to his animal imagery another set of similes and metaphors having to do with colors:

> After a moment the window brightened as if the four panes of it had been stained with blood, and a quick ear might have been led to imagine the fire-imps calling and calling, clan joining clan, gathering to the colors. . . . No one could have heard this low droning of the gathering clans. . . . Suddenly the panes of the red window tinkled and crashed to the ground, and at other windows there suddenly reared other flames, like bloody spectres at the apertures of a haunted house. This outbreak had been well planned, as if by professional revolutionists. (201–2)

This redness as evil, along with sapphire blue (could he have in mind national colors, red and blue, blue and gray?), reappears in the colors of the chemicals spilled in Dr. Trescott's lab during the fire, and which reflect, ironically, the "color" that undoes Johnson, "colored" and arrayed in the colorful garments of "the dude." It also appears in the closing scene, with the red furnace of the Trescotts: "Seeing that the door of the little drawing-room was open, he entered. The room was bathed in the half-light that came from the four dull panes of mica in the front of the great stove. As his eyes grew used to the shadows he saw his wife curled in an arm-chair. He went to her" (247). Most of the color imagery is associated with Johnson or with fire, irretrievably linking them together, and throwing more blame on Johnson. The town ostracises Dr. Trescott because he is now touched by color. As long as color was controlled, with Johnson's bright clothes the reflection of his stereotyping and a false sign of power and respectability, as read by the whites, the situation was static. When real color intrudes and controls, almost like a supernatural force (but also a scientific one), Johnson "reverts" to primitive fear upstairs in the burning house, but he overcomes his fears and still attempts to act rationally.

After Johnson's disfiguration, he is seen as out of control. He fought "color" and showed his power in facing nature in a way none of them can imagine, and so he must be shunned. His "color" has diminished them. In effect he has "run away" from his colored place, and, like a runaway slave, is not to be tolerated; he becomes dangerous as "colored." Where he has gone none can follow, and with his face and his identity removed, he is even more feared as the "Other," the black "beast" of racist propaganda. How little they know of him, like the villagers terrified of Frankenstein's Creature. In the fire scene, the metaphor of the ladder is deployed to suggest how Johnson "rises above" his race in facing his fears and saving Jimmie; but the ladder image more pointedly foreshadows his descent from man to monster, the way the town becomes a jungle of depraved fears based on racism, and Johnson's failure to attain selfhood, let alone be recognized as a selfless hero, just because he is a black man (Wilson-Jordan 50). In a strange way, he seems above all of this; indeed, as Wilson-Jordan observes, "If Henry had enacted his prescribed role, Jimmie would have died" (55).

Crane's intentions and his obfuscations are found in animal and color imagery, as described above, connected to race. Words like "swinging" and "snake" connect to the animal imagery—with the "swinging" monkey fighting for survival against the figurative betrayal of the "mystic" snake—while "slavery," "the negro wail that had in it the sadness of the swamps" and "in the manner of his race" point to Johnson's lowly status (205–6). But as Johnson "faces" "color," the townspeople are entertained by the spectacle and speculate about its facts: "They did not particularly want to have anybody's house burn, but still it was fine to see the gathering of the companies, and amid a great noise to watch their heroes perform all manner of prodigies" (208).

The townspeople form their own spectatorship and narrative of Johnson. Alek Johnson hopes to make money off of him. Little girls scream in fright at him. Little boys tease each other in contests of bravery with him. The town secretly wants him dead or at least removed from the town where he has lived all of his life. During the many discussions between townspeople and Dr. Trescott, as well as those going on in kitchens and parlors all over town, varying justifications for getting rid of Johnson are voiced: "A man who had not heretofore spoken said, solemnly, 'It's the women'" (245). And he repeats it—the old excuse for running off—or lynching—Negro men. To his credit, Dr. Trescott stands firm. His support costs him a lot, and this puzzles him, but his case for Johnson hinges not on natural human sympathy or the attempt to make Johnson seem just as human as any of the townspeople, let alone arguing against racism, but upon his own duty, which of course reflects on him.

The narrative of descent is experienced by Johnson and the Trescotts, but it is more the town's. Nearly all of them behave irrationally and destructively. The reader sees the potential for a tragic point of view of Johnson, but the story's irony prevents it, even as it undercuts and questions its own aims. Johnson's heroism, even in the racist sense of overcoming his race, is an ascent but is treated as a descent; a hero a monster. The town, like Twain's Hadleyburg, thinks it represents the most ascendant values in society, but it has sinned against one of its own, and a favorite at that. According to James Nagel, Johnson is "nearly perfect" in his heroism, which further exposes the racial prejudice of Whilomville as "fundamentally corrupt, ethnically reductive, morally offensive" (54). The story is a sardonic meditation on criminality: by an act of selfless virtue Johnson becomes criminalized because the town assumes at first he set the fire. Who is the criminal here? The town thinks the judge is, but to the reader the townspeople are. Yet this promising argument against racism is, as noted above, circumvented by Crane's troubling racial metaphors of monkeys and Watermelon Alley. One wants to search his intentions, but as these are not known, we are left with some provocative fictional contradictions about justice, race, and human nature.

From paired images of laboratory jars and fire to that of teacups and fire, the rawness of Johnson's empty state is grotesquely contrasted with the doctor's professional quandary and his wife's loss of social status. All the faces, glass surfaces, performances, and hypocrisy expressed in the story amount to a critique of the reflection or image of Whilomville. As in Norris's satire of "teacup tragedies," "The Monster" is a parody of society, an attack on its "parenting" of African Americans, and a savage critique of Whilomville's ideas of science, parenting, family, Howellsian middle-class values, race, community, as well as a systematic failure of institutions: blacks' freedom, the town, the fire departments, the ladies, science, the family.

JACK LONDON: "THE CHINAGO"

London handled race rather differently than other writers of his day, including the other naturalists. Norris could without apology describe the "old Jew" Zerkow in *McTeague* as having "the thin, eager cat-like lips of the covetous; eyes that had grown keen as those of a lynx from long searching amidst muck and debris; and claw-like, prehensile fingers—the fingers of a man who accumulates but never disburses. It was impossible to look at Zerkow and not know instantly that greed—inordinate, insatiable greed—was the dominant passion of the man" (32–33), but in most of London's nearly two hundred short stories, the hero is most often of another race, and London's narrators identify with him. It is this act of cross-identification that sets London apart; it is easy to either disdain or sympathize with the racially oppressed, but it is quite another thing consistently to imagine being another race or telling a story from another race's point of view. The difference is partly due to

London's lower-class and mixed racial background as compared with those of the other naturalists; that is, like racial passing, London was class-passing. Other well-born popular writers such as Owen Wister did not feel obligated to think critically about race, as the crude racial stereotypes in his *The Virginian* (1902) confirm. London's interrogations of race stand in sharp contrast to the self-righteous bigotry and gratuitous violence of Thomas Dixon in *The Clansman* (1905) and D. W. Griffith's film version, *Birth of a Nation* (1915). London's psychological, class, and racial struggles through his characters resemble those of more racially aware writers of his day such as Charles Chesnutt, James Weldon Johnson, Pauline Hopkins, Sui Sin Far, and Abraham Cahan rather than his fellow naturalists. Because he was anxious about his own racial origins, his illegitimacy, and his being raised largely by an African American foster mother when his own mother rejected him, London "immigrated" to the middle class, as it were, and also immigrated into middle-class whiteness in both the social and psychological sense.

Norris was a child of the upper middle class, born in Chicago, who lived in San Francisco and New York City and went to the University of California at Berkeley and then to Harvard. Crane came from New Jersey and New York, his parents a Methodist clergyman and clergyman's daughter, of a middle-class small-town family. In contrast, London emerged from the working class, and he never identified with the middle class or its pretensions. He was an alcoholic and a gang member at the age of fifteen. A few years later, he was arrested as a vagrant and imprisoned in the Erie County Penitentiary. As a youth, he went to sea and became an oyster pirate on San Francisco Bay. These factors, plus his authorial anxieties, gave him a different perspective on matters of race, criminality, vocation, and social class. It almost seems unfair to compare London with the other naturalists on the subject of race; where they were confused or indifferent, he was obsessed with race both personally and artistically. London wrote dozens of stories besides "The Chinago" with non-white heroes, told from their perspectives and containing attacks on white racism. London was thus the only one of the naturalists to write from a non-white perspective and to treat non-white characters with the required depth so that readers could identify with their perspective. London's other well-known stories adopting the perspective of another race include "The House of Pride," "Chun Ah Chun," "Koolau the Leper," "Mauki," and "The League of the Old Men." That London's racial orientations are conflicted is a problem—he could be a white supremacist, but he grew out of that for the most part—at the same time as he was writing stories critical of white racism. In most of his South Seas stories, the author's and narrator's intentions are clear: to expose the banality of evil in the colonial setting and more broadly acknowledge that survival depends upon knowledge as cultural and based in language, not on some essential racial trait.

"The Chinago" (1911) is a story of innocence cruelly destroyed by the stupidity and greed created by the colonial system; if not tragic, then it is naturalistic and also tragically absurd. Here, "race" is constructed by culture and language; racial essentialism is overturned by the possibility of linguistic understanding. London constantly returns to the theme of the limitations and dangers of not knowing the other's language in his writings about Asia and the South Pacific, from his Russo-Japanese War correspondence to essays like "The Yellow Peril" and especially "The Language of the Tribe." During his 1915 stay in Honolulu, London delivered his lecture "The Language of the Tribe" at the Outrigger Club, sponsored by the Pan-Pacific League. London emphasized that English is "composed of hundreds of thousands of words; the Japanese language [is] the same, and yet these great peoples are narrow and limited and they prevent the man who knows only English from understanding the man who knows only Japanese. The 'language of the tribe' I referred to was the world language—the cosmic language" (117).

Just as with Norris and Crane, criminality is tied to race in "The Chinago," but it is eventually clear in the story that the "raced" Chinese criminal is innocent and his white European accusers guilty, and that the trial is a semiotic and linguistic mistake on the whites' part. Ah Cho is an innocent victim of first mistaken identity and more broadly of the crime of slavery. All the Chinese fieldworkers in Tahiti, called by the Tahitians "Chinagos," are by definition criminals by virtue of being Chinese. London deftly reverses this racist stereotype by pinning the moral blame in the story on Ah Cho's French and German masters and the English company which owns the plantation. In doing so, he also reverses the old stereotype of Asians being "inscrutable" by sharing with us Ah Cho's clear and rational thoughts against those of the whites, whose thoughts seem to Ah Cho to be inscrutable.

When, in the beginning of the story, the crime of murder of one of the coolies is discovered, Ah Cho knows he did not commit the murder and so is unconcerned. He knows that another coolie named Ah Chow is the murderer. His attitude resembles the innocent but fatally uninformed attitude of Buck in the beginning line of *The Call of the Wild*: "Buck did not read the newspapers, or he would have known that trouble was brewing, not alone for himself, but for every tide-water dog, strong of muscle and with warm, long hair, from Puget Sound to San Diego. Because men, groping in the Arctic darkness, have found a yellow metal" (25). Ah Cho's very strength, his philosophical view of life, turns out to be an evolutionary hindrance to his survival, in the sense that he should have been wiser about the white masters' likely response to the murder.

It is primarily the barrier of language that acts to condemn to death the innocent Chinago. In addition to English, Gary Riedl and Tom Tietze point out, the story presents seven other languages from the court proceedings in "unceasing, explosive French" to the various dialects spoken by the workers. "Universal misinterpretation and confusion" instead of understanding erupt (507). The first and last sentences of the story involve knowing: "Ah Cho did not understand French" (1405) and "[t]hat much he knew before he ceased to know" (1417). Each section of the story presents "racial" knowledge as either wrong (despite the central motif of the trial as a way to find out truth), misinterpreted, or deliberately covered up. As he sits in the courtroom, Ah Cho muses, "There was no understanding these white devils. . . . There was no telling what went on at the back of their minds. . . . They grew angry without apparent cause, and their anger was always dangerous. They were like wild beasts at such times. There was a curtain behind the eyes of the white devils that screened the backs of their minds" (1408–9). Later, just before his execution, he reflects, "They could never understand the white dogs any more than could the white dogs understand them" (1414). Such a reversal of the Asian stereotype of inscrutability and the imputation of devilishness to the whites would not have been ignored by London's readers, for these notions violated the Euro-American racialistic views of the South Seas and Asia.

All the coolies anywhere near the murder are rounded up and thoroughly beaten. After three weeks in prison, Ah Chow's marks are still unhealed, so he is the one marked to die, while Ah Cho receives only twenty years in the penal colony on New Caledonia. But through another series of interpretive mistakes, Ah Cho is mistaken for Ah Chow and taken out to the guillotine. London's insistence on having linguistic confusion twice condemn Ah Cho makes the irony inescapable (Riedl and Tietz 508–10). As in the other stories, London questions the limitations of language and interpretation, but the author himself is not confused about those limitations and presents them objectively. Unlike stories by other naturalists, in this one the author is able fully to develop the interiority of his protagonist.

According to the narrator, Ah Cho is content with little things and simple pleasures: "The hush and quiet in the cool of the day after the blazing toil in the cotton field was to him an infinite satisfaction. He could sit for hours gazing at a solitary flower and philosophizing about the mysteries and riddles of being" (1407). But such reserve is no match for his foreman:

> Schemmer, Karl Schemmer, was a brute, a brutish brute. But he earned his salary. He got the last particle of strength out of the five hundred slaves; for slaves they were until their term of years was up. Schemmer worked hard to extract the strength from those five hundred sweating bodies and to transmute it into bales of fluffy cotton ready for export. His dominant, iron-clad, primeval brutishness was what enabled him to effect the transmutation. Also, he was assisted by a thick leather belt, three inches wide and a yard in length, with which he always rode and which, on occasion, could come down on the naked back of a stooping coolie with a report like a pistol-shot. (1407–8)

Ah Cho's other antagonist, the gendarme Cruchot, "had seen twenty years of service in the colonies, from Nigeria and Senegal to the South Seas, and those twenty years had not perceptibly brightened his dull mind. He was as slow-witted and stupid as in his peasant days in the south of France" (1410). Cruchot is the one who tells Ah Cho the guillotine will not hurt:

> "Don't be afraid," said Cruchot, with the philanthropic intention of making it easier for his prisoner. "It is not difficult to die that way." He snapped his fingers. "It is quick—like that. It is not like hanging on the end of a rope and kicking and making faces for five minutes. It is like killing a chicken with a hatchet. You cut its head off, that is all. And it is the same with a man. Pouf!—it is over. It doesn't hurt. You don't even think it hurts. You don't think. Your head is gone, so you cannot think." (1412)

When it is discovered that they have the wrong man, Cruchot assesses the situation based not on justice but racism: "What if he was the wrong man and they cut his head off? It was only a Chinago when all was said, and what was a Chinago, anyway? Besides, it might not be a mistake. He did not know what went on in the minds of his superiors. They knew their business best. Who was he to do their thinking for them?" (1413). Like the town of Whilomville, he goes along with social prejudices and his superiors' goal of sensationalizing the story of the lynching. The master of the plantation and the gendarme confer and decide that they are wasting field time for the coolies and that they will go ahead and execute an innocent man. The narrator notes, "They spoke in French, and Ah Cho, who did not understand a word of it, nevertheless knew that they were determining his destiny. He knew, also, that the decision rested with the sergeant, and he hung upon that official's lips. 'All right,' announced the sergeant. 'Go ahead with it. He is only a Chinago'" (1416).

At the point of death, Ah Cho finally sees through all the lies of the whites: he "opened his eyes. Straight above him he saw the suspended knife blazing in the sunshine. He saw the weight which had been added, and noted that one of Schemmer's knots had slipped. Then he heard the sergeant's voice in sharp command. Ah Cho closed his eyes hastily. He did not want to see that knife descend. But he felt it—for one great fleeting instant. And in that instant he remembered Cruchot and what Cruchot had said. But Cruchot was wrong. The knife did not tickle. That much he knew before he ceased to know" (1417).

Norris's mixed message on masculine sexuality and the racial "Other" and Crane's seemingly at-odds purposes in "The Monster" would not, despite the dramatic complexities of their tales, seem to bode well for how naturalism could address racism and racialism. Not until London's dozens of short stories with nonwhite protagonists do we see a future for naturalism's treatment of race relations. Among these three naturalists' satiric treatments of race, only London's speaks on behalf of the victims of Euro-American exploitation.

This discussion of naturalist short fiction and race, especially of "The Chinago," raises the question of what happened to naturalism. Did it resurface in Hemingway? It did in a sense, but Hemingway's characters resist the truths of naturalism with their codes of conduct and firmly support racial and cultural stereotypes. Faulkner? Perhaps, especially his idea that the South is afflicted with a spiritual illness that will allow no one to develop as "Nature intended." He creates characters driven by forces beyond their control, such as Joe Christmas in *Light in August*. Also, Faulkner brings sex in as a biological determinant, as in Popeye's background and Temple's nymphomania in *Sanctuary*, but it all becomes gothic melodrama instead of imitating the cool detachment of Zola. Faulkner's work is also influenced by symbolism, modernism, complexity of methods, mythology, a sense of history, and, most significantly, the importance of the individual, who, if doomed, at least recognizes it in himself as well as in his society—as with Pizer's analysis of the doomed but self-aware naturalist hero. But Faulkner loves his characters in a non-naturalist way, their faults as much individual as they are human. If they are victims, these characters are not passive. Erskine Caldwell might be viewed as more naturalistic. But most significantly, naturalism was practiced by African American writers such as

Charles Chesnutt, James Weldon Johnson, Paul Laurence Dunbar, and Richard Wright. Naturalism should not lose its sense of outrage and social satire, and it didn't with these writers; their fictional realities closely involve criminality, race, and social justice. These protest writers are thus the rightful inheritors of naturalism. It was up to them to specifically and inarguably conjoin naturalism with their modern critique of racism in the United States. And then, of course, it was up to African American women writers, Toni Morrison and so many others, to redefine race and naturalism once again. Naturalism has a brilliant future, but it must be able to examine race like so many other "hereditary" influences upon a hero with an objective eye, a human sensitivity, a sense of identification, and a responsive voice to any social injustice.

WORKS CITED

Bower, Stephanie. "Dangerous Liaisons: Prostitution, Disease, and Race in Frank Norris's Fiction." *Modern Fiction Studies* 42 (1996): 31–60.

Cleman, John. "Blunders of Virtue: The Problem of Race in Stephen Crane's 'The Monster.'" *American Literary Realism* 34 (2002): 119–34.

Crane, Stephen. "The Monster." *Great Short Works of Stephen Crane.* Ed. James B. Colvert. New York: Harper & Row, 1968. 190–247.

Dudley, John. "Inside and Outside the Ring: Manhood, Race, and Art in American Literary Naturalism." *College Literature* 29 (2002): 53–82.

Goldsby, Jacqueline. *A Spectacular Secret: Lynching in American Life and Literature.* Chicago: University of Chicago Press, 2006.

London, Jack. *The Call of the Wild.* New York: Macmillan, 1903.

———. "The Chinago." 1911. *The Complete Short Stories of Jack London.* Ed. Earle Labor, Robert C. Leitz III, and I. Milo Shepard. 3 vols. Stanford: Stanford University Press, 1993. 1405–17.

———. "The Language of the Tribe." *Mid-Pacific Magazine* 10 (Aug. 1915): 117–20.

McElrath, Joseph R., Jr. *Frank Norris Revisited.* New York: Twayne, 1992.

Mitchell, Lee Clark. "Face, Race, and Disfiguration in Stephen Crane's 'The Monster.'" *Critical Inquiry* 17 (1990): 172–92.

Nagel, James. "The Significance of Stephen Crane's 'The Monster.'" *American Literary Realism* 31.3 (1999): 38–57.

Norris, Frank. "Among Cliff Dwellers: A Peculiar Mixture of Races from the Four Corners of the Earth." 1897. *The Apprenticeship Writings of Frank Norris, 1896–1898.* Ed. Joseph R. McElrath, Jr. and Douglas K. Burgess. Vol. 1: 1896–1897. Philadelphia: American Philosophical Society, 1996. 262–65.

———. "A Case for Lombroso." 1897. *The Apprenticeship Writings of Frank Norris, 1896–1898.* Ed. Joseph R. McElrath, Jr. and Douglas K. Burgess. Vol. 2: 1897–1898. Philadelphia: American Philosophical Society, 1996. 127–32.

———. *McTeague: A Story of San Francisco.* Ed. Carvel Collins. New York: Rinehart, 1958.

Pizer, Donald. "Late Nineteenth-Century American Naturalism." *Realism and Naturalism in Nineteenth-Century American Literature.* Rev. ed. Carbondale: Southern Illinois University Press, 1984. 9–30.

Riedl, Gary, and Thomas R. Tietze. "Misinterpreting the Unreadable: Jack London's 'The Chinago' and 'The Whale Tooth.'" *Studies in Short Fiction* 34 (1997): 507–18.

Todorov, Tveztan. "'Race,' Writing, and Culture." Trans. Loulou Mack. *Critical Inquiry* 13 (1986): 171–82.

Wilson-Jordan, Jacqueline. "Teaching a Dangerous Story: Darwinism and Race in Stephen Crane's 'The Monster.'" *Eureka Studies in Short Fiction* 8 (2007): 48–61.

CHAPTER 17

NATURALISM AND COMMODITY CULTURE

MARY E. PAPKE

THREE orphaned siblings, still clad in mourning, wander lost and fearful through the maze of Parisian streets in search of their last living relative. Their situation is dire, their future bleak. Yet, in the very first moments of their adventure, they find unexpected comfort and distraction from their plight—The Ladies' Paradise, a department store in which they see the surreal, seductive, excessive display of goods, a spectacle that renders the novel's protagonist, Denise Baudu, "excited, fascinated, oblivious to everything else" (Zola, *Au Bonheur* 4). While Denise Baudu's subsequent relationships with and in this department store provide the bare bones for a plot, it is the overripe, sumptuous flesh of things, the almost hysterically detailed descriptions of saleable goods and the process by which they are marketed, that demands most attention from the reader. Zola's *Au Bonheur des dames* (*The Ladies' Paradise* [1883]), part of his magisterial Rougon-Macquart series, reminds us throughout of his first principles of naturalism—the deterministic import of heredity and environment, the necessity for scientific documentation of particular cases of evolution and devolution; more important, for this essay, it also reveals Zola's equal fascination with how the modern French commodity culture of manufactured needs and desires necessarily destroyed the old mercantile culture and created a new breed of buyers and sellers, workers and overseers. Even Zola's pure and compassionate heroine comes to recognize this consumer culture as the new religion for the masses that is good both for buyers and sellers, though its making requires her "to witness to the bitter end the inexorable workings of life, which requires the seed of death for its continual renewal" (385). Eschewing the hard determinism of *Germinal* or *L'Assommoir*, this transitional work offers us virtue wedded to profit-making both in terms of the love plot and the betterment of some workers' lives as a precondition for another person's economic success; yet despite the happy ending for Denise, the economic evolution toward commodity culture that is the central story is signified repeatedly as a *mise en abîme* of vampiric feeding over which the pure Denise bemoans "the sight of warblers eating spiders who, in their turn, were eating flies" (375) while the venal Mouret, Denise's would-be seducer and eventual faithful lover, celebrates to the end his ability "to let the strong devour the weak," "this new way of applying the struggle for survival" (35, 36).

NATURALISM AS CRITIQUE OF COMMODITY CULTURE

Commodity culture, not surprisingly, is also central to much of American literary naturalism. Emerson famously lamented in his "Ode, Inscribed to William H. Channing" that "Things are in the saddle, /And ride mankind." Realist writers typically incorporated the drive for acquisition of things to motivate their plots. Naturalism, however, would take the focus on things to an entirely new level, that of the Zolaesque scientific documentation of commodities as markers of personal and social valuation and of fetishistic obsession with things reified to extraordinary degrees. Naturalism would catalog in sometimes excruciating detail how things ride the characters to their overdetermined fates. Zola's *Au Bonheur des dames* boldly emphasized the centrality of commodity culture to individuation and self-satisfaction; the American naturalists, from Rebecca Harding Davis to Theodore Dreiser and beyond, followed suit by illustrating in intricate detail the hold of commodity culture on American life. They document through meticulous attention to the phantasmagoric value of things the ways we continue to pay for America's emergence in the nineteenth century as the leading capitalist, industrial power in the world.

Certainly among the forces that gave rise to literary naturalism in America, commodity culture provided perhaps the richest material to fashion into fiction. One might go so far as to claim, indeed, that American naturalism is itself an inevitable by-product of commodity culture because it is simultaneously a diagnosis of it. As virtually all overviews of American realism and naturalism recite, from 1860 to 1900, the population of the United States doubled, primarily due to the influx of immigrants, many of whom were recruited as workers for the new industries in fast-growing metropolitan centers such as Chicago, New York, Pittsburgh, and Cleveland, and who were promised the American Dream with all the things that the Dream entailed as their just deserts. At the same time, emigration from rural to urban sectors further swelled city populations and centralized the marketing of goods. Scientific developments created new systems of categorization and presentation of matter that trickled down from academies of science and the medical schools to the quotidian display of goods in venues ranging from Carrie Meeber's first department store to the Metropolitan Museum, curiously similar institutions that both began to accrue considerable profit once they registered as part of what some critics have called the new exhibitionary landscape of the late nineteenth century. With the intense industrialization of the 1870s following the closing of the frontier and completion of the transcontinental railroad in 1869, the national identity was effectively transfigured from that of a country peopled by self-reliant farmers and shopkeepers to that of a monopolistic or oligopolistic capitalist state in which robber barons would boast of hiring one half of the working class to kill the other half. The accumulation of heretofore-unimaginable wealth in the hands of the few created a sharp divide between the haves and have-nots that inescapably restructured social relations even as the economics of simple supply and demand was supplanted by an economics of multiple and ever-unsatisfiable desires that suggested the leveling of social distinctions through a democratization of the availability of luxury products or their reproductions to all classes. As both economic desire and social Darwinism exponentially raised the value of having things as a marker of self-worth, the new scientific determinism of Herbert Spencer and Charles Darwin, as its upper-class interpreters would argue, boldly proclaimed ruthlessness and voraciousness, gross appetite and the desire for self-satisfaction as simply natural law. For many, it was the best of times; for at least as many, if not more, it was the worst.

As Anne Mayhew explains, the dominant economic narratives generated in the late nineteenth century comprise a matrix of sharply competing versions. Economic historians, for example, view the period as one of steadily increasing incomes and prosperity for the majority, while other economists and historians note the several economic downturns that affected all but the most wealthy, though these economic reversals are rarely described as catastrophic. Fiction writers, and the naturalists in particular, focused on a distinctly different set of scenarios, most often describing the period "as a time of hardship, economic unhappiness, and not infrequent destitution" (1). It was, Mayhew goes on to argue, a period of abundance in which for some the foremost question became how that abundance, the ever-increasing output of goods and services, would be distributed. In short, who would profit, how would they profit, and at what cost to others would they profit?

Rebecca Harding Davis's "Life in the Iron-Mills" (1861), a transitional naturalist work like Zola's novel, captures well this new industrialscape in which ownership of commodities, including one's labor, rather than character or will, determines fate. The novella illustrates the accumulation of capital trumping both the idealist sensibilities evident in the last gasps of transcendentalist rhetoric and the sense of moral responsibility for the less fortunate promoted by utopian socialist philosophies. The story, interrupted repeatedly by the narrator with apologies for the subject matter and the demands placed on the reader to interpret it correctly, centers on Hugh Wolfe, a mill worker trapped in an animal-like existence with seemingly no hope of reprieve, his one protest against his overly determined fate literally embodied in the sculptures he cuts out of the waste product of the mill. One night a group of moneyed men on a touristic jaunt through the mills stumble upon his latest creation cut out of korl, what Hugh calls a starving woman, and its display becomes the occasion for the men to speculate on art as they define it as well as the worker's lot and their relationship to it (this group is comprised of symbolic authority figures—the mill owner's son, a doctor, the press—those, in short, who profit from another's labor). In a striking reversal of the process of interpellation central to the theories of Louis Althusser, Hugh's stature as a man to whom attention should be paid is repeatedly denied, a process already begun by Hugh's fellow workers who have emasculated him by renaming him "Molly" because of his finer artistic sensibilities. On this night of specularization, speculation, and irruption of the uncanny into the ordinary, Hugh is cast out by the alpha wolves clad in fur and bejeweled with blood-red rings who seem to sympathize with Hugh's case but reject any possibility of their having responsibility for alleviating his suffering. Hugh's naturalistic art is deemed incompetent by the medical man, ugly by those who, admittedly like Hugh himself, buy into narrow romanticized definitions of womanly beauty, and, more importantly, as without either use- or exchange-value, for as a commodity without capital to back it, it is, as its literal materiality announces, pure waste. Indeed, from the vantage point of the mill owner's son and his entourage, the statue could signify a type of theft through the misuse of labor capacity that is embodied in the worker and on which the mill owner depends for his profit-making. Not only does Hugh lack the fiduciary capital necessary for broadcasting his self-expression, but the impossibility of establishing productive social relations between workers and capitalists suggests the lack of cultural capital Hugh and his interlocutor possess at this historical moment: they can neither represent the reality of certain lives fully nor, the narrator fears, manipulate signs correctly so as to force recognition of the virtually unspeakable truth. Or, to put it another way, if Hugh's story, his pathetic attempt at self-construction, is denied legitimacy, authority, and authenticity, then there is little possibility of any other outcome than Hugh's subsequent complete erasure. While Davis's story ends on a salvific note, critic Sharon M. Harris makes clear in her *Rebecca Harding Davis and American Realism*, as do other readers of the story, the centrality of commodification both to Davis's plot and her aesthetic agenda to represent truthfully what had not heretofore been admitted as material for fiction. Davis attempted to reimagine fiction's ability to interpellate a new type of reader who would welcome realism depicted across class lines. That attempt failed, however, in that the novella was quickly forgotten, an erasure also forestalling any thick description of the rise of naturalism until the late twentieth-century feminist recuperation of women writers.

Simultaneous with the transmogrification of national identity was the reorganization and reconceptualization of literary culture as a commodity accessible to the masses, foreshadowed as necessary for the common good by Davis's apologetic narrator, effected in the commercial realm of literary production primarily by William Dean Howells and his entourage. As his own career proved, once the Brahmin Boston culture chiefs were dethroned by age, mental incapacity, and rejection by the then-limited readership, and once-ordinary men of no particular social privilege could work their way into positions of leadership in the field of cultural production, then a more capacious, democratic type of literature—by, for, and about the American people—might emerge and be promoted as high art. Ralph Waldo Emerson, one of the Brahmins, had called for a new poet who would represent all of America—from the commercial to the spiritual—to itself and the world, but it required a man of the middle class, of the middle states, of middling education but of liberal generosity to aspiring writers like himself to bring that new art into being. Indeed, as his *A Hazard of New Fortunes* (1890) illustrates, a demand for a new type of fiction could be created by and for, and marketed to, a growing readership across class, gender, and race lines. While Howells could not himself capture more than a traveler's view of subaltern cultures—the slums, the working class—his literary call for truth in representation required his support of a new realism considerably harsher in its import than his own genteel novels and theories of art. Yet however much his democratization of realism through his own writing and his editorial work enabled representations of subaltern experiences to emerge, he himself never overcame a certain ambivalence or reticence toward this savage new art form. Neither could he escape the contemporary urge to categorize, compartmentalize, classify, and then to present, or sell, products for certain audiences and needs. Our conceptualization of the early canon of naturalist literature is therefore forever colored by his desire to promote but simultaneously to set apart fiction by women, blacks, and ethnic writers from that of white male writers. While he did include women writers in his anthology of "modern" stories, in much of his critical writing he favored white male writers. Later, there would be a qualitative shift in the work of proletarian critics such as Vernon L. Parrington and Granville Hicks who would focus in the main on male writers to the virtual exclusion of minority and women authors, especially, in the case of the latter, if they were of the upper class. And, thus, in their rudimentary analyses of naturalism, Parrington and Hicks set a precedent that precluded the inclusion of women and minority writers as practitioners of naturalism or even of having been influenced by the naturalist agenda created by white men. Students of naturalism, then, are necessarily recuperating the body of works even as they study naturalism as a discrete cultural product.

One key element of naturalism is the depiction of the social relations that organize a capitalist consumer society precisely through documentation of that by which a capitalist system is most readily defined—commodity exchange and fetishism. Materialist philosophers predating Zola's call for a scientific literature had already observed in detail the inescapable determinism of modern life. Marx, for instance, in his *The Eighteenth Brumaire of Louis Napoleon* noted that "[m]en make their own history, but they do not make it just as they please; they do not make it under circumstances chosen by themselves" (10). In addition to "the tradition of all the dead generations" that Marx posits as central to our understanding of our own self-construction in *Capital*, his conception of commodity as it developed in industrial capitalism emphasizes that the importance of capitalism's reconceptualization of use value cannot be understated if we wish to understand the realm of social relations in which we believe we create ourselves. Marx is, of course, himself drawing upon the tradition of all the dead generations as far back as Plato's originary account of the consequences of mistaking the material for the ideal, the illusion of reality for the truth, the birthing of false consciousness out of the womb of our desires and fantasies. Several of the naturalists certainly point us in this direction as well through staged scenarios in which their protagonists take up or aspire to the position of the men in Plato's cave of illusions. It is not difficult to overlay Plato's primal scene on the Dantesque rendering of the mill in Davis's work, and there are clearly references to Plato's cave in Upton Sinclair's *The Jungle* (1906), Edith Wharton's 1905 *The House of Mirth* (and, in what seems to me her wholesale and satiric rewriting of the myth for a modern audience, her "The Valley of Childish Things, and Other Emblems" [1896]), Elizabeth Maddox Robert's "Death at Bearwallow" (1926), and Ann Petry's "The Witness" (1971), to name just a few examples. The exposition of false consciousness cannot alone determine whether a work is naturalist, as the term is used to describe a movement and body of work definable through shared principles. It nevertheless provides the subject matter upon which the naturalist work rests and most often depends upon for its interrogation of the new realm of social relations experienced with the rise of industrial capitalism.

June Howard's *Form and History in American Literary Naturalism* offers us a helpful reading of the aesthetic features by which we might recognize a text as naturalistic as well as gesturing toward the moral agenda that distinguishes naturalism from contemporary movements. Howard argues that "[n]aturalism is not just deterministic fiction or realism in a pessimistic mood. These characterizations point toward some of the qualities of naturalist novels, but they do not enable us to penetrate analytically the way in which the novels reinvent the possibilities of narrative at their historical moment" (182). Naturalist works, she insists, are built upon the concentrated and freestanding presentation of facts and things, of one thick slice of life, Zola's *tranche de vie*, offered for the reader's delectation, followed by another slice and then yet another, a continual accretion of facts the documentary logic of which obviates neat closure and promotes instead a contiguous relation of the work in hand to that which it preserves for our observation. It is, further, a form of literary production that, while it reassembles elements from previous genres that remain useful as recognizable and effective literary hooks, is nevertheless profoundly different from the literary products that have come before it precisely in terms of its intense engagement with lived experiences of the real, and it thus provides readers with endless "facts" in which "the detail signifies not only reality but the rigorous investigation of reality" (147). It is "knowledge work" the consequence of which—whether to imagine reformist measures out of literary depictions of despair or simply to acknowledge the limitations that we daily confront—depends on the reader and what knowledge work she or he chooses to accomplish with the text. It is knowledge work for and by its audience that because of the polyvalent perversity of the genre is remarkably open to misprision. Recall here Sinclair's dismay at the public's misreading of his moral agenda in *The Jungle* or Georg Lukács's wholesale dismissal of naturalism as anemic documentary and passive voyeurism. More recent critics have persuasively argued that even the most seemingly nihilist of works have the potential to promote a new structure of feeling, to use Raymond Willams's rich phrase, the nascence of a political consciousness that would demand the making of a less alienating system of social relations than that depicted in the text in question. As Howard so astutely observes, "Naturalism is not a fashionable genre"; nevertheless, she insists, it does demonstrate "a dynamic solution to the problem of generating narrative out of the particular historical and cultural materials that offered themselves to these writers" (xi). Perhaps it might be more profitable simply to think of a spectrum of naturalism—thus my use of qualifiers such as "transitional" or "hard"—and to get on with the great amount of knowledge work we have yet to do to understand the attraction to and repulsion from naturalism that so many readers experience.

Naturalist texts are inventions, sometimes interventions, occasioned by particular sociohistorical developments and a reflection upon and interrogation of those developments, and most share a careful attention to the commodity culture of the time and the costs of that culture to the characters in the works, a culture of reification, objectification, and self-alienation. Characters see themselves swallowed up in machines, as trapped insects tearing themselves to pieces, as objets d'art the only meaning of which is to be made worthy for use by the greatest collectors. There is an intense focus, in other words, on things, including the commodified self, not simply as archaeological artifacts but as vessels of ideological interpellation that simultaneously effect group identification and signal self-fragmentation. The things in these works speak deeply to the characters; indeed, they often speak the characters and the self-alienation and atomization experienced by those whose desires can be expressed only through the commodities in which they invest, commodities which in turn create a false sense of self that occludes the experience of self-commodification that they are forced to suffer because of historical and biological circumstance. Marx's definition of "commodity" reminds us that this simple term is itself a matrix of competing narratives; he writes, "A commodity appears, at first sight, a very trivial thing, and easily understood. Its analysis shows that it is, in reality, a very queer thing, abounding in metaphysical subtleties and theological niceties" (*Capital* 81). Marx goes on to describe in detail the process whereby commodity emerges and, in turn, as exchange value becomes further estranged from use value, translates into commodity fetishism, in which the thing is no longer of value strictly in and of itself but for what it has come to represent in terms of social relations within capitalist society. Think here of Maggie's pathetic cretonne lambrequin, McTeague's canary, or even Lily Bart's display of herself as collectable art. Each object expresses a desire for or reminder of social inclusion, acceptance, and agency. In the case of each such object, then, the material is meant to represent the ideal but just as often is simply mistaken for it. Hugh Wolfe's statue has extraordinary value for himself as an expression of his alienated labor and the hell in which he exists; however, it speaks to and of him but not in the way it will be received by the class who in essence own him. And while it speaks to and of him, it also keeps him quiet and distanced from any social action that might conceivably improve his situation and that of his tribe.

While Dreiser's Carrie is the American character most often recognized as spoken to, seduced by, and indistinguishable from commodities, other works illustrate just as well in more compact form the inherent nature of commodities to divorce one from apprehension of material reality through the momentary ecstasy of a delusory self-possession that commodities enable. Naturalist texts document, that is, the false consciousness on which the success of commodity culture depends and which, in turn, often serves as yet another element that determines the trajectory of character in naturalist fiction. Kate Chopin's "A Pair of Silk Stockings" (1897) comes immediately to mind, reading almost like a scene lifted from Zola's *Au Bonheur des dames* itself. A poor widow and sole provider for too many dependents somewhat miraculously comes into possession of what Hugh Wolfe lacked—money, not a great amount, but if spent carefully, it can provide much needed articles for all her family save herself. One simple gesture, however, proves her undoing: she leans against a counter of silk stockings and rests a weary hand on them. The silk stockings then "glide serpent-like through her fingers," arousing her—"two hectic blotches came suddenly into her pale cheeks"—and seducing her into partaking of them (501). The phrase "it becomes her"—to describe the relationship between an accessory and its owner—does not begin to do justice to the desacralized transubstantiation that occurs as she unconsciously takes in the promise of the thing on which her hand rests. Like Zola's Denise Baudu, she is immediately comforted as she is hailed into the realm of commodity fetishism in which, Neil Cummings and Marysia Lewandowska contend, the desired things both "(over)compensate for the missing whole" and act as "a marking of the site of loss, of alienated lack. . . . Forever out of context, the object is a relic of a past wholeness it—or its purchaser—could never obtain" (138). The thing, the commodity itself—or, that is, what the commodity represents to her—almost immediately, without involving rational thought, transports her into a state of false consciousness, the thing calling her to identify with, partake in, and, inevitably pay for, inclusion into a particular class group for whom money is not an issue, sensuality is a right, not a privilege, and the desire for such privilege trumps one's having to think of one's moral responsibility even to one's own children. It simultaneously reminds her of better times and allows her or causes her to forget her present social reality. Chopin's prescient analysis of the instantiation that commodities promise the consumer, the commanding language with which they speak to us, thus both echoes Zola's continual rehearsal of the power of commodities to move humans to destroy themselves in their quest for things that would identify them as replete, enviable, and invulnerable, and foreshadows Theodor Adorno's attack on the cultural forgetting commodity culture effects. We are indeed transported deep into Plato's cave—in this work perhaps overtly signified in the theatre scene—when we open a naturalist work, itself yet one more matrix of narratives competing for our attention but one in which the language of commodity culture continually redounds and in which we can begin to imagine, even as through a glass darkly, what its bound prisoners are forced to see and mistake for both their concrete reality and the ideals to which they might aspire.

Why, then, if commodity culture is such perfect material for naturalism's documentary logic has it not already been exhaustively investigated? One reason is that naturalist texts are themselves matrices of competing narratives, and any one narrative thread—reading the scientific, the philosophical, the economic, the aesthetic—requires careful contextualization and study. Further, excavating nineteenth-century (and even twentieth-century) social practices as these are figured though commodification and consumerism in literature requires the sort of interdisciplinary work that has not until relatively recently been deemed acceptable in a field traditionally paralyzed by periodization, genre boundaries, and disciplinary expectations that precluded too much work outside the texts themselves and certainly not the type of work better left to sociologists, economic historians, or anthropologists. The advent of British cultural studies in the post–World War II period did not translate easily into American critical practices at that time; outlier critical modes such as materialist—and certainly Marxist—analyses similarly met with considerable resistance in American settings less politically charged toward radical reformism than the classrooms of Birmingham, the academies of Frankfurt, or one cell within an Italian prison. Formalist criticism refused to see the text as itself a cultural product and insisted that evaluation of the text in and of itself, in accordance with a set of abstract descriptors, the elaboration of which afforded enormous cultural capital to the critic, required no thick contextualization of the sort mandated in cultural studies. Further, as I have already noted, the study of naturalism in America had from early on its own dominant narrative—often contested but until fairly recently holding firm—that privileged the study of white male authors who shared a particular fascination with male characters whose acts were profoundly conditioned by environment, heredity, biological drives, and chance and seemed subject to an injurious fatalism that precluded individual moral agency. While this narrative sometimes acknowledged the pull of things on male protagonists, it did not, on the whole, concern itself with the centrality of commodities or self-commodification to the blighted social contracts naturalism documents so forcefully, perhaps because even early theories of consumer culture engendered it as feminine. This critical narrative of what constitutes naturalism, like other types of compartmentalization, categorization, and evaluation characteristic of modern commodity culture, is thus constrained by the limitations inherent in its historical provenance, the number of artifacts available for investigation, and readers' desire for definitude and closure, moral agency and individual autonomy, elements that June Howard, Lee Clark Mitchell, and other critics have argued are profoundly antithetical to the naturalist project as conceived by the writers who created "the period's most characteristic texts" (Mitchell 121). Cultural study such as the investigation of commodity culture as it is transfused throughout naturalist texts requires, then, a great deal of work for which literary scholars have had insufficient training, resources, and compensation. Nevertheless, important work in this subfield of naturalism studies during the last thirty years has enhanced in significant ways our understanding of a continually growing body of texts deemed naturalist and why they mattered at the moment of their creation and why they continue to matter in this our postmodern, late capitalist, hypermaterialist global village.

CRITICISM OF NATURALISM AS COMMODITY CULTURE CRITIQUE

The task of the critic investigating naturalism's contiguity with commodity culture has been made immeasurably easier by the appearance of several works that provide a bedrock foundation on which to base superstructural analysis. I purposely introduce here first the terms of classical Marxism to indicate the importance of determinist philosophies such as those found in *Capital* and Thorstein Veblen's *The Theory of the Leisure Class* to numerous early and even more recent readings of naturalism and commodity culture even as I acknowledge the sometimes reductive instrumentality of their formulations. Indeed, my dependence throughout on Marxist terminology and definitions should by no means suggest a defense of the overall Marxist worldview but merely an acknowledgment of the continued utility of the Marxist assessment of the rise of commodity culture and the terms it generated that enable thick description of social relations as they emerged in the early period of industrial capitalism. Michael Spindler's *American Literature and Social Change: William Dean Howells to Arthur Miller* (1983), while it does not focus solely on naturalism, presents a basic reading of the shift from production-oriented culture as it is made evident in the works of Howells, Norris, Dreiser, and Sinclair to the consumption-oriented culture depicted in Dreiser's late novels as well as in works by Fitzgerald, Lewis, Dos Passos, and Miller. His focus necessarily includes an overview of American economic change and consequent shifts in the social construction of power relations as seen through a rudimentary Marxist lens. Basic information about socioeconomic and historical influences on the development of American naturalism is readily available in such standard compendiums of essays as those edited by Donald Pizer, Robert Paul Lamb and G. R. Thompson, and Emory Elliott. Sarah Way Shulman's "Mapping the Culture of Abundance: Literary Narratives and Consumer Culture" (2005) in the Lamb and Thompson volume offers, for example, like Spindler's study, an overview of cultural shifts that play out in texts ranging from *Walden* to Dreiser's novels and a most helpful bibliography of secondary sources; whereas the section "Becoming Cultured and Culture as Commodity" in *The American 1890s* (2000), edited by Susan Smith and Melanie Dawson, provides contemporary documents that address commodity culture. David Shi's *Facing Facts: Realism in American Thought and Culture, 1850–1920* (1995) also provides helpful general background on the period in which naturalism first appeared, including the emergence and effects of consumer culture on literary practices.

David Hawkes's *Ideology* (2003), in turn, offers an important overview of the development of idealist, liberal, and materialist philosophies that are reflected in the naturalist texts themselves and that can inform a certain type of ideology critique of those texts. While my own analysis throughout has leaned heavily toward the early period of naturalist emergence, there is a direct link between the theories of Marx and Veblen to the theoretical formulations of Benjamin, Gramsci, Adorno, Debord,

Baudrillard, and others in any continuing investigation of consumer culture, and many of the texts I will now cite borrow liberally from a variety of theoretical standpoints to make their case. James C. Davis, in his *Commerce in Color: Race, Consumer Culture, and American Literature, 1893–1933* (2007), for instance, opens with a condensed summary of critical formulations most conducive to the study of consumer culture; similarly, Rachel Bowlby in her *Just Looking: Consumer Culture in Dreiser, Gissing and Zola* (1985) focuses our attention on materialist theories of consumer culture that she then employs in her close readings of these three naturalists. Indeed, virtually every extended analysis of consumer culture as it is reproduced in naturalist texts offers some sort of theoretical glossary that models the concentrated knowledge work demanded of commodity culture critique.

For a similarly basic grounding in the history of commodity culture in America, one should turn to T. J. Jackson Lears's *No Place for Grace: Antimodernism and the Transformation of American Culture, 1880–1920* (1994), Alan Trachtenberg's *The Incorporation of America: Culture and Society in the Gilded Age* (1982), and the essay collection edited by Lears and Richard Fox entitled *The Culture of Consumption: Critical Essays in American History 1880–1980* (1983). While the following sources do not address naturalism in particular, John Frow's *Time and Commodity Culture: Essays in Cultural Theory and Postmodernity* (1997) and the essay collection *The Social Life of Things: Commodities in Cultural Perspective* (1986), edited by Arjun Appadurai, are most often cited as primary texts in the cultural study of the commodity. Most commodity culture critiques also mention *The World of Goods* (1996), by Mary Douglas and Baron Isherwood, particularly their argument that consumption operates outside social logic and constructs its own, a logic we see at work in the Chopin story referred to above, as well as at least a gesture toward the work of Marcel Mauss on gift exchange with which to contrast the effects on social relations of a shift to commodity exchange. And for further discussion of the "high-culture-low-culture pas de deux" between department stores and museums, see *The Value of Things* (2000), by Neil Cummings and Marysia Lewandowska, as well as Michael Kimmelman's "Art in Aisle 3, by Lingerie, And Feel Free to Browse" (1995).

Just as Marx's work is considered crucial to any understanding of the nature of commodity capitalism, Thorstein Veblen's *The Theory of the Leisure Class* (1899) is typically cited as the originary critique of American consumerism. Rarely is Veblen's entire theoretical construct invoked, though it could be argued that his overarching theory of modern society's reenactment of barbaric tribal traditions is literally demonstrated in certain naturalist texts. I think, for example, of the opening fight scene in Crane's *Maggie* (1983) and the unchanging primitivism of Jimmie's relation of self to others. Wharton similarly depicts modern New York society, in her case the upper class, as a meeting of the tribes, some more savage than others and therefore more successful in the struggle to survive and dominate. Whatever the degree of one's investment in Veblen's worldview, his concepts of conspicuous consumption and waste, pecuniary emulation, and leisure have proven utile for literary critics, and the application of these terms to literary texts has been particularly resonant for feminist scholars. As I noted before, and as other critics such as Rachel Bowlby have discussed at length, modern consumerism was engendered early on as female work, and Veblen's text supports—perhaps provides the basis for—such an assertion. Feminist critics have certainly capitalized on that social construction, as have critics more generally concerned with the subjugation of women and the supposed hyper-masculinity of naturalism. Ruth Bernard Yeazell's "The Conspicuous Wasting of Lily Bart" (1992) is a classic example of such a critique as is Anne-Marie Evans's analysis of conspicuous consumption in works by Wharton and Glasgow. Other critics have more broadly applied Veblenian concepts to literary critique. Claire Eby, for instance, reads instances of pecuniary emulation and invidious comparison in Dreiser's work; Andrew Lawson investigates emulation in Crane's fiction; Mario Varricchio focuses on conspicuous consumption and waste in Sinclair's work; and, quite inventively, Myles Weber employs Veblenian principles to argue that Norris's Vandover fails precisely because he is not barbaric enough to achieve admission into the savage leisure class.

A great deal of critical work on commodity culture and naturalism has depended on various materialist theories that expand upon straightforward Marxist and Veblenian protocols while always gesturing back to those seminal theories. For instance, analysis employing Bourdieu's concepts of distinction, field, and capital, such as Carol J. Singley's essay on Wharton's work, clearly extends and complicates earlier theorization of the same by Veblen. Wai-chee Dimock's immensely influential essay on *The House of Mirth* depends on the Marxist conceptualization of exchange and investment even as it refuses to be constrained by Marx's prognostications concerning social relations. My own focus on the social fiction of Chopin and Wharton in *Verging on the Abyss: The Social Fiction of Kate Chopin and Edith Wharton* (1990), to a much lesser degree of influence than Dimock's work, seeks to trace the economic narrative thread in their texts that one picks up almost too easily by finding and citing references to commodity exchange and moral bankruptcy.

New historicist analyses, in turn, offer a thick description of the ways in which the economic discourse of commodity fetishism is made to appear, is replicated in, and is then transmitted in literary texts, fiction by no means privileged over complementary contemporary legal, anthropological, and scientific texts but which serves merely as the ground from which the traces of economic discourse can be excavated and reconstituted. The most famous of these analyses is, without doubt, Walter Benn Michaels's *The Gold Standard and the Logic of Naturalism* (1987), a most provocative elaboration of commodity fetishism as it appears in works by Crane, Dreiser, and, most intensely, Norris. New historicist analysis is particularly adept at revealing why things in naturalist (or realist) texts should matter to us rather than simply determining the instrumentality of the objects within the confines of the texts themselves. Bill Brown's *A Sense of Things: The Object Matter of American Literature* (2003) models such an approach to literary texts and provides thick description of commodity forms bordering on the archaeological, at times at the expense of the literary aspect of the critique.

Other approaches resembling archival anthropology have been played out through investigation of particular commodity forms in literary texts. A perfect example is Cristina Giorcello's study of hats in works by Wharton, Chopin, and

Dreiser—who wears them, what kind do they wear, and why—or Bill Brown's research into the popular entertainment form of staged disasters as it obtains to Crane's "The Open Boat" ("Interlude"). Similarly, Lori Merish demonstrates the centrality of commodity spectacle to naturalist texts, while Robert Dowling drills down to determine the particular popular spectacle forms that influenced Crane's depiction of commodity culture in slum life. Other critical investigations into the use of urban culture forms within naturalism include Nancy Von Rosk's work on the emergence of black consumer culture in Paul Laurence Dunbar's *The Sport of the Gods* and Kecia Driver McBride's reading of the compulsion toward consumption emphasized in Ann Petry's *The Street*; these essays along with Dowling's were collected in my *Twisted from the Ordinary: Essays on American Literary Naturalism* (2003).

More general takes on commodity culture and naturalism include Lois Tyson's reading of *The House of Mirth* that focuses on woman figured as commodity fetish and attempts to determine the cost of such an alienatory process to women and men alike; Sara Quay's study of the effect of materialism upon character in *McTeague*; Robert Shulman's study of the effects of the market on social relations in *The House of Mirth*; Joseph A. Ward's work on the moral barrenness of the hotel as a commodified setting in James, Dreiser, and Wharton; and Philip Fisher's lengthy study of the objectification of self in urban capitalism as it is figured in the American novel. Stanley Corkin directs our attention back to the importance of objects in self-construction in his analysis of *Sister Carrie*. And Edith Wharton's fiction continues to be eminently amenable to examination through the lens of commodification and consumption; see, in particular, the essays collected in Gary Totten's *Memorial Boxes and Guarded Interiors: Edith Wharton and Material Culture* (2007). The perceived centrality of commodity culture to naturalism has even served to renegotiate who belongs in the naturalist canon. Donna Campbell and Jennifer Fleissner have used the engendering of consumer culture, albeit in very different ways, to argue that beneath the hypermasculinity of naturalist texts there is always necessarily the story of a woman. And because of the centralization of commodity culture in the urbanscape and the centrality of commodity culture to naturalism, Seokwon Yang confidently argues for Howells's nomination for a seat, if not precisely in that canon, then closer to it than where his reputation now rests.

The critical work cited above makes a strong case for reimagining naturalism's inventiveness in the representation of social relations and conflict and its necessary attention to issues of race, gender, class, and sex. The body of critical work on naturalism is not comprised of competing narratives except insofar as they vie for our attention; rather, they serve as complementary documentation of the continued relevance of the value of studying the naturalism of the past and into the present. Excavation of the relationship between naturalism and commodity culture paradoxically frees the naturalist label from the moment of its determination and brings naturalism out of the historical record of the late nineteenth century and into our own time. Marx argued that as long as commodity fetishism obtained, then the mass of men—and women—would lead overdetermined lives of alienation and suffering. Our susceptibility to the allure of commodity culture deepens our vulnerability to the matrix of social forces that we neither understand nor control, the matrix of forces that we find so thoroughly documented in naturalism. We can only hope that an understanding of commodity culture's appeal will allow us to loosen its grip on our imaginations. It behooves us, then, to reconsider from every possible angle these perversely dark, sadly plaintive, fantastically cynical scenarios of the human capacity for moral agency, however limited that might be, in contest with the enforced and continual overdetermination of the socialized self, in part effected through commodity fetishism, for which there will be no end in the multinational capitalist worldscape constructed out of glut, guts, and dreams.

WORKS CITED

Appadurai, Arjun. *The Social Life of Things: Commodities in Cultural Perspective.* Cambridge: Cambridge University Press, 1986.

Bowlby, Rachel. *Just Looking: Consumer Culture in Dreiser, Gissing and Zola.* New York: Methuen, 1985.

Brown, Bill. "Interlude: The Agony of Play in 'The Open Boat.'" *Arizona Quarterly* 45 (1989): 23–46.

———. *A Sense of Things: The Object Matter of American Literature.* Chicago: University of Chicago Press, 2003.

Campbell, Donna M. *Resisting Regionalism: Gender and Naturalism in American Fiction, 1885–1915.* Athens: Ohio University Press, 1997.

Chopin, Kate. "A Pair of Silk Stockings." 1897. *The Complete Works of Kate Chopin.* Ed. Per Seyersted. Baton Rouge: Louisiana State University Press, 1969. 500–4.

Corkin, Stanley. "*Sister Carrie* and Industrial Life: Objects and the New American Self." *Modern Fiction Studies* 33 (1987): 605–19.

Cummings, Neil, and Marysia Lewandowska. *The Value of Things.* London: Birkhäuser, 2000.

Davis, James C. *Commerce in Color: Race, Consumer Culture, and American Literature, 1893–1933.* Ann Arbor: University of Michigan Press, 2007.

Davis, Rebecca Harding. *Life in the Iron Mills, or the Korl Woman.* 1861. Old Westbury, N.Y.: Feminist Press, 1972.

Dimock, Wai-chee. "Debasing Exchange: Edith Wharton's *The House of Mirth.*" *PMLA* 100 (1985): 783–92.

Douglas, Mary, and Baron Isherwood. *The World of Goods: Towards an Anthropology of Consumption.* New York: Routledge, 1996.

Dowling, Robert M. "Stephen Crane and the Transformation of the Bowery." Papke 45–62.

Eby, Claire Virginia. "The Psychology of Desire: Veblen's 'Pecuniary Emulation' and 'Invidious Comparison' in *Sister Carrie* and *An American Tragedy.*" *Studies in American Fiction* 21 (1993): 191–208.

Elliott, Emory, gen. ed. *The Columbia Literary History of the United States.* New York: Columbia University Press, 1988.

Evans, Anne-Marie. "Shopping for Survival: Conspicuous Consumerism in Edith Wharton's *The House of Mirth* and Ellen Glasgow's *The Wheel of Life*." *Edith Wharton Review* 22.2 (2006): 9–15.

Fisher, Philip. *Hard Facts: Setting and Form in the American Novel*. Oxford: Oxford University Press, 1985.

Fleissner, Jennifer L. *Women, Compulsion, Modernity: The Moment of American Naturalism*. Chicago: University of Chicago Press, 2004.

Frow, John. *Time and Commodity Culture: Essays in Cultural Theory and Postmodernity*. New York: Oxford University Press, 1997.

Giorcello, Cristina. "Tra costume e letteratura: I cappelli femminili negli Stati Uniti (1878–1914)." *Abito e identità: Ricerche di storia letteraria e culturale*. Rome: Ila Palma, 2004. 105–64.

Harris, Sharon M. *Rebecca Harding Davis and American Realism*. Philadelphia: University of Pennsylvania Press, 1991.

Hawkes, David. *Ideology*. New York: Routledge, 2003.

Howard, June. *Form and History in American Literary Naturalism*. Chapel Hill: University of North Carolina Press, 1985.

Kimmelman, Michael. "Art in Aisle 3, by Lingerie, and Feel Free to Browse." *New York Times* 19 March 1995: sec. 2, 43.

Lamb, Robert Paul, and G. R. Thompson. *A Companion to American Fiction, 1865–1914*. Oxford: Blackwell, 2005.

Lawson, Andrew. "Class Mimicry in Stephen Crane's City." *American Literary History* 16 (2004): 596–618.

Lears, T. J. Jackson. *No Place for Grace: Antimodernism and the Transformation of American Culture, 1880–1920*. Chicago: University of Chicago Press, 1994.

Lears, T. J. Jackson, and Richard Fox, eds. *The Culture of Consumption: Critical Essays in American History 1880–1980*. New York: Pantheon, 1983.

Marx, Karl. *Capital: A Critique of Political Economy*. 1867. New York: Modern Library, 1906.
———. *The Eighteenth Brumaire of Louis Napoleon*. 1852. Moscow: Progress, 1934.

Mauss, Marcel. *The Gift: Forms and Function of Exchange in Archaic Societies*. Trans. Ian Cunnison. Intro. E. E. Evans-Prichard. London: Cohen and West, 1954.

Mayhew, Anne. *Narrating the Rise of Big Business in the USA: How Economists Explain Standard Oil and Wal-Mart*. New York: Routledge, 2008.

McBride, Kecia Drive. "Fear, Consumption, and Desire: Naturalism and Ann Petry's *The Street*." Papke 304–22.

Merish, Lori. "Engendering Naturalism: Narrative Form and Commodity Spectacle in U.S. Naturalist Fiction." *Novel* 29 (1996): 319–45.

Michaels, Walter Benn. *The Gold Standard and the Logic of Naturalism: American Literature at the Turn of the Century*. Berkeley and Los Angeles: University of California Press, 1987.

Mitchell, Lee Clark. *Determined Fictions: American Literary Naturalism*. New York: Columbia University Press, 1989.

Papke, Mary E. *Verging on the Abyss: The Social Fiction of Kate Chopin and Edith Wharton*. New York: Greenwood, 1990.
———, ed. *Twisted from the Ordinary: Essays on American Literary Naturalism*. Knoxville: University of Tennessee Press, 2003.

Pizer, Donald, ed. *The Cambridge Companion to American Realism and Naturalism: Howells to London*. New York: Cambridge University Press, 1995.

Quay, Sara E. "American Imperialism and the Excess of Objects in *McTeague*." *American Literary Realism* 33 (2001): 209–34.

Rosk, Nancy Von. "Coon Shows, Ragtime, and the Blues: Race, Urban Culture, and the Naturalist Vision in Paul Laurence Dunbar's *The Sport of the Gods*." Papke 144–68.

Shi, David E. *Facing Facts: Realism in American Thought and Culture, 1850–1920*. New York: Oxford University Press, 1995.

Shulman, Robert. "Divided Selves and the Market Society: Politics and Psychology in *The House of Mirth*." *Perspectives on Contemporary Literature* 11 (1985): 10–19.

Shulman, Sarah Way. "Mapping the Culture of Abundance: Literary Narratives and Consumer Culture." Lamb and Thompson 318–39.

Singley, Carol J. "Bourdieu, Wharton, and Changing Culture in *The Age of Innocence*." *Cultural Studies* 17 (2003): 495–519.

Smith, Susan, and Melanie Dawson, eds. *The American 1890s: A Cultural Reader*. Durham: Duke University Press, 2000.

Spindler, Michael. *American Literature and Social Change: William Dean Howells to Arthur Miller*. London: Macmillan, 1983.

Totten, Gary, ed. *Memorial Boxes and Guarded Interiors: Edith Wharton and Material Culture*. Tuscaloosa: University of Alabama Press, 2007.

Trachtenberg, Alan. *The Incorporation of America: Culture and Society in the Gilded Age*. New York: Hill and Wang, 1982.

Tyson, Lois. *Psychological Politics of the American Dream: The Commodification of Subjectivity in Twentieth-Century American Literature*. Columbus: Ohio State University Press, 1994.

Varricchio, Mario. "The Wasteful Few: Upton Sinclair's Portrait of New York's High Society." *Public Space, Private Lives: Race, Gender, Class, and Citizenship in New York 1890–1929*. Ed. William Boelhower and Anna Scacchi. Amsterdam: VU Press, 2004. 242–61.

Veblen, Thorstein. *The Theory of the Leisure Class*. 1899. Oxford: Oxford University Press, 2009.

Ward, Joseph A. "'The Amazing Hotel World' of James, Dreiser, and Wharton." *Leon Edel and Literary Art*. Ed. Lyall H. Powers. Ann Arbor: University of Michigan Press, 1988. 151–60.

Weber, Myles. "Lacking Brutish Conviction: Vandover's Tumble from the Leisure Class." *Studies in American Fiction* 31 (2003): 221–33.

Williams, Raymond. *Marxism and Literature*. Oxford: Oxford University Press, 1977.

Yang, Seokwon. "Howells' Realism Reconsidered: Representing the Unrepresentable in *A Hazard of New Fortunes*." *Journal of English Language and Literature* 49 (2003): 845–70.

Yeazell, Ruth Bernard. "The Conspicuous Wasting of Lily Bart." *ELH* 59 (1992): 713–34.

Zola, Émile. *Au Bonheur des dames*. 1883. Trans. Brian Nelson as *The Ladies' Paradise*. Oxford: Oxford University Press, 1995.

CHAPTER 18

NATURALISM AND CLASS

JUDE DAVIES

REBECCA Harding Davis's prototypical naturalist novella "Life in the Iron-Mills" (1861) opens with a long description of the dirt and fog produced by heavy industry, in which are glimpsed "masses of men, with dull besotted faces bent to the ground" (40). Davis goes on to announce what would become a typical if deceptively simple authorial strategy, urging the reader to "hide your disgust, take no heed to your clean clothes, and come right down with me,—here, into the thickest of the fog and mud and foul effluvia" (41). This definition of the naturalist author as mediating the experience of an industrial, often immigrant working class for the middle-class reading public would solidify in the central works of naturalist literature, helping define it as a literary form. As a pioneer, Davis writes with more intensity than would be the case in the canonical naturalist works of the turn of the century, works that perhaps are more valued because of their apparent ease in accomplishing what in Davis had to be done dramatically and explicitly. But her example highlights the work necessary to produce and substantiate naturalist writing's negotiation of American class divisions. Notwithstanding the class background or political affiliations of their authors, Stephen Crane's *Maggie: A Girl of the Streets* (1893), Frank Norris's *McTeague* (1899), Theodore Dreiser's *Sister Carrie* (1900), and even overtly socialist-identified work such as Jack London's *The People of the Abyss* (1903) and Upton Sinclair's *The Jungle* (1906) in one way or another interpolate readers as fellow members of the middle-class and offer them access to the public, domestic, and laboring spaces of those who work manually or who are unemployed. As claims for the innovatory status of this writing were predicated upon its mediation of class experience, its authors were credentialed by their detailed observation of urban life, whether as newspaper reporters (Crane, Dreiser, Sinclair, and David Graham Phillips, author of *Susan Lenox: Her Fall and Rise* [1917]), through deliberate passing as a member of the underclass (Crane in "An Experiment in Misery" [1894] and

London in *The People of the Abyss*), or by former membership in the working class (London and Sinclair and, more obliquely, Dreiser). Naturalism's engagement with class, then, allowed for authors' diverse responses to a nation perceived to be divided by class as never before in its history, the centrifugal force of which was contained by its framing as the representation by and to the middle class of its "other half."

This mediating project aligns naturalism with the political and cultural main-stream of the progressive era, situating it within the broader move to manage the tensions and conflicts engendered by the United States' rapid industrialization and urbanization and its changing ethnic make-up due to mass immigration.[1] Across a broad spectrum of political and cultural discourses, a key element of this project tied the representation of the urban poor to the emergence of a new middle class. Alongside reporter and slum reformer Jacob Riis in *How the Other Half Lives: Studies Among the Tenements of New York* (1890) and President Theodore Roos-evelt, who in December 1901 used his first annual message to Congress to warn of the "very serious social problems" posed by "the growth of cities" and the "startling increase . . . in the number of . . . very large fortunes" (13), naturalism played a sig-nificant role in forging this new middle-class sensibility. Like Riis and Roosevelt, Dreiser, Norris, Crane, and even the overtly left-wing Sinclair and London helped shape and solidify this class and ultimately enabled its self-recognition as the cul-tural and political mainstream, a position it retains. Typical naturalist texts helped define an aspirational middle class against existing elites and the industrial working class through their subject matter and mode of address. Looking upward and back-ward, naturalism catered to a literary taste that thought of itself as displacing the "genteel" realism associated with Boston and of which William Dean Howells became, somewhat unfairly, the epitome. Looking downward, the naturalist text differentiated its readers from its typical subjects precisely by virtue of their implied capacity for self-determination, in contrast to the Maggies, McTeagues, Carries, Hurstwoods, and others, whose narratives are determined by social and biological forces.

Hence, though naturalism broke with picturesque, sentimental, and sensation-alistic depictions of poverty, its embrace of environmental determinism tended to objectify its working-class and underclass subjects.[2] For this reason, direct represen-tations of the agency of workers as a class are found more frequently during this period in other literary forms, especially at the historical remove of utopian and dystopian fiction such as Ignatius Donnelly's *Caesar's Column* (1890) and Jack Lon-don's hybrid utopian/naturalistic novel *The Iron Heel* (1908). While Donnelly expresses both intoxication with and fear of mass action as irrational and uncontrol-lable, London contains revolutionary class action within a complex narrative frame. *The Iron Heel* is presented as a manuscript written by one Avis Cunningham, which describes at first hand a revolt against the capitalist plutocracy of the immediate future. Breaking off abruptly in 1932, the manuscript is annotated by Anthony Mer-edith, an editor living in a utopian commonwealth seven hundred years distant from the action of the narrative, who discloses from the outset that the revolt failed, pro-voking a fascistic backlash known as the "iron heel," which intensified and prolonged plutocratic power for three hundred years. Through Avis, a professor's daughter who is attracted to and later marries a labor leader, Ernest Everhard, London provides an exemplary narrative of a shift from middle-class to working-class political outlook, while her middle-class sensibility, refracted especially through the novel's diction, is aimed at satisfying readers' literary preferences. Filtered through Avis's political education at the hands of Ernest Everhard, London depicts the violence visited upon working-class people through recognizable naturalistic narrative strategies, ranging from the physical damage to workers inflicted by avoidable industrial accidents to the repression organized to protect the plutocracy when its power is threatened. From a socialist perspective, naturalism proves a useful vehicle to depict the injuries of class, while the novel's evocation of revolutionary social change remains abstract. Though Ernest Everhard is a working-class hero combining intellectual, physical, and political leadership rarely glimpsed in straightforwardly naturalist texts, readers are aware of his failure and execution from the start, and the novel's title reflects its main focus.

The narrators of more typical naturalist texts rarely go even this far in envisioning working-class agency, while tending at the same time to avoid attributing constraints upon individual agency to economic class. Determination and constraint are registered instead as biological, ethnic, and psychological degeneration, and shifts in individual class position operate as indices of these other "forces." Thus Frank Norris's *McTeague* details the economic, moral, and physical downfall of a set of characters who, like McTeague himself, cannot control the "brute that . . . lay so close to the surface" (234). In *Maggie: A Girl of the Streets* Stephen Crane makes a young Irish slum girl's romantic dreams of middle-class domesticity the means of her seduction, abandonment, and death. Crane effectively suspends middle-class judgment upon his underclass characters, adopting what Keith Gandal terms an "ethnographic" approach to social forms (53) that neither excuses, blames, nor exactly sympathizes. Individuals of any class may "stupidly," as Crane puts it elsewhere, believe that social forms are immutable laws, or just as stupidly, like Maggie, fail to understand the social codes by which they are to be judged. Still, it is the stupidity of the Tenderloin and the Bowery, not the drawing room, which mostly interests Crane as a writer, and in part *Maggie* dramatizes how the penalties for violating social forms vary considerably according to class and gender. Class is central to these canonical naturalist texts, but as Crane's understanding of stupidity as classless suggests, their narrative dynamics lie at a tangent to class.

Despite naturalism's hesitation over working-class agency, its depiction of the "other half" is not reducible to objectification in the service of defining a middle-class observer. In *Labor's Text: The Worker in American Fiction*, a monumental history of the worker in American fiction, Laura Hapke hails turn-of-the-century naturalism and realism as exhibiting "the first positive interest in the artistic uses of working-class subject matter" in American literature (97), albeit an interest that would not come to fruition until the very different circumstances of the 1930s and later. An understanding of naturalism in solely middle-class terms cannot explain why writers like Crane and Dreiser would serve as enabling models for later generations intent on depicting working people from the inside and as a distinct class, often alongside ethnic and racial difference. Itself intermediate between contemporaries Jacob Riis and Theodore Roosevelt and later writers like Abraham Cahan, James T. Farrell, Michael Gold, Agnes Smedley, John Fante, Richard Wright, Richard Price, and Joyce Carol Oates, naturalism's mediation of class embraces a complicated set of affiliations and disaffiliations and alternative perspectives.

Even when viewed through the lens of its participation in the formation of middle-class consciousness, naturalism brought to the surface doubts and anxieties that were repressed in the reformist discourse of progressive politics. The strained, even melodramatic evocation of class difference in the antebellum "Life in the Iron-Mills" exemplifies this particularly clearly. Extrapolating Alexis de Tocqueville's fear that "at the very time at which the science of manufactures lowers the class of the workmen, it raises the class of masters" (86), Davis's novella depicts class difference in absolute terms, contrasting the cultured, leisured middle class (including by implication her readers) with workers whose daily struggle to survive renders them wage slaves. Davis tropes this class binary according to a racial dualism of the free and the unfree that is suggested by the smoky, blackening nature of industrial labor, which is signaled in the opening paragraphs by connecting the spectacle of laborers going to work, the "slow stream of human life creeping past, night and morning, to the mills" with the narrator's childhood fancy of "a look of weary, dumb appeal upon the face of the negro-like river slavishly bearing its burden day after day" (40). Later, the narrator slips into the account of a touristic visit to the mill by a group of middle-class men a reference to Virginia's status as a "Slave State" (51). This tendency to project class difference on to a black/white binary of race is also found in later naturalist texts, as will be seen,[3] but its evocation in "Life in the Iron-Mills" is particularly forceful. Hugh Wolfe, its flawed hero, apprehends class as an "order of being" (49), feeling that his own existence is close to nothingness in comparison to the freedom and autonomy enjoyed by the middle-class visitors, a view corroborated by the narrative of his moral temptation, imprisonment, and suicide. The racial trope reinforces Wolfe's narrative of degeneration, defining the workers as being so degraded as to be beyond the reach of either national democratic traditions or sociopolitical reform. Instead of these, Davis offers redemption in spiritual and religious form, following the story of Hugh Wolfe's death with a brief account of how his widow Deborah Wolfe is befriended and introduced to Quakerism by the narrator. In the closing pages of "Life in the Iron-Mills," the light/dark metaphor shifts from a racial register to that of Christian symbolism, as Davis invokes "God['s] . . . promise of the Dawn" (74) in an effort to imagine class reconciliation.

In *Playing in the Dark*, Toni Morrison has shown how blackness is often used figuratively to work through tensions and contradictions in American literature. Davis's metaphorical invocation of slavery effects a symbolic erasure of African American experience (and the need to address problems of race as well as class) along the lines traced by Morrison, though in doing so it works not toward ideological coherence but to undermine eighteenth- and early nineteenth-century ideas of American classlessness. The novella goes so far as to depict the rhetoric of self-improvement as itself an instrument of mystification, self-consciously exploding beliefs that "the American system" is "a ladder that any man can scale" (54), as mill-owner Kirby glibly states. These and other more well-meaning middle-class pronouncements in the face of structural economic inequality, Davis suggests, put Hugh Wolfe in the impossible position for which the only resolution is suicide. Unable to fulfill his potential as a sculptor or as a man, by the grind of work and the impossibility of class mobility, Wolfe is particularly excited by the urgings of the good-hearted but ineffectual Doctor May, one of the group of visitors to the mill who act as mouthpieces for various middle-class perspectives on poverty. "Make yourself what you will. It is your right" (56), urges May, in words that echo through Wolfe's mind over several pages, determining his fateful decision to keep the pocket-book stolen by Deborah. Though the effect is ultimately softened by Davis's Quaker jeremiad, "Life in the Iron-Mills" portrays the discourse of classlessness as making the crisis of democracy worse. In other words, the absolute class difference depicted in the novella is not simply attributable to the direct environmental constraints imposed upon the mill workers, which by themselves could be considered aberrations from traditions of American classlessness, requiring only the restoration of such traditions. Rather, Davis shows the chasm of class being deepened by a rhetoric of rights and self-determination that is completely decoupled from economic, legislative, or political reality.

This quite-radical suggestion of the invidious effects of democratic and aspirational discourses in the absence of actual working-class agency is touched upon by Crane in *Maggie* and is the subject of sustained treatment by Dreiser in *An American Tragedy* (1925) as well as in essays such as "Life, Art and America" (1917) and "More Democracy or Less? An Inquiry" (1919). The latter essay discusses the problem of working-class agency in terms of politics, implicitly rejecting the spiritual resolution that Davis had invoked. Dreiser thus entertains the very different possibility that, given the weakness of organized labor, some kind of autocracy might be necessary to curb corporate power. Dreiser's novels also reiterate Davis's dualistic sense of class, repeatedly depicting the experience of class difference in absolute terms, as felt lack and imagined presence. Animated by what Dreiser's narrator calls "the old definition: 'Money: something everybody else has and I must get'" (*Sister Carrie* 45), Carrie Meeber's social rise is predicated on chasing the feelings of satisfaction and contentment that she believes are possessed only by members of the middle class. Whether faced with the patrons of Chicago's department stores, the inhabitants of North Shore Drive mansions, behind whose "richly carved entrance ways" Carrie imagines there was "happiness" and "neither care nor unsatisfied desire" (86), or the parade of fashionable socialites on Broadway (227), Carrie associates middle-class identity with the satisfaction of desire and her own status as utterly lacking.[4]

Dreiser's best-known novels, *Sister Carrie* and *An American Tragedy*, no doubt owe some of their popularity to this foregrounding of desire and lack in the experience of class difference. Other Dreiser texts uncover the formation of dualistic notions of class, often by reference to race, since Dreiser tends to position the racial troping of class at one or more removes from the authorial persona. The opening chapter of *The Financier* (1912) contains one of the most famous naturalistic passages in American literature where, as a young boy, the future millionaire Frank Cowperwood learns a social Darwinist lesson by watching the struggle between a lobster and a squid. What is often missed in readings of this passage is how Frank immediately redacts this lesson from the natural world into an understanding of racial tension within the antebellum United States. His understanding of "how life is organized" derives not directly from the lobster's victory over the squid but from the awareness of slavery and one-sided racial conflict to which his mind immediately connects it: "That was it! Sure, men lived on men. Look at the slaves. They were men. That was what all the excitement was about these days. Men killing other men—negroes" (5). It is this consciousness of the historical acceptability of slavery that legitimates for the adult Cowperwood the view of finance capitalism as an arena for the ruthless pursuit of self-interest. At another social level, in the 1911 story "The Mighty Rourke," Dreiser has an Irish foreman call Italian workers "nagurs" to express the immutability of their subordinate status as mere laborers. Though the first-person narrator questions this, he is able only to correct Rourke's terminology (to "negroes" and then "blacks"), not his racialized conception of a fundamental difference between foreman and laborer (291).

The twist in the tail of "The Mighty Rourke" is that this "dogmatic and unreasoning" foreman eventually sacrifices himself to protect his team of workers when a building collapses under them. It is one of several stories and essays in which Dreiser interrogates the class binary by reference to figures who directly mediate between capital and labor. Several of these emanate from his own experience working as what he called "an amateur laborer" for the New York Central Railroad between June and December 1903 as he recovered from a mental and physical breakdown, and it was a topic Dreiser revisited in 1924–25, while composing *An American Tragedy*. Of these, "The Mighty Rourke," a later reworking of the same material in "The Irish Section Foreman Who Taught Me How to Live" (1924), and "St. Columba and the River" (1925) offer broadly celebratory accounts of such mediators. By contrast, "The Toil of the Laborer" (1913), a combination of autobiographical fiction and philosophical meditation on industrial work, describes how, when made foreman, the narrator drives his team of laborers still harder than did his hated predecessor. A particularly interesting aspect of "The Toil of the Laborer" is that it works a distinct Dreiserian trope, the urban scene at "quitting time," from the perspective of the internalization of class power, in direct contrast to its typical association with what critic Robert Seguin terms "middle-class fantasy." As Seguin has observed, in *Sister Carrie* the evocation of this moment, at which work is done and leisure is anticipated, encodes a kind of "urban pastoral" through which can be glimpsed, with a little interpretive effort, a utopian vision of unalienated labor (19–27, 42). While Seguin's reading of this formation in *Sister Carrie* is enlightening, the same logic is comprehensively rejected in "The Toil of the Laborer." There, "quitting time" evokes the contrast between railroad passengers glimpsed through windows reclining in warmth and comfort, and the worn-out Italian immigrant workers, "all trudging patiently on like cattle." Contrasting "the weariness of their labor with the flower which it had produced," the narrator resolves to have no more part in this exploitative system, "even though by quitting I could not relieve the situation of its pain" (11).

These stories and essays, formally on the periphery of naturalism, complicate naturalism's habitual binarizing of class difference and implicitly contest its popularizing, even in a way universalizing, of a middle-class perspective. They present the "middle-ness" of the middle-class as problematic, interstitial, and even torn between irresolvable affiliations. Sharing a common concern with the foreman figure as a kind of mediator between classes, they evoke various understandings of class relations. Rourke epitomizes a tough, working-class masculinity that understands implicitly the responsibilities that come with leadership; the world of "The Mighty Rourke" is exclusively working class, with little reference to the wider social and economic contexts that, in the last analysis, determine the hazards encountered on the job. McGlathery in "St. Columba and the River" gropes uncertainly toward a similar ideal of the foreman who protects his team, while this story complicates matters by widening the context to include another level of mediators, engineers who promise to make tunneling safer for the workers, and the economics of danger by which a higher rate of pay lures McGlathery back underground after successive accidents. The autobiographical narrator of "The Toil of the Laborer," however, ends up negating the role of the foreman completely, as one required by corporate ethics to extract maximum profit from those whose share in it is negligible.

These differing, and to an extent conflicting, evocations of class in the work of a single author underline that naturalism's project of class mediation is unstable and diverse, its varied depictions of the "other half" clashing against its invocation of the binary distinction encapsulated by Riis's resonant phrase. Even Upton Sinclair, who identified himself as "proletarian" and intended that *The Jungle* portray the Lithuanian workers of Chicago's Packingtown "from the inside," addressed the novel's readers as if they were ignorant of industrial working conditions. Though dedicated "To the Workingmen of America," *The Jungle* presents itself as another window on the "other half" both in its book publication and its serialization in the socialist *Appeal to Reason* in 1905–6. The magazine had a circulation of 300,000 at the time—according to Michael Brewster Folsom, the largest working-class socialist readership of any publication in the history of the American left. Yet as Folsom points out, Sinclair stated his belief in an open letter to the magazine that "the majority of the *Appeal* readers are ignorant" of the "system that prevails in Packingtown" (506), and Sinclair researched and presented his exposé accordingly, immersing himself in Packingtown, gaining access to the meat-processing yards disguised as an inspector, and attending the Lithuanian *veselija* or wedding feast that gave rise to the novel's first chapter, all of which is registered through the perspective of the novel's guiding authorial persona, who at times refers to himself explicitly as a "visitor" questioning the "residents" (*Jungle* 30).

This middle-class positioning allowed *The Jungle* to reach beyond the socialist movement into the progressive mainstream. Sinclair's dealings with President Theodore Roosevelt in the wake of the publication of *The Jungle* have been well documented. The arch-mediator of the period, Roosevelt responded to the furor touched off by the novel, as Robert M. Crunden describes, by assuming a "sincere and characteristic pose, that of the interested and aroused citizen holding off the radicals and lecturing them while trying in all honesty to get the facts so he could act sanely" (455). This was Roosevelt's way of dealing with more radical demands for reform, epitomized by the journalism he himself stigmatized as "muck-raking." Roosevelt's highly personalized self-presentation as performing this mediating role has not only helped shape the personae expected of presidents, but it has also helped orchestrate progressive reform around an emergent American middle class. His appeal was a grander version of Jacob Riis's, installing the middle class at the political center in opposition to a small, corrupt corporate elite and as guardians of the welfare of a large, powerless urban class. Roosevelt's political rhetoric could always go further than naturalist literature in framing middle-class agency around the activities of reform and management, rather than, simply, observation. Conversely, the naturalists explored what Roosevelt could only hint at: that the urban poor served not only as passive recipients of influence, but also, at least some of them—the Rourkes, the Jurgis Rudkuses, the Martin Edens—as limit cases of the national ideology of democratic individualism.

The popularity of *The Jungle* gave Upton Sinclair unprecedented access, for a novelist, to Roosevelt's White House as industrial legislation was being drafted. Yet he was famously frustrated at the book's influence being confined to the regulation of meat-processing hygiene rather than as an indictment of "what [the country's] industrial masters were doing to their victims" (Sinclair, "What Life" 351). Sinclair's well-known comment in a 1906 article that "I aimed at the public's heart, and by accident I hit it in the stomach" ("What Life" 351) is one of the most striking examples of how the consumption of naturalism was determined by progressive-era class formations. It also typifies the widespread concern displayed by naturalist writers with the interpretive frameworks of their texts, made manifest in their numerous narrative interventions, prefaces, and commentaries within, at the margins, and outside their literary works: the scene-setting introduction of "Life in the Iron-Mills"; the intrusive philosophical commentaries in Dreiser's *Sister Carrie*; the overtly pedagogical positioning of the lobster and the squid episode in *The Financier*; London's variously fictionalized and direct explanations of himself and his views in *The Iron Heel*, *Martin Eden*, and *John Barleycorn* (1913); and in Stephen Crane's description of his intent in writing *Maggie*, inscribed in copies of the first edition sent to literary figures and reformers "to show that environment is a tremendous thing in the world and frequently shapes lives regardless." Rather at odds with the mock-heroic tone and the episodic, proto-modernist organization of the novella, Crane suggests that his aim has been to make "room in Heaven for all sorts of souls (notably an occasional street girl) who are not confidently expected to be there by many excellent people" ("*Maggie* Inscription" 1).

Why would naturalist writers feel such an urge to supplement their fictions with explanation? One answer is provided by the proliferation of what naturalist writers regarded as misinterpretations of their depictions of class and of politics.

London, for example, responded in public to criticism of *Martin Eden* by Oakland pastor Reverend Charles R. Brown. He further intended to correct misreadings of the novel in the "alcoholic memoirs" *John Barleycorn*, since despite its depictions of literary production as turning the writer into a "work-beast," prevalent literary taste as utterly bankrupt, and literary success as an illusion bringing only despair and ultimately leading to suicide, some readers had insisted on reading *Martin Eden* as a kind of Horatio Alger self-help book for aspiring writers. Yet these misinterpretations also suggest a dialogism in naturalist texts that is often concealed by naturalistic metaphors—for example, readers' assumptions that Dreiser and his narrator share Cowperwood's interpretation of the lesson of the lobster and the squid. This is, in part, Jennifer Fleissner's point when she argues for an expanded "*natural-ism*" animated by "the sense of the natural and the social as intertwined and yet distinct, thus calling for ongoing theorization of their interconnection," in contradistinction to "the social Darwinist view that the social world turns out to be simply *equivalent* to, a mirror of, an already grasped natural world of predator and prey" (22). It is surely arguable that for the most part, naturalist texts are at their least persuasive when they inject narrative explanations about natural science. Such authorial explanations are less convincing than the strong appeal of class as visual spectacle—the authentic snapshot of the "other half" like a Riis photograph—and the engaging narrative of class mobility, whether as decline, ascension, compulsion, or constraint. *Martin Eden* itself can be seen as exemplifying this hierarchy, notwithstanding London's unusual (among naturalist writers) interest in narrative over spectacle. When the young Martin Eden encounters his former girlfriend, the working-class Lizzie Connolly, while out walking with his middle-class love interest Ruth Morse, Martin explains with absolute authority to Ruth how the "hardness" visible in the working-class girl's eyes results from long hours of machine labor and the need for self-reliance (92). Where the novel utterly lacks authority (and herein lies much of its interest for readers) is in the management of Martin's own ascension narrative, which requires a great deal of brutalizing labor, only for him to be utterly disillusioned by success and middle-class life. Herbert Spencer offers no help whatsoever in negotiating this disillusionment, neither for Eden, who commits suicide, nor perhaps for London, for whom Eden was clearly, but in complex and contradictory ways, a surrogate self.[5]

The naturalists' apparent need for extra-diegetic explanation might therefore be taken as an attempt to resolve the tension generated by the form's simultaneous commitment to spectacle, with its promise that an energetic middle class will reintegrate society, and to narratives that disrupt this integration. Frank Norris's *The Octopus* (1901) provides a case in point. This substantial novel narrates the conflict between the Pacific and South Western Railroad and a group of Californian ranchers who are destroyed morally, politically, and economically. What is distinctive about *The Octopus* is less its implicit nativism and ethnic chauvinism than its overt use of post-Darwinian ideas to reinvigorate an earlier mode of social integration, one whose passing was marked by the progressive era's acknowledgement of class. As the novel draws to a close, Norris alternates powerfully between depicting a sumptuous dinner party given by a railroad vice-president, and the grinding down of a rancher's widowed family into prostitution and starvation. Norris's protagonist Presley, a guest at the dinner who has hitherto sided with the ranchers, has a "fancy" of the railroad's activities as "unspeakable cannibalism" (608), which seems to be confirmed when Norris narrates how the guests discuss the freshness of their asparagus (brought by rail so that it can be consumed within twenty hours of being cut), while outside Mrs. Hooven starves to death on the streets of San Francisco, with her young child in tow. Norris's indictment of the railroad at this point is so strong that Upton Sinclair included the passage in his 1915 anthology of social protest literature, *The Cry for Justice*. And before the end of the novel, Norris has S. Behrman, another railroad executive who has orchestrated its strategy against the ranchers, fall into the hold of the cargo ship *Swanhilda*, where he suffocates in a load of wheat being loaded for transportation to India. Though certainly un-American, and Norris's nativism is evident in his casting a Jew in this role, Behrman is not simply a scapegoat for the evils of capitalism. In the novel's conclusion, Presley, aboard the same vessel, experiences a revelation about the globalization of capital that renders immaterial the "welter of blood" and "sham charity and shallow philanthropy" of the preceding 650 pages (651). The circumstances of the wheat's production may have been violent and oppressive, but because the laws of supply and demand dictate that the wheat will be shipped to the starving in India, "in a far distant corner of the world a thousand lives are saved" (652). According to this "larger view" (652), Behrman may well be regarded as being punished, not for his role in the "years of extortion and oppression" (608), but for his hubris—"I guess there ain't nothing can touch me" (627), he tells Presley after having beaten and humiliated the ranchers— in assuming that he can control the "force" of nature. Though Behrman is a minor character, the similarity to Captain Ahab in Melville's *Moby Dick* is telling, for Norris recasts the American "romance" for a post-Darwinist sensibility. With Behrman's death and the novel's conclusion, Norris refracts a naturalist sense of class conflict through the literary tradition of the earlier nineteenth century. That tradition, as Myra Jehlen has argued, resulted from the historical integration of the United States as a nation in middle-class terms in contrast to, for example, European societies in which the middle class came to power through insurgency against older elites. Human nature and society were therefore conceptualized as being essentially in harmony, and the universe itself was imagined as a kind of natural marketplace. Yet individualism itself constituted a paradox with which, Jehlen argues, the "romance" tradition wrestles: while "individualistic ambition" was natural, its realization was taboo, since it would violate for others the open future upon which it depends (54–55). In *The Octopus*, Norris restores a sense that "America's growth" was "the unfolding realization of its inherent form and meaning" (Jehlen 53) precisely by associating that growth with a naturalized vision of global capitalism. The "colossal indifference" of nature, that had earlier seemed so devastating to Presley, becomes in the novel's conclusion a token of its ability—and that of the capitalism that has merged with it—to transcend class. To achieve this transcendence, *The Octopus* pushes the naturalist project of mediation to its extreme. The novel retains both naturalism's orientation of integrative spectacle and disintegrative narrative, as well as its privileging of the former, while shifting their content. Narrative encodes social disruption, not only in the struggle between railroad and ranchers that is the novel's basic theme, but also as cause and effect: the Hooven family are defeated by the railroad, expelled from the land, and fall into destitution, prostitution, and death. But this narrative logic is outflanked by Norris's transcendentalist reworking of naturalist spectacle, which dispenses with the "other half" and instead takes "the larger view"—a global perspective.

Fainter echoes of the romance's dilemma of individualism can also be seen in the subgenre of naturalist novels that engages simultaneously with popular narratives of ascension: the class-mobility stories of the age of the robber barons, such as Dreiser's *Sister Carrie* and the Cowperwood trilogy *The Financier* (1912), *The Titan* (1914), and *The Stoic* (1947), as well as London's *Martin Eden* and *Burning Daylight* (1910). London's first capitalist hero, Elam Harnish, known as "Burning Daylight" for his energy, is rescued from the romantic dilemma by his immersion in a kind of prototypical ecological consciousness at his Sonoma County ranch, together with a bourgeois romance narrative culminating in marriage. Dreiser has Cowperwood, whose motto is "I satisfy myself," neither seek nor find any such redemption, though at the end of the trilogy, his widow finds some satisfaction in Eastern mysticism.

Concerned as much with the workings of finance capitalism and the psychological effects of the success ethic as they are with class, these narratives of social mobility return us to the formation of the "other half." Jacob Riis's work continues to act as a touchstone for understandings of naturalism and class because it foregrounds naturalism's dualistic framing of the "other half" as simultaneously limit cases of the national ideology of democratic individualism and as objects of fascination for the middle-class gaze. Thus Riis is seen on the one hand as initiating the humanitarian tradition of documentary photography that would become more socially conscious in the hands of Lewis Hine and in 1930s work by Dorothea Lange, Walker Evans, and other New Deal photographers. Yet on the other hand, as Maren Stange has remarked, Riis's work employs "the controlling gaze as middle-class right and tool" (23). Like his political hero and sometime-mentor Theodore Roosevelt, whose photograph appears as the frontispiece to *The Battle with the Slum* (1902), Riis moved from a concern with eliminating urban corruption to an overt program of "Americanization." Unlike Roosevelt, however, Riis rejected nativism, arguing that immigration should be unrestricted as to ethnicity and geographical origin. Riis's work abounds in descriptions of individuals who are asserted to be "representative" of ethnic groups, but this superficial sense of ethnic determinism is undermined, especially in his late work, by an understanding of ethnicity as a momentarily historicized form of environmental determinism. Riis depicts the determining effects of ethnicity (as he sees it) and environment as precursors to the transforming power of assimilation and a positive environment. Implicit in the reform agenda surrounding *How the Other Half Lives*, this strategy is made explicit in its sequels *A Ten Years' War* (1900) and *The Battle with the Slum* (1902), in which Riis argues against any bars to immigration on ethnic or geographical criteria and looks specifically to working-class Jewish and Italian immigrants as prime "material for citizenship" (*Battle* 192).

Naturalist writers such as Dreiser and Crane echoed Riis's rage against a privileged class complicit in maintaining the status quo, and his address to an emergent middle class which is differentiating itself from the leisure class on the one side and the inhabitants of the slum on the other. Their embrace of various reforming and political projects also links Dreiser, Sinclair, and London with Riis. (As editor of the women's magazine the *Delineator* from 1907–10, Dreiser obtained contributions from Riis.) But what marks the naturalists as different from other reformers is their comparative lack of faith in the program of "Americanization" that Riis commends as a means of enabling immigrants to climb in American society. Rather, naturalists ran the gamut of the mixed and conflicted notions of class characterizing the Janus-faced era of progressivism. Politically, as has been seen, they could outflank Riis to the left, with the socialism that Sinclair and London sought to express in their fiction, or to the right, with the nativism and social Darwinism codified in London's animal fictions *The Call of the Wild* (1903) and *White Fang* (1906) and in Norris's *McTeague*, or with the naturalist/transcendentalism of *The Octopus*. Crane, whose politics are least explicit, is stylistically closest to Riis, a congruence noted by contemporary reviewers who described *Maggie* as a series of "instantaneous literary photographs of slum life" (qtd. in Hayes 8), an explicit echo of Riis's 1888 article in the *New York Sun* that launched his career as a photographer and reformer.

Crane, despite the overt leftist positioning of Sinclair, London, and the later Dreiser, is also perhaps the strongest link with later writers who tried, in more favorable circumstances, to depict working-class experience from the inside. In *Jews Without Money* (1930) for example, one of the strongest assertions of the determining power of class in American writing, Michael Gold adapts many of the tropes used by Crane to depict the Bowery in order to portray the Jewish Lower East Side situated, Gold explains, only a block away (13). Reminiscing about the 1890s and 1900s—every saloon displays a chronotype of Theodore Roosevelt—Gold like Crane presents the episodic drama of the street, with its protagonists and its viewers and its recurring vignettes of poverty: the violent street games, the young prostitute, and the boy decapitated while playing under a horse-car. Like Crane, in part Gold considered himself to be picturing the effects of an "environment" of material deprivation, and like Crane he felt the need to draw attention to this aim outside the text in a preface added to the book in 1935 under the shadow of Nazi anti-Semitism.

By registering the injuries of class as a constraint upon the autonomy of working-class subjects, naturalism in the 1890s and the 1900s tended to attribute agency only to the exceptional individual who ascends the social ladder out of poverty. Gold, by contrast, reserves an acid portrayal for the middle-class Jews who have left the ghetto. Describing a visit to Borough Park, a new suburb being built in Brooklyn, Gold opens a paragraph, "Mrs. Cohen, a fat, middle-aged woman, lay on a sofa. She glittered like an ice-cream parlor. Her tubby legs rested on a red pillow. . . . She looked like some vulgar, pretentious prostitute, but was only the typical wife of a Jewish *nouveau rich*" (217). Stylistically echoing Crane, Gold also points to the emergence of new spaces where class began to be made visible later in the twentieth century. While many writers in the naturalist tradition have continued to figuratively "go down into the mud," suburbia may have emerged as a key site of the continuing negotiation of class and *natural-ism* alike, not least because its utopian promise and dystopian menace both depend upon environmental determinism. In Richard Yates's *Revolutionary Road* (1961), Frank Wheeler remarks when viewing the suburban house into which he and his family will move that "I don't suppose one picture window is necessarily going to destroy our personalities" (29). The personalities of Frank and April Wheeler are indeed destroyed during the course of the novel. And like his predecessors at the turn of the century, Yates felt the need to elucidate his view of environmental determinism outside the literary text. As he put it in a 1972 interview: "The book was widely read as an anti-suburban novel, and that disappointed me. The Wheelers may have thought the suburbs were to blame for all their problems, but I meant it to be implicit in the text that that was *their* delusion, *their* problem, not mine" (Henry and Clark 1).

Such have continued to be the problems, possibilities, and productivity of naturalist depictions of class.

NOTES

1. Here I am in part echoing June Howard's sense of the naturalist writer as playing "the role of the readers' guide and interpreter in an alien land" (that is, working-class experience), which, she claims, betokens "the fundamental structural similarity . . . between naturalism and progressivism" (159, 160). Howard's highly influential work has inspired critics such as Keith Gandal and Robert Seguin to explore in more detail naturalism's complicities with progressivism, especially in relation to the culture and psychology of the twentieth-century American middle class. My argument emphasizes that naturalist works were not predetermined to conform to mainstream progressive ideology and suggests that they tend to exceed the containing observational, diagnostic, and reformist elements of progressive discourse. Naturalism both promulgated and undermined the middle-class perspectives associated with progressivism, sometimes, as with Dreiser's *Sister Carrie* and Sinclair's *The Jungle*, in the same text.

2. "Picturesque" and "sensationalistic" are drawn from Gavin Jones's observations on the reputation of Crane and Dreiser as innovators in *American Hungers* (37). Jones, however, disputes that naturalism was either formally or politically innovatory, emphasizing its tendencies to reinforce contemporary middle-class assumptions about poverty.

3. For example, Upton Sinclair recounted conceiving of *The Jungle* as the equivalent of Harriet Beecher Stowe's abolitionist *Uncle Tom's Cabin* for wage-slaves ("What Life" 350–51).

4. Carrie's dualistic understanding of class in terms of desire and lack contrasts somewhat with that of the novel's other major protagonist, George Hurstwood, whose status as a bar manager brings with it a sense of class as a "finely graduated scale" (32). However, after Hurstwood falls into poverty in New York, he adopts a similar dualism of have and have-not.

5. During the novel, Martin engages in a fabulously overwrought debate over the true social and political significance of Herbert Spencer, in which he accuses the progressive Judge Blount of talking individualism while enacting socialistic measures in restraint of corporations. Professing the credo of individualism (as did London, alongside his socialism), Eden is unsurprised when the capitalist press subsequently describes him as a socialist (272–77). On the parallels between London and Eden, especially in the context of the now largely discredited possibility that London himself committed suicide, see Raskin 206–10.

WORKS CITED

Crane, Stephen. "The *Maggie* Inscription to Hamlin Garland." *The Portable Stephen Crane.* Ed. Joseph Katz. New York: Penguin, 1969. 1.

Crunden, Robert M. "Muckraking, Progressivism, and the Pure Food and Drug Law." Sinclair, *Jungle* 445–59.

Davis, Rebecca Harding. *Life in the Iron-Mills.* Ed. Cecelia Tichi. Boston: Bedford/St. Martin's, 1998.

Dreiser, Theodore. *The Financier.* New York: Horace Liveright, 1912.

——. "The Irish Section Foreman Who Taught Me How To Live." *Hearst's International* 46 (Aug. 1924): 20–21, 118–21.

——. "Life, Art and America." *Seven Arts* 1 (Feb. 1917): 363–89.

——. "The Mighty Rourke." *Twelve Men.* New York: Horace Liveright, 1919. 287–319.

——. "More Democracy or Less? An Inquiry." *Hey Rub-a-Dub-Dub: A Book of the Mystery and Wonder and Terror of Life.* New York: Boni and Liveright, 1920. 225–37.

——. *Sister Carrie.* Ed. Donald Pizer. 3rd ed. New York: Norton, 2006.

——. "St. Columba and the River." *Chains: Lesser Novels and Stories.* New York: Boni and Liveright, 1927. 98–132.

——. "The Toil of the Laborer." New York *Call* 13 July 1913: 11.

Fleissner, Jennifer L. *Women, Compulsion, Modernity: The Moment of American Naturalism.* Chicago: University of Chicago Press, 2004.

Folsom, Michael Brewster. "The Development of *The Jungle.*" Sinclair, *Jungle* 503–12.

Gandal, Keith. *The Virtues of the Vicious: Jacob Riis, Stephen Crane, and the Spectacle of the Slum.* New York: Oxford University Press, 1997.

Gold, Michael. *Jews Without Money.* New York: Horace Liveright, 1930.

Hapke, Laura. *Labor's Text: The Worker in American Fiction.* New Brunswick: Rutgers University Press, 2001.

Hayes, Kevin. J. Introduction: Cultural and Historical Background. *Maggie: A Girl of the Streets.* By Stephen Crane. Ed. Kevin J. Hayes. Boston: Bedford/St. Martin's, 1999. 3–23.

Henry, DeWitt, and Geoffrey Clark. "Interview with Richard Yates." *Ploughshares* 1.3 (1972): http://pshares.org/issues/article.cfm?prmArticleID=128.

Howard, June. *Form and History in American Literary Naturalism.* Chapel Hill: University of North Carolina Press, 1985.

Jehlen, Myra. *Readings at the Edge of Literature.* Chicago: University of Chicago Press, 2002.

Jones, Gavin. *American Hungers: The Problem of Poverty in U.S. Literature, 1840–1945.* Princeton: Princeton University Press, 2008.

London, Jack. *Martin Eden*. Harmondsworth: Penguin, 1967.

Morrison, Toni. *Playing in the Dark: Whiteness and the Literary Imagination*. Cambridge: Harvard University Press, 1992.

Norris, Frank. *McTeague: A Story of San Francisco*. New York: Penguin, 1982.

———. *The Octopus: A Story of California*. New York: Penguin, 1986.

Raskin, Jonah. Introductory Note to *Martin Eden*. *The Radical Jack London: Writings on War and Revolution*. Ed. Jonah Raskin. Berkeley and Los Angeles: University of California Press, 2008. 206–10.

Riis, Jacob A. *The Battle with the Slum*. Mineola: Dover, 1998.

———. *How the Other Half Lives: Studies Among the Tenements of New York*. Mineola: Dover, 1971.

Seguin, Robert. *Around Quitting Time: Work and Middle-Class Fantasy in American Fiction*. Durham: Duke University Press, 2001.

Sinclair, Upton. *The Jungle*. Ed. Clare Virginia Eby. New York: Norton, 2003.

———. "What Life Means to Me." Sinclair, *Jungle* 348–53.

Stange, Maren. *Symbols of Ideal Life: Social Documentary Photography in America, 1890–1950*. Cambridge: Cambridge University Press, 1989.

Roosevelt, Theodore. "State of the Union Address, December 3, 1901." *State of the Union Addresses*. Whitefish, Mont.: Kessinger Publishing, 2004.

Tocqueville, Alexis de. "That Aristocracy May Be Engendered by Manufactures." Davis 85–88.

Yates, Richard. *Revolutionary Road*. London: Methuen, 1986.

CHAPTER 19

THE GROTESQUE CITY, THE CITY OF EXCESS, AND THE CITY OF EXILE

JAMES R. GILES

To a large degree, the American city was the creation of diverse social, economic, and political forces that dominated the nation immediately after the Civil War, and, since the late nineteenth century, the city has evoked widely disparate responses in the American mind. Especially in the late nineteenth century, it embodied, for impoverished rural and small-town Americans and Europeans, the promise of sudden wealth and luxury. For many, the city offered the allure of capitalist excess, the enshrinement of the commodity. But the 1890s brought an economic depression in America, the depths of which would not be equaled until the 1930s. The depression was especially severe in the agrarian Midwestern and Western regions of the nation; and, for many farmers and small-town dwellers in these areas, the city, especially the Eastern city, functioned as a symbolic scapegoat for their desperation.

Yet a newly emerging urban America experienced its own economic desperation, exacerbated by the national economic reversal and by factors unique to the city. The rapid and uncontrolled growth of the city resulted in severe infrastructure and sanitation problems.[1] Extreme poverty and violence characterized the urban ghetto, the inner cities that resulted from unchecked growth and economic exploitation. The urban population explosion in America in the years between 1870 and 1920 was, in part, the result of waves of new immigrants, especially from Eastern Europe. African Americans fleeing the brutal circumstances of life in the post-Reconstruction South were an added ingredient in an unstable ethnic mix. Thus arose the phenomenon of the ethnic ghetto—isolated enclaves within the city populated by non-English-speaking immigrants. June Howard points out that "in 1880, 80 percent of the population of New York was foreign-born or born of immigrants; in Chicago the figure was 87 percent; in Detroit, 84 percent; in St. Louis and San Francisco, 78 percent" (33). The isolated ghettos were perceived as threatening by middle- and upper-class Americans, as well as by the urban Irish, themselves still trapped in oppressive social and economic conditions.

American literary naturalism, to a significant extent, emerged in the 1890s in response to the phenomenon of the new American city. Like other Americans, the classic naturalists reacted to it in quite different ways; but they were, above all, determined not to ignore it. Stephen Crane and Frank Norris were two of the first American naturalists to treat the city, and their responses to it reflected the complex national view of urban America. For Crane and Norris, of middle- and upper-class backgrounds, respectively, the city was both fascinating and disturbing in its foreignness. Both perceived intuitively that this new American space could not be approached from the perspective of the realism associated with William Dean Howells and Henry James, that on a crucial level it was inherently and profoundly irrational. In their attempts to capture this irrationality, Crane and Norris both focused on impoverished areas within the city. What results is a radically new aesthetic, labeled "naturalist gothic" by Christophe Den Tandt: "instead of panoramas of crowds and speculation, urban gothic offers a grim vitalist portrayal of the abject psychologies and living conditions of city dwellers" (42). In such an aesthetic, the city inevitably functions as symbol as well as space. To some extent, the ethnic ghetto functions for Crane and Norris, as well as for later naturalists, as a metonym for the nightmare world of the unconscious, the most frightening of all irrational spaces.

Crane appears to have found inspiration for his approach to the city in Jacob Riis's *How the Other Half Lives* (1890).[2] Riis's text, in its incorporation of personal observation, sociological data, and photography, constituted, in itself, a new genre of American writing. The central intent of *How the Other Half Lives* was to expose the inhuman living conditions found in the tenement world that mushroomed in New York City after 1870, and his text resulted in some meaningful reform. Unfortunately, Riis chose to organize his text around discussions of specific ethnic groups during which he frequently lapses into condescension and stereotype. The result is a peculiar form of sympathetic witnessing undercut by narrative distance. Moreover, a hardly relevant motif of Christian melodrama, which seems designed to appeal to secure middle- and upper-class communities, runs throughout *How the Other Half Lives*. As I have observed elsewhere, "Riis . . . seems to be trying to have it both ways—emphasizing the exciting foreignness of eastern and southern immigrants while distancing himself from any appeal that might emanate from that foreignness" (20).

Narrative distance also characterized Crane's path-breaking first novel, *Maggie: A Girl of the Streets* (1893). Distance in it results both from Crane's version of the urban gothic and his emphasis on environmental determinism. The narrative perspective of *Maggie*, as in *How the Other Half Lives*, is that of a tour guide presenting the grotesque reality of New York City's Bowery district to the reader. Crane's embrace of the urban gothic is most obvious in the abrupt appearance of the grotesque "fat man" in the original 1893 version of the novel. The fat man seems to leap from the nightmare realm of the unconscious into Crane's text. Whether he murders Maggie or not, he is clearly associated with her death, the ultimate surrender to the irrational. The ending of *Maggie* encapsulates the emphasis upon the irrationality of violence that is central to subsequent naturalist texts.

Violence is pervasive in Crane's text, and the opening scene makes it clear that it will continue to be so. The battle for turf between the young boys of Rum Alley and Devil's Row is revelatory of a morality rooted in conflict and neighborhood warfare. While Crane in part envisions the pervasive violence of the text as symptomatic of the desperate poverty of the inhabitants of the Bowery, it feels more metaphoric than systemic. The names, Rum Alley and Devil's Row, are laden with gothic connotations, especially when one remembers the popular term *demon rum*.

Moreover, Crane's narrative of the struggle is intensely ironic. His references to Jimmie Johnson as "the little champion of Rum Alley" in combat with the "true assassins" evokes a grotesquely inappropriate code of medieval chivalry for what is, in fact, an episode of gang warfare (11). Moreover, the young boys' attempt to possess this turf is inherently absurd. On an economic scale, the turf, as part of the ghetto of the Bowery, is virtually worthless, and its true owners exist in a realm far beyond the comprehension of the embattled "young urchins." Crane's mock-chivalric language calls attention to the implied narrator's role as tour guide of a distinctly foreign ghetto, and the condescension inherent in such language further distances the narrator from the world he observes for the middle-class reader.

Though idealized as "a most rare and wonderful product of a tenement district, a pretty girl" (29), Maggie herself is not free from associations with the grotesque even before her descent into prostitution and death. Maggie first observes the bartender Pete when he is engaged in a ludicrous bragging contest with her brother Jimmie, and her reaction could hardly seem more ridiculous: "Maggie perceived that here was the ideal man. Her dim thoughts were often searching for far-away lands where the little hills sing together in the morning. Under the trees of her dream-gardens there had always walked a lover" (32). While Crane insists that "none of the dirt of Rum Alley seemed to be in her veins" (29), she, in her "dim thoughts," is very much a product of the grotesque world of her environment. This is especially apparent in the theater scene, after which Pete brings Maggie to "the gruesome doorway" (40) of her home; in the popular melodrama during which Maggie sits enthralled, "unmistakably bad men evinced an apparently sincere admiration for virtue. The loud gallery was overwhelmingly with the unfortunate and the oppressed" (44). Of course, Maggie is one of the most "unfortunate and oppressed," but her ability to simultaneously empathize with, and distance herself from, the characters of the melodrama parallels the novel's narrative perspective. Neither she nor Pete could ever comprehend that the melodrama is the dominant culture's mode of controlling the poor by distancing them from their own suffering. Nell, the cynical prostitute, often seems the most intelligent character in Crane's novel, and it is thus appropriate that she first mocks Maggie and then robs a drunken Pete.

The narrative distance inherent in Crane's naturalist gothic is augmented by his philosophical commitment to environmental determinism. In *Maggie*, the ghetto is depicted as a grotesque space that relentlessly molds and controls the lives of those trapped in it. No character ultimately possesses the power of ethical choice, and thus all are naturalistic victims. This vision of the ghetto as determinist force recurs throughout urban naturalism. Ultimately, in *Maggie* and later urban naturalistic texts, the middle-class reader is relieved to complete the tour of a grotesque space and return to a world in which exists at least the possibility of choice.

Maggie is a prime example of what Blanche Gelfant, in her classic study *The American City Novel*, described as an "ecological novel," a text that narrows its perspective to a relatively small, isolated area of the city (12–13). The larger city, and especially the New York of capitalist luxury, seems, despite Maggie's brief appearance in the theater district, impossibly distant from the gothic world of the Bowery. In this context, it is important to remember that Maggie is a native of the Bowery. She does not come to the city seeking escape from agrarian American or European poverty, though it is likely that her ancestors did. For Maggie, any dream of capitalist luxury has been debased to the hope of marriage to Pete, a barely literate slum bartender. Despite *Maggie*'s narrative immersion in the claustrophobia of the Bowery, it is not primarily concerned with such practical matters as inadequate infrastructure and sanitation. Rather, it conveys a vision of the city as metonym for a nightmare world of oppression and violence.

Though in different ways, Frank Norris's *McTeague* (1899) is also an example of the naturalist gothic. A fascination with the grotesque runs throughout the novel, which culminates in violence. McTeague is an unnatural graft upon the city. Time itself distances him from the San Francisco in which he finds himself; finally, McTeague is an atavistic throwback to the Western pioneers. In addition, he grew up in the California gold mines, his immense strength enabling him to succeed in that dangerous world even as a child. His mother incongruously apprenticed him into the dental profession, but Norris signals early in the novel his inadequacy for this, and probably for any other, professional career: "he had read many of the necessary [dental] books, but he was too hopelessly stupid to get much benefit from them" (2). Ultimately, it is the sheer incomprehensibility of the city that destroys McTeague.

Implicit in *McTeague* is a contrast between the Big Dipper mine, where gold is a tangible mineral in the process of being extracted from the earth, and San Francisco, where it has become the abstract base of a capitalist system that valorizes commodification. Ultimately, in the form of Trina's gold coins, it becomes in itself a commodity. Ironically, with the exception of McTeague and his longed-for gold tooth, neither of the novel's main characters, though living in an urban center whose prominence was based on dreams of capitalistic excess, truly desires commodities. Gold is not for them a means of owning things, an unnatural response to urban life that dooms them.

McTeague is initially quite content with his concertina, his engraving of the court of Lorenzo de Medici, and his canary. Even though he ultimately murders for the bag of gold, he does not desire the gold coins as a means of purchasing material objects, but rather as a guarantee of survival and a mode of revenge on Trina. Walter Benn Michaels links Trina's erotic response to the coins to her masochism:

> We have no reason, after all, to believe that Trina finds any of the "qualities" that usually "inspire affection" exciting, including the male genitalia. The bag can only become exciting because it contains money that hasn't been, and won't be, spent, and the genitalia themselves can only become exciting insofar as they become symbolic, of saving for the sake of saving or submitting for the sake of submitting. (120–21)

The abnormality of the response of both characters to the coins is magnified by the urban space in which they find themselves. In San Francisco, gold symbolically supports an elaborate system of capitalist exchange that is, and must remain, abstract and impersonal. The city magnifies McTeague's and Trina's highly personal, and thus inappropriate, responses to the gold until they are driven to madness and mutual destruction. Marcus Schouler, who apparently understands the city sufficiently to bring about McTeague's banishment from the dental profession, nevertheless allows himself to become so enraged by losing lottery money (not Trina) that he, too, descends into madness. Sexual imagery, usually denoting perversion, dominates much of the novel. It is as if Norris envisions the city as a stimulus for McTeague's repressed sexuality, a sexuality that, in keeping with biological determinism, awakens the atavistic brute within the once-innocent mine carboy.[3] The union in the novel of sexuality and gold is depicted from the perspective of an urban nightmare.

Before the novel opens, McTeague has found a sanctuary from San Francisco's valorization of capitalist excess and greed in the microscopic world of Polk Street. The neighborhood of Polk Street is an area dominated by small shops and lower-middle-class workers and small businessmen. The modes of capitalist exchange in it are sufficiently basic that they do not overwhelm McTeague. But Polk Street's status as a boundary between the comfortable middle-class sections of the city and the dehumanizing world of the ghetto signals the tentative nature of McTeague's sanctuary. Moreover, the destructive greed of the larger city has invaded it even before the novel opens in the forms of Maria Macapa, Zerkow, and especially Marcus. Maria Macapa's story of the lost, and perhaps imaginary, gold plate serves as a metonym for the city's abstract system of capitalist excess. The greed and jealousy of Marcus, the ambitious though unsuccessful political hack, will ultimately trigger his destruction, as well as McTeague's and Trina's.

The invasion is completed by McTeague's marriage to Trina Sieppe, the descendant of German-Swiss peasants, and the wedding party scene, an exercise in the comic grotesque. In Norris's novel, Crane's urban fat man has moved across the continent to San Francisco, a Western city that emerged as a response to the promise of easily acquired wealth and the luxury of excess. Donald Pizer has noted that American literary naturalists have historically practiced an aesthetic distinguished by "the contemporary, low, and sensational" (110), and the low and sensational are certainly present in *McTeague*.

As McTeague's surrender to the brute within and Trina's greed intensify, the novel's setting declines from the lower-middle-class Polk Street to the depths of urban squalor. Soon they are living in a ghetto neighborhood that Maggie Johnson would have had no trouble in recognizing. But the ghetto is no more foreign to McTeague than the rest of San Francisco outside Polk Street, as is clear in his fruitless searches for lasting employment after the city denies him the right to practice dentistry. "You can't make small of me" is McTeague's regular refrain when he is confronted by the intricacies of the city, but in fact the city does diminish him. McTeague's embarrassing experience while purchasing theater tickets demonstrates his inability to comprehend the nuances of urban life.

After murdering Trina, McTeague flees the foreign space of the city and returns to the Big Dipper mine, the scene of his childhood innocence. He is attempting to escape not only the bewildering complexity of urban existence but the disastrous results of his awakened sexuality as well. In the mines, he ironically returns to the womb from which his mother banished him. At home in a space where gold is extracted from the womb of the earth, he briefly flourishes. The extraction of gold was always a more promising pursuit for McTeague than the extraction of teeth; inside the mines, he does not feel that anyone can "make small" of him.

But San Francisco's reach is extensive, and Marcus Schouler, the personification of urban greed and treachery, tracks him down. The novel ends with McTeague doomed to die of thirst and starvation in the middle of Death Valley, a metonym for the ground zero of his urban nightmare. Once grafted onto the city, McTeague can never truly escape it. The fat man tracks him down, and he is destroyed by the urban grotesque.

Norris's posthumously published *Vandover and the Brute* (1914) contains a comparable vision of San Francisco as an implacable space of humiliation and destruction. *Vandover* is, in fact, replete with examples of grotesque incident and scenes of degradation. In a freakish incident, Vandover's virginal friend Dolly Haight is infected with syphilis by a prostitute; and, in the novel's last scene, the once socially prominent Vandover, now reduced to the status of handyman, retrieves "an old hambone covered with a greenish fuzz" from beneath a sink, while being mocked by a young boy (351). The most shocking passages in the novel are those describing the effects on Vandover of the lycanthropy that he contacts after years of drunken debauchery:

> At long intervals he uttered a sound, half word, half cry, "Wolf—wolf!" but it was muted, indistinct, raucous, coming more from his throat than from his lips. It might easily have been the growl of an animal. . . . Naked, four-footed, Vandover ran back and forth the length of the room. (310)

In discussing *Vandover*, Warren French observes that "the city, in Norris' work . . . is an unnatural place, where the innocent suffer, the susceptible go astray, and the corrupt flourish" (60). One can perhaps relate Norris's vision of the city as urban nightmare to what June Howard has described as the naturalist "fear of *proletarianization*" (95), a terror of exclusion from the security of the middle and upper class.

When Norris was twenty-four, his parents divorced and his prosperous father remarried, changing his will in the process. The experience was unsettling for Norris on several levels, including the financial.

Elements of the naturalist gothic are also present in Upton Sinclair's *The Jungle* (1906) and are once again rooted in a tour-guide narrative perspective. The extended narration of the brutal lives of Lithuanian immigrants trapped in Packingtown opens the novel and is certainly its most successful segment. In a manner somewhat comparable to Jack London's submersion in the East End of London before writing *The People of the Abyss* (1903), Sinclair, the son of a Baltimore liquor salesman, spent seven weeks exploring the lives of native and foreign workers in Packingtown. Still, as Jacqueline Tavernier-Courbin points out, Sinclair remained "a spectator rather than a participant" in the lives of Chicago's stockyard workers (251). An ironic kind of narrative distance emerges in the novel largely because of the seemingly endless disasters that befall the novel's protagonist, Jurgis Rudkus, and his extended family and because of the passionate call for socialist revolution that dominates the last half of the novel.

To forward his political agenda, Sinclair ultimately envisions a number of urban spaces in the novel that will be subsumed in two enveloping visions of the city—a cynical and decidedly corrupt capitalist city as manifested in Chicago, and a just, humane socialist city as yet unrealized. In fact, Sinclair portrays the capitalist city as corrupt even before Jurgis and his extended family arrive in Chicago. Having been seduced by images of America as a land of abundant opportunity for well-remunerated work, they are exploited by a corrupt agent upon arriving in New York City.

Largely because of Sinclair's extensively detailed account of the unsanitary working and living conditions in Packingtown, the dangerous working environment of the stockyards, and the cynical exploitation of immigrant workers by corrupt agents of capitalism, it is the Packingtown section that readers most remember. As has been pointed out by critics and by Sinclair himself, the reception of the novel was ironic, with middle-class readers outraged by the text's extensive and, to be sure, nauseating descriptions of the reckless and dangerous excesses practiced in the processing of meat, but not by the inhumane living conditions experienced by immigrant laborers.

The naturalist gothic motif of the novel emerges most strongly in Sinclair's detailed account of these excesses, including this description of the various diseases that the workers in Packingtown contract:

> There were the men in the pickle rooms, for instance . . . scarce a one of these that had not some spot of horror on his person. Let a man so much as scrape a finger pushing a truck in the pickle rooms, and he might have a sore that would put him out of the world; all the joints of his fingers might be eaten by the acid, one by one. . . . There were the wool pluckers, whose hands went to pieces, even sooner than the hands of the pickle men; for the pelts of the sheep had to be painted with acid to loosen the wool, and then the pluckers had to pull out this wool with their bare hands, till the acid had eaten their fingers off. (101)

The most famous example of the urban grotesque in *The Jungle* is, of course, its descriptions of workers falling into vats of lard.

But for a full exposé of the corrupt capitalist city, Sinclair had to extend his vision outside Packingtown. Thus, other Chicago spaces come to the forefront in the last half of the novel, and, in keeping with his description of the city as a "great sore" that had "spread itself over the surface of the prairie" (33), they are all literally unsanitary, profoundly dehumanizing, and morally degraded. Ultimately, Sinclair envisioned Chicago, just as Nelson Algren would, as a space originating in, and devoted to, greed and the "hustle," in Algren's words "a city on the make."

The tour on which Sinclair's narrator conducts the reader becomes overtly Dantesque at times, for instance, in his description of the steel works and its fire-breathing Bessemer furnace, and of the underground world in which Jurgis briefly works laying telephone wires. Fittingly, his sojourn underground only comes about as a result of a corrupt deal made by the city government. In addition, the narrator provides a detailed description of the insect-infested city jail.

Physical spaces give way to more abstract ones in the last half of the novel when Jurgis becomes involved first in Chicago's criminal subculture and then as a subordinate employee of its corrupt political structure. Ultimately, all the novel's spaces expand into the vast Darwinian space of American capitalism, which further expands to include the entire nation, itself supported by corporate dishonesty and exploitation of the worker: "the great corporation which employed you lied to you, and lied to the whole country—from top to bottom it was nothing but one gigantic lie" (78).

Despite his distance from the working class, Sinclair's depiction of the physical spaces of Chicago is memorable. One can hardly find a more unnerving motif of the naturalist gothic than in the descriptions of working conditions in Packingtown. In these, the fat man of grotesque naturalism reappears, especially in the novel's account of the fertilizer works in meat-packing plants, a submersion into filth that leaves those who work there with an ineradicable stench. He is less successful in his analysis of the expanding capitalist city, simply because it is so rooted in abstraction, and he fails aesthetically in his concluding prophecy of a future socialist city. Rushed to finish the novel, Sinclair, in the last few chapters, stops writing fiction and lectures the reader endlessly about socialist theory. Tavernier-Courbin correctly points out that Sinclair's vision of the city was characterized by "horror" (258); and, when it abandons the horror of the specific for abstract political outrage, its power is lost.

In some memorable naturalistic fiction published later in the twentieth century, the tour-guide perspective would undergo a significant shift. In *Maggie, McTeague*, and *The Jungle*, this perspective is clearly external in nature, resulting in the narrative distance that characterizes all three novels. In contrast, the narrators of Michael Gold's *Jews Without Money* (1930), Richard Wright's *Native Son* (1940), and Hubert Selby Jr.'s *Last Exit to Brooklyn* (1940) merge with their ghetto protagonists, resulting in an internal perspective. As a result, the naturalist gothic in these novels assaults the reader on an immediate, visceral level. In all three novels, the inner city is dominant, and, while *Native Son* does reach out to include an upper-class white enclave of the city as well as its downtown during the trial scene, the African American ghetto is always the novel's controlling space.

Jews Without Money is a central text in the canons of the American immigrant novel and the Jewish American novel. It delineates the tenement culture that emerged in New York City's Lower East Side after the Civil War. Fleeing poverty, discrimination, and oppression so extreme that it not infrequently took the form of bloody pogroms, Jews from Eastern Europe were drawn to promises of freedom and wealth in the United States. After generally debasing experiences in Ellis Island's way station to America, many, lacking any material resources and not speaking English, settled in crowded, unsanitary tenement buildings where they underwent a new form of oppression.

Michael Gold (born Itshok Isaac Granich) was the child of immigrants who grew up in the East Side tenement world. *Jews Without Money* is so closely based on Gold's childhood and young adulthood that critics have debated whether it should be labeled a memoir or a novel.[4] The sufferings of Gold's Jewish Americans are not as extreme as those of Sinclair's Lithuanian Packingtown immigrants, but because of the novel's internal perspective and because they are not so relentlessly detailed, they seem more plausible and thus engage the reader more successfully. Nevertheless, Gold's Lower East Side contains its own horrors. What Sinclair touches on only briefly, the criminal subculture that extreme poverty inevitably produces, is a major focus in *Jews Without Money*. Prostitution is open and ubiquitous in the novel, and one of the closest friends of the first-person narrator, who is simply called Michael, constantly tempts him to turn to petty crime.

In addition, Gold focuses on the deplorable sanitary conditions that existed in the tenement world. In *The Historical Atlas of New York City*, Eric Homberger, after exploring one tenement building, writes that "the inadequate provision of sewerage and the difficulty of airing out mattresses, explained the building's terrible mustiness. A closer inspection revealed the overwhelming presence of vermin and lice" (110). In this regard, one especially memorable example of the naturalist gothic in *Jews Without Money* is Michael's description of the bedbugs that plague the Lower East Side tenements: the bedbugs "have a peculiar nauseating smell of their own; it is the smell of poverty. They crawl slowly and pompously, bloated with blood, and the touch and smell of these parasites wakens every nerve to disgust" (71). In addition, there is his account of the practice of tenement housewives of throwing garbage out of windows onto the streets below: "in summer the East Side heavens rained with potato peelings, coffee grounds, herring heads and dangerous soup bones. Bang, went a bundle, and the people in the street ducked as if a machine gun sounded" (59). In *Jews Without Money*, the fat man of grotesque urban naturalism assumes the form of bedbugs and garbage.

Like Jurgus Rudkus, Michael experiences a sudden conversion to socialism at the end of the novel. But in Gold's novel, the conversion is literally the end and is barely one page long. If it is no more convincing than Jurgus's epiphany, it is certainly less tedious. Gold does not lecture the reader about an envisioned city of socialist perfection.

Chicago provides the setting of Wright's *Native Son*, and it is a city both like and unlike Sinclair's. As a Marxist protest novel, Wright's novel follows in the path marked out by *The Jungle* and *Jews Without Money*. Moreover, it focuses on the African Americans concentrated in Chicago's South Side ghetto, a minority group perhaps even more marginalized than Sinclair's Lithuanian immigrants and Gold's tenement-dwelling Jewish Americans. From a contemporary perspective, the most unfortunate passages in *The Jungle* are those in which Sinclair, in unapologetically racist language, attacks the African American scabs recruited by the meat packers during the novel's big strike.

For much of the time, *Native Son*'s narrative perspective alternates between two Chicago spaces that, while geographically close, are economically and culturally worlds apart. Most memorably, there is the impoverished and embittered African American South Side. The novel introduces it on a jarring note in the famous first scene with its loudly jangling alarm clock and the large rat that invades the cramped living quarters of the Thomas family. Wright's South Side emerges as an island of urban poverty surrounded by an ocean of white power. Book One of the novel, en-titled "Fear," establishes the degree to which its protagonist, the nineteen-year-old South Side gang leader, is the psychological product of fear and hatred of the white world that surrounds the ghetto and severely limits the potential of its inhabitants. Bigger's fear outweighs his hatred, and he does not want to leave the narrow enclave of economic oppression where he has established a limited, and largely illusionary, power over his gang.

He is forced nonetheless by the economic system to do precisely that, being expelled into the Daltons' world of capitalistic excess and privilege. Bigger could scarcely feel more foreign if he had abruptly been transported to the moon than he does inside the Dalton household. For the first time, he finds himself in a space crowded with capitalist commodities. While fascinated by all the expensive objects that he observes, he can, at least initially, scarcely be said to covet them precisely because what they represent is so foreign to all that he has known. But as Alan W. France has noted, Bigger, at first on a subconscious level, sexually responds to Mary Dalton, turning her into the most forbidden of all commodities. In the extended passage in which Bigger accidentally suffocates Mary and then burns her body in the furnace in the basement of the Dalton house, Wright turns to an extreme of the naturalist gothic. He records in detail Bigger's difficulties in getting the body inside the furnace, necessitating its beheading, with all this happening under the watchful eyes of the Daltons' white cat, an animal with supernatural overtones. In this scene, Crane's urban fat man merges with Edgar Allan Poe.

After the killing of Mary, Bigger, in flight, returns to the South Side and this time to a unique manifestation of the results of African American poverty, the extensive space of abandoned tenements inside the African American community. The power of the white establishment is illustrated in the map of derelict buildings used by the city to track Bigger down. Previously invisible to the white city, Bigger, having unintentionally violated the most sacred of taboos, can no longer escape its relentless observation.

The trial scene introduces another urban space, that of the city's political and legal establishment. In the context of Wright's novel, it is inevitable that this crucial space should be exclusively white except for Bigger and his family members and the body of his girlfriend Bessie, whom he raped and quite deliberately and savagely murdered. The use to which Bessie's body is put in the scene, besides serving as another example of the naturalist gothic, encapsulates the exploitive relationship between the ghetto and the white power structure. The district attorney introduces the body as evidence that Bigger murdered Mary Dalton, Bessie's brutal death viewed as being, in itself, irrelevant. In the white-controlled Chicago of Wright's novel, the black South Side is irrelevant except when it crosses its assigned boundaries and thereby violates taboos, and when it is politically useful.

Wright knew Chicago's African American ghetto quite well, and his account of it is powerful and convincing. He is also successful in depicting the downtown courtroom and the jail in which Bigger is incarcerated, while somewhat less so in his description of the Dalton family mansion. Like Sinclair, he does weaken his novel with an extensive Marxist lecture in Max's defense summary, but he compensates for it by having Bigger reject the central implications of the lecture. Ultimately, Wright's Chicago is just as oppressive and dehumanizing as Sinclair's.

Still, no urban space in an American novel is as horrific as Brooklyn's lower-working-class neighborhood in Hubert Selby's *Last Exit to Brooklyn*. Selby's perspective is internal and unmediated, thus eliminating any significant distance between narration and reader. The novel reads as if its rage-filled characters are shouting at an implied middle-class reader. One can find, in fact, few more compelling examples of fiction as controlled assault than *Last Exit to Brooklyn*.

For Selby, Brooklyn, and especially the neighborhood of Red Hook, is a sterile, degraded space, a nightmarish wasteland. *Last Exit* takes the urban gothic of earlier naturalist novels to its extreme. Violence and mindless brutality are commonplace throughout the novel, and any affirming impulse is immediately assaulted and crushed. Moreover, the claustrophobia of the novel is enhanced by Brooklyn's isolated status. Except for some brief excursions, the rest of New York, especially Manhattan, is foreign, unexplored territory for Selby's characters. Unlike Sinclair, Gold, and Wright, he is not concerned with establishing the debased setting of his novel as part of a larger, subsuming urban structure.

Gerd Hurm observes that the five main sections of the text take place during the late 1940s, while the "Landsend" coda is set in the late 1950s (280). American soldiers sometimes intrude upon Brooklyn space and are treated as an invading army, robbed and savagely assaulted. This trope of warfare serves as a metaphor for daily life in the Brooklyn of the novel.

Selby has been described as the leading voice of urban rage in American fiction,[5] and his prose is a direct reflection of that rage. *Last Exit* is unified by a savage white street gang that extracts punishment on those characters who violate Red Hook's taboos, especially when searching for love or even some comforting gentleness. Richard A. Wertime views the street gang members as "psychic avengers," the embodiments of the hidden areas of the characters' subconscious that abruptly surface and negate any affirmative emotions they may feel. Even more completely than *Maggie* and *McTeague*, *Last Exit to Brooklyn* is an exercise in naturalist gothic, an invocation of the space of nightmare.

Affirmative emotions have destructive results for the novel's three most memorable characters. The drag queen Georgette is debased and humiliated when she seeks love from one of the street gang members; Harry Black, a self-hating lathe operator and minor union official, is crucified against a billboard when he gives in to his repressed homosexual desires; and Tralala, a rapacious prostitute, descends into self-destruction and suffers a prolonged gang rape followed by death after an army officer offers her love instead of cash for sex.

It would be difficult to find a more relentlessly brutal piece of writing than "Landsend," the novel's coda, which describes the dehumanized existence of the inhabitants of a housing project. The very name of the housing project, Landsend, emphasizes the dead-end existence of those entrapped there.[6] Selby's Landsend represents a doomed attempt by the city of New York to provide a livable space for Brooklyn's lower classes. What results instead is a gothic world of grotesque cruelty. One passage in "Landsend" describes the reactions of a group of female residents of the housing project after they see an unattended baby on a fourth floor ledge of the building: "the women watched the baby as it crawled around on the ledge and window sill. Maybe he thinks hes a bird. Hey, ya gonna fly? Laughter. . . . The women continued to laugh and wonder when it would fall" (281). It would seem that the motif of the urban gothic, the incarnation of Crane's fat man, has culminated in "Landsend."

Elements of the grotesque are present in two other canonical naturalistic novels, Theodore Dreiser's *Sister Carrie* (1900) and John Dos Passos's *Manhattan Transfer* (1925); but, in these two texts, they are subordinated to evocations of the city of capitalist excess and the city of economic exile. Dreiser's novel famously opens with its female protagonist, Carrie Meeber, entering Chicago on a train in August 1889. The innocent Carrie envisions Chicago as a site of vaguely realized future conquest: "a half-equipped little knight she was, venturing to reconnoitre the mysterious city and dreaming wild dreams of some vague, far-off supremacy which should make it prey and subject, the proper penitent, groveling at a woman's slipper" (4). Carrie will, in fact, conquer the city, though it will be New York rather than Chicago.

Still, Dreiser's narration of Carrie's train journey contains a succinct summary of the essential quality that will allow her to triumph in urban America: "self-interest with her was high, but not strong" (4). In Dreiser's late nineteenth-century urban America, as in Dos Passos's vision of New York during the first two decades of the twentieth century, an emotionless self-interest and sheer luck are the essential ingredients of success. Carrie, in addition, embodies desire on several levels. Philip Gerber argues that Carrie knows exactly what she wants: "comfort, money, security" (26). Walter Benn Michaels modifies this argument: "Carrie's definition of money, like everything else about her, includes the element of desire; money for her is never simply a means of getting what you want, it is itself the thing you want" (33–34). In fact, Carrie intuitively understands that a materialism based on the possession of commodities is the foundation of urban American culture. Her desire for comfort, security, and things subsumes the other levels of her desire, including the sexual. Thus, she passively enters into her relationships with both Drouet and Hurstwood and apparently never feels strong desire for either of them.

Dreiser emphasizes that money and the comfort and security symbolized by materialist possession are central to both Chicago and New York. He conveys the importance of money in both cities through a number of urban spaces that are defined by the presence or absence of money. Hurstwood's luxurious home on Chicago's North Side, Carrie's rooms at the Waldorf Hotel, and the expensive world of the New York theater are the novel's prime examples of conspicuous consumption. It is hardly surprising that Drouet is enchanted by Carrie's presence in the last two spaces: "ah, what a prize, he thought. How beautiful, how elegant, how famous. In her theatrical and Waldorf setting, Carrie was, to him, the all-desirable" (475). She is, in fact, all desire. Drouet's Chicago apartment and the New York flat on 78th Street that Hurstwood rents for himself and Carrie are solid middle- to upper-middle-class spaces, while their second New York flat represents a step down the socioeconomic ladder. The Hanson flat in Chicago is emblematic of the dehumanized lives of those in the working class, as is Carrie's experience in the shoe factory.

The most memorable evocation of the city of economic exile, however, is Dreiser's account of Hurstwood's disintegration in New York. As critics have long noted, Hurstwood's fate epitomizes Dreiser's vision of the role of chance and accident in human life. The narration of Hurstwood's economic and spiritual desperation clearly signifies that *Sister Carrie* is an example of what Eric Carl Link calls "'dark' or 'negative' literary naturalism" (69). The chance inherent in Hurstwood's fall calls into question the central mythology of the American success ethic.

Two scenes in the novel involving an exchange of money dramatize the polarities of Dreiser's binary vision of the American city as a space of consumerist excess and a space of economic exile. In the first, Carrie, in the fourth day of futilely searching for a job that will provide her with the luxury of a new hat, encounters Drouet for the first time since they entered the city together. He takes her to dinner in "a large, comfortable" restaurant (58) and then afterward gives her "two soft, green, handsome, ten-dollar bills" (62). While the sexual overtones of the scene are clear, it is not Drouet but the ten-dollar bills that seduce Carrie by their promise of comfort and security.

The second money exchange scene occurs late in the novel and concerns Hurstwood after he has been reduced to begging. He meets "a comfortable-looking gentleman" leaving "a fine barber shop" "clean-shaven" and asks for "a little something": "The gentleman looked him over and fished for a dime. Nothing but quarters were in his pocket. 'Here,' he said, handing him one to be rid of him. 'Be off now'" (492). At one time back in Chicago, Hurstwood might have been the "comfortable-looking gentleman," but, now destitute, he is exiled from the city of material comfort. Dreiser is unstinting in his description of the stages of Hurstwood's descent from working as a scab during a strike to his humiliation on the streets of New York as one of the Captain's starving band and finally his suicide in a flophouse. While Carrie triumphs in the city of capitalist excess, Hurstwood is exiled from it into the sordid world of urban poverty. Both Dreiser's city of capitalist excess and his city of economic exile exist outside morality. The novelist viewed the city as a force as inherently immoral as nature: "nature is so grim. The city, which represents it effectively, is also grim. It does not care at all. It is not conscious. The passing of so small an organism as that of a man or a woman is nothing to it" (107).

The city of capitalist excess, the grotesque city, and the city of exile are also manifestations of John Dos Passos's New York in *Manhattan Transfer*. Dos Passos's technique in the novel is distinctly modernist, but his underlying vision is essentially naturalistic, and quite similar to Dreiser's, in its emphasis upon the city as a force that controls the lives of those within it. As the title, a reference to a train station on the New York route, signals, the city of *Manhattan Transfer* is a bewildering space of rapid social, economic, and spiritual change. The novel's numerous characters exist in transitory states, continually moving up and down the socioeconomic ladder, nearly always suffering spiritual wounds in the process. Dos Passos's modernist technique is manifested in his rapidly shifting point of view and in his use of parallel scenes and recurrent symbols to convey his image of New York. He introduces each chapter of the novel with a brief segment that usually conveys the historical time frame of what follows. One of these describes an old man and a young man watching the arrival of a ship of immigrants, probably from Eastern Europe:

> "I'd give a million dollars," said the old man . . . "to know what they come for."
> "Just for that pop," said the young man. . . . "Aint it the land of opportoonity?"
> "One thing I do know" said the old man. "When I was a boy it was wild Irish came in the spring with the first run of shad. . . . Now there aint no more shad, an them folks, Lord know where they come from."
> "It's the land of opportunity." (49)

It is, in fact, the land of opportunity for Congo Jake, a French immigrant who intuitively understands the essentially amoral nature of the city and how to exploit it. But for the rest of the characters, social advancement comes only at great emotional and spiritual cost, if it comes at all.

This scene is juxtaposed to a later one describing a ship transporting political deportees to Russia. Here political exile is transformed into grotesque theater: "'Take a look at the deportees. . . . Take a look at the undesirable aliens,' shouted the man with the telescopes and fieldglasses" (290). The grotesque dominates other moments in the novel: for instance, the scene in which the old pedophile preaches the doom of the city to two young boys and the scene in which a drunken party of plutocrats ends when a Broadway star accidentally kicks one of them in the eye. Fire threatens the city throughout the novel, a motif that culminates in the climatic conflagration that leaves Anna Cohen disfigured; and prophecies of its doom are replete in the novel, most of them taken from the old pedophile's speech.

Two recurrent symbols that represent the absence of stability in the city are the rollercoaster and the revolving door. Congo Jake and Ellen Thatcher ride the rollercoaster to the top, though Ellen is transformed into a "tin mechanical toy, all hollow inside" (375) in the process. Joe Harland descends from the top of the rollercoaster as the one-time "King of the Curb [Market]" to the bottom as a drunken exile from his family. In contrast, Bud Korpenning never ascends above the ride's bottom level, dying without finding "the center of things" in the city.

The novel's revolving-door scene focuses on Jimmy Herf, Dos Passos's clearly autobiographical protagonist, as he decides not to enter the Merivale business and social world. Dos Passos effectively merges the revolving-door metaphor with an allusion to the stock market to convey the sacrifice of individualism that succumbing to the Merivale temptation would entail: "[bodies] fed in two endless tapes through the revolving doors out into Broadway, in off Broadway. Jimmy fed in a tape in and out the revolving doors, noon and night and morning, the revolving doors grinding out his years like sausage meat. All of a sudden his muscles stiffen. Uncle Jeff [Merivale] and his office can go plumb to hell" (120). Jimmy thus rejects the city of capitalist excess personified by the Merivales and, at the conclusion of the novel, chooses voluntary exile from the city.

Dreiser and Dos Passos effectively convey the allure of the city of capitalist excess, a space that is absent in most naturalistic urban novels. As *Sister Carrie*, *McTeague*, *The Jungle*, and *Last Exit to Brooklyn* illustrate, the grotesque city, the naturalistic gothic, appears frequently in texts associated with the genre of naturalism. Crane's, Norris's, and Sinclair's fascination with the emerging American inner city and the violent, sordid lives of those trapped within it resulted in a dominant subgenre of American naturalism. For writers devoted to observing grotesque spectacle, recording taboo subject matter, and depicting marginal characters surrendering to "the beast within," the ghetto proved irresistible. Thus, Crane's fat man is a familiar figure in the world of urban naturalism, while characters like Carrie Meeber, Congo Jake, and Ellen Thatcher who ride to the top of the capitalist rollercoaster seem exotic visitors there. They, too, are victims of deterministic forces, but the cost that the city extorts from them is internal.

NOTES

1. According to the *World Almanac and Book of Facts 2002*, between 1850 and 1900 New York City's population increased from 700,000 to approximately 3.5 million; that of Philadelphia from 120,000 to approximately 1.3 million; while Boston saw an increase from 136,000 to 560,000. In the Midwest, the urban centers of Cleveland and Chicago seemed to mushroom over night: Cleveland's population rose from 17,000 to almost 382,000 and, even more spectacularly, Chicago's from 30,000 to almost 1.7 million.

2. For an incisive discussion of the respective approaches to the ghetto of Riis and Crane, see Gandal.

3. For an extensive discussion of the interrelationship of urban capitalism, gold, and perverted sexuality in *McTeague*, see Michaels 139–80.

4. See, for instance, Guttman as well as Tuerk.

5. See, for instance, my chapter, "The Game of Mum as Theme and Narrative Technique in Hubert Selby's *Last Exit to Brooklyn*," in *The Naturalistic Inner-City Novel in America*.

6. Gerd Hurm argues that Landsend is based on a low-income housing project built during the 1950s in the Red Hook neighborhood of Brooklyn near the Gowanus Canal (280).

WORKS CITED

Crane, Stephen. *Maggie: A Girl of the Streets*. Ed. Thomas A. Gullason. New York: Norton, 1979.

Den Tandt, Christophe. *The Urban Sublime in American Literary Naturalism*. Urbana: University of Illinois Press, 1998.

Dos Passos, John. *Manhattan Transfer*. Boston: Houghton Mifflin, 1953.

Dreiser, Theodore. *Sister Carrie*. New York: Penguin, 1981.

France, Alan W. "Misogyny and Appropriation in Wright's *Native Son*." *Modern Fiction Studies* 34 (1988): 413–23.

French, Warren. *Frank Norris*. New York: Twayne, 1962.

Gandal, Keith. *The Virtues of the Vicious*. New York: Oxford University Press, 1997.

Gelfant, Blanche H. *The American City Novel*. Norman: University of Oklahoma Press, 1954.

Gerber, Philip. *Theodore Dreiser*. New York: Twayne, 1992.

Giles, James R. *The Naturalistic Inner-City Novel in America*. Columbia: University of South Carolina Press, 1995.

Gold, Michael. *Jews Without Money*. New York: Carroll and Graf, 1984.

Guttmann, Allen. *The Jewish Writer in America: Assimilation and the Crisis of Identity*. New York: Oxford University Press, 1971.

Homberger, Eric. *The Historical Atlas of New York City*. Rev. ed. New York: Holt, 2005.

Howard, June. *Form and History in American Literary Naturalism*. Chapel Hill: University of North Carolina Press, 1985.

Hurm, Gerd. *Fragmented Urban Images: The American City in Modern Fiction from Stephen Crane to Thomas Pynchon*. New York: Peter Lang, 1991.

Link, Eric Carl. *The Vast and Terrible Drama: America Literary Naturalism in the Late Nineteenth Century*. Tuscaloosa: University of Alabama Press, 2004.

Michaels, Walter Benn. *The Gold Standard and the Logic of Naturalism*. Berkeley and Los Angeles: University of California Press, 1987.

Norris, Frank. *McTeague*. New York: Holt, Rinehart, and Winston, 1950.

———. *Vandover and the Brute*. New York: Doubleday, 1914.

Pizer, Donald. *Realism and Naturalism in Nineteenth-Century American Fiction*. Carbondale: Southern Illinois University Press, 1984.

Selby, Hubert, Jr. *Last Exit to Brooklyn*. New York: Grove, 1965.

Sinclair, Upton. *The Jungle*. New York: Signet, 1962.

Tavernier-Courbin, Jacqueline. "*The Call of the Wild* and *The Jungle*." The Cambridge
    Companion to American Realism and Naturalism: Howells to London. Ed. Donald
    Pizer. Cambridge University Press, 1995. 236–62.
Tuerk, Richard. "*Jews Without Money* as a Work of Art." *Studies in American Jewish
    Literature* 7 (1988): 67–79.
Wertime, Richard A. "Psychic Vengeance in *Last Exit to Brooklyn*." *Literature and
    Psychology* 24 (1974): 153–66.
World Almanac and Book of Facts 2002. New York: World Almanac, 2002.

CHAPTER 20

....

NATURALISM AND CRIME

....

GARY SCHARNHORST

Stealing a man's wife, that's nothing, but stealing his car, that's larceny.

　　　　—James M. Cain, *The Postman Always Rings Twice*

Both utopian writers and literary naturalists at the turn of the twentieth century believed that crime was a "disease" that could be eradicated. The parlor socialist Edward Bellamy, for example, predicted in *Looking Backward, 2000–1887* (1888) that prisons would soon become obsolete. "All cases of atavism are treated in the hospitals," as Bellamy's hero discovers. In the future crime will be "looked upon as the recurrence of an ancestral trait" (121). Similarly, as one of the "Over Mothers" in Charlotte Perkins Gilman's feminist fantasy *Herland* (1915) remarks, "We have preventive measures and cures" for crime; "sometimes we have to 'send the patient to bed,'" but "it's only part of the treatment" (112).

HEREDITARY DETERMINISM

....

Like the utopian writers, the earliest literary naturalists held that most criminals were atavists or evolutionary throwbacks with a hereditary predisposition to commit crime. That is, criminals inherited bestial traits from their ancestors and could not be blamed for their antisocial behavior. The two groups differed, however, in the "nature versus nurture" debate. Whereas the utopians believed that criminals could be "cured," the early naturalists believed that criminal diseases could only be bred out of the human stock over generations, much as an epidemic may be controlled and slowly ameliorated over time. Predictably, the scientists who influenced these early naturalists—among them Francis Galton, Richard Louis Dugdale, and the Italian criminologist Cesare Lombroso—were eugenicists or advocates of selective breeding. In *The Jukes: A Study in Crime, Pauperism, Disease, and Heredity* (1877), Dugdale studied seven generations of an upstate New York family and concluded that criminals, no less than paupers and the congenitally ill, were predestined by their ancestry. According to Lombroso in *Criminal Man* (1876), most criminals were degenerates who exhibited such physical stigmata as square jaws, brutish postures, oversized ears, and flat noses. As Donald Pizer explains, "The Lombrosian criminal was a member of a distinct and anomalous human subspecies" (560). In other words, "criminal types"—habitual or natural-born criminals—not only were predetermined to suffer inexorable destinies but they could be readily identified by their physiognamy. Their fates could be read in their faces.

The French novelist Émile Zola, a pioneering literary naturalist, famously traced the transmission of biological traits through four generations in his twenty-volume Rougon-Macquart cycle published between 1871 and 1893. More to the point, Zola argued in *Nana* (1880) and *La Bête humaine* (1890) that heredity was a source of such crimes as prostitution and murder. The American novelist Frank Norris was influenced by Lombroso's theory of criminality, as is evident in such stories and essays as "Lauth" (1893), *Vandover and the Brute* (written 1894–95, published 1914), "A Reversion to Type" (1897), "New Year's at San Quentin" (1897), "Little Dramas of the Curbstone" (1897), and "A Case for Lombroso" (1897). In "A Reversion to Type," for example, a timid clerk in a department store suddenly regresses to "a freebooter seven feet tall, with a chest expansion of fifty inches" (93), and he soon accosts and kills a man while trying to rob him. Norris combined Lombroso's criminal theories and Zola's literary theories to characterize the eponymous hero of *McTeague* (1899). He repeatedly refers to McTeague's "square-cut" and "angular" head (6, 23, 53, 79, 102, 109, 166, 187, 199), his "big red ears" (166), his "enormous" or "huge mouth" (45, 97, 167), his "heavy," "protruding," or "salient jaw" (6, 53, 98, 103, 106, 132, 165, 166, 199), or "massive, protruding chin" (166)—in all, facial traits resembling those of a carnivore. An atavistic Irishman or "white Negro" according to the criminal anthropology of the period, McTeague is destined from the first pages of the novel to commit horrific crimes. He figuratively rapes his future wife Trina while she is anesthetized in his dental chair by kissing her "grossly, full on the mouth" (22). In an editorial aside, Norris both indicts McTeague's "evil instincts" and absolves him of responsibility for them: "Below the fine fabric of all that was good in him ran the foul stream of hereditary evil, like a sewer. The vices and sins of his father and of his father's father, to the third and fourth and five hundredth generation, tainted him. The evil of an entire race flowed in his veins" (22). Slowly stripped of his civilized veneer, "lapsing back to his early estate" (183), McTeague eventually steals Trina's lottery winnings and ruthlessly tortures and murders her in a fit of alcohol-fueled rage. Tracked to the middle of Death Valley by Trina's cousin, who wants to avenge Trina's murder but mostly to recover the stolen loot, McTeague beats him to death in a struggle over the money. A natural-born criminal without agency or volition or remorse, McTeague can no more escape his destiny than a leopard can change its spots. Or as Malcolm Cowley explains, "The effect of naturalism as a doctrine is to subtract from literature the whole notion of human responsibility" (417).

The rhetoric of regression, or the notion that all criminals are atavists, permeates turn-of-the-twentieth-century American literature. In *Susan Lenox: Her Fall and Rise* (1917), for example, David Graham Phillips asserts that bootleg whiskey "produces in anyone who drinks it a species of quick insanity, of immediate degeneration—a desire to commit crime" (2: 237). Though rarely regarded as a work of literary naturalism, Mark Twain's *Pudd'nhead Wilson* (1894) may also be discussed as a study of criminal atavism. The usurper Tom Driscoll, born a slave by a fiction of law but raised a freedman as the result of legal subterfuge, not only becomes a petty thief but sells his emancipated mother down the river and kills his adopted father to secure his inheritance. Some characters in the novel, whether they know his racial history or not, attribute his antisocial behavior to atavism. Pudd'nhead Wilson calls him a "degenerate remnant of an honorable line" (68), for example, and his mother Roxy complains that he has regressed to the level of an ostensibly inferior race: "Thirty-one parts o' you is white, en on'y one part nigger, en dat po' little one part is yo' *soul*" (75). The scabs who are employed to break a Packingtown strike in Upton Sinclair's *The Jungle* (1906) "contained an assortment of the criminals and thugs of the city, besides Negroes and the lowest foreigners—Greeks, Roumanians, Sicilians, and Slovaks" (255–56). The playwright Eugene O'Neill deploys the trope of racial atavism in *The Emperor Jones* (1920), a late naturalistic work (albeit one that points in the direction of modernism). In the course of eight scenes, the brutish Brutus Jones, a former Pullman porter who has become the self-styled emperor of a West Indies island, regresses through his personal and racial history, shedding identities like a peeled onion. Resplendently dressed in military uniform in scene 1, he is clad only in a breech cloth in the final tableau. He too is a natural-born killer: he has murdered two men back in the United States:

> "When I cotches Jeff cheatin' wid loaded dice my anger overcomes me and I kills
> him dead! Lawd, I done wrong! When dat guard hits me wid de whip, my anger
> overcomes me, and I kills him dead. Lawd, I done wrong! And down heah whar
> dese fool bush niggers raises me up to the seat o' de mighty, I steals all I could
> grab. Lawd, I done wrong!" (31)

Simply put, O'Neill's script poses a rhetorical question about Brutus Jones: "Is you civilized, or is you like dese ign'rent black niggers heah?" (29). The only answer the play permits, however repugnant it may be to modern audiences, is the latter.

Environmental Determinism

Most American literary naturalists emphasized training or environmental factors rather than heredity in the shaping of character. As Stephen Crane often wrote on the flyleaf of copies of his novella *Maggie, a Girl of the Streets* (1893), the story of a slum girl who becomes a prostitute,

[i]t is inevitable that you will be greatly shocked by this book, but continue, please, with all possible courage to the end. For it tries to show that environment is a tremendous thing in the world, and often shapes lives regardless. If one proves that theory, one makes room in Heaven for all sorts of souls (notably an occasional street girl) who are not confidently expected to be there by many excellent people. (*Correspondence* 1: 52–53)

Like others who believed that environment creates criminals or that, in the essentialist view, poverty causes crime, Crane in effect composed a brief in defense of Maggie. She "blossomed in a mud puddle" (16) before she is seduced by her dreams and a coarse, penny-ante bartender. By the close of the novella, he has abandoned her and she has been expelled from her home. Desperate, she becomes a "girl of the painted cohorts" (52) and "the crimson legions" (53) and drowns in the East River, perhaps a suicide, perhaps murdered by one of her johns, but in either case a victim of her fatal environment. Her failure is in stark contrast with the success of Nell, "a woman of brilliance and audacity" (55), a prostitute who cons her customers and lives lavishly. Cowley later noted that Crane harbored "an obsessive notion about the blamelessness of prostitutes that affected his career from beginning to end; it caused a series of scandals, involved him in a feud with the vice squad of Manhattan, and finally led him to marry the madam of a bawdy house in Jacksonville" (380).

"Fallen women" portrayed in other works of American naturalism are cut from the same cloth: they turn tricks simply to survive. Minna Hooven in Frank Norris's *The Octopus* (1901) confesses she has "gone to hell" because "it was either that or starvation" (414). In Sinclair's *The Jungle*, the Lithuanian immigrant Ona Lukoszaite Rudkis is forced to work in a whorehouse some nights by her foreman in a Chicago packing plant in order to keep her job. "He told me—he would have me turned off. He told me he would—we would all of us lose our places" (146), she cries. Ona's friend Marija Berczynskas loses her job in a packinghouse, is abandoned by her fiancé, and eventually must turn to prostitution in order to earn a livelihood and support her family. "I had to live," she explains, "and I couldn't see the children starve. . . . When people are starving . . . and they have anything with a price, they ought to sell it." She pays fifteen dollars a week to feed the family and "so the children can go to school." Nor is it anything "to be ashamed of—we can't help it," she insists (275–77, 281). The police raid the brothel, but only to shake down the madam. The crime scene reopens in the morning. Anna Christie, the title character of O'Neill's 1921 play, has also become a prostitute. After working as a "dirty slave" (110) on a farm, she "got the chance—to get into that house. And you bet your life I took it! . . . It was all men's fault—the whole business. It was men on the farm ordering and beating me—and giving me the wrong start. . . . It wasn't none of my fault" (64, 110). Susan Lenox, a "love child" spurned by her family, is driven by "the irresistible pressure of economic forces" (2: 124) to sell her body. "I was dirty—and I wanted to be clean," she asserts. "I was hungry—and I wanted food. I was cold— that was the worst. I was cold, and I wanted to get warm" (1: 463). Prostitution is permitted to exist in the major cities, as Phillips explains, through an elaborate system of organized graft, "one of those general words that mean everything and nothing. What is graft and what is honest income? Just where shall we draw the line between rightful exploitation of our fellow-beings through their necessities and their ignorance of their helplessness, and wrongful exploitation?" (2: 174). Phillips wrote the novel in 1910, the same year Congress passed the Mann Act outlawing interstate trafficking for purposes of prostitution.

Thieves exercise no more agency than prostitutes in the amoral universe of literary naturalism. The engineer Dyke in Norris's *The Octopus* is fired and blacklisted by the railroad and his farm financially ruined by an increase in shipping rates. As the narrator explains, "He had been merely the object of a colossal trick, a sordid injustice, a victim of the insatiate greed of the monster, caught and choked by one of those millions of tentacles suddenly reaching up from below, from out the dark beneath his feet, coiling around his throat, throttling him, strangling him, sucking his blood" (249).Maddened by bankruptcy and drink, Dyke holds up a train, steals five thousand dollars in gold, and kills the brakeman. As another of the characters complains to an agent for the railroad:

> "You and your gang drove Dyke from his job because he wouldn't work for starvation wages. Then you raised freight rates on him and robbed him of all he had. You ruined him and drove him to fill himself up with Caraher's whiskey. He's only taken back what you plundered him of, and now you're going to hound him over the State, hunt him down like a wild animal, and bring him to the gallows at San Quentin." (298–99)

Dyke's mother also rallies to her son's defense: "He was driven to it. They hounded him down, they wouldn't let him alone. He was not right in his mind. They hounded him to it. . . . They drove him and goaded him till he couldn't stand it any longer" (305). Dyke is finally cornered and captured, tried and convicted, and sentenced to life in prison, after having been "driven to outlawry and a jail" (425) by the rail company's mendacity. The Octopus "had hounded Dyke from his legitimate employment and had made of him a highwayman and criminal" (457).

Similarly, Jurgis Rudkis is driven to crime in Sinclair's *The Jungle*. After he has been twice jailed, the first time for beating the foreman who forced Ona into prostitution, the second for attacking a bartender who cheated him, he becomes a petty thief, the accomplice of a mugger he met in prison. "Before long Jurgis would think no more of" assaulting and robbing pedestrians, the narrator adds, than the "knockers" in the stockyards thought of killing steers with a sledge hammer (240). In a dog-eat-dog world, Jurgis merely earns a modest living.

The most provocative and ambiguous depiction of a theft in American literary naturalism, however, appears in Theodore Dreiser's *Sister Carrie* (1900). George Hurstwood, the hail-fellow-well-met, unhappily married manager of Fitzgerald and Moy's, a high-class bar in downtown Chicago, becomes infatuated with Carrie and entices her to run away with him. While closing the bar for the last time, he robs the safe—or does he? Certainly Hurstwood takes the money, but Dreiser is careful to describe his actions as indecisive and the event as accidental. His crime is unintentional, or so it seems. Hurstwood discovers the safe is unlocked and counts the bills. A page or so later he "decided he would take them," but they don't fit in his pocket. He puts the cash in a satchel, then decides to return it to the safe. "Think of what a scandal it would make" if he stole the money. "The police! They would be after him." He returns the money, then realizes he may have "put the sums in the wrong boxes," so he "opened the door again. . . . While the money was in his hand the lock clicked" and, too late now to return it, "he became the man of action" (193). To be sure, he keeps the money, but only after the safe is locked. As Leonard Cassuto remarks, "The scene of George Hurstwood before the open safe in *Sister Carrie*, agonizing over whether to take the money inside, is a masterpiece of mixed motivation and inner equivocation, culminating in an impulsive crime" (197). Is he guilty? Not beyond a reasonable doubt, on the basis of the evidence in Dreiser's narrative. But would he be convicted of the crime? No doubt.

The pattern of exonerating or at least suspending judgment of so-called lawbreakers in works of American literary naturalism based on extenuating circumstances extends to virtually all types of crime. The only significant exception to this generalization is rape or sexual assault. While they may pardon prostitutes, murderers, and thieves, many naturalists presume agency on the part of the rapist (e.g., the rapist and murderer of Angelé in Norris's *The Octopus*, Wolf Larsen's attempted rape of Maud Brewster in Jack London's *The Sea-Wolf* [1904], Bigger's rape and murder of Bessie in Wright's *Native Son* [1940]). Henry Fleming in Crane's *The Red Badge of Courage* (1895) worries whether he will stand and fight in battle. He expects "many men of courage . . . to desert the colors and scurry like chickens" (50), and he concludes "that the only way to prove himself was to go into the blaze, and then figuratively to watch his legs to discover their merits and faults" (11). In only his second skirmish, he panics, throws down his rifle, and runs "like a rabbit" or "a proverbial chicken" (31) before the advancing Confederate army—a crime for which a military tribunal might have sentenced him to death. When he learns his army had held its position, in fact, Fleming "cringed as if discovered in a crime" (34). Yet he believes that nature shows him a sign when he throws a pine cone at a squirrel and it runs away. All he has done in fleeing the battle, he rationalizes, is to heed the instinct of self-preservation like an animal.

Frank Cowperwood is charged with larceny in Dreiser's *The Financier* (1912), though he too justifies his crime as necessary in order to survive and succeed.

> Law, if you had asked him, . . . was a mist formed out of the moods and the
> mistakes of men, which befogged the sea of life and prevented plain sailing for the
> little commercial and social barques of men; it was a miasma of misinterpretation
> where the ills of life festered, and also a place where the accidentally wounded
> were ground between the upper and the nether millstones of force or chance; it
> was a strange, weird, interesting, and yet futile battle of wits where the ignorant
> and the incompetent and the shrewd and the angry and the weak were made
> pawns and shuttlecocks for men. . . . In the hands of the strong, like himself when
> he was at his best, the law was a sword and a shield, a trap to place before the feet
> of the unwary; a pit to dig in the path of those who might pursue. It was anything

you might choose to make of it—a door to illegal opportunity; a cloud of dust to be cast in the eyes of those who might choose, and rightfully, to see; a veil to be dropped arbitrarily between truth and its execution, justice and its judgment, crime and punishment. (290–91)

Even after he is convicted and sent to prison, Cowperwood "did not think he was evil. As he saw it, he was merely unfortunate" (386).

Sam Spade, the detective-hero of Dashiell Hammett's *The Maltese Falcon* (1930), explains the insignificance of anti-bigamy laws in a parable he tells femme fatale Brigit O'Shaughnessy. (More than a comment about marriage law, the story is a key to understanding the novel as a whole.) A realtor named Charles Flitcraft left his office in Tacoma for lunch one afternoon and never returned. He disappeared "like a fist when you open your hand," Spade explains (62). Five years later, he surfaced a few miles away in Seattle, where he owned an automobile agency and a new house and lived under a new name with a new wife and son. "His second wife didn't look like the first," Spade notes, "but they were more alike than they were different" (64). As it happened, Flitcraft had been nearly struck and killed by a falling beam at a construction site as he walked to lunch five years earlier. "He felt like somebody had taken the lid off life and let him look at the works. . . . The life he knew was a clean orderly sane responsible affair," and "a falling beam had shown him that life was fundamentally none of these things." If "life could be ended for him at random," then "he would change his life at random" (63–64). He drifted for a couple of years and then settled in Seattle "into the same groove he had jumped out of in Tacoma." Put another way, like a Darwinian creature in a world of chance, he "adjusted himself to beams falling, and then no more of them fell, and he adjusted himself to them not falling" (64). Not that he is prosecuted as a bigamist, however. He and his first wife were quietly divorced "and everything was swell all around" (63).

Murder is usually represented in literary naturalism as an impulsive act of retaliation, an instinctive act of self-defense, or an act of kindness, if the killer exercises any agency at all. Toward the close of Crane's "The Blue Hotel" (1898), a gambler kills a drunken Swede who has grabbed him "frenziedly at the throat and was dragging him from his chair" (352). He is convicted of murder but given a lenient sentence. John Steinbeck's *The Grapes of Wrath* (1939) opens with Tom Joad's release on parole from the Oklahoma state prison where he has been jailed for killing a man (though in self-defense) during a drunken fight. Later, Tom assaults a deputy sheriff who has shot a homeless woman in a Hooverville, though Jim Casy takes the rap to save Tom from a parole violation. Still later, when Jim is murdered by a goon during a strike, Tom retaliates by killing his killer and becomes a fugitive from "justice." In context, however, each of Tom's and Jim's actions is justified. As Pa Joad explains when the family buries Grampa illegally because they cannot afford a funeral, "Sometimes the law can't be foller'd no way. . . . Not in decency, anyways. They's lots a times you can't. . . . Sometimes a fella got to sift the law" (190–91). In Steinbeck's *Of Mice and Men* (1937), the feeble-minded Lennie inadvertently breaks the neck of Curley's wife when she begins to scream. "Lennie never done it in meanness" (90), he merely didn't know his own strength, as his partner George understands, but George resolves not to permit Lennie to be jailed or "put in a cage" (92) where he would starve. He kills Lennie with a bullet to the brain rather than allow him to be arrested and prosecuted for murder or worse. Similarly, the physician who narrates Edwin Arlington Robinson's dramatic monologue/sonnet "How Annandale Went Out" (1910) rationalizes euthanasia, his mercy-killing of a suffering and terminally ill patient, and concludes, "You wouldn't hang me? I thought not" (346). And in Willard Motley's *Knock on Any Door* (1947), the protagonist Nick Romano is prosecuted for murder after he robs a tavern and kills a police officer who is chasing him—a cop who had beaten him when he was younger. His lawyer defends Nick on the grounds he is the victim of his surroundings; that is, he is only guilty of "having been reared in desperate poverty in the slums of a big city. He is guilty of having had the wrong environment and the wrong companions. He is guilty of the poolrooms and the taverns whose doors were open to him from the time he was fifteen" (442). Not that the defense succeeds: Nick is convicted and executed in the electric chair.

Motley's novel recapitulates many of the ideas that appeared in Richard Wright's *Native Son* (1940). As Wright explains in his essay "How Bigger Was Born," often reprinted as an introduction or afterword to the novel, "I began to see and understand the environmental factors which made for this extreme conduct" (515). His black protagonist Bigger Thomas is the "product of a dislocated society; he is a dispossessed and disinherited man . . . resentful toward whites, sullen, angry, ignorant, emotionally unstable, depressed and unaccountably elated at times" (521, 523). Hired to work on the Hyde Park estate of a rich white family in Chicago, Bigger is patronized by their daughter and her communist lover. After the three of them go "slumming" in the ghetto one evening, Bigger carries the drunken Mary to her bed and, when her blind mother enters the room, accidentally suffocates her while trying to muffle her voice. Bigger incinerates the body in the furnace he has been hired to tend and, when her bones are about to be discovered, he runs for his life in a "passion of fear" (Grenander 225). "Though he had killed by accident, not once did he feel the need to tell himself that it was an accident," Wright explains. "He was black and he had been alone in a room where a white girl had been killed; therefore he had killed her" (119). While on the lam, Bigger hooks up with his girlfriend Bessie, whom he rapes and then kills to prevent her from snitching on him: "He could not take her and he couldn't leave her; so he would have to kill her. It was his life against hers" (273). Bigger neither raped Mary "nor killed her intentionally," as John P. McWilliams Jr. notes, but "he bullied Bessie into an abandoned house, forced himself upon her sexually, and then, with malice aforethought, bludgeoned her to death with a brick" (99). Ironically, when he is finally arrested, he is prosecuted not for the crimes he committed (the rape and murder of a black woman) but for the alleged crimes he did not commit (the rape and murder of a white woman). Wright rarely rises above agitprop in the trial scene; his defense attorney Boris Max, hired by the local chapter of the Communist Party, offers no real defense—he even has Bigger (the "boy") plead guilty—but simply "addresses the court as a criminologist whose assumptions about causation are fundamentally Marxist" (McWilliams 103).

Poverty causes crime, according to Max (= Marx). The "cramped environment" of the slums (225) had produced a killer. On the other hand, the district attorney mostly offers racial slurs and panders to the lowest prejudices of the jury in prosecuting Bigger: "Every decent white man in America ought to swoon with joy for the opportunity to crush with his heel the woolly head of this black lizard" (373).

Criminal Innocence versus Guilt

The deterministic argument that criminals are created by their environments suggests, as a logical next step, that there is no fundamental difference in character between criminals and non-criminals, those in prison and those without. More exactly, the difference is that most criminals have not been caught, most crimes have not been detected, and/or most people have not been placed in circumstances in which they would have broken the law. As Clarence Darrow, the most renowned defense attorney of his generation, declared in an address to the prisoners in the Cook County jail in 1902,

> I really do not in the least believe in crime. There is no such thing as a crime as the word is generally understood. I do not believe there is any sort of distinction between the real moral conditions of the people in and out of jail. One is just as good as the other. The people here can no more help being here than the people outside can avoid being outside. I do not believe that people are in jail because they deserve to be. They are in jail simply because they cannot avoid it on account of circumstances which are entirely beyond their control and for which they are in no way responsible. (qtd. in Weinberg 3–4)

Dreiser shared Darrow's point of view. In his memoir *A Hoosier Holiday* (1916), Dreiser reminisced about his friend Red Brogan, who had been physically abused as a child, turned to robbery as an adult, and was eventually executed for murder. "If you want to know of a fairly good boy who died a criminal in the chair owing to conditions over which he had no least control or certainly very little," Dreiser opined, "this was one" (418).

When he became a journalist in the early 1890s, Dreiser began to collect newspaper accounts of a recurrent type of crime—the murder of a young woman by an ambitious young man (Moers 192–205). Often the woman was pregnant. In the early 1920s, Dreiser began to research in earnest a novel about such a crime, taking as his model the celebrated murder of Grace ("Billy") Brown by Chester Gillette in upstate New York in 1906. "In my examination of such data as I could find in 1924 relating to the Chester Gillette–Billy Brown case," he explained, "I became convinced that there was an entire misunderstanding, or perhaps I had better say non comprehension, of the conditions or circumstances surrounding the victims of that murder *before* the murder was committed" ("I Find" 88). His plan for the novel was "not to moralize" but "to give, if possible, a background and a psychology of reality

which would somehow explain, if not condone, how such murders happen—
and they have happened with surprising frequency in America as long as I can
remember" (*Letters* 2: 458). Much as Norris based McTeague's murder of Trina on
the murder of a charwoman in San Francisco in 1893 and Wright based some details
of the murder of Mary Dalton on the Robert Nixon case in Chicago in 1936, Dreiser
modeled the murder of Roberta Alden in *An American Tragedy* (1925) on Gillette's
murder of Grace Brown.

An American Tragedy is Dreiser's masterpiece and perhaps the greatest work of
literature (not only crime literature) by an American literary naturalist. The first of
three sections details the adolescence of Clyde Griffiths, who will eventually be
charged with murder. In order to understand the crime literally and figuratively at
the center of the novel, Dreiser insists, the reader must recognize all the forces and
influences that shape Clyde's character, from his "impractical and materially ineffi-
cient" father (8) and his parents' evangelical faith to his sexual desires, malleable
temperament, innate paganism, "exotic sense of romance" (14), and overweaning
ambition. Robert Bone, among many others, compares *An American Tragedy* to
Native Son. Both novels "make use of criminality as their chief dramatic device, and
in each case the crime is the natural and inevitable product of a warped society.
Both authors draw the data for their trial scenes, in classic naturalist fashion, from
authentic court records. . . . Both authors advance a guilt-of-the-nation thesis as a
corollary to their environmentalist view of crime" (142–43).

In the final pages of Book I, about a fifth of the way into the two-volume novel,
Clyde and some of his pals steal a car and take it joyriding. After drinks, they speed
"at almost forty miles an hours" (139) back to the hotel where several of them work.
Before the joyride is over, however, "a child had been killed; a car stolen and wrecked;
[Clyde's] job was most certainly lost," and the police are pursuing them (141).
Though Clyde escapes the dragnet, the driver is captured. But the driver is soon
convicted not of murder or manslaughter but of car-theft and illegal driving (166–67),
much as Bigger is convicted of crimes he did not commit (Mary Dalton's rape and
murder) rather than the crimes he committed (Bessie's rape and murder). In *An
American Tragedy*, the explanation is class difference; in *Native Son*, it is racial
difference. More to the point, the incident foreshadows Clyde's craven behavior
throughout the rest of the novel.

In the final pages of Book II, slightly over halfway through the novel, occurs the
"crime" that is its axis. Clyde has drifted into an intimate relationship with Roberta
Alden, one of the workers he manages in his uncle's collar factory, and she becomes
pregnant. Roberta's unwanted pregnancy is the result, Dreiser makes clear, of ignorance and the unavailability "of more than the simplest, and for the most part unsatis-
factory, contraceptive devices" (368). Clyde accompanies Roberta to the house of a
doctor who "had assisted in extricating from the consequences of their folly several
young girls of good family who had fallen from grace and could not be otherwise rescued," but the doctor refuses to perform an illegal abortion for Roberta because the
procedure "was not heavily sponsored by others" (400). Dreiser was not opposed to
abortion, whether legal or illegal, but he protested its availability only to the upper class.

Meanwhile, like Hurstwood to Carrie, Clyde has been attracted to the rich and beautiful Sondra Finchley, the "perfect girl" (308) and daughter of one of the first families of the city. In order to pursue Sondra, however, Clyde must first dispose of Roberta, and he gradually decides to stage her "accidental, unpremeditated drowning" in a lake (440). As Cassuto explains, "Clyde does not decide to kill Roberta so much as edge toward the idea, approaching and retreating from it" (203). Clyde's plans are prompted by the whisperings of a "Giant Efrit" or "the genie of his darkest and weakest side" (471, 464). On their ostensible wedding journey Clyde rows Roberta to a secluded cove. But at "the cataclysmic moment," he suffers "a sudden palsy of the will—of courage" (491). Roberta reaches to touch him, but Clyde—less a proper noun than the unspoken object of a gerund in the scene— "flinging out at her, but not even then with any intention to do anything but free himself of her," accidentally strikes her in the face with the camera slung around his neck. She screams and he stands up, "in so doing completely capsizing the boat— himself and Roberta being as instantly thrown into the water" (492–93). Clyde might save her, but "the voice at his ear" persuades him to let her drown: "An accident—an accident—an unintentional blow on your part is now saving you the labor of what you sought, and yet did not have the courage to do!" (493). Like Hurstwood's theft of money from the safe in *Sister Carrie*, Clyde's murder of Roberta might best be described as a premeditated accident. Dreiser consulted with lawyers while writing *An American Tragedy* and, according to C. R. B. Dunlop, "in the murder scene, he created a situation so ambiguous that it is almost impossible to decide whether, legally or morally, Clyde is guilty" (393).

In Book III, Dreiser criticizes the investigation of the crime and Clyde's subsequent trial. Because he planned the "murder" so poorly, he is arrested almost immediately. But by describing the background of so many of the officials involved in the investigation, Dreiser details their own prejudices and aversions. "Almost without exception," Dunlop avers, "Dreiser depicts the functionaries of the legal system, whether police, lawyers, officials, or judges, as being brusque, inhuman, secretive, and corrupt" (383). Even the jailhouse lawyer Clyde later meets in prison is, ironically, a jailed lawyer. The ambiguity of the scene in which Roberta drowns is irrelevant to Clyde's trial. His defense lawyers assume that he is guilty. Neither the prosecution nor the defense presents a case based on facts; instead, as Dunlop adds, both sides "break the law with impunity, create false evidence, and coach their witnesses in fabricated stories" (384). The courtroom becomes a stage, the trial a theater. Clyde is found guilty on perjured evidence, including a strand of hair planted on the camera that struck Roberta's face. In turn, the jurors vote their rural prejudices. In the end, neither the judge, the prosecutors, nor the defense attorneys try the case fairly. Clyde's appeal to a higher court costs a small fortune, arduously raised by his mother—justice depends upon the ability to pay, Dreiser demonstrates—and the appeals court merely affirms the original verdict; that is, it finds no legal irregularities in Clyde's trial. The state's governor refuses to commute Clyde's sentence for the same reason. Like Darrow in his address to the Cook County inmates in 1902, Dreiser fundamentally questions the guilt of all prisoners.

Each of the inmates on Death Row, including Clyde, Dreiser suggests, "had responded to some heat or lust or misery of his nature or his circumstances" (767). "*An American Tragedy* is not a pamphlet advocating political or legal reforms," Dunlop contends; "it is a plea for compassion to those who commit crimes because they are driven to do so" (397). It is only incidentally an indictment of capital punishment.

Six years after the publication of his novel, Dreiser attempted to force changes in the script of a motion picture based on it. In *Dreiser v. Paramount Publix Corporation*, he claimed that the novel was "an indictment of our social system under which individuals are overwhelmed by forces outside themselves, react in certain ways which are due largely to their background and environment, and individually pay the penalty." He further maintained that the novel presented "the situation of an ordinary but weak youngster named Clyde Griffiths, who, through the vicissitudes of life, over which he had little or no control, was gradually forced to one position after another, until he became involved in a great tragedy" ("Murder Trial"). Significantly, Dreiser did not use either of the words "crime" or "murder" in his summary of the plot.

In his novel *The Postman Always Rings Twice* (1934), James M. Cain gives an ironic twist to Dreiser's representation of murder in *An American Tragedy*. The protagonist/narrator plots with his lover to kill her husband in a staged "accident." Despite the suspicions of the authorities, they pull off the murder. But then he accidentally kills her in a car wreck and is indicted and executed for her murder. On Death Row he encounters another inmate convicted of first-degree murder, who

> says he didn't really do it, his subconscious did it. I asked him what that meant, and he says you got two selves, one that you know about and the other that you don't know about, because it's subconscious. It shook me up. Did I really do it, and not know it? . . . To hell with the subconscious. I don't believe it. It's just a lot of hooey, that this guy thought up so he could fool the judge. You know what you're doing, and you do it. I didn't do it, I know that. (119)

This final sentence is as ambiguous as Clyde's responsibility for Roberta's death. He didn't do "it," the crime for which he is convicted; but he did do "it," the murder he had earlier planned and executed to perfection. Cain's killer is as guilty/innocent and/or no less guilty/innocent as Clyde.

HARD-BOILED CRIME FICTION

The hard-boiled crime fiction of the 1920s and 1930s, born in the pages of *Black Mask* and other pulp magazines, was a spin-off of the naturalistic crime novel. Dashiell Hammett, Raymond Chandler, and other writers in the genre in effect prove Darrow and Dreiser's point that there is no essential difference between those in and out of prison. The methods employed by such working-class detectives as

Sam Spade, Mike Hammer (spades and hammers are workers' tools), and Philip Marlowe in solving crimes are often indistinguishable from the methods of the criminals. Their tales, often told in the first person, focus less on solving mysteries than surviving in a hostile and corrupting environment, the "mean streets" of San Francisco, Los Angeles, and other cities. In Hammett's *The Maltese Falcon*, for example, the tough-minded Spade, who resembles "a blonde Satan" (3), must fend off the inept police and district attorney as well as the conniving crooks. He illegally searches the apartment of the femme fatale and, after referring the wife of his partner (who is also his mistress) to his personal lawyer, persuades the lawyer to violate attorney-client privilege by telling him what she said. He brags that his reputation for blurring the line between law and outlaw enables him better to "deal with the enemy" (215)—both cops and criminals. He avenges his partner's murder if only for business reasons—"when one of your organization gets killed it's bad business to let the killer get away with it. . . . I'm a detective and expecting me to run criminals down and then let them go free is like asking a dog to catch a rabbit and let it go" (214). In short, Spade inhabits a "wild and unpredictable" world (211), as he illustrates in the Flitcraft parable, and he aims not for justice but mere survival. Or as John G. Cawelti explains, "More than any other hard-boiled writer, Hammett's work reflects the vision of a godless naturalistic cosmos ruled by chance, violence, and death" (173). The brutish killer Moose Malloy in Chandler's *Farewell, My Lovely* (1940) is a fraternal twin of Steinbeck's Lennie, as Cawelti observes, in his "epic strength" (180):

> "You killed a woman," I said. "Jessie Florian. That was a mistake."
> He thought. Then he nodded, "I'd drop that one," he said quietly.
> "But that queered it," I said. "I'm not afraid of you. You're no killer. You didn't mean to kill her. The other one—over on Central—you could have squeezed out of. But not out of beating a woman's head on a bedpost until her brains were on her face."
> "You take some awful chances, brother," he said softly.
> "The way I've been handled," I said, "I don't know the difference any more. You didn't mean to kill her—did you?" (216)

Little wonder that hard-boiled crime novels—for example, *The Maltese Falcon*, *The Glass Key* (1931), *The Big Sleep* (1939), and *Farewell, My Lovely*—were adapted to film noir or that Chandler's *Playback* (1958), originally written as a screenplay, was later converted into a hard-boiled detective novel without significant revision. The amoral universe of the literary naturalist corresponds exactly to the bleak world of the hard-boiled or "tough guy" crime novelist and his film noir cousin.

WORKS CITED

Bellamy, Edward. *Looking Backward, 2000–1887*. Ed. Robert C. Elliott. Boston: Houghton Mifflin, 1966.

Bone, Robert. *The Negro Novel in America*. New Haven, Conn.: Yale University Press, 1965.

Cain, James M. *The Postman Always Rings Twice*. New York: Vintage, 1962.

Cassuto, Leonard. "Dreiser and Crime." *The Cambridge Companion to Theodore* Dreiser. Ed. Leonard Cassuto and Clare Virginia Eby. New York: Cambridge University Press, 2004. 196–213.

Cawelti, John G. *Adventure, Mystery, and Romance*. Chicago: University of Chicago Press, 1976.

Chandler, Raymond. *Farewell, My Lovely*. New York: Pocket, 1943.

Cowley, Malcolm. "'Not Men': A Natural History of American Naturalism." *Kenyon Review* 9 (1947): 414–35.

Crane, Stephen. "The Blue Hotel." *Great Short Works of Stephen Crane*. New York: Perennial, 2004. 325–54.

———. *The Correspondence of Stephen Crane*. Ed. Stanley Wertheim and Paul Sorrentino. New York: Columbia University Press, 1988. 2 vols.

———. *Maggie: A Girl of the Streets*. Ed. Thomas A. Gullason. New York: Norton, 1979.

———. *The Red Badge of Courage*. Ed. Donald Pizer. 3rd ed. New York: Norton, 1994.

Dreiser, Theodore. *An American Tragedy*. New York: Signet, 1981.

———. *The Financier*. New York: Signet, 1967.

——— *A Hoosier Holiday*. New York: John Lane, 1916.

———. "I Find the Real American Tragedy." *Mystery Magazine* 11 (Feb. 1935): 9–11, 88–90.

———. *Letters of Theodore Dreiser*. Ed. Robert Elias. Philadelphia: University of Pennsylvania Press, 1959. 3 vols.

———. *Sister Carrie*. Ed. Donald Pizer. New York: Norton, 1970.

Dunlop, C. R. B. "Law and Justice in Dreiser's *An American Tragedy*." *University of British Columbia Law Review* 6 (1971): 379–403.

Gilman, Charlotte Perkins. *Herland*. New York: Pantheon, 1979.

Grenander, M. E. "Criminal Responsibility in *Native Son* and *Knock on Any Door*." *American Literature* 49 (1977): 221–33.

Hammett, Dashiell. *The Maltese Falcon*. New York: Vintage, 1989.

McWilliams, John P., Jr. "Innocent Criminal or Criminal Innocence: The Trial in American Fiction." *Law and American Literature: A Collection of Essays*. New York: Knopf, 1983. 45–124.

Moers, Ellen. *Two Dreisers*. New York: Viking, 1969.

Motley, Willard. *Knock on Any Door*. New York: Appleton-Century, 1947.

"The Murder Trial of Chester Gillette." *The Historical Society of the Courts of the State of New York*. http://www.courts.state.ny.us/history/gillette.htm.

Norris, Frank. *McTeague*. Ed. Donald Pizer. 2nd ed. New York: Norton, 1997.

———. *The Octopus*. New York: Signet, 1981.

———. "A Reversion to Type." *The Third Circle*. New York: John Lane, 1909. 89–100.

O'Neill, Eugene. *Anna Christie, The Emperor Jones, The Hairy Ape*. New York: Vintage, 1995.

Phillips, David Graham. *Susan Lenox: Her Fall and Rise*. New York: Appleton, 1917. 2 vols.

Pizer, Donald. "Evolutionary Ethical Dualism in Frank Norris' *Vandover and the Brute* and *McTeague*." *PMLA* 76 (1961): 552–60.

Robinson, Edwin Arlington. "How Annandale Went Out." *Collected Poems of Edwin Arlington Robinson*. New York: Macmillan, 1954. 346.

Sinclair, Upton. *The Jungle*. Ed. Clare Virginia Eby. New York: Norton, 2003.

Steinbeck, John. *The Grapes of Wrath*. New York: Viking, 1939.

———. *Of Mice and Men* and *Cannery Row*. New York: Penguin, 1973.

Twain, Mark. *Pudd'nhead Wilson and Those Extraordinary Twins*. Ed. Sidney E. Berger. 2nd
    ed. New York: Norton, 2005.
Weinberg, Arthur. *Attorney for the Damned*. New York: Simon & Schuster, 1957.
Wright, Richard. "How Bigger Was Born." *Native Son*. New York: HarperPerennial, 1993.
    505–40.
———. *Native Son*. New York: HarperPerennial, 1993.

PART V

NATURALISM AND
THE MARKETPLACE

CHAPTER 21

···

NATURALIST AUTHORS AND THE AMERICAN LITERARY MARKETPLACE

···

CHARLES JOHANNINGSMEIER

To those Americans who aspired to become full-time, self-supporting fiction authors in the late 1880s through early 1900s, when most naturalist writers were beginning their careers, the literary marketplace must have appeared to promise almost unlimited opportunity. The demand for fiction was expanding exponentially, with the number of publication outlets growing at a rapid pace. Numerous new book-publishing firms were being established each year, and consequently the total number of books—many of them novels or short-story collections—published in the United States doubled between 1890 and 1910 (Lichtenstein 45). Magazines and newspapers—most of which printed fiction—were also virtually omnipresent, since the number of non-newspaper periodicals in the United States rose from 3,300 in 1885 to 5,500 in 1900, and 6,000 in 1905 (Mott 11), while the number of daily newspapers increased from 1,731 in 1890 to 2,226 by 1899 (Johanningsmeier 17). The audience for fiction was growing concomitantly, too: bestselling novels during this era typically sold in the hundreds of thousands, with the most popular periodicals regularly selling at least 500,000 copies per issue after 1895, and over one million copies per issue after 1905 (Sedgwick 408). The extraordinary increase in demand for fiction encouraged more and more people—including well-known naturalist authors such as Stephen Crane, Theodore Dreiser, Paul Laurence Dunbar, Hamlin Garland, Jack London, Frank Norris, and Edith Wharton—to forsake working regular jobs as newspaper reporters, farmers, editors, schoolteachers, elevator operators, sailors, and so forth, and to attempt to make their living producing this commodity.

Also substantially contributing to the flood of literary aspirants was the portrayal in the popular press and elsewhere of literary success—and its accompanying financial rewards—as relatively easy to achieve. Newspapers and magazines were full of stories about authors whose books sold in previously unheard of numbers or whose works commanded high prices from magazine editors and newspaper syndicators. Details of the substantial, sumptuously furnished houses and comfortable lifestyles enjoyed by successful authors could be found in countless articles and books. A few commentators did counter that earning one's living as a fiction writer was not quite as easy as commonly thought and that such successes were rare, but their warnings generally went unheeded; the appeal of the imagined "easy" fiction-writer's life was simply too strong.

Authors were further encouraged because most of these articles and books implied it was no longer necessary to have "Imagination" or "Genius" to achieve such success; instead, they suggested that success resulted from methodically and persistently following a set of guidelines laid out by the nascent "literary advice" industry. A plethora of books and magazines advised authors how to prepare their manuscripts, send them to editors, have them accepted, and get paid well for them; these publications contributed substantially to what scholar Christopher Wilson has termed the "professionalization" of fiction writing during this period (*Labor* 15). Even an author whose work tended to fly in the face of social and literary conventions could have been forgiven for believing that, with a little hard work and adherence to the advice and guidelines proffered by these publications, he or she could, before long, begin to enjoy a lifetime of independent work and a genteel lifestyle.

Despite the seemingly unlimited promise and easy achievability of success offered by the American literary marketplace, however, it disappointed most naturalist authors—at least initially. Most had to pay much higher dues during their early careers than they had been led to anticipate, and as they went through this stage almost all complained mightily about their perceived "mistreatment" at the hands of those whom they believed controlled the marketplace: editors, publishers, and readers. Not surprisingly, given the propensity among naturalists to see the individual in modern society as being at the mercy of large, powerful societal and environmental forces, they often cast themselves in letters, essays, and elsewhere as heroic truthtellers who were engaged in a mighty struggle against a publishing industry that they described in bestial or mechanistic terms, and whose sole concern, they believed, was making money by catering to the philistine, prudish American reading public. In their own minds they were, in short, Davids battling multiple Goliaths.

With very few exceptions, academic commentators since the 1920s have accepted these authors' critiques of the American literary marketplace, possibly because literary scholars naturally have a strong affinity with the authors whose creations they admire. As a result, the marketplace during this period has been painted with broad strokes and in starkly contrasting colors as a battle between valiant, avant-garde naturalist authors with proletarian affinities and a bourgeois, morally conservative American publishing industry and audience. A more accurate portrayal of how naturalist authors interacted with the marketplace, however, requires more subtle brush work. Detailed examination of naturalist authors' experiences with editors, publishers, and readers reveals that one depiction does not fit all; the evidence suggests that instead of a "hidden hand" hegemonically controlling the publishing industry, multiple groups of interested parties—whose memberships were constantly changing—negotiated over the publication terms of each naturalist text. Each author, and indeed, each work, consequently has its own history and deserves its own investigation.

Naturalist Authors, Factory Work, and "The Iron Madonna"

Naturalist authors, reflecting their philosophical predispositions and the rapid industrialization taking place in the late nineteenth and early twentieth centuries, complained about their treatment by editors and publishers in a slightly different manner than earlier authors had. For instance, they frequently compared editors and publishers to animals. In a letter to Hamlin Garland, Stephen Crane described magazine publisher and newspaper syndicator S. S. McClure, to whom he had submitted the manuscript of *The Red Badge of Courage*, as having been "a Beast about the war novel" (1: 79); later, he would complain about how constraining his contract with McClure was and call him a "Scotch ass" (1: 327). Jack London, through his supposed doppelgänger Martin Eden, protagonist of London's eponymous novel, also thought of editors and publishers as animals and contended that their power was contrary to evolution: "Every portal to success in literature is guarded by those watch-dogs. . . .The editors, sub-editors, associate editors, most of them, and the manuscript-readers for the magazines and book-publishers . . . of all creatures under the sun the most unfit, are the very creatures who decide what shall and what shall not find its way into print" (*Martin Eden* 796).

Many naturalist authors also accused editors and publishers of acting increasingly like factory foremen and owners who were reducing naturalist authors to serving as proletarian laborers who had little control over the products of their labor, their work schedule, or their wages. London has Martin Eden, for example, depict editors as part of an "inhuman editorial machine" (737) and declare to himself (and the reader): "Surely there were no live, warm editors at the other end. It was all wheels and cogs and oil-cups—a clever mechanism operated by automatons" (737). Like any factory worker, Eden is constantly frustrated at the seemingly inexplicable decisions and delays made by his "bosses," the editors, as well as the low pay for his work. Frank Norris also employed the industrial-worker analogy, writing to a friend in 1898 about "the difficulty of keeping up . . . with the hammer and tongs work of a New York publication such as the McClure Magazine and syndicate" (*Collected Letters* 47). In one 1902 essay, Norris argued that modern editors and publishers were essentially akin to foremen in factories run according to Tayloristic principles. Writing with the authority of an "insider" (Norris had worked for the McClure periodical and book-publishing firms in various capacities and for book publishers Doubleday, Page and Co.), he alleged: "No one not intimately associated with any one of the larger, more important 'houses' can have any idea of the influence of the publisher upon latter-day fiction. More novels are written—practically— to order than the public has any notion of. The publisher again and again picks out the man (one speaks, of course, of the younger generation), suggests the theme, and exercises, in a sense, all the functions of instructor, during the period of composition" ("Salt and Sincerity" 198).

Not only did naturalist authors complain about editors and publishers, but they also loudly and frequently criticized the people whom they believed exerted the most influence over their decisions: the allegedly politically and morally conservative American reading public, which naturalist authors generally believed only wanted to be entertained by fiction, not edified by it. They were not the first American authors to complain about the American audience for fiction. Novelist Hjalmar Hjorth Boyesen had protested mightily in 1887 against the power of the female reading public, whom he represented as "the Iron Madonna, who strangles in her fond embrace the American novelist, the Moloch upon whose altar he sacrifices, willingly or unwillingly, his chances of greatness" (618–19). William Dean Howells in 1891 offered his judgment that magazine editors "will print nothing which a father may not read to his daughter, or safely leave her to read herself" (75). Norris echoed Boyesen and Howells, writing in 1902: "One may go so far as to say that the figure of the Amiable Young Girl throws its shadow over the whole scope and range of our latter-day fiction. This fiction is *about* Amiable Young Girls; it is addressed *to* Amiable Young Girls; and—save the mark—is written *by* Amiable Young Girls" ("Salt and Sincerity" 206). Not surprisingly, London's Martin Eden rails against the reading public that won't accept his view of "reality," telling Ruth Morse, the fictional representative of the Iron Madonna or Amiable Young Girl: "The bourgeois spirit hates realism. The bourgeoisie is cowardly. It is afraid of life" (915). And Edith Wharton, in a 1903 essay entitled "The Vice of Reading," further argued that the marketplace was dominated by what she called "the sense-of-duty reader" (99) or "mechanical reader" (100) who read whatever the "*vox populi*" (102) said it should. Wharton condemned these readers for not being independent enough or sufficiently appreciative of fine literary art, concluding that when this type of reader "invades the domain of letters—discusses, criticises, condemns, or, worse still, praises . . . the vice of reading becomes a menace to literature" (100).

THE AUTHOR AS "COG IN THE MACHINE"

Thus far, almost all academic commentators have concurred with the naturalists' assessment of the literary marketplace during this period. One of the first to portray the publishing industry as akin to a factory, with editors and publishers acting as foremen and factory owners and authors as proletariat workers, was historian Nelson Lichtenstein, who in 1978 argued that the low-priced, mass-market magazines introduced in the late 1880s and early 1890s, such as *Cosmopolitan, Munsey's, Ladies' Home Journal*, and the *Saturday Evening Post*, were largely responsible for the publishing industry's rapid transformation (42); many others have since concurred.

To support their contention that editors heavy-handedly controlled literary production, a number of scholars have cited the aforementioned passage from Frank Norris's "Salt and Sincerity" and come to very negative conclusions about editors and publishers. Daniel Borus, for instance, in *Writing Realism: Howells, James, and Norris in the Mass Market*, opines, "Publishers commanded a coordinated package. Writers were an important, but by no means sole, cog in the machine" (48). Christopher Wilson, whose *The Labor of Words: Literary Professionalism in the Progressive Era* almost single-handedly established the prevailing scholarly paradigm about the relationship of naturalist authors to the marketplace, charges that Jack London, Upton Sinclair, and David Graham Phillips were "pressured to prefabricate their writing to meet certain editorial prescriptions. Editors proved more than willing to take 'inspiration' off writers' hands. . . . The professional author had to negotiate an editorial idea that had been assigned in advance, an editorial demand for a trademark style for which a writer was well known" (*Labor* 200). Wilson elsewhere argues that such editorial direction, which subordinated both authors *and* readers to their designs ("Rhetoric" 42–44), simply emulated the rules governing efficient factory operations; it "was a matter of making the production process more predictable at both ends" ("Rhetoric" 48).

How accurate, though, are such portrayals of editors, publishers, authors, and readers? When pressed to provide concrete examples of how the operating conditions of the literary marketplace in the 1890s and early 1900s affected naturalist authors, scholars have generally referred to a relatively small sampling of prominent instances in which editors and/or publishers, supposedly acting on the behalf of the reading public, negatively interfered with the publication of works now regarded as literary masterpieces. Stephen Crane's difficulties getting both *Maggie: A Girl of the Streets* (1893) and *The Red Badge of Courage* (1895) published are often cited, as are the alleged censorship of Theodore Dreiser's *Sister Carrie* (1900), the suppression of *The "Genius"* (1915), and the excision of the scene in Norris's *McTeague: A Story of San Francisco* (1899) in which Auguste Sieppe wets his pants.

Scholars have further posited that even when editors didn't actively wield their blue pencils, naturalist authors and others self-censored their works before submission according to what they believed editors and their readers wanted. Ellery Sedgwick has recently contended that "most writers consciously adapted their production to the requirements of the editors and readers who constituted the magazine market" (402). Frequently cited supporting evidence includes London's difficulties breaking away from writing Yukon stories; Dunbar's supposed inability to publish something other than humorous dialect poetry; and London's own *Martin Eden* (1909), commonly regarded as a thinly veiled, yet accurate, autobiography of London's early years as a struggling author.

Most strongly castigated by scholars, however, is the marketplace's alleged strict control over the treatment of sex and adultery in fiction. As John Tebbel writes, for instance, the *Saturday Evening Post* under George Horace Lorimer "hid its head in the sands of convention wherever sex was involved" (49). Donald Sheehan contends that this general "prohibition" can be largely ascribed not only to readers' perceived sensitivity but also to publishers' fears of being prosecuted under the Comstock Laws (107–9).

Overall, the prevailing academic paradigm about the interaction between the literary marketplace and fiction authors—especially naturalist ones—at the end of the nineteenth and the beginning of the twentieth centuries positions authors as poorly paid workers who possessed very little control over their fictions. Naturalist works were also supposedly rejected by the readers of their time; as Donald Pizer has recently asserted, because of "the powerful radical center of naturalistic expression" (191), they were "frequently assailed for their seemingly over-critical and thus negative view of the ills of American society" (189). Those naturalist authors who did "succeed" financially by gaining a large readership, it is implied, were able to do so only because they "sold out" their artistic vision to the bourgeois marketplace.

To what extent, though, did naturalist authors actually lose control over their texts before, during, and after composition? And were their cutting-edge works indeed completely rejected by editors, publishers, and readers? A few examples must here suffice to demonstrate that one needs to look past the conventional depiction of authors as heroic saints, editors and publishers as villainous demons, and readers as wholly conservative, in order to get more accurate answers to these questions.

STEPHEN CRANE: NEOPHYTE IN THE MARKETPLACE

One of the most apocryphal stories about a naturalist author's battle to maintain control over his text involves Stephen Crane's widely recounted difficulties finding a publisher for *Maggie: A Girl of the Streets*. According to the usual scholarly account, Crane submitted the manuscript of *Maggie* to Richard Watson Gilder, editor of the prestigious *Century* magazine, in late 1892 or early 1893 (Crane 1: 40), who rejected it for its immorality and foul language. Crane then allegedly took matters into his own hands by paying to have *Maggie* privately published under the name of Johnston Smith. Lacking the marketing support of a major publisher, the book went largely unnoticed until D. Appleton, riding the wave of Crane's fame after *The Red Badge of Courage*, published a version of *Maggie*, albeit a bowdlerized one, in 1896. This narrative has typically been used to demonstrate the conservative, censorious nature of the marketplace with which naturalist authors were forced to contend. Gilder, so this line of argument goes, was a typical editor who represented the professional self-conception of all magazine editors when he wrote in 1896 that to fulfill their civic duty, editors needed to fight "[s]alaciousness and gross sensationalism" (1670).

Typically overlooked in this narrative, however, is that the evidence used to support it is tenuous at best. Scholars have assumed, for instance, that one undated note from Hamlin Garland to Gilder recommending a manuscript by Crane referred to *Maggie*; however, Garland many years later stated that he did not read *Maggie* until after it had been published, which would mean that Garland's note had referred to a different Crane text (Garland 191–92). Assertions about how and why Gilder— along with, supposedly, other editors—rejected *Maggie* have been based solely on the extremely dubious recollections of his friends Willis Fletcher Johnson (Sorrentino 36–37), Post Wheeler (Sorrentino 27), and Willis Brooks Hawkins (Sorrentino 167). Also frequently cited is Thomas Beer's undocumented, frequently inaccurate 1923 account in *Stephen Crane: A Study in American Letters* (80–102). After having spent years investigating the circumstances of *Maggie*'s publication, noted scholar Stanley Wertheim recently concluded that circumstantial evidence suggests Crane did, indeed, submit the manuscript of *Maggie* to Gilder and the *Century*, but "[t] here isn't a shred of evidence that *Maggie* was submitted to any other publisher" (Wertheim). Based on what is currently known, then, it is very difficult to support any assertion that "the marketplace" rejected Crane's first novel.

Even if Crane did submit his manuscript of *Maggie* to Gilder, I would suggest that one should blame Crane just as much as Gilder for its rejection because Crane should have known that the *Century* was a wholly inappropriate venue for such a novel. Gilder and Robert Underwood Johnson, his associate editor, were widely known among writers as being more conservative and moralistic than most other editors. Fiction author James Lauren Ford, writing in *The Literary Shop and Other Tales* in 1894, recalled that although he had succeeded in placing his work in other magazines, "I soon found that every literary man of my acquaintance was fully aware of his [Johnson's] feelings in the matter [of fiction that treated of unseemly subjects], and therefore took pains not to introduce into a story any scenes or characters which might serve to render the manuscript unsalable in the eyes of the *Century* editors" (69). An intelligent response by Crane to this apparently widely known information should have been to first submit *Maggie* to a different magazine.

One might further ask why Crane, a penurious young author, moved so quickly to pay for *Maggie*'s publication instead of submitting it to other magazines. Again, the answer would appear to be his naïveté about the literary marketplace. There were certainly other editors who would have welcomed the opportunity to pay Crane for serial or book rights to the novel. One obvious outlet would have been the *Arena* magazine and book-publishing firm in Boston, which Crane, in close contact with Hamlin Garland, who had published many works with them by 1893, should have known did not shy away from social-activist literature. Its publisher, Benjamin Flower, had even explicitly told Garland on 30 April 1890: "In writing for the Arena either stories or essays I wish you always to feel yourself thoroughly free to express any opinions you desire or to send home any lessons which you feel should be impressed upon the people. I for one do not believe in mincing matters when we are dealing with the great wrongs and evils of the day and the pitiful conditions of society and I do not wish you to feel in writing for the Arena at any time, the slightest constraint" (qtd. in Newlin 138). Moreover, Garland knew that the *Arena* paid the same rates as the *Century* and did so promptly. It is unknown whether Garland had the opportunity to advise Crane specifically about *Maggie* before Crane paid to have it published, but one would assume that Garland had at some point mentioned to Crane his success with the Arena company and the liberality of its publisher. In any case, Flower apparently read the 1893 *Maggie* shortly after its publication and approved of it, evidently leading him to write to Crane and praise the book, for in April 1893, Crane wrote to Lily Brandon Munroe that "B. O. Flower of the 'Arena' has practically offered me the benefits of his publishing company for all that I may in future write" (1: 55). Unfortunately, while Crane seems to have arranged for the Arena Publishing Company to reprint *Maggie*—probably in unexpurgated form— sometime in 1893, for some reason this never happened (Crane 1: 58 n4). In sum, the account offered here of *Maggie*'s early publication history at the very least suggests that the responsibility for its not being brought out by a regular magazine or book publisher until 1896, and even then only in amended form, belongs not just to one conservative editor but also to Crane himself.

Paul Laurence Dunbar: Race-Champion or Poet-for-Hire?

Much of the scholarship concerning Paul Laurence Dunbar's career has thus far asserted that he was in control of neither his subject matter nor narrative treatment and was constrained by the white-controlled publishing industry to produce humorous Negro dialect poetry in order to please white readers. According to one of Dunbar's early biographers, the demand of the white audience for such poetry, his great need for the money such work earned him, and the imperative that he himself be presented as "a simple-minded child, a buffoon" (Gayle xiv), was what eventually drove him to drink and to his death (Gayle xiii–xiv). Dunbar himself once wrote, "I am tired, so tired of dialect. I send out graceful little poems [in standard English], suited for any of the magazines, but they are returned to me by editors who say, 'we would be very glad to have a dialect poem, Mr. Dunbar, but we do not care for the language compositions'" (qtd. in Gayle 123). Such constraints allegedly extended to the production of his more naturalistic and critical 1902 novel *Sport of the Gods*, a view that can be partially supported by Dunbar's statement about writing it: "Last spring, when filling an order for a prose composition for *Lippincott's Magazine*, I wrote fifty thousand words in thirty days, but I have never recovered from the strain of it" (qtd. in Brawley 89). Dunbar's case thus might appear to be another demonstration of the dominance of the marketplace—comprised of white editors, publishers, and audiences—and how it eventually transformed a talented writer into a machine-like laborer turning out the non-threatening entertainment demanded by his bosses.

Closer examination of Dunbar's career, however, complicates this simplistic depiction. The white-dominated marketplace certainly strongly desired Dunbar's dialect poetry. Yet it could also be very receptive to such texts as the strongly and explicitly anti-lynching poem "The Haunted Oak" (1900), which was published in no less a publication than *Century* magazine. As biographer Benjamin Brawley notes, "Some reviewers wondered that the *Century*, known for its gentle literary flavor, would dare to print a piece so intensely realistic; and the fact that it appeared shows that Mr. Gilder, the editor, and his associates were open-minded and ever ready to consider Dunbar's best work" (88–89). Dunbar was also incredibly successful in placing his later short stories in a variety of other prominent magazines such as *Cosmopolitan*, *Lippincott's*, *Independent*, and the *Saturday Evening Post*. In part this was probably because Dunbar's fiction, unlike Crane's, did not depict whites transgressing established standards of sexual and marital behavior, instead focusing mostly on social and political issues.

Significantly, to be published in such venues Dunbar was not forced to produce the types of bland stories about African Americans that most white editors and readers would have wanted. Many of Dunbar's serialized stories, including "Mr. Cornelius Johnson, Office Seeker" (*Cosmopolitan*); "The Conjuring Contest," "The Strength of Gideon" and "The Finish of Patsy Barnes" (*Saturday Evening Post*), as well as stories in his popular collections *The Strength of Gideon and Other Stories* (1900), *In Old Plantation Days* (1903), *The Heart of Happy Hollow* (1904), and the novel *Sport of the Gods*, were very critical of whites and of racist ideologies. As Dunbar's biographer astutely notes, "The disappointments, the bitterness, the hostility—all were to be found . . . neatly tucked between the narratives of the plantation tradition" (Gayle 131). Increasingly, in fact, scholars are beginning to recognize that far from being a compliant producer of "Plantation School" fictions, Dunbar achieved great success in the marketplace while "signifying" on his audiences, and that he "used his literature to promote covert and overt forms of resistance and racial protest" (Best 3).

Jack London: Crafting the Proletariat Myth

The case of Jack London, who complained mightily about being a beset proletarian worker while simultaneously becoming America's first millionaire author, is a curiously contradictory one. Some scholars conclude, as Wilson does, that "even as

London signified the American writer's new market power, he also became an example of how one might be victimized by it" (*Labor* 96). Yet, as numerous others have noted, most especially Jonathan Auerbach, London's portrayal of himself in published essays and private letters as a strong, masculine, proletarian writer fighting against the bourgeois publishing Machine was an important part of his self-conception (9, 20), and one should always question the veracity of someone with so much at stake in such a portrayal.

What most scholars have cited as particularly representative of London's own interactions with the literary marketplace are Martin Eden's experiences in his eponymous 1909 novel. Encountering the seemingly machine-like modern literary marketplace personified by magazine editors, Eden nearly starves to death before they start accepting his work. Even then, they often purportedly "slaughter" his texts before publishing them (784) and don't pay him what he thinks they are worth. Eventually becoming a huge success, Eden ascribes this neither to the editors' recognition of his genius nor to his own hard work; instead, it is a matter either of "the smooth-running editorial machine" breaking down (747) or "sheer jugglery of fate" (877); "[f]awn or fang," he asserts, "it was all a matter of chance" (897).

Eden's fictional experiences—which make for great drama—were, however, not wholly accurate depictions of London's real-life experiences. To support their portrayal of London as a Martin Eden–like hero battling against bourgeois commercialism, scholars frequently cite a 1907 letter to editor George Brett of Macmillan's in which London lashes out at the allegedly conservative, censoring editors at *McClure's Magazine* for their poor treatment of him from 1900 to 1902 (*Letters* 2: 675). Yet in February 1900, London gleefully wrote to his friend Cloudesley Johns about his growing success with *McClure's Magazine*. They had, as he told Johns, recently accepted a story of his ("The God of His Fathers") about "a minister who apostasizes . . . and the vile sinner who did not" (*Letters* 1: 153). According to London, "*McClure's* accepted it if I would agree to the cutting of the opening and the elimination of certain swear-words. Of course I agreed, as it was an affair of 6000 words" (*Letters* 1: 153). He further added that the firm was also enthusiastic about— and accepted—"that socialistic essay I read to you ["Question of the Maximum"]. What do you think of that for a rather conservative house? I mean conservative politically" (*Letters* 1: 153). Just a few days later, on 13 February 1900, London, almost giddy with the beginnings of literary success, wrote to Anna Strunsky about the acceptance of "The God of His Fathers": "*McClures*' [sic] have become interested in my work, and are begging me to give them first glance at whatever I write. They accepted a 6000 word story of mine the other day on condition that I should change the opening and eliminate the profanity. I agreed, telling them to go ahead and do it them selves. Gave them *carte blanche*, in fact" (*Letters* 1: 157). A publisher who "begs" does not appear to be in a position of power. As in Crane's case, the editor— in this case, the magazine's managing editor, John Phillips—was clearly objecting only to the language used, not to the ideological content of the fiction itself. In fact, as James Williams perceptively writes, despite other scholars' charges about *McClure's*, he has "not found documentary evidence that someone at the magazine asked London to downplay or eliminate his socialism and that London was angry" (234n). Audiences, too, did not reject London's texts for their socialistic themes; instead, as London once wrote to Cloudesley Johns, "I flatter myself that I am one of the rare socialists who have ever succeeded in making money out of their socialism" (*Letters* 1: 226).

It is thus very difficult to accept London's depiction of himself as a poorly paid, disempowered factory laborer. Especially after he was better known, London not only wrote about whatever he wanted, and in whatever way he wished, but he also retained firm control over his production schedule and his texts, voluntarily giving editors permission to edit as they saw fit. London appears to have been an author who neither worried very much about the integrity of his works' political "messages" nor about their actual texts; instead, he was more interested in making money from his writing in order to live an independent life. As he told Johns in 1900 about his sales to *McClure's*, "Why certes, if they wish to buy me, body and soul, they are welcome—if they pay the price" (*Letters* 1: 164).

Edith Wharton: Mastering the Marketplace

Edith Wharton certainly did not turn to writing as a means of avoiding manual labor, gaining more control over her time, or earning a living. In recent years, however, Wharton has increasingly been recognized as a naturalist author who, in her own way, confronted head-on the relationship between the individual—most often the female—and the environment in the modern age. And although she didn't focus on the urban, industrial proletariat, Wharton nonetheless wrote a number of "radical" fictions that called for social change. She also had to fight against conservative ideologies of gender and class in order to pursue her career as a writer, a struggle manifested in the way a number of her earlier stories dealt "with professional integrity, [and] the betrayal of the artist's true self or the loss of privacy in the literary marketplace" (Lee 189).

Unlike some other naturalists, though, Wharton's fictions were not rejected by the marketplace, even at the outset of her career. Despite the fact that, as Hermione Lee notes, many of Wharton's stories from the early years of her career display a naturalistic outlook—"there is a feeling of being stuck inside a dilemma from which there is no exit" (189)—Wharton experienced no difficulty placing her works with magazine and book publishers. While her "default" place of publication was the conservative *Scribner's Magazine*, she also published stories and serials in *Youth's Companion*, *Harper's Monthly*, *Collier's*, and the *Atlantic Monthly*. To be sure, she did have some difficulty publishing some of her more radical stories. For instance, her story "The Bunner Sisters," written in 1891 or 1892, about a woman who is seduced by a man who turns out to be a drug addict, loses her baby, and then dies, was initially turned down by Edward Burlingame of *Scribner's Magazine* and not serialized in *Scribner's* until October and November 1916 (Lee 185). Yet the reason given for its rejection was not its sordid subject matter but rather its length. Wharton remembered editor Roger Burlingame telling her that it was "too long for one number of the magazine, & unsuited for serial publication"; otherwise, she said, he "spoke otherwise very kindly of it" (*Letters* 31). "Souls Belated" (1899), which depicts a woman who has left her husband for another lover, was also not serialized (Lee 188).

Despite its naturalistic elements and depiction of unpunished adultery, however, when *The House of Mirth* was accepted for serialization in *Scribner's Monthly* between January 1905 and November 1905, there is no evidence that anyone at the magazine asked her to make it less "naturalistic" in any way, such as by making Lily have more control over her fate or by writing a more optimistic ending. Once again, this case demonstrates that naturalistic texts were largely exempt from editorial intervention as long as they did not contain overly objectionable language or explicit depictions of sexual behavior (although one might argue that descriptions of Lily's body at the *tableaux vivants* borders on the prurient). In addition, Wharton exercised a great deal of control over the novel's production. Although she only reluctantly agreed to let the book be illustrated (*Letters* 94), she did approve of the frontispiece (*Letters* 95) and, because she thought the epigraph from Ecclesiastes made the book seem too moralistic, she blue-pencilled it out (*Letters* 94). When she objected to the copy on the book's dust jacket, Scribner's had all of the jackets removed (Garrison 78).

Although some readers disliked Selden's "weakness" (Waid 164) and the ending of *The House of Mirth* (Blair), the serial and book were smashing popular successes. It appears that at least some readers were actually attracted by the naturalistic elements of this novel. At one Los Angeles women's book club, for instance, *House* was one of two books "taken up [for discussion] as being the narrated illustrations of the influence of environment"; when one woman "read extracts from various commentators [on *House*] . . ., the storm of discussion that threatened was stopped for lack of time" ("Women's Clubs" 114). The book, released in October 1905, proved to be a bona fide bestseller, selling 30,000 copies during the first three weeks after its release; by early 1906 it had sold over 100,000 copies (Blair 149), earning Wharton approximately $20,000 (Lee 205). Thus, the supposedly conservative, prudish American reading public wholeheartedly embraced this naturalist work.

Finally, one should note that after *The House of Mirth*, Wharton became an even more confident, empowered agent in the literary marketplace. Its great popularity as a serial led Wharton to confidently negotiate a higher royalty for her next novel (Waid 164). And when faced with a large monetary offer from William Randolph Hearst's *Cosmopolitan* magazine for her novel *Summer* in 1916, Wharton wrote, "What I hate is taking money from such a hound, & helping 'boom' his magazine" (*Letters* 382). As a result, on her own she sold the serial rights of *Summer* to *McClure's Magazine* for $7,000 (*Letters* 331). When Charles Scribner wrote to complain about Wharton's apparent desertion of the firm, she coolly and confidently replied that she had disposed of the book rights of *Summer* to Appleton's and serial rights to *McClure's* (*Letters* 387) because Scribner had told her earlier that he didn't have room in *Scribner's* for a serial. Wharton certainly cannot be regarded as having been an author at the mercy of the beasts and industrial machinery of the publishing world.

CONCLUSION

The histories offered above of a selected group of naturalist authors and texts are intended neither as comprehensive nor complete (Dreiser, Norris, and Garland, for instance, are mentioned only briefly); instead, they are intended to suggest questions about naturalist authors and the American literary marketplace that deserve further investigation. What is evident even from the examples given here is that the experiences of naturalist authors with the literary marketplace were quite diverse and cannot be comprehended by a single narrative.

Furthermore, one cannot simply demonize all editors and publishers of this era. The risks—financial and otherwise—that they took to publish naturalist fictions, as well as the constraints they operated under, deserve to be taken more fully into account. There might have been a few "beasts" or "machine-like" editors and publishers, or ones that turned down fictions because they worried about their readers' reactions and low sales, but for each one of these, there was another willing to provide a struggling naturalist author with a much-needed advance, provide a part-time job that allowed an author plenty of time to develop his or her writing skill, or take a chance offending his readers. Examples abound of cases in which Crane, Dunbar, London, Garland, and Norris benefitted from editors' and publishers' liberal treatment. S. S. McClure, for instance, generously advanced Crane a great deal of money early in his career on the promise of future short stories and/or novels. And without Irving Bacheller's syndicated newspaper serialization of *The Red Badge of Courage*, even in its truncated form, as well as his financing of Crane's travels to the West and Mexico in early 1895, the latter might have sunk into obscurity before his career had really taken off. One can also ascribe much of Jack London's success to S. S. McClure's and George Brett's willingness to offer him advances, jobs, and long-term contracts.

The success of Frank Norris, too, depended heavily on McClure, who in 1898 agreed to publish some of his early attempts at novels, gave him a relatively easy job in New York where he could do a variety of editorial tasks and work on his own fiction, and in early 1899 advanced him the money to do research for what would become *The Octopus* (McElrath and Crisler 334–35). Norris eventually left McClure's employ and joined the new firm of Doubleday, Page, and Co. But shortly after he did so, he wrote to *McClure's Magazine* managing editor John Phillips, "In deciding as I have, I have not overlooked a single instance of your kindness to me. I remember perfectly well that as far as 'getting on' is concerned I practically owe you everything. . . . I owe my start to you and whatever measure of success I have achieved so far" (Norris, *Collected Letters* 102). One should remember, too, that it was Doubleday, McClure, and Co. that had assumed the risk of publishing *McTeague*. A few years later, Doubleday, Page, and Co. gave Norris a book manuscript reading job that didn't even require him to come to the office every day (McElrath and Crisler 363).

Counterbalancing these acts of kindness is the fact that at least in the 1890s, editors and publishers do appear to have enforced a fairly strict, industry-wide "prohibition" against overt depictions of sexuality, positive—or even unpunished—depictions of adultery, and excessive use of profanity. This interdiction seems to have loosened somewhat slightly after the turn of the century, as seen in the cases of Edith Wharton's *The House of Mirth* and *Summer*. Nonetheless, as late as 1915 Theodore Dreiser's *The "Genius"* could still run afoul of the New York Society for the Suppression of Vice, the organization originally founded by Anthony Comstock. Designating many parts of the novel as obscene, blasphemous, "lewd," and "profane," and threatening to sue the publisher for sending obscene materials through the mails, this group forced Dreiser's publisher, John Lane, to withdraw the book from stores just as it was becoming popular (Loving 254–62).

Overall, one must carefully distinguish between naturalistic ideology—which succeeded quite well in the marketplace among editors, publishers, and readers — and naturalistic depictions of sex and language, which were generally scorned. It was not for their "radical," anti-bourgeois, deterministic, pessimistic philosophy that naturalistic works were sometimes resisted by editors, publishers, and readers. Stephen Crane was free to criticize the modern industrial war machine in *The Red Badge of Courage*, or in "The Open Boat" (1897) point out the absence of a benign deity and undercut prevailing theories about the rewards of individual effort. Jack London could challenge the prevalent idea that humans were better than animals, question whether a divine being existed, attack capitalism, and promote socialism, and the marketplace rewarded him munificently. Naturalist works also found their way into many public libraries both large and small, where even more readers welcomed them. Frank Norris optimistically opined in 1902: "Say what you will, the People, the Plain People who Read, do appreciate good literature in the end. One must keep one's faith in the People,—the Plain People, the Burgesses, the Grocers,—else of all men the artists are most miserable and their teachings vain" ("Salt and Sincerity" 210).

Naturalist authors of the late nineteenth and early twentieth centuries, despite their vociferous complaints, can thus not in any way be confused with poorly paid, oppressed factory workers. As historian Borus succinctly puts it, "Unlike the emerging industrial proletariat [of this era], writers did not suffer erosion of work skills, sell their labor, punch a time clock, or toil under direct supervision. For all the editorial intervention of the Gilded Age, they kept control of their work process and retained the ability to initiate production" (66). Ultimately, what most empowered naturalist authors was the rapidly proliferating choice of possible publishing outlets available in the literary marketplace to which they could send their short-story or novel manuscripts; because of this, no one editor or publisher—or group thereof—had the power to dictate terms to all authors. Such a conclusion in many ways contradicts previous depictions of naturalists' place in the marketplace. Literary scholars have generally shared, as Christopher Wilson admits he does, "many of the naturalists' original aspirations for a more democratic and realistic American literature" (*Labor* xv), as well as Wilson's conclusion that "[b]y the testimony of the authors themselves, the design of the new marketplace jeopardized the entire project of literary democracy" (*Labor* xvi). Such sympathies, however, should not keep future scholars from acknowledging the many benefits the new marketplace held for authors and from taking into account testimony by those other than frustrated, disgruntled authors early in their careers. Only by more fully incorporating the voices of agents, editors, publishers, readers, as well as by more closely interrogating the testimony of the naturalist authors themselves, will a more complex and complete understanding of how naturalist authors interacted with the American literary marketplace be created.

WORKS CITED

Auerbach, Jonathan. *Male Call: Becoming Jack London*. Durham: Duke University Press, 1996.

Beer, Thomas. *Stephen Crane: A Study in American Letters*. New York: Knopf, 1923.

Best, Felton. *Crossing the Color Line: A Biography of Paul Laurence Dunbar, 1872–1906*. Dubuque, Iowa: Kendall/Hunt, 1996.

Blair, Amy. "Misreading *The House of Mirth*." *American Literature* 76 (2004): 149–75.

Borus, Daniel H. *Writing Realism: Howells, James, and Norris in the Mass Market*. Chapel Hill: University of North Carolina Press, 1989.

Boyesen, H[jalmar] H[jorth]. "Why We Have No Great Novelists." *Forum* 2 (Feb. 1887): 615–22.

Brawley, Benjamin. *Paul Laurence Dunbar: Poet of His People*. 1936. Port Washington, N.Y.: Kennikat, 1967.

Crane, Stephen. *The Correspondence of Stephen Crane*. Ed. Stanley Wertheim and Paul Sorrentino. 2 vols. New York: Columbia University Press, 1988.

Ford, J[ames] L[auren]. *The Literary Shop and Other Tales*. New York: G. H. Richmond, 1894.

Garland, Hamlin. *Roadside Meetings*. New York: Macmillan, 1931.

Garrison, Stephen. *Edith Wharton. A Descriptive Bibliography*. Pittsburgh: University of Pittsburgh Press, 1990.

Gayle, Addison. *Oak and Ivy: A Biography of Paul Laurence Dunbar*. Garden City, N.Y.: Doubleday, 1971.

Gilder, Richard Watson. "An 'Open Letter' about Editing." *Independent* 48 (1896): 1669–70.

Howells, W[illiam] D[ean]. *Criticism and Fiction and Other Essays*. Ed. Clara Marburg Kirk and Rudolf Kirk. New York: New York University Press, 1959.

Johanningsmeier, Charles A. *Fiction and the American Literary Marketplace: The Role of Newspaper Syndicates in America, 1860–1900*. Cambridge: Cambridge University Press, 1997.

Lee, Hermione. *Edith Wharton*. New York: Knopf, 2007.

Lichtenstein, Nelson. "Authorial Professionalism and the Literary Marketplace, 1885–1900."
     American Studies 19 (1978): 35–53.

London, Jack. *The Letters of Jack London*. Ed. Earle Labor, Robert C. Leitz III, and I. Milo
     Shepard. 3 vols. Stanford: Stanford University Press, 1988.

London, Jack. *Martin Eden. Novels and Social Writings*. Ed. Donald Pizer. New York:
     Library of America, 1982. 552–931.

Loving, Jerome. *The Last Titan: A Life of Theodore Dreiser*. Berkeley and Los Angeles:
     University of California Press, 2005.

McElrath, Joseph R., Jr., and Jesse S. Crisler. *Frank Norris: A Life*. Urbana and Chicago:
     University of Illinois Press, 2006.

Mott, Frank Luther. *A History of American Magazines, 1885–1905*. Vol. 4 of 5. Cambridge:
     Belknap Press of Harvard University Press, 1957.

Newlin, Keith. *Hamlin Garland, A Life*. Lincoln: University of Nebraska Press, 2008.

Norris, Frank. *Collected Letters*. Compiled and annotated by Jesse S. Crisler. San Francisco:
     Book Club of California, 1986.

———. "Salt and Sincerity." *The Literary Criticism of Frank Norris*. Ed. Donald Pizer. Austin:
     University of Texas Press, 1964. 195–231.

Pizer, Donald. "Late Nineteenth-Century American Literary Naturalism: A Re-Introduction."
     American Literary Realism 38 (2006): 189–202.

Sedgwick, Ellery. "Magazines and the Profession of Authorship in the United States,
     1840–1900." *Papers of the Bibliographical Society of America* 94 (2000): 399–425.

Sheehan, Donald. *This Was Publishing: A Chronicle of the Book Trade in the Gilded Age*.
     Bloomington: Indiana University Press, 1952.

Sorrentino, Paul, ed. *Stephen Crane Remembered*. Tuscaloosa: University of Alabama Press, 2006.

Tebbel, John. *George Horace Lorimer and The Saturday Evening Post*. New York: Doubleday,
     1948.

Waid, Candace. "Building *The House of Mirth*." *Biographies of Books. The Compositional
     Histories of Notable American Writings*. Ed. James Barbour and Tom Quirk. Columbia:
     University of Missouri Press, 1996. 160–86.

Wertheim, Stanley. "Re: Publication Information about *Maggie*." Message to Charles
     Johanningsmeier. 4 May 2009. E-mail.

Wharton, Edith. *The Letters of Edith Wharton*. Ed. R. W. B. Lewis and Nancy Lewis. New
     York: Scribner, 1988.

———. "The Vice of Reading." 1903. *The Uncollected Critical Writings*. Ed. Frederick
     Wegener. Princeton: Princeton University Press, 1996. 99–106.

Williams, James. "Commitment and Practice: The Authorship of Jack London." *Rereading
     Jack London*. Ed. Leonard Cassuto and Jeanne Campbell Reesman. Stanford: Stanford
     University Press, 1996. 10–24.

Wilson, Christopher. *The Labor of Words: Literary Professionalism in the Progressive Era*.
     Athens: University of Georgia Press, 1985.

———. "The Rhetoric of Consumption: Mass-Market Magazines and the Demise of the
     Gentle Reader, 1880–1920." *The Culture of Consumption: Critical Essays in American
     History, 1880–1980*. Ed. Richard Wightman Fox and T. J. Jackson Lears. New York:
     Pantheon, 1983. 39–64.

"Women's Clubs." *Los Angeles Times* 16 Jan. 1906: 114.

CHAPTER 22

CONSOLATION, AFFIRMATION, AND CONVENTION: THE POPULAR RECEPTION OF AMERICAN NATURALIST TEXTS

CAROL S. LORANGER

THE works of early pioneers of American literary naturalism received a varied response by readers in proportion to their being in advance of the mores of the times, though a writer's willingness to affirm certain cultural truisms, the restraining hand of an editor, or the general resemblance of a work to popular genre fiction of the day often compensated for the authors' adventurousness. Critical reception is less easy to characterize because it varied depending on the venue and critic. Early newspaper reviewers, for example, tended to be less enthusiastic in their regard for literary naturalism than reviewers in the major literary and social affairs magazines of the day. Having a champion among reviewers might not significantly affect an author's sales or reputation, but a positive review could have a psychological benefit, especially for a young writer. A publisher's efforts, or lack of effort, in promoting a novel would also have a significant effect on reception. In general, though, each new naturalist text, even when it failed to find a receptive audience, pushed farther the boundaries of what the general reading public considered to be appropriate subject matter for fiction. American literary naturalists were very much in the business of educating American readers in how to respond to innovations in fiction.

Stephen Crane's first book, *Maggie: A Girl of the Streets (A Story of New York)*, offers a useful handhold for grasping the reception history of individual works of American literary naturalism: writers who negotiated the tricky balancing act of combining popular story elements with sensational subject matter that pushed the boundaries of decorum enjoyed popular and critical success, while writers who ignored or overturned popular literary conventions while also flouting conventional moralities invited condemnation or neglect.

Maggie's inauspicious debut in March 1893 is representative. Unable to interest publishers, and unwilling to risk his future reputation by linking his name to a potential failure, Crane self-published under the name "Johnston Smith," planning to reveal himself as the author if the book somehow became a sensation. Only a few volumes of *Maggie*'s initial run found space on New York City bookstore shelves, and fewer still sold. Looking back on the experience two years later, after the wild success of *The Red Badge of Courage* (1895), Crane wrote that his "first great disappointment was in the reception of 'Maggie, A Girl of the Streets.' I remember how I looked forward to its publication, and pictured the sensation I thought it would make. It fell flat. Nobody seemed to notice it or care for it" (*Correspondence* 1: 232). Indeed, *Maggie* registered so little on the public consciousness in 1893 that upon its republication in 1896, the *New York Times* claimed it "had never been actually published before, even in serial form" (Weatherford 42).

What was wrong with *Maggie*? Crane was not breaking new ground as to subject matter: "slum novels" had become increasingly popular over the preceding two decades in the United States. Sentimental and prurient interest in our native slums had already been aroused by such social and moral tracts as Charles Loring Brace's *Dangerous Classes of New York* (1872) and Thomas DeWitt Talmage's *Abominations of Modern Society* (1872) and *Night Side of City Life* (1878) and by muck-raking reportage such as Jacob Riis's *How the Other Half Lives* (1890). Tastefully presented stories of the suffering of the virtuous poor were staples of magazine fiction and popular drama in the last decades of the nineteenth century. The lugubrious ends meted out to fallen women were likewise served up as standard fare in popular drama and in sentimental songs such as "The Picture that Is Turned to the Wall" and "She May Have Seen Better Days." As Frank Norris observed, the cast of *Maggie* were already "old acquaintances in the world of fiction" (qtd. in Benfey 64). The difference was that Crane resisted the consolatory mode of these popular texts: no good happens to his characters to compensate them for their suffering, nor does Crane attempt to make his victims admirable: neither Maggie nor Jimmie is presented as a better person than their circumstances would warrant.

Instead, Crane's narrator maintains an uncompromising distance from characters (not even named in early drafts) who were unlikely to warm a reader's heart toward the tale. When Crane showed a draft to family friend Richard Watson Gilder at the *Century* in March 1892, Gilder's response was characteristic of other readers' views: Gilder found Maggie honest but lacking in saving sentiment (Stallman 67). Hamlin Garland, whose acquaintance Crane had recently made, read a subsequent revision in which the characters bore names. The "scrap" between Jimmie and the "mick" from Devil's Row impressed him "with so much insight and with such unusual and vivid use of English that [he] became very much excited about it" (qtd. in Stallman 71). Garland sent the book to William Dean Howells, who urged Crane to persevere. Howells championed *Maggie* as he had other underappreciated works. Though he deplored its profanity, Howells would ultimately rate *Maggie* and the lesser known *George's Mother* (1896) above Crane's more popular *The Red Badge of Courage*: "As a piece of art they are altogether superior to [*Red Badge*], and as representations of life their greater fidelity cannot be questioned. The advance is relentless; the atmosphere is transparent; the texture is a continuous web where all the facts are wrought with the unerring mastery of absolute knowledge" (*New York World*, 26 July 1896: 18; qtd. in Weatherford 47)

Over the long term, Howells's and Garland's support would be important to Crane, but it was not sufficient to save this first incarnation of *Maggie*. Crane's popular reception suffered exactly in proportion as *Maggie* resisted the pull of sentiment, decorum, and the undercurrent of progressivism that had been typical of nineteenth-century realism and the contemporary muck-raking slum exposé. Even Crane's early champion, Garland, in one of the few reviews to mark *Maggie*'s first appearance, regretted Crane's rejection of the conventions of genre. After calling *Maggie* "the most truthful and unhackneyed study of the slums I have yet read," in his June 1893 *Arena* review, Garland added, "It is typical only of the worst element of the alley. The author should delineate the families living on the next street, who live lives of heroic purity and hopeless hardship" (Weatherford 38). E. J. Edwards in the *New York Press* agreed. Crane's realism was "cold, awful, brutal" and his artistry praiseworthy, but Edwards wished the young writer were "not so shocking" (qtd. in Stallman 72). Another review in the *New York Times* left open the "question if such brutalities are wholly acceptable in literature. Perhaps, as Mr. Howells says, they will be before long" (qtd. in Stallman 72).

In 1893, American readers were still looking for a kind of affirmation of democratic and progressive principles of individual self-worth (as reflected in Garland's comment about "heroic" families down the street), wrapped up in a sentimental package of holy motherhood and damsels who remain sexless ("pure") even though fallen, which Crane did not give them. Though Crane's presentation is by modern-day standards quite mild, Maggie clearly exhibits unladylike sexual interest in Pete, drawn by the hairy virility of his "oiled bang" and his "bristling moustache of short wire-like hairs" and by the threat of violence of his "shoes . . . like murder-fitted weapons" (19). Crane's novel was neither conventionally artistic nor conventionally elevating.

But before Howells's prophesy could be tested, Crane did the one thing that could cause the reading public to reevaluate *Maggie* without also reevaluating conventional pieties: he launched a bestseller and became famous. Throughout 1894 and 1895, Crane was diligently writing and increasingly successful in placing journalism, essays, interviews and short stories in magazines and newspapers such as *Arena*, *McClure's*, *Truth*, and the *New York Press*. Through the good offices of Garland and Howells, he was able to secure a publisher for his collection of poems *The Black Riders and Other Lines* (1895) and, more importantly, syndicated publication of an abridgement of his forthcoming novel, *The Red Badge of Courage*, in a half dozen journals and newspapers including the *Philadelphia Press*, *New York Press* and *San Francisco Examiner* (Werthheim and Sorrentino 116–17). Early in 1895, Crane secured Appleton and Company as publishers for the novel, with a fall release scheduled. With the way paved by the earlier buzz raised by the syndicated version, sales of *The Red Badge of Courage* were brisk, and complimentary comparisons to Tolstoy and to Zola frequent (Davis 127). In those venues that kept track of such things—New York City, Denver, Cleveland—*The Red Badge of Courage* was a best-seller well into 1896 (Davis 129).

Compared to *Maggie*, *The Red Badge of Courage* is arguably the more approachable novel. Crane does not sentimentalize young Henry Fleming, but he does give him a personality, treating him less like a specimen under a microscope and more like a character with a psychology and a future. While *Red Badge* also transgresses some of the limitations imposed by the recognizable genres it inhabits—the war story, the novel of education—it does not ask the popular reader to set aside taboos on the handling of female sexuality, nor hold the reader's focus relentlessly on the "worst elements" of the alley.

Buoyed by this success, Crane revised *Maggie* for publication by his then-publisher Appleton in 1896. Much of the revision was to take out or soften the vulgar language that had so put off the first reviewers; Crane wrote in February that he had "toned it somewhat at the request of the Appletons" (*Correspondence* 1: 206). Reviews of the second incarnation of *Maggie* improved, as did its sales, but the novel was never to become a beloved popular text, nor indeed the one most associated in the popular mind with Stephen Crane. It is revealing that, while many of Crane's works—including *The Red Badge of Courage*, "The Blue Hotel" (1898), and "The Bride Comes to Yellow Sky" (1898)—have, like much of the naturalist canon, made the leap to film and television, *Maggie* never has.

Recalling how *The Red Badge of Courage* erupted onto the literary scene in 1895, H. L. Mencken would conflate its arrival with that of two ships into the San Francisco Bay two years later bearing news of the discovery of gold in the Klondike: "Who was this astonishing young man? A drunken newspaper reporter in New York? One of [Richard Harding] Davis's heroes! The miracle lifted newspaper reporting to the level of a romantic craft, alongside counterfeiting and mining in the Klondike" (qtd. in Davis 129). Mencken's conflation of the Yukon with the tapping of a literary motherlode was apt. Out of the Klondike would arise a very hero out of Richard Harding Davis: Jack London, a writer of strenuous outdoorsy novels and tales laced with distinct naturalist values, who would manage, despite his own sexual and personal unconventionalism, to satisfy American readers' appetites for affirmation of their conventional mores and tap into a growing appetite for depictions of the outdoors as holding the path to individual salvation.

Although London too had had some difficulties finding an audience early on—one magazine editor had "advised London to forget about a writing career" (Lundquist 39)—the boom in magazine publishing at the turn of the century and a seemingly insatiable appetite for tales and sketches of the Klondike in the years immediately following the gold rush, combined with London's consistent theme of struggle as essential to growth at a time when Americans were rediscovering the outdoors as a salvation for the neurasthenic middle classes and their children, increased demand for London's fiction. By 1897, London was publishing tales and sketches regularly in high-profile general-interest national magazines like *Overland Monthly*, *McClure's*, and *Atlantic Monthly*, as well as in niche publications like *American Agriculturalist*. Reviewers were admiring: "I would rather have written 'The White Silence,'" effused one, "than anything that has appeared in fiction in the last ten years" (qtd. in Lundquist 39). The magazine stories of these years, gathered into the 1901 volume *The Son of the Wolf*, sold very well.

During these successful early years, London developed professional habits that would serve him well—he delivered on time and was generally willing to accept magazine editors' advice to cut and soften scenes—as well as a following among magazine readers and editors that translated into book sales. *McClure's* essentially put him on retainer in 1901, with a "125-dollar monthly advance against future work" (Lundquist 47), a move followed by Macmillan, which upped the ante to $150, in 1902. By 1903, London was able to sell the serial rights to *The Call of the Wild*, an unlikely short novel with a dog for a protagonist, to *The Saturday Evening Post* for $750 and the American book rights to Macmillan's for another $2,000. This was an excellent investment for the publisher: the first edition of 10,000 copies sold out in a single day (O'Connor 176). Reviewers were almost universally complementary; comparisons to Kipling, to Stevenson, and to Crane (the Crane of *The Red Badge of Courage* and "The Open Boat" [1897], not the Crane of *Maggie*) abounded. London's novel was an ideal book for marketing in America: accessible to adults and youths alike, it offered a view of self-sufficiency attainable by even the most pampered, an acknowledgement that though the world was a hostile place, the innate superiority of American bourgeois individuals (whether human or canine), when tapped, might not prevent them from being scarred, but would eventually raise them to a position where those scars would become badges of success. *The Call of the Wild* also quietly affirmed contemporary social prejudices: women and natives are put in their places, American exceptionalism and manifest destiny, in the person of Buck, are affirmed. So popular was it that D. W. Griffith would shoot a one-reel treatment of the novel as early as 1908, while the first of many full-length films of the novel would debut in 1923.

The Call of the Wild announced London's most enduring theme and further opened publishers' doors to the product of his pen. At the end of 1903, the *Century* paid $4,000 for serial rights to London's next novel, *The Sea-Wolf*, when the second half was still in outline form. When Macmillan released the novel in 1904, the publisher was able to pre-sell 40,000 copies (O'Connor 199). As in *The Call of the Wild*, the protagonist of *The Sea-Wolf* is a pampered child of civilization, Humphrey Van

Weyden, who, like Buck the dog, finds himself in a situation that tests his mettle and perfects his latent will to survive. Unlike Buck, for whom the "dominant primordial beast" is the realization of his highest self, the strength and will Van Weyden develops as Wolf Larsen's captive/protégé on the *Ghost* are modified by altruism, circumspection, and love to produce a civilized human variant.

London has a great deal of fun setting up his narcissistic, slightly effete protagonist in the opening pages of the novel, making good use of the first-person narrative to invite readers to hope for his immediate comeuppance. When first seen, Van Weyden, nicknamed "Sissy" by his female relatives, lounges and preens about the passenger deck of a ferry, proudly ignorant of the men's work going on around him, prouder still of his recently published *Atlantic* article on Poe. When the ferry capsizes, "Sissy" shrieks "like a woman" and flails helplessly in the water unable to save himself. The narrative perspective is that of the future, evolved Van Weyden who both invites readers to be critical of his earlier self and simultaneously voices the irritatingly smug self-regard of his former "Sissy" self. A popular writer in America can never go wrong by enlisting his audience's latent anti-intellectualism, and London lays it on pretty thickly in the opening pages. His readers were sure to recognize in Van Weyden the deplorable figure of ease painted by Theodore Roosevelt in his oft-reprinted 1899 speech "The Strenuous Life": a "cumberer of the earth's surface . . . [unfit] to hold his own with his fellows" or "for serious work in the world" (3). Once his experiences on the *Ghost* under the brutal tutelage of the more manly Wolf Larsen have transmuted "Sissy" into the self-sufficient, masculine "Hump," the novel provides him with a suitably strenuous mate, "strong and brave and high-minded" (Roosevelt 4). Here is a source of this novel's success, and London knew it; he had already considered deeply how to "dream romances for other people and transmute them into bread & butter" (*Letters* 1: 313). *The Sea-Wolf* combines London's trademark tale of individual growth with a love story, plenty of action, and a distinct appeal to popular mores. He had promised Macmillan's a tale "which shall have adventure, storm, struggle, tragedy, and love." The "love-element" would "run throughout . . . but the human motif underlying all [would be] mastery." Showing an acute sense of his readership, London added, "The superficial reader will get the love story & the adventure; while the deeper reader will get all this, plus the bigger thing underneath" (*Letters* 1: 337–38). Indeed, London plays up the melodrama: Maud (author of the poem "The Kiss Endured") is sexually endangered by the predatory Larsen; she and Van Weyden escape to a handy island where they begin to build a little grass-hutted lover's paradise. This paradise is briefly threatened by Larsen, who is abandoned by his crew and shipwrecked there; but a subsequent stroke weakens him, and Maud and Hump become his caretakers while they use their newly acquired survival skills to repair the *Ghost* and sail away to civilization, mated for life.

London assured *Century* editor Richard Watson Gilder (the same editor who had found Maggie both shocking and cruel) that he would be most circumspect: "American prudes will not be shocked by the last half of the book" (*Letters* 1: 383), but he acceded in advance to any editorial changes. As a result of this circumspection, the physical brutality of the novel violated no contemporaneous standards for the depiction of masculine characters and Larsen's attempted rape of Maud is handled in two sentences, ending with her chastity preserved. Once alone on their island sanctuary, Hump and Maud sublimate their passion for each other with work, learning to sail and building adjoining huts with the ardor of a pair of athletic nuns. In short, there was nothing to offend and everything to confirm conventional pieties. The result may have been something of a fiasco from an artistic standpoint—both London and reader Ambrose Bierce would agree that the novel's handling of the sexual attraction between the characters was harmed by the bourgeois proprieties of magazine publishing: "The 'love' element, with its absurd suppressions and impossible proprieties, is awful," wrote Bierce. "I confess to an overwhelming contempt for both sexless lovers" (qtd. in O'Connor 198). But the majority of reviewers and readers did not mind. The *New York Herald* termed it "a superb piece of craftsmanship" (qtd. in O'Connor 198). Bierce himself admired London's accomplishment with the creation of Wolf Larsen and referred to *The Sea-Wolf* privately as "a rattling good story" (qtd. in Kershaw 152). The *New York Times Book Review* noted the brutality of the tale but concluded that London gave his "monsters" "considerable literary value" and lauded "excellent word pictures of storm and calm at sea; the reader feels sure of the reality of many things Mr. London writes about" ("The Sea-Wolf" 689). Financially, *The Sea Wolf* was London's greatest success. Together with *The Call of the Wild* and his visible exploits stemming from his reports of the Russo-Japanese conflict the following year, *The Sea-Wolf* marked London as both a writer and a celebrity, virtually guaranteeing him a warmly receptive audience for the remainder of his career.

Both Crane and London attained popular and/or critical success after short apprenticeships. Theodore Dreiser, whose early career neatly coincides with the careers of both Crane and London—journalism and the odd short fictional piece in the 1890s, followed swiftly by a novel—would not find popular success for several decades. Dreiser's experience with the reception of *Sister Carrie*, his first novel, was much like Crane's with *Maggie*: disappointing. Though, like Crane, Dreiser would early on earn the regard and support of cognoscenti—Frank Norris and Mencken, for example, though not, unfortunately, Howells—it would be almost two decades before a novel of his received both critical and popular acclaim.

The story of the devastating flop of *Sister Carrie* in 1900 is a familiar one and told elsewhere in this volume. The experience put a serious crimp in Dreiser's productivity as a novelist. Though he came to view the episode as an unjust suppression of his work by moral prudes, he was initially devastated. Dreiser returned to magazine journalism and eked out a living in various editorial positions while licking his wounds. A somewhat more successful second release of *Sister Carrie* by a new publisher in 1907 returned him to the public eye, and *Carrie* was followed shortly by four novels: *Jennie Gerhardt* (1911), *The Financier* (1912), *The Titan* (1914), and *The "Genius"* (1915). But none of these was significantly popular, and reviews for the first three were moderate to mixed. Dreiser's handling of the fallen woman in *Jennie* is more observant of conventional pieties than was Crane's with *Maggie*, perhaps because his editor at Harper's, Ripley Hitchcock, who had also edited the

1896 *Maggie*, seems to have had a good understanding of the limits of the American public's tolerance (Loving 204). Though *Carrie* would be more highly regarded by critics, *Jennie* remained more popular with the common reader. The first two Cowperwood novels, increasingly long and lacking the potentially sympathetic female subject, earned critical praise but low royalties, so, midway into his second decade as a novelist, popular success still eluded Dreiser, though his critical admirers were steadfast. With *The "Genius,"* however, Dreiser experienced the full force of popular disapproval and a shaking of his critical support.

Probably his most thorough-going fictional exploration of his own theories of male and female sexuality, *The "Genius"* draws liberally and, even sympathetic readers thought, uncritically on Dreiser's own complex sexual history to flesh out a lengthy, rambling portrait of the sexually voracious and self-consumed artist Eugene Witla. Viewed from a century's distance, Dreiser's handling of sex in *The "Genius"* seems almost quaint, but in the eyes of public moralists the novel was pornographic. Upon its release by publisher John Lane in 1915, the novel was attacked by the New York and the Western Societies for the Suppression of Vice as immoral, citing some ninety-seven pages of the novel as either lewd or profane (Loving 260). The publisher quietly stopped selling the book, denying Dreiser both the solace of heightened sales in the wake of a scandal and a formal obscenity trial to settle the matter. Reviews of the book ranged from lukewarm to hostile, on artistic, moral, and even patriotic grounds. Even the support of the Author's League of America, which petitioned against the Society's "attempt to ferret out blasphemy and indecency where they are not, and to condemn a serious artist under a law aimed at common rogues" ("Protest" 803), strained at the content and artistry of the novel that Mencken, who organized the petition, referred to in his *Smart Set* review as "the longest and damnedest of his novels. . . . as shapeless as a Philadelphia pie-woman" (Salzman 239, 241). Hamlin Garland, who had praised Maggie even while deploring Crane's narrow representation of slum life, and who had been encouraging throughout Dreiser's early career, refused to become one of the petition's five hundred signers, along with William Dean Howells and poet Joyce Kilmer, among others (Loving 261–62).

The disappointing outcome of this episode in his career stalled Dreiser's production of novels for the next decade. He regularly turned out plays, short stories, essays, and autobiographical writings, settling into the role of "a famous man of letters, highly respected by some [but] regularly reviled for the 'immorality' of his naturalistic subject matter and vision" (Orlov 39). The vast reading public saw Dreiser as both difficult and immoral, and his readership remained small in relation to his level of fame or notoriety. Only with *An American Tragedy* (1925), arguably a franker, more relentless exposé of the tawdry collision of American material and sexual appetites, would Dreiser grab a wide popular readership, some twenty-five years after the publication of his first novel.

Sex, ambition, and reckless consumption form the central thematic trinity of much of Dreiser's oeuvre. As Donald Pizer has pointed out, Dreiser's interest in the American myth of success frequently expressed itself in tales linking aspirational hypergamy and criminality. Pizer identifies at least three "abortive" attempts by Dreiser at this theme, each based on an actual criminal case, before he embarked on *An American Tragedy* (205). Based loosely on the famous Chester Gillette–Grace Brown murder investigation and trial of 1906, *An American Tragedy* follows the rise and fall of Clyde Griffiths in an inverted reworking of the Horatio Alger plot familiar to Dreiser's generation. Through a combination of pluck and luck, Clyde raises himself from demeaning circumstances as the child of itinerant, uncultured street missionaries, sheds family entanglements, flees the repercussions of various social and sexual missteps, and lands temporarily on his feet as a foreman in the Lycurgus, New York, collar factory of a long-lost uncle. There, though he has his eyes on forming a rich alliance with a girl of his uncle's economic class, Clyde nonetheless satisfies his immediate sexual and emotional appetites by initiating a relationship with Roberta Alden, one of his uncle's employees in the factory. When Roberta's inevitable pregnancy threatens Clyde's budding relationship with Sondra Finchley, a cultured young woman in his uncle's circle, Clyde attempts first to have the baby aborted, then decides to remove the impediment by eliminating Roberta. His decision notwithstanding, Clyde suffers a case of indecision in the boat with poor pregnant Roberta at Big Bittern Lake and, as Dreiser renders it, it is not clear to the reader whether Clyde deliberately knocks her out of the boat or simply decides not to aid her when she tumbles overboard. Regardless, Clyde is caught, after a brief run, and in the last quarter of the novel he is tried, convicted, and sentenced to death.

The novel is laced throughout with a deliberately unromantic attitude toward sex, and it is difficult to see how Dreiser and his publisher could have expected *An American Tragedy* to fall any more gratefully into the hands of the American reading public than had his earlier works. The sexual longing and frustration of the characters is palpable, even though Dreiser observed a certain amount of post-*"Genius"* restraint in his handling of Clyde and Roberta's amours. But as might be expected of the author of "A Word Concerning Birth Control," Dreiser had made prevention of pregnancy an overt concern for his doomed lovers, and their panicked efforts at undoing Roberta's pregnancy get an extended treatment across several chapters. There is much talk of missed periods; Clyde haunts drugstores hoping to find a miracle pill or prescription to bring off the pregnancy and ultimately escorts Roberta to a doctor whom he has heard may perform the "contraceptal operation" both desire. Despite his overall frankness, Dreiser does not use the word "abortion" anywhere in these scenes. Dreiser makes clear, though, how Roberta's pregnancy almost immediately strips her of entitlement to Clyde's regard, even beyond his determination to move up to a higher-class mate, and he shows Roberta's awareness of Clyde's disregard: she remarks to herself when he leaves her outside the doctor's office that he has lost his "spontaneous enthusiasm" for her (458). Even in her panic and misery, Roberta attains a kind of gravity and superiority in this moment, in her embrace of her utter isolation. How far we have come from Maggie, in whose shame Crane seems, in retrospect, complicit, or from the unsexed mate-woman London conjures up for Van Weyden. Dreiser's handling of Roberta's consultation with the abortion doctor flouts every possible taboo in a world in which the Comstock Act of 1873 had essentially placed all contraception outside the law and in which abortion was a crime. This is some of his finest writing, but it was not the sort of stuff readers typically rewarded. At best, *An American Tragedy* should have been yet another financially unremunerative succès d'estime.

This seems to have been what Dreiser anticipated. The novel was heavily rewritten and revised by him over the five or so years of its composition (Pizer 228), with Dreiser frequently worrying over just such scenes and setting the novel aside to work on other projects. In its final version, Book One, covering Clyde's formative years up through the car accident that propels him out of the Midwest and the into arms of Hortense and then into the bosom of the Lycurgus Griffiths family, remained loose and episodic as well as didactic—a flaw noted by Mencken in his March 1926 *American Mercury* review—but Books Two and Three exerted a compensatingly inexorable pull on readers. Boni and Liveright's editor-in-chief, Thomas R. Smith, reported reading these sections "with real agony. The slow, fatal working-up to the death of Roberta is one of the grimmest and most gripping tragedies that I have read in years" (qtd. in Loving 308).

The book remained long, despite a series of deep cuts by Dreiser, weighing in at 400,000 words and over 800 pages in the published version (Pizer 230). Boni and Liveright issued the novel in two volumes, at the hefty price of five dollars, another factor that Dreiser feared would lessen sales. But despite its length, price, and sexual frankness, *An American Tragedy* was an immediate bestseller upon its publication in November 1925. Thirteen thousand copies sold in the first two weeks, fifty thousand copies in its first year, netting Dreiser close to $46,000 (Loving 318). Not content simply to leave the book to succeed on its own, Boni and Liveright aggressively marketed it, even sponsoring an essay contest: "Was Clyde Griffiths guilty of murder in the first degree?" Reviewers, with some exceptions, were enthusiastic. Stuart P. Sherman in the *New York Herald Tribune*, a severe critic of Dreiser's earlier works, praised him for leaving behind his "naïve naturalism" and acquiring "detachment" (Salzman 443); Joseph Wood Krutch, reviewing for *The Nation*, found *An American Tragedy* to be "the greatest of its author's works . . . the greatest American novel of our generation" (Salzman 471). In *Century Magazine*, Carl Van Doren compared Dreiser's achievement in *An American Tragedy* to the recently reevaluated *Moby Dick*, in that it progressed "with the same fateful tread, carrying all its documents on its back" (Salzman 495). There were complaints in some quarters about the book's immoral content and attempts to ban it in Boston. Besides its sexual content, the book was deemed to argue for wider availability of contraceptives to married and unmarried people. Beyond contraception was the lengthy, nonjudgmental treatment of abortion as a last-ditch preventive and Roberta's unsentimental openness to the procedure. Boni and Liveright, who seem to have understood the temper of the times, shrewdly exploited these incidents: the publishers arranged to have a representative arrested and tried "for corrupting the morals of youth" in 1927 for attempting to sell a copy of the book in Boston (Swanberg 319). Far from driving away the reader of 1925, as it might have the reader of 1900 or 1894, the attention made *An American Tragedy* a cause célèbre, much like *Lolita* (1955) or *Portnoy's Complaint* (1969) would be for future generations.

That Dreiser had become, with *An American Tragedy*, our greatest moralist while avoiding moralizing in a book chock-full of immoral behaviors is one of the great paradoxes of American literary history. The successful mingling of genres (coming-of-age tale, crime story, courtroom drama), his deft handling of his fully sexualized characters (Roberta in particular has a depth and gravity Dreiser's other female characters only hint at and Crane and London never came near), and the novel's willingness to treat social issues, such as access to contraception, very close to his reader's own concerns, seems to have offered just the right combination for all but the most censorious. That, added to his publisher's willingness to capitalize on, rather than run from, the whiff of scandal contributed to the wild success of *An American Tragedy*. With sales, film rights, and (as had been the case with Crane) a renewed appetite for his earlier works, the novel made Dreiser a comparatively rich man.

Published some fifteen years later, Richard Wright's *Native Son* (1940) similarly navigated the stormy channel between sensation and popular mores with success. Wright's close early associations with the John Reed Club and the Federal Negro Theatre and Illinois Writer's Project in 1930–31 found him his first audience, the progressive and leftist readers of *New Masses*, *Left Front*, and, later, the *Daily Worker*, which published his early essays and stories, four of which become *Uncle Tom's Children* in 1938. As with Jack London, having a specific periodical audience to write for—albeit a very different group from the readers of the *Saturday Evening Post*—helped Wright hone his skills. Over the decade of the 1930s, Wright had developed strict habits, making him both highly productive and one of the Left's most celebrated young writers, able to give readers of these magazines absorbing stories that knitted Marxist ideals into a fabric exotically, but not overly, racial. *Uncle Tom's Children* would earn Wright a Guggenheim Fellowship in 1939—funding of inestimable value for a young writer in Depression-era America—which allowed him to complete *Native Son*, begun in 1937, within the year.

Early reviews of *Native Son* noted similarities between it and *An American Tragedy*. Its overall critical reception repeats several of the patterns already established for naturalist fiction by the reception of Crane, London, and Dreiser. For example, editorial input by the Book-of-the-Month Club led Wright to tone down the more charged scenes, much as input from Gilder had restrained London's hand on *The Sea-Wolf*: not just long portions of Max's courtroom speech, but also Wright's explicit handling of Bigger's sexual nature, his masturbation in the theater and desire for Mary Dalton, and Mary's own libidinous behavior, specifically her willingness to engage in extended sex play with her boyfriend in the back seat of the car as Bigger drives, was reduced to some innocuous kissing. Even the term "spooning" did not survive the editorial board's blue pencil (Rowley 181–82).

Though Dreiser had broken many sexual boundaries in *The "Genius"* and *An American Tragedy*, the mix of race and sex in Wright's novel went a long step farther for contemporary readers. Even such toned-down representations of Bigger's rampant

black male sexuality and Mary Dalton's ambiguously interracially oriented eroti-
cism were potentially offensive to the 1940s white bourgeois reader, the typical sub-
scriber to the Book-of-the-Month Club. Also, Wright risked alienating other crucial
audiences: the black bourgeoisie, who throughout the first half of the century
objected to the airing of the race's "dirty laundry" in print, and the American Communist Party, which might, and in part did, object to his critique of the party's often-
exploitive handling of victims of American racial politics. By his own account,
Wright had set out to offend these three readerships: his earlier popular success
with the collection of linked stories in *Uncle Tom's Children* convinced him that he
had overestimated readers' capability of understanding his intent: "When the
reviews of that book began to appear," he wrote in "How Bigger Was Born" in 1940,
"I realized that I had made an awfully naïve mistake. I found that I had written a
book which even banker's daughters could read and weep over and feel good about.
I swore that if I ever wrote another book, no one would weep over it; that it would
be so hard and deep that they would have to face it without the consolation of tears"
(qtd. in Kinnamon 1). Nonetheless, he did accede to the Book-of-the-Month Club's
editorial requests, with impressive sales results. The imprimatur of the club, which
had a reputation as a reliable supplier of quality fiction for half a million subscribers,
together with the promise of exciting, topical subject matter, pushed sales phenom-
enally: the first printing sold out in a matter of hours. Accounts vary depending on
data sets, but bookstore sales together with advance sales and Book-of-the-Month
Club orders totaled something between 215,000 and 250,000 in the first few weeks
(Kinnamon 4; Butler 13).

Like *An American Tragedy*, *Native Son* had its genesis in a real murder and trial.
Like Dreiser, Wright saw the case as neatly encapsulating the elements of his social
critique. In Chicago in 1938, Robert Nixon, eighteen-years-old and black, bludgeoned a white woman to death with a brick (the same implement Bigger would use
on his girlfriend Bessie). This was the last of a string of bludgeoning murders in
1937–38. The racial element played large in the news accounts, supplied to Wright at
his request by friend and future biographer Margaret Walker and which Wright
studied carefully, remarking on the intense racial invective contained in these
accounts (Walker 121). Like Bigger, Nixon seems to have been a stunted person,
intellectually and emotionally; newspaper accounts of the crime referred to him as
"the Brick Moron."

Organized in three parts whose titles—Fear, Flight, Fate—emphasize Bigger's
animal nature and Wright's naturalist approach to his characters, *Native Son* begins
and ends with the killing of vermin. In the morning of the day that comprises all of
Book One, Bigger kills a rat with a skillet in his family's slum apartment. At novel's
end, Bigger, convicted of the murder of his employer's daughter, is sent to the electric
chair, the state's somewhat tidier means of removing noxious or loathsome "animals."
Between these events, Bigger plans a robbery, finds a job, kills, dismembers, and
attempts to burn the corpse of the drunken Mary Dalton, and rapes and murders
his girlfriend Bessie and throws her body down an airshaft. Though Wright makes
clear that Bigger's individual pathology—his lack of affect or empathy, his inability

to plan or to hold a thought, his reactive violence and uncontrolled sexual response—is produced by the culture's own racial and economic pathologies that have combined to manufacture, as Sterling Brown put it in his *Opportunity* review, "the outcast, the disinherited, the generation lost in the slum jungles of American civilization" (Reilly 96), he nonetheless refuses to grant Bigger a single positive characteristic with sufficient consistency to arouse reader sympathy. Through this relentless characterization of his social victim, Wright joins Crane and Dreiser in refusing to offer a sop to sentiment. Despite an occasional glimmer of self-awareness, Bigger goes out the way he came in, ignorant and fearful.

For early reviewers, *Native Son* invited comparisons to other literary touchstones: *Crime and Punishment*, *The Grapes of Wrath*, and *An American Tragedy* being the most frequently cited. *The New York Times*'s Charles Poore noted Wright's "Dreiserian" method (also his Dostoievskian scale), but unsurprisingly found Wright the better stylist: "he has written his American tragedy in a notably firm prose. He knows how to tell a story" (Reilly 44). The lengthier review, by Peter Monro Jack, in the *New York Times Book Review* of the same week adumbrated the similarities:

> Both are tragedies and Dreiser's white boy and Wright's black boy are equally
> killed in the electric chair not for being criminals—since the crime in each case
> was unpremeditated—but for being social misfits: The pattern in both books is
> similar. . . . The conclusion in both is that society is to blame, that the environment
> into which each was born forced upon them their crimes, that they were the
> particular victims of a general injustice. (Reilly 53)

Reviewers in *Commonweal* and the *New York World Telegram* concurred: Wright had written a new *American Tragedy*. The "startling difference" between the two tomes, reviewers noted, arose from the racial dimension: Clyde Griffiths's pathology "represents a social 'complex' that could be reasonably taken care of" (Reilly 62), whereas Bigger Thomas's "tragedy is to be born into a black and immutable minority race, literally, in his own words, 'Whipped before you born'" (Reilly 54). The racial dimension, especially as it related to the place of *Native Son* and its author in the American literary consciousness, was not far from the minds of reviewers from the very first. The African American press hosted "lively" debates about Wright's accomplishment and his handling of racial themes (Kinnamon 3). In his announcement for the *Book-of-the-Month Club News* in February 1940, Henry Seidel Canby laid out the limiting terms of subsequent reviewers' racial discourse: *Native Son* was "a novel which only a Negro could have written" and "certainly the finest novel as yet written by an American Negro" (Reilly 39), a sentiment echoed by the *New York Sun* and the *Crisis*. The influential African American weekly *Chicago Defender* was almost alone in removing the qualifying word "Negro" from its encomium: Wright was, simply, "a novelist of the first magnitude" whose novel, the reviewer hoped, "shall not only focus attention upon the evils which are visited upon us, but [shall] by the very urgency of its message, transform a rotten social, economic system into a living democracy for all" (Reilly 65).

Dreiser's reviewers, even while applauding his moral force in *An American Tragedy*, stopped short of calling for social reform. Their concern was mainly with his literary achievement and the accuracy of his moral eye. With the possible exception of making contraceptives more widely available, reviewers did not regard *An American Tragedy* as suggesting how America might do away with sexual hypocrisy or economic privilege. But reviewers in both the African American and leftist press found in *Native Son* a powerful and needed critique. Samuel Sillen's review in the *New Masses* and Ben Davis Jr.'s in the *Sunday Worker*, as well as the unsigned *Chicago Defender* review quoted above, focused at length on the novel as critique: "a terrific indictment of capitalist America, which deliberately robs vast Negro communities and holds them in subjection . . . under appalling conditions of misery and discrimination" (Reilly 69) and "a brilliant analysis of the interplay of social and psychological factors" (Reilly 60). These reviewers also rejected, strongly, Canby's suggestion that Wright was satirizing radicals in his characterization of Mary's lover Jan and the Communist lawyer Max, who pleads Bigger's case. Sillen argues, with some justice, that these two radicals are "the only ones who make Bigger aware of his dignity as a human being" (Reilly 60).

Not all reviewers were pleased with *Native Son*, of course. Howard Mumford Jones in the *Boston Evening Transcript* found it "imperfect and uneven," an overblown murder story with an unpleasant protagonist and "a thesis" to illustrate (Reilly 47). The *Saturday Review of Literature*, too, would have preferred "a headlong hard-boiled narrative" to a tract on race relations (Reilly 51). Perhaps the harshest criticism came from the staunchly anti-Communist Burton Rascoe in *American Mercury*, who found the novel and its reviewers "juvenile" and "confused" and its novelist guilty of violating the Aristotelian unities and of making too much money from the novel. Rascoe, speaking no doubt for a swath of readers uncomfortable with confronting race, took Bigger personally:

> Bigger, I have been amply convinced, wouldn't hesitate two minutes to shoot me
> or his lawyer or his author, even if we were going about business and paying him
> no mind. I don't like the idea of being shot, even fictionally, just because my
> color is not like Bigger's. I wouldn't like it even if I knew that all the Bigger
> Thomases think I am somehow responsible because life hasn't been cushy for
> them. (Reilly 90)

(It should be noted that in enthusiastically reviewing *An American Tragedy* for the *New York Sun* in 1926, Rascoe had not once fearfully fantasized about being pushed out of a rowboat by a class-jumping white boy.) *Atlantic Monthly*, frequently home to socially conservative book reviewers, lectured Wright and his critical supporters on the cheery state of Negro civil rights circa 1940: "In all of the non-Southern states, Negroes have complete political rights, including the suffrage, and even in the South Negro suffrage is constantly being extended," wrote Mississippian David L. Cohn. So much political power were African Americans possessed of, Cohn argued, that, "in closely contested Presidential elections the Negro vote may decide who shall become President of the United States" (Reilly 91; also Kinnamon 3).

Native Son was considered but rejected for a Pulitzer Prize, and it is worth mentioning, in light of the overall discomfort with Wright's handling of race and sex among even his supporters, that no prize was awarded in 1941, the year of *Native Son's* eligibility. But negative reviews and the absence of a Pulitzer did not significantly affect *Native Son's* sales or interest for audiences of multiple media. Wright collaborated on a stage version of the novel in 1940, and in 1951, following Jack London's lead with *The Sea-Wolf*, he appeared in a film of *Native Son* as Bigger himself.

The above snapshots suggest that critical esteem alone was not sufficient to propel a work of literary naturalism into the public's embrace, though for Crane and Dreiser it had the effect of buoying them through periods of neglect or outright hostility, while for London and Wright the regard of specific publishing houses and critics led to more material financial support early in their careers. On the other hand, violating conventional sexual or social pieties would not in itself hurt popular reception, so long as other pieties or desires—for instance, London's offers of attainable masculinity and affirmations of American exceptionalism and strenuous style—were observed or satisfied, or, as in the case of *An American Tragedy* and *Native Son*, the violation occurred within a work that otherwise appeared to conform to recognizable conventions of genre or that, particularly in the case of *Native Son*, but also *An American Tragedy*, gave readers a means for tackling emergent social issues of immediate concern to them. Crane's *Maggie*, that early experiment in American literary naturalism with which we began, demonstrates the peril of violating both the pieties and the conventions of genre while at the same time refusing to offer the reader a consolatory handhold or energizing call to reform. Stripped bare of all of these, *Maggie*, like its protagonist, had nowhere to go. The measure of the popular success of later works of American literary naturalism would be proportionate to their willingness to inhabit genre or to offer either consolation or a call to arms.

WORKS CITED

Benfey, Christopher. *The Double Life of Stephen Crane*. New York: Knopf, 1992.

Butler, Robert. *The Critical Response to Richard Wright*. Westport, Conn.: Greenwood, 1995.

Crane, Stephen. *The Correspondence of Stephen Crane*. Ed Stanley Wertheim and Paul Sorrentino. 2 vols. New York: Columbia University Press, 1988.

———. *Maggie: A Girl of the Streets and Other New York Writings*. New York: Modern Library, 2001.

Davis, Linda H. *Badge of Courage: The Life of Stephen Crane*. New York: Houghton Mifflin, 1998.

Dreiser, Theodore. *An American Tragedy*. New York: Library of America, 2003.

Kershaw, Alex. *Jack London: A Life*. New York: St. Martin's, 1997.

Kinnamon, Kenneth, ed. *Critical Essays on Richard Wright's* Native Son. New York: Twayne, 1997.

London, Jack. *The Letters of Jack London*. Ed. Earle Labor, Robert C. Leitz III, and I. Milo
    Shepard. 3 vols. Stanford: Stanford University Press, 1988.
Loving, Jerome. *The Last Titan: A Life of Theodore Dreiser*. Berkeley and Los Angeles:
    University of California Press, 2005.
Lundquist, James. *Jack London: Adventures, Ideas, and Fiction*. New York: Ungar, 1987.
O'Connor, Richard. *Jack London: A Biography*. Boston: Little, Brown, 1964.
Orlov, Paul A. *An American Tragedy: Perils of the Self Seeking Success*. Lewisburg: Bucknell
    University Press, 1998.
Pizer, Donald. *The Novels of Theodore Dreiser: A Critical Study*. Minneapolis: University of
    Minnesota Press, 1976.
"A Protest Against the Suppression of Theodore Dreiser's *The 'Genius.'*" *Dreiser-Mencken
    Letters: The Correspondence of Theodore Dreiser and H. L. Mencken, 1907–1945*. Ed.
    Thomas P. Riggio. 2 vols. Philadelphia: University of Pennsylvania Press, 1986. 2:
    802–4.
Reilly, John M., ed. *Richard Wright: The Critical Reception*. New York: Burt Franklin, 1978.
Roosevelt, Theodore. "The Strenuous Life." *The Strenuous Life: Essays and Addresses*. New
    York: Century, 1905. 1–21.
Rowley, Hazel. *Richard Wright: The Life and Times*. Chicago: University of Chicago Press,
    2001.
Salzman, Jack, ed. *Theodore Dreiser: The Critical Reception*. New York: David Lewis, 1972.
"The Sea-Wolf." Rev. of *The Sea-Wolf*. *New York Times Book Review* 12 Nov. 1904: 768–69.
Stallman, R. W. *Stephen Crane: A Biography*. New York: George Braziller, 1968.
Swanberg, W. A. *Dreiser*. New York: Scribner, 1965.
Walker, Margaret. *Richard Wright: Daemonic Genius*. New York: Amistad, 1988.
Weatherford, Richard M., ed. *Stephen Crane: The Critical Heritage*. Boston: Routledge, 1973.
Wertheim, Stanley, and Paul Sorrentino, eds. *The Crane Log: A Documentary Life of Stephen
    Crane, 1871–1900*. New York: G. K. Hall, 1994.

CHAPTER 23

EDITING NATURALISM

KEVIN J. HAYES

WHEN Ripley Hitchcock died suddenly on 4 May 1918 at a Park Avenue hotel banquet, American literature lost one of its most influential behind-the-scenes figures. At the time of his death Hitchcock was working as director and literary adviser for Harper and Brothers, a firm he had been with since 1906. Earlier, from 1890 to 1903, he had served as literary adviser to D. Appleton and Company, another prominent New York publisher. Describing Hitchcock's responsibilities at Appleton, Arthur Stedman blandly identified him as the "manager of this firm's departments relative to the acceptance and publication of books" (192). When Hitchcock left Appleton, "The Lounger" offered a more spirited comment to describe the reputation he had established there: "His record as a discoverer of authors and a suggester of popular books generally is not second to that of any literary adviser in America" (Gilder and Gilder 483). These comments indicate what literary advisers did for the publishers who employed them. They discovered new authors and devised new ideas for books that could make money.

Francis Halsey, who took over as literary adviser at Appleton upon Hitchcock's departure, discussed his professional responsibilities in *The Building of a Book*, a collection of essays directed toward would-be authors. Though intended as practical advice, Halsey's essay is remarkably vague when it comes to delineating the literary adviser's precise responsibilities. Halsey reiterates the importance of discovering new authors. He also explains that the adviser, whose duties "should pertain almost exclusively to the manuscripts," functions as "an intermediary between the publisher and the author." According to Halsey, the adviser's primary responsibility is "to preserve and to create good-will from authors toward the house which employs him, for that good-will is an asset of the first importance to a publishing house" (16, 22). Halsey does not explain how the literary adviser promotes such goodwill—or why promoting goodwill should be such an important duty. The absence of specifics is frustrating, but what Halsey seems to be saying is that advisers must stroke the egos of their authors to make them more amenable to the changes that commercial demands may impose upon their texts.

Clarence Clough Buel, a good friend of Hitchcock, offered a tribute to him in a letter to the *New York Times Book Review*. Buel recognized the role of literary adviser as the defining feature of Hitchcock's career: "After ten years of journalism he began his real life work as literary adviser with the old and highly respected house of Appleton. No other position in a great publishing business is so interesting as that of the literary guide and spiritual artificer, or calls for so much moral devotion and thankless drudgery" (5). Buel reveals in this tribute what Halsey had hesitated to say in his essay, namely, that literary advisers must read, and revise, manuscripts with scrupulous moral devotion: an effort that authors could find objectionable.

The era of American literary naturalism was a time when authors were willing to write what publishers were unwilling to publish: a situation scarcely conducive to goodwill between them. The literary adviser took on a crucial role in the production of naturalistic texts because he—almost always a he—became the person who smoothed the rough edges from the gritty originals to make them palatable to a popular readership. Generally, authors disliked the way advisers tinkered with their texts. As Buel observed, authors often "revert ruefully to the prunings that have been cast into the fire" (5). The story of how American literary naturalism has been edited is a two-part story, the first part telling how diligent, sometimes overzealous literary advisers pruned away some of the boldest and most innovative aspects of their authors' work and cast them into the fire, the second part relating the efforts of modern textual scholars to rescue those prunings from the flames.

Second Thoughts and First Editions

Francis Halsey estimated that an American publishing house large enough to employ a full-time literary adviser at the turn of the century received at least one thousand unsolicited manuscripts per year. Of these only about one and a half percent were accepted for publication (17). These odds are sufficient to intimidate any would-be author. Take Stephen Crane for example. After completing his first book-length work, *Maggie: A Girl of the Streets (A Story of New York)*, he showed the manuscript to Hamlin Garland, who thought quite highly of it. Garland recommended it to Richard Watson Gilder, editor of *Century Magazine*, who rejected it.

With its daring subject matter and numerous instances of "damn" and "hell" throughout, *Maggie* did not find in Gilder a sympathetic reader. In "An 'Open Letter' about Editing," Gilder emphasized the importance of toning down foul language when editing realist and naturalist fiction for publication. Gilder saw the editor as a combatant in the "battle for decency in literature," someone whose blue pencil is his best weapon (2). Gilder may have told Crane that no publisher would be willing to publish the narrative as it stood with its profanity and graphic detail. Consequently, Crane decided against submitting the manuscript to a commercial house. Instead, he exhausted a small legacy and financed the publication himself (Hayes, Introduction 3–4).

When word later got around that numerous publishers had turned down *Maggie*, Crane let the reading public know that *Maggie* "was not refused by a long list of publishers, for the reason that he never offered it to any of them, but published it himself" ("Literary" 7). Issued pseudonymously under the name "Johnston Smith," the first edition of *Maggie* appeared in 1893. By publishing it himself, Crane avoided the literary adviser's blue pencil and escaped the revisions typically imposed by someone like Gilder or Hitchcock, editors who saw their professional work as an act of moral responsibility. Save for several annoying typographical errors, the text of *Maggie* turned out just as Crane wanted it. That was the advantage of publishing the book himself. The disadvantage: he had no publicity beyond what he could personally muster. The great benefit of a commercial press, after all, is the massive amount of publicity it can use to puff a book. People buy what they are told to buy, and a commercial publisher can summon a huge amount of promotional material: feature stories, interviews, library tie-ins, magazine advertisements, newspaper advertisements, posters, review copies. Crane's personal efforts to promote *Maggie* largely involved sending inscribed copies to influential literary figures who might review the book, men like Hamlin Garland and William Dean Howells. Both diligently noticed the book in the press, but few other contemporary reviews of the first edition of *Maggie* appeared. One perceptive early reviewer did appreciate the work's "daring and terrible directness," finding it "iconoclastic in its bearing, and indicative of the free, rugged strength of young genius" ("Of Books" 6).

Disappointed with the commercial failure of his first novel, Stephen Crane remained undaunted. He completed *The Red Badge of Courage*, arranged publication of an abridged version for newspaper syndication, and sought a publisher for the complete work. While *Red Badge* ran in syndication, Crane approached Ripley Hitchcock, who clearly remembered their first meeting:

> It was in December, 1894, that Mr. Crane came to the editorial office of
> D. Appleton and Company, bringing two short stories as examples of the work
> which he was then doing for the newspapers. The impression made by the stories
> was so strong that Mr. Crane was asked if he had a story long enough for
> publication in book form. He replied hesitatingly that he had written one rather
> long story, which was appearing in a Philadelphia newspaper, and "some of the
> boys in the office seemed to like it." (Hitchcock v–vi)

By approaching Hitchcock, Crane faced up to a discouraging truth: to succeed, novelists had to place their works with a commercial press and had to accept, however begrudgingly, the alterations literary advisers might impose. For the most part, Hitchcock did not alter the text of the *Red Badge* manuscript himself. Rather, he left that task to Crane, essentially letting him know that the book would not be published unless he made certain changes. With boxes and boxes of unsold copies of *Maggie* littering his seedy New York apartment, Crane reluctantly agreed. Years after the book appeared, he still grumbled about the alterations Hitchcock imposed upon *Red Badge*, telling his wife Cora that Hitchcock made him change its text (*Correspondence* 1: 173).

In Crane's original version, Henry Fleming, his young soldier-protagonist, runs away from battle and gets away with desertion. Hitchcock recognized that this sardonic portrayal of combat would antagonize contemporary readers and doom the book to commercial failure. After all, many veterans of the Civil War were alive and well in the 1890s, and many Civil War books were being published, books like highly romanticized regimental histories (Hayes, *Stephen Crane* 83). Hitchcock shrewdly understood contemporary tastes; the huge commercial success of *Red Badge* validated his role as literary adviser.

Anxious to capitalize on the success of *Red Badge*, Hitchcock agreed to issue a trade edition of *Maggie* but insisted Crane revise the first-edition text significantly. As Crane informed his British publisher William Heinemann, "I have toned it somewhat at the request of the Appletons" (*Correspondence* 1: 206). Crane's correspondence generally indicates what Hitchcock asked him to change. Marking up a copy of the 1893 *Maggie* in February 1896, he "dispensed with a goodly number of damns" and "carefully plugged at the words which hurt" but hesitated to make more significant changes, fearing larger excisions would compromise the work's integrity (*Correspondence* 1: 197, 200). The most significant change Hitchcock insisted on occurs in chapter 17, which describes Maggie's last night. The following paragraph was omitted entirely:

> When almost to the river the girl saw a great figure. On going forward she
> perceived it to be a huge fat man in torn and greasy garments. His grey hair
> straggled down over his forehead. His small, bleared eyes, sparkling from amidst
> great rolls of red fat, swept eagerly over the girl's upturned face. He laughed, his
> brown, disordered teeth gleaming under a grey, grizzled moustache from which
> beer-drops dripped. His whole body gently quivered and shook like that of a dead
> jelly fish. Chuckling and leering, he followed the girl of the crimson legions. (89)

The appearance of this gross fat man is what precipitates Maggie's suicide in the 1893 text. Without it, it is unclear precisely why Maggie drowns herself in the river or that she drowns herself. Once Hitchcock finished editing the book, Crane could hardly look at it. "The proofs make me ill," he said (*Correspondence* 1: 224).

Crane did much of the revising and proofreading outside of New York. When he returned to the city in April 1896, the Lantern Club hosted a dinner for him. Howells delivered a rousing speech on the future of American literature. The more skeptical labor journalist John Swinton spoke after Howells. Swinton's comments, which concerned the editorial process, seem directed toward Hitchcock, also in attendance. Swinton "declared that over every American writer hangs the fear of the editorial blue pencil, and that not until men dare to be themselves and not the echoes of others can the country hope for a literature that will compare favorably with that of England and France" (qtd. in "Howells" 9). Swinton's remarks apparently had no impact on Hitchcock's editorial practice.

Appleton's watered-down edition of *Maggie* appeared in June. Some reviewers condemned Crane's stark portrayal of Maggie's life, but the book generally received positive notices. One anonymous review formerly attributed to Frank Norris praised Crane's "habit and aptitude for making phrases—short, terse epigrams struck off in the heat of composition, sparks merely, that cast a momentary gleam of light upon whole phases of life" ("Stephen Crane's Stories" 151; McElrath, "Stephen Crane" 2). This reviewer did not find Crane's choice of subject matter startling, however. *Maggie* was one of many slum novels to have appeared in recent years.

Frank Norris faced difficulties with publishers similar to Crane's. While a student at Harvard during the 1894–95 school year, Norris had written tales and sketches he would later incorporate as parts of two novels, *McTeague* and *Vandover and the Brute*. After finishing *McTeague* in 1897, he had difficulty finding a publisher. His hard-hitting style, deterministic outlook, and fascination with the lowly and downtrodden repelled publishers. In frustration, Norris wrote an adventure tale more certain to capture the public fancy, *Moran of the Lady Letty*, which Doubleday and McClure published in 1898. In that year, S. S. McClure also hired Norris to read manuscripts for all three facets of his publishing business: his newspaper syndicate, *McClure's Magazine*, and his book division, Doubleday and McClure. Norris's position created new opportunities, and Doubleday and McClure soon accepted *McTeague*, which it released in 1899.

Reviews were mixed, but even those who critiqued *McTeague* could not deny that it was a work of power. Norris's explicit detail was too much for some readers, however. Many disliked the scene at the theater where little Owgooste Sieppe wets his pants:

> But at this moment a dreadful accident happened to Owgooste; his distress reached its climax, his fortitude collapsed. What a thing beyond words! For a moment he gazed wildly about him, helpless and petrified with astonishment and terror. Then his grief found utterance, and the closing strains of the orchestra were mingled with a prolonged wail of infinite sadness.
>
> "Owgooste, what is ut?" cried his mother, eyeing him with dawning suspicion; then suddenly, "What haf you done? You haf ruined your new Vaunteroy gostume!" Her face blazed; without more ado she smacked him soundly. Then it was that Owgooste touched the utter limit of his misery, his unhappiness, his horrible discomfort; his utter wretchedness was complete. He filled the air with his doleful outcries. The more he was smacked and shaken, the louder he wept. (85)

This scene seems fairly innocuous by today's standards, but contemporary readers felt a novel was no place for a description of urination. Grant Richards, Norris's British publisher, insisted he rewrite the scene for the British edition. American reprints followed the rewritten version. This scene was not restored to the text of *McTeague* until 1941 (McElrath, *Frank Norris* 44).

With the success of *McTeague*, Norris submitted *Vandover and the Brute* to Doubleday and McClure, which rejected this brutal tale of a young San Francisco man unable to cope with the cultural, moral, and social forces that doom him to disaster. Norris tried other publishers with no better luck. Grant Richards rejected it, and so did William Heinemann (McElrath and Crisler 326). Having written *Vandover and the Brute* before coming to work for S. S. McClure, Norris now had a better idea of the kinds of books that would sell. He shelved this early novel and turned his attention to other projects.

Never fully satisfied with his position with McClure, Norris went with Frank N. Doubleday, who split to form Doubleday, Page and Company with Walter Hines Page and others. Besides being junior partner, Page also served as literary adviser, deciding acquisitions based on advice from his readers (Marcosson 37). Norris's responsibilities at the new firm were much more clearly defined than they had been with McClure. He worked half-time as one of Page's readers, enabling him to spend the other half of his time on his own writing, to which Doubleday, Page and Company would have exclusive rights (McElrath and Crisler 363).

It is crucial to realize that Norris was reading and evaluating the manuscripts of others while working on his own novels, *The Octopus* (1901) most importantly. He developed a keen understanding of what publishers and the public wanted. Norris himself wanted very much to be a successful novelist. His experience with Doubleday, Page and Company let him know what he could or could not get away with in his writing. To write books acceptable to a wide readership, he had to soften his brutality, to omit text liable to offend, to give his writing a surer moral basis, and to revert to safer modes of storytelling. Norris's experience as a publisher's reader turned him into his own censor. *The Octopus* proved to be a popular success, but the hard-hitting frankness and uncompromising detail make *McTeague* his masterpiece.

In early 1900, Norris read a manuscript by an unknown author named Theodore Dreiser. Writing to Dreiser the last week of May, Norris said *Sister Carrie* was the best novel he had read in manuscript since coming to work for Doubleday, Page and promised to do all he could to make sure the firm accepted the book. Before Norris received Dreiser's manuscript, its text had already gone through a rigorous editorial process. Dreiser's wife Sara and his friend Arthur Henry provided extensive, yet sometimes ill-considered, editorial advice throughout its composition. The typists he hired made further changes to the work (West, Berkey, and Winters 503–19). Once they finished the typescript, Dreiser sent it to Harper and Brothers, which declined the manuscript because of its slow narrative pace and overt sexuality. Dreiser sought Arthur Henry's help again. Henry reread the manuscript, marking blocks of text to delete. Dreiser accepted virtually all of Henry's suggestions, cutting some 36,000 words from the work. But Henry was not as careful a reader as Dreiser thought, and these block cuts introduced many textual anomalies and removed much explanatory detail (Hayes, "Textual" 54).

The version Norris read for Doubleday, Page was shorter and tamer than the version his counterpart at Harper had read. Norris showed it to Page, who approved the work. Frank Doubleday, in Europe at the time, was shocked when he read *Sister Carrie* upon his return. He did not want to publish the book at all; his attorneys told him he had to publish it but did not have to promote it (West, Berkey, and Winters

524–25). Doubleday insisted Dreiser make further changes. The surviving manuscript contains a copious number of blue pencillings throughout. Though Doubleday refused to promote the book, Norris did what he could, sending out dozens of review copies. Regardless, the few sales of *Sister Carrie* proved to be a major disappointment to its author.

Longing to republish *Sister Carrie* properly, Dreiser sought a publisher who would offer him a two-book deal for a new edition of *Sister Carrie* and the first edition of his next novel, which would eventually appear as *Jennie Gerhardt* in 1911. He approached several publishers in 1901 with no luck, but late that year he received a letter from Ripley Hitchcock, still literary adviser at Appleton, praising *Sister Carrie* and expressing interest in Dreiser's next novel. But Hitchcock wanted a "less drastic" novel, meaning one that would not offend conservative literary tastes (West, "Composition" 425). Dreiser got a bad feeling about what Hitchcock wanted and did not pursue a deal with Appleton. After Hitchcock left Appleton to become literary adviser at A. S. Barnes and Company, Dreiser, still hoping for a two-book deal, contacted him in 1905. To drum up support for Dreiser at Barnes, Hitchcock sent a copy of *Sister Carrie* to A. R. Cross, one of the firm's readers. But Cross strongly disliked the book. He told Hitchcock that *Sister Carrie* had so offended him that he "put it in the fire, not wishing anyone to see such a book in my house and believing it would do more harm than good in the village library" (qtd. in West, "Composition" 429). Dreiser ultimately arranged for B. W. Dodge and Company to rerelease *Sister Carrie* in 1907, at which time he had yet to finish *Jennie Gerhardt*.

Hitchcock kept his eye on Dreiser. When he moved to Harper to become director and literary adviser there, Hitchcock was finally in a position to offer Dreiser the two-book agreement he desired. In 1910, he wrote to tell Dreiser the good news. Pleased with a possible deal at long last, Dreiser finally finished *Jennie Gerhardt* in January 1911. Hitchcock still had to work hard to convince Harper to publish the book, but he ultimately succeeded, apparently by promising that he would rework the manuscript significantly to make it more palatable for general readers. Though Dreiser considered *Jennie Gerhardt* finished, Hitchcock saw the manuscript as merely the raw material from which he could fashion a commercially viable product. Dreiser's agreement with Harper allowed the publisher to revise the text thoroughly and excise any offensive material (West, "Composition" 434).

Hitchcock ultimately cut sixteen thousand words from Dreiser's manuscript and made thousands of changes to the remaining text. He deleted nearly all mention of sex, minimized Dreiser's social commentary, and considerably shortened lengthy passages of description. The revisions flatten Jennie's character and sentimentalize the story. Learning of Hitchcock's thoroughgoing changes to the text of *Jennie Gerhardt*, Dreiser's good friend H. L. Mencken observed, "Such ruthless slashing is alarming. The chief virtue of Dreiser is his skill at piling up detail. The story he tells, reduced to a mere story, is nothing" (18–19). Dreiser agreed. He could have broken the contract with Harper and taken the book elsewhere, but *Jennie Gerhardt* had been eleven years in the making already. How many more years would it take to find another publisher, if he would be able to find one at all? He stuck with Harper, and *Jennie Gerhardt*, a shadow of its former self, appeared in October 1911.

The Canonization of Naturalist Texts

Despite the travesties they suffered at the hands of zealous literary advisers, editors, and publishers, enough of these naturalist texts remained intact to prompt succeeding generations of readers to recognize them as powerful contributions to literary history, and the published texts were canonized as classics of American literature. Behind the scenes, however, friends and collectors understood that the public versions did not tell the whole story of these works. Surviving manuscripts, typescripts, and obscure first editions contained the raw material to understand them more thoroughly, and these textual artifacts gathered value over time.

When the *Bookman* announced the publication of the revised edition of *Maggie* in 1896, it suggested that the value of the first edition would increase significantly: "*Maggie: A Girl of the Streets* is to be wholly revised and largely rewritten before it is published by the Appletons, so that possessors of the original edition, and we presume they are few, may consider that they own a prize" ("Chronicle" 11). Even before Crane's death, a Brooklyn collector with a copy of the 1893 *Maggie* was looking to trade it for a set of back issues of *Saturday Night*, the rare weekly Philadelphia newspaper (Monteiro 38). In 1914, a New York dealer was aggressively seeking a copy of the first edition of *Maggie* ("Books" 1124). By the 1930s, the 1893 *Maggie* was being called the rarest book in modern American literature (Stallman 329–30).

Crane held onto the manuscript of *The Red Badge of Courage* until after the English edition of the book appeared but decided to give it to his New York friend Willis Brooks Hawkins in 1896. Crane had planned to spend much time in the city that year, but the noise and the crowds sent him scurrying to the countryside. Consequently, he had been unable to see Hawkins as much as he had wished. From the country, he wrote, "I am expressing you the original ms of The Red Badge. Thought maybe you'd like it" (*Correspondence* 1: 189). Crane's actions indicate the social value a literary manuscript held. He sent the *Red Badge* manuscript to his friend as a stand-in for himself. The gift reinforced their friendship and compensated for Crane's inability to see Hawkins in person. By 1931, A. S. W. Rosenbach had acquired the manuscript, eventually selling it to Virginia bibliophile Clifton Waller Barrett in 1951. It now forms a highlight of the Barrett Collection at the University of Virginia.

Frank Norris's manuscript texts survived in different states after his death. He held onto the *Vandover* manuscript, which he mined for other novels, sometimes taking whole scenes from it to use in other books. For example, Norris took a description of a parlor and incorporated in his 1899 novel *Blix* (Pizer 1217). At the time of his death in 1902, the whereabouts of the *Vandover* manuscript remained uncertain. When Doubleday, Page published it for the first time in 1914, the firm had a special dust-jacket printed for the advance edition, the cover of which displays a letter from the publishers printed to resemble handwriting, a nice touch, subtly emphasizing the newly rediscovered manuscript of the book. The explanatory note on the cover also softens the story's brutality:

> The Ms of this story was found in a box of Frank Norris's personal effects that survived both the San Francisco earthquake and fire.
>
> We are sending this advance copy to you, first because of the interest that attaches to the author's unrevised draft, and second, because this tremendous piece of realism conveys a moral lesson that no one who reads it can forget. If, like Arthur of old, you are engaged as a minister or layman in making the sway of the Brute grow less and less in the land, then this story has a message for you—as it has for every human being who fights the eternal fight between good and evil in his own soul. (qtd. in McElrath, *Frank Norris* 153–55)

Writing an introduction to this edition, Frank Norris's brother Charles, himself a novelist, reiterated the earthquake story but later recanted it, explaining that his brother's widow had retained the manuscript for years. Preparing *Vandover and the Brute* for publication, Charles Norris significantly edited the manuscript, trimming foul language and removing a long early chapter that depicts Vandover drunk. He even added about five thousand words of his own (Pizer 1217). After Doubleday, Page published *Vandover and the Brute* in 1914, the manuscript mysteriously disappeared. Charles Norris apparently destroyed it to obscure the extent of his revisions to his brother's work. The manuscript of *McTeague* remained intact until 1928, when Doubleday, Doran published *The Argonaut Manuscript Limited Edition of Frank Norris's Works*, a sumptuous ten-volume edition bound in simulated vellum, which included a leaf of the holograph manuscript in the first volume of each of the 245 sets of the edition. Norris scholars have patiently sought to reconstitute the manuscript, but so far have recovered only around one hundred leaves.

In 1914, Theodore Dreiser presented the manuscript of *Sister Carrie* to his friend H. L. Mencken. Like Crane's gift to Hawkins, Dreiser's gift indicates the social value of literary manuscripts. Mencken had been extremely supportive of Dreiser throughout the composition of *Jennie Gerhardt*; giving him the *Sister Carrie* manuscript, Dreiser offered a heartfelt expression of their friendship. Mencken ultimately deposited the manuscript at the New York Public Library, where it remains today. Both Crane and Norris died before they had much time to think about the disposition of their literary remains or before literary manuscripts had much monetary value, but Dreiser lived long enough to recognize both the monetary and scholarly value of his manuscript material. In 1922, he sold the *Jennie Gerhardt* manuscript to collector W. W. Lange, who, in turn, sold it in 1928 to the Phoenix Book Shop, where it was purchased by R. Sturgis Ingersoll. Before Dreiser died in 1945, he arranged to have the University of Pennsylvania library acquire his literary papers. With the Dreiser Collection established, Ingersoll magnanimously donated the *Jennie Gerhardt* manuscript to the University of Pennsylvania.

By the mid-twentieth century, surviving manuscripts and other documentary material were ready for scholars to examine and, in so doing, to reconsider the compositional history of naturalist texts, but professors of literature were strangely reluctant to do so. The 1950s was the heyday of New Criticism, a critical approach to literature maintaining that history, biography, and textual variation do not matter. All that matters is the text itself, which, the New Critics naïvely believed, came ready-made for critical interpretation. Professors of literature wrote and published critical studies of, say, Stephen Crane's ambiguity in *The Red Badge of Courage*, unaware that the work's ambiguity was largely imposed by Ripley Hitchcock, for Crane's surviving *Red Badge* manuscript depicts him as a cravenly soldier who never really matures in the end.

While New Criticism raged, a new approach to textual editing emerged. The general goal of this approach was to produce eclectic texts, meaning texts that combined elements from different versions of the same work to form a sort of ideal text. Those who followed this approach did not seem bothered by its ahistorical approach. Theirs was the editorial equivalent to New Criticism. Both the New Critic and the New Editor believed in the self-sufficient nature of the text (McKenzie 15). Editors of eclectic texts could apply their editorial formulae to any literary work regardless of time period or the types of evidence that survive. Starting from W. W. Greg's classic essay, "The Rationale of Copy-Text," Fredson Bowers, the don of this new editorial approach, developed it as a method of editing Renaissance texts before turning his attention to American literature. Ignoring the fact that much fuller evidence survives to guide editorial decisions regarding works published since Christopher Marlowe's *Dr. Faustus*, Bowers rigidly applied his method to the works of Stephen Crane—with disastrous results (Parker and Higgins).

The eclectic approach basically involves choosing a copy-text, which forms the basis of an edition, and then emending that text by comparing it with other authorial versions of the work: surviving drafts, page proofs, and revised editions published during the author's lifetime. For *Maggie*, Bowers chose the 1893 first edition as copy-text. So far so good. But then he emended from the 1896 version, arguing that changes to the text in the second edition represent Crane's final intentions, ignoring the evidence contained in Crane's letters, evidence such as Crane's statement that reading the page proofs of the 1896 edition made him ill. Released in 1969 as part of the first volume of the University of Virginia Edition of the Works of Stephen Crane, Bowers's *Maggie* was lambasted in the press, but Bowers, an editing juggernaut, continued to *Red Badge*. As it had developed since the early 1960s, the eclectic method of editing typically shied away from using manuscripts as copy-texts (Parker 19). Complete manuscripts, however, more accurately represent an author's vision of a work before the intrusion of literary advisers and commercial editors. Despite the survival of a near-complete manuscript, Bowers chose the 1895 first edition as his copy-text. He examined the manuscript for minor variants but ignored the fact that the manuscript contained an extra chapter in the middle of the work, which completely changed the tone and tenor of the story.

Bowers's version of Ripley Hitchcock's version of *The Red Badge of Courage* appeared in 1975 as the second volume of the Virginia Edition. Bowers would oversee the complete Virginia Edition, which ran to ten volumes, the last of which appeared in 1976. Other Crane editors also hesitated to base their editions on the surviving manuscript. Preparing *Red Badge* for the Norton Critical Edition in 1962, Sculley Bradley, Richmond Croom Beatty, and E. Hudson Long printed passages from the manuscript as an appendix but based their text on the 1895 Appleton edition, asserting that the numerous changes to the text did not alter the meaning of the novel. Donald Pizer prepared the second edition of the Norton Critical Edition in 1976. Though a facsimile edition of the *Red Badge* manuscript had appeared in 1973, Pizer set aside the manuscript and chose to follow the 1895 first-edition text.

With no one else interested in the task, Hershel Parker, then at the University of Southern California, asked his student Henry Binder to edit *Red Badge* from the surviving manuscript. Binder reconstructed the text of *Red Badge* as it stood after Crane first finished the work yet before Ripley Hitchcock got his hands on it. He completed the edition as his doctoral dissertation in 1978. Parker subsequently helped Binder arrange publication with Norton, the reconstructed text to appear initially in first edition of *The Norton Anthology of American Literature* (1979) and to be separately published later. A founding editor of this landmark textbook, Parker saw the *Norton Anthology* as an ideal way to disseminate the reconstructed text, to assure that college students across the nation reading *Red Badge* for the first time would be reading *Red Badge* as Crane really wrote it. Parker's goal of disseminating the text as widely as possible was well intended, but for the most part it went unappreciated. Many college professors felt Parker had pulled a fast one. Used to teaching *The Red Badge of Courage* the same way they had taught it for years, these professors suddenly had to rethink and even reread the book.

In early 1982, Norton published a trade edition of the reconstructed text to widespread critical acclaim. Reviewers across the nation applauded Binder's efforts to restore the text of *Red Badge*. But Norton found itself in an odd situation. With the release of the new edition, it suddenly had two very different versions of *Red Badge* in print, the Binder edition and the Norton Critical Edition. As part of an established and well-respected series, the Norton Critical Edition stayed in print; Henry Binder's edition went out of print. Norton sold the paperback rights to Avon, which released its edition in 1983 (dated 1982), rereleased it in 1987, but let it go out of print soon thereafter. Critical and textual studies continued to demonstrate the subtlety of the Binder text (Hayes, "How"; Mitchell). But from the late 1980s to the late 1990s, the Binder edition was marginalized. Meanwhile, the Norton Critical Edition of *Red Badge* went into a third edition. Norton ultimately resecured the paperback rights to the Binder edition and reprinted the reconstructed text in 1999. Norton recently commissioned the fourth edition of the Norton Critical Edition of *Red Badge*, which appeared in 2008. Since Norton now owns the paperback rights to the reconstructed text, the editors could have used the Binder text, but instead they decided to use the 1895 Appleton edition as their copy-text. Sadly, it has become easy to ignore the Binder edition.

The rollout of the reconstructed text of *Sister Carrie* has been much more successful. Whereas Binder did not publish his edition of Crane's classic war story until after *Red Badge* appeared as part of the University of Virginia Edition, James L. W.

West published his reconstructed version of *Sister Carrie* in 1981 as part of the Pennsylvania Edition of Theodore Dreiser. The University of Pennsylvania Press then sold the trade paperback rights to Penguin, which released an inexpensive photo-offset reprint of the Pennsylvania Edition with an introduction by the renowned Alfred Kazin. To reinforce the significance of the reconstructed text, West published *The Sister Carrie Portfolio* in 1985, a handsome coffee-table book that reproduces documents pertaining to the reconstructed text.

West's edition of *Sister Carrie* did meet some resistance, however. His toughest decision involved the book's ending. The 1900 Doubleday, Page text ends with the beautiful, if melancholy, image of Carrie, successful but alone, rocking back and forth in her rocking chair, a movement which mimics the oscillations her life has taken: "In your rocking-chair, by your window dreaming, shall you long, alone. In your rocking-chair, by your window, shall you dream such happiness as you may never feel" (557). As Dreiser had originally written the book before Sara Dreiser and Arthur Henry changed it, *Sister Carrie* ended with Hurstwood's suicide. His life having spiraled downward since meeting Carrie, Hurstwood ends up in a New York flophouse, tucks his coat along the crack under the door of his room, and turns on the gas. Here's the last sentence of the reconstructed text: "'What's the use,' he said wearily, as he stretched himself to rest" (499). In the 1900 text, this episode had appeared earlier.

Disagreements over the differences between the first edition and the reconstructed version of *Sister Carrie* are understandable. But Dreiser's editors, by strategically placing their work in both the scholarly realm and the commercial arena, have made the Pennsylvania text impossible to ignore. Reprinted by Penguin, the Pennsylvania text can be found in bookstores and classrooms across the nation. The Pennsylvania editors have accomplished with *Sister Carrie* what Hershel Parker only dreamed of doing with *Red Badge*: to make sure that people coming to the work for the first time would read the reconstructed text.

CONCLUSION

In the late nineteenth and early twentieth centuries, literary advisers like Ripley Hitchcock had commercial reasons for altering their authors' work. They saw an author's manuscript as raw material, something they could mold into a viable product that would yield a profit for their companies. Though motivated by monetary gain, they also had personal reasons that inspired their work. Hitchcock's ego partly motivated him. He very much enjoyed his reputation for discovering new literary talent. The changes he imposed on *Maggie*, *Red Badge*, and *Jennie Gerhardt* seem heavy-handed in retrospect, but there can be no denying his responsibility in bringing these works before the public. The scholarly editor, with little or no commercial interest in his work, would seem to have more altruistic motivations: to produce a text true to its author's intentions. Yet egos also intervene. To read the contentious articles about editorial procedure written by Fredson Bowers and those by Hershel Parker is to witness a clash of titans. Throughout his life, the strong-willed Bowers kept his eclectic approach in the forefront of literary editing, but with his passing in 1991, the eclectic approach has fallen from favor. Scholarly editors now understand that there is no magic formula that can be applied to all literary texts. They must evaluate each text individually and take into account all surviving evidence, not just a work's text, but letters, diaries, reminiscences of friends and family, newspaper articles, anything that bears on the history of a work's composition and publication. Only by taking all evidence into account can scholarly editors hope to produce responsibly edited texts.

WORKS CITED

"Books Wanted." *Publishers' Weekly* 28 March 1914: 1117–25.
Buel, Clarence Clough. "A Friend's Tribute to Ripley Hitchcock." *New York Times Book Review* 26 May 1918: 5.
"Chronicle and Comment." *Bookman* 3 (1896): 97–112.
Crane, Stephen. *The Correspondence of Stephen Crane.* Ed. Stanley Wertheim and Paul Sorrentino. 2 vols. New York: Columbia University Press, 1988.
———. *Maggie, A Girl of the Streets.* New York: D. Appleton, 1896.
———. *Maggie, A Girl of the Streets (A Story of New York).* [New York: The author,] 1893.
———. *Maggie: A Girl of the Streets (A Story of New York).* Ed. Kevin J. Hayes. Boston: Bedford, 1999.
———. *The Red Badge of Courage: A Facsimile of the Manuscript.* Ed. Fredson Bowers. Washington, DC: NCR / Microcard Editions, 1973. 2 vols.
———. *The Red Badge of Courage: A Norton Critical Edition.* Ed. Donald Pizer. 2d ed. New York: Norton, 1976.
———. *The Red Badge of Courage: A Norton Critical Edition.* Ed. Donald Pizer. 3d ed. New York: Norton, 1994.
———. *The Red Badge of Courage: A Norton Critical Edition.* Ed. Donald Pizer and Eric Carl Link. 4th ed. New York: Norton, 2008.
———. *The Red Badge of Courage: An Episode of the American Civil War.* Ed. Henry Binder. New York: Norton, 1982.
———. *The Red Badge of Courage: An Episode of the American Civil War.* Ed. Henry Binder. 1982. New York: Avon, 1987.
———. *The Red Badge of Courage: An Episode of the American Civil War.* Ed. Henry Binder. 1982. New York: Norton, 1999.
———. *The University of Virginia Edition of the Works of Stephen Crane.* Ed. Fredson Bowers. Charlottesville: University Press of Virginia, 1969–1976. 10 vols.
Dreiser, Theodore. *Jennie Gerhardt: A Novel.* New York: Harper and Brothers, 1911.
———. *Jennie Gerhardt.* Ed. James L. W. West III. Philadelphia: University of Pennsylvania Press, 1992.
———. *Sister Carrie.* New York: Doubleday, Page, 1900.
———. *Sister Carrie.* New York: B. W. Dodge, 1907.

————. *Sister Carrie*. Ed. James L. W. West III, John C. Berkey, Alice M. Winters, and Neda M. Westlake. Philadelphia: University of Pennsylvania Press, 1981.

————. *Sister Carrie*. Ed. James L. W. West III and Neda M. Westlake. New York: Penguin, 1981.

[Gilder, Jeanette L., and Joseph B. Gilder.] "The Lounger." *Critic* 42 (1903): 483–98.

Gilder, Richard Watson. "An 'Open Letter' about Editing." *Independent* 48 (1896): 1669–70.

Greg, W. W. "The Rationale of Copy-Text." *Studies in Bibliography* 3 (1950–51): 19–36.

Halsey, Francis W. "The Literary Adviser." *The Building of a Book: A Series of Practical Articles Written by Experts in the Various Departments of Book Making and Distributing*. Ed. Frederick H. Hitchcock. New York: Grafton, 1906. 16–24.

Hayes, Kevin J. "How Stephen Crane Shaped Henry Fleming." *Studies in the Novel* 22 (1990): 296–307.

————. Introduction: Cultural and Historical Background. Crane, *Maggie* 3–23.

————. *Stephen Crane*. Tavistock, Northumberland: Northcote House in association with the British Council, 2004.

————. "Textual Anomalies in the 1900 Doubleday, Page *Sister Carrie*." *American Literary Realism* 22 (1989): 53–68.

Hitchcock, Ripley. Preface. *The Red Badge of Courage: An Episode of the Civil War*. New York: D. Appleton, 1917. iii–x.

"Howells Lauds Crane." *Boston Daily Advertiser* 10 April 1896: 9.

"Literary Littlebits." *Idaho Avalanche* 10 July 1896: 7.

McElrath, Joseph R., Jr. *Frank Norris: A Descriptive Bibliography*. Pittsburgh: University of Pittsburgh Press, 1992.

————. "Stephen Crane in San Francisco: His Reception in *The Wave*." *Stephen Crane Studies* 2.1 (1993): 2–18.

McElrath, Joseph R., Jr., and Jesse S. Crisler. *Frank Norris: A Life*. Urbana: University of Illinois Press, 2006.

McKenzie, D. F. *Bibliography and the Sociology of Texts*. New York: Cambridge University Press, 1999.

Marcosson, Isaac F. *Adventures in Interviewing*. New York: John Lane, 1920.

Mencken, H. L. *Letters of H. L. Mencken*. Ed. Guy J. Forgue. New York: Knopf, 1961.

Mitchell, Lee Clark, ed. *New Essays on* The Red Badge of Courage. New York: Cambridge University Press, 1986.

Monteiro, George. "Another Copy of the 1893 *Maggie*." *Stephen Crane Studies* 15 (2006): 38.

Norris, Frank. *McTeague: A Story of San Francisco*. New York: Doubleday and McClure, 1899.

————. *McTeague: A Story of San Francisco*. London: Grant Richards, 1899.

————. *McTeague: A Story of San Francisco*. Ed. Jerome Loving. New York: Oxford University Press, 1995.

————. *Moran of the Lady Letty: A Story of Adventure off the California Coast*. New York: Doubleday and McClure, 1898.

————. *The Octopus: A Story of California*. New York: Doubleday, Page and Company, 1901.

————. *Vandover and the Brute*. Ed. Charles G. Norris. New York: Doubleday, Page and Company, 1914.

"Of Books and Their Authors." *North American* [Philadelphia] 6 July 1895: 6.

Parker, Hershel. *Flawed Texts and Verbal Icons: Literary Authority in American Fiction*. Evanston: Northwestern University Press, 1984.

Parker, Hershel, and Brian Higgins. "The Virginia Edition of Stephen Crane's *Maggie*: A Mirror for Textual Scholars." *Bibliographical Society of Australia and New Zealand Bulletin* 19 (1995): 131–66.

Pizer, Donald. "Note on the Texts." *Novels and Essays*. By Frank Norris. Ed. Donald Pizer. New York: Library of America, 1986. 1217–22.

Stallman, R. W. *Stephen Crane: A Critical Bibliography*. Ames: Iowa State University Press, 1972.

Stedman, Arthur. "New York Topics." *Dial* 16 (1894): 192.

"Stephen Crane's Stories of Life in the Slums: *Maggie* and *George's Mother*." *Maggie: A Girl of the Streets (A Story of New York)*. By Stephen Crane. Ed. Thomas A. Gullason. New York: Norton, 1979. 151–52.

West, James L. W., III. "The Composition and Publication of *Jennie Gerhardt*." *Jennie Gerhardt*. Ed. James L. W. West III. Philadelphia: University of Pennsylvania Press, 1992. 421–60.

———. *A Sister Carrie Portfolio*. Charlottesville: University Press of Virginia, 1985.

West, James L. W., III, John C. Berkey, and Alice M. Winters. "*Sister Carrie*: Manuscript to Print." Dreiser, *Sister Carrie* 501–41.

CHAPTER 24

....

REFASHIONING AMERICAN LITERARY NATURALISM: CRITICAL TRENDS AT THE TURN OF THE TWENTY-FIRST CENTURY

....

CHRISTOPHE DEN TANDT

NATURALISM'S POSTMODERN TURN

....

In literary critical debates, American naturalism has, to paraphrase the protagonist of Alfred Hitchcock's *Psycho*, not quite been itself in the last twenty-five years. Neo-Marxist, neo-historicist, multiculturalist, or feminist essays of the 1980s and 1990s, which for brevity's sake I will call postmodernist, have subjected it to a defamiliarizing transfiguration, refashioning its literary features, scrutinizing its politics, and redrawing its canon. Until the 1960s, critical discussions worked within the confines of what we might call the classical definition of naturalist writing. The latter was formulated with remarkable clarity in the 1920s by Vernon Parrington: naturalism, he writes, is "a pessimistic realism, with a philosophy that sets man in a mechanical world and conceives of him as victimized by that world" (325). For critics at the mid-twentieth century, Parrington's definition compellingly summarized the ambitions of novelists such as Stephen Crane, Hamlin Garland, Theodore Dreiser, Frank Norris, Jack London, or Upton Sinclair. The latter writers, these readers concurred, aimed to write novels capturing what Norris calls "the complications of life"

("Fiction" 51) in the uncompromising light of scientific doctrines aligning human beings with "the brute" (Norris, *Vandover* 213). This literary practice, modeled on that of French novelist Émile Zola, seemed apt to expose the social wrongs of the Gilded Age. The unappetizing realities of this era—the coexistence of extreme wealth and abject poverty—had, according to the champions of naturalism, been overlooked not only by upper- and middle-class readers favoring popular romances but even by realists such as William Dean Howells, whose humanistic earnestness was shackled by Victorian pieties (Kazin 33). By contrast, naturalism was portrayed as the scourge of puritanical censorship and of the politically corrupt "plutocracy" (Parrington 118). Small wonder that critics emulating Parrington—Alfred Kazin and Warner Berthoff, for instance—should have depicted it as an effective tool of socio-literary investigation, and that they should have located it within a political dynamic striving toward "liberalism and democracy" (Berthoff iii).

The postmodernist characterization of naturalism contradicts the classical definition in all respects. In June Howard's, Walter Benn Michaels's, Amy Kaplan's, Rachel Bowlby's, or Mark Seltzer's essays, naturalism no longer demystifies the hardships of urban capitalism: it glorifies the culture of consumerism. Instead of charitably expanding the scope of literary representation in order to include depictions of urban poverty, it portrays subaltern populations as subhuman, ethnically alien outcasts. Postmodernist scholars also object to the naturalist representation of women's condition. Politically naïve readers might believe that Dreiser's *Sister Carrie* (1900), London's *The Iron Heel* (1908), or David Graham Phillips's *Susan Lenox* (1917), which feature inventive and resilient heroines, are meant to chart paths of feminine empowerment. They would therefore credit American naturalism for emulating classics of nineteenth-century European fiction such as Gustave Flaubert's *Madame Bovary* (1857) or Henrik Ibsen's *Hedda Gabler* (1890), reputed to expose the alienation of upper- and middle-class women trapped in patriarchal marriages. Neo-Marxist or neo-historicist readers, on the contrary, contend that naturalism only exacerbates patriarchy: it condones the roles ascribed to women in the culture of consumerist commodification or deploys a social Darwinian discourse of male supremacy of unprecedented harshness. In postmodernist readings, the naturalist reworking of social Darwinian discourse betokens no genuine attempt to ponder the mysteries of sociobiological determinism: it serves instead as matrix for a discourse of gender and racial supremacy whose presence in the texts few previous critics had acknowledged. Predictably, this pessimistic assessment prevents postmodernist critics from portraying Crane and his peers as countercultural heroes. Previously praised as authors of "social novels" (Kazin 25), they now appear as professionals in an expanding editorial market, astutely devising new ways of acquiring cultural capital.

Above all, postmodernist criticism proves defamiliarizing because its reexamination of naturalist politics is grounded in poststructuralist theories contradicting deeply entrenched assumptions about the relation of text and world. Neo-Marxists and neo-historicists reject the reflectionist concept of realistic mimesis endorsed both by naturalist novelists and by their twentieth-century readership. In so doing, postmodernist criticism relinquishes the hope that novels may be effortlessly referential—that they may "get to the places where things are real," as Frank Norris puts it in his 1898 *Moran of the Lady Letty* (309). According to poststructuralist semiotics, texts never neutrally hold up the mirror to nature: they actively construct the social reality they claim to reproduce. Thus, naturalist novels, by virtue of the very signifying practices of the realist tradition, are bound to act as hypocritical tools for the perpetuation of power relations. Cloaked in the prestige of scientific objectivity, they construct fictional universes where ideology is disguised as reality itself.

This essay aims to clarify the stakes of the recent critical revision of naturalism and to determine how durably its shift in methodological practice and thematic focus has affected literary scholarship. There has, I believe, been no overall return to previous classical orthodoxies. Issues such as gender and race have gained a permanent standing in the critical landscape. Still, studies focusing on more traditional issues—determinism and the literary appropriation of science, notably— have been published throughout the neo-Marxist/neo-historicist refashioning of the field. Likewise, scholarship has kept developing in ways unrelated to postmodernist theory. The 1981 publication of the restored text of *Sister Carrie* indicated how classical scholarship still had the capacity to set the terms of the critical debate. Additionally, advances in literary historical research have brought into the circle of critical discussion ever more texts deserving inclusion into the naturalist corpus. These developments further the emergence of what we might call a postclassical definition of naturalism. The latter term is relevant to discussions of naturalism that integrate the critical input of postmodernism without reducing turn-of-the-twentieth-century texts to test cases for theoretical paradigms. Postclassical scholarship, unlike some essays of the 1980s and 1990s, handles naturalism as a genre with its specific history, thematics, and discursive features.

THE NEW NATURALIST ECONOMY

Admittedly, the paradigm shift triggered by postmodernist scholarship is depicted above in excessively contrasted terms: the classical definition of naturalism had already been redrawn before the 1980s. In the 1950s and 1960s, Charles Child Walcutt and Donald Pizer charted for naturalism a literary genealogy that shifted the genre away from realism: they emphasized the continuity linking Crane, Norris, and Dreiser to the canonically prestigious romance tradition of the American Renaissance (Walcutt 9–29; Pizer, "Frank Norris's Definition" 107–9). While this romance reading of naturalism is corroborated by the discursive features of the texts themselves, it also constituted a salvage operation justified by the context of the 1950s. On the one hand, it made naturalism palatable to post–World War II academics raised on the principles of the New Criticism and therefore supposedly averse to the documentary naïveté, pathos, and violence of Dreiser's generation. On the other, Pizer points out that linking naturalism to the romance tradition amounted to a gesture of political rehabilitation. The commitment of second-generation naturalists (John Steinbeck, Richard Wright, James T. Farrell, Michael Gold, etc.) to the proletarian politics of the 1930s had rendered the naturalist corpus unpalatable to post–World War II readers aware of Stalinist repression (Pizer, "Is American" 390). It was therefore essential to show that naturalism was not bound to a chapter in political history that readers were eager to leave behind and to proclaim that Crane, Norris, and Dreiser held a rightful place in the tradition of U.S. literary art. Still, compared to neo-Marxist and neo-historicist essays, Pizer's and Walcutt's rereading effects only a partial overhaul of the genre: naturalism, in Walcutt's terms, appears as a "divided stream" (Walcutt 17); its documentary dimension is not denied but rather is placed in interaction with romantic and idealist dimensions of the texts.

By the early 1980s, several essays were published indicating that Pizer's and Walcutt's reevaluation of naturalism would in later scholarship be complemented, even superseded, by a reexamination of the novels' mode of insertion in their historical context. Ronald E. Martin's *American Literature and the Universe of Force* (1981) initiated a new approach to the link between naturalism, social Darwinism, and Nietzscheism. Similarly, Richard Lehan, in a 1984 article, argued that the previous attention devoted to naturalist determinism should give way to readings of the texts as "social/historical/cultural" responses to a new stage of capitalism and empire (529). The major thematic and methodological break came, however, with the publication of Eric J. Sundquist's *American Realism: New Essays* (1982). This collection included contributions by Michaels, Seltzer, and Philip Fisher that transposed the reading practices of poststructuralism and postmodernism to Dreiser, Norris, and Henry James, thus anticipating similar critical efforts by Howard, Bowlby, and Kaplan.

The reevaluation of turn-of-the-twentieth-century fiction initiated by these critics marks a moment not only in the critical reception of naturalism but also in the history of postmodernist/poststructuralist theory. Up to the late 1970s, the label "postmodernism" had been relevant mostly to the post-1950s avant-garde (see Hassan, *Postmodern* 46–83). Likewise, French poststructuralist theorists focused on the modernist canon. Conversely, the formalist approaches that gave birth to (post) structuralism had handled realist/naturalist writing dismissively. In this context, Howard's, Michaels's, Seltzer's, Bowlby's, or Kaplan's essays had the appeal of innovative scholarship dragging an unmanageable object into a new theoretical perimeter.

The mixture of deconstruction and political scrutiny characterizing postmodernist scholarship was provocatively illustrated in the reassessment of naturalist attitudes toward capitalism and progressivism. The critics who undertook this critical endeavor contend that key naturalist texts—Dreiser's *Sister Carrie* and Norris's *McTeague* (1899) and *The Octopus* (1901)—not only fail to live up to their reputation as critiques of Gilded-Age capitalism but embody the logic of acquisitiveness in their textual mechanisms. In a landmark reading of *Sister Carrie*, Michaels contends that Dreiser's novel refrains from castigating desire—particularly the yearning after money and items that make up the spectacle of consumption. The open-ended drift of desire constitutes instead the novel's narrative driving force. Carrie starts out as a young woman fascinated by the promise of the big city and ends up a successful actress fantasizing over her further personal aggrandizement. In this, Michaels points out, Dreiser contradicts Howells's realist ethos. For Howells, realism implies the refusal of capitalist speculation, an ideal of economic scarcity, the debunking of sentimental fantasies, and the celebration of character anchored in the work-ethic tradition (Michaels 41). Admittedly, Dreiser pays lip service to this asceticism: in *Sister Carrie*, these values are voiced by Robert Ames, an electrical engineer Carrie admires (Michaels 41–42). Yet Ames's admonitions have no hold on the heroine's behavior, nor are they corroborated by the passages where the narrator expatiates on the opportunities of city life (Michaels 48). Bowlby elaborates on Michaels's argument by showing how deeply entangled Dreiser's writing practice is with the novelist's fascination for nascent consumerism. She shows for instance that *The "Genius"*—Dreiser's 1915 novel of artistic education—reads like a celebration of commercial art (Bowlby 128).

Seltzer reaches similar conclusions in his reading of Norris's *The Octopus*—the first installment of the California novelist's unfinished "The Epic of Wheat." He contends that, contrary to what earlier critics believed, the novel cannot be read as a pro-Populist anti-trust statement. While the text initially positions the reader on the side of California farmers struggling against the railroad trust, it eventually develops an economic vision that sanctions the inevitability of corporate expansion and voids of its substance any gesture of political opposition. Characters are puppets of the mystical power of the Wheat, which co-opts all other forms of human agency and fulfills the agenda of imperialist capitalism (Seltzer 44). Michaels's take on Norris is more nuanced than Seltzer's. The gold imagery of *McTeague*, Michaels indicates, reshuffles the antithetical standpoints of Populists and advocates of the gold standard without ever settling on one set of positions (176). *The Octopus*, in Michaels's reading, explores a philosophical issue that fascinated economists and jurists who witnessed the development of monopolies—whether corporations should be granted the status of persons. In this case, Michaels concludes that Norris's economic mysticism does settle the issue in favor of the monopoly.

In *Form and History in American Literary Naturalism* (1985), Howard explores the underside of naturalism's supposed complicity with turn-of-the-twentieth-century political conservatism. Her argument anchors naturalism's quasi-scientific discourse in attempts by the early twentieth-century middle classes to contain the supposed threat of the new immigrant working classes. Drawing upon Algirdas Julien Greimas's structuralist semantics, Howard reexamines classical discussions of naturalist determinism. She discerns in Dreiser, Norris, and London a common pattern of meaning that opposes, on the one hand, aspirations toward free will, manhood, and mastery, and, on the other, the behavior of beastlike brutes, unpredictably shuttling between violence and passivity (91). These elements form the matrix of naturalist narratives of instinctual and social decline—Hurstwood's path to suicide in *Sister Carrie* or the artistic and biological degeneration of the eponymous protagonist of Norris's *Vandover and the Brute* (1914). In Howard's reading, such stories express fears of proletarianization affecting middle-class authors in a period of mass immigration (95). In addition to registering these anxieties, naturalism sets up structures of management and control. In this light, naturalism's documentary strategies—the elaboration of a quasi-scientific apparatus of literary spectatorship—positions supposedly threatening members of the underclass in a subordinate position. This ideological apparatus, Howard argues, matches the reform agenda of Progressive-era reformers (136). The latter professed to embark on what historian Robert Wiebe calls a "search for order" (iii): the rational adaptation of U.S. society to urban-industrial conditions. Yet in Howard's view, the rise out of the late nineteenth-century social crisis allowed upper- and middle-class experts to exert their hegemony over lower-class subjects—a gesture anticipated in the scientifically validated fictions of naturalism (140).

EXCLUDED MARGINS: GENDER AND RACE

When reading postmodernist interpretations, one wonders how previous scholars could have blinded themselves to naturalism's capitalist and anti-proletarian proclivities. This hermeneutic chasm is due in the first place to a reconfiguration of the politics of literary studies, leading to a reevaluation of the interface between culture and politics. Most classical studies were written by left-wing liberal critics who did view political issues as relevant to fiction but who did not regard literary discourse as inherently constitutive of political practices (see Parrington 325, 351, 353; Kazin 291–92). For them, novels were able to reflect the class struggle, but they could not stage what Stuart Hall felicitously calls a "class struggle in language" itself (79). Postmodernist academics, on the contrary, were trained during the period of the civil rights movement, 1960s New-Left radicalism, and the resurgence of feminism. In this new context, culture and politics seemed nearly undistinguishable: all sign systems came to be regarded as arenas of political gestures. These critics therefore gained a hermeneutic perspective enabling them to discern within turn-of-the-twentieth-century literature elements that could not be viewed critically in the authors' own time. Conversely, they have sometimes ignored the issues that did fire up the naturalists' political enthusiasm—the struggle against moral and sexual censorship, or the empowerment achieved by writing about current socioeconomic conditions.

Second, one must reckon with changes in the understanding of how texts produce meaning. Classical interpretations have a secure sense of what realism and naturalism should be: they discard whole dimensions of the novels as literarily inappropriate. Kazin dismisses as "sentimental mysticism" the elements of Norris's novels that later critics will interpret as pro-monopoly (77). Likewise, Berthoff condemns Dreiser's "Trilogy of Desire" as flawed novels spreading a pseudo-Nietzschean pro-business "immoralism" (242). Postmodernist scholars, by comparison, handle the novels with a paradoxical mixture of deference and skeptical scrutiny. On the one hand, they cannot stoop to sort the naturalist grain from the sentimental chaff. On the other, they endorse deconstructionist guidelines that, to previous readers, tear the novels apart. Among the most general of these, one may mention the belief that texts are inherently self-contradictory; that these contradictions are ideologically symptomatic; that texts construct their meaning more often through latent discursive strategies than through overt thematic content; that such meaning is often constructed independently of the author's conscious decision; and that literary works are meaningful by virtue of their insertion within an intertextual field where they interact with non-literary texts. Neo-Marxist scholars such as Howard and Bowlby, while accepting these tenets, also presuppose that literary texts enact a semiotic struggle circumscribed within the terms of Marxist sociology: neo-Marxism, Fredric Jameson remarks, cannot ignore institutional frameworks such as the unequal hierarchy of labor and capital or the rise of monopoly capitalism and consumerism (35–37). By comparison, neo-historicist scholars such as Michaels assume that texts enact negotiations of power unconstrained by an axiomatic philosophy of history. Also, neo-historicists reject the belief that literature may be more perceptive to hidden social tensions than the non-literary signifying practices in which it is embedded (Veeser xi). Fiction, in this view, deploys semiotic mechanisms of the same type as, for instance, economic treatises or advertising copy.

Concretely, the politico-semiotic struggle waged by 1980s and 1990s critics manifests itself in their refusal to privilege what previous scholars regarded as naturalism's core elements—the thematics of determinism—over what was supposedly marginal or literarily irrelevant—gender and race. Overall, gender has arguably received the highest degree of attention in recent interpretations. Its analysis has been carried out along two main axes. First, critics have focused on what might be called the gendering of the naturalist economy—the representation of economic production and exchange as sexual processes. Second, they have analyzed the novels' elaboration of profiles of literary manhood. Michaels's reading of Dreiser's *The Financier* (1912) reveals what is at stake in the gendering of the economy. Dreiser's titular hero Frank Cowperwood, Michaels argues, associates his own marriage to the stability of the traditional economy of producers. His relation to his mistress, on the other hand, displays the fascinating unpredictability of financial speculation (65). As is his custom, Michaels shows that neither Dreiser's novel nor nonfiction texts of the period—Ida Tarbell's *History of the Standard Oil* (1904) or John D. Rockefeller's *Random Reminiscences of Men and Events* (1909)—manage to endorse these gender/economic poles consistently: they end up representing nature itself as a reproductive matrix whose behavior alternatively sanctions and castigates speculation (Michaels 83). Seltzer's discussion of power strategies in Norris follows similar lines. For him, naturalism's depiction of a social field where economic and gender energies morph into each other constitutes the very mechanism by which the texts negate the agency of oppositional subjects. The gendered economic field sets up a "flexible and totalizing machine of power" (Seltzer 44) that merges the public and the private,

economic structures and individuality, leaving no vantage point from which protest may express itself.

Scholars of the 1980s and 1990s have interpreted naturalism's gendered economy
as the literary expression of a far-reaching reconfiguration of gender relations—a
"crisis of masculinity" (Gammel 77) or a panic over "overcivilization" (Den Tandt,
"Amazons" 641; see also Lears 103–4). Historian Anthony Rotundo contends that
the late nineteenth century witnessed the passage from an entrepreneurial model of
masculinity anchored in the principles of the work ethic to more aggressive and
exuberant profiles extolling the "barbarism" of male passion (253). Recent readings
of naturalism suggest that this psychological shift responds both to specific changes
in gender relations—the rise of the New Woman, particularly—and to broad
economic shifts. To late nineteenth-century observers, writers included, the development of monopoly capitalism, speculation, consumerism, and the professionalization of middle-class careers seemed to threaten the foundations of masculinity.
These factors triggered fears that culture and the economy might become feminized, a threat against which new modes of behavior had to be devised. In a few
cases, the naturalist response to overcivilization looks forward to the gender eman-
cipation of modernism: Dreiser, Michaels indicates, relishes the labile intensities of
speculation, which his texts depict as feminine (64). He also occasionally champions androgyny as the proper profile for artists in the speculative field (see Den
Tandt, "Amazons" 659). Yet Dreiser's *Sister Carrie*, Irene Gammel contends, stirs the
more conservative echoes of the crisis of masculinity. The novel depicts an urban
economy where the heroine prospers by putting her body on display while her
lovers end up diminished or dead (Gammel 78). In London and Norris, the most
common response to the crisis of masculinity is the endorsement of the aggressive
stances mentioned by Rotundo. Kaplan, in a reading of late nineteenth-century historical romances, notices a motif that encapsulates the ambiguities of this masculine
game of one-upmanship—a gendered performance she calls the "spectacle of masculinity" ("Romancing" 665). Male characters, Kaplan indicates, are often called to
perform their exploits in front of female audiences—an anxiety-ridden configuration. The spectacle of masculinity makes visible both men's strenuous will to perform
and their anxiety of meeting with an indifferent audience response. Accordingly, it
captures the situation of weakened economic actors in a context whose instability is
perceived as unmanning.

The specific instance of the spectacle of masculinity that has retained the attention of many scholars of naturalism is the gendered construction of literary authorship. Such discussions begin with the analysis of the literary gesture by which
realism separated itself out from sentimental fiction. Alfred Habegger indicates
that, to Howells and the early James, endorsing realism represented a career choice
that helped them manage their presumed status as literary "sissies" (56). On the one
hand, Howells and James selected for their novels the subject matter of popular
mid-nineteenth-century sentimental domestic fiction—the thematic field of authors
whom Nathanael Hawthorne called "scribbling women" (qtd. in Pattee 110). On the
other, Howells and James depicted this feminine environment from a demystifying,

male-connoted point of view. The choice of realism as a manly literary genre, Habegger contends, was therefore meant to render acceptable a career choice—novel writing—that was regarded as improper for real men (62).

With the advent of naturalism, gender discourse veers toward plain masculinist bombast. For Frank Norris, Donna Campbell notes, the appropriation by male realists of the feminized discourse of domestic fiction only yields a literary idiom comparable to what Norris called "the drama of a broken teacup" (Norris, "Plea" 76)—a metaphor later taken up by Sinclair Lewis in his uncharitable characterization of Howells as "a pious old maid whose greatest delight was to have tea at the vicarage" (qtd. in Campbell, *Resisting* 5). Ironically, Michael Davitt Bell contends, this masculinist stance, far from generating a plainer documentary discourse, led to rhetorical flourishes egregiously illustrated in Norris's prose. With his uncompromising devotion to things that are "real" (Bell 118), Norris meant to stage "a revolt against style" (Bell 115)—that is, against the supposedly feminized realm of idealist aesthetics. Yet the novelist, as he switched from his early romances to naturalism, produced a fictional idiom that was "literary in the very worst sense of the term" (Bell 130): it constructed a "'reality' that is in fact a tissue of the very crudest fantasy" (Bell 130).

The naturalist paeans to what late nineteenth-century critic James Lane Allen calls the "Masculine Principle" (qtd. in Campbell, *Resisting* 60) gave rise to a literary game of self-definition and competitive positioning analyzed by Campbell, Christopher Wilson, and John Dudley. Naturalist writers, Campbell argues, wished to distance themselves from the predominantly feminine—and commercially successful—tradition of 1880s local color realists. These writers—Sarah Orne Jewett, Mary Wilkins Freeman, or Rose Terry Cooke—responded to post–Civil War urbanization and the correlative decline of small-town life by developing a literature emphasizing "continuity, community, reverence for the past, and . . . endurance" (Campbell, *Resisting* 8). By comparison, the naturalist choice to privilege the depiction of inarticulate characters in the urban scene appears as a gesture of masculine defiance.

Wilson analyzes the masculinization of authorship among writers who contributed to what he calls "popular naturalism" (xii)—London, Sinclair, Lincoln Steffens, and Phillips. These writers, he contends, charted a path between nonfiction, muckraking journalism, and politically committed novels. He shows that they viewed the male-connoted prerogative to investigate the public sphere as a guarantee of personal autonomy—a practice that allowed them to stake out their independence with regard to such institutional players as publishers and literary editors (197). Likewise, Dudley argues that "the masculinist discourse of the Progressive Era"—expressed notably in the competitive ideology of sports and the rhetoric of imperialism—is "an essential element in the formation of American literary naturalism (14). The latter genre, he argues, defined a hypermasculine profile of authorship whose legacy extends as far as Ernest Hemingway and Norman Mailer.

Though scholars of naturalism condemn the novels' gender discourse, they often emphasize its complexity and inventiveness. The naturalist representation of race seems crude, by comparison. In the demystifying perspective of neo-Marxism and neo-historicism, naturalism duplicates the stereotypes of nativist politics and social Darwinian pseudo-science. In a landmark reading of Howells's *A Hazard of New Fortunes* (1890), Kaplan sketches out the genealogy of this racial discourse. She points out how late nineteenth-century texts articulate racial otherness with regard to modes of perception of the new urban sphere. The main characters of *Hazard*, Basil March and his wife Isabel, are genteel Bostonians transplanted to New York. In their approach to the immigrant metropolis, Kaplan shows, they adopt a strategy of domestication: they test whether the new environment is compatible with upper-middle-class family values, and thus, in terms of literary discourse, whether it lends itself to the gaze of domestic realism (*Social* 48). The Marches' efforts as amateur sociologists achieve mixed results. On the one hand, they perceive immigrant neighborhoods as a picturesque showcase of human diversity—a spectacle that serves as the object of Basil's illustrated journalistic sketches. On the other, when viewing the slums from the safe remove of an elevated train window, the Marches see the multicultural metropolis dissolve into a threatening blur (Kaplan, *Social* 52).

One might have expected naturalist authors, who pride themselves on their ability to provide literary snapshots of slum life, to help dispel the sense of befuddlement experienced by Howellsian observers. Neo-Marxist and neo-historicist criticism suggests, however, that this is seldom the case. While Howells inscribes boundaries of class and race by reducing otherness to picturesque local color or by giving voice to the social panic of middle-class characters, Norris and London transfigure race and ethnicity into the gothic features of what Howard calls the naturalist brute (78). The proletarian monster that stands at the heart of naturalist sociology is indeed not only a class fiend but also an ethnic Other (Howard 85)—an "exotic immigrant," as James R. Giles puts it in a discussion of naturalist city novels (30). Fashioned by the clichés of scientific hereditarianism and social Darwinism, the frightening figure appears as an atavistic threat—a throwback to the Stone Age (Howard 101). Thus, Howard contends, naturalist novels reveal aliens in full close-up yet also as abstract threats: the racial discourse they elaborate is not ethnically specific. Similarly, Kenneth Warren writes that "brute forces rule" (13) in the fiction of Dreiser and Norris, so that institutions, including those that perpetuate racism, "seem merely to glance off the individuals they touch, hardly changing their trajectories" (Warren 13). Even authors such as London and Norris, who explicitly develop nativist and white-supremacist rhetoric, use otherness as a generic threat—a metaphorical condensation for the perils of the city's destabilizing economy. The multi-ethnic San Francisco cast of Norris's *McTeague*, the Lithuanian immigrants of Upton Sinclair's *The Jungle* (1906), the Portuguese-born California farmers in London's *The Valley of the Moon* (1913), or even the Chinese immigrants Jacob Riis observes in downtown New York in his 1890 *How the Other Half Lives* (78–80) share the overall strangeness of this unfamiliar environment respectively as slum denizens, exploitable labor force, practitioners of speculative methods of scientific agriculture, or suspects in criminal traffics (see Den Tandt, *Urban* 138–50). Never is ethnicity viewed in the determinate sense noticeable in later writers influenced by the politics of identity, where difference implies specific traditions and history.

FROM A DIALOGICAL TO A POSTCLASSICAL DEFINITION OF NATURALISM

Neo-Marxist and neo-historicist naturalism scholarship relies on a conception of the dynamics of culture shaped by the postmodernist/poststructuralist concepts of intertextuality and dialogism. These terms, elaborated by Mikhail Bahktin, Julia Kristeva, and Roland Barthes, imply that the meaning of literary works and genres is constructed by virtue of their interaction with all signifying processes: texts build their meaning, not by their relation to the extra-linguistic world, as realist episte- mologies imply, but by virtue of their position on a cultural chessboard. Dialogism requires therefore that texts be interpreted as sites of connectedness—interwoven strands in what Roland Barthes calls "a fabric of voices" (27).

Dialogism has triggered many critical breakthroughs. It has made it easier for critics to investigate the historical processes that render meaningful the often-noted heterogeneity of naturalism—its hesitation between realism and sentimentalism, documentary objectivity and the gothic. In a dialogical perspective, what Sara Britton Goodling calls naturalism's "silent partnership" with sentimentalism, romance, or symbolism ceases to be a parasitical feature or, conversely, a felicitous literary histor- ical coincidence (1). Georg Lukács's argument castigating Zola's naturalism for resort- ing to symbolist metaphors becomes groundless ("Narrate" 131). Nor is it necessary to contend, as Walcutt does, that American naturalism's capacity to merge scientific realism and romance is "an exercise of creative intelligence" (29). Instead, the two phenomena appear as direct offshoots of the dialogical configuration of turn-of-the- twentieth-century literary field. Second, dialogism—voiced as the neo-historicist precept that "literary and non-literary 'texts' circulate inseparably" (Veeser xi)— underlies the 1980s and 1990s reexamination of the anchorage of naturalism in turn- of-the-twentieth-century popular culture, politics, and economic discourse. Without endorsing dialogism, it would have been difficult for Habegger, Kaplan, Bell, Wilson, and Campbell to understand the role of naturalism as a vehicle of literary masculin- ity, ostensibly opposed, yet in fact deeply linked to late nineteenth-century feminine culture. Similarly, Michaels's, Kaplan's, Bowlby's, and Howard's essays, which take for granted that naturalist novels unfold on the same cultural plane as treatises in eco- nomics or the social sciences, would lack a proper theoretical grounding.

The dialogical model raises, however, almost impassable difficulties regarding the very definition of naturalism. In a poststructuralist perspective, intertextuality precludes genre definition since the tangle of cultural interactions it takes into con- sideration is too fluid to accommodate presumably stable constellations of texts: genres have no legitimacy in a field where literary works themselves have no fixed outline (see Howard 7–10). Michaels's *Gold Standard* offers the most symptomatic instance of this dialogical blurring. In this essay, naturalist novels interact with obscure economic tracts such as William H. Harvey's *Coin's Financial School* (1894) or Thomas Nast's 1876 *Robinson Crusoe's Money* (145–46). *The Gold Standard* even traces intertextual links between, on the one hand, Howells's, Norris's, and Dreiser's works and, on the other, the seemingly remote aesthetic issues of late nineteenth-century *trompe l'oeil* painting and 1950s abstract expressionism (Michaels 163). Michaels's Foucaultian premises justify the interfacing of such scattered cultural practices. Power, according to Michaels, is constructed by a discursive apparatus cutting across texts and genres, with only a limited regard for a landscape of recognizable institutions. A consistent definition of naturalism has no purchase in this economy of power.

In spite of their belief in the dissemination of cultural processes, postmodernist essays do yield two tentative yet important conceptualizations of what the term "naturalism" designates. On the one hand, naturalism is depicted not only as a proper target for deconstruction, but, because of its inscription in a heterogeneous dialogical network, as a proto-deconstructionist writing practice itself. Naturalism, in this view, feigns to endorse but in fact subverts the assumptions of realism. This argument has been developed most explicitly by David Baguley, who contends that naturalism's obsession with thematics of social entropy—"heredity, illness, [and] sexuality" (208)—precipitates a breach of realist narrative codes. In this, Baguley echoes several essays of the 1980s. Kaplan argues that Howells's and Dreiser's novels expose "the way in which the terms of the realistic debate have become polarized rather than resolved," and that they accordingly stage "a debate with conflicting definitions of reality" (Kaplan, *Social* 160). Michaels's *Gold Standard* contrasts the rigidities of Howellsian realism with the semiotic instability of naturalism. Likewise, "The Naturalist Machine" depicted by Seltzer is a discursive apparatus that, in deconstructionist fashion, erases binary oppositions. Later essays develop the naturalism-as-deconstruction thesis from other theoretical or thematic angles. Lee Clark Mitchell contends that the often-derided inarticulateness and repetitiousness of naturalist prose enact the erasure of the self under the pressure of determinism and mock any attempt to reconstruct causal chains compatible with the theories of free will endorsed by realist writers (x–xi). William Dow describes Rebecca Harding Davis's, Crane's, and Norris's works as performative texts that do not "define the world" (25) but stage "the appearance of something that cannot become manifest or completed" (34). Patrick Brady discerns in naturalist texts a dynamic to which only chaos theory can render justice, making Zola's tradition a stepping stone toward postmodernism (90).

On the other hand, postmodernist critics depict naturalism in terms that paradoxically hearken toward classical historicism: they suggest, in an apparent breach of postmodernist orthodoxy, that the fiction of Crane, Norris, and Dreiser might express what Jameson calls the "unified inner truth" of a historicist moment (27). Postmodernist essays indeed portray naturalism as an economic episteme—a political and economic field structured by specific semiotic mechanisms. Crane's, Norris's and

Dreiser's fiction, in this view, enact the signifying logic of urban-based, corporate, consumerist capitalism—the system that took hold in the United States after the Civil War
or the Haymarket riots. Michaels makes this point by suggesting that the key debate
staged in naturalism concerns "representation" (158), namely the belief in the validity,
both in the cultural and the economic fields, of conventional, as opposed to natural,
signs. Realists, in this logic, are in implicit agreement with gold-standard advocates
because they contend that the value of art (or money) is not conventional but is instead
anchored in nature (Michaels 145): in the same way as realist art aims to be mistaken
for nature, gold is "money itself" (Michaels 159). Naturalists, on the contrary, admit of
the possibility that "anything can be money" (Michaels 159), or, in cultural terms, that
art is not consubstantial with its purported object. Likewise, Howard's discussion of
the naturalist brute is semiotically based: it reveals that a binary opposition of determinism and free will underlies the naturalist characterization of proletarian brutes,
upper-middle-class experts, and scientifically informed novelists. Ironically, while the
very notion of a consumerist episteme gestures toward postmodernist arguments by
Michel Foucault and Jean Baudrillard, it is also compatible with Lukács's orthodox
Marxist claim that Zola's fiction marks the early stage of modernist "anti-realism" and
is as such complicit in the deployment of capitalist reification (Lukács, *Meaning* 17; see
also Lukács, "Narrate" 132). Still, 1980s arguments avoid reverting to Lukács's historicism by identifying an unstable signifying practice as the core of naturalist writing. In
this fashion, naturalism can still be viewed as a contested signifying field, not as a
homogeneous moment in the deployment of the spirit of history.

Intriguingly, the two postmodernist characterizations of naturalism—as proto-
deconstruction or as the episteme of consumerism—make it more difficult to regard
Crane's or Dreiser's fiction as the literary practice against which modernism defined
itself: naturalism, in the 1980s account, seems more semiotically inventive than champions of modernism traditionally acknowledge (see Bradbury and McFarlane 25).
Still, merely absorbing naturalism into (post)modernism is counterproductive: there
are contexts in which critics need criteria enabling them to distinguish, say, Norris's
McTeague from Jean Toomer's *Cane* (1923) and Gertrude Stein's *Ida: A Novel* (1941).
For instance, canon expansion—one of the chief concerns of recent scholarship—
requires finer generic distinctions than what the broad (neo)-historicist portrayal of
naturalism affords. The evolution of literary studies toward feminism and multicul-
turalism, but also the intrinsic dynamic of scholarly research, has indeed led critics of
naturalism to examine how the corpus of turn-of-the-twentieth-century fiction could
be broadened to include authors previously sidelined on account of their ethnic and
gender profile or because of the lower status of their literary practice in the hierarchy
of cultural capital. Campbell, we noted above, investigates the interaction of naturalism with the fiction of local colorists. Goodling points out the naturalist dimension
of authors—Rebecca Harding Davis and Elizabeth Stuart Phelps—previously
regarded as sentimentalists (2). Elizabeth Ammons positions within the field of
realism and naturalism non-white women writers such as Zitkala-Ša (Gertrude
Simmons Bonnin), Pauline Hopkins, and Sui Sin Far (97). Bernard Bell and Nancy
Von Rosk analyze the realist and naturalist credentials of African American authors

such as Charles Waddell Chesnutt, Paul Lawrence Dunbar, James Weldon Johnson, and W. E. B. Du Bois (Bell 79; Von Rosk 144–45). Peter J. Conn has attracted critical attention to writers of the pre–World War I decade such as muckraker David Graham Phillips, socialists Charlotte Teller, Arthur Bullard, and Ernest Poole, as well as anti-socialist polemicist David Perry (83–118).

In keeping with the principles of dialogism, few of the above-mentioned studies—except, perhaps, Campbell's vindication of Phillips's *Susan Lenox* (see Campbell, "Bitter Taste" 238)—claim to unearth neglected masterpieces of unadulterated naturalism. Instead, canon revisers endorse Thomas O. Beebee's view that a text's meaning is not contained "in any specific genre category, . . . but rather in the play of differences between its genres" (249–50). Accordingly, they position minority or lesser known authors with regard to the main landmarks of turn-of-the-twentieth-century fiction—sentimentalism, local color, realism, naturalism, emergent modernism—and determine how each text integrates these discourses in varying degrees of dominance. Inspiring research has been accomplished along those lines. Ammons, in her plea for the "multicultural construction of American realism" (105) indicates that, in the late nineteenth-century field, "William Dean Howells's prescriptions for realists" (103) competed with Chesnutt's and Zitkala-Ša's radically different visions of the real. In a complementary perspective, Warren argues that Chesnutt, whose politics aimed at "African American liberation" (13), privileged the realism of James and Howells over Dreiser's and Norris's naturalism, because the former idiom entertains "the belief that . . . properly functioning social institutions possess the potential to shape or reform the individual" (13). Conversely, Bernard W. Bell and Von Rosk evaluate how naturalism proved both an asset and a liability for Dunbar, Johnson, and Du Bois. On the one hand, it opens up the literary text to social and political arguments tuned to the realities of black urban America. On the other, it follows a model of psychological determinism that condemns characters to perdition or the isolation of "a white culture that privileges the individual" (Von Rosk 166).

Still, even an approach presupposing that texts are inherently multivocal must identify the strands out of which textual fabrics are woven: the landmarks that structure the cultural field not only need to be located but also scanned and tagged. Dialogical discussions of naturalism may therefore ultimately not elude genre definition. The task involved therein requires in the first place vindicating the possibility of realism itself—the term to which naturalism is always more or less closely linked. Second, it entails charting a conceptually valid boundary between these interlocked literary practices. I noted above that some recent scholarship takes on this unpopular assignment: it gestures toward the elaboration of a postclassical definition of naturalism integrating postmodernist concerns without losing track of naturalism's periodization and specific thematics.

Within postmodernism itself, the possibility of realism has been reexamined by critics dissatisfied with the persistently anti-referential drift of their own theoretical field. Lacanian literary theoretician Catherine Belsey stigmatizes the "culturalist insouciance" (10) of radical constructivists who fail to distinguish between "what exists" (the real) and "what we know" (culture, texts; 12). Likewise, pioneer critic of postmodernism Ihab Hassan contends that realism may be reclaimed in the name of an attitude of pragmatically based "cognitive trust" rejecting "falsity and pretence" ("Beyond" 206, 208). Hassan's allusion to trust-based cognition reads like an endorsement, if not of naturalism, at least of classical realism—the idiom of Jane Austen and Howells. Kaplan argues indeed that Howellsian realism, derived from domestic fiction, focuses on "knowable communities" (47)—a term used by sociologist of culture Raymond Williams in order to designate human groups bound by "mutual social recognition" (Kaplan, *Social* 47). Similarly, Brook Thomas describes realism as based on "the promise of contract" (11)—the commitment that truth can be sustained by immanent social bonds. Howellsian realism, in this view, is the literary idiom that renders an account of a familiar social perimeter. Even though realist texts are expected to deliver demystifying reports of such knowable worlds, their claims are ultimately validated by the communicational trust binding the community's members. Thus defined, Pam Morris remarks, realism finds its epistemological validation in the concepts of "interpretive charity" developed by American philosopher Donald Davidson (147) and in the practice of communicative action delineated by German philosopher Jürgen Habermas (149–51).

Scholarship old and new reveals, however, that naturalism focuses precisely on objects that challenge cognitive trust. Crane's *Maggie* (1893), Norris's *McTeague*, and Dreiser's *Sister Carrie* differ from Howells's *A Modern Instance* (1882) or Jewett's *The Country of the Pointed Firs* (1896) because they peer beyond the perimeter within which the dominant forms of communicative action are acted out—indeed beyond the round of life of upper- and middle-class readers and writers. Naturalist texts shine their literary light into the slums (however confusedly), on the mystifying corporate economy, and on the alienated deterministic self. In so doing, they produce, to use an often-quoted formula from Norris's criticism, a picture of life "twisted from the ordinary" (Norris, "Zola" 72), slipping into hyperbole, excess, the gothic, or sentimentality. Thus, as we shift from Howells to Crane, Norris, and Dreiser, realist trust-based cognition gives way to the deconstruction of realism discussed above. The grotesque or hyperbolic accents through which the novels' pessimistic thematics are conveyed reveal that the texts enact a crisis of cognitive skepticism. Their seemingly parasitical multivocalism and their somber thematics are the residue of a failed attempt to grasp a segment of the social field broader than the commonsense perimeter of realist writing (see Den Tandt, *Urban* 27–31).

Admittedly, defining naturalism by reference to its breach of realist cognitive trust leads us back to the naturalism-as-deconstruction thesis, blurring the line between naturalism and modernism. I suggested above that this boundary cannot merely be erased. Postclassical definitions of the genre should acknowledge both the continuity of realism and naturalism—the effort to anchor characters in their social background; the refusal of moral idealism and supernaturalist epistemologies—as well as naturalism's refusal of key modernist tenets such as the pursuit of formal consistency for its own sake. A few recent critical contributions propose an inventive remapping of nineteenth- and twentieth-century literature that achieves this difficult balance. These arguments propose what we might call transhistorical or "long" (that is, chronologically extended) definitions of realism and naturalism. Classical scholarship did take into account late nineteenth- and twentieth-century developments of naturalism, defining the 1890s and the 1930s as the primary and secondary peaks of the genre (see Parrington; Kazin 291–93; Pizer, *Twentieth*). Recent essays broaden the scope even further. In the field of French literature, Jacques Dubois's study of "the novelists of the real" includes not only early nineteenth-century realists such as Stendhal and Balzac but also naturalist Zola, modernist Marcel Proust, and mid-twentieth-century existentialist crime-fiction writer George Simenon (11). Likewise, in American literature, Goodling and Dow contend that Davis's "Life in the Iron Mills" constitutes an instance of naturalism published before Zola gave the movement its name (Goodling 2; Dow 25). Conversely, Pizer suggests that turn-of-the-twenty-first-century authors such as Raymond Carver, Paul Auster, and Don DeLillo, in spite of their ostensible anchorage in postmodernism, prolong naturalism: they presuppose that human beings are "not only inseparable from the material, social, and intellectual world in which [they] live but [are] deeply and often irrevocably limited in [their] actions and beliefs by that world" ("Is American" 391). Other critics—such as Lana A. Whited and James Naremore—highlight the naturalistic features of popular genres—true crime (see Whited 324) or hard-boiled detective fiction (see Naremore 50–54).

For this "long" definition to be workable, one needs to define how naturalism interlocks with (post)modernism without relinquishing its function as socially referential literature. Recent reevaluations of the scientific relevance of naturalism indicate how the first half of these preconditions may be fulfilled. Philip Gerber, Lee Clark Mitchell, Patrick Brady, and Mohamed Zayani suggest that even texts enacting a cognitive crisis may fit Zola's ideal of the experimental novel. These new pleas for a scientifically informed naturalism are based, first, on the acknowledgment of the historicity of scientific theories. Deterministic approaches have changed in the course of a century, so that, Gerber contends, contemporary naturalist fiction might develop on a new scientific basis (380–83). Second, Zayani and Mitchell argue that scientific reason is not necessarily oriented toward closure, monovocalism, and the absence of discursive self-reflexiveness. Twentieth-century science, Zayani points out, studies "the changing relation between order and disorder" (Zayani 349; see also Mitchell xiv–xvi). Chaos theory, which has attracted the attention of postmodernist theorists such as Jean-François Lyotard, is in Zayani's view a proper model for naturalist texts that not only reproduce but renew the reader's concept of what is real (363).

Second, in order to establish naturalism's capacity to offer what London calls "a new and awful revelation of life" (49), the genre's "long" definition requires what might be called a referential contract, binding writers, readers, and critics. Literary works indeed do not acquire the prerogative to map the social world on the basis of intrinsic discursive features alone. Texts claiming to designate the real are empowered by a social pact established through writers' discussions of their own practice (one thinks of Howells's or Norris's criticism), readers' feedback, and reviews—indeed through all ideological debates about "conflicting definitions of reality" (Kaplan, *Social* 160). In classical realism, this contract is often tacitly established by the text's capacity to mimic the procedures ensuring cognitive trust in everyday situations: they form the basis of what Ian Watt calls the novel's "formal realism," its principles of verisimilitude (35). However, the corpus covered by naturalism's "long" definition, since it is not restricted to works offering a "mimetic" mapping of society (Zayani 363), needs a more explicitly stated contract, relying on less conventional characterizations of the genre—those developed in Pizer's and Zayani's recent essays in the volume edited by Papke, for instance. Still, these critical redefinitions would miss their target if they generated a "long" definition encompassing the whole twentieth-century literary field. André Breton's statement praising surrealism's capacity to reach "absolute reality" (qtd. in Kolocotroni 308) is unlikely to fulfill naturalism's contractual requirements, for instance. It could hypothetically do so only if it were validated by dialogical communicative action, thus by a socially mediated process that cannot be imposed by individual decree, be it a writer's or a critic's.

The postclassical definition adumbrated above admittedly remains within the bounds of postmodernism. It retains from neo-Marxism and neo-historicism the acknowledgment that naturalism, even in its early manifestations, displays deconstructive, metadiscursive dimensions. Yet it places this insight within an approach that does justice to the genre's historical continuity and to its efforts at sociological mapping. Pizer's comments on Auster and DeLillo corroborate this interpretation ("Is American"). His reading ascertains what I called above the referential contract of postmodern novels—their ability to address the situation of characters within contemporary history and culture. Conversely, Zayani's and Brady's arguments imply that the metafictional strategies developed by the two turn-of-the-twenty-first-century novelists—their reflections on writing or their performative deconstruction of authorship—also add to their novels' naturalist credentials. These experimental elements, supposedly the hallmark of postmodernism, can indeed be interpreted as functional equivalents of the gothic or sentimental slippages of classic naturalism, since both sets of devices mark out—implicitly in one case, explicitly in the other—the text's cognitive limits, its difficulties in charting its environment. In this light, Parrington's 1920s definition is amended, not abolished. Naturalism appears as a pessimistic form of meta-realism. It includes past and present novels that capture the actions of individuals under the constraints both of nature and culture, and that do so, contrary to other varieties of realism, within a pessimistic vision motivated not only by the nature of their object but also by the awareness of the incompleteness and diversity of the strategies of representation required for the task.

WORKS CITED

Ammons, Elizabeth. "Expanding the Canon of American Realism." *The Cambridge Companion to American Realism and Naturalism: Howells to London.* Ed. Donald Pizer. Cambridge: Cambridge University Press, 1995. 95–114.

Baguley, David. *Naturalist Fiction: The Entropic Vision*. Cambridge: Cambridge University Press, 1990.

Barthes, Roland. *S/Z*. Paris: Seuil, 1970.

Beebee, Thomas O. *The Ideology of Genre: A Comparative Study of Generic Instability*. University Park: Pennsylvania State University Press, 1994.

Bell, Bernard W. *The Afro-American Novel and Its Tradition*. Amherst: University of Massachusetts Press, 1989.

Bell, Michael Davitt. *The Problem of American Realism: Studies in the Cultural History of a Literary Idea*. Chicago: University of Chicago Press, 1993.

Belsey, Catherine. *Culture and the Real: Theorizing Cultural Criticism*. Milton Park, U.K.: Routledge-Taylor and Francis, 2005.

Berthoff, Warner. *The Ferment of Realism: American Literature 1884–1919*. New York: Free Press, 1965.

Bowlby, Rachel. *Just Looking: Consumer Culture in Dreiser, Gissing, and Zola*. New York: Methuen, 1985.

Bradbury, Malcolm, and James McFarlane. "The Name and Nature of Modernism." *Modernism, 1890–1930*. Eds. Malcolm Bradbury and James McFarlane. Harmondsworth, U.K.: Penguin, 1976. 19–55.

Brady, Patrick. "La théorie du chaos et le texte naturaliste." *Les cahiers naturalistes* 65 (1992): 89–103.

Campbell, Donna M. "The 'Bitter Taste' of Naturalism: Edith Wharton's *The House of Mirth* and David Graham Phillips's *Susan Lenox*." Papke 237–59.

———. *Resisting Regionalism: Gender and Naturalism in American Fiction, 1885–1915*. Athens: Ohio University Press, 1997.

Conn, Peter J. *The Divided Mind: Ideology and Imagination in America, 1898–1917*. Cambridge: Cambridge University Press, 1983.

Den Tandt, Christophe. "Amazons and Androgynes: Overcivilization and the Redefinition of Gender Roles at the Turn of the Century." *American Literary History* 8 (1996): 639–64.

———. *The Urban Sublime in American Literary Naturalism*. Urbana and Chicago: University of Illinois Press, 1998.

Dow, William. "Performative Passages: Davis's *Life in the Iron Mills*, Crane's *Maggie*, and Norris's *McTeague*." Papke 23–44.

Dubois, Jacques. *Les romanciers du réel: De Balzac à Simenon*. Paris: Seuil, 2000.

Dudley, John. *A Man's Game: Masculinity and the Anti-Aesthetics of American Literary Naturalism*. Tuscaloosa: University of Alabama Press, 2004.

Gammel, Irene. *Sexualizing Power in Naturalism: Theodore Dreiser and Frederic Philip Grove*. Calgary: University of Calgary Press, 1994.

Gerber, Philip. "Whither Naturalism?" Papke 367–89.

Giles, James R. *The Naturalistic Inner-City Novel in America: Encounters with the Fat Man*. Columbia: University of South Carolina Press, 1995.

Goodling, Sarah Britton. "The Silent Partnership: Naturalism and Sentimentalism in the Novels of Rebecca Harding Davis and Elizabeth Stuart Phelps." Papke 1–22.

Habegger, Alfred. *Gender, Fantasy, and Realism in American Literature*. New York: Columbia University Press, 1982.

Hall, Stuart. "'The Rediscovery of 'Ideology': Return of the Repressed in Media Studies." *Culture, Society and the Media*. Ed. Michael Gurevitch. New York: Methuen, 1982. 56–57.

Hassan, Ihab. "Beyond Postmodernism: Toward an Aesthetic of Trust." *Beyond Postmodernism: Reassessments in Literature, Theory, and Culture*. Ed. Klaus Stierstorfer. Berlin: De Gruyter, 2003. 199–212.

———. *The Postmodern Turn: Essays in Postmodern Theory and Culture.* Columbus: Ohio State University Press, 1987

Howard, June. *Form and History in American Literary Naturalism.* Chapel Hill: University of North Carolina Press, 1985.

Jameson, Fredric. *The Political Unconscious: Narrative as a Socially Symbolic Act.* Ithaca: Cornell University Press, 1981.

Kaplan, Amy. "Romancing the Empire: The Embodiment of American Masculinity in the Popular Historical Novel of the 1890s." *American Literary History* 2 (1990): 659–90.

———. *The Social Construction of American Realism.* Chicago: University of Chicago Press, 1988.

Kazin, Alfred. *On Native Grounds: An Interpretation of American Prose Literature.* 1942. New York: Reynal & Hitchcock, 1956.

Kolocotroni, Vassiliki, Jane Goldman, and Olga Taxidou, eds. *Modernism: An Anthology of Sources and Documents.* Edinburgh: Edinburgh University Press, 1998.

Lears, T. J. Jackson. *No Place of Grace: Antimodernism and the Transformations of American Culture 1880–1920.* New York: Pantheon, 1981.

Lehan, Richard. "American Literary Naturalism: The French Connection." *Nineteenth-Century Fiction* 38 (1984): 529–57.

London, Jack. *The Iron Heel.* 1908. Ed. Jonathan Auerbach and Jordan Schugar. New York: Penguin, 2006.

Lukács, Georg. *The Meaning of Contemporary Realism.* London: Merlin, 1963.

———. "Narrate or Describe." *Writer and Critic and Other Essays.* New York: Grosset & Dunlap, 1970. 110–48.

Martin, Ronald E. *American Literature and the Universe of Force.* Durham: Duke University Press, 1981.

Michaels, Walter Benn. *The Gold Standard and the Logic of Naturalism: American Literature at the Turn of the Century.* Berkeley and Los Angeles: University of California Press, 1987.

Mitchell, Lee Clark. *Determined Fictions: American Literary Naturalism.* New York: Columbia, 1989.

Morris, Pam. *Realism.* London: Routledge, 2003.

Naremore, James. *More Than Night: Film Noir in Its Contexts.* Berkeley and Los Angeles: University of California Press, 1998.

Norris, Frank. "Fiction is Selection." Norris, *Literary Criticism* 50–53.

———. *The Literary Criticism of Frank Norris.* Ed. Donald Pizer. Austin: University of Texas Press, 1964.

———. *Moran of the Lady Letty.* 1898. *The Complete Works of Frank Norris.* Vol. 3. Garden City, N.Y.: Doubleday, 1928. 176–326.

———. "A Plea for Romantic Fiction." Norris, *Literary Criticism* 5–78.

———. *Vandover and the Brute.* 1914. Lincoln: University of Nebraska Press, 1978.

———. "Zola as a Romantic Writer." Norris, *Literary Criticism* 71–72.

Papke, Mary E., ed. *Twisted from the Ordinary: Essays on American Literary Naturalism.* Knoxville: University of Tennessee Press, 2003.

Parrington, Vernon Louis. *The Beginnings of Critical Realism in America, 1860–1920.* New York: Harcourt, Brace, 1930.

Pattee, Fred L. *The Feminine Fifties.* New York: Appleton-Century, 1940.

Pizer, Donald. "Frank Norris's Definition of Naturalism." *Realism and Naturalism in Nineteenth-Century American Literature.* Rev. ed. Carbondale: Southern Illinois University Press, 1984. 107–11.

———. "Is American Literary Naturalism Dead? A Further Inquiry." Papke 390–404.

———. *Twentieth-Century American Literary Naturalism: An Interpretation*. Carbondale: Southern Illinois University Press, 1982.

Riis, Jacob A. *How the Other Half Lives: Studies Among the Tenements of New York*. 1890. New York: Dover, 1971.

Rotundo, E. Anthony. *American Manhood: Transformations of Masculinity from the Revolution to the Modern Era*. New York: Basic/HarperCollins, 1993.

Seltzer, Mark. "The Naturalist Machine." *Bodies and Machines*. New York: Routledge, 1992. 25–44.

Sundquist, Eric J., ed. *American Realism: New Essays*. Baltimore: Johns Hopkins University Press, 1982.

Thomas, Brook. *American Realism and the Failed Promise of Contract*. Berkeley and Los Angeles: University of California Press, 1997.

Veeser, H. Aram. Introduction. *The New Historicism*. Ed. H. Aram Veeser. New York: Routledge, 1989. ix–xxvi.

Von Rosk, Nancy. "Coon Shows, Ragtime, and the Blues: Race, Urban Culture, and the Naturalist Vision in Paul Laurence Dunbar's *The Sport of the Gods*." Papke 144–68.

Walcutt, Charles Child. *American Literary Naturalism: A Divided Stream*. Minneapolis: University of Minnesota Press, 1956.

Warren, Kenneth. *Black and White Strangers: Race and American Literary Naturalism*. Chicago: University of Chicago Press, 1993.

Watt, Ian. *The Rise of the Novel: Studies in Defoe, Richardson and Fielding*. Harmondsworth, U.K.: Penguin, 1983.

Whited, Lana A. "Naturalism's Middle Ages. The Evolution of the American True Crime Novel." Papke 323–43.

Wiebe, Robert. *The Search for Order: 1977–1920*. New York: Hill & Wang, 1967.

Wilson, Christopher P. *The Labor of Words: Literary Professionalism in the Progressive Era*. Athens: University of Georgia Press, 1985.

Zayani, Mohamed. "From Determinism to Indeterminacy: Chaos Theory, Systems Theory, and the Discourse of Naturalism." Papke 390–404.

PART VI

NATURALISM AND THE OTHER ARTS

CHAPTER 25

SAD ENDINGS AND NEGATIVE HEROES: THE NATURALIST TRADITION IN AMERICAN DRAMA

ROBERT M. DOWLING

In December 1905, Clyde William Fitch, at the time America's most famous living dramatist, knocked at the front door of 884 Park Avenue, Edith Wharton's New York residence. Wharton's first bestseller *The House of Mirth* (1905) had just appeared, and Fitch, a flamboyant and prolific playwright rumored to have enjoyed "relations" with Oscar Wilde in the early 1890s, asked if he might persuade her to collaborate on a stage adaptation of her new novel. She accepted the offer, if with a good deal of reservation. Wharton had previously tried to win over theatergoers with original plays, but she could never descend low enough for the average audience and rebuffed her friend Walter Berry's advice that if she wanted a hit play, she should consider the century-old costumes and "society gags" that ensured one (Lee 181). Numerous fiction writers before her had tried their hand on the boards from the 1880s to the early 1900s—Henry James, William Dean Howells, Mark Twain, Bret Harte, Mary Wilkins Freeman, Hamlin Garland, Mary Austin, Hjalmar Hjorth Boyesen, and Jack London, among others—none of them successfully. "Forget not," James ridiculed the profession of playwrighting, "that you write for the stupid" (qtd. in Murphy 58).

Departing the Savoy Theater after the New York premiere of Fitch's *The House of Mirth* on 22 October 1906, Wharton remarked to her escort William Dean Howells, "What the American public always wants is a tragedy with a happy ending."

"I now doubt if that kind of play," she admitted after several poor reviews, "with a 'sad ending,' and a negative hero, could *ever* get a hearing from an American audience" (qtd. in Lewis 172). Nearly three decades later, Wharton agreed to another collaboration, this time with the forward-thinking playwright Zoë Akins, based on Wharton's novella *The Old Maid* (1924). *The Old Maid* was a resounding success, and it beat out Lillian Hellman's thematically parallel *The Children's Hour*, Maxwell Anderson's *Valley Forge*, and Clifford Odets's and Robert Sherwood's Depression plays *Awake and Sing!* and *The Petrified Forest*, respectively, for the 1935 Pulitzer Prize for drama.

The following year, playwright Eugene O'Neill, the Irish-American "master of the misbegotten," having already won three Pulitzers in the 1920s alone (a fourth would be granted posthumously in 1956 for his autobiographical masterpiece *Long Day's Journey into Night*) emerged as the only American dramatist to date to win the Nobel Prize in literature. It was an honor, he told the Swedish Academy in his acceptance letter, that spoke to the evolution of American theater as a whole: "This highest of distinctions is all the more grateful to me because I feel so deeply that it is not only my work that is being honored, but the work of all of my colleagues in America—that this Nobel Prize is a symbol of the recognition by Europe of the coming-of-age of the American theatre . . . worthy at last to claim kinship with the modern drama of Europe, from which our original inspiration so surely derives" ("Nobel Prize" 427). Whatever one's prejudice toward the Nobel and the Pulitzer, by the 1930s, naturalistic American plays with sad endings and negative heroes had found their hearing.

In any discussion of American drama and the naturalist tradition, Eugene O'Neill must necessarily take center stage. "O'Neill gave birth to the American theatre," Tennessee Williams once said, "and died for it" (qtd. in Isaac 129). In his letter to the Nobel Prize committee, O'Neill suggests the extraordinary and permanent effect of European influence on American drama, an influence that should not be underestimated or read as mere lip service to the Swedes. French writer Émile Zola's dramatization of his novel *Thérèse Raquin* (1873) was likely the first consciously naturalistic play ever produced (Strindberg, "On Modern Drama" 76), and the movement was popularized later by André Antoine's Théâtre Libre during the 1880s, and by plays like Henry François Becque's *Les Corbeaux* (1882) and *La Parisienne* (1885), August Strindberg's *The Father* (1887) and *Miss Julie* (1888), and Maxim Gorky's *The Lower Depths* (1902). Henrik Ibsen memorably drew the demarcation line between his own social dramas and Zola's naturalism: "When I go into the sewer, I go to clean it out. When Zola goes into the sewer, he takes a bath" (qtd. in Miller and Frazer 32). Zola countered such attacks by citing the French physiologist Claude Bernard, who when asked about his "sentiments on the science of life" explained that "it is a superb salon, flooded with light, which you can only reach by passing through a long and nauseating kitchen" (qtd. in Farrell, "Some Observations" 253). In his famous preface to *Miss Julie*, subtitled "A Naturalistic Tragedy," Strindberg encapsulates the naturalistic spirit of future trends in twentieth-century drama:

My souls (characters) are conglomerates of past and present stages of culture, bits out of books and newspapers, scraps of humanity, torn shreds of once fine clothing now turned to rags, exactly as the human soul is patched together, and I have also provided a little evolutionary history. . . . The type [of Miss Julie's character] is tragic, offering the spectacle of a desperate struggle against nature, a tragic legacy of Romanticism, which is now being dissipated by Naturalism. . . . [Miss Julie is] a relic of the old warrior nobility that is now giving way to the new aristocracy of nerve and brain; a victim of the discord which a mother's "crime" has implanted in the family; a victim of the errors of an age, of circumstances, and of her own deficient constitution, which together form the equivalent of the old fashioned concept of Fate or Universal Law. (61)

In spite of Strindberg's rigorous attempts to formulate a workable definition of naturalism, theater critics often admit a distinction between realism and naturalism, but then deliberately ignore it. In the United States, the source of this uncertainty might in part be found in theater giant David Belasco's conflation of the terms in his backward-looking treatise *The Theatre Through Its Stage Door* (1919). Once an indomitable force on the American stage, Belasco claimed that "both as playwright and producer I am a realist" (52); he then proposed "naturalism" as the aim of any self-respecting director, producer, or actor (as in "act natural"). His chapter "Holding the Mirror up to Nature" misconstrued naturalism, however, as "the art of reflecting life and nature in their true and normal aspects" (233), and he declared that he "went direct to nature" for his inspiration (236). In fact, Belasco misidentified the movement flourishing in Europe as "impressionism," to his mind led by "a bunch of faddists who are always ready to fancy that they discern sublime truth in things that to normal eyes are grotesque and unreal" (167–68).

Frank Norris's widely known definition of naturalism paradoxically calls to mind Belasco's definition of impressionism. Norris was an acolyte of Zola, and he insisted that unlike pedestrian realism (which he derided as "crises involving cups of tea"), in a naturalistic tale "everything is extraordinary, imaginative, grotesque even, with a vague note of terror. . . . It is all romantic, at times unmistakably so . . . closely resembling the work of the greatest of all modern romanticists, Hugo. . . . It is a school by itself, unique, somber, powerful beyond words. It is naturalism" (1107, 1108). Norris correctly suggests that the term "naturalism" derives in part from Victor Hugo, whose oft-cited preface to his historical play *Cromwell* (1827) renounced the dramatic unity of classical Greek tragedy in favor of a new kind of theater reflecting the truer laws of nature (Törnqvist 29). But the term was more clearly defined later by Zola and Strindberg. Along with Zola's signature emphasis on heredity and environmental determinism, in his volume *Naturalism in the Theatre* (1881), he specified that for the stage "the simple formula of naturalism" consists of "great things with the subjects and characters that our eyes, accustomed to the spectacle of the daily round, have come to see as small" (364); and in Strindberg's seminal essay "On Modern Drama and Modern Theatre" (1889), the Swedish playwright disabused his readers of the idea that naturalism "simply consisted in copying a piece of nature in a natural way." He steadfastly insisted that

this definition "is the kind of misconceived Naturalism . . . not the greater naturalism which seeks out those points where the great battles take place, which loves
to see what one does not see every day, which delights in the struggle between
natural forces, whether these forces are called love and hate, the spirit of revolt, or
social instincts, which is not concerned whether something is beautiful or ugly, as
long as it is great" (78).

Donald Pizer, furthermore, could well have been discussing drama rather than
fiction when he observed that although scholars continue to debate the division
between realism and naturalism, the latter has enjoyed a more "enduring presence
in twentieth-century American fiction." "Nor has American naturalism been static
or monolithic in theme and form since its origin in the 1890s," Pizer continues.
"Indeed, one of the striking characteristics of the movement has been its adaptability to fresh currents of idea and expression in each generation while maintaining
a core of naturalistic preoccupations." This thematic core of naturalist texts "appears
to rest on the relationship between a restrictive social and intellectual environment
and the consequent impoverishment both of social opportunity and of the inner
life" (13). Joseph R. Roach similarly observes that "Realism and Naturalism have a
sharply different appearance . . . when they are viewed, not from the perspective of
what they have become, but from the perspective of what they were attempting to
subvert" (44). Naturalism was thus well-suited for export to the United States from
continental Europe because it is an inherently democratic literary form, postulating
social variation and personal freedom while at the same time representing the overwhelming restrictions imposed upon individuals by forces of intolerance and economic control. In a review of John Dos Passos's first play *The Moon is a Gong* (1925;
also called *The Garbage Man*), for instance, the critic unknowingly characterized
the whole of serious American drama after World War I when he wrote that the
play's "central theme is the conflict between the individual and society, between the
'society misfit' who wants to lead his own life, and organized society, forcing him to
fit into its groove" (qtd. in Ludington 237).

By the mid-1920s, amid the critical ferment of American theater's most experimental and productive period, Eugene O'Neill was indisputably the nation's foremost playwright, and he responded to Belasco's *Theatre Through the Stage Door* in a
note to his most experimental mask play, *The Great God Brown* (1925):

> This play is not merely realistic or naturalistic. . . . Life in terms of the theatre, as
> an art separate and distinct from the simulacra of what we term reality, may find
> expression for the great forces of which that reality is but a doughy symbol.
> Naturalism and realism, even at their deepest are so circumscribed by their limits
> that their articulateness is bound to be inarticulate. . . . Holding the mirror of a
> soul up to Nature is one thing. Holding the kodak of a mind is quite another—an
> infinitesimally lesser. . . . And if we have no gods, or heroes to portray we have the
> subconscious the mother of all gods and heroes. But for this realism is
> insufficient. ("Great God" 52)

Unwittingly perpetuating Belasco's conflation, O'Neill reworded this sentiment
and admitted his confusion over the terms (despite his familiarity with Zola and

Strindberg) in a statement used for the playbill of the Provincetown Player's 1924
American premiere of Strindberg's *The Spook Sonata* (1907):

> The old "naturalism"—or "realism," if you prefer (I would to God some genius
> were gigantic enough to define clearly the separateness of these terms once and
> for all!)—no longer applies. It represents our fathers' daring aspirations toward
> self-recognition by holding the family kodak up to ill-nature. But to us their old
> audacity is *blague*, we have taken too many snapshots of each other in every
> gracious position. We have endured too much from the banality of surfaces.
> ("Strindberg" 108–9)

In 1924, O'Neill even renounced his Pulitzer-Prize winning *"Anna Christie"* (1920),
not only for widespread failures of critical interpretation but for its naturalism
(which he defined simplistically as "true to life"). "Naturalism is too easy," he told a
reporter in a *New York Times* interview:

> It would, for instance, be a perfect cinch to go on writing *Anna Christies* all my
> life. I could always be sure of the rent then. . . . Because you can say practically
> nothing at all of our lives since 1914 [referring to the disillusionment prompted by
> World War I] through that form. The naturalistic play is really less natural than a
> romantic or expressionistic play. That is, shoving a lot of human beings on a stage
> and letting them say the identical things in a theatre they would say in a drawing
> room or a saloon does not necessarily make for naturalness.

"It's what those men and women do not say," O'Neill contended, "that usually is
most interesting" (qtd. in Kantor 48). In a similar way, when asked about realism
and naturalism in a 1981 interview, playwright Edward Albee sidestepped the issue
by incongruously applying the terms to his abstract play *Tiny Alice* (1964) and "all of
Beckett's plays" because they have "three things going on at the same time. There is
what is being said, what is not being said, and the implications of what is not being
said" (qtd. in Krohn and Wasserman 11), a statement that ironically echoes O'Neill's
earlier definition of what realism and naturalism are not.

Recognition as a serious playwright came to O'Neill with his two tragic plays
Beyond the Horizon (1918) and *"Anna Christie,"* each of which won the Pulitzer Prize
(1920, 1922), and each of which comes very close to what Strindberg described as
"the struggle between natural forces" for a naturalist play. O'Neill's autobiographical
protagonist Robert Mayo in *Beyond the Horizon* perpetuates what critic Travis
Bogard coined the "Horizon Syndrome," an endemic American obsession with a
futile yearning to discover what exists "beyond the horizon," connoting in fiction,
drama, poetry, and elsewhere a "boundless aspiration for a somewhat vaguely
defined freedom of spirit" (125). O'Neill explained to H. L. Mencken that his early
sea plays "deal with merchant-sailor life on a tramp steamer as it really is—its sor-
didness inexplicably touched with romance by the glamour of the horizons" (qtd. in
Richter 146). Bogard turns to the American playwright Edward Sheldon's *The High
Road* (1912) as a probable source of this "syndrome," but O'Neill likely derived much
of it from Jack London's equally autobiographical protagonists in the novels *Martin
Eden* (1909) and *The Valley of the Moon* (1913). Robert's dream of viewing life

"beyond the horizon" is dashed by his more powerful drive to explore a sexual relationship with the Strindbergian "female destroyer" Ruth Atkins, whose name significantly calls to mind Martin Eden's genteel love interest Ruth Morse. Both Martin and Robert die in the final scene—Martin by suicide, Robert by tuberculosis—conscious of their undeserved failures among the living.

"*Anna Christie*" charts the story of Anna Christopherson, a young prostitute who reunites with her seafaring father, Chris Christopherson, then sails with him on his barge from New York to Boston. Trapped in a fog bank off the Massachusetts coast, they rescue a shipwrecked Irish sailor named Mat Burke, and he and Anna fall in love. In the final scene, both men have signed on for a deep-sea voyage, with Chris cursing "dat ole davil, sea," and Anna soon to be left ashore to her own devices (1027). Audiences applauded the notoriously morbid playwright's apparent happy ending, but O'Neill claimed they missed the point, insisting that the final scene represents the sea's pitiless grip on its victims. Few critics walked out with the sense of tragic fate that O'Neill intended, with the exception of famed theater critic Alexander Woollcott, who observed, "O'Neill seems to be suggesting to the departing playgoers that they can regard this as a happy ending if they are short-sighted enough to believe it and weak-minded enough to crave it" (30).

Plays concerning prostitution, a topic novelists like Stephen Crane and David Graham Phillips, among others, had employed as a vehicle to challenge the boundaries of morality, had previously received harsh responses from the censors. That theater audiences, even as late as 1921, would accept a respectable marriage as a happy ending for a "girl gone bad" is therefore a remarkable development (see Johnson), and Zoë Akins's prostitution drama *The Varying Shore* also appeared that year. Though "*Anna Christie*" was a failure in O'Neill's mind, the play marks a clear shift in the kind of subject matter American audiences were willing to accept, along with a tolerance for staged naturalism that grew rapidly into box-office demand.

Also in 1921, the Provincetown Players produced Theodore Dreiser's full-length *The Hand of the Potter* (discussed below) on the same bill as O'Neill's *The Hairy Ape* and Susan Glaspell's two plays *The Verge* and *Chains of Dew* for their sixth season at New York's Playwrights' Theatre. Although best known for his fiction, Dreiser experimented with the dramatic arts at least as early as 1893 when he penned his first play *Jeremiah I* while serving as theater critic for the *St. Louis Globe-Democrat*. His collection *Plays of the Natural and Supernatural* (1916) significantly appeared the same year as O'Neill's legendary initiation at Provincetown, Massachusetts, where he was first discovered by the Provincetown Players. Dreiser's volume contains three plays with realistic settings: *The Girl in the Coffin* (loosely based on the Paterson Silk Workers' Strike of 1913), *The Light in the Window*, and "*Old Ragpicker*." But like *The Hand of the Potter* (1918), each play reveals, in Dreiser's words, "the inscrutability of life and its forces and its accidents" (qtd. in Newlin and Rusch, Introduction xxvi)—a notable approximation of O'Neill's later spoken desire to uncover the "inscrutable forces behind life" in his own work (Letter to Barrett Clark; *Selected Letters* 87). But even Dreiser's "supernatural" plays treat the naturalistic "'chemical' forces that Dreiser believed to be responsible for human behavior and action" (Newlin and Rusch, Introduction xvii). O'Neill himself was then writing in his self-styled "super-naturalist" method of the 1920s (by and large, he gets the credit for coining the term; but as we see above, it was Dreiser's, not O'Neill's), wherein playwrights "may express in the theater what we comprehend intuitively of that self-obsession which is the particular discount we moderns have to pay for the loan of life" (qtd. in Clark 86).

O'Neill continued to read Zola throughout his life, but more important, he read Strindberg, who also made the logical move from naturalism to "expressionism," a form characterized by characters' violent emotional states, grotesque exaggerations of the outer world, and the distorted psychological fantasies of the characters and writers through whom we perceive that world. By way of expressionism, Strindberg and O'Neill both reached "a heightened naturalism designed to express 'inner spiritual forces'" (Styan 133). Other early twentieth-century American dramatists such as Elmer Rice, John Howard Lawson, and Sophie Treadwell followed suit by infusing naturalistic elements in otherwise expressionistic dramas. With O'Neill's pronounced emphasis on the "subconscious" as "the mother of all gods and heroes" ("Great God Brown" 52), which he applied to his most accomplished plays of his experimental period—*Desire Under the Elms* (1924), *Strange Interlude* (1927), and *Mourning Becomes Electra* (1931)—O'Neill's distaste for naturalism was not for naturalism per se but for which forces determined characters' fates. Thus emerged a trend in American drama toward psychological determinism that powerfully resonates in the plays of Arthur Miller (whose working title for *Death of a Salesman* [1949] was "In His Head"), Tennessee Williams, LeRoi Jones, and Edward Albee, among many others. Dreiser evolved in the direction of psychological determinism as well. In a letter to Clifford Odets, he criticized the dramatist's limited naturalism in his play *Paradise Lost* (1935), writing that although he was "greatly impressed" with the play, "personally, I would not agree that the neuroses from which a number of your characters were certainly suffering were the result [as Odets implies] of the economic order alone" (*Letters* 3: 756).

Along with psychological themes, drama critics often perceive symbolism to be in opposition to naturalism even though, as Christopher Innes points out, "the major plays of the naturalistic canon are structured around symbols" (25). Both O'Neill and James T. Farrell, for instance, considered Irish playwright John Millington Synge's *The Riders of the Sea* (1904) and *The Playboy of the Western World* (1907) literary models for their own work; more specifically, each identified the Abbey Theatre's 1911 and 1938 American tours' melding of "symbolism and realism" as watershed moments in their artistic development (Farrell, "Diary Note" 176). Indeed, Joseph R. Roach argues that what ties the naturalism of Zola to the symbolism of Brecht and other late modernists is that each offers "strategies of performance that historicize, criticize, and contest dominant and oppressive ideologies" (52; see also Rundle 92–93). Regardless of his 1920s-era renunciation of the writing of naturalistic plays as "too easy," O'Neill's late masterpieces of the 1930s and early 1940s fit squarely in the naturalist tradition, each with strong symbolic undertones—*Mourning Becomes Electra* (1931), *The Iceman Cometh* (1940), *Long Day's Journey into Night* (1941),

Hughie (1941–42), and *A Moon for the Misbegotten* (1943). Brenda Murphy identifies the Great Depression as the landmark historical event that brought this "naturalist subtext" back to his later plays, along with others from the period by Odets, John Steinbeck, Irwin Shaw, and especially Sidney Kingsley (148). "In Kingsley's world," she writes, "there are no choices. Every detail of his picture suggests inevitable destruction by social and economic forces. . . . Kingsley's is theatrical realism as Zola described it—realism with a program" (149).

American playwrights also repeatedly invoke the theories of Darwin and Spencer, equating what Strindberg considered the outdated concepts of "Fate and Universal Law" with what O'Neill called "man's biological past creating the present" ("Neglected Poet" 125). "The fact of the matter is," Strindberg proclaimed, "'Darwinism' has existed in every age, ever since Moses's successive history of creation from the lower animals up to man; it is just that we have discovered and formulated it now!" (Preface 59–60). On the significance of such naturalistic atavism to O'Neill's plays, Egil Törnqvist writes that "from naturalism O'Neill overtook the modern, 'scientific' view of heredity and environment as the powers determining man's fate. With Darwin and Zola he revealed the beast in man, seeing him as a victim of his own biological past, of his own animal instincts or of a corrupt society" (29).

Naturalistic plays are generally infused with such "zoocentric rhetoric," as Roach calls it. "Darwinism provided Naturalism with a language to define itself in radical opposition" to theatrical conventions, he writes, "for to adopt its zoocentric constructions was to identify with its subversive agenda" (50–51). Biological regression thus plays a vital thematic role in the development of American theater history, and the examples are legion: the portraits of Darwin and Spencer hanging on the farmhouse wall in the stage directions of William Vaughn Moody's *The Faith Healer* (1910) and Robert "Yank" Smith's descent to the zoo in O'Neill's *The Hairy Ape*—the stokers on his steamship are described as so dehumanized by industrial labor as to resemble "*those pictures in which the appearance of the Neanderthal Man is guessed at*" (121; see Rundle for a thorough analysis of Darwinism and *The Hairy Ape*). Amanda Wingfield in Tennessee Williams's *The Glass Menagerie* (1944) responds to her son Tom's explanation that his late-night meanderings are a result of animal "instinct": "Don't quote instinct to me!" Amanda snaps. "Instinct is something people have got away from! It belongs to animals! . . . Only animals have to satisfy instincts! Surely your aims are somewhat higher than theirs! Than monkeys—pigs—" (150). Blanche Dubois in Williams's *A Streetcar Named Desire* (1951) pleads with her sister Stella to leave Stanley Kowalski because "there's even something—subhuman—something not quite to the stage of humanity yet! Yes, something—ape-like about him, like one of those pictures I've seen in anthropological studies. . . . *Don't hang back with the brutes!*" (83). And symbolic regression into Afrocentric primitivism is present in O'Neill's *The Emperor Jones* (1920), Lorraine Hansberry's *A Raisin in the Sun* (1961), and LeRoi Jones's *Dutchman* (1964), among countless other examples.

Out of this zoocentric rhetoric emerges the ever-present "sins of our fathers" motif in American drama that perpetually informs the actions of its characters in the language of physiology. "Sons are always their fathers," O'Neill wrote in his Pulitzer Prize–winning *Strange Interlude*. "They pass through the mother to become the father again" (817). Decades later, Sam Shepard's negative hero Weston in *The Curse of the Starving Class* (1976) believes his blood to be "infected" by his father's poison (167), just as Vince Tilden in Shepard's Pulitzer-winning *Buried Child* (1979) experiences a revelation while staring at his reflection in his car windshield that he cannot escape the physiological legacy of his forebears: "And then his [Vince's] face changed. His face became his father's face. Same bones. Same eyes. Same nose. Same breath. And his father's face changed to his Grandfather's face. And it went on like that. Changing. Clear on back to faces I've never seen before but still recognized. Still recognized the bones underneath. The eyes. The breath. The mouth" (130).

Albee's slippery reconfiguration of realism and naturalism—"there is what is being said, what is not being said, and the implications of what is not being said" (qtd. in Krohn and Wasserman 11)—still situates what most people consider to be his "absurdism" in the desire to unlock grander truths linked to atavism and instinct that social mores continue to suppress. Although *Tiny Alice* investigates the challenges of arriving at "truth," it is perhaps typical of Albee's elusiveness in interviews that he didn't address the atavism of his most acclaimed play *The Zoo Story* (1959), which, along with its prequel *At Home at the Zoo* (2004; originally titled *Peter and Jerry*), engages atavism at its most elemental. *The Zoo Story* presents a bourgeois Everyman named Peter, who is cross-examined in Central Park by Jerry, a probing, nihilistic truth-seeker. Jerry's process of revealing through harsh dialogue and physical duress the "truth" of Peter's falsifying bourgeois existence releases his subject's basest animal instincts by eventually goading Peter into murdering him. As Rose A. Zimbardo succinctly breaks down the thematic structure of the play, "While Peter is one of the 'people' who is separated from the animal in himself and others, Jerry is an animal (he knows his own nature) who fights separation from the other animals. In part his isolation is forced upon him. But in large measure it grows out of his need for truth. He is determined to discover the essential nature of the human condition" (11–12).

This narratological quest for "truth" took wing in the late 1920s and 1930s, when playwrights sought to express what Murphy calls a "neonaturalism shot through with Freudianism"; after Freud, she professes, even an American play "would not have seemed realistic to its audience if sufficient attention had not been paid to personality" (161). But as powerfully influenced by Freud's psychological theories as modern drama had become by the 1920s, Elmer Rice still specified that the "conduct" of his dehumanized and spiritually bankrupt character Mr. Zero in *The Adding Machine* (1923) "is determined by hereditary influences, childhood environment, education and social inheritance, but more particularly it is influenced by the state of his digestion, the weather, his internal secretions and the multitudinous sensory stimuli of light and sound, touch and temperature, taste, motion and pain" (qtd. in Murphy 150). Hence there's little reason to ignore the effect of naturalism on later, more psychological, "supernatural," expressionistic, or symbolic experimental plays—*The Adding Machine*, Treadwell's *Machinal* (1928), Steinbeck's figuratively staged dramatization *Of Mice and Men* (1937), and Albee's later absurdist dramas—wholly outside the traditional purview of the naturalist tradition. As Darwin himself wrote in *The Expression of the Emotions in Man and Animals* (1872), "He who admits on general grounds that the structure and habits of all animals have been gradually evolved, will look at the whole subject of Expression in a new and interesting light" (qtd. in Roach 50).

Biological regression, ancestral heritage, and environmental and psychological determinism importantly form the basis for the morally relativistic attitude of major twentieth-century American dramatists. Whether to blame (melodrama, comedy, and realism) or not to blame (naturalism) has been the question for most of these writers. And by the 1930s, given staggering innovations in the fields of physiology, sociology, and psychology, the best of them chose the latter. As early as 1908, in Edward Sheldon's *Salvation Nell*, the title character tells her drunken, abusive lover Jim, "You an' me didn't have no chance—did we, Jim? An' it ain't all our fault if we don't come quite up ter the mark" (128). When Chris Christopherson apologizes to his fallen daughter in *"Anna Christie"* for abandoning her at an early age, thus initiating her descent into a life of prostitution, she retorts in street-wise dialect, "Don't bawl about it. There ain't nothing to forgive, anyway. It ain't your fault, and it ain't mine. . . . We're all poor nuts, and things happen, and we yust get mixed in wrong, that's all." "You say right tang, Anna, py golly!" Chris agrees. "It ain't nobody's fault!" (1015). Two decades later, in *Long Day's Journey Into Night*, the morphine-addled Mary Tyrone recasts Anna's absolution in an upper-middle-class Irish context by submitting that the Tyrone family's dysfunctional pathologies are not their fault: "None of us can help the things life has done to us. They're done before you realize it, and once they're done they make you do other things until at last everything comes between you and what you'd like to be, and you've lost your true self forever" (749). Later still, Willie Loman's stalwart neighbor Charley iterates "nobody dast blame this man" *twice* at Willie's funeral following his suicide in the final "Requiem" section of Arthur Miller's *Death of a Salesman* (111).

Such lines reverberate throughout American drama by a host of varied characters from diverse milieus, ultimately manifesting what critic Sophus Winther calls a "naturalistic ethics." "If no one is to blame," he writes, "then moral certainty cannot exist." Though naturalistic plays more often than not incorporate melodramatic elements (see Newlin, "Ten" 14), naturalistic ethics are unbound by the notions of good and evil one finds in traditional melodrama; rather, they combine to form a relativistic worldview and consciousness of the ever-changing standards of morality. Winther adds that O'Neill pushes the boundaries "even further in that he condemns a fixed standard as destructive of life, holding that in the last analysis it will lead to false pride, arrogant and cruel behavior, hypocrisy and a destructive fanaticism" (123). In kind, Strindberg argued that composing a believable character demands roundness of personality, of course, but also of moral judgment: "There is no such thing as absolute evil. . . . The summary judgments that authors pass on people—this one is stupid, that one brutal, this one jealous, that one mean—ought to be challenged by naturalists, who know how richly complicated the soul is, and who are aware that 'vice' has a reverse side, which is very much like virtue" ("On Modern Drama" 57, 59). Tennessee Williams summed up the general American theatrical trend of naturalistic ethics decades later in his 1957 self-interview entitled "The World I Live In": "I don't believe in 'original sin.' I don't believe in 'guilt.' I don't believe in villains or heroes—only right or wrong ways that individuals have taken, not by choice but by necessity or by certain still-uncomprehended influences in themselves, their circumstances, and their antecedents" (184). Playwrights in the United States not only adopted and modified the scientific attitudes of self-identified naturalist writers like Zola, Strindberg, Norris, and Dreiser, but the fundamental ethics of naturalism as well—the rejection of the false dichotomies of good and bad, hero and villain, right and wrong—a stance that permeates the whole of twentieth-century American drama.

Dreiser audaciously tested the boundaries of naturalistic ethics with *The Hand of the Potter*, an openly sympathetic treatment of a murderous child molester named Isadore Berchansky (based on the actual pedophilic murderer Nathan Swartz; see Newlin and Rusch, Introduction xx–xxii). Isadore brutally rapes and murders a young girl in the first act of the play, prior to which the character showed obvious signs of a terrifying psychopathology. But in the final scene, the character Dennis Quinn, an Irish-American journalist with a deep brogue, serves as a mouthpiece for Dreiser's own ethical view of Isadore's actions, dictated as they are by the biological imperatives that drove him to the crime:

> Most people have a few rules, a pattern, an' everybody's supposed to be like that. Well, they're naht. An naathin' will ever make 'em exactly alike, ayther—ayther aal good or aal bad, or a little ave waan or the other, accordin' to anybody's theory. Nature don't work that way. An' nature makes people, me young friend, me an' you [*he taps him on the chest*], an' every waan else, an' she don't aalways make us right ayther, by a damned sight. . . . Sometimes they're made to do things—lots ave thim—by forces over which they have no control. (277)

This extreme line of naturalistic ethics came too early for audiences in 1921. H. L. Mencken, a critic best known for his defense of artistic freedom, deplored the play as a vehicle for "shocking the numskulls for the mere sake of shocking them" (qtd. in Newlin and Rusch, Introduction xxvii). But although he was also embroiled in a controversy over publication of his decadent autobiographical novel *The "Genius"* (1915), Dreiser mulishly refused to bury the play, even if the warning to do so came from straight from Mencken, one of his greatest champions.

How the legal system treats the forces over which characters have no control (in Isadore's case, the physiological role of "hormones" [274]) thus serves as another vital theme in American drama. Strindberg wrote of the staged tension between naturalistic forces and the penal system that "the naturalist has erased guilt along with God, but he cannot erase the consequences of an action—punishment, prison, or the fear of it—for the simple reason that these consequences remain, whether or not he acquits the individual" ("On Modern Drama" 61). In *The Hand of the Potter*, legal consequences assume an important role in illuminating the disjunction between the laws of courts and the truer laws of nature, history, and circumstance. Dreiser presents the "truth" that his prosecutor and jury seek as superficial at best.

In the courtroom scene, the prosecutor demands from his witnesses "the truth, the whole truth, and nothing but the truth" before ordering the fugitive Isadore to the electric chair (239). But the facts of the case don't account for "truth" in Dreiser's larger naturalistic sense; the play ends with Isadore's suicide and policemen judging his guilt by a legal system that profoundly contrasts with Dreiser's laws of nature.

Treadwell's *Machinal* (1928) also includes a courtroom scene, entitled "The Law," in which her generic Young Woman's true motivations for murdering her husband—the living death of a loveless marriage—is never borne out. After she's found guilty and sentenced to death, in the final scene, "A Machine," the Young Woman's last words signify an inability to redress this absence of truth amid the indomitable "machine" of symbols about her—the traditional family (her mother), the church (a priest), the community (reporters), and the law (the jailers)—crying out "Somebody! Sombod—*Her voice is cut off*" (83). Elmer Rice covered similar ground with his breakout play *On Trial* (1914), a work that importantly introduced the flashback as a narrative device; *The Adding Machine*, in which the antihero Mr. Zero is put on trial for murdering his boss; and his Pulitzer Prize–winning *Street Scene* (1929), about a bullying tenement man who kills his unfulfilled wife and her lover. Maxwell Anderson's 1935 masterpiece *Winterset*, a verse-play about the 1920 Sacco and Vanzetti trial, offers a historically grounded example as well. O'Neill ended many plays with policemen confronting his negative heroes, scenes that stress the insignificance of the legal system when compared to the laws of environment and natural desire—*The Web* (1913), *The Dreamy Kid* (1919), *Desire Under the Elms* (1924), *The Great God Brown* (1926), and *The Iceman Cometh* (1946). In the final scene of *The Great God Brown*, for instance, common law melds with extraordinary lives when, after gunning down the soul-searching William Brown, a policeman asks, notebook in hand, "Well, what's his name?" "Man!" a prostitute responds. "How d'yuh spell it?" (533).

The influence of *The Hand of the Potter* on American theater was negligible at best, given its lackluster production by the Players and incendiary subject matter, but what is certain is that in the first decades of the twentieth century, American playwrights and fiction writers became increasingly influenced by each others' naturalistic visions. They frequently corresponded with one another, sharing ideas and charting each others' progress in letters, reviews, and articles. Throughout their collaboration, Wharton and Akins conducted a lengthy discourse over the use of dialogue in drama as opposed to fiction (see Kreizenbeck). O'Neill was the first sustained American practitioner of European expressionism, but Keith Newlin credits Dreiser's *Laughing Gas* (1916) for being the first expressionistic play ever produced in the United States ("Expressionism"), and also for anticipating Thornton Wilder's work by staging, as Richard Goldstone writes, "scenes of continuous and even simultaneous action" (qtd. in Newlin and Rusch, "Productions" 348). Wilder expanded on two naturalistic themes from Dreiser's otherwise expressionistic *The Spring Recital* (1916) and *Laughing Gas* for his Pulitzer-winning *Our Town* (1938) and *The Skin of Our Teeth* (1942)—in the playwright's words, they were "the ecstasy of being alive, as seen through the eyes of those who no longer have life, and the repetitive, cyclical history of mankind" (qtd. in Newlin and Rusch, "Productions" 348).

Along with O'Neill's adoption of Dreiser's term "super-naturalism," Rice cited *Plays of the Natural and Supernatural* as influencing *The Adding Machine*, and Dos Passos testified that his 1925 play *The Moon is a Gong* was inspired by the premiere of O'Neill's *The Emperor Jones* five years earlier (Ludington 201). In his essay "Is the 'Realistic' Theatre Obsolete?" (1925), Dos Passos noted that "the throb of the drum in *The Emperor Jones* cleared many a pair of ears that had been until that time tuned only to suburban comedy. The chesty roar of *The Hairy Ape* made several people forget to read how The Well Dressed Man would wear his cravat" (593). He also warned that if theater was to survive as an art form, it must progress in the ways O'Neill demonstrated in *The Emperor Jones* and *The Hairy Ape* and that John Howard Lawson revealed in *Processional* (1925), a play Lawson himself described in naturalistic terms as offering "the grotesque of the American environment, the colorful exaggeration of the American language" (qtd. in Ludington 236).

O'Neill dedicated his Nobel Prize to his "master" August Strindberg ("Nobel Prize" 428), but he emphatically believed the prize should have been awarded to Dreiser. When the announcement came that O'Neill had won, Dreiser wrote the playwright a congratulatory note, to which O'Neill responded with both heartfelt thanks and a touch of contrition: "You are one of the very few I really wanted to hear from. . . . I can say to you with entire sincerity and truth, from my head and heart both, that I would take a great deal more satisfaction in this prize if you were among those who had had it before me. As it is, I have a sneaking feeling of guilt—as if I had pinched something which I know damned well should, in justice, be yours" (*Selected Letters* 458). Upton Sinclair, who described himself as a fervent admirer of O'Neill's, sent the playwright scripts for his plays *Hell* (1923) and *Singing Jailbirds* (1924) for critical feedback and production help. O'Neill responded with enthusiasm: "I'm sure glad to know you're a 'fan.' It's sure reciprocated, believe me: I've been one of yours ever since way back in 'Jungle' days, and I think I've read everything of yours—except 'The Goose Step'—since then. All sincere appreciation and respect to you!" (*Selected Letters* 182). He considered *Singing Jailbirds* "fine stuff—strong and true" and was "deeply moved by it" (Letter to Sinclair, 22 Aug. 1924), but he was unable to find Sinclair a producer; by that time, August 1925, the Provincetown Playhouse, headed by James Light, was strictly "supposed to do the more radical and experimental things" (Letter to Sinclair, 22 Aug. 1925).

Along with Dreiser and Sinclair, O'Neill corresponded with naturalist fiction writer James T. Farrell, and the two Irish Americans explored naturalistic themes in remarkably analogous ways. O'Neill wrote Farrell that he viewed his *Studs Lonigan* trilogy (1932, 1934, 1935) with "great admiration" as a "splendid piece of work," and he railed against the American Library Association's decision to include it on their list, only to remove it in an overt demonstration of the kind of censorship he had been struggling against the length of his career (and that Dreiser had earlier lampooned in his play *The Court of Progress* [1916]).O'Neill fumed in a letter to James Henle of the Vanguard Press that "to include it and then suddenly withdraw it for no real reason except an evasive impulse toward moral censorship strikes me as a deliberate insult to a widely known American writer of genuine artistic integrity and high accomplishment, and to a splendid novel of American life."

How these cross-genre interactions played out on the stage was not lost on their critics. Following the 1946 premiere of O'Neill's masterpiece *The Iceman Cometh*, Mary McCarthy published a notoriously unflattering comparison between O'Neill and other naturalist writers. In her derisive *New York Times* review entitled "Eugene O'Neill—Dry Ice," McCarthy chastised O'Neill for belonging to "that group of American authors, which includes Farrell and Dreiser, whose choice of vocation was a kind of triumphant catastrophe" (31). What follows is a litany of abuse aimed at the three naturalists—at naturalism in general, in fact: it is "tone deaf," "didactic," "pulpy in detail"; it exhibits a "strange, blank nihilism" and a tendency to "drive an idea or a theme step by step to its brutal conclusion with the same terrible force they have brought to bear on their fugitive profession . . . [with] no curtain of decency to drop on their heroes' remains" (32). McCarthy meant to be unkind, but her analogy is sound nonetheless. And she couldn't have known that over the years, the targets of her scorn had been cultivating longstanding artistic bonds.

Few American plays following World War II can be considered purely naturalistic, but the tenets of naturalism have been studied, modified, and developed by American playwrights throughout the last century and into our own. While acknowledging drama critic Eric Bentley's verdict that "as modern persons we are willy-nilly under the spell of Naturalism," Jordan Y. Miller and Winifred L. Frazer in their comprehensive study *American Drama Between the Wars* contend that they "can state with reasonable accuracy that the predominant style of American drama between the wars was *realistic*" (169). "Realism," broadly speaking, refers to the nineteenth-century revolt against melodrama and romanticism toward a theatrical form that ends with calculated ambiguity and reflects the contemporary lives of run-of-the-mill characters who exhibit free will. "Naturalism," on the other hand, vaguely connotes a grittier, more perverse form of realism in common theater parlance. But as shown above, once we remove realistic "slice of life" plays that share the fourth-wall illusion of most naturalistic dramas, it does adhere to the term's tangible definition in fiction studies: a literary tradition that demonstrates a predilection for sad endings and negative heroes, sublime truths existing beneath surface realities, and the philosophical position that individual fates are determined by biological, historical, circumstantial, and psychological forces beyond their control.

Throughout the process of tackling the "semantic problem" with the proper definitions outlined above—"is this or that play realistic or naturalistic, or something of both" (171)—Miller and Frazer find strains of naturalism in the works of American playwrights Elmer Rice, Clifford Odets, George Kelly, Sidney Kingsley, Lillian Hellman, and in John Steinbeck's dramatization of his fiction, but in the end they favor ignoring the difference as essentially irrelevant:

> Realism-Naturalism. Is it worth the effort to keep them apart? . . . Natural
> determinism and lack of free will may make these plays *naturalistic*;
> independence of fate and exertion of free choice may make them *realistic*; but in

their final analysis as successes or failures, it probably doesn't really matter at all. From Odets to Steinbeck, these dramatists were often able to thwart the critics' insistence on sticking on labels, and they created a body of serious drama with memorable characters and action. The universality of their best efforts makes those works relevant to any era—call them what you will. (208–9)

Strindberg and Norris took issue with this argument, as we have seen, but Miller and Frazer's point is well taken. It would be reckless to disagree with their conclusion that a "hard-and-fast distinction may not always be possible" (163). But equally reckless would be to abandon the term "naturalism" in drama studies outright, just as it would in fiction studies. However incautiously, playwrights and novelists historically appropriated naturalism and other methods for well over a century to explain their art. When used judiciously, such labels can also offer audiences and critics a generalized understanding of intent—who or what playwrights were rebelling against historically and artistically, their worldviews, even their frequent attempts to thwart labels themselves.

In his 1950 essay "Some Observations on Naturalism, So-Called, in Fiction," James T. Farrell posited an important rhetorical question: "What insights do we gain by linking them [Flaubert, Zola, Crane, Dreiser, and Dos Passos] together in terms of a watered down generalization?" Farrell categorically responds that we link them because they are part of a "tradition . . . written in the spirit of truth. If they are part of a tradition, that tradition has had more force and more impact, and has been able to nourish and give more energy to successive generations than any other tradition" (258). The conflation of naturalism with other techniques, particularly expressionism, symbolism, and absurdism, comes to characterize the American style of drama that triumphs in the last century, but the naturalist tradition nearly always predominates. The diverse group of writers discussed above unleashed fresh perspectives on this ever-evolving tradition, and they set the stage for the next gifted generation—August Wilson, Wendy Wasserstein, David Henry Hwang, Tony Kushner, John Guare—each of whom, in their own unique ways, pushed forward with their forbears' exploration of "the inscrutable forces behind life."

WORKS CITED

Belasco, David. *The Theatre Through Its Stage Door*. Ed. Louis V. Defoe. New York: Harper & Brothers, 1919.

Bogard, Travis. *Contour in Time: The Plays of Eugene O'Neill*. Rev. ed. New York: Oxford University Press, 1988.

Cargill, Oscar, N. Bryllion Fagin, and William J. Fisher, eds. *O'Neill and His Plays: Four Decades of Criticism*. New York: New York University Press, 1961.

Clark, Barrett H. *O'Neill: The Man and His Plays*. 1929. New York: Dover, 1947.

Dos Passos, John. "Is the 'Realistic' Theatre Obsolete? Many Theatrical Conventions Have Been Shattered by Lawson's 'Processional.'" 1925. *Travel Books and Other Writings, 1916–1941*. Ed. Townsend Ludington. New York: Library of America, 2003. 591–95.

Dreiser, Theodore. *The Collected Plays of Theodore Dreiser*. Ed. Keith Newlin and Frederic
 E. Rusch. Albany, N.Y.: Whitston, 2000.

———. *The Hand of the Potter*. 1921. Dreiser, *Collected Plays* 188–282.

———. *Letters of Theodore Dreiser*. Ed. Robert H. Elias. 3 vols. Philadelphia: University of
 Pennsylvania Press, 1959.

Estrin, Mark W., ed. *Conversations with Eugene O'Neill*. Jackson: University of Mississippi
 Press, 1990.

Farrell, James T. "Diary Note." 9 Aug. 1938. *On Irish Themes*. Ed. and intro. Dennis Flynn.
 Foreword William V. Shannon. Philadelphia: University of Pennsylvania Press, 1982:
 176–78.

———. "Some Observations on Naturalism, So-Called, in Fiction." 1950. *Documents of
 American Realism and Naturalism*. Ed. Donald Pizer. Carbondale and Edwardsville:
 Southern Illinois University Press, 1998. 251–69.

Floyd, Virginia, ed. *Eugene O'Neill at Work: Newly Released Ideas for His Plays*. New York:
 Ungar, 1981.

Innes, Christopher. *A Sourcebook on Naturalist Theatre*. New York: Routledge, 2000.

Isaac, Dan. "Founding Father: O'Neill's Correspondence with Arthur Miller and Tennessee
 Williams." *Eugene O'Neill Review* 17 (1993): 124–30.

Johnson, Katie N. "'Anna Christie': The Repentant Courtesan, Made Respectable." *Eugene
 O'Neill Review* 26 (2004): 87–104.

Kantor, Louis. "O'Neill Defends His Play of the Negro." Estrin 44–49.

Kreizenbeck, Alan. *Zoë Akins: Broadway Playwright*. Westport, Conn.: Praeger, 2004.

Krohn, Charles, and Julian N. Wasserman. "An Interview with Edward Albee, March 18,
 1981." *Edward Albee: An Interview and Essays*. Ed. Julian N. Wasserman. Houston:
 University of St. Thomas Press, 1983. 1–28.

Lee, Hermione. *Edith Wharton*. New York: Knopf, 2007.

Lewis, R. W. B. *Edith Wharton: A Biography*. New York: Harper and Row, 1975.

Ludington, Townsend. *John Dos Passos: A Twentieth Century Odyssey*. New York: Dutton,
 1980.

McCarthy, Mary. "Eugene O'Neill—Dry Ice." *A Bolt from the Blue and Other Essays*. Ed. A.
 O. Scott. New York: New York Review of Books, 2002.

Miller, Arthur. *Death of a Salesman: Certain Private Conversations in Two Acts and a
 Requiem*. 1949. Intro. Christopher Bigsby. New York: Penguin, 1998.

Miller, Jordan Y., and Winifred Frazer. *American Drama Between the Wars: A Critical
 History*. Boston: Twayne, 1991.

Murphy, Brenda. *American Realism and American Drama, 1880–1940*. Cambridge:
 Cambridge University Press, 1987.

Newlin, Keith. "Expressionism Takes the Stage: Dreiser's 'Laughing Gas.'" *Journal of
 American Drama and Theater* 4 (1992): 5–22.

———. "Ten Questions with Keith Newlin." *ALN: The American Literary Naturalism
 Newsletter* 4.1–2 (2009): 12–14.

Newlin, Keith, and Frederic E. Rusch. Introduction. Dreiser, *Collected Plays* ix–xxxvii.

———. "Productions of Dreiser's Plays." Dreiser, *Collected Plays* 331–48.

Norris, Frank. "Zola as a Romantic Writer." 1896. *Novels and Essays*. Ed. Donald Pizer.
 New York: Library of America, 1986. 1106–8.

O'Neill, Eugene. "*Anna Christie*." 1920. *Complete Plays, 1913–1920*. Ed. Travis Bogard. New
 York: Library of America, 1988. 957–1027.

———. *Complete Plays, 1920–1931*. Ed. Travis Bogard. New York: Library of America, 1988.

———. *The Great God Brown*. 1925. O'Neill, *Complete Plays* 469–535.

———. "The Great God Brown: Author's Forward." Floyd 52.

———. *The Hairy Ape*. 1921. O'Neill, *Complete Plays* 119–63.

———. Letter to James Henle. 24 Nov. 1942. Eugene O'Neill Foundation, Tao House Library and Yale University Beiniecke Rare Book and Manuscript Library.

———. Letter to Upton Sinclair. 22 Aug. 1924. Eugene O'Neill Foundation, Tao House Library and Yale University Beiniecke Rare Book and Manuscript Library.

———. Letter to Upton Sinclair. 22 Aug. 1925. Eugene O'Neill Foundation, Tao House Library and Yale University Beiniecke Rare Book and Manuscript Library.

———. "Neglected Poet." Letter to Arthur Hobson Quinn. Cargill 125–26.

———. "The Nobel Prize Acceptance Letter." *The Unknown O'Neill: Unpublished or Unfamiliar Writings of Eugene O'Neill*. Ed. Travis Bogard. New Haven: Yale University Press, 1988. 427–28.

———. *Selected Letters of Eugene O'Neill*. Ed. Travis Bogard and Jackson R. Bryer. New Haven: Yale University Press, 1988.

———. *Strange Interlude*. 1927. O'Neill, *Complete Plays* 629–818.

———. "Strindberg and Our Theatre." 1924. Cargill 108–9.

Pizer, Donald. Introduction: The Problem of Definition. *The Cambridge Companion to American Realism and Naturalism: Howells to London*. Ed. Donald Pizer. Cambridge: Cambridge University Press, 1995. 1–18.

Richter, Robert A. *Eugene O'Neill and Dat Ole Davil Sea: Maritime Influences in the Life and Works of Eugene O'Neill*. Mystic, Conn.: Mystic Seaport, 2004.

Roach, Joseph R. "Darwin's Passion: The Language of Expression on Nature's Stage." *Discourse* 13.1 (1990–91): 40–58.

Rundle, Erika. "The Hairy Ape's Humanist Hell: Theatricality and Evolution in O'Neill's 'Comedy of Ancient and Modern Life.'" *The Eugene O'Neill Review* 30 (2008): 48–144.

Sheldon, Edward. *Salvation Nell*. 1908. *50 Best Plays of the American Theatre*. Vol. 1. Selected by Clive Barnes and with Individual Play Introductions by John Gassner. New York: Crown, 1970. 88–148.

Shepard, Sam. *Buried Child*. 1979. *Seven Plays*. Intro. Richard Gilman. New York: Dial, 2005. 61–132.

———. *The Curse of the Starving Class*. 1976. *Seven Plays*. Intro. Richard Gilman. New York: Dial, 2005. 133–200.

Strindberg, August. "On Modern Drama and Modern Theatre." 1889. *Selected Essays*. Ed. Michael Robinson. Cambridge: Cambridge University Press, 1996. 73–86.

———. Preface. *Miss Julie: A Naturalistic Tragedy*. 1888. Trans. Michael Robinson. New York: Oxford University Press 1998. 56–68.

Styan, J. L. *Modern Drama in Theory and Practice*. Vol.1. Cambridge: Cambridge University Press, 1981.

Törnqvist, Egil. *A Drama of Souls: Studies in O'Neill's Super-Naturalistic Technique*. New Haven: Yale University Press, 1969.

Treadwell, Sophie. *Machinal*. 1928. Intro. Judith E. Barlow. London: Nick Hern, 1993.

Williams, Tennessee. *The Glass Menagerie*. 1944. *50 Best Plays of the American Theatre*. Vol. 3. Selected by Clive Barnes and with Individual Play Introductions by John Gassner. New York: Crown, 1970. 137–74.

———. *A Streetcar Named Desire*. 1947. Intro. Arthur Miller. New York: New Directions, 2004.

———. "The World I Live In." Williams, *Streetcar* 181–84.

Winther, Sophus Keith. *Eugene O'Neill: A Critical Study*. New York: Random, 1934.

Woollcott, Alexander. "Second Thoughts on First Nights." *New York Times* 13 Nov. 1921; rpt.
     in *The Critical Response to Eugene O'Neill.* Ed. John H. Houchin. Westport, Conn.:
     Greenwood, 1993. 29–30.
Zimbardo, Rose A. "Symbolism and Naturalism in Edward Albee's *The Zoo Story.*"
     Twentieth Century Literature 8.1 (1962): 10–17.
Zola, Émile. "From *Naturalism in the Theatre.*" 1881. *The Theory of the Modern Stage: An
     Introduction to Modern Theatre and Drama.* Ed. Eric Bentley. New York: Penguin,
     1968. 351–75.

CHAPTER 26

NATURALISM AND POETRY

CHRIS BEYERS

IN his essay, "The Responsibilities of the Novelist," Frank Norris remarked that Marlowe and Shakespeare were the spokesmen for their era, and Pope and Dryden for theirs, while novelists spoke for the modern age. He continues, "if the matter could be in any way statisticized, the figures would bear out" his assumption, since novels are "essential" in that they "express modern life" more truthfully and authentically than poetry and other genres (176). Because Norris is considered to be an important theorist of American literary naturalism, when he says "novelist," most interpret him to mean "naturalist writer." For Norris, naturalist works are inherently written in prose.

Norris's view of poetry and naturalism has often been echoed; Donald Pizer, the movement's most persistent critic and historian, defines naturalism as a "vital stream in American fiction" (ix), and time and again, when critics talk about naturalism, they address novels and short stories exclusively. Few if any poets claim the title of naturalist, and critics have infrequently used the word to describe poetry. Consequently, there are no manifestos to read, no prefaces to consult, and no critical tradition to summarize. If Norris is right, naturalism and poetry are mutually exclusive. However, if we consider the ways that naturalism is generally defined, there is a body of poetry that can profitably be looked at as naturalist.

American literary naturalism is generally considered a subgenre of the realist fiction of the late nineteenth and early twentieth century. Finding its inspiration in the novels and theories of Émile Zola, such novelists as Stephen Crane, Frank Norris, Theodore Dreiser, Jack London, and John Dos Passos seek to document, more or less objectively, the material forces shaping humankind, examining the lives of people circumscribed by biological, social, economic, and political systems. Complicating this view of naturalism is Charles Child Walcutt's "divided stream" thesis, which identifies a more hopeful branch of naturalism that valorizes "intuition" and promotes a more progressive, even radical ideal; the other stream, Walcutt argues, goes through the "dark canyon of mechanistic determinism" (vii–viii). His example of a darker, deterministic stream is Dreiser's *An American Tragedy* (1925), in which its protagonist, Clyde Griffiths, "is powerless to choose at the very climax of the action" (26). He finds the more optimistic, ideal stream in such novels as London's *The Sea-Wolf* (1904), in which "the movement of the plot depends on acts of self will and in no sense embodies the operation of external determining forces" (113), and in Frank Norris's *The Octopus* (1901), where the Vanamee subplot expresses the "fruitfulness and benign natural force" (146). Walcutt argues that the two branches are rarely completely separate, so that the more idealist naturalist works typically contain significant materialist elements.

This generally accepted definition helps explain why comparatively little poetry is written in the naturalist mode. Since the eighteenth century, writers seeking to document material conditions have usually chosen prose. A realist novel frequently introduces characters by describing their upbringing, their experiences, and their world as a way of explaining their character. While the modernist poets who were contemporaries of the naturalist novelists do try to represent their world, they usually represent it using symbol, implication, and other sorts of truncation.

More fundamentally, modernist poets typically do not accept the category "reality" as posited by the naturalists. Consider, for example, the tryst between the typist and the carbuncular clerk in part III of T. S. Eliot's *The Waste Land* (1922)—the type of scene (often considered sordid in its day) that might appear in a naturalist novel. In Eliot's poem, a figure out of classical mythology narrates the episode; subsequent elaborations of the idea rely on allusions to the operas of Richard Wagner and to fertility myths. Thus it seems that, for every contemporary gesture in modernist poetry, there is a counter-gesture toward the universal and transhistorical. Moreover, modernist poets like Eliot question the naturalist presumption of objectivity. When naturalist writers seek to document the world "scientifically," they typically take for granted a notion that the conditions and events they describe can be verified objectively and, for that reason, peruse newspapers and other documents in order to report, truly, things that happened in the world. Their facts can be easily verified. For example, Dreiser carefully studied newspaper articles on Chester Gillette while writing *An American Tragedy*, just as Norris studied newspaper reports about a sensational San Francisco murder when drafting *McTeague*. Modernist poets, however, tend to question what we mean by "the world" as well as the notion that their works should be based on verifiable evidence. What is the factual source for Eliot's depiction of the encounter between the typist and the clerk? Even if we are to accept it as something that actually happened, how should we interpret the scene? To what extent is the evidence mediated by its mythic, Greek teller?

A good touchstone for modernist poetry's attitude toward the objective world occurs in canto LXII of Ezra Pound's *Cantos* (1938), when the speaker remarks that Alexander Hamilton "was the Prime snot in ALL American history," followed by the phrase, "ego scriptor cantilenae" (Latin for "I, the writer of these cantos" [350]). Although Pound believed his judgment valid, the fact that he must announce that he is offering his own opinion indicates that most of what is said in the *Cantos* is not his opinion—instead, the long poem constantly introduces voices that speak from other subjectivities. Indeed, when modernist writers do incorporate documents that might seem to represent objective reality, they typically fragment them or in other ways present them as rooted ineluctably in their own historicity and subject to reinterpretation.

A final stumbling block to a truly naturalist verse is the fact that poets have been less likely to embrace the sense of futility sometimes associated with naturalism, partly because of the liberating sense that the speaker's voice tends to give a poem. This is particularly notable for poets who embrace the poetry of witness, a politically engaged mode seeking to articulate perspectives that they feel have been ignored by previous generations. A good illustration can be seen by comparing Adrienne Rich's early poem, "Aunt Jennifer's Tigers" (1951), with her later poem, "Hunger" (1978). In the former poem, the narrator describes a woman burdened by the "massive weight of Uncle's wedding band." The narrator remarks that she is "mastered by" the "ordeals" she must endure (4). That is to say, she is caught, as so many naturalist characters are, in an oppressive patriarchal system. However, two decades later, the narrator in "Hunger" remarks, "They can rule the world while they can persuade us / our pain belongs in some order" (230). In the poem, the antecedent for the "They" is never firmly established. It would seem that Rich wants the reader to understand the "They" as the agents and beneficiaries of the patriarchal, capitalist system that seeks to control all of us. While Aunt Jennifer has been persuaded that her pain is justified, in "Hunger" the statement's very articulation demonstrates that the speaker is *not* so persuaded, that the reader should not be so persuaded, and that *we* can avoid being mastered by refusing to be persuaded. The poem puts human choice, freely made and defiant, at the fulcrum of human society; it seems to make change possible, even imminent.

Thus, the main intellectual trends of twentieth-century poetry are inimical to a naturalist verse tradition. On the other hand, nothing in the generally assumed definition disqualifies poetry from the genre. Regarding naturalist poetry in terms of genre, a rather clear narrative comes into view: naturalist poets began by critiquing convention, as naturalist novelists did, and went on to adopt modernist techniques to reflect the changing notion of what constitutes reality. Common to all is an enduring strain exploring the severe restraints on human possibility.

STEPHEN CRANE

Probably more than any other poet, Stephen Crane's two startling books of poetry—*The Black Riders* (1895) and *War Is Kind* (1899)—offer a clear challenge to convention. This is clear even in the typography of the early editions of *The Black Riders*, where the poems were printed without titles and with all words in small capitals.

This sets a fitting tone for the volume. Capitalization and titles establish hierarchies among words in a poem; they can also help suggest frames of interpretation. Crane's poetry, above all else, questions established hierarchies, a stance that became a dominant naturalist tendency.

For example, in poem IV of *The Black Riders*, the speaker challenges the prevalent notion of the transcendent truth of poetic language. The speaker says that he has "a thousand tongues / And nine and ninety-nine lie." He chooses to sing with the one truthful tongue yet struggles because this honest impulse "will make no melody at my will" (1300). Crane thus establishes a dichotomy between truthful saying and the false sonorities of verse. Perhaps John Keats found Beauty and Truth synonymous, but Crane did not. This is made even clearer in a lyric unpublished during Crane's life that parodies Henry Wadsworth Longfellow's once-universally-known poem, "The Psalm of Life":

> Tell me not in joyous numbers
> We can make our lives sublime
> By—well, at least, not by
> Dabbling much in rhyme. (Crane 1347)

Seventy years earlier, Longfellow said that we could reach sublimity by following in the footsteps of those who have gone before us. Crane mocks Longfellow's strenuous didacticism, suggesting that the traditional music of poetry willfully falsifies the real conditions of human experience for the tune's sake.

Crane's divergence from tradition is especially noticeable in his many poems that are essentially theological anecdotes. In them, Crane presents an unlikely God that resembles the Judeo-Islamic-Christian deity only in name. For instance, in poem VI of *The Black Riders*, God "carefully" makes "the ship of the world," using "the infinite skill of an all-master." But when he turns his head to attend to some "wrong," the ship escapes his grasp, and "forever rudderless" (1300) moves in its arbitrary patterns while "many in the sky" laugh at the sight (1301). The God of this poem is capable of error and distraction and is either powerless to control his creation or so indifferent that he just does not do it. The angels in heaven seem to think the whole thing is amusing, though the world's inconstancies and vagaries cause great suffering.

The view of God here is greatly at odds with the conception of God as all-loving, all-powerful, and all-knowing. While it is not unusual to come across agnostic poets looking at empty skies or atheist poets who deny a deity, Crane confidently asserts a peculiarly unconventional, uncomforting God. His main target is the problem addressed by religious apologists: how to square the conception of a loving God with natural catastrophes and more generally with the fact that evil does not seem to be hindered or punished. In this regard, Crane takes an empirical approach. Observing human pain and its causes, he asks, "What sort of god created this?" Crane's poems can be seen as little existentialist sermons, refusing to make the leap of faith, asserting the world's absurdity, and forging a kind of faux theology based on observable evidence.

As Crane emphatically rejected a conventional God, so his nature poems turn their back on romantic nature. Wordsworth saw the natural world as a restorative, giving us a glimpse of something greater to buoy us as we trudge on in this vale of tears. In a famous lyric, however, Crane describes the universe of London's "To Build a Fire" or his own "The Open Boat":

> A man said to the universe:
> "Sir, I exist!"
> "However," replied the universe,
> "The fact has not created in me
> "A sense of obligation." (1335)

The tart response tells us that, from the universe's viewpoint, human existence is neither particularly interesting nor obliges it to anything. Someone seeking to find truth in the natural world is like the person chasing the horizon in poem XXIV of *The Black Riders*: a fool desiring a beautiful illusion.

Taken as a whole, the salient point of Crane's poetry is not the positions it takes but the skeptical stance it assumes. A consistent butt of satire are those who adhere rigidly to their ideas despite disastrous results. In poem V from *The Black Riders*, for instance, incalculable blood is shed as a result of people who obey a man demanding that the whole world be arranged in rows; in a later poem, a youth cheerfully allows himself to be assassinated because it is being done in accordance with "the best legends" (1308). Similarly, Crane's war poems depict, time and again, the dangers of believing false ideas. The first poem in *War is Kind*, for instance, relentlessly juxtaposes the pain and suffering of war with the rhetoric used to justify it. After describing "a thousand corpses," the speaker admonishes the weeping survivors that "[w]ar is kind" because it gives the fallen soldiers a "splendid shroud" (1325). His ultimate message, then, seems to presage the message that Adrienne Rich articulated nearly a century later: they can control you so long as you believe that your pain belongs to some transcendent order. Crane's poetry tries to get the reader to see just how improbable and self-serving these conceptions of order are.

CARL SANDBURG

Although Carl Sandburg wrote a great deal for over fifty years, *Chicago Poems* (1916) best demonstrates his naturalist tendencies toward critiquing the social and economic forces that entrap humans, tendencies that are most evident in the works he wrote before becoming the self-appointed celebrator of all things American. While some poems in the volume do not fit in well with the traditions of naturalism, others clearly do. The poem "Mamie," for instance, recounts the life of a female figure who, like Dreiser's Carrie Meeber, dreams of something better, yet like Crane's Maggie Johnson, ends up defeated by economic realities. There are, in fact, a number of sympathetic poems documenting the plight of women caught in economic systems that do not offer social mobility and that encourage disregard for their well-being. "Onion Days" is one of the more hopeful poems, describing a pregnant immigrant onion-picker who looks forward to the birth of her child—that is to say, her happy dreams may be realized since they do not involve economic or social advance. Other characters are like "Anna Imroth," the "factory girl" (33) who died because the sweathouse where she worked did not have a fire escape.

The men in these poems do not fare much better. In "Muckers," for instance, the speaker describes the terrible working conditions of the men digging ditches for new gas mains. While ten men wipe their brows and say, "O, it's a hell of a job," as many say, "Jesus, I wish I had a job" (21). Although a poem like "Mag"—in which the speaker regrets getting married and having children—portrays the breakdown of familial feeling also seen in Upton Sinclair's The Jungle (1906), more often Sandburg portrays those who have not been dehumanized by conditions. For instance, in three successive poems, "The Shovel Man," "A Teamster's Farewell," and "Fish Crier," workers retain their humanity and sense of self despite enervating work. Sandburg rather scrupulously avoids the Victorian implication that hard work is, itself, morally uplifting. In fact, in poems like "Dynamiter," "Ice Handler," "Masses," and "I am the People, the Mob," Sandburg's endorsement of Marx's vision of proletarian revolution (and Marx's romantic notion of an ideal future) disqualify him from endorsing the sublime resignation to nature and global systems that Norris seems to endorse at the end of The Octopus. Sandburg's poetry tends to the forward-thinking, ameliorationist impulse—we are encouraged to see that, for example, the deaths of people like Anna Imroth can be avoided by perfectly enactable measures like building codes.

Though Sandburg's poetry fits well within the naturalist impulse to describe the forces that constrict human life, he is always a little resistant to the more determinist strains. Take, for example, "Skyscraper." Skyscrapers at the time were quickly becoming the visible emblems of major cities, sources of civic pride and testaments to engineering. The designs of architects like Louis Sullivan frequently highlighted vertical lines to give buildings that were already unprecedentedly tall an even taller feel. As such, these buildings functioned as self-regulated, self-sufficient, massive systems. "Skyscraper" makes gestures in this direction, describing the long elevators, the girders used to hold up the frame, the "hundreds of names" on office doors, the "tons of letters" that circulate every day, and the "master-men who rule the building" (66). But for all this, Sandburg does not give in to pessimism. The poem's refrain is that the building has a "soul," and its final scene is of a "young watchman" (67) hopefully looking out a window at the city lights below. One senses that, had Sandburg written An American Tragedy, Clyde Griffiths would have been able to make parole.

EDGAR LEE MASTERS

Both in subject matter and philosophical orientation, Edgar Lee Masters's *Spoon River Anthology* (1915) strongly reflects the influence of American literary naturalism, particularly its skepticism regarding convention, its concern for documenting the lives of the lower classes, and its depiction of the ways in which social and economic forces constrain human aspirations. The book's main conceit is that of a graveyard tour where, at each gravesite, a dead person rises to speak. Like the disembodied voices of *The Greek Anthology* that inspired Masters, the poems are short, generally lyric, and most often consist of the dead person's reflections on life. Masters updated the *Anthology* by locating the speakers in a small town in Ohio, so that the volume anticipates the perspective of works like *Main Street* (1920), *Babbitt* (1922), and *Winesburg, Ohio* (1919).

Spoon River also has a strong allegiance to the first third of *The Divine Comedy* (1321). Like the denizens of Dante's Inferno, the spirits who tell their stories in *Spoon River* find that their translation to the next realm has not taken away their personalities, passions, or prejudices. Masters's volume begins with a poem about the great leveler, death, listing people up and down the social scale, followed by the refrain, "*All, all, are sleeping on the hill*" (11), yet the spirits themselves seem surprised by this fact—those of high social standing, such as Judge Somers, are disgusted that they must rest for eternity next to ne' er-do-wells. Idlers and thieves like Chase Henry and Hod Putt find death's disregard for position and rank very amusing, a cosmic practical joke on their more respectable neighbors.

In *Spoon River*, the characters are generally defined not so much by the facts of their lives, but by the part of their lives they choose to narrate and how they explain, apologize, exult upon, or try to excuse their actions. Often the same event is narrated by more than one spirit, introducing a dynamic perspectivism that would become the hallmark of modernist art. For instance, Knowlt Hoheimer explains he enlisted in the Civil War to avoid going to prison for hog-stealing and pointedly asks the reader what the phrase, "Pro Patria," on his tombstone means. However, the next speaker, Lydia Puckett, tells us that Hoheimer really went off to fight because she broke up with him. Which is the right version of events? Is Puckett revealing Hoheimer's real motivation, or are we to see her assertion as an example of her overweening pride? Are both telling the truth? Neither?

Puckett's claim also highlights one reason why the book is less popular with academics than it was fifty or sixty years ago: her entire speech is about Hoheimer's supposed affection for her. Indeed, very few of *Spoon River*'s women define themselves except in terms of the men they love or who love them; even fewer suppose any identity except that as lover, wife, or mother. The men, it is true, frequently focus on their personal relationships as their lives' defining aspect, but they just as often talk about their professions, their political and social aspirations, or their philosophical ideas. What keeps the women from being merely cultural stereotypes, however, is the way that their poems express frustration over their circumscribed lives. In this, the poems reflect naturalism's general attitude that social institutions hinder rather than promote happiness.

The problem of marriage is one aspect of the greater naturalist theme in *Spoon River*—how corrupt human institutions and narrow social ideologies deprive human beings of happiness. Spoon River is filled with people whose lives have been inhibited. Both Serepta Mason and Mabel Osborne in fact describe themselves as stunted flowers, and readers hear from a frustrated inventor (Franklin Jones), frustrated politicians (most pathetically, Enoch Dunlap), a frustrated philanthropist (Seth Compton), frustrated scientists (Perry Zoll and Alfonso Churchill), and frustrated artists (Margaret Fuller Slack and Archibald Higbie). Abel Melveny believes himself to be "a good machine / That Life had never used" (168).

Some of Spoon River's denizens blame their frustration on life itself or fate. Robert Fulton Tanner explains that life is nothing other than a rat trap, seemingly offering something only to use that to ensnare us, whereas Cassius Hueffer and Henry Layton assert the biological argument that since they are made of such incompatible elements, their failure was inevitable. Aner Clute and Griffy the Cooper articulate socially deterministic points of view—the former explains that, if enough people decide a boy is or will be a thief, that boy will grow up to be a thief, and Griffy says that we are all constrained by "[t]aboos and rules and appearances" (77).

In addition to social and religious taboos, the spirits in Spoon River frequently point to a small group of men who enriched themselves and kept the rest from opportunity: Thomas Rhodes, who owned the bank and worked for the railroads; Coolbaugh Whedon, editor of the newspaper, *The Argus*; Rev. Abner Peet; and A. D. Blood, the mayor. The corrupting influence of these men is mentioned even by people who were not directly hurt by them. However, in their own epitaphs, only Whedon admits any wrongdoing; in his monologue, he says that he was able to "see every side of every question" (137), which apparently led to a moral relativism directed by whatever was convenient and profitable for him at the moment. His disgust is directed partly at himself, as he acknowledges the "base designs" his newspaper promoted, and partly at Spoon River, which he sees as a sewer of illicit activities and not worth saving.

While Rhodes mocks the "liberals" and offers his own life devoted to getting money as "self-contained, compact, harmonized" (115) as opposed to the messy and unsuccessful lives of his detractors, the other powerful characters do not bother to address their detractors. They either do not recognize or refuse to admit the suffering they caused. An instructive group of epitaphs in this regard is the sad story of Minerva Jones, who was born with some sort of birth defect that left her with a "heavy body, cock-eye, and a rolling walk" (32), yet she also wrote poetry for the *Argus*. One day, "Butch" Weldy hunted her down and brutally raped her, leaving her with Dr. Meyers, who tried, unsuccessfully, to save her life. After she died, Meyers was indicted for the murder and vilified by the *Argus*, which presumably implied that she died because he tried to abort a child that he had engendered. His wife, Meyers explains, died of "a broken heart" (34), and he himself by pneumonia.

After Jones and Meyers tell their stories, Weldy tells his—and yet he does not even mention the incident. He only describes how he "got religion and settled down" (36) and was blinded in an accident in the canning works. While his actions on that one night constituted the defining, tragic moment for three other people, it does not seem to have been particularly remarkable or important to him. Moments such as this in *Spoon River* suggest that human society is, as Thomas Rhodes suggested liberals are, just "cellular atoms," interacting randomly according to no grand scheme.

Indeed, the only characters satisfied with their lives are the ones who believe in conventional religion or in some spiritual substitute and who have given up worldly success. They find satisfaction in life because they expect nothing from it. While the town is full of frustrated and discouraged women, an exception is Lois Spears who is the "happiest of women, / As wife, mother, and housekeeper" (62), occupations that brought no joy to Margaret Fuller Slack. Spears finds these tasks fulfilling because she was born blind and thus (given the cultural milieu) grew up assuming she would be an old maid. Likewise, Fiddler Jones rejects the opportunity to labor on a farm and instead spends his life fiddling for dances and picnics. His epitaph ends,

> I ended up with a broken fiddle,—
> And a broken laugh, and a thousand memories.
> And not a single regret. (71)

The moral seems to be that the world's systems are corrupt and like Tanner's rat trap. The reasonable person does not go for the bait.

THEODORE DREISER

Theodore Dreiser's verse, more than any other of the works in this survey, exemplifies the justice of Walcutt's divided-stream argument—yet both streams are rarely present in the same poem. *Moods, Philosophic and Emotional, Cadenced and Declaimed* (1935) can be neatly divided between poems on theological and spiritual themes and poems portraying the sort of stunted lives found in *Spoon River*.

The realist, documentary impulse can be seen in "Geddo Street," which juxtaposes the "Bleary dwellings, / Dreary dwellings" and the "open saloons at every corner" of the ghetto, with the "splendid machines, / That never pause, / Speeding to the west" (66)—trains—to dramatize economic inequality. "Flaherty Junction" offers brief sketches of a "bearded German and his wife," a frazzled station agent, a tramp, a "lout," and a Swede, all accompanied by details Dreiser might have used in one of his novels. However, these sorts of poems are in the minority, probably because when Dreiser was adopting this sort of documentary approach, he typically thought in terms of prose.

More generally, Dreiser emphasizes the fruitless hopes of people bumping their heads against economic systems and social prejudices. In "The Factory," for example, the workers are but cogs in a huge machine, their "deepest, darkest moods repressed" (107). There are only a few that dream, laugh, or sing; what everyone believes, the narrator explains, is that if the workers do not hasten in their work, they will be impoverished and lose "the respect of men" (108). In "The Victim Speaks," a boy who has lost his hand in a railroad accident complains that he is exactly the same person he was before the accident, yet now "All men withdraw from me / As though they feared contagion" (173). The theme of the futility of hope is emphasized by the last poem in *Moods*, "As with a Finger in Water," which informs its readers that "The aspirations, / The dreams, / And the achievements / Of men" (423) are as significant and lasting as a finger in water, chalk on a chalkboard, and breath misting a windowpane.

This fatalistic view is countered by poems that articulate the spiritual beliefs Dreiser associates with Eastern religion. In "Brahma," for instance, the speaker perceives

> Dim
> But persistent images
> Of sloughing mortal, meaty flesh,
> For the pure fire of energy and thought. (21)

Later in volume, "Sutra" offers an *"Improvisation upon the Upanishad"*—a loose interpretation of a text held holy by Hindus—which suggests an "absolute" behind all earthly appearances (316).

Dreiser seems to prize these non-Western conceptions of the divine as an arational antidote to the repressive conceptions he finds in conventional religion, which are almost always the butt of satire. In "Sailor," for instance, the sailing speaker walks on "the deck of dogma, / Steering by the light of faith" and yet finds his conceptions are inadequate for his actual experiences in the world. In a poem reminiscent of one of Crane's metaphysical lyrics, the God in "Toymaker" describes the "chemism"—human beings—which he created and for which he does not "provide / Enough" (12). God finds his toy entertaining and laughable.

This mechanistic view of human existence, which ultimately lampoons the Enlightenment's Clockmaker God, is addressed in "Martyr," the story of a Christian martyr in Roman times who, facing imminent death, begins a series of metaphysical and theological reflections. He begins "Proud of what I thought was true" but comes to a less certain belief. He asks whether he is just "a mathematical, / Or shall I say, / Electro-chemical formula" (114), but rejects this notion, ultimately arriving at the same reality that René Descartes did: the self, the ego, the "I." While the martyr is unsure, finally, of his Savior, he does affirm the self that desires (and perhaps invented) such a savior.

Like Crane, Dreiser seems either incapable of, or more likely, uninterested in providing a consistent and coherent theology or metaphysics, but instead wants to affirm the human desire for something greater and to attack narrow points of view. Thus, we can see the strain of naturalist agnosticism and skepticism running through Dreiser's verse; like Crane, sometimes he seems to believe and sometimes he seems to deny, and overall the only thing a reader can confirm is his spiritual questioning.

ROBINSON JEFFERS

Jeffers's corpus can be seen as one long demonstration of the naturalist notion that human beings are unable to alter the social, economic, and natural forces which determine their lives. In "The Purse-Seine," for example, the speaker likens schools of sardines caught in a net to all of Western civilization, telling the reader that, like the fish, our "interdependence" will lead to our ultimate destruction. The speaker does not warn but prophesizes: "There is no escape," the speaker remarks dispassionately; didn't we know "that cultures decay, and life's end is death" (62)?

Moreover, the poem constitutes a rejection of romantic nature even more emphatic than anything in Crane. Wordsworth's revelation at the top of Mount Snowdon gives him sudden insight about his relationship with the world, with the God of which the natural world is a manifestation, and with all other humans. Jeffers's speaker, also looking down from a height, likewise gains insight into his relations with the world, God, and other people, but he finds the symbols point to human futility, not to the infinite reaches of human possibility. The interdependence which Wordsworth hails as a foundation of moral life Jeffers sees as the inevitable cause of decay. The lesson the natural world teaches us is how far civilization has taken us from the primal impulse of free growth, independent direction, and passionate creativity.

Unlike Crane and Dreiser, who are generally content to critique the limitations of traditional religion, in his longer poems Jeffers proposes a quasi-religious outlook that embraces the physical world and rejects human institutions. This is most evident in his strange and disturbing narrative, *The Roan Stallion* (1925), which features a young mother whose name, California, and parentage (she is one-fourth Scottish, one-fourth Native American, one-fourth Spanish, and one-fourth unidentified) alert the reader to her allegorical importance. Jeffers describes California as an ideal woman: she is "nobly formed," as "strong as a new tower; the features stolid and dark, / But sculpted into a strong grace," not unlike the stone cottage and tower Jeffers built overlooking Carmel Bay. She is carved out of local materials, with an intrinsic nobility befitting her rough-hewn dignity. Her brutal, alcoholic husband, Johnny, on the other hand, is an "outcast Hollander; not old but shriveled with bad living." He is the worst of a dying civilization and controls California by violence and by withholding money. Their daughter, Christine, is close to her mother but has "inherited" her father's "race blue eyes" (15). She sees the world, in a fundamental way, as her father does, partly because she is a Christian. The main characters, then, are products of their heredity, environment, and history. They are initially positioned, that is, as if they were characters in a novel by Zola.

As the narrative opens, Johnny, drunk as usual, returns home in the early hours of the morning, bringing a stallion he has won in a poker game. This earns California's silent disgust, since it is not a working horse and has no utility; the narrator later tells us that "she hated him for his uselessness, serving nothing / But Johnny's vanity" (21). She worries that the stallion will eat up all the barley normally given to their "buckskin," a mare and workhorse. As he stumbles to bed, she gets up to go to Monterey to buy presents for Christine since the next day will be Christmas. She rides on the buckskin, whose hard life, patient nature, and unstinting work ethic cause her to identify with the horse. The poem, then, portrays her as virtually the property of her vicious patriarch, who uses her with as much compassion as he uses his workhorse. At the beginning of the poem, she is very much like Rich's Aunt Jennifer.

Together, the two make the arduous journey to town, nearly dying on their return, since a rainstorm swells the river they must ford. The connection between California and the buckskin is made even more directly in this scene, since to coax the animal across and preserve her presents (including Johnny's whiskey), she must lead the horse by hand and strap the burden on herself: she is literally the pack animal. Thus, the first half of the narrative posits essential, racial character and examines the brutal, hopeless life of the underclass. But Jeffers is uninterested in the larger economic conditions that led to her victimization, as the narrative's second half demonstrates. Startlingly, the second part of the narrative aligns itself with the intuitional, idealist stream of naturalism without relinquishing the pessimism that is often seen as accompanying the materialist stream.

After Johnny leaves again and Christine is put to bed, California goes out into the night, seeking to understand the sense of a transcendence she experienced while fording the river. She climbs a mountain and has a vision in conjunction with the Roan Sstallion, whose natural power and reckless freedom represent everything that her life lacks: he is the "savage and exultant strength of the world" (27). Her mystical vision includes a "crucified man," yet California sees this as one of the "racial myths" that are "the phantom rulers of humanity" (29). The narrator had earlier explained what California learns: "I say / Humanity is the mould to break from, the crust to break through, the coal to break into fire, / The atom to be split" (24). In her encounter with the Roan Stallion, California learns to embrace what Jeffers would later call the gospel of Inhumanism, which urges us to break free of human solipsism and accept the transhuman magnificence that our humanistic beliefs have caused us to discount or allegorize into something else. That is why the racial myths are "phantoms": they are fictions that we invent in an attempt to render transcendent truth into human categories. Thus, while *The Roan Stallion* exemplifies both tributaries of Walcutt's divided stream, it does so by advocating a kind of idealism that, like the universe in Crane's lyric, is unimpressed with human aspiration and unmoved by human suffering.

Nowhere is this more evident than in the poem's final, climatic scene. Johnny, drunk again, instructs his dog to track California down so that he can have sex with her. Driven by her night-time experience, she hides in the stallion's corral, but the dog picks up the trail and follows her to the corral where the stallion, agitated by the dog, begins to paw the ground. Johnny, fearing injury to his dog and his stallion, enters the corral, while California doubles back to the house to get a rifle. The powerful stallion is upset by the snarling dog and the tense human. By the time California returns, Johnny has been injured and is crawling slowly back to the fence around the corral. California, "without doubting, without hesitance," shoots the dog. She then lowers the rifle and watches while the horse rears up and kills Johnny, leaving "nothing alive but teeth" (33).

As dreadful as this scene is, it is made even more terrible because Christine has witnessed the entire thing, crying out when her mother killed the dog (though California claims, dishonestly, it was a mistake), and then watching in silent horror as the stallion kills her father. With such a witness, California then feels compelled to act. Jeffers's description is disconcerting. California, "moved by some obscure human fidelity," takes up her rifle and draws a bead on the stallion:

> Each separate nerve-cell of her brain flaming the stars fell from their
>   places
> Crying in her mind; she fired three times before the haunches crumpled
>   sidewise, the forelegs stiffening,
> And the beautiful strength settled to earth; she turned then on her little
>   daughter the mask of a woman
> Who has killed God. (33–34)

California, driven by her ideological identification with "the human," her notions of what is expected of a mother and wife, and the Christian religion, kills the transhuman, untamed, and vital spirit. Given the chance to burst out of her skull and break the mould, she instead chooses to deny her true self and adopt the mask. She feels she must act against what she knows instinctively, in a way that she has been told is "good," and thus destroys the actual spirit manifesting itself.

From Jeffers's perspective, the deaths of Johnny and his dog are not tragic. The dog, after all, lives to please the man. And Johnny represents the last, degenerate dregs of a Dutch race that flourished in the seventeenth and eighteenth centuries but now has spent its force. Allowing the stallion to kill him only hastens what was already happening. When California kills the horse, though, she tragically chooses that branch of the human family tree that will lead to our demise. Her name identifies her as an emblem of the last frontier in America; her action symbolizes the national acquiescence to values that will cause us all, in the not-too-distant future, to be caught up in the sardine net. In the end, she cannot break from the systems and the beliefs that naturalist writers from Zola to Jeffers insist have subjugated us.

The poem also reveals Jeffers as taking the naturalist view of nature to an extreme beyond that which was envisioned by London or Crane. By the eighteenth century, poets like Alexander Pope, James Thomson, William Cowper, and count-less others established the practice of relentlessly allegorizing the natural world. The romantic writers changed the meaning of these allegories, but time and again, the reader finds out that natural phenomena are significant because of the greater truths they point to, generally some version of a divine plan. In naturalist works, however, the natural world functions not as a symbol but as the reality to which symbols point. In Crane and London, for instance, we are left with the realization that, despite the universe's impressiveness, it has no interest in furthering human philosophical enlightenment. Still, these works leave us with the notion that it is a shame that we live in such a world, that it would be so much nicer and more com-fortable if only we lived in the purposeful universe of Thomson and Wordsworth. Jeffers, however, is one of the first to take the perspective of the astrophysicist or archaeologist—human life comes and goes, civilizations rise and fall, and every-thing develops and decays inevitably. Jeffers is unusual in asserting that the fall of great civilizations, and of humanity in general, is a good thing, since these human beings are constantly distracted from the vital, the beautiful, the clean, the absolute, and the lasting. It is a lonely cosmology, to be sure, but, Jeffers would have us know, it is the only one that has any claim to truth.

Robert Lowell, Sylvia Plath, and Sharon Olds

Naturalist poetry generally went the way of naturalist fiction, becoming subsumed into the evolution of realism into modernism, remaining a stream but rarely so purely expressed as it was in the late nineteenth century and the early twentieth century. Naturalist religious skepticism helped lay a foundation for the twentieth-century poet's quest for a new, individualistic, more satisfying spirituality (even if the answer turned out to be a healthy dose of atavism), and poets have remained interested in the underclass. However, the naturalist poetical works that seemed daring and new in the teens began to seem old-fashioned by the avant-garde poets who became more interested in ever-more-radical experiments in poetic form (and in the ideologies implicit in these forms) than in documenting the material realities of life. Moreover, the grounds of what writers began to consider "reality" started to undergo a seismic shift that was almost lethal to the Zolaesque naturalists. The assumptions fundamental to the objective, "scientific" approach, such as the validity of "race" and social Darwinism, began to seem much less tenable. Poets, in general, became more preoccupied with uncertainly and subjectivity.

    Paradoxically, this preoccupation helped give rise to an impressive body of poetry with strong naturalist tendencies in the 1950s and 1960s. Since naturalist poets and novelists were grounded in nineteenth-century speculation, they were apt to talk about "character," but they were often trying to understand something that nowadays would be called psychology. Freud and others revolutionized how we thought about the mind, personality, and the motivations for human behavior, sometimes in positing rather deterministic paradigms. For this reason, the poetic movement that most markedly exhibits naturalist tendencies is the intensely subjective confessional poetry.

For instance, in *Life Studies* (1959), Robert Lowell narrates his own life in "91 Revere Street," which shows that the troubled and damaged persona of the volume is the result of growing up in household where life was made uncomfortable by his mother's insistent though undirected sense that she deserved something better, and by the way his father miserably failed in doing the things that his wife demanded and he thought he was obligated to do. The family became financially insecure and emotionally unbalanced. In short, Lowell shows how he was created by his environment.

Writing about himself as a character controlled by environmental forces led Lowell into the habit of seeing everyone so controlled. In "Memories of West Street and Lepke," for instance, the speaker remarks, "These are the tranquillized fifties" (85). That is, he implies that his view from the roof of the West Street Jail is more generally the view of his generation, and that the final image of a lobotomized "Czar Lepke"—the nickname of an infamous crime syndicate leader—is only an exaggerated image of us all, since we are all seemingly incapable of any "agonizing reappraisal" (86).

Similarly, in one of Lowell's finest poems, "Skunk Hour," the speaker, alone at night, observes the world in a car overlooking a point where teenagers park to make out. The "radio bleats / Love, O careless Love"—a song about how love is doomed and destroys the lives of those in its throes. However, the speaker and the various characters he describes are too lifeless even to experience the agonies of passion. The speaker's attitude anticipates postmodernism: we are all spectators rather than actors, imagining (probably wrongly) that other people live more fully and have more meaningful contact with one another than we do.

The poem's one nondespairing image is only a cause for greater despair. The poem concludes with a description of a mother skunk and her kittens rooting through the garbage. However disgusting, life is going on for the skunk, who, upon being spotted, "drops her ostrich tail, / And will not scare" (90). The skunk—capable of resistance, procreation, and self-assertion—can find her way in a modern landscape, mainly because she is not human and thus not bedeviled with self-consciousness. She cannot hear the song "Careless Love" and reflect on her own lack. Her stubborn fecundity, then, only foregrounds the unbridgeable difference between the natural world and the world humans have made for themselves. For all its modernist trappings, the poem reflects the naturalist, anti-romantic conception of the natural world.

Sylvia Plath's poetry similarly depicts the plight of its persona caught in a hostile world and in the remorseless operations of her own mind, a terrible drama depicted time and again in her greatest work, *Ariel* (1965). In what is today perhaps her most famous poem, "Daddy," the speaker speaks, impossibly, futilely, to her dead father, venting her rage at his early death and what she describes as his "Fascist" manners when he was alive. She admits to attempting suicide in order to "get back, back, back to you," but "they" wouldn't let her die (58).

The speaker's irrational vehemence invites the reader to ask what conditions cause her to think these thoughts. These conditions include the social pressures placed on women, as is made clear on a series of poems Plath wrote about bees ("The Bee Meeting," "The Arrival of the Bee Box," "Stings," "The Swarm," and "Wintering"), all of which explore the paradox that even the most powerful female bee, the queen, is caught in a system, a "honey-machine" (70) that will eventually serve as her "mausoleum" (71)—just as, implicitly, women are trapped in their role of baby-making machine and nurturer.

In addition to manifesting the naturalist impulse to social criticism, Plath's poetry is laced with despair regarding human possibility. At the end of "Daddy," the speaker claims to be "through" with her father, but it is hard to credit this assertion since she does not seem to have gained the self-understanding that would allow her, in good Freudian style, to put the past safely in the past and begin living in the present. Plath's characters, like Lowell's, have an enduring argument with the past, and for this reason, the argument cannot be resolved. A poem to an ex-lover may spark a reply, even a change of heart, but dead people do not write poems, answer phone calls, or amend their actions.

The contemporary confessional poet Sharon Olds carries on these naturalist tendencies of the poets of the 1950s and 1960s, but she has carved out a less desperate persona. This is especially evident in the conclusion to *The Father* (1992), a book of poems that describes a grown woman watching her aged father, beset with incurable illness, slowly degenerate and die. The father is ill, vulnerable, helpless, trying to hold on to something as he "moves, hour by hour, head-first / toward death" (6). As such, he is pitiable, except for one thing: he lived an alcoholic, abusive, and violent life, married to a woman who was unable to defend herself. To her credit, Olds does not forget this aspect of her past relationship with her father in order to make it an easier book to write or a more empathetic portrayal of illness and death. Instead, in the concluding poems of the book, she asks with increasing intensity, what is my connection with this person? Clearly her relationship has not been what a father-daughter relationship "should" be, what everybody assumes it "really is," what people tend to assume all father-daughter relationships, at some deep level, "are." At every turn, she rejects metaphysical consolation, the idea that his abusive past does not matter any more, and the notion that, like Tolstoy's Ivan Illych, his illness and suffering have moralized him.

What, then, is there to love? In the final poem, Olds lists the things she loves—which all turn out to be body parts. Even his brain is lovable, not because of its thoughts, but for its "halves and silvery folds" (78). She decides she loves her biological connection to her father, an attachment with none of the traditional, nostalgic pull of other sorts of bonds, but a connection she finds real and compelling nonetheless. As she looks down at the body of her dead father, she finds it saying to her:

> I am matter,
> your father, I made you, when I say now that I love you
> I mean look down at your hand, move it,
> that action is matter's love, for human
> love go elsewhere. (79)

In these lines, Olds affirms a strong attachment that is in part the human desire for love (even for the despicable) and in part DNA. She affirms the worth of this need, and she attempts to push her desire for physical connection out into the world in which we live so that it might have some tangible positive influence.

This ending makes the poem perhaps the supreme naturalistic philosophical poem. Naturalist poets typically struggle mightily between Walcutt's two "streams"—that is, between a relentless materialism which seems, ineluctably, to lead to determinism, and the idealist impulse which tends toward transcendent hope. Some poets, like Crane, give in to one strain, resorting to satire and anecdotes of futility, while others, like Dreiser, schizophrenically dabble in both streams. Jeffers cast his lot with the rocks and oceans and rather insouciantly bids goodbye to all messy humanity. While Jeffers found a formulation that is idealist and pessimistic, Olds found one that is nearly diametrically opposite. She crafts a position that is both material and progressive. The end of *Father* indicates that our positive values come from paying attention to what Blake, two centuries earlier, called "minute particulars"—small things like the hands of a dead man. Taken as a whole, her poetry attests to the enduring legacy of a naturalist poetic tradition.

WORKS CITED

Crane, Stephen. *Prose and Poetry*. New York: Library of America, 1984.

Dreiser, Theodore. *Moods, Philosophic and Emotional, Cadenced and Declaimed*. New York: Simon & Schuster, 1935.

Jeffers, Robinson. *Selected Poems*. New York: Vintage, 1965.

Lowell, Robert. *Life Studies and For the Union Dead*. New York: Farrar, Straus & Giroux, 1964.

Masters, Edgar Lee. *Spoon River Anthology*. New York: Signet, 1992.

Norris, Frank. "The Responsibilities of the Novelist." *Documents of American Realism and Naturalism*. Ed. Donald Pizer. Carbondale: Southern Illinois University Press, 1998. 175–78.

Olds, Sharon. *The Father*. New York: Knopf, 1992.

Pound, Ezra. *The Cantos of Ezra Pound*. New York: New Directions, 1986.

Pizer, Donald. *Twentieth-Century American Literary Naturalism*. Carbondale: Southern Illinois University Press, 1984.

Plath, Sylvia. *Ariel*. New York: Harper-Perennial, 1975.

Rich, Adrienne. "Aunt Jennifer's Tigers." *The Fact of a Doorframe*. New York: Norton, 1984. 4.

———. "Hunger." *The Dream of a Common Language*. New York: Norton, 1978. 12–14.

Sandburg, Carl. *Chicago Poems*. Urbana and Chicago: University of Illinois Press, 1992.

Walcutt, Charles Child. *American Literary Naturalism, A Divided Stream*. Minneapolis: University of Minnesota Press, 1956.

CHAPTER 27

NATURALISM AND THE VISUAL ARTS

DONALD PIZER

By "naturalism" in my title, I mean American fiction of the 1890s and 1930s that was committed to the depiction of hardship, poverty, and other forms of deprivation and of the inability both of the individual and of society to overcome these conditions. By "visual arts," I mean both the graphic arts of painting and various kinds of drawing and the more recently developed art of photography. I will devote my attention to two ways in which the visual arts and naturalistic expression are interrelated during the 1890s and 1930s. The first stems from the immersion of both visual artists and writers in a similar social and artistic milieu, one which encouraged expression to take roughly parallel form and shape in both areas of expression. The second concerns a more specific act of borrowing from a visual form by a writer. I will initially discuss the impact of a 1890s school of New York urban realism in photography and the graphic arts on Theodore Dreiser's *Sister Carrie* (1900) and the relationship of Stephen Crane's writing to photography and impressionism. I will then examine the influence of 1930s documentary photography on John Steinbeck's *The Grapes of Wrath* (1939).

Almost all of these instances of a naturalist writer's indebtedness to a visual art form confirm the truism that naturalists usually viewed themselves as playing a mediating role between social reality and need on the one hand and the reader on the other. There is a social condition—for example, the slums or migrant exploitation—and the naturalist writer seeking to represent it is almost inevitably drawn to parallel efforts by visual artists. The specific instances of this attraction in the three writers I examine, however, should also demonstrate that the truism is useful only as far as it goes, which is not very far at all in comparison to the richness and variability of the specific instance. Indeed, a realization of the full dimensions of these instances should cast far more light on each individual writer's distinctive qualities of mind and art than that provided by the commonplace about a naturalist's preference for visual arts with a social realism bias.

THEODORE DREISER

Ellen Moers once noted that Dreiser's lengthy article "Curious Shifts of the Poor," published in November 1899, can scarcely be separated from his "first contribution to the literature of realism, *Sister Carrie*" (57). Moers in part means by this remark that Dreiser's extensive early career as a newspaper reporter, editor, and magazine writer from 1892 to 1899 had revealed little inclination toward the kind of subject matter present initially in "Curious Shifts" and shortly thereafter in *Carrie*, which he began writing in the fall of 1899. True, he had expressed a conventional kind of dismay over the condition of the working poor of New York in several of his *Ev'ry Month* editorials, but these accounts lacked any element of the pictorial—of the physical actuality of poverty and hardship. "Curious Shifts," however, aside from a shift into Dreiser's philosophical voice at its close, is very different. The article consists of four sketches describing in concrete detail the desperate efforts of New York's down-and-out homeless to stay alive during the depths of a hard winter. The sketches are laced with tropes of coldness—of snow and freezing temperatures—and of men standing in line as they seek out the meager charities available to them. In this effort, the poor are herded as groups but are in isolation from each other, and every haven from the weather and starvation is clearly a temporary one. Dreiser was to use large sections of the article verbatim in the closing chapters of *Sister Carrie*, but, as I will point out, his entire account of the final phase of Hurstwood's life is permeated with both its material actuality and emotional ethos.

How did Dreiser, with little or no prior indication of an interest in or an ability for this kind of urban pictorial realism, "suddenly" (it would seem) blossom into "Curious Shifts"? For an answer to this question, it is necessary to turn to two significant developments in the New York art world during the 1890s, both stressing the art-worthiness of the New York scene, that impinged on Dreiser's consciousness in the closing years of the decade.[1] The first, chronologically speaking, was the photography of Alfred Stieglitz, the second the sketches and painting of the group of artists who came to be known as the Ash Can School.[2]

Stieglitz had from the early 1890s pioneered through his own work and that exhibited by the Camera Club, a photography cooperative led by him, a new kind of urban photography, one which ignored the conventional subjects of the grandiose and picturesque for commonplace scenes of New York life. There was nothing "candid" about his shots of either people or scenes; many were studies in composition and also frequently suggested the "poetic" in their manipulation of light and focus. But they were nevertheless striking efforts to render quotidian New York as worthy of artistic representation. Stieglitz's work was increasingly known throughout the decade after he achieved a notable success in 1893 when he exhibited "Winter on Fifth Avenue," no doubt the best-known photograph of this phase of his career (figure 27.1). Dreiser published three articles between June 1899 and May 1902 about either Stieglitz or the Camera Club.[3] Although these are conventional pieces of popular journalism and offer little insight into Dreiser's personal response to Stieglitz's work, his article of October 1899 does contain a notable admiring brief comment on "Winter on Fifth Avenue." "The driving sleet," Dreiser wrote, "and the uncomfortable atmosphere issued out of the picture with uncomfortable persuasion" ("Camera Club" 85)

Although many commentators on this phase of Dreiser's career claim that Stieglitz's New York scenes played a major role in the emergence of the urban realism of *Sister Carrie*, the more likely scenario is that his work served as a precursor for the more significant and extended role of the later-to-appear Ash Can figures and especially of Everett Shinn. Most of the Eight (another term for the Ash Can School) were Philadelphia-bred and trained newspaper illustrators who

Figure 27.1   Alfred Stieglitz, "Winter on Fifth Avenue" (1893)

migrated to New York toward the end of the decade, where they drifted first into magazine illustrating and then full-fledged independent art careers. The figures included Shinn, John Sloan, George Luks, George Bellows, and William Glackens. Dreiser came to know Shinn, Luks, and Glackens, but it was Shinn who played the major role in his thinking about urban realism. Even before Shinn's appearance in New York in 1898, however, Dreiser had been exposed to the principal thrust of the Ash Can School by his acquaintance during the mid-1890s, when he was editing *Ev'ry Month*, with the artist W. L. Sonntag, Jr. Sonntag, who died of illness while reporting the Spanish-American War, was memorialized by Dreiser in an 1901 article called "The Color of To-Day." He recalled Sonntag showing him Greeley Square at night, a scene alive with crowds and lights, and Sonntag exclaiming, "It's a great spectacle! . . . It's got more flesh and blood in it than people usually think" ("Color" 277). "Spectacle" and "flesh and blood" and Dreiser's own "color of to-day"[4] are the key terms connecting Sonntag's beliefs and the ideas and practice of the Ash Can School. New York, from posh upper Fifth Avenue to the slums of the lower East Side, was a great spectacle, full of vibrant life of every kind. It is sometimes believed that the artists holding this belief concentrated on the poor and downtrodden, as is suggested by the term Ash Can School as a designation for the group. But in fact, their work ranged over the full face of New York life, from immigrants to the wealthy and from popular entertainments to street accidents, though they tended in all their efforts toward depicting groups of people in vibrant interaction. The point was to communicate the "color"—the variety and richness—of urban life whatever its social level or its lack of a traditional role in art representation.

Dreiser probably came to know Shinn in 1898, when both he and Shinn were contributing regularly to *Ainslee's*—Dreiser poems and articles, Shinn covers. (The link between them may well have been Dreiser's close friend Richard Duffy, who was then an editor at *Ainslee's*). Shinn's first one-man show occurred during February and March 1900 when he exhibited forty-four pastels of New York scenes at the Boussod-Valadon Galleries (Wong 37–38). A *New York Times* reviewer described the exhibition as consisting of "pastel colored drawings, for the most part scenes on Union and Madison Squares and Fifth Avenue on the afternoons and early evenings of Winter snowstorms . . ." ("Week"). Shinn's "Fifth Avenue Coach, Winter" (1899) was among these pastels referred to by the reviewer (Deshazo 39), and there is considerable evidence from Dreiser's *The "Genius"* that he saw the drawing at that time or perhaps even earlier when Shinn was preparing his work for the exhibition. Indeed, Shinn recalled much later in life that he immediately recognized, on reading *The "Genius"* (1915), that Dreiser's description of Eugene Witla's first New York show contained descriptions of many of the pastels he had exhibited in February 1900 (Kwiat, "Dreiser's *The 'Genius'*" 17).

Dreiser's use of Shinn as a model for Witla's career in *The "Genius"* is probably the best evidence of the significance of Shinn's work in his own writing. (Witla, it should be clear, is based on Shinn only insofar as Witla's work as an artist is concerned; the account of Witla's personal experience in the novel stems from Dreiser's own life.) Witla arrives in New York having worked as an illustrator but still unformed as an artist. He is soon drawn, however, to the vitality and richness of the New York world all around him and attempts to communicate these qualities in his work, concentrating during this early phase on industrial cityscapes and lower-class street life. Among his various paintings of this period, two stand out in their connection both to Shinn and Dreiser. The bread line at Fleischmann's Vienna Style Café is one of Witla's subjects (232). Shinn himself did a notable pastel of this well-known New York institution, also in 1899, and Dreiser devotes one of the sketches in "Curious Shifts" to its depiction.[5] And Shinn's pastel of "Fifth Avenue Coach, Winter" (figure 27.2) is described in detail by M. Charles, the director of the gallery where Witla is having his first show. He is "struck by the force" of the "team of lean, unkempt, bony horses."

> He liked the delineation of swirling, wind-driven snow. The emptiness of this thoroughfare, usually so crowded, the buttoned, huddled, hunched, withdrawn look of those who traveled it, the exceptional details of piles of snow sifted on to window sills and ledges and into doorways and on to the windows of the bus itself, attracted his attention.
>
> "An effective detail," he said to Eugene, as one critic might say to another, pointing to a line of white snow on the window of one side of the bus. Another dash of snow on a man's hat rim took his eye also. "I can feel the wind," he added.
> (227–28)

Most of M. Charles's account is clearly related to Shinn's pastel, which, as I have noted, was one of the New York winter scenes shown at his February 1900

Figure 27.2   Everett Shinn, "Fifth Avenue Coach, Winter" (1899)

exhibition. The large vehicle dominating the drawing is a coach (the opening letters of the coach-line's name, METRO, can be made out on its side), and the matching lines of snow on the coach window and on the pedestrian's bowler that Charles
admired are also evident. But another element in the painting admired by Charles—
the emptiness of the street compared to its usual bustle—is perhaps better commu-
nicated by the wider focus of the Stiegliz photograph. In brief, Dreiser may well
have blended aspects of the scene as portrayed by Stieglitz and Shinn into his own
conception of how a pictorial work devoted to the scene might best serve his needs.
Thus, when writing his account of Witla's painting more than a decade after viewing
Stieglitz's photograph and Shinn's pastel, Dreiser was describing in 1912 his later
realization that work of this kind constituted the best tendencies both in the turn-
of-the-century New York art scene and his own emerging realistic aesthetic of the
late 1890s.[6]

I am drawn to this interpretation both because it suggests how Dreiser, and
how indeed most authors, are influenced—not by exact copying of a single source
but by a variety of sources feeding into a depiction—and because it says something of value about the portrayal of Hurstwood's New York decline in *Sister Carrie*. As several commentators have noted, whenever Dreiser shifts during the
closing portion of the novel from accounts of Carrie's rise to fame and fortune to
Hurstwood's drift toward complete physical and psychological collapse, the
weather also shifts from spring or summer to winter. (An exception is our final
glimpse of Carrie.) The Hurstwood depicted at this point in the novel is an approximation in prose narrative of the scenes portrayed by Stieglitz and Shinn, and
especially by Shinn. Hurstwood is in a sense the man with the bowler in the Shinn
pastel: alone, insufficiently dressed, struggling to make his way in the snow against
a strong wind while the business of the city goes on around him. I of course do not
mean a literal relationship between the two, but rather one of suggestive implications in the pictured scenes of how the writer might depict in his own fictional
portrayal the often-losing struggle to stay alive in the inhospitable environment of
a great metropolis in the midst of a winter storm. Stieglitz's and Shinn's winter
scenes are therefore reflected in specific passages describing New York in a snowstorm during Hurstwood's final days in the city, as in the paragraph in chapter 47,
which begins:

> It was truly a wintry evening. . . . Already, at four o'clock, the sombre hue of night
> was thickening the air. A heavy snow was falling—a fine picking, whipping snow,
> borne forward by a swift wind in long, thin lines. The streets were bedded with
> it—six inches of cold, soft carpet, churned to a dirty brown by the crush of teams
> and the feet of men. Along Broadway men picked their way in ulsters and
> umbrellas. Along the Bowery, men slouched through it with collars and hats
> pulled over their ears. (348)

The composite scene rendered by Stieglitz and Shinn also constitutes what can be
considered the backdrop setting of the stage on which is played out the entire
sequence of Hurstwood's decline in the period after he and Carrie part.

STEPHEN CRANE

Although both Stephen Crane and Theodore Dreiser responded to 1890s developments in photography and the graphic arts, the difference in the ways they did so
illustrates the great variety in the kinds of impact that visual art can make upon
written expression. Dreiser often seized upon specific aspects of specific art works
for inspiration, and it is thus possible, as I have attempted to do, to trace suggestive
connections between particular photographs and drawings and particular moments
in his fiction. Crane's relationship to the visual arts, however, remains—despite valiant efforts over the years by both art and literary historians—amorphous and fuzzy.
There is little doubt that there are links between his fiction and contemporary visual
art and that it is critically profitable to explore them, but it is also necessary to
acknowledge that it is difficult if not impossible to tie down with any certainty their
precise nature.

I will discuss two aspects of the relationship of Crane's work to the visual arts of
his time: the connection between *Maggie: A Girl of the Streets* (1893) and Jacob Riis's
photographs of the slums in his *How the Other Half Lives* (1890), and the relationship between *The Red Badge of Courage* (1895) and impressionism in painting. These
are not the only ways of discussing Crane and the visual arts. There has been interest,
for example, in the possible impact of Thomas Brady's Civil War photographs on the
Red Badge as well as in the relationship between Crane's fiction and later schools of
pictorial surrealism and expressionism. But the two aspects of Crane's connection
with visual expression that I will be taking up have the advantage of engaging us
both in central aspects of his fictional themes and method and in major art movements of his own time.

Riis's *How the Other Half Lives* was widely discussed on its appearance as a pioneering exposé of New York slum conditions.[7] It continues today to receive much
attention, especially as one of the first American works to exploit the possibilities of
photojournalism and because of Riis's problematical ethnic and racial beliefs. Riis's
distinction was that he not only engaged in a great deal of first-hand investigation
of almost every aspect of slum life—from horrendous housing and sweatshop conditions to the neglect of the young, elderly, and sick—but that he also did so with
camera in hand and thus recorded both verbally and visually what he had found. He
was aided in this breakthrough by developments in the mechanics of taking and
reproducing photographs. The Eastman Kodak Company had recently produced a
small camera which, since it was hand (rather than tripod) held and functioned
with dry rather than wet plates, could easily be transported to almost any site.
(Indeed, it was often informally given the name "detective camera.") Most important for Riis's purpose, a magnesium flash device had also recently been developed
as a means of taking photographs in semidarkness—that is, in the light available in
most dwellings, workplaces, and similar enclosed settings. Along with these striking
developments in facilitating the taking of photographs without the elaborate

preparations and cumbersome equipment previously required, the half-tone process for reproducing photographs in print mediums had been sufficiently advanced to make possible the ready and cheap duplication of photographic images in newspapers, magazines, and books.

There is little doubt that Crane knew of Riis's book before undertaking *Maggie*, given its notoriety and Crane's realization that he and Riis was engaged in similar enterprises. In addition, he attended one of Riis's lantern slide lectures on the slums during early July 1892. Crane was working that summer on the Jersey shore as a stringer for the New York *Tribune* and wrote a brief account of the occasion for the *Tribune* in which he commented on the nature of Riis's lecture (Stallman 49; Crane, "Summer Dwellers" 514–15).[8]

Writing about New York slum life before *How the Other Half Lives* tended toward either the sentimental and picturesque (slum types and conditions as a form of local color) or the moralistic (the fallen creatures of the slums require salvation). Riis, however, a former newspaper police reporter, sought to render the authentic in slum conditions—what it was like to live and die in that world—and he marshaled as irrefutable evidence of the realities of the slum his own first-hand explorations, a large body of statistics, and visual reproduction of specific slum scenes. Roughly speaking, Crane was also attempting in *Maggie* to go beyond the usual conventions in the representation of the slum and to render truthfully its life, though his method—unlike Riis's—also included an ironic inversion of those conventions within the plot and themes of *Maggie*. The extent of Crane's slum "fieldwork" during his visits to New York in the early 1890s before undertaking the novel is not known. But it is known that somewhat later in his career, in 1894 when writing for New York newspapers, Crane appears to have modeled himself closely on Riis's practice. In such sketches as his "An Experiment in Misery," he consciously adopts, as did Riis, the role of an outsider who ventures into the often-ignored depths of slum life to record accurately its conditions.

Running through all of Riis's close study of slum conditions is the thesis that those living in these conditions are its victims, that individual volition plays very little role in their fate. "To a certain extent," Riis states flatly toward the close of *How the Other Half Lives*, "we are all creatures of the conditions that surround us, physically and morally" (265). Although Riis does not study slum prostitution at length—the subject of prostitution was still largely unacceptable in books intended for the general public—his occasional references to its widespread prevalence in the slums strongly echo Crane's treatment of Maggie, a girl who "blossomed in a mud-pile" morally pure, works in a sweat shop, is seduced and then abandoned by a lover who initially appears to offer her a better life, becomes a prostitute, and dies a suicide in the East River. Thus, as one of the "unfathomable mysteries of life," Riis offers the evidence that "it is not an uncommon thing to find [in the slums] sweet and innocent girls, singularly untouched by the evil around them . . ." (161). But for most young women bred in the slum, Riis writes at a later point, the daily grind of sweatshop labor followed by a tenement existence almost guarantees their acceptance of prostitution as an alternative life:

> To [the tenement after a day's labor] come the young with their restless yearnings,
> perhaps to pass on the threshold one of the daughters of sin, driven to the
> tenement by police when they raided her den, sallying forth in silks and fine attire
> after her day of idleness. These in their coarse garments—girls with the love of
> youth for beautiful things, with this hard life before them—who shall save them
> from the tempter? (164)

Indeed, Crane stated in several inscriptions to *Maggie* a conception of the novel's
subject matter and theme similar to Riis's belief that it is the specifics of a slum environment that cause its initially "pure" young girls to turn to prostitution. The
novel, he wrote,

> tries to show that environment is a tremendous thing in the world and frequently
> shapes lives regardless. If one proves that theory, one makes room in Heaven for
> all sorts of souls (notably an occasional street girl) who are not confidently
> expected to be there by many excellent people. (Crane, *Correspondence* 1: 53)

However, despite these similarities in method and theme, anyone turning to
the photographs of *How the Other Half Lives* expecting to find there scenes
resembling those depicted in *Maggie* will be disappointed.[9] First of all, there are
not that many photographs. Of the book's forty-three illustrations, just sixteen
are half-tone photographs. The remainder are conventional drawings. And since
the half-tone process was still in its infancy, the photographs themselves, in the
1890 edition, are not clear and sharp. Finally, few come close to rendering specific moments of the novel. Perhaps the ones that come nearest are shots of small
street boys ("Didn't Live Nowhere") and of a group of youths consuming a large
can of beer ("A Growler Gang in Session"). Both pertain to the street gangs that
Jimmie belongs to, the first as a boy, the second as a youth. But neither photograph reflects anything specific in the portrayal of any character or scene in the
novel.

What, then, is the connection between Riis's photographs of New York slum
conditions in *How the Other Half Lives* and Crane's depiction of similar circumstances in *Maggie*? I suggest that the photographs played the same role in Crane's
thinking about the slums that Riis wished them to play in the minds of all his
readers. The photographs, amateurish by most standards and crudely reproduced in
the form that Crane saw them, nevertheless catch the eye and the imagination. Yes,
we instinctively feel, these are flesh and blood people—not statistical enumerations
or verbal accounts—and these are the miserable conditions they live in, the crowded
and filthy tenements, dark alleyways, airless sweatshops, and noxious dives. Each
face looking out at us is thus a story to be told of a body wasted and hope blighted,
of a life going nowhere but downward. Crane had a number of sources other than
How the Other Half Lives for the subject matter of *Maggie*, and the novel of course
also contains his own distinctive mix of irony and striking metaphor. But he appears
to have found in Riis's ideas about the slum as social reality and in the photographs
enforcing the validity of these ideas a vivifying catalyst in his effort to bring to life
his own vision of how the other half lives.

There has been a great deal written about Crane and impressionism, including James Nagel's excellent 1980 study *Stephen Crane and Literary Impressionism* as well as several first-rate essays by other critics. The notion that Crane's style owes something to the impressionistic movement in painting has been present in Crane criticism from its onset, since there is a great deal of evidence in his career to suggest the validity of the idea. By the 1890s, French impressionism was having a major impact upon American artists, and Crane spent much of his time in New York during the early 1890s living and associating with young artists. In addition, Hamlin Garland, his literary mentor during that time, was a staunch proponent of impressionism in painting, and indeed in 1894 was to publish—in the chapter "Impressionism" in his *Crumbling Idols*—one of the first extended explanations and defenses of the movement to appear in America. Finally, Crane's extraordinary color sense—color both as metaphor and as literal rendering—appears to suggest a direct link between his work and an art movement which revolutionized painting by emphasizing color as the principal vehicle of pictorial representation.

Yet, as I suggested earlier, the impact of impressionism upon Crane is still unclear. The difficulty in coming to grips with the subject lies in the fact that the relationship is one posited on a transference of ideas relating to how paint is applied to canvas to ideas about how words shape a narrative. Dreiser and Crane (in *Maggie*) in their response to pictorial representations of New York snowstorms and slums were undoubtedly drawn to these visual representation by their subject matter; they were engaged in writing about snowstorms and the slums, and the pictorial depiction of these scenes appears to have stimulated a greater realization of the possibilities for depiction of similar scenes in their own work. This kind of postulation can not be offered for Crane and impressionism, since there is little reflection of conventional impressionistic themes in his writing. Rather, it is argued, it was the way the impressionists painted—not their subject matter—that stimulated him to seek an approximation of that painterly style in his own prose and narrative styles.

This critical attempt to describe Crane's impressionism has produced a great deal of absorbing and often valuable commentary. Such aspects of Crane's style as his seeking to render the flux of a scene—its basic instability rather than its static condition—and his complementary effort to suggest the immense difficulties inherent in attempting to know what is occurring in experience—these and several other important areas of Crane's fictional center have been traced to similar concerns of impressionist painters.[10] But in the end, these comparisons are just that. They may indeed usefully help explain Crane's concerns as a writer by relating them to similar concerns by artists working with paint and canvas, but they do not explain the specific source of these ideas—what painter, what art works?—and thus leave the door open for the possibilities that Crane either derived these notions from other sources or that they were in large part sui generis.

Nevertheless, I believe that there is one aspect of Crane's putative debt to impressionism that is both traceable to a specific source and powerfully exemplified in a major work—that is, the way Crane uses Henry Fleming as a center of consciousness in *The Red Badge of Courage*. Let me begin with the issue of how Crane himself conceived of impressionism, since an understanding of this matter will provide a way into his possible use of an impressionistic method.

Many writers about Crane and impressionism have quoted the passage in his late work "War Memories" in which he mentions "French impressionists," since it is one of the few instances in which a specific awareness of impressionism appears in his writing. The passage requires quoting at length, because if one cites merely the phrase in which "French Impressionists" occurs (as is usually the case), its full meaning is obscured. Crane is recalling a scene during the Spanish-American War when he encountered a village church that had been transformed into a hospital for the Spanish wounded.

> The interior of the church was too cavelike in its gloom for the eyes of the operating surgeons, so they had the altar-table carried to the doorway, where there was a bright light. Framed then in the black archway was the altar-table with the figure of a man upon it. He was naked save for a breech-clout, and so close, so clear was the ecclesiastic suggestion, that one's mind leaped to a fantasy that this thin pale figure had just been torn down from a cross. The flash of the impression was like light, and for this instant it illumined all the dark recesses of one's remotest idea of sacrifice, ghastly and wanton. I bring this to you merely as an effect—an effect of mental light and shade, if you like; something done in thought similar to that which the French impressionists do in color; something meaningless and at the same time overwhelming, crushing, monstrous. ("War Memories" 254)

The passage richly suggests not only the special meaning that "impressionism" held for Crane but also the heart of his own fictional method. First, it is clear that Crane in this passage is not thinking of impressionism as a subject matter but as a technique. The technique itself consists of two components—an initial act of visual perception and a complementary act of mental realization of the implications of the perception. In this instance, these resolve themselves into the narrator's perception of the wounded man on the altar-table and then his realization that this image can be related to the archetypal image of Christ's sacrifice on the cross. The crucial aspect of this interaction between a perception of a visual image and the realization of its meaning is that the two are in ironic interplay. The church as a Christian sanctuary and place of worship is in ruins; what remains has been transformed into a hospital to save those injured in warfare; and thus the visual perception and its intellectual conception interplay to produce an ironic commentary on the present status of the meaning of Christ's sacrifice.

This particular example of Crane's ironic use of Christ's sacrifice is of course not unique. One recalls especially Jim Conklin's death in the *Red Badge* as a parallel instance. But the point I am making here is not that this form of irony is a common theme in Crane's work but that its method of interlacing a striking visual moment with its ironic implication is central to Crane's literary imagination, and that he here attaches this method to that of the French impressionists. It should also be noted that there is nothing in French impressionist painting which resembles what Crane seeks to render in this account. Not only did the impressionists avoid this kind of sensationalist subject matter, since it harkens back to what they considered the excesses of a previous generation of painters—to Géricault, for example—but their work usually also lacks the ironic dimension central to Crane's depiction.

So the first question to be tackled in dealing with Crane's idiosyncratic notion of impressionism is: what is its source? A possible answer to this question lies in his relationship to Hamlin Garland, a writer to whom Crane noted an intellectual debt on several occasions.[11] The best source of Garland's ideas on impressionism in the visual arts is the chapter in *Crumbling Idols* that I previously noted, a chapter based on a lecture that Garland prepared in response to having seen a number of impressionistic paintings during the summer of 1893 at the Chicago World's Columbian Exposition.[12] Crane and Garland, it will be recalled, saw a good deal of each other in New York during 1893 and 1894.

Garland in his account of impressionism identifies its major characteristic as the artist rendering a specific scene from life as it appears to him at a specific moment. But he is also at pains to place impressionism within his more inclusive category of "veritism," his coined term for an art that commits all artists, whatever their medium, to the ideal of fidelity both to nature and to themselves. Thus, impressionists are not "delineating a scene; they are painting a personal impression of a scene, which is vastly different" (133). As he also argued elsewhere in *Crumbling Idols*, "Impressionism, in its deeper sense, means the statement of one's own individual impression of life and nature, guided by devotion to truth" (50). This notion, I would argue, is very close to Crane's explanation at the close of the passage from "War Memories" that I have quoted. Since literary expression functions in time rather than space, Crane first presents us with the "flash of the impression" of the scene (the wounded man on the altar-table), which is then followed by what it "illumined" (the Christ parallel), the two combining for "an effect of mental light and shade" (that is, the prose equivalent of paint on a canvas). Of course, Garland himself did not conceive of his veritistic or impressionistic formula as a means toward the kind of irony which Crane exploits within the seemingly neutral idea of "effect." But given Crane's inherent inclination to adopt an ironic stance in interpreting all experience, his introduction of an ironic dimension into Garland's conception of impressionism was an almost inevitable step.

The second question to be faced is: how does this idiosyncratic idea of impressionism, one which in Garland's version stresses personal vision and which in Crane's version extends the personal in an ironic direction, find expression in the *Red Badge*? The answer lies in Crane's deployment of Henry Fleming, the novel's protagonist, as its center of consciousness. Within this role, Henry has an impressionistic eye for the scene before him and is especially brilliant in recording on his consciousness the vibrant variations in movement and color that characterize a battlefield. But also embedded in his visual record are his thoughts and feelings about the scene before him and above all about his role in each central event of the two days of combat as the battle unfolds. And often, especially at moments either of crisis or of self-evaluation, there is clearly an ironic disconnect between the actuality of the moment and Henry's conception of it. The irony present in the scene from "War Memories" that I have quoted arises from the narrator's perception of the disparity between ancient and contemporary versions of Christ's sacrifice, while that in the *Red Badge* stems from Henry's failure to realize the frequent disparity between what he sees and records and what he thinks or feels. But both devices are similar in that they render a distinction between the raw actuality of a scene and its interpretation. Crane, while relying on Garland's basic formulation, has also realized the ironic possibilities inherent in a perverse subjectivism. To Garland, there was no apparent problem in rendering an "individual impression" of a scene while being "guided by a devotion to truth." To Crane, on the other hand, and especially in the *Red Badge*, in the instance of a soldier beset by demons of self-doubt, the two goals are irreconcilable, and Crane's dramatic rendering of this truth is one way to describe both the method and the theme of the novel. Henry seeks to be true both to his impressions of the scene before him and to his role in it, but he lacks both the maturity and the insight into his own motives to achieve this goal. Crane may have believed that he was using an impressionistic technique in his fiction, but he also appears to have had grave doubts about the efforts by most men to rely on their understanding of the world around them.

John Steinbeck

The relationship between John Steinbeck's 1930s fiction and the documentary photography of the period—and, more particularly, between *The Grapes of Wrath* and the work of Dorothea Lange—is of great interest not only in its own right but because one of its most significant elements also characterizes a central aspect of 1930s American naturalistic fiction in general. To be an artist, it was widely accepted during this period of social upheaval, was to document the social conditions of one's own time. The most blatant version of this belief was the Soviet Union's doctrine of socialist realism, in which the state actively suppressed all art that did not aid in achieving its political goals. Few 1930s American writers of importance shared this view, but few also failed to respond positively to the premise that it was a function of the writer to document objectively the deplorable conditions prevalent in many areas of American life. The inherent paradox in this premise was the tension between the ideal of documentary objectivity and the very nature of art, especially art produced during a period when art sought above all to affect belief and thus action. And nowhere was this tension played out more clearly than in the relationship between the seeming objectivity of the photograph and the social and political leanings that both a photographer and a writer relying upon photographic images can express through these images.

Although both Lange and Steinbeck lived and worked in the San Francisco area during the late 1930s, and indeed though both were also deeply troubled by the condition of migrant farmers in California's agricultural industry from the mid-1930s onwards, they did not in fact meet until after the publication of *The Grapes of Wrath* in early 1939. Nevertheless, there is considerable evidence that Steinbeck viewed significant examples of Lange's extensive efforts to document in photographs the dire circumstances of California's migrant farm population, and that his knowledge of her work enters into his portrayal of similar conditions in *The Grapes of Wrath*.[13] Migrants from western prairie farms began to arrive in California in early 1935, driven out of their homes by drought, dust storms, and mechanized farming ("tractored over" was the common phase). Their presence in large numbers and their powerlessness made them vulnerable to exploitation, and their conditions in the shanty and tent camps that sprang up throughout the agricultural heartland of California quickly became deplorable. In the summer of 1936, Steinbeck was asked by the San Francisco *News* to write a series of articles about the migrants, and the seven articles he prepared appeared in October. He was sufficiently stimulated by his first-hand study of the migrant problem to plan and begin work on a novel dealing with the phenomenon, but the project stalled. In the late summer of 1937, however, he determined to return to it. After additional first-hand research that fall and winter, he began writing *The Grapes of Wrath* in May 1938 and completed it in October of that year (Parini 192, 200–2).

Lange, who had begun her career in photography as a portraitist, became absorbed in the documentation of the consequences of the Depression, and by the early 1930s had already done major work in this area, including her well-known "White Angel Bread Line" of 1933 (Meltzer). She began photographing migrant conditions in early 1935, working with Paul Taylor, a Berkeley economics professor. For several years, beginning in mid-1935, their efforts were sponsored by the Resettlement Administration, headed by Paul Stryker, which in 1937 became the Farm Security Agency. Stryker's announced goal was to influence social policy by the documentation of social misery, and to this end he enlisted a notable group of photographers, which included not only Lange but also such figures as Walker Evans, Carl Mydans, and Arthur Rothstein (Hurley; Wilkinson). During this period, Lange's photographs appeared in two significant publications. In early 1938, Archibald MacLeish published his book-length poem about the effects of the Depression on American farm life, *Land of the Free*, which contained eighty-eight photographs, thirty-three of which are by Lange. And in 1939, Lange and Taylor published *An American Exodus: A Record of Human Erosion*, a volume consisting of Lange's photographs and Taylor's captions and introductory passages.

Although *An American Exodus* appeared too late for Steinbeck to examine it before he began writing *The Grapes of Wrath*, he had several other opportunities to study Lange's migrant photographs while preparing and writing the novel. It is known that he consulted the Farm Security Administration's extensive collection of photographs in mid-1937 not long after he and his wife returned to the United States from a European holiday. Since he had decided to turn once again to a novel about California migrants, he stopped off in Washington on his way west after his European trip to get advice and aid from the Farm Security Administration on his plan to visit the government-run camps that were now helping California's migrant farm labor. Taking advantage of the occasion, he also took several days to view the agency's file of photographs, a file later deposited in the Library of Congress (Kehl 2; Hurley 140). In addition, during the summer of 1938, as he was engaged in writing *The Grapes of Wrath*, his earlier newspaper articles of mid-1936 were collected in a pamphlet, *"Their Blood Is Strong,"* which contains a number of Lange's photographs. Finally, he may well have even examined *Land of the Free*, since it appeared in April 1938, just before he began writing *The Grapes of Wrath*. In the discussion which follows, I will focus on Lange's untitled cover photograph for the *"Their Blood Is Strong"* (figure 27.3), since it offers a specific and resonant example of the possible ways in which Steinbeck was influenced by Lange's work as he wrote the novel.

Lange's photographs of the "American Exodus" occupy niches in what constitutes a full narrative of the 1930s migration westward of prairie farmers preserved in the photographs of the event commissioned by the Farm Security Administration (Ohrn). Each stage in the migration has its repetitive iconic images—the tractored-over land, now emptied of farm houses; the displaced farmers sitting idly on their haunches in prairie towns; the jalopies transformed into overburdened trucks; the makeshift camps of tents and shanties—that render both the story of these displaced farm families and the meaning of that story. The story is that of a western migration that reverses the expectations of the myth. Seeking a better life in the west, the migrants find only hardship and misery. The photographs not only document the

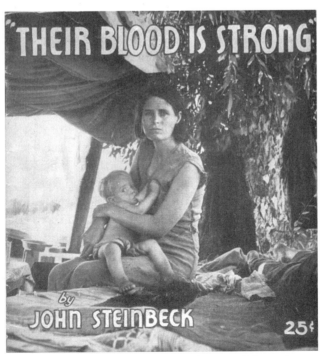

Figure 27.3   Dorothea Lange, untitled cover photograph from the pamphlet by
John Steinbeck, *"Their Blood Is Strong"* (1938)

stages in this ironic reversal but also interpret it. The farm families are almost always white and from the older strains of the American settlement. Their bodies give evidence of lives of hard labor, but they have little to show for their efforts and will soon be reduced to having nothing. Yet—and this is an important "yet" for Lange's photographs—they have not given up all hope. There is some ineluctable source of inner strength that they continue to draw upon and that will see them through. As Robert Coles noted, Lange's migrant photographs "attest to a vitality, a perseverance, a willfulness of purpose" (177). This quality of mind and spirit, however, needs nurturing, and it is the California government camps that complete the narrative in that they offer some hope of recovery and perhaps eventual renewal.

This is of course also Steinbeck's narrative and theme in *The Grapes of Wrath*, and it is thus not surprising that scholars have identified specific Lange photographs with specific portraits and scenes in the novel.[14] The photograph I will discuss, that of a nursing mother and child on the cover of *"Their Blood Is Strong,"* is not the only such Lange image. Her 1936 "Migrant Mother," perhaps her most famous photograph other than "White Angel Bread Line," though similar in subject matter to the pamphlet cover, also differs significantly. Its mother is considerably older and more worn than the woman depicted on the cover, and there is less of what can be identified as an enduring will in her countenance. She appears to be merely suffering. Both shots seem to be unposed photographs of opportunity—we are viewing a bit of actuality caught on the run, as most actuality is encountered. But in fact here and elsewhere Lange was guided by a series of selective devices that comprise a powerful interpretive tool. Most prominent of these was the choice of a nursing mother in miserable surroundings as the subject of the portrait, a subject loaded with deep and powerful religious and natural allusive strains. We as a nation, photographs of this kind say, have travestied the fecundity we celebrate as a nation when we allow it to occur within settings of this kind.[15] In addition, Lange almost always took a series of photographs of a particular scene (as she did for both "Migrant Mother" and the cover photograph), and then selected one for distribution that best suited her purpose. And finally, she cropped a great many of her photographs as a form of editorial emphasis. So, for example, the cover photograph is one of a series of the same nursing mother, a series that reveals that a man is lying next to her. Lange, however, has cropped that portion of the photograph for the cover (one can now only see the man's feet to the right of the shot) in order to make the woman and child central to the image.[16]

The principal image of a nursing mother in *The Grapes of Wrath* occurs in the final scene of the novel. A flood of Biblical proportions has enveloped the remnants of the Joad family just as Rose of Sharon gives birth to a stillborn child. The family takes refuge in a barn, where a man lies dying of starvation. Encouraged by her mother, the stalwart Ma Joad, Rose agrees to nurse the stranger, and the novel ends with her doing so. Rose and Ma Joad have had the instinctive wisdom and strength to realize the transcendent virtue of preserving life by whatever form this act requires, a realization that crystallizes our recognition both of what they are and of what we owe them. Just as the Lange cover photograph encapsulated the central thrust of what Steinbeck had to say about the migrant experience in the reportage of a pamphlet entitled *"Their Blood Is Strong,"* so it seems to have served a similar role in informing the fictional portrayal of a migrant mother in the final scene of *The Grapes of Wrath.*

NOTES

I would like to thank Ron Parsley for his aid in preparing for publication the illustrations used in this essay.

1. There has been considerable discussion about the possible influence of Stephen Crane's 1894 sketch "The Men in the Storm" on Dreiser's depiction in "Curious Shifts of the Poor" of a similar scene involving men waiting in a snowstorm to be admitted to a lodging house (see, for example, Moers 60–68). I do not myself take up this possibility since my emphasis here is on the relationship of "Curious Shifts" and *Carrie* to visual expression.

2. For Dreiser and Stieglitz, see Greenough and Hamilton; Haines; Moers; Rabb; and Shloss. For Dreiser and the Ash Can School, see Kwiat ("Dreiser and the Graphic Artist" and "Dreiser's The 'Genius'"); Moers; and Zurier (*Metropolitan Lives* and *Picturing the City*).

3. See Dreiser's "A Master of Photography," "The Camera Club of New York," and "A Remarkable Art: Alfred Stieglitz."

4. Dreiser was later to publish his own collection of New York sketches under the title *The Color of a Great City* (1923).

5. See Pizer, "The Bread Line," which also contains a reproduction of the drawing.

6. It may be helpful to summarize the chronology that I have posited for the relationship of Stieglitz's and Shinn's New York work to *Sister Carrie*:

- Stieglitz exhibits his New York–based photographs in the mid-1890s; Dreiser's first article on Stieglitz appears in June 1899. Dreiser comments on Stieglitz's "Winter on Fifth Avenue" in an article published in October 1899.
- Shinn and Dreiser meet in 1898. Most of Shinn's New York street-scene pastels are dated 1899 by him and are probably based on winter scenes of early 1899. Dreiser's "Curious Shifts of the Poor," which is published in November 1899, was written in the spring or summer of 1899 and is thus no doubt also based on winter scenes of early 1899. Both Shinn's work of this period and "Curious Shifts of the Poor" include sketches of Fleischmann's bread line. Shinn's show at the Boussod-Valadon Galleries opens in late February 1900.
- Dreiser begins writing *Sister Carrie* in September 1899, but having stopped work on the novel several times, does not reach the portion devoted to Carrie and Hurstwood in New York until February 1900. He includes in this portion of the novel almost all of "Curious Shifts of the Poor."

7. For Riis and Crane, see Gandal; Giamo; Hales; Leviatin 36–37; and Orvell.

8. Gullason notes Crane's report of the lecture and also several later occasions (after the publication of *Maggie*) when Crane and Riis met in New York.

9. It should be clear that there is a significant difference between the photographs reproduced in many modern editions and discussions of *How the Other Half Lives* (for example, see Gandal and the 1996 Bedford edition of *How*) and those in the original 1890 edition. The former derive from prints preserved in the Museum of the City of New York

and are much clearer and larger than the prints in the 1890 edition.

    10. See especially Bergon and Nagel.

    11. See, for example, Crane to Lucy Brandon Monroe, April 1894 (*Correspondence* 1: 63).

    12. See Pizer, *Hamlin Garland's Early Work* 133–43.

    13. See Runge and Shloss for the fullest accounts of Lange's influence on Steinbeck.

    14. See especially Kehl and Valenti.

    15. Steinbeck himself discusses at some length in *"Their Blood Is Strong"* (8, 22–23) the prevalence of stillbirths and infant mortality in the migrant camps.

    16. An uncropped photograph from this same series (*Dorothea Lange* 35) contains a man, with his face to the camera, in the foreground of the photograph, thus dominating it.

WORKS CITED

Bergon, Frank. *Stephen Crane's Artistry.* New York: Columbia University Press, 1975.

Coles, Robert. *Doing Documentary Work.* New York: Oxford University Press, 1997.

Crane, Stephen. *The Correspondence of Stephen Crane.* Ed. Stanley Wertheim and Paul Sorrentino. 2 vols. New York: Columbia University Press, 1988.

———. "Summer Dwellers at Asbury Park and Their Doings." *The Works of Stephen Crane.* Vol. 8. Ed. Fredson Bowers et al. Charlottesville: University Press of Virginia, 1973. 514–15.

———. "War Memories." *The Works of Stephen Crane.* Vol. 6. Ed. Fredson Bowers et al. Charlottesville: University Press of Virginia, 1970. 222–63.

Deshazo, Edith. *Everett Shinn 1876–1953: A Figure in His Time.* New York: Clarkson S. Potter, 1974.

Dorothea Lange. Millerton, N.Y.: Aperture, 1981.

Dreiser, Theodore. "The Camera Club of New York," *Ainslee's* 4 (Oct. 1899): 324–35; rpt. in Hakutani, *Theodore Dreiser* 80–92.

———. "The Color of To-Day." *Harper's Weekly* 45 (14 Dec. 1901): 1272–73; rpt. in Hakutani, *Selected* 267–78.

———. "Curious Shifts of the Poor." *Demorest's* 36 (Nov. 1899): 22–26; rpt. in Dreiser, *Sister Carrie* 403–12 and Hakutani, *Selected* 170–80.

———. *The "Genius."* New York: John Lane, 1915.

———. "A Master of Photography." *Success* 2 (10 June 1899): 471; rpt. in Hakutani, *Selected* 248–53.

———. "A Remarkable Art: Alfred Stieglitz." *Great Round World* 19 (3 May 1902): 430–34; rpt. in Hakutani, *Theodore Dreiser* 112–21.

———. *Sister Carrie.* Ed. Donald Pizer. 3rd ed. New York: Norton, 2006.

Gandal, Keith. *The Virtues of the Vicious: Jacob Riis, Stephen Crane, and the Spectacle of the Slum.* New York: Oxford University Press, 1997.

Garland, Hamlin. *Crumbling Idols.* Chicago: Stone and Kimball, 1894.

Giamo, Benedict. *On the Bowery: Confronting Homelessness in American Society.* Iowa City: University of Iowa Press, 1989.

Greenough, Sarah, and Juan Hamilton, eds. *Alfred Stieglitz, Photographs and Writings.* Washington, D.C.: National Gallery of Art. 1999.

Gullason, Thomas A. "The Sources of Stephen Crane's *Maggie.*" *Philological Quarterly* 38 (1959): 497–502.

Haines, Robert E. *The Inner Eye of Alfred Stieglitz.* Washington, D.C.: University Press of America, 1982.

Hakutani, Yoshinobu, ed. *Selected Magazine Articles of Theodore Dreiser: Life and Art in the American 1890s.* Vol. 1. Rutherford, N.J.: Fairleigh Dickinson University Press, 1985.

———, ed. *Theodore Dreiser: Art, Music, and Literature, 1897–1902.* Urbana: University of Illinois Press, 2001.

Hales, Peter B. *Silver Cities: The Photography of American Urbanization, 1839–1915.* Philadelphia: Temple University Press, 1984.

Hurley, F. Jack. *Portrait of a Decade: Roy Stryker and the Development of Documentary Photography in the Thirties.* Baton Rouge: Louisiana State University Press, 1972.

Kehl, D. G. "Steinbeck's 'String of Pictures' in *The Grapes of Wrath.*" *Image* 17 (1974): 1–10.

Kwiat, Joseph J. "Dreiser and the Graphic Artist." *American Quarterly* 3 (1951): 127–41.

———. "Dreiser's *The 'Genius'* and Everett Shinn, The 'Ash-Can' Painter." *PMLA* 67 (1952): 15–31.

Lange, Dorothea, and Paul S. Taylor. *An American Exodus: A Record of Human Erosion.* New York: Reynal & Hitchcock, 1939.

Leviatin, David. "Framing the Poor: The Irresistibility of How the Other Half Lives." *How the Other Half Lives: Studies among the Tenements of New York.* New York: Bedford, 1996. 1–50.

MacLeish, Archibald. *Land of the Free.* New York: Harcourt, Brace, 1938.

Meltzer, Milton. *Dorothea Lange: A Photographer's Life.* New York: Farrar, Straus, Giroux, 1978.

Moers, Ellen. *Two Dreisers.* New York: Viking, 1969.

Nagel, James. *Stephen Crane and Literary Impressionism.* University Park: Pennsylvania State University Press, 1980.

Ohrn, Karin Becker. *Dorothea Lange and the Documentary Tradition.* Baton Rouge: Louisiana State University Press, 1980.

Orvell, Miles. *The Real Thing: Imitation and Authenticity in American Culture, 1880–1940.* Chapel Hill: University of North Carolina Press, 1989.

Parini, Jay. *John Steinbeck: A Biography.* New York: Henry Holt, 1995.

Pizer, Donald. "The Bread Line: An American Icon of Hard Times." *Studies in American Naturalism* 2 (2007): 103–28.

———. *Hamlin Garland's Early Work and Career.* Berkeley and Los Angeles: University of California Press, 1960.

Rabb, Jane M. *Literature and Photography: Interactions, 1840–1990.* Albuquerque: University of New Mexico Press, 1995.

Riis, Jacob. *How the Other Half Lives: Studies among the Tenements of New York.* New York: Scribner, 1890.

Runge, Evelyn. *John Steinbeck, Dorothy Lange, und die Grosse Depression.* Munich: Martin Meidenbaur, 2006.

Shloss, Carol. *In Visible Light: Photography and the American Writer, 1840–1940.* New York: Oxford University Press, 1987.

Stallman, Robert W. *Stephen Crane: A Biography.* New York: Braziller, 1968.

Steinbeck, John. *"Their Blood Is Strong."* San Francisco: Simon J. Lubin Society, 1938.

Valenti, Peter. "Steinbeck's Ecological Polemic: Human Sympathy and Visual Documentary in the Intercalary Chapters of *The Grapes of Wrath.*" *Steinbeck and the Environment:*

Interdisciplinary Approaches. Ed. Susan F. Beegel. Tuscaloosa: University of Alabama Press, 1997. 92–112.

"The Week in Art." *New York Times* 3 March 1900, Book Sec.: 11.

Wilkinson, Sean. "The Story in Pictures: Ray Stryker and the Farm Security Administration Photography Project." *University of Dayton Review* 23 (1995): 62–79.

Wong, Janay. Introduction. *Everett Shinn: The Spectacle of Life.* New York: Berry-Hill Galleries, 2000.

Zurier, Rebecca. *Picturing the City: Urban Vision and the Ashcan School.* Berkeley and Los Angeles: University of California Press, 2006.

———, et al. *Metropolitan Lives: The Ashcan Artists and Their New York.* Washington, D.C.: National Museum of American Art, 1995.

CHAPTER 28

AMERICAN LITERARY NATURALISM AND FILM NOIR

JEFF JAECKLE

ONE of the major expressions of American literary naturalism occurred in the cycle of Hollywood films made during the 1940s and 1950s commonly referred to as film noir. These films revisit and adapt nineteenth-century naturalist narratives via characters constrained by the forces of material environments, past experiences, instinctual urges, and mysterious fates. Even a cursory review of film noir titles reveals these movies' concerns with what Donald Pizer calls "the tragic nature of life because of the determining forces of experience" (Postscript 151). These titles include *Out of the Past* (1947), *No Way Out* (1950), *No Escape* (1953), *Caught* (1949), *Caged* (1950), *Possessed* (1947), *Spellbound* (1945), *Cornered* (1945), *The Dark Corner* (1946), *One Way Street* (1950), *Force of Evil* (1948), *Touch of Evil* (1958), *Born to Kill* (1947), and *Gun Crazy* (1950). The plots and characters of films noirs echo the dominant conventions of 1890s literary naturalism, which Pizer succinctly summarizes in "Three Phases of American Literary Naturalism":

> Naturalistic writers found that the poor—in education, intellect, and worldly goods—are indeed pushed and forced, that the powerful do control the weak, that few men can overcome the handicaps imposed upon them by inadequacies of body and mind, and that many men have instinctive needs that are not amenable to moral suasion or rational argument. (20)

Like the literary naturalist characters that preceded them, the protagonists of films noirs are constrained: they are poor, unemployed, or work unsatisfying jobs; they are trapped in failed relationships or marriages of convenience; they have powerful yet culturally inappropriate urges; and they are surrounded by characters who are better off, better educated, and happier. These pressing situations often propel the characters into states of obsession in which they desire gold, wealth, and fame; crave sex or infidelity; are consumed with jealousy; and are drawn to violence and destruction. Like the naturalist novel's plot of decline, these characters succumb to their urges and wind up imprisoned, dying, or dead.

Apart from conveying a mood of pessimism, these film noir narratives echo the central features of American literary naturalism and thus testify to the movement's adaptability from page to screen. It might come as a surprise, then, to learn that few scholars have investigated in any serious detail the parallels between literary naturalism and film noir. This critical gap is especially remarkable given the wealth of existing scholarship on the origins of film noir. Scholars readily acknowledge that film noir—whether categorized as a genre, cycle, or style—is the culmination of several filmic, literary, and cultural influences, most notably German Expressionism, 1930s Hollywood gangster films, hardboiled detective fiction, existentialist philosophy, and psychoanalysis. Most scholars make only passing observations, however, about the influence of literary naturalism. James Naremore, for instance, credits Theodore Dreiser's *An American Tragedy* (1925) as "a source for films noirs" and notes that the "influence of Dreiser on noir persists down to the present day" (279). Yet other than a brief reference to Woody Allen's *Match Point* (2006), which he considers a Dreiserian neo-noir, Naremore does not explain how Dreiser—or naturalism—shaped film noir narratives. Carl Richardson draws parallels between the "unflattering views" of humanity in both naturalism and noir but then suggests that the former "was more scathing an attack on society than *film noir* would ever be" (23). Like Naremore, Richardson leaves the details of these cultural critiques unexplored.

One reason for this relative critical silence is that naturalism seems insignificant as a literary precursor to film noir in comparison to the more obvious choice of hardboiled fiction. Writers such as Dashiell Hammett, Raymond Chandler, and James M. Cain contributed the novels, short stories, and screenplays to the period's defining films, including *The Maltese Falcon* (1941), *Double Indemnity* (1944), *Mildred Pierce* (1945), *The Postman Always Rings Twice* (1946), and *The Big Sleep* (1946). These writers' use of first-person narrators, contemporary slang, witty dialogue, detective and femme fatale characters, and sensationalist narratives of crime and sex laid the foundations for these films. In striking contrast, naturalist works such as *McTeague* (1899) and *Sister Carrie* (1900)—with their detached third-person narrators, stilted and sprawling prose, and characters that verge on the symbolic or allegorical—seem to bear little relation to the fast-paced and gripping features commonly associated with film noir. Not surprisingly, scholars often point to these stylistic distinctions when arguing for the influence of hardboiled fiction over naturalism. In *The Dark Side of the Screen: Film Noir*, one of the few studies to discuss the influence of naturalism in any depth, Foster Hirsch acknowledges that literary naturalism, film noir, and hardboiled fiction share concerns with the harsh and suffocating effects of urban life. He also claims that "[f]ate in the naturalist novel is as dark and as relentless as in the grimiest crime novel or *film noir*" (49). Yet Hirsch undercuts these parallels when criticizing literary naturalist prose as "laborious and flat-footed" in comparison to the sleek hardboiled style. He also disparages naturalist characters as simplistic, claiming "everyone was a victim of heredity and environment" (49, 51). These criticisms ultimately elevate hardboiled fiction as the primary literary source of film noir while minimizing the contributions made by naturalist novels. Indeed, Hirsch frames this section with the caveat that film noir drew "marginally" on literary naturalism by using some of its narrative conventions, though on a notably "smaller, less bombastic scale" (49).

Despite these fleeting and dismissive comments that downplay naturalism's influence on film noir, scholars have in fact drawn repeated, though implicit, parallels between the two movements. Time and again, scholars have referred to the centrality of determinism—be it fate, environmental constraints, instinctual urges, or atavism—in film noir narratives yet have failed to identify these conventions as naturalist. Kelly Oliver and Benigno Trigo, for instance, comment on film noir's determinist plots in which "everyday people come to bad ends in spite of their best efforts because of this fate beyond their control" (89). Steven M. Saunders echoes this argument when identifying the "sense of doom that makes film noir *noir*": a sense that the characters are "trapped in circumstances that they did not wholly create and from which they cannot break free" (96, 93). Paul Schrader looks to the constraining effects of physical environments in films noirs: "When the environment is given an equal or greater weight than the actor, it, of course, creates a fatalistic, hopeless mood. There is nothing the protagonists can do; the city will outlast and negate even their best efforts" (104). Andrew Dickos examines the determining effects of behavior in film noir, noting that "characters are doomed by temperament and consequence to face irrevocable consequences for bad actions" (97). Jean Pierre Chartier goes a step further by identifying these actions as atavistic, arguing that noir characters are "monsters, criminals, or victims of illness; nothing excuses them, and they act as they do simply because of a fatal, inner evil" (27). Finally, R. Barton Palmer underscores the sheer complexities of these determining influences when observing, "noir characters usually act from inchoate, unknown, or pathological motives" (*Hollywood's Dark Cinema* 19). Collectively, these arguments tacitly suggest that the plots, settings, and character types of films noirs draw heavily upon the core conventions of naturalist fiction. It stands to reason then that—without denying its numerous other origins—film noir is a cinematic incarnation of naturalism.

To date, the most extensive articulation of this idea is Christopher Orr's "Cain, Naturalism, and Noir."[1] Drawing on examples from the film adaptations of Cain's novels, *The Postman Always Rings Twice* and *Double Indemnity*, Orr points to the naturalist elements of film noir, which include the femme fatale as a force of sexual determinism; camera techniques, such as close-ups, that emphasize instinctual urges; and voiceover narration as an indicator of doom. Orr also deflates the primacy of the hardboiled fiction/film noir connection by demonstrating that both movements owe their developments in part to literary naturalism. In the case of Cain, Orr notes that the author's characters are models of naturalism: "regardless of

486   NATURALISM AND THE OTHER ARTS

how they see themselves, [they] are nevertheless, victims of forces beyond their control" (49).[2] Furthermore, instead of agreeing with Hirsch that naturalist conventions diminish when adapted from page to screen, Orr insists, "Chandler and Wilder's *Double Indemnity* is actually a stronger example of naturalism than Cain's 1936 novel" (49). Orr's chief contribution, then, is that he makes explicit what scholars have often left implicit: the plots, character types, visual styles, and aural patterns of these movies suggest that film noir is not merely an inheritor of literary naturalism but, more significantly, a form of cinematic naturalism.

A close analysis of two of the most central and critically acclaimed films noirs, *The Maltese Falcon* (1941) and *Double Indemnity* (1944), reveals that these films often blend naturalist narrative conventions with key cinematic devices: environmental constraints, emphasized through staging, high-contrast lighting, and low-angle cinematography; instinctual urges, emphasized through dialogue, costuming, blocking, and close-ups; and fate as a determining force, emphasized through dialogue, voiceover, and flashbacks. These conventions and devices find concrete expression in the thoughts and actions of the films' protagonists, who negotiate their desires for money and sex in the contexts of harsh environments, such as the criminal underworld, the private-detective business, an unsatisfying job, or a failed marriage. These negotiations often conclude with the characters succumbing to their greed and sinking into depravity or death; on rare occasions, however, these negotiations end with a hazy yet significant glimmer of hope. In each case, these movies attest not only to the power of film noir but also to the richness of cinematic naturalism.

THE MALTESE FALCON

John Huston's *The Maltese Falcon* is often described as the "first" film noir. Although the Dashiell Hammett novel had been adapted on two previous occasions—in 1931 under the same title and again in 1936 as *Satan Met a Lady*—the Huston version was arguably the first to combine the core elements of film noir: detective and femme fatale characters, emphases on sex and violence, high-contrast and low-angle cinematography, a convoluted narrative, and a mood of uncertainty. These elements were so pronounced that French critic Georges Sadoul proclaimed, "*The Maltese Falcon* creates, in one fell swoop, the conventions of *film noir*" (qtd. in Borde and Chaumeton 34). *The Maltese Falcon* is also a key example of cinematic naturalism. Indeed, these classifications tend to go hand-in-hand: the more a film can be described as noir, the more it tends to fit the category of naturalist. The dominant naturalist conventions in *The Maltese Falcon* are psychological obsessions with money and sex and an emphasis on greed as the cause of destructive behavior. In tandem with these constraining forces, however, is a counterbalancing vision of hope. According to Pizer, hope is the latter half of naturalism's two-part definition.

Despite the bleak and often doomed nature of their lives, these "limited and deprived characters still struggle to stay afloat in a world of violent destructiveness" ("Contemporary" 185). Although their efforts are often misguided and rarely successful, naturalist characters remain hopeful that they will one day gain control of their lives and improve their situations. Robert G. Porfirio echoes this sentiment in the context of film noir: "Set down in a violent and incoherent world, the *film noir* hero tries to deal with it in the best way he can, attempting to create some order out of chaos, to make some sense of his world" (127). In the context of *The Maltese Falcon*, the deteriorating effects of the golden falcon on Kasper Gutman (Sydney Greenstreet) and the overwhelming influence of the femme fatale on Miles Archer (Jerome Cowan) stand in stark contrast to Sam Spade's adherence to his detective code, which emerges as a form of naturalist hope.

Although the two most commonly discussed characters in *The Maltese Falcon* are the noir detective Sam Spade (Humphrey Bogart) and the femme fatale Brigid O'Shaughnessy (Mary Astor), the film's most quintessentially naturalist character is Kasper Gutman, whose seventeen-year quest to possess the fabled gold-and-jewel-encrusted Maltese falcon has deprived him of any moral or ethical compass. Like the Zerkow character in Frank Norris's *McTeague*, Gutman's all-consuming greed defines his existence. Both men are intent on possessing a legendary golden treasure: Zerkow desires the gold service that supposedly belonged to Maria Macapa's family, while Gutman desires the Maltese falcon reportedly given to Emperor Charles of Spain. These powerful urges gradually taint every aspect of the characters' lives. Their bodies, for instance, blatantly reflect their greed. The novel's narrator tells us that Zerkow's "claw-like, prehensile fingers" reveal that "greed—inordinate, insatiable greed—was the dominant passion of the man" (28). Gutman's uncontrollable appetite comes across not only through his name and nickname in the film ("the fat man") but also through techniques of costuming and cinematography. Sydney Greenstreet's vertically striped trousers accentuate his already rotund body, which reportedly weighed 300 lbs during the film's production, as does the low-angle camerawork that causes his gut to fill the lower third of the frame. (See fig. 28.1.) These techniques create the physical symbol of an enormous gut as a corollary to Gutman's psychological greed.

Apart from their physical appearances, the characters' dialogue highlights their obsessions. Because the golden objects they desire currently exist more as myths than as facts, both Zerkow and Gutman take avid pleasure in recounting their histories. Immediately after Maria rehearses the story of the gold service, Zerkow insists, "let's have it all over again. Polished like a mirror, hey, and heavy? Yes, I know, I know. A punch-bowl worth a fortune. Ah! and you saw it, you had it all!" (31). During Gutman's second meeting with Spade, he regales him with the full history of the legendary bird, from its initial creation up to its last-known location. Not only does Gutman's otherwise measured speech increase in pace as the story unfolds, it also becomes peppered with exclamations of sheer delight, such as the story being "the most astounding thing you've ever heard!" and the bird as a "glorious golden falcon," all of which he insists are "facts, historical facts."

Figure 28.1   Vertically striped trousers and low-angle camerawork accentuate Kasper
Gutman's character-defining greed in *The Maltese Falcon* (Warner Bros., 1941)

These characters' obsessions are so pervasive that, as Pizer observes, the men
are no longer "amenable to moral suasion or rational argument" ("Three Phases"
20). Zerkow's obsession with Maria's fabled gold service prompts him to propose to
her. According to their neighbor Trina, "he's going to marry her just so's he can hear
that story every day, every hour" (122). This arrangement appears to work until
Maria, grieving the death of her newborn child, forgets the story of the gold service.
Believing that she is lying in order to conceal the treasure's whereabouts, Zerkow
goes into a rage and pries up the floorboards in search of the service. When his
efforts prove futile, he murders Maria by slitting her throat. Later that evening, he is
found dead and clutching a sack of rusty dishes and pans. Gutman pursues a similar
morbid trajectory. After seventeen years of tracking the elusive falcon, he believes
he has located it in San Francisco, whereby he dispatches agents to recover it by any
means, including bribery, extortion, arson, and murder. Gutman is entirely unfazed
by these methods, viewing them as acceptable means to fulfill his quest, which has
even placed him beyond the reach of human affection. When negotiating with
Spade over who will take the fall for several recent murders, Gutman willingly offers
his secretary and bodyguard Wilmer (Elisha Cook, Jr.). Although Gutman initially
dismisses Spade's suggestion to frame Wilmer, noting that he feels "toward Wilmer
here just exactly as if he were my own son," he quickly changes his mind when his
emotions threaten to deprive him of the bird. Upon leaving Wilmer to fend for
himself, Gutman reveals the extent of his obsession: "if you lose a son, it's possible
to get another. There's only one Maltese falcon." To Gutman's chagrin, the falcon he
recovers is a lead forgery. However, still in the grip of his insatiable greed, he leaves
immediately for Istanbul on the trail of yet another lead, oblivious to the destruction left in his wake.

The epic nature of Gutman's greed contrasts sharply with the roughly eight-
hour obsession the married Miles Archer has for his client Brigid O'Shaugnessy.

Whereas Gutman's behavior is determined by his desire for gold and jewels, Miles's downfall is his sexual urge for Brigid, whose allure is established in the film's opening scene when Spade's secretary Effie (Lee Patrick) bluntly remarks, "She's a knockout." Miles's gestures reveal that he evidently agrees. He smiles and his eyes widen after he shakes Brigid's hand; he also leans across Spade's desk to be closer to Brigid and stares longingly at her with an open mouth. After agreeing to shadow Floyd Thursby, the man suspected of kidnapping Brigid's sister, Miles verbalizes his attraction: "You don't have to look for me. I'll see you all right." Brigid does not deflect Miles's attention but rather manipulates his sexual urges, which is a key tactic of the femme fatale. Although scholars typically associate this character type with film noir, Orr locates its origins in literary naturalism. He argues, "the noir femme fatale heroine does not signal a disavowal of naturalism but rather a somewhat new development within that tradition in which we sympathize primarily with the male protagonist who is not only a victim of his own desires and environment but also of a predatory female" (58). Indeed, the emphasis on fate in the term "femme fatale" underscores this character's determining power: she controls the lives of those under her influence.

This reading bears out in the case of Miles Archer, whose sexual desire for Brigid overwhelms his detective skills and leads to his death. Spade offers a similar interpretation when charging Brigid with Miles's murder. He first questions the official story that Thursby killed Miles by shooting him at close range. Spade highlights Miles's competence, noting that he had "too many years experience as a detective to be caught like that by a man he was shadowing up a blind alley with his gun on his hip and his overcoat buttoned." Yet he also recognizes that Miles's attraction to Brigid made him easy prey. Like Zerkow and Gutman, Miles's desire makes him incapable of rational thought. Spade criticizes Brigid on this point: "But he'd have gone up there with you, angel. He was just dumb enough for that. He'd have looked you up and down and licked his lips and gone, grinning from ear to ear." Indeed, only seconds before Miles's death, the medium shot shows him smiling while he stands surrounded by darkness and, unwittingly, face-to-face with a murderer. Miles's look of shock when Brigid suddenly shoots him underscores both her determining influence and the all-consuming power of his sexual urges.

Brigid's murder of Miles is only one example of the pervasive pessimism in *The Maltese Falcon*, which includes Gutman's obsession with the falcon, Spade's affair with Miles's wife Iva, and Wilmer's murder of Floyd Thursby and Captain Jacoby; the film also features numerous incidents of lying and physical abuse. Yet, despite this mood of pessimism, *The Maltese Falcon* does offer a glimmer of hope, signaled by Spade's decision to turn in Brigid for Miles's murder. Like Miles, Sam is sexually aroused by Brigid and has in fact acted on that urge already; however, unlike Miles, he overcomes her determining influence and remains rational. When Brigid begs him to save her by framing someone else for Miles's murder, Sam stays clearheaded and insists, "I won't because all of me wants to, regardless of consequences." Sam also asserts the primacy of his detective code over his sexual passions:

> When a man's partner's killed he's supposed to do something about it. It doesn't make any difference what you thought of him. He was your partner and you're supposed to do something about it. And it happens we're in the detective business. Well, when one of your organization gets killed it's bad business to let the killer get away with it. Bad all around. Bad for every detective everywhere.

Sam's personal decision to turn in Brigid has universal significance in that he believes it assures the future security of the detective business and "every detective everywhere." Though he is certainly motivated by a desire for self-preservation (i.e., not wanting to become Brigid's next victim), Sam's concern for his fellow investigators demonstrates his capacity for unselfish behavior—a capacity that almost every other character in the film lacks. Moreover, Sam's actions not only put an end to cycles of violence and deceit, they also assert a measure of control over his sexual urges and the destructive elements in his society. He therefore represents hope in an otherwise bleak naturalist world by demonstrating that the forces of biological and environmental determinism do have limits and can be bested, if only by a select few.

DOUBLE INDEMNITY

Whereas Huston's *The Maltese Falcon* is often described as the first film noir, Raymond Chandler and Billy Wilder's *Double Indemnity* has the honor of being the paradigmatic film noir. According to Naremore, "Few would deny that *Double Indemnity* is a definitive film noir and one of the most influential movies in Hollywood history" (81). Raymond Durgnat echoes this accolade and provides a justification: "*Double Indemnity* is perhaps *the* central *film noir*, not only for its atmospheric power, but as a junction of major themes, combining the vamp (Barbara Stanwyck), the morally weak murderer (Fred MacMurray) and the investigator (Edward G. Robinson)" (93). *Double Indemnity* is also a prototypical naturalist narrative.[3] Like *The Maltese Falcon*, *Double Indemnity* locates sex and money as the primary causes of ruin, depicts the femme fatale as the human agent of destruction, and offers a glimmer of hope amidst rampant pessimism. Yet *Double Indemnity* goes even further, pushing the envelope of cinematic naturalism with voiceover narration that highlights the protagonist's doom and explicitly frames fate as a dominant force of determinism. An appropriate tagline for the film could be Walter's voiceover commentary just prior to murdering his client: "The machinery had started to move and nothing could stop it." This sense of inevitability not only adds to the narrative tension, but it also underscores the film's naturalist ethos.

The protagonists of *Double Indemnity*, Walter Neff and Phyllis Dietrichson, are classic naturalist characters: ordinary people who find themselves constrained and discontented. Walter has worked a mundane job as an insurance salesman for eleven years, while Phyllis has been trapped in an abusive marriage with no hope of divorce or economic freedom after her husband's death. Under the present circumstances,

Walter's only future is a promotion to a desk job as claims manager, an even more unsatisfying (and lower paying) professional reality; Phyllis's only recourse is to distract herself by using the remainder of her husband's fortune to buy clothing and accessories. As a romantic couple, however, Walter and Phyllis envision other prospects. By having an affair with Phyllis, his client's wife, Walter has an opportunity for excitement and sexual satisfaction; Phyllis can exact revenge on her husband by making him a cuckold. The couple's affair also holds darker possibilities that revolve around money and murder. Once they become lovers, Walter and Phyllis scheme to defraud his insurance company for $100,000 by murdering Mr. Dietrichson (Tom Powers) and staging his death as a business-related accident (a fall from the back of a moving train). This scheme provides Walter with another form of excitement: the realization of a longtime fantasy to "crook the house" by beating his insurance company at its own game. For Phyllis, her husband's death would release her not only from a failed marriage but also from economic dependence.

As is typical of naturalist narratives, these intersecting plots of sex, money, and murder fail to bring about the desired outcomes. Although Walter and Phyllis successfully murder Dietrichson, they are unable to stage it convincingly as an accident, so they do not receive the insurance money. Moreover, the sheer stress of the murder scheme and their compulsions to complete it overwhelm the couple's sexual desires, thereby ruining the basis of their relationship and transforming them into mortal enemies. In the end, Walter discovers that Phyllis used his sexual urges to manipulate him; she neither loved him nor remained faithful. Walter reacts by murdering Phyllis, but not before she shoots him in the left shoulder. In the film's final scene, a bloody Walter slumps in a doorway near his office while his boss and best friend Barton Keyes calls the paramedics and police.

Wilder's use of voiceover narration underscores the characters' psychological obsessions and reinforces their inevitable doom. A dominant aural convention of film noir, often presented in first person from the protagonist's perspective, voiceover narration allows for subtle manipulations of time and space that both deepen character psychology and complicate a film's narrative arc. In *Invisible Storytellers: Voice-Over Narration in American Fiction Film*, Sarah Kozloff describes voiceover narration as "oral statements, conveying any portion of a narrative, spoken by an unseen speaker situated in a space and time other than that simultaneously being presented by the images on the screen" (5). Voiceover in films noirs tends to accompany flashbacks, so that the protagonist occupies a present location while narrating the past events that led to his current situation. Given the naturalist inclinations of film noir, this narration tends to emphasize the protagonist's determined existence. According to Orr, "As a rhetorical device, voiceover narration . . . implies a premonition of doom, the foreboding of the inevitable unhappy ending" (54). For Schrader, voiceover "creates a mood of *temps perdu*: an irretrievable past, a determined fate, and an all-enveloping hopelessness" (104). In *Double Indemnity*, voiceover effectively forecloses any possibility that Walter and Phyllis will find the money or happiness they seek by reminding audiences of the characters' unstoppable movement toward death.

The film establishes this pessimistic narrative framework in its opening scene via Walter's physical appearance and dialogue. The movie opens as Walter's car races down the street toward his office at the Pacific All-Risk Insurance Company. Once inside, the sweating and visibly shot Walter switches on the Dictaphone and begins recounting, to his boss and friend Barton Keyes, the steps that led to his murder of Dietrichson. Walter eliminates any mystery about his possible innocence in the criminal events that follow when he confesses, "I killed Dietrichson. Me, Walter Neff." He also undermines any hope of his scheme's success when reflecting on his motivations: "I killed him for money and for a woman. I didn't get the money, and I didn't get the woman." These admissions of guilt and failure cast a shadow over the entire film, so that when the story shifts into the modes of flashback and voiceover, audiences are already keenly aware that everything they are seeing and hearing eventually leads to a scene of powerlessness.

This sense of doom is particularly strong in regard to Walter's relationship with Phyllis. Like Miles Archer in *The Maltese Falcon*, Walter's sexual desire for the femme fatale clouds his professional judgment and ultimately leads to his demise. Viewers of *Double Indemnity*, however, are privy not only to Walter's dialogue and gestures, as they are with Miles's, but also to his voiceover thoughts, which reveal the sheer extent of the femme fatale's power. Walter and Phyllis first meet when he visits the Dietrichson home to convince Mr. Dietrichson to renew an auto insurance policy. Instead he finds Phyllis, wearing nothing but a towel and a gold anklet. Drawn by Phyllis's sexual allure, Walter makes a series of thinly veiled verbal passes that reveal his sense of confidence and control. Upon driving away, his voiceover confirms this optimism, indicating that he felt "like a million" and enjoyed the wafting scent of honeysuckle along the road. Yet the voiceover also highlights his obliviousness to Phyllis's intentions. In recounting his experiences, Walter benefits from hindsight: "How could I have known that murder can sometimes smell like honeysuckle? Maybe you would have known, Keyes, the minute she mentioned accident insurance. But I didn't." During the couple's second encounter, Phyllis again mentions accident insurance, explicitly requesting that Walter write a policy for her husband without his knowledge. In response, Walter's gestures and dialogue again suggest his sense of control: he denies Phyllis's request, insists that he's not "a dope," and storms out. As earlier, however, his retrospective voiceover undermines his forceful display, revealing instead that Phyllis's grip was already firmly established. After drinking a beer and bowling in an attempt to rid his mind of Phyllis, Walter concedes defeat: "I was all twisted up inside and I was still holding on to that red-hot poker. And right then it came over me that I hadn't walked out on anything at all. That the hook was too strong. That this wasn't the end between her and me. It was only the beginning." Notable here are the images of torture that characterize the femme fatale's power: a red-hot poker that burns Walter and a hook that entraps him. His claim to self-awareness, however, seems to convey a sense of autonomy. Unlike the previous scene in which Walter admits his ignorance of Phyllis's intentions, here he insists that knowledge came "right then." He therefore purports to be aware of the femme fatale's determining influence, not retrospectively, but in the moment she acted upon him.

Because naturalist characters are often depicted as unwitting victims of forces beyond their control, Walter's claim to self-awareness in *Double Indemnity*, a quintessential film noir, suggests a core structural difference between literary naturalism and film noir. Walter is arguably a non-naturalist character because he recognizes both the presence and power of these determining forces, a recognition that eludes classic naturalist characters. These distinctions are most apparent when the constraining influence is force itself—not a human agent of constraint, but rather a supernatural agent of fate. In Theodore Dreiser's classic naturalist novel *Sister Carrie*, for instance, the protagonist Carrie Meeber, along with her lovers Drouet and Hurstwood, are oblivious to the surrounding forces that influence their behaviors. They are therefore pawns in a cosmic game of manipulation. Walter Neff, by contrast, repeatedly articulates the constraining power of fate in his decisions and actions; from his perspective, fate can both forestall and compel specific events in his life. While these perceptual differences between Carrie and Walter ostensibly divide naturalism from noir, they are actually part of a continuum that links the two movements. Just as the femme fatale marks a development in naturalism, so too does Walter's self-aware voiceover narration chart new territory. This innovation exists in the clever coupling of Walter's awareness and subsequent actions: even though he can name the sources of his constraint, Walter remains a determined character who is unable to act successfully upon this knowledge. His fate thus suggests an even bleaker reality than Carrie's, in which there is no escape even for those aware of their entrapment.

As a means of comparison, consider first the characters' sheer lack of knowledge in *Sister Carrie*. The novel's narrator subscribes to a bleak and all-encompassing view of fate that renders the protagonist as little more than a pawn, epitomized in the opening chapter's subtitle "A Waif Amid Forces." This image of engulfment complements the narrator's detached perspective, which enables quick shifts from the particulars of people and places, such as Carrie Meeber and Chicago, to distanced pronouncements about "a girl" and "the city" with its "wholly superhuman forces" that tempt and allure even the "most cultured human" (1, 2). The narrator pairs this distanced perspective with relentless judgments of Carrie as both ignorant of and vulnerable to these surrounding forces. While describing her early job searches, the narrator remarks on Carrie's "helplessness amid so much evidence of power and force which she did not understand" (12). The narrator applies these judgments as well to the social status of Carrie's lover, Drouet: "Deprived of his position, and struck by a few of the involved and baffling forces which sometimes play upon a man, he would have been as helpless as Carrie—as helpless, as non-understanding, as pitiable, if you will, as she" (48).

This ignorance is so pervasive that the characters remain unaware not only of the surrounding forces but also of their own motivations and desires. When Carrie's second lover, Hurstwood, has an opportunity to steal $10,000 from his employer, his actions are partially out of his control. Apparently manipulated by an unknown "stern hand" and "solemn voice," Hurstwood's body and mind betray him, thus eliciting a series of uncertainties: he "did not know why" he wished to look into the safe; he wonders, "What was this thing, making him suspicious? Why did he wish to move about so quietly" (191). Even the act of theft appears external to him. After deciding not to steal the money, he finds "the lock clicked. It had sprung! Did he do it?" (193). A similar lack of awareness consumes Carrie, who despite her rise to fame as an actress in Chicago and New York has no grasp on her actual desires but finds herself controlled by vaguely defined instincts. Toward the novel's conclusion, the narrator reemphasizes Carrie's ignorance by once more drawing on the metaphor of forces: "And it must be remembered that reason had little part in this. Chicago dawning, she saw the city offering more loveliness than she had ever known, and instinctively, by force of her moods alone, clung to it" (368). Thus, the novel closes with the palpable sense that knowledge has been deferred. In all cases—be it success, ruin, or even death—the characters fail to grasp the full extent of the forces that shape their lives.

In stark contrast to Carrie, who sits in her rocking chair waiting futilely for some shred of enlightenment, Walter Neff of *Double Indemnity* is keenly self-aware, knowing all too well that he is an adulterer, defrauder, and serial murderer who will soon die, either from the gunshot wound in his shoulder or in a gas chamber in San Quentin. Because Walter narrates his own story, he appears more self-aware and less constrained than his literary counterparts. His voiceover, however, actually underscores his determined existence. Even though he is aware, for instance, of Phyllis's manipulations—evident in his metaphors of red-hot pokers and hooks— Walter nonetheless agrees to write the insurance policy and stage the murder as an accident, going so far as to murder Dietrichson for her. Moreover, after being compelled by Phyllis to hatch this scheme, Walter appears to lose any control over it, admitting in his voiceover: "That was it, Keyes. The machinery had started to move and nothing could stop it."

This same irony holds true for Walter's knowledge of fate: even though he can perceive the determining forces of fate in his life, he is unable to act upon this knowledge and free himself. When Dietrichson breaks his leg just prior to his scheduled business trip, for instance, Walter takes it as a sign. He notes, "I kept telling myself that maybe those fates they say watch over you had gotten together and broken his leg to give me a way out." Walter responds to this sign by canceling the murder scheme, not because he makes an active decision, but because he believes an external force willed it. By the same token, when Dietrichson decides to take the train trip despite his leg cast, Walter passively resumes the murder scheme in response to a perceived will of fate. He comments resignedly in his voiceover, "Those fates I had been talking about had only been stalling me off. Now they had thrown the switch. The gears had meshed. The time for thinking had all run out." Despite his concoction of a complicated murder plot, Walter assigns his ultimate decision to kill a human being to the fates. It was "they" who threw the switch, not he; in fact, he ceases "thinking" altogether, becoming more like the unstoppable machines and gears he describes. In response to the fates, Walter follows through with the plan: he kills Dietrichson, impersonates him on the train, jumps off, and plants the corpse along the tracks. Even though these actions suggest that he is in precise command of the events that occur, Walter's voiceover exposes the dominating effects of forces beyond his control. Immediately after completing the scheme, he is overcome by a feeling of total powerlessness, which he expresses through voiceover:

> Nothing had slipped. Nothing had been overlooked. There was nothing to give us away. And yet, Keyes, as I was walking down to the street to the drugstore, suddenly it came over me that everything would go wrong. It sounds crazy, Keyes, but it's true, so help me. I couldn't hear my own footsteps. It was the walk of a dead man.

Once again, Walter gains knowledge not retrospectively but in the moment when it "suddenly came over" him that his scheme would fail. Although his thoughts are prescient, Walter's knowledge proves futile. He is unable to claim the insurance money or save his relationship with Phyllis. Even his decision to murder Phyllis proves useless as a means of protecting himself, given that he immediately drives to his office to record his involvement in acts of murder and fraud. Thus, as Walter's story unfolds and the blood drains from his body, it becomes increasingly apparent that he is doomed to imprisonment or death. The only lingering question at the film's conclusion is which fate will come first.

Despite the sheer bleakness of Walter's portrait of decline, *Double Indemnity* does offer a glimmer of hope through the character of Barton Keyes. Like Sam Spade in *The Maltese Falcon*, Barton is a professional investigator who spends his days tracking down criminals, specifically perpetrators of insurance fraud. He lives by a rigorous code of ethics that makes it impossible for him to tolerate deceit of any kind in others. Barton is keenly aware of this personality trait, which he defines as his "little man"—a form of conscience that manifests physically via indigestion. A major downside of the little man is its negative effects on Barton's relationships with others. Apart from condescending to suspected clients, he once canceled a wedding engagement after discovering that his fiancée had concealed that she dyed her hair and was previously married. Regardless of these personality quirks that show him to be overly committed to his job and his principles, Barton is capable of true affection, which he repeatedly shows to Walter. Unlike every other relationship in the film, which either begins or ends in betrayal, Barton maintains his friendship to Walter, despite his coworker's duplicitous and criminal actions that go against everything for which he stands. In the film's final scene, as Walter slumps in the office doorway, too weak to light the match for his cigarette, the two men share their feelings. After Walter comments that Barton didn't solve the case because the murderer sat directly across from him, Barton insists that he was in fact "closer than that," which prompts Walter's response and the film's final line, "I love you, too." Coupled with one of the film's closing images, that of Barton lighting the dying Walter's cigarette, this example of loyalty emerges as the one bright spot in a world otherwise populated with cheating wives, unfaithful lovers, corrupt employees, and fraudulent customers.

These readings of *The Maltese Falcon* and *Double Indemnity* suggest that film noir is a form of cinematic naturalism replete with the same harsh urban environments, constrained characters, and cruel fates found in classic naturalist novels. While these paradigmatic films certainly attest to the fact that literary naturalism shaped the narrative, visual, and aural designs of films noirs, much work remains to be done. Just as Donald Pizer's groundbreaking scholarship expanded notions of naturalism from a nineteenth-century literary curiosity to a vast and perennial movement with three distinct waves in the 1930s, 1940s, and 1950s, so too has scholarship on film noir expanded the movement's conventional boundaries (1941–58) to encompass both proto-noirs and the ever-growing list of neo-noirs. If film noir is indeed a form of cinematic naturalism, then these historical expansions suggest that naturalism's influence on cinema is potentially much greater—in both breadth and scope—than scholars currently recognize. It would seem then that the next step is a full-scale analysis of literary naturalism's influence not just on film noir but the entire history of cinema. Apart from explicit adaptations of literary naturalist works, these analyses could consider the ways in which naturalist principles (aesthetic, philosophical, and cultural) have pervaded cinema from its earliest inceptions to present-day films. Inklings of this scholarship already exist in Tony Williams's work on naturalism and the horror genre, Anna Gural-Migdal and Robert Singer's anthology on Émile Zola's influence on silent cinema, and Lea Jacobs's study of naturalism and sentimentality in 1920s Hollywood films. These contributions suggest that criticism of cinematic naturalism will increasingly rival that of literary naturalism as scholars come to appreciate the sheer adaptability and resilience of the naturalist movement.

NOTES

1. For a brief discussion of the parallels between naturalism and noir, see Singer 200, 205.
2. See also James Naremore's comments on Cain's naturalism (83, 279).
3. Orr argues that Émile Zola's naturalist novel *Thérèse Raquin* (1867) is the master plot for Cain's *Double Indemnity* and *The Postman Always Rings Twice* (49).

WORKS CITED

Borde, Raymond, and Etienne Chaumeton. *A Panorama of American Film Noir: 1941–1953.*
    Trans. Paul Hammond. Intro. James Naremore. San Francisco: City Lights, 2002.
Chartier, Jean Pierre. "The Americans Are Making Dark Films Too." Palmer, *Perspectives*
    25–27.

Dickos, Andrew. *Street With No Name: A History of the Classic American Film Noir*. Lexington: University Press of Kentucky, 2002.

Double Indemnity. Screenplay by Raymond Chandler and Billy Wilder. Dir. Billy Wilder. Paramount, 1944.

Dreiser, Theodore. *Sister Carrie*. Ed. Donald Pizer. 2nd ed. New York: Norton, 1991.

Durgnat, Raymond. "Paint It Black: The Family Tree of Film Noir." Palmer, *Perspectives* 83–98.

Gural-Migdal, Anna, and Robert Singer, eds. *Zola and Film: Essays in the Art of Adaptation*. Jefferson, N.C.: McFarland, 2005.

Hirsch, Foster. *The Dark Side of the Screen: Film Noir*. 2nd ed. New York: Da Capo, 2001.

Jacobs, Lea. *The Decline of Sentiment: American Film in the 1920s*. Berkeley and Los Angeles: University of California Press, 2008.

Kozloff, Sarah. *Invisible Storytellers: Voice-Over Narration in American Fiction Film*. Berkeley and Los Angeles: University of California Press, 1988.

The Maltese Falcon. Dir. John Huston. Warner Bros, 1941.

Naremore, James. *More Than Night: Film Noir in Its Contexts*. Updated and exp. ed. Berkeley and Los Angeles: University of California Press, 2008.

Norris, Frank. *McTeague: A Story of San Francisco*. Ed. Donald Pizer. 2nd ed. New York: Norton, 1997.

Oliver, Kelly, and Benigno Trigo. *Noir Anxiety*. Minneapolis: University of Minnesota Press, 2003.

Orr, Christopher. "Cain, Naturalism, and Noir." *Film Criticism*. 25.1 (2000): 47–64.

Palmer, R. Barton. *Hollywood's Dark Cinema: The American Film Noir*. New York: Twayne, 1994.

———, ed. *Perspectives on Film Noir*. New York: G. K. Hall, 1996.

Pizer, Donald. "Contemporary American Literary Naturalism." Pizer, *Twentieth-Century* 167–86.

———. Postscript. Pizer, *Twentieth-Century* 150–52.

———. "The Three Phases of American Literary Naturalism." *The Theory and Practice of American Literary Naturalism*. Carbondale: Southern Illinois University Press, 1993. 13–35.

———. *Twentieth-Century American Literary Naturalism: An Interpretation*. Carbondale: Southern Illinois University Press, 1982.

Porfirio, Robert G. "No Way Out: Existential Motifs in the Film Noir." Palmer, *Perspectives* 115–28.

Richardson, Carl. *Autopsy: An Element of Realism in Film Noir*. Metuchen, N.J.: Scarecrow, 1992.

Saunders, Steven M. "Film Noir and the Meaning of Life." *The Philosophy of Film Noir*. Ed. Mark T. Conrad. Lexington: University Press of Kentucky, 2006. 91–105.

Schrader, Paul. "Notes on Film Noir." Palmer, *Perspectives* 99–109.

Singer, Robert. "'At the Still Point': Framing the Naturalist Moment." *Zola and Film: Essays in the Art of Adaptation*. Gural-Migdal and Singer 194–205.

Williams, Tony. *Hearths of Darkness: The Family in the American Horror Film*. Cranbury, N.J.: Associated University Presses, 1996.

INDEX

....

Abrahams, Roger, 267
Adler, Alfred, 182, 191–93
Adorno, Theodor, 298, 300
Aesop, 279, 280
African Americans, 63
    abolition of slavery and, 261
    blues narratives and, 264–66
    histories of Native Americans and, 173
    identities redefined, 267
    as inferior and menacing, 173–74
    intelligentsia, 262
    journalism and stories about, 261, 264
    lynching and, 261–64, 268, 280
    manhood, violence and, 266–68
    marginalization of writers and, 92
    as minstrel figures, 280
    mob violence against, 261, 262–63
    narrator as spectator/brute and, 263–64
    poets, 265
    racial evolution theory as liberating for, 58, 66
    racism against, 64
    sexual selection and, 269, 270
    as subhuman, 279–80
    trauma theory and, 264
    writers and naturalism, 257–71
The Age of Innocence (Wharton), 210, 211, 226,
    227, 233
Ahnebrink, Lars, 3
Akins, Zoë, 427, 438
Alas, Leopoldo, 78
An Albany Trio: Legs (Kennedy), 251–52
Albee, Edward, 431, 433, 434, 436
Alden, Roberta, 348
Alexis, Paul, 22
Alger, Horatio, 315, 381
Algren, Nelson, 49
Allee, W. C., 212
Allen, James Lane, 245, 412
Allen, Woody, 484
altruism, 189, 211–12, 215, 216, 218
An American Exodus: A Record of Human Erosion
    (Lange and Taylor), 476
An American Tragedy (Dreiser), 45, 109, 110, 111,
    113, 168, 183, 446
    class in, 311
    criminal innocence v. guilt and, 348–50
    psychology, love and death in, 196–99
    sexuality and violence in, 250–51
    as source for film noir, 484

American Hungers (Jones), 319n2
American Literary Naturalism: A Divided Stream
    (Walcutt), 3, 82
"American Literary Naturalism and the
    Humanistic Tradition" (Pizer), 123
American Literary Realism, 1865–1910, 54
*American Literature and Social Change: William
    Dean Howells to Arthur Miller* (Spindler),
    300
American Literature and the Universe of Force
    (Martin), 407
American Temperance Union, 163
The American City Novel (Gelfant), 325
Ames, Robert, 408
Ammons, Elizabeth, 416, 417
"Among Cliff Dwellers" (Norris), 276
Anderson, Maxwell, 427, 438
Anderson, Sherwood, 57–58, 183
    male sexuality and, 66
    psychology, masculine protest and, 191–93
Anesko, Michael, 93
Anglican Church, 161
animals, 57
    baboon defense and sacrifice, 217
    female intrasexual competition in, 210–11
    fictional characters portrayed as, 282–83,
    284
    gender role plasticity in, 209
    as vicious predator or dumb brute, 230
Anna Christie (O'Neill), 342, 431–32
Anna Karenina (Tolstoy), 105
The Annals of 'Steenth Street (Dunbar-Nelson),
    236
Anselm (saint), 157
antiheroes
    literary noir and, 49
    sad endings, negative heroes and, 427–41
anti-Semitism, 318
Antoine, André, 428
Appadurai, Arjun, 301
Aquinas, Thomas (saint), 157
architects, 450
Ardrey, Robert, 217
Ariel (Plath), 459–60
Aristotle, 86, 157, 386
Arius, 158
Arnold, Matthew, 135, 169
"Art in Aisle 3, by Lingerie, And Feel Free to
    Browse" (Kimmelman), 301

Ash Can School, 464
    influence on Dreiser, Theodore, 465–68
    members, 465–66
Asian Americans, 63
L'Assommoir (Zola), 23–24, 25, 26
atavism
    crime as, 339–41
    degeneration and, 172–80
    men's power over women and, 279
At Fault (Chopin), 225, 233
"At the Pit Door" (Crane), 280
Auerbach, Erich, 95
Auerbach, Jonathan, 366
Augustine, 157
"Aunt Jennifer's Tigers" (Rich), 447
Austen, Jane, 56, 96, 418
Auster, Paul, 419, 420
Austin, Mary, 230, 427
authors. *See* writers
autobiographies, 139, 143, 169–70
Autobiography (Mill), 124–25
The Autobiography of an Ex-Colored Man
        (Johnson), 262, 263, 264, 269
The Awakening (Chopin), 225–26
    childbirth and, 235
    homoeroticism in, 252–53
    marital infidelity plot in, 246
    as naturalistic, 237n3
    sexual selection in, 60

Babcock, B. W., 114, 115
Bacheller, Irving, 369
Baetzhold, Howard G., 133
Baguley, David, 415
Bahktin, Mikhail, 414
Baker, Houston, 265
Baldwin, James, 258
Balzac, Honoré de, 15, 38, 42, 49, 80, 419
Baraka, Amiri, 265
Barash, David, 213
Barash, Nanelle, 213
Barren Ground (Glasgow), 183, 193–96, 228
Barrett, Clifton Waller, 396
Barthes, Roland, 49, 414
"Bâtard" (London), 178
The Battle with the Slum (Riis), 317
Baudrillard, Jean, 300, 416
Beatty, Richmond Croom, 399
beauty
    evolutionary feminism and, 206–8
    human standards of, 58
    sexy son hypothesis and, 204–6
Becker, George, 81
Beckett, Samuel, 100
"Becoming Cultured and Culture as
        Commodity" (Smith and Dawson), 300
Becque, Henry François, 428
Beebee, Thomas O., 417
Beer, Thomas, 363

Before Adam (London), 114, 115, 177
behavioral genetics, 128–29
Belasco, David, 429, 430
Bell, Bernard, 416, 417
Bell, Michael Davitt, 143, 412, 414
Bellamy, Edward, 46, 73, 339
Bellow, Saul, 4
Bellows, George, 466
Belluscio, Steven, 269
Belsey, Catherine, 417
Bender, Bert, 151, 212, 217, 230, 237n3, 269
Bentley, Eric, 440
Bentley, Nancy, 226
Berger, John, 108
Bergson, Henri, 57, 66, 81
Berliner, Jonathan, 151
Bernard, Claude, 22, 78, 127
Berry, Walter, 427
Bertalanffy, Ludwig von, 50
Berthoff, Warner, 405, 409
Bester, Alfred, 73
La Bête humaine (Zola), 25–26, 340
Beyond the Pleasure Principle (Freud), 197, 198
the Bible, 270
Bierce, Ambrose, 135, 378
The Big Sleep (Chandler), 351, 484
biology
    destiny of race and, 173
    evolutionary, 66
birdsong, 57
Birth of a Nation (film), 285
Birthright (Stribling), 66
*Black and White Strangers: Race and American
        Literary Realism* (Warren), 257
Black Mask, 350
The Black Riders (Crane), 164, 447–49
Blake, William, 461
Blood Meridian (McCarthy), 252, 253
the blues. *See also* music
    music and, 59, 62
    narratives, 264–66
"The Blue Hotel" (Crane), 345
Boas, Franz, 268
bodies
    childbirth and laboring, 235
    disabled, 234
    expendable female, 251
    grotesque, 233
    obese, 233–34
    spectacle of women's, 231–33
Boeckmann, Cathy, 257
Bogard, Travis, 431
Bonaparte, Napoleon, 123
Bone, Robert, 348
Au Bonheur des dames (Zola), 25–26, 298
Boodin, John Elof, 212
Booth, Michael, 9, 16n2
Born to Kill (film), 483
Borus, Daniel, 361, 370

Boussod-Valadon Galleries, 466, 479n6

Bower, Stephanie, 276

Bowers, Fredson, 398–99, 401

Bowlby, Rachel, 301, 405, 407, 408, 410, 414

Boyesen, Hjalmar Hjorth, 360, 427

Boyle, Robert, 156

Boyle, T. C., 67

Brace, Charles Loring, 374

Bradley, Sculley, 399

Brady, Patrick, 415, 419

Brady, Thomas, 469

"Brahma" (Dreiser), 454

Brawley, Benjamin, 365

Brecht, Bertolt, 433

Breton, André, 420

Brett, George, 366, 369

Breuer, Josef, 190

Bridle, Augustus, 111

Brill, A. A., 196, 198

Brogan, Red, 347

Brooke-Rose, Christine, 100

Brooks, Peter, 11, 14, 15, 24–25

Brown, Bill, 230, 302, 303

Brown, Charles R., 315

Brown, Grace "Billy," 111, 113, 347, 348, 381

Brown, Sterling, 265, 385

brutes, 408, 416
    animals as dumb, 230
    narrator as spectators and, 263–64
    naturalist, 413

Buckland, William, 159

Bucknell Review, 83

Buel, Clarence Clough, 390

Bullard, Arthur, 417

"Bunner Sisters" (Wharton), 230

burden of proof, pessimism and, 130–31

Burhans, Clinton S., 133

Burlingame, Edward, 368

Burning Daylight (London), 317

Burton, Richard, 76–77

Buss, David, 207

By the Light of the Soul (Freeman), 233

Cady, Edwin, 82

Caesar's Column (Donnelly), 46, 308

Caged (film), 483

Cahan, Abraham, 74, 285, 310

Cain, James M., 48, 49, 135, 339, 350, 484, 485, 496n3

"Cain, Naturalism, and Noir" (Orr), 485

California, as woman, 455–57

The Call of the Wild (London), 109, 112, 115, 177, 286, 318, 377, 379

Campbell, Donna, 4, 85, 183, 303, 412, 414, 416, 417

Camus, Albert, 48

Canby, Henry Seidel, 385

Cantos (Pound), 446–47

Capital (Marx), 295, 300

capital punishment, 347, 350

Capote, Truman, 252–53

Cargill, Oscar, 81

Carter, Everett, 82

Carus, Paul, 133

Caruth, Cathy, 264

Carver, Raymond, 419

Casanova, Pascale, 98

"A Case for Lombroso" (Norris), 276–79, 340

Cather, Willa, 66
    as journalist, 225
    naturalism, women writers and, 223–36
    transformed naturalistic romance and, 230

Catholicism, 139, 156, 157–58, 163, 168, 169

Caught (film), 483

Cawelti, John G., 351

Céard, Henri, 22

Center for Naturalism, 54, 67

Chandler, Raymond, 49, 350, 351
    film noir and, 484, 486, 490–96

Channing, William H., 292

chaos theory, 127–28, 140, 419

Charles, M., 467

Chartier, Jean Pierre, 485

Chase, Richard, 11, 83

Chesnutt, Charles W., 54, 58, 74, 258, 260–61, 267, 268, 269, 271, 285, 289, 417

Chevrel, Yves, 26

Chicago Poems (Sandburg), 449

childbirth, 235, 245, 460

Children of the Night (Robinson), 74

"The Chinago" (London), 284–89

choice. *See* sexual selection

"The Choice" (Wharton), 60–61

Chopin, Frederic, 57

Chopin, Kate, 3, 56, 65, 74, 135, 301, 302
    commodity culture and, 298
    evolutionary biology and, 66
    marital infidelity plot and, 246–47
    naturalism, women writers and, 223–36
    plot of decline and, 230
    on sexuality, 242
    sexuality and, 241
    sexual selection and, 57, 60
    as writer in initial group of 1890s naturalists, 241
    Zola's influence on, 224–25

Christianity, 310
    cooperation and, 156
    Eucharistic ritual in, 165
    sexuality, repression and, 242

Christian Science, 169

"Chun Ah Chun" (London), 285

cities
    of excess, 331–34
    of exile, 334–36
    foreign space of, 325–27
    grotesque, 323–30
    overview of ethnic ghettos and, 322–23
    population growth, 1850–1900, in, 336n1

Civello, Paul, 4, 85

civilized society, 53
Civil War, 38, 50, 140, 279, 412, 469
The Clansman (Dixon), 173–74, 268, 285
class, 319n3
    class-passing and, 284–85
    naturalism and, 307–20
    urban poor to new middle, 308
    violence, 309
Cleman, John, 280–81
Cleopatra, 211
Cloudstreet (Winton), 99
Cohn, David L., 386
Coles, Robert, 478
Collins, Carvel, 11
Collins, Patrick, 109–10
The Color of a Great City (Dreiser), 479n4
Commerce in Color: Race, Consumer Culture, and
    American Literature, 1893–1933 (Davis),
    301
commodity culture
    criticism of naturalism as critique of, 300–304
    explanation of, 291–92
    naturalism and, 291–304
    naturalism as critique of, 292–99
compatibilism, 124–26
Comstock, Anthony, 370
Conder, John J., 81, 123
Conklin, E. G., 64
Conn, Peter J., 417
A Connecticut Yankee in King Arthur's Court
    (Twain), 46
Conrad, Joseph, 48
"The Conspicuous Wasting of Lily Bart"
    (Yeazell), 302
Constantine (emperor), 158–59
Cooke, Jay, 45
Cooke, Rose Terry, 230, 412
Cooper, Anna Julia, 262
Copernicus, 155, 156
copyrights, 114
Corkin, Stanley, 303
Cornered (film), 483
The Dark Corner (film), 483
The Cost (Phillips), 228
Council of Nicaea, 159
courtship plot
    female power of choice in, 56, 59–63
    male's passion/combativeness in, 56–58
    music and dance in, 57–58
    naturalism, sexual selection and, 56–63
Cowley, Malcolm, 6, 81, 342
Cowper, William, 458
Crane, Stephen, 3, 16n1, 72, 73, 74, 80, 83, 105, 132,
    134, 154, 155, 183, 223, 224, 225, 227, 235, 265,
    266, 267, 404, 454–55, 458, 461
    African Americans as minstrel figures and, 280
    cities and, 323
    class and, 307, 308, 309, 311
    commodity culture and, 301, 302, 303

dialogism and, 415, 416, 418
early life of, 285
editing naturalism, publishing and, 390–93,
    396, 398–99
environmental determinism and, 341–42, 344,
    345
environment as crushing influence and, 64
evolution of literary naturalisms and, 48
French origins and, 21
human nature and, 65
James, William, and, 184–87
journalism and, 107, 110–11, 280, 469
laboring body and, 235
literary marketplace and, 357, 359, 369
literary realism and, 82
lynching and, 280
male gaze and, 232
nature in naturalism and, 52, 53, 56
as neophyte in literary marketplace,
    362–64
plays and, 432
poetry and, 447–49
popular reception of naturalist texts and,
    374–76, 379
race and, 268
race, criminality and, 274–75
race and naturalism in short fiction of,
    279–84
religion and, 163–65
sexual selection and, 57
social mechanism as monster and, 33–34
typology of documentary and, 110
unromantic machines and, 32
use of stoical force and, 47
visual arts and, 463, 469–75, 479n1
as writer in initial group of 1890s naturalists, 241
Zola's outlook mirrored in work by, 27
Crane, William, 280
Creative Evolution (Bergson), 66
Crime: Its Causes and Remedies (Lombroso),
    174
crime/criminality
    in "A Case for Lombroso," 276–79
    in "The Chinago," 284–89
    criminal innocence v. guilt and, 347–50
    degeneration and, 174–76
    environmental determinism and, 341–47
    hard-boiled crime fiction and, 350–51
    hereditary determinism and, 339–41
    in "The Monster," 279–84
    naturalism and, 339–51
    race and, 274–75, 276–84
criminal innocence, guilt and, 347–50
Criminal Man (Lombroso), 64, 340
Criminal Sociology (Ferri), 133
Cross, A. R., 395
Crumbling Idols (Garland), 8, 242, 474
Crunden, Robert M., 314
The Cry for Justice (Sinclair), 316

culture
  identity and degeneration of Anglo-American, 172–80
  naturalism and commodity, 291–304
The Culture of Consumption: Critical Essays in American History 1880–1980 (Lears and Fox), 301
Cummings, Neil, 298, 301
Cummins, Denise, 210
"Curious Shifts of the Poor" (Dreiser), 464, 467, 479n6
custom, tyranny of, 85–88
The Custom of the Country (Wharton), 246

"Daddy" (Plath), 460
Dalton, Mary, 348
The Damnation of Theron Ware (Frederic), 163, 243
dance, courtship plot and, 57–58
The Dance of Life (Ellis), 58
Dark Laughter (Anderson), 58
Dark Princess (Du Bois), 59, 62
The Dark Side of the Screen: Film Noir (Hirsch), 484
Darrow, Clarence, 245, 347, 349
Darwin, Charles, 4, 5, 139, 142, 145, 146, 155, 157, 159, 166, 188, 203, 223, 224, 225, 293, 407, 436
  altruism and, 211–12
  drama and, 434
  ecological web and, 66–67
  evolution and, 53–54
  on free will, 131–32
  group values and, 141
  human nature and, 63–66
  literary naturalism and, 38–39, 71–72
  on male sexual agency, 245
  racial evolution theory and, 58, 66
  religion and, 160–62, 164
  repression and, 65
  on role of men/women in sexual selection, 211
  sexual selection and, 55, 56–63, 254n5, 269
Darwinism and Divinity: Essays on Evolution and Religious Belief (Durant), 160–61
The Data of Ethics (Spencer), 151, 188
Davidson, Donald, 418
Davis, Ben, Jr., 386
Davis, James C., 301
Davis, Rebecca Harding, 73, 163, 164, 233, 234, 235, 292, 293, 296, 415, 416, 419
  class and, 307, 310–11
Dawkins, Richard, 212
Dawson, Melanie, 300
death
  death-in-life ending and, 248
  tragedy, love and, 196–99
Defoe, Daniel, 96
Degeneration (Nordau), 64
degeneration, atavism and, 172–80
DeLillo, Don, 3, 50, 74, 252, 419, 420
Dell, Floyd, 191, 196

Den Tandt, Christophe, 264, 323
Descartes, René, 156, 158
The Descendant (Glasgow), 228
The Descent of Man (Wharton), 225
The Descent of Man, and Selection in Relation to Sex (Darwin), 39, 53, 57, 60, 141, 245
Desire Under the Elms (O'Neill), 191
Determined Fictions: American Literary Naturalism (Mitchell), 4
determinism
  crime and environmental, 341–47
  crime and hereditary, 339–41
  free will, moral responsibility and, 121–36
  Freud on, 182–83
  naturalistic writers and, 131–36
  quantum mechanics, chaos theory and, 127–28
  Zola on, 182
DeWall, Nathan C., 205
Dick, Philip K., 73
Dickos, Andrew, 485
Dimock, Wai-chee, 302
disease
  crime as, 339
  love as, 277–78
The Divine Comedy (Dante), 451
Dixon, Thomas, Jr., 263, 268, 271, 285
  degeneration, atavism and, 173–74
  racism and, 63
Documentary Expression and Thirties America (Stott), 104
documentary method
  definition and uses of, 104
  factual research in, 108–11, 113, 114, 115, 116
  London, Jack, plagiarism problem and, 111–16
  strategies of naturalism, 104–16
  typology of, 105–11
Donnelly, Ignatius, 46, 308
Dooley, Patrick K., 184
Dos Passos, John Roderigo, 4, 48, 74, 300, 333, 336, 430, 439, 445
Doubleday, Frank N., 394
Double Indemnity (Cain), 484, 485, 496n3
Double Indemnity (film), 484, 486, 490–96
Douglas, Mary, 301
Douglass, Frederick, 259–60
Dow, William, 415, 419
Dowling, Robert, 257, 303
drama, naturalism and, 427–41
Draper, John William, 155
Dreiser, Emma, 42
Dreiser, Sara, 394, 400
Dreiser, Theodore, 3, 72–74, 80, 83, 123, 132, 154–55, 163, 184, 191, 223–24, 228, 235, 236, 241, 271, 292, 404, 407, 437, 440, 445–46, 450
  Ash Can School's influence on, 465–68
  autobiography of, 139, 143, 169–70
  cities and, 333–35
  class and, 307, 308, 309–10, 311–12, 317, 318
  commodity culture and, 297, 300–302

Dreiser, Theodore (*continued*)
   criminal innocence v. guilt and, 347–50
   degeneration, criminality and, 176
   dialogism and, 415–16, 418
   editing naturalism, publishing and, 394–96,
      397, 400
   environmental determinism and, 343, 344–45
   evolution of literary naturalisms and, 38–39
   factual research and, 108, 113, 115, 116
   female sexuality and, 254n3
   film noir influenced by, 484, 493
   financial markets and, 45–46
   French origins and, 21
   on Freud, 190
   gender, race and, 409, 411, 413
   internal conflict and, 183
   journalism and, 347–48
   as journalist, 107, 111
   literary conventions and, 16n1
   literary marketplace and, 357, 361
   lynching and, 268
   male gaze and, 232
   male sexuality and, 66
   melodramatic vision and, 10–11, 15
   on moral responsibility, 134–35
   morality and, 140, 147
   naturalistic imagination and, 6–7
   nature in naturalism and, 52
   plagiarism and, 111
   plays and, 432
   poetry and, 453–55
   popular reception of naturalist texts and,
      379–83, 386
   power of sympathy and, 188–90
   psychoanalysis and, 196
   psychology, love, death and, 196–99
   race and, 261
   religion and, 168
   on sexuality, 242, 243
   sexual selection and, 61
   social mechanism as monster and, 33–34
   Stieglitz and Shinn's influence on, 479n6
   truth, art and, 266
   typology of documentary and, 105–106, 109
   unromantic machines and, 32
   use of conciliatory forces and, 40, 42–43
   visual arts and, 463, 464–68, 469, 479n1, 479n4
   on writers and truth, 266
   Zola's outlook mirrored in work by, 27
Dreiser v. Paramount Publix Corporation, 350
Drop City (Boyle), 67
Dryden, John, 445
Dubois, Jacques, 419
Du Bois, W. E. B., 58–59, 62, 258, 259, 262, 268,
   270, 271, 417
Dudley, John, 4, 84, 230, 245, 276, 412
Dugdale, Richard Louis, 340
Dunbar, Paul Laurence, 74, 135, 235, 258, 262,
   265–66, 289, 303, 357, 369, 417

Dunbar-Nelson, Alice, 236
Dunlop, C. R. B., 349
Durant, John, 160–61
Durgnant, Raymond, 490
Durkheim, Émile, 41

Eastman Kodak Company, 469
Eby, Clare Virginia, 237n10, 302
ecological web, human nature and, 66–67
economics
   literary naturalism and, 45–47
   new naturalist economy and, 406–9
Eddy, Willard O., 127
editing naturalism
   canonization of naturalist texts and,
      396–400
   conclusions, 400–401
   explanation of, 389–90
   second thoughts, first editions and,
      390–96
Edwards, E. J., 375
The Ego and the Id (Freud), 195
the Eight, 465–66. *See also* Ash Can School
Elbert, Monika, 230
Eliot, T. S., 114–15, 446
Elliott, Emory, 300
Ellis, Havelock, 57, 58, 61, 244–45
Ellison, Ralph, 265
Elsie Venner (Holmes), 73, 79
Emerson, Ralph Waldo, 53, 292, 295
The Emperor Jones (O'Neill), 341
England
   Industrial Revolution in, 28
   man-made monsters in U.S., and, 27–29
   naturalism's influence in, 21–22
English, Daylanne, 270
the Enlightenment, 158
environmental determinism
   crime and, 341–47
   prostitution and, 164, 251, 316, 317, 324, 340,
      342–43, 470–71
EP. *See* evolutionary psychology
Epicurus, 157, 158
Episcopalians, 165–66
Epoques de la nature (Leclerc), 159
Esau, 270
Ethan Frome (Wharton), 209–10, 211, 226,
   227
ethics, 124–26, 134–35. *See also* moral
   responsibility
   naturalist fiction and evolutionary,
      142–52
Eucharistic ritual, 165
eugenics, 64, 340
Evangelical Protestantism, 169
Evans, Anne-Marie, 302
Evans, Walker, 317, 476
Evidence as to Man's Place in Nature (Huxley),
   53, 59

evolution. *See also* Darwin, Charles
  evil and, 57
  influence on cultural/intellectual life, 88
  racial theory of, 58
  sexual selection and, 56–63
  theory of, 39, 53–54
evolutionary biology, 66
evolutionary feminism, 206–8
evolutionary morality
  debate over, 140–42
  naturalism and, 139–52
evolutionary psychology (EP)
  altruism/reciprocity and, 211–12
  evolutionary feminism in "Roman Fever" and,
    206–8
  explanation of, 203–4
  family and, 212–13
  Machiavellian intelligence, competition for
    mates and, 208–11
  naturalism and modern, 203–18
  reciprocity and, 211–12, 213–15
  sexy son hypothesis, Wharton and, 204–6
An Examination of Sir William Hamilton's
  Philosophy (Mill), 125–26
experimental novel, problems of, 21–24, 99–100
"The Experimental Novel" (Zola), 127, 182
The Expression of the Emotions in Man and
  Animal (Darwin), 53, 57, 65
extra-pair copulation
  men and, 207–8
  women and, 205

Fabi, M. Giulia, 269
Facing Facts: Realism in American Thought and
  Culture, 1850–1920 (Shi), 300
facts
  distinguishing between fiction and, 113–14
  documentary method, research and, 108–11,
    113, 114, 115, 116
  science and technical, 108–9
  truth and, 156
family, EP and, 212–13
Fante, John, 310
Faraday, Michael, 156
Farewell, My Lovely (Chandler), 351
Farm Security Administration, 476, 477
Farm Security Agency, 476
Farrell, James, 73, 74, 130, 135, 241, 310, 433, 439, 440, 441
fatalism
  free will, chance and, 126–29
  Zola on, 127
"The Fate of a Voice" (Foote), 230
The Father (Olds), 460–61
Faulkner, William, 288
Felski, Rita, 100
females. *See also* women
  animals and intrasexual competition in, 210–11
  courtship plot and power of choice by, 56, 59–63
  expendable bodies and, 251

objectification of, 33
sexuality, 66, 226, 246–48
women's body as spectacle and, 231–33
feminism
  evolutionary, 206–8
  sex-centric movement and, 243–44
femme fatales, 49, 345, 484, 486, 490–96. *See also*
  film noir
Ferngren, Gary B., 155
Ferri, Enrico, 133
fiction
  creative nonfiction and, 110
  distinguishing between fact and, 113–14
  evolutionary ethics in naturalistic, 142–52
  hard-boiled crime, 350–51
  journalism's influence on, 101, 105, 106–11, 276,
    280, 308, 347–48, 469, 476, 477
  race and naturalism in short, 274–89
  science of, 28
  women valuing knowledge gained from, 100
Fielding, Henry, 96
"Fifth Avenue Coach, Winter" (Shinn), 467f
Figg, Robert, 83
Fillebrown, Thomas, 108
film noir. *See also* Cain, James M.; Chandler,
  Raymond; Hammett, Dashiell; *specific film*
  noir titles
  Double Indemnity and, 484, 486, 490–96
  femme fatales and, 484, 486, 492–93
  hard-boiled crime fiction and, 351
  heroes, 487
  Kasper Gutman in, *488*
  literary naturalism and, 483–96
  The Maltese Falcon and, 484, 486, 490, 492, 495–96
  roots, 484
  sense of doom in, 492
  sexuality in, 484, 489, 490, 492–93
  vamps in, 490
  voiceover narration in, 491
The Financier (Dreiser), 45, 228, 410
  class in, 312, 314, 317
  environmental determinism in, 344–45
  sexuality in, 243
First Idea, 38
First Principles of a New System of Philosophy
  (Spencer), 39–40, 139, 143, 160, 168
Fisher, Philip, 303, 407
Fisher, Rudolph, 59, 62–63
Fishkin, Shelly Fisher, 110
Fiske, John, 144
Fitch, Clyde William, 427
Fitch, M. H., 133
Fitzgerald, F. Scott, 54, 57, 64, 66, 300
Flaubert, Gustave, 80, 246, 405
The Flea Palace (Shafak), 99
Fleissner, Jennifer, 4, 26, 84, 183, 230, 231, 254n4,
  257, 303
  class and, 315
  on sexuality, 245

Flower, Benjamin, 363
Floyd, Samuel, 265
Folsom, Michael Brewster, 313
Foote, Mary Hallock, 230, 231
Force of Evil (film), 483
forces
    in literary naturalism, 38–39, 40–47
    as power, 45
    types of, 44
Ford, James Lauren, 363
The Ford (Austin), 230
*Form and History in American Literary
        Naturalism* (Howard), 4, 104, 296, 408
Foucault, Michel, 242, 254n2, 415, 416
Fox, Richard, 301
France
    impressionism, 469, 471–75
    naturalism's origins in, 21–24, 54, 77–78, 98
    Second Empire, 26–27
Frazer, Winifred L., 440
Frederic, Harold, 53, 74, 135, 163
    literary realism and, 82
    sexuality and, 243
    sexual selection and, 57, 60–61
    as writer in initial group of 1890s naturalists,
        241
free love, 244
Freeman, Mary E. Wilkins, 230, 233, 235, 412, 427
free will, 408
    determinism, moral responsibility and, 121–36
    fatalism, chance and, 126–29
    libertarian, 125, 131
French, Warren, 327
Freud, Sigmund, 57, 61, 62, 63, 65, 196, 197,
        198–99, 434, 459, 460
    on determinism, 182–83
    early Freudian age and, 190–91
    mental functioning and, 194
    pre-Freudian psychology and, 183–84
    psychoanalysis and, 190–91, 193–96
    sublimation and, 195
Frow, John, 301
The Fruit of the Tree (Wharton), 234
Fuller, Henry Blake, 74
Fulton, David Bryant, 261

Galilei, Galileo, 155, 156
Gallagher, Catherine, 96, 100
Galton, Francis, 340
Gammel, Irene, 411
Gandal, Keith, 319n1
Garland, Hamlin, 3, 74, 231, 359, 404, 427
    critical reception and, 375, 376, 380, 390, 391
    impressionism and, 472, 474
    literary marketplace and, 357, 363–364, 369
    melodramatic vision and, 14, 15
    naturalistic imagination and, 6, 7, 8
    sexuality and, 242, 243
Garland-Thomson, Rosemary, 234

Gassendi, Pierre, 157–58, 158
Gates, Elmer, 108
"Geddo Street" (Dreiser), 453
Gelfant, Blanche, 325
Gemeinschaft (community), 41
gender
    excluded margins, race and, 409–14
    role plasticity in animals, 209
Gendin, Sidney, 134
genres
    defining literary naturalism and, 71–88
    difficulties of defining, 93–94
    disbelief, speculation and, 96
    documentary strategies of naturalism and,
        104–16
    naturalism and other, 92–101
George, Henry, 15
George's Mother (Crane), 266, 267
Gerber, Philip, 333, 419
Géricault, Théodore, 474
German Expressionism, 484
Germinal (Zola), 25, 26
Gesellschaft (society at large), 41
Giddings, Franklin, 172–73
Gilder, Richard Watson, 362, 363, 365, 374–75,
        378, 383, 390–91
Giles, James, 4, 413
Gillette, Chester, 113, 347, 348, 381, 446
Gilman, Charlotte Perkins, 73, 74, 339
    sexuality and, 243–45
    as writer in initial group of 1890s naturalists,
        241
Giorcello, Cristina, 302
Gissing, George, 28, 32, 33–34, 301
Gitelman, Lisa, 101
Glackens, William, 466
Glasgow, Ellen, 74, 183, 191, 302
    on Jung's contribution to novels, 193–94
    marital infidelity plot and, 246
    naturalism, women writers and, 223–36
    repression and, 193–96
    South's obsession with heredity and, 230,
        237n5
    as writer in initial group of 1890s naturalists,
        241
Glaspell, Susan, 432
The Glass Key (Hammett), 351
Glazener, Nancy, 224
God, 123, 144, 162, 448–49, 454, 455
    as Creator, 161
    as punitive, 164
    as warrant for empirical inquiry, 158
Gold, Michael, 310, 318–19, 330
Golden Rule, 212. *See also* reciprocity
Goldsby, Jacqueline, 264, 280
gold standard, 45, 81, 408, 416
Goldstone, Richard, 438
The Gold Standard and the Logic of Naturalism
        (Michaels), 4, 302

Goodling, Sara Britton, 235, 414, 416, 419
Gorky, Maxim, 428–29
Gosse, Edmund, 76
Gramsci, Benjamin, 300
The Grapes of Wrath (Steinbeck), 204, 463
    altruism and reciprocity in, 211–12
    environmental determinism in, 345
    Lange's influence on, 475–79
The Greek Anthology, 451
Greenstreet, Sydney, 487, *488*
Griffith, D. W., 285, 377
Griggs, Sutton, 258, 262–63, 264, 268, 270, 271
Grimsted, David, 10, 12
group values, 141. *See also* moral responsibility
Gruber, Laura, 230
Guare, John, 441
guilt, 347–50. *See also* crime/criminality
Gun Crazy (film), 483
Gural-Migdal, Anna, 496
Gurney, Edmund, 57
Gutman, Kasper (fictional character), *488*

Habegger, Alfred, 411, 412, 414
Habermas, Jürgen, 418
habits, 182, 184
Haeckel, Ernst, 57, 59, 63, 64, 149, 223, 225, 269
Hagar's Daughter (Hopkins), 270
The Hairy Ape (O'Neill), 64, 176–77, 432
Hall, G. Stanley, 245
Hall, Stuart, 409
Halsey, Francis, 389–90
Hamilton, Alexander, 446
Hamilton, Clayton, 8
Hamilton, W. D., 212–13
Hamilton, William, 125–26
Hammett, Dashiell, 49, 135, 350, 351
    environmental determinism and, 345
    film noir and, 484, 486–90
The Hand of the Potter (Dreiser), 111, 176, 196, 438
Hansberry, Lorraine, 434
Hapke, Laura, 309
Hardy, Thomas, 22–23, 32, 34
    historical genesis of monster machine and, 28–29, 30
    science of fiction criticized by, 28
Harlem Renaissance, 257, 270. *See also* African Americans
    courtship and women's power of choice in, 61–62
    music and human nature in, 58–59
    racial evolution theory and, 66
    sexual primitivism and, 58
Harper, Frances E. W., 262
Harris, Sharon, 235, 294
Harris, Trudier, 262
Harte, Bret, 107, 427
Harvey, William H., 415
Hassan, Ihab, 418
Hawkes, David, 300

Hawkins, Willis Brooks, 363, 396, 397
Hawthorne, Nathaniel, 143, 411
Haymarket riots, 416
A Hazard of New Fortunes (Howells), 295, 413
Hearst, William Randolph, 368
Hebert, Ernest, 99, 100
Hedda Gabler (Ibsen), 405
Heilman, Robert B., 12, 13
Heinemann, William, 392, 394
Hellman, Lillian, 427, 440
Hemingway, Ernest, 3, 74, 288, 412
    literary noir and, 49
    male sexuality and, 66
    primitive/civilized contrasted and, 48
Henle, James, 439
Hennique, Léon, 22
Henry, Arthur, 394, 400
Henslow, John Stephens, 161
hereditary determinism, 64, 73, 339–41
Herland (Gilman), 73, 244, 339
heroes
    antiheroes and, 49
    film noir, 487
    negative, 427–41
Herrick, Robert, 74, 228
Herschel, William, 140
heterosexuality, 243
Hicks, Granville, 295
Higgins, William, 110
Himes, Chester, 258
The Hindered Hand (Griggs), 262, 263, 264
Hinduism, 454
Hine, Lewis, 317
Hirsch, Foster, 484–85
Hitchcock, Alfred, 404
Hitchcock, Cora, 392
Hitchcock, Ripley, 379, 389–90, 391, 392, 395, 398, 399, 400
Hobbes, Thomas, 81, 126
Hochman, Barbara, 230
Hofstadter, Richard, 188
Hollywood. *See* film noir
Holmes, Oliver Wendell, 73, 79, 114, 135
Holyfield, Evander, 88
Homberger, Eric, 330
The Home: Its Work and Influence (Gilman), 244
Home to Harlem (McKay), 59
A Hoosier Holiday (Dreiser), 347
Hopkins, L. A., 42
Hopkins, Pauline, 74, 258, 262, 268, 270, 285, 416
Hosseini, Khaled, 100
The House Behind the Cedars (Chesnutt), 269
The House of Mirth (Wharton), 33, 145–47, 226, 227, 296, 302, 303, 368, 427
    male gaze in, 232
    marital infidelity plot in, 246
    projected titles for, 237n4
"The House of Pride" (London), 285
The House of Seven Gables (Hawthorne), 143

Howard, Bronson, 10
Howard, June, 4, 84, 104, 107, 296, 299, 319n1, 323,
        327, 405, 407, 408, 409, 410, 414
    narrator as brute/spectator and, 263–64
    on naturalism, 297
Howe, Irving, 26
Howells, William Dean, 73, 74, 76, 78, 80, 81, 86,
        88, 95, 96, 243, 294, 300, 303, 323, 405, 415,
        427
    class and, 308
    courtship plot, sexual selection and, 57, 60
    critical reception and, 375, 376, 380, 391
    gender, race and, 413
    human nature and, 65, 66
    literary marketplace and, 360
    naturalistic imagination and, 7–8
    nature in naturalism and, 53
    realism and, 408, 411, 417, 418
    typology of documentary and, 106, 107
How the Other Half Lives: Studies Among the
        Tenements of New York (Riis), 308, 317, 323,
        413, 469, 479n9
Hughes, Langston, 265
Hugo, Victor, 78, 429
human nature
    behavioral genetics and, 128–29
    ecological web and, 66–67
    environment's influence on, 64
    evolutionary roots of, 203
    Harlem Renaissance and, 58–59
    hereditary determinism and, 64, 73
    novels as scientific case studies of, 77–78
    related elements in puzzle of, 63–66
Hume, David, 132, 134
Huret, Jules, 22
Hurm, Gerd, 332, 337n6
Hussman, Lawrence, Jr., 144
Huston, John, 486, 490
Huxley, Julian, 54, 55, 203, 224, 225
Huxley, Thomas Henry, 53, 59, 132, 133, 141, 143
Huysmans, Joris-Karl, 22
Hwang, David Henry, 441
Hyde, George Merriam, 71

Ibsen, Henrik, 405, 428
identity
    degeneration of Anglo-American culture and,
        172–80
    determined at moment of conception, 64
    poetry and women's, 451
    racial, 263
    redefining African-American, 267
Ideology (Hawkes), 300
If I Don't Six (Reid), 98–99
immigrants, 413. See also class
    ethnic ghettos and, 322–23
    as inferior race, 173, 276
Imperium in Imperio (Griggs), 268
impressionism, 469, 471–75

Incidents in the Life of a Slave Girl (Jacobs), 259
In Cold Blood (Capote), 252–53
The Incorporation of America: Culture and Society
        in the Gilded Age (Trachtenberg), 301
industrialism. See also the monster machine
    shift from agrarian society to, 26, 27, 38, 39
Industrial Revolution, 28
Ingersoll, R. Sturgis, 397
Innes, Christopher, 433
innocence. See crime/criminality; criminal
    innocence
An Inquiry Concerning Human Understanding
        (Hume), 132
insanity
    bootleg whiskey and, 341
    love as disease and, 277–78
    mental disorders and, 183–84, 197–98
Invisible Storytellers: Voice-Over Narration in
        American Fiction Film (Kozloff), 491
"The Irish Section Foreman Who Taught Me
        How to Live" (Dreiser), 312
The Iron Heel (London), 167, 405
    class in, 308–9, 314
    economic power in, 46–47
Isherwood, Baron, 301

Jack, Peter Monro, 385
Jackson, Gregory, 94, 97
Jacobs, Harriet, 259–60
Jacobs, Lea, 496
Jacobson, Karen F., 129
James, George Wharton, 167
James, Henry, 15, 53, 56, 60, 65, 74, 80, 81, 86, 135,
        140, 142–43, 323, 407, 427
    as naturalist, 54–55
    review of Zola, 52
    sexual selection and, 57
James, William, 53, 55–56, 141–42, 183
    depth psychology and, 190
    on habits, 182, 184
    on link between experience and action, 184
    psychology, Red Badge of Courage and, 184–87
Jameson, Fredric, 410, 415
jazz age, 57. See also music
Jeffers, Robinson, 123, 455–58, 459–61
Jennie Gerhardt (Dreiser), 236, 395–96, 397, 400
Jewett, Sarah Orne, 412, 418
Jews, 63, 64, 318
Jews Without Money (Gold), 318, 330
Jim Crow laws, 258, 263, 265
John Barleycorn (London), 314, 315
Johns, Cloudesley, 133, 149, 367
Johnson, B. S., 99–100
Johnson, James Weldon, 74, 258, 262, 263, 264,
        269, 270, 285, 289, 417
Johnson, Robert Underwood, 363
Johnson, Willis Fletcher, 363
Jones, Alexander, 132–33
Jones, Gavin, 319n2

Jones, Howard Mumford, 386
Jones, LeRoi, 433
Joule, James, 156
journalism, 243
    African American stories and, 261, 264
    fiction influenced by, 101, 105, 106–11, 276, 280,
        308, 347–48, 469, 476, 477
    muck-raking, 314
    photo, 308, 310, 314, 315, 317, 464–65, 468, 469,
        475–79
    writers and, 107, 109, 110–11, 225, 276, 280,
        347–48, 469, 476, 477
The Jukes: A Study in Crime, Pauperism, Disease,
    and Heredity (Dugdale), 340
Jung, Carl, 168, 191
    novels and, 193–94
The Jungle (Sinclair), 106, 296, 319n3, 413, 450
    class in, 307, 313–14
    criminality in, 341
    environmental determinism in, 342, 343–44
Jurnak, Sheila Hope, 16n1

Kane, Robert, 126
Kaplan, Amy, 101, 405, 407, 411, 413, 414, 418
Kazin, Alfred, 81, 83, 400, 405, 409
Keats, John, 448
Kelley, Edith Summers, 231, 235, 241, 246–47
Kelly, George, 440
Kennedy, Tanya Ann, 229
Kennedy, William, 49, 251
Kepler, Johannes, 156
Kerouac, Jack, 49
Kidd, Benjamin, 149
Kilmer, Joyce, 380
Kim, Sharon, 146
Kimmelman, Michael, 301
Kingsley, Charles, 161
Kingsley, Sidney, 434, 440
"The King's Favor" (Crane), 280
Kipling, Rudyard, 377
The Kite Runner (Hosseini), 100
"The Knife" (Crane), 280
Knock on Any Door (Motley), 346
"Koolau the Leper" (London), 285
Kozloff, Sarah, 491
Kristeva, Julia, 414
Krutch, Joseph Wood, 382
Ku Klux Klan, 173–74
Kushner, Tony, 441

Labor, Earle, 149
Labor's Text: The Worker in American Fiction
    (Hapke), 309
The Lady of the Aroostook (Howells), 57
Lamarck, Jean Baptiste de, 140, 155, 157, 159, 160
Lamarckian principle, 63, 140, 145, 148, 268, 270
Lamb, Robert Paul, 300
Landmarks in the Struggle between Science and
    Religion (Simpson), 155

Land of the Free (MacLeish), 476, 477
Lane, John, 370, 380
Lange, Dorothea, 317, 475–76, 478–79, 480n16
    "Untitled," *477*, 478
Lange, W. W., 397
Laplace, Pierre-Simon, 123, 140
Lars, Åhnebrink, 81
Larsen, Nella, 61–62, 235, 236, 241, 270
    death-in-life ending and, 247
    sexuality and race as signifiers of value and, 233
Last Exit to Brooklyn (Selby), 332, 336
Lawson, Andrew, 302
Lawson, John Howard, 433, 439
"The Law of Life" (London), 179
"The League of the Old Men" (London), 285
Lears, T. J. Jackson, 301
Lecky, W. E. H., 225
Leclerc, Georges Louis, 159
LeConte, Joseph, 41, 57, 63, 133–34, 147, 149, 165,
    166, 245, 269
Lee, Hermione, 367
Lehan, Richard, 27, 28, 85, 145, 198, 230, 234, 266,
    407
The Leopard's Spots (Dixon), 173, 263, 268
Leopold, Aldo, 67
Leopold, Nathan F., 113
Levine, Lawrence, 267
Lewandowska, Marysia, 298, 301
Lewis, Robert, 280, 300
Lewis, Sinclair, 74, 412
libertarian free will, 125, 131
Lichtenstein, Nelson, 361
"Life in the Iron-Mills" (Davis), 73, 233, 235, 293
    class in, 307, 310–11, 314
Life Studies (Lowell), 459
Light, James, 439
Lilly, W. S., 77
Lincoln, Abraham, 217
Linderg, David C., 155
Link, Eric Carl, 4, 29, 92, 95, 121, 230
Liszt, Franz, 57
literary devices, 11
literary marketplace
    crafting proletariat myth, London, Jack, and,
        365–67
    Crane as neophyte in, 362–64
    Dunbar as race champion or poet for hire in,
        364–65
    explanation of, 357–59
    naturalist writers and, 357–71
    Wharton mastering, 367–69
    writer as cog in machine and, 360–62
    writers, factory work, "The Iron Madonna"
        and, 359–60
literary naturalism
    core naturalistic novel and, 38
    Darwin and, 38–39, 71–72
    definition of, 71–72
    degeneration and atavism in, 172–80

literary naturalism (*continued*)
  determinism, free will, moral responsibility
    and, 121–36
  dialogical to postclassical definition of, 414–20
  economic power and, 45–47
  explanation of, 71
  film noir and, 483–96
  forces in, 38–39, 40–47
  gender, race and, 409–14
  identifying literary naturalists in, 72–74
  individual and community's place in, 40–42
  in late nineteenth century, 75–79
  literary noir and, 49
  neo-realism's roots in, 47–48
  new naturalist economy and, 406–9
  as offspring of transcendentalism, 82
  as part of narrative mode, 38
  as pessimistic realism, 81–82
  postmodern turn of, 404–6
  pre-Freudian psychology and, 183–84
  as product of social era, 49–50
  psychology and, 182–99
  refashioning, 404–20
  return to First Idea in, 38
  sexuality and, 241–54
  structuralism and, 49
  Technocracy and, 46
  as transformed literary movement, 37–51
  in twentieth/twenty-first centuries, 79–85
  tyranny of custom and, 85–88
  wheat as economic symbol and, 45
literary noir
  antiheroes in, 49
  femme fatales in, 49, 345
literature
  naturalism as future of, 22
  obscenity in, 21–22
  philosophy and, 121–24
"Little Dramas of the Curbstone" (Norris), 340
The Little Lady of the Big House (London), 191
Locke, Alain, 61
Loeb, Jacques, 134–35
Loeb, Richard Albert, 113
The Log from the Sea of Cortez (Steinbeck), 67
Lombroso, Cesare, 64, 110, 174–75, 176, 340
London, Charmian, 168
London, Jack, 3, 72, 73, 74, 80, 83, 105, 132, 154, 155,
    163, 204, 223, 224, 226, 241, 266, 271, 404, 427,
    431, 445, 446, 458
  atavism and, 177–80
  belief in survival of fittest creation and, 114
  class and, 307–9, 314–15, 317, 318
  class-passing and, 284–85
  ecological web and, 66–67
  economic power, political force and, 46–47
  environment as crushing influence and, 64
  factual research and, 113, 114–16
  on free will, 133
  gender, race and, 411, 412, 413

  human nature and, 65
  as journalist, 107
  laboring body and, 235
  literary marketplace and, 357, 359, 361, 369
  in literary marketplace crafting proletariat
    myth, 365–67
  male sexuality and, 66
  melodramatic vision and, 15
  morality and, 140, 149–150, 151, 152
  naturalistic imagination and, 6, 7
  nature in naturalism and, 52, 54
  plagiarism problem and, 111–16
  popular reception of naturalist texts and,
    376–79, 383
  possible suicide and, 320n5
  primitivism and, 267
  psychoanalysis and, 190–91
  race, criminality and, 274–75
  race and naturalism in short fiction of, 284–89
  on sexuality, 243
  sexual selection and, 61
  "survival of the fittest" and, 166–68
  typology of documentary and, 109
Long, Hudson E., 399
Long, Lisa, 92, 94
Longfellow, Henry Wadsworth, 448
Looking Backward, 2000–1887 (Bellamy), 46, 73,
    339
Lorimer, George Horace, 362
A Lost Lady (Cather), 232
"Lost in the Land of the Midnight Sun" (Bridle
    and Macdonald), 111–12, 114, 115
Lourdes (Zola), 225
love
  as disease and insanity, 277–78
  free, 244
  plot, 291–92
  tragedy, death and, 196–99
Lovejoy, Arthur, 85
"Love of Life" (London), 111–12, 115. *See also*
    plagiarism
Lowell, Robert, 458–59
Lukács, Georg, 26, 97, 105, 296, 414, 416
Luks, George, 466
Lutherans, 169
Lutz, Tom, 183
Lyell, Charles, 52–53
Lyell, George, 140
lynching, 261–64, 268
"The Lynching of Jube Benson" (Dunbar), 262
Lyotard, Jean-François, 419

Macdonald, J. K., 111
Machiavellian intelligence, men and women,
    competition for mates and, 208–11
machines. *See also* industrialism; the monster
    machine
  as mythic monster, 30
  unromantic, 32–35

MacLeish, Archibald, 476
Madame Bovary (Flaubert), 246, 405
*Madame Bovary's Ovaries: A Darwinian Look at
    Literature* (Barash and Barash), 213
Maggie, A Girl of the Streets (Crane), 27, 33, 73,
    164, 227, 233, 265, 301, 318, 362, 390, 400, 418
    African Americans as minstrel figures in, 280
    class in, 307, 309, 311
    environmental determinism in, 341–42
    grotesque city in, 323–25
    male gaze in, 232
    popular reception of naturalist texts and, 374–79
    prostitution in, 432, 436
    sexuality in, 248, 250
    use of force in, 47
    visual arts, Riis, and, 469–71
Mailer, Norman, 4, 412
Maimonides, Moses, 157
Main-Travelled Roads (Garland), 6, 231
male gaze, 232–33
males. *See also* men
    blue-gilled perch as "cheater," 209
    courtship plot and passion/combativeness of,
        56–58
    physical strength and, 234
    sexuality, 66, 245, 248–51
    as spectators and male gaze, 232–33
    violence and African-American, 266–68
    Winesburg, Ohio, masculine protest and, 191–93
The Maltese Falcon (film)
    film noir and, 484, 486–90, 492, 495–96
    Kaspar Gutman in, *488*
The Maltese Falcon (Hammett), 351
    environmental determinism in, 345
    film noir and, 484, 486–90
Malthus, Thomas, 159
Maner, John K., 205
Manly, Alexander, 261
*The Man-Made World or, Our Androcentric
    Culture* (Gilman), 244
Mann Act, 343
"Mapping the Culture of Abundance: Literary
    Narratives and Consumer Culture"
    (Shulman), 300
Marais, Eugene, 217
Margraf, Erik, 237n3
marital infidelity plot, 246–47
The Market-Place (Frederic), 60–61
Marlowe, Christopher, 398, 445
The Marrow of Tradition (Chesnutt), 261, 267,
    268, 269
Martin, Jay, 182
Martin, Ronald, 6, 149, 407
Martin Eden (London), 12, 13, 150, 152, 190, 314,
    315, 317, 320n5
Marx, Karl, 46, 49, 84, 149, 295, 297, 299, 300, 301,
    302, 303, 409, 416
masculine protest, 191–93
Masters, Edgar Lee, 74, 451–53

Match Point (film), 484
Maudesly, Henry, 184
"Mauki" (London), 285
Maupassant, Guy de, 224, 226
    Medan group and, 22
    on Zola, 22
Mauss, Marcel, 301
"Maverick" (Foote), 230
Maxwell, James Clarke, 156
Mayhew, Anne, 293
The Mayor of Casterbridge (Hardy), 28–29
McBride, Kecia Driver, 303
McCarthy, Cormac, 3, 73, 74, 251, 253, 440
McCarthy, Mary, 440
McClure, Samuel S., 112, 114, 359, 369, 393
McElrath, Joseph, 133–34, 276
McKay, Claude, 59
McTeague (Norris), 74, 129, 165, 225, 284, 303,
    413, 418
    atavism and, 175
    blues narrative and, 265
    class in, 307, 309
    criminality in, 340–41, 446
    documentary, plagiarism and, 113
    editing process and, 393, 397
    evolution of literary naturalisms and,
        41–44
    film noir and, 484, 487
    human nature and, 63
    melodramatic vision and, 11, 12–13, 14
    mental disorders in, 184
    morality and, 148
    as naturalistic gothic, 325–27
    naturalistic imagination and, 6
    new naturalistic economy and, 407
    racism in, 63–64, 276
    sexuality in, 248–50
    typology of documentary and, 106, 109
Medan group, 22
media, fiction influenced by, 101
melodrama, normal world v. world of, 16n2
Melville, Herman, 65, 73, 160, 163, 316
The Memoirs of an American Citizen (Herrick),
    228
"Memories of West Street and Lepke" (Lowell), 459
men
    antiheroes and, 49
    courtship plot and passion/combativeness of,
        56–57
    Darwin on role of sexual selection and, 211
    evolutionary feminism and influence on,
        206–8
    extra-pair copulation and, 207–8
    Machiavellian intelligence and competition for
        mates between women and, 208–11
    paternity question and, 205–6, 209
    power over women and atavism in, 279
    sexuality and, 244
    sexy son hypothesis and, 204–6

Mencken, H. L., 376, 379, 380, 382, 395, 397, 431, 437
Mendel, Gregor, 39, 54, 63
Mennonites, 169
mental functioning, 194
Mephisto Walzer (Liszt), 57
Merish, Lori, 303
mermaids, 57
Methodists, 163
Mexican Americans, 63
Meyer, George W., 127
Michaels, Walter Benn, 4, 84, 234, 302, 333, 405, 408, 410, 411, 414, 415, 416
Michelangelo, 164
"The Mighty Rourke" (Dreiser), 312–13
"Migrant Mother" (Lange), 478
Mildred Pierce (film), 484
Mill, John Stuart, 124–26, 131
Miller, Arthur, 433, 436, 441
Miller, Jordan Y., 440
Mimesis (Auerbach), 95
minstrel figures, 280
Mitchell, Lee Clark, 4, 84, 130, 280, 299, 415, 419
Mob Rule in New Orleans (Wells), 261
mob violence, 261, 262–63
Moby-Dick (Melville), 160, 163, 316, 382
A Modern Instance (Howells), 66
A Modern Lover (Moore), 21
Moers, Ellen, 464
the monster machine
    as consequence of science, 25
    Crane and, 27
    French origins, experimental novel and, 21–24
    Hardy and historical genesis of, 28–29, 30
    man-made monsters in England, U.S., and, 27–29
    Norris and, 29–32
    unromantic machines and, 32–35
    Zola and, 24–27
"The Monster" (Crane), 233, 268
    naturalism and race in, 279–84
Montgomery, C. W., 110
Moods, Philosophic and Emotional, Cadenced and Declaimed (Dreiser), 453–54
Moody, William Vaughn, 434
Moore, George, 21, 23, 28
moral responsibility
    compatibilism, ethics and, 124–26
    free will, determinism and, 121–36
Morgan, Thomas, 266
Morgan, William, 94
Morris, Pam, 418
Morrison, Toni, 289, 310
Motley, Willard, 346
"Muckers" (Sandburg), 450
A Mummer's Wife (Moore), 28
Munroe, Lily Brandon, 364
murder. *See also* crime/criminality; film noir
    capital punishment and, 347

as self-defense/act of kindness, 345–46
Murphy, Brenda, 434
Murphy, Edward, 110
music
    birdsong and, 57
    blues, 59, 62, 264–66
    courtship plot, sexual selection and, 57–58
    Harlem Renaissance and, 58–59
Mydans, Carl, 476
My Dogs in the Northland (Young), 109, 112, 114

NAACP. *See* National Association for the Advancement of Colored People
Nagel, James, 472
Nana (Zola), 52, 105, 340
Naremore, James, 419, 484, 490, 496n2
Narrating the News (Roggencamp), 101
Narrative of the Life of Frederick Douglass, An American Slave Written By Himself (Douglass), 259
narrators
    as bystander and spectator, 263–64
    class and, 309
    double-consciousness of, 264
    film-noir voiceover, 491
The Narrow House (Scott), 235
Nast, Thomas, 415
National Association for the Advancement of Colored People (NAACP), 261
Native Americans, 53, 63, 167, 173, 225, 455
Native Son (Wright), 111, 113, 346–47, 348
naturalism. *See also* literary naturalism
    African American writers and, 257–71
    class and, 307–20
    commodity culture and, 291–304
    commodity culture critique and criticism of, 300–304
    crime and, 339–51
    as critique of commodity culture, 292–99
    documentary strategies of, 104–16
    drama and, 427–41
    editing, 389–401
    evolutionary morality and, 139–52
    French origins of, 21–24, 54, 77–78, 98
    industrialization/urbanization's influence on, 26, 27, 38, 39
    misconceptions about, 236
    modern EP and, 203–18
    nature in, 52–68
    and other genres, 92–101
    poetry and, 445–61
    religion and, 154–70
    in science and theology, 157–62
    short fiction, race and, 274–89
    in transatlantic context and monster machine, 21–36
    visual arts and, 463–80
    women's writing and characteristics of, 229–36
    women writers and, 223–36

Naturalism in American Fiction (Conder), 124
"The New Naturalism" (Lilly), 77
Natural Theology; Evidences of the Existence and Attributes of the Deity (Paley), 159
nature. *See also* animals
    courtship plot, sexual selection and, 56–63
    ecological web and human, 66–67
    in naturalism, 52–68
    naturalism and explanation of, 52–56
    related elements in puzzle of human, 63–66
    soul transcending, 53
negative heroes, sad endings and, 427–41
"The Negro in Art: How Shall He Be Portrayed?" (Du Bois), 58
neo-realism, 47–48
neurasthenia, 183
The Neurotic Constitution (Adler), 191
New Grub Street (Gissing), 28, 33–34
Newlin, Keith, 438
Newspaper Days (Dreiser), 139, 143
The New Negro (Locke), 61
New Thought Movement, 242
Newton, Isaac, 156, 158
"New Year's at San Quentin" (Norris), 340
Nichols, Mary Gove, 244
Nicodemus, 168
Nietzsche, Friedrich, 149, 150, 151, 167, 168, 191, 407, 409
nineteenth century, literary naturalism in late, 75–79
"91 Revere Street" (Lowell), 459
Nixon, Robert, 348, 384
No Escape (film), 483
noir. *See* film noir; literary noir
nonfiction, creative, 110
No Place for Grace: Antimodernism and the Transformation of American Culture, 1880–1920 (Lears), 301
Nordau, Max, 64, 110
Norris, Charles, 397
Norris, Frank, 3, 72, 74, 80, 83, 86, 122, 129, 132, 140, 154, 155, 163, 223, 226, 230–31, 259, 284, 404, 415, 418, 437, 441
    blues narrative and, 265
    as "Boy Zola," 21, 87
    cities and, 323
    class and, 307, 308, 309, 315–16
    commodity culture and, 300, 302
    courtship plot, sexual selection and, 62
    on crime, 340
    criminal innocence v. guilt and, 348
    definition of naturalism and, 429
    on degeneration and criminality, 174–76
    determinism and, 133–34
    early life of, 285
    editing naturalism, publishing and, 393–95, 396
    environmental determinism and, 342, 343
    evolution of literary naturalisms and, 40
    factual research and, 108–9, 113

film noir and, 487
gender, race and, 412, 413
human nature and, 65
journalism and, 107, 109, 276
literary marketplace and, 357, 359, 361, 369
literary realism and, 82
lower-class protagonists in, 236
masculine sexuality and, 288
melodramatic vision and, 10, 12–15
mental disorders and, 183–84
monster machine and, 29–32
music and, 57
naturalist gothic and, 325
naturalistic imagination and, 6–7
nature in naturalism and, 52
new naturalist economy and, 406–7
poetry and, 445, 446
primitivism and, 267
progressive evolutionary development and, 147–49
race, criminality and, 274–75
race and naturalism in short fiction of, 276–79
racism and, 63–64
religion and, 165–66
romance and, 97
on sexuality, 243
sexual selection and, 57
typology of documentary and, 105–6
use of combative force and, 41–45, 47
on violence, 263
as writer in initial group of 1890s naturalists, 241
on Zola as romantic, 22, 79
Zola's outlook mirrored in work by, 27–28, 29–32
Norton Anthology of English Literature, 126
novels
    antagonism between romance/naturalism in, 76
    buddy, 213
    degrees of truth in, 97, 100
    experimental novel and problems of, 21–24, 99–100
    Glasgow on Jung's contribution to, 193–94
    without monster machines, 32–35
    ongoing, nonlinear, repetitive motion in, 230
    as scientific case studies of human nature, 77–78
    social realism and, 83
    source materials for, 111–13
    utopian, 73
"The Novel with a 'Purpose'" (Norris), 10
No Way Out (film), 483
Numbers, Ronald L., 155

Oakley, John M., 276
Oates, Joyce Carol, 3, 49, 74, 310
    factual research and, 113, 115
    sexuality and, 251
obscenity, Zola and, 21–22
O'Connor, Flannery, 279

The Octopus (Norris), 62, 86, 149, 166, 231, 233,
    315, 316, 318, 407, 446
    environmental determinism in, 342, 343
    monster machine in, 27–28, 30–32
    use of force in, 47
    Vanamee subplot in, 31–33
Odets, Clifford, 428, 433, 434, 440
Odysseus, 211
Oedipus Complex, 191
Of Mice and Men (Steinbeck), 204, 217
    altruism and reciprocity in, 211–12
    environmental determinism in, 345–46
    reciprocity in, 211–12, 213–15
Olds, Sharon, 458, 460–61
The Old Man and the Sea (Hemingway), 67
Oliver, Kelly, 485
O'Neill, Eugene, 176–77, 191, 436, 438
    drama and, 428, 430, 431, 432, 433–35, 439–40
    environmental determinism and, 342
    environment as crushing influence and, 64
    racial atavism and, 341
One Way Street (film), 483
"Onion Days" (Sandburg), 450
*On the Origin of Species by Means of Natural
    Selection* (Darwin), 39, 53, 56, 139, 159,
    160–61, 225
"The Open Boat" (Crane), 47, 52, 110, 165, 303
O Pioneers! (Cather), 229, 231
originality, writers and, 115–16. *See also* plagiarism
Orr, Christopher, 485–86, 491, 496n3
Osborne, Theodore, 77
Outlines of Cosmic Philosophy (Fiske), 144
Out of the Past (film), 483
*The Oxford Handbook of American Literary
    Naturalism*, 4, 93

Page, Thomas Nelson, 268
Page, Walter Hines, 394
Paine, Albert Bigelow, 132
paintings, 114, 471–75
"A Pair of Silk Stockings" (Chopin), 298
Paley, William, 159
Palmer, R. Barton, 485
Papke, Mary E., 130, 230, 302, 420
Parker, Hershel, 399, 401
Parrington, Vernon Louis, 80, 83, 84, 85, 295, 404,
    405, 420
    pessimistic realism and, 81–82
Passing (Larsen), 233, 237n9, 270
Pater, Walter, 48
paternity questions, 205–6, 209
The Pathology of Mind (Maudesly), 184
Peattie, Elia, 230, 231
The People of the Abyss (London), 151, 307
Perry, David, 417
perversion, sexual, 254n2
pessimism, burden of proof and, 130–31
Petry, Ann, 236, 241, 258, 296, 303
    naturalism, women writers and, 230, 234

sexuality and, 248
Phelps, Elizabeth Stuart, 234, 235, 416
Phillips, David Graham, 50, 74, 228, 235, 361, 412,
    417, 432
    class and, 307
    on criminality, 341
    environmental determinism and, 342–43
    male gaze and, 232
Phillips, John, 366, 369
philosophy, literature and, 121–24
Philosophy of "As If" (Vaihinger), 191
photojournalism, 308, 310, 314, 315, 469
    Brady and, 469
    Evans and, 317, 476
    Lange and, 475–79
    Stieglitz and, 464–65, 468
physical strength, 234
The Physical Basis of Mind and Morals (Fitch), 133
Pierce, James, 79, 80
Pieta, 164
The Pit (Norris), 45, 57, 86, 236
Pizer, Donald, 4, 6, 83–84, 85, 129, 133–34, 230,
    234, 237n3, 237n6, 362, 380, 399, 406–7, 419,
    420, 430, 496
    on crime, 340
    on definition of naturalism, 445
    on film noir, 483, 486
    on internal conflict, 183
    on misconceptions about naturalism, 236
    on naturalist writers, 258
    sexuality and, 241
    on study of naturalism, 121–25, 274–75
plagiarism
    London, Jack, and problem of, 111–16
    paintings, copyright and, 114
    as survival of fittest creation, 114–15
Plath, Sylvia, 458, 459–60
Plato, 157, 295–96, 298
Playback (Chandler), 351
Playing in the Dark (Morrison), 310
plays. *See* drama, naturalism and
playwrights. *See* drama, naturalism and; *specific
    playwrights*
Playwrights' Theatre, 432
Plessy v. Ferguson, 258
plots
    of decline, 223, 230
    film noir, 483–96
    ironic, 230
    love, 291–92
    marital infidelity, 246–47
    sexual selection and courtship, 56–63
The Pluralistic Philosophy of Stephen Crane
    (Dooley), 184
Poe, Edgar Allan, 160, 378
poetry
    Crane and, 447–49
    Dreiser, Theodore, and, 453–55
    Jeffers and, 455–58, 459–61

poetry (*continued*)
    Lowell and, 458–61
    Masters and, 451–53
    naturalism and, 445–61
    Olds and, 458, 460–61
    Plath and, 458, 459–60
    Sandburg and, 449–50
poets, 265. *See also specific poets*
Poole, Ernest, 417
Poore, Charles, 385
Poovey, Mary, 96
Pope, Alexander, 445, 458
Porfirio, Robert G., 487
The Portion of Labor (Freeman), 235
The Portrait of a Lady (James), 57
Possessed (film), 483
Post-Historic Man (Seidenberg), 40
The Postman Always Rings Twice (Cain), 48, 339,
    350, 484, 485, 496n3
postmodernism, naturalism and, 404–6, 407
Pot-Bouille (Zola), 99
Pound, Ezra, 446–47
poverty, 308
    "Curious Shifts of the Poor" and, 464
    slum conditions and, 469
power
    as force, 45
    lynching's "terribly real," 264
    of men over women, 279
    sexy son hypothesis and women's, 204–6
    of sympathy, 188–90
    wheat's mystical, 408
    will to, 191
The Power of Music (Gurney), 57
Presbyterians, 194
Price, Richard, 310
Primer of Philosophy (Carus), 133
primitive society, 53, 58
The Princess Casamassima (James), 54, 142–43
Principia philosophiae (Descartes), 158
Principles of Geology (Lyell), 52–53
Principles of Psychology (Spencer), 141, 189
The Principles of Psychology (James), 53, 184, 188
prisons. *See also* crime/criminality
    criminal innocence v. guilt and, 347, 349–50
    as obsolete, 339
"The Problem of Philosophy in the Naturalistic
    Novel" (Pizer), 122–23
prostitution
    drama and, 432, 436
    as environmental determinism, 164, 251, 316,
        317, 324, 340, 342–43, 470–71
    Mann Act and, 343
protagonists, fated to die, 142–43
Protestants, 163, 169
Proust, Marcel, 419
Provincetown Players, 432, 439
"The Psalm of Life" (Longfellow), 448
Psychanalysis (Brill), 196

Psycho (film), 404
psychoanalysis, 190–91, 193–96. *See also* Freud,
    Sigmund
psychology
    An American Tragedy and, 196–99
    depth, 190
    early Freudian age and, 190–91
    James, William, *Red Badge of Courage* and,
        184–87
    literary naturalism and, 182–99
    literary naturalism and pre-Freudian, 183–84
    naturalism and modern evolutionary, 203–18
    repression, *Barren Ground* and, 193–96
    Sister Carrie, Spencer and, 188–90
    somatic style of, 183
    Winesburg, Ohio, masculine protest and, 191–93
Psychology: Briefer Course (James), 184
Psychology of the Unconscious (Jung), 168, 191
The Psychopathology of Everyday Life (Freud), 198
publishing
    editing naturalism and, 389–401
    literary marketplace and, 357–71
    popular reception of naturalist texts and,
        373–87
Pudd'nhead Wilson (Twain), 341
Pure Food and Drug Act of 1906, 106
Puritans, 190
"The Purse-Seine" (Jeffers), 455
Pynchon, Thomas, 135

Quakers, 163, 169, 310
quantum mechanics, 127–28
Quay, Sara, 303
Questionable Charity (Morgan), 94
The Quest of the Silver Fleece (Du Bois), 259, 268,
    270
Quicksand (Larsen), 235, 237n6, 237n9
    courtship plot and women's power of choice
        in, 61–62
    death-in-life ending in, 248

race. *See also* racism
    biology as destiny of, 173
    criminality and, 274–75, 276–84
    degeneration of Anglo-American culture and,
        172–80
    excluded margins, gender and, 409–14
    fetishization of Anglo-Saxon, 227
    identity and, 263
    immigrants as inferior, 173, 276
    riots, 261
    sexuality as signifier of value with, 233
    short fiction, naturalism and, 274–89
    skin color and, 58
    stratification of higher and lower, 173
    sub-human state and issues of,
        63–64
race suicide, 173, 269
racial evolution theory, 58, 66

racism
    Anglo-Saxon supremacy and, 63–64
    badman as heroic as counterforce to, 267
    degeneration, atavism and, 172–80
    difference between racialism and, 275
    psychological effects of, 263
Radano, Ronald, 264
Radway, Janice, 100, 101
Rahv, Philip, 81, 83
Railsback, Brian, 212
railways
    clock time standardized by, 27
    as monster machines, 25–26, 30–31
Raine, Anne, 230
Rainsford, William S., 166
Rampersad, Arnold, 62
Raper, Julius Rowan, 237n5
Rascoe, Burton, 386
Rawlings, Marjorie Kinnan, 241, 246
readership, signifying function of, 230
Reading the Romance (Radway), 100
realism, 22
    defining, 71, 76, 80, 94, 95, 100–101, 106
    first realists and, 65
    literary naturalism as pessimistic, 81–82
    neo-, 47–48
    social, 83
    urban pictorial, 464–66
Realism and Naturalism in Nineteenth-Century
    American Literature (Pizer), 4
reality television, 95
reason, altruism and, 189
The Reasonableness of Faith (Rainsford), 166
Rebecca Harding Davis and American Realism
    (Harris), 294
reciprocity
    altruism and, 211–12
    in Of Mice and Men, 213–15
A Red Record (Wells), 261
Red Rock (Page), 268
The Red Badge of Courage (Crane), 65, 86, 163,
    165, 183, 195, 375–76, 391, 398–99
    environmental determinism in, 344
    psychology, James, William, and, 184–87
    use of force in, 47
    visual arts, impressionism and, 469,
    471–75
Reesman, Jeanne Campbell, 149
the Reformation, 156, 163
Reid, Elwood, 98–99
religion. See also specific religions
    Dreiser, Theodore, and, 139
    and literary naturalists, 162–70
    naturalism and, 154–70
    the Renaissance, 159
repression, 65
    psychology and, 193–96
    sexual, 194
    sexuality and Judeo-Christian, 242

research, documentary method and factual,
    108–11, 113, 114, 115, 116
Resettlement Administration, 476
Resisting Regionalism: Gender and Naturalism in
    American Fiction (Campbell), 4
"A Reversion to Type" (Norris), 340
Revolutionary Road (Yates), 319
Rice, Elmer, 433, 434, 438, 439, 440
Rich, Adrienne, 447
Richards, Grant, 393–94
Richardson, Carl, 484
The Riddle of the Universe (Haeckel), 59, 64
Riedl, Gary, 286
Riis, Jacob, 308, 310, 314, 315, 317–18, 323, 374, 413,
    469–71, 479n8
Riley, James Whitcomb, 107
Rise of the Novel (Watt), 95
The Rise of Silas Lapham (Howells), 95, 106
Roach, Joseph R., 430, 433, 434
The Road (McCarthy), 252, 253
The Roan Stallion (Jeffers), 455–57
Robert, Elizabeth Maddox, 296
Roberts, John W., 267
Robinson, Edwin Arlington, 74, 346
Rockefeller, John D., 410
Rockwell, Norman, 88
Rodin, 176
Roggencamp, Karen, 101
Rohrbach, Augusta, 270
"Roman Fever" (Wharton), 204, 211
    evolutionary feminism in, 206–8
Le Roman expérimental (Zola), 22, 23, 24, 77–78,
    98
    science as subservient in, 25
romanticism, 76
    defining, 71
    as hereditary virus, 22
    Zola and, 22–23, 78–79
The Romantic Comedians (Glasgow), 233
romantic virus, 22
Roosevelt, Theodore, 50, 267, 308, 310, 313–14,
    317, 378
Rosenbach, A. S. W., 396
Rosenberg, James L., 7
Ross, Edward, 172–73
Rossetti, Gina, 230
Rothstein, Arthur, 476
Rotundo, Anthony, 411
Rougon-Macquart (Zola), 25–26, 98, 291, 340

sadism, 278–79
Sadoul, Georges, 486
"St. Columba and the River" (Dreiser), 312–13
St. Jean, Shawn, 135
Saltus, Edgar, 76
Sanctuary (Faulkner), 288
A Sand County Almanac (Leopold), 67
Sandburg, Carl, 449–50
Sapphira and the Slave Girl (Cather), 234

"Sarrasine" (Balzac), 49
Satan Met a Lady (film), 486
Satter, Beryl, 254n3
Saunders, Steven M., 485
Saussure, Ferdinand de, 49
Sawaya, Francesca, 231
Scarborough, Dorothy, 241, 246
Schrader, Paul, 485, 491
Schriber, Marysue, 146
Schudson, Michael, 107
science
    behavioral genetics and, 128–29
    chaos theory, quantum mechanics and, 127–28
    evolution as savior of modern, 59
    of fiction, 28
    monster machines as consequence of, 25–26
    naturalism in theology and, 157–62
    physiology of, 182
    as subservient, 25
    technical facts based on, 108–9
Science and Religion: A Historical Introduction (Ferngren), 155
Scopes, John Thomas, 54, 155
Scott, Evelyn, 235, 236, 241
Scott, Howard, 45–46
Scribner, Charles, 368
"The Sculptor's Funeral" (Cather), 231
The Sea-Wolf (London), 6, 86, 151–52, 167–68, 226, 377–79, 446
Sedgwick, Adam, 161
Seguin, Robert, 312, 319n1
Seidenberg, Roderick, 40–41
Selby, Hubert, 332, 333
Seltzer, Mark, 84, 245, 405, 407, 408, 415
sex-centric movement
    feminist views of, 243–44
    masculinist views of, 243
sexuality, 253n1
    female, 66, 226, 246–48
    female marital infidelity and, 246
    in film noir, 484, 489, 490, 492–93
    Judeo-Christian repression and, 242
    literary naturalism and, 241–54
    male, 66, 245, 248–51
    moderate/right-wing conservatives and, 242–43
    perversion and, 254n2
    race as signifier of value with, 233
    sadism and, 278–79
    sex-centric reformist movement and, 243
    triangular situations and, 250–51
    violence and, 250–51, 252–53, 261
    women's marital entrapment and, 246–47
sexual primitivism, 58
sexual repression, 194
sexual selection, 55, 254n5
    African-American writers and, 269, 270
    birdsong and music in, 57
    naturalism, courtship plot and, 56–63

primitive society and, 58
sexual struggle, components of, 56
sexy son hypothesis, 204–6
Seyersted, Per, 237n3
Shack People, 99–100
Shafak, Elif, 99, 100
Shakespeare, William, 445
    plagiarism and, 111
    pre-Darwinian courtship and, 56
Sharratt, Bernard, 16n2
Shaw, Irwin, 434
Sheehan, Donald, 362
Sheldon, Edward, 431, 436
The Sheltered Life (Glasgow), 246
Shepard, Sam, 434
Sherman, Stuart P., 83, 382
Sherwood, Robert, 428
Shi, David, 300
Shinn, Everett, 465, 466, 467, 468, 479n6
Shulman, Robert, 303
Shulman, Sarah Way, 300
The Silent Partner (Phelps), 235
Sillen, Samuel, 386
Simenon, George, 419
Simmel, Georg, 41
Simpson, J. Y., 155
Sinclair, Upton, 3, 6, 74, 106, 109, 235, 296, 300, 302, 316, 361, 404, 412, 413, 439, 450
    class and, 307, 308, 313–14, 318, 319n3
    criminality and, 341
    environmental determinism and, 342, 343
    naturalistic gothic and, 328–29
Singer, Robert, 496
Singley, Carol J., 302
Sister Carrie (Dreiser), 183, 231, 303, 317, 395, 405
    canonization of, 397, 399
    cities and, 333–35
    class in, 307, 311, 312, 314
    crime and, 349–350
    environmental determinism in, 343–44
    film noir and, 484, 493
    gender, race and, 411
    immediate/omniscient voice in, 143–44
    male gaze in, 232
    man-made monsters and, 27
    melodramatic vision and, 10–11
    new naturalist economy and, 407, 408
    popular literary conventions in, 16n1
    power of sympathy, Spencer and, 188–90
    religion and, 168, 169
    sexual selection in, 61
    social class and, 319n3
    Stieglitz and Shinn's influence on, 479n6
    typology of documentary and, 106–107
    unromantic machines and, 33–34
    visual arts and, 463, 464, 468
    women as naturalist writers and, 236
Skaggs, Peggy, 237n3
"Skunk Hour" (Lowell), 459

"Skyscraper" (Sandburg), 450
slavery, abolition of, 261
Sloan, John, 466
Slumming in New York: From the Waterfront to Mythic Harlem (Dowling), 257
Smedley, Agnes, 310
Smith, Johnston. *See* Crane, Stephen
Smith, Robert "Yank," 434
Smith, Susan, 300
Smuts, Jan Christian, 212
Social Purity Movement, 243
Social Statics (Spencer), 141, 188
The Social Life of Things: Commodities in Cultural Perspective (Appadurai), 301
society
    grotesque body as threat to, 233
    industrialism and shift from agrarian, 26, 27, 38, 39
    primitive and civilized, 53
sociobiology, 254n8
Les Soirées de Médan (Medan group), 22
soliloquy, 11
somatic style, 183
Sonntag, W. L., Jr., 466
soul, transcending nature, 53
Soul of the Ape (Marais), 217
The Souls of Black Folk (Du Bois), 59, 258, 262
source materials. *See also* plagiarism
    as fair game for creative work, 114
    for novels, 111–13
Southern Horrors: Lynch Law in All Its Phases (Wells), 261
South Moon Under (Rawlings), 246
"South of the Slot" (London), 178–79
spectators
    double-consciousness of, 264
    narrators as brutes and, 263–64
Spellbound (film), 483
Spencer, Herbert, 4, 155, 157, 159, 168, 184, 203, 223, 225, 269, 270, 434
    altruism, reason and, 189
    altruism and, 212
    class and, 315
    Darwinism and, 39
    evolutionary development and, 160
    evolutionary morality and, 140–41
    on free will, 132, 133
    individual, community and, 40–41
    individualism and, 150
    melodramatic vision and, 11
    morality and, 139, 142, 149, 151
    naturalistic imagination and, 8–9
    nature's conflicting forces and, 40, 42–43
    scientific determinism and, 293
    scientific physiology and, 182
    Sister Carrie, power of sympathy and, 188–90
    social and political significance of, 320n5
    "survival of the fittest" and, 140

Spindler, Michael, 300
Spoon River Anthology (Masters), 74, 451–53
The Sport of the Gods (Dunbar), 235, 265, 266–67, 303
Stalin, Josef, 407
Stange, Maren, 317
The Star Rover (London), 73
Stedman, Arthur, 389
Steffens, Lincoln, 412
Stein, Gertrude, 416
    female sexuality and, 66
    racism and, 64
Steinbeck, John, 3, 4, 67, 74, 135, 204, 351, 434, 463, 480n15
    altruism and, 211–12
    drama and, 434, 440–41
    environmental determinism and, 345–46
    journalism and, 476, 477
    reciprocity and, 211–12, 213–15
    visual arts and, 475–79
Stendhal, 419
Stephen Crane and Literary Impressionism (Nagel), 472
"Stephen Crane's Own Story" (Crane), 110
Stepto, Robert, 263
Stevens, Wallace, First Idea and, 38
Stevenson, Robert Louis, 107
Stieglitz, Alfred, 464–65, 468, 479n6
Stockham, Alice, 243
The Stoic (Dreiser), 317
Stokes, George Gabriel, 156
The Story of Ab (Waterloo), 114, 115
Stott, William, 104
Stowe, Harriet Beecher, 319n3
The Street (Petry), 236, 237n10, 303
    "catalogue of refuse" in, 230
    sexuality in, 248
    spectacle of desire/repulsive truth-teller in, 234
strength, physical, 234
Stribling, T. S., 61, 66
Strindberg, August, 428, 431, 432, 433, 434, 436, 437, 439, 441
structuralism, 49
Strunsky, Anna, 366
Stryker, Paul, 476
Studies in the Psychology of Sex (Ellis), 58, 244
Styron, William, 4
sublimation, 195
Sui Sin Far, 74, 285, 416
Sullivan, Louis, 450
Sumner, William Graham, 245
    degeneration, atavism and, 172–73
Sundquist, Eric, 257, 260, 407
The Sun Also Rises (Hemingway), 48, 57
"Superman," 168
"survival of the fittest," 140, 166–67
Susan Lenox: Her Fall and Rise (Phillips), 232, 341, 405
Swinton, John, 392

sympathy, power of, 188–90
Synge, John Millington, 433
Synthetic Philosophy (Spencer), 188
Sypher, Wylie, 9
A System of Logic (Mill), 125

Talmage, Thomas DeWitt, 374
Tarbell, Ida, 410
Taylor, Paul, 476
Tebbel, John, 362
Technocracy, 46
Teller, Charlotte, 417
Tennyson, Alfred (lord), 65
La Terre (Zola), 21
Terrell, Mary Church, 262
Tess of the d'Urbervilles (Hardy), 28
A Text-book of Operative Dentistry (Fillebrown), 108
theater. *See* drama, naturalism and
Théâtre Libre, 428
"Their Blood Is Strong" (Steinbeck), 477, 479, 480n15
them (Oates), 251
theology, naturalism in science and, 157–62
The Theory of the Leisure Class (Veblen), 300, 301
Thérèse Raquin (Zola), 98, 278, 496n3
Thomas, Brook, 418
Thompson, G. R., 300
Thompson, Maurice, 88
Thomson, James, 458
Thomson, William, 156
Thoreau, Henry David, 53
Three Contributions to the Theory of Sex (Freud), 195
Tietze, Tom, 286
Tillman, Ben, 263, 268
time, standardization of, 27
Time and Commodity Culture: Essays in Cultural Theory and Postmodernity (Frow), 301
The Titan (Dreiser), 45, 228
    class in, 317
"To Build a Fire" (London.), 52, 179–80
Tocqueville, Alexis de, 310
Todorov, Tzvetan, 275
To Have and Have Not (Hemingway), 49
"The Toil of the Laborer" (Dreiser), 312–13
"Told in the Drooling Ward" (London), 179
Tolstoy, Leo, 80, 105
Tompkins, Jane, 7
Tonnies, Ferdinand, 41
Toomer, Jean, 416
Totten, Gary, 303
Touch of Evil (film), 483
To Wake the Nations: Race in the Making of American Literature (Sundquist), 257
Trachtenberg, Alan, 301
The Traitor (Dixon), 173, 174, 268
transcendentalism, 82
trauma theory, 264
A Traveler from Altruria (Howells), 73

Treadwell, Sophie, 433, 438
Trigo, Benigno, 485
Trilogy of Reconstruction (Dixon), 173–74
Trivers, Robert, 212–13, 215
"True Art Speaks Plainly" (Dreiser), 242
truth
    fact and, 156
    obese bodies as repulsive tellers of, 233–34
    Plato's illusion of reality for, 296
    writers and, 266
Turner, Frederick Jackson, 50
Turner, James, 155
Twain, Mark, 46, 74, 132, 133, 284, 341, 427
Twentieth-Century American Literary Naturalism: An Interpretation (Pizer), 4
twentieth/twenty-first centuries
    literary naturalism in, 79–85
    transcendentalism in, 82
Twisted from the Ordinary (Papke), 230, 303
tyranny, 85–88
Tyson, Lois, 303
Tyson, Mike, 88

Uncle Tom's Cabin (Stowe), 319n3
Under the Gaslight (Daly), 111
"Under the Lion's Paw" (Garland), 15
The Unfortunates (Johnson), 99–100
United States
    industrialization's influence in, 27
    man-made monsters in England and, 27–29
Unnatural Selections: Eugenics in American Modernism and the Harlem Renaissance (English), 270
"Untitled" (Lange), 477, 478
urbanization, 27, 38
USA (Dos Passos), 48
utopian novels, 73

Vaihinger, Hans, 191
Valley of the Moon (London), 229
The Valley of the Moon (London), 61, 66–67
The Value of Things (Cummings and Lewandowska), 301
vamps, film noir, 490
Van Doren, Carl, 382
Vandover and the Brute (Norris),
    atavism, degeneration and, 175–176, 267, 408
    canonization and, 396–97
    "catalogue of refuse" in, 230
    city as dangerous trap and, 266
    crime and, 340
    devolution and, 226
    editing process and, 393, 394
    grotesque cities and, 327
    literature, philosophy and, 122
    melodramatic vision and, 12, 13–14
    religion and, 165
    sexuality in, 243
Varricchio, Mario, 302

The Vast and Terrible Drama: American Literary Naturalism in the Late Nineteenth Century (Link), 4
Veblen, Thorstein, 41, 300, 301–2
Verging on the Abyss: The Social Fiction of Kate Chopin and Edith Wharton (Papke), 302
Victorian Age, 154–55
violence, 408
   African-American manhood and, 266–68
   class, 309
   homoerotic, 252–53
   lynching, 261–64, 268, 280
   mob, 261, 262–63
   murder and, 345–46
   sexuality and, 250–51, 252–53, 261
   trauma theory and, 264
The Virginian (Wister), 285
visual arts. *See also* paintings; photojournalism
   Crane and, 469–75
   Dreiser, Theodore, and, 464–68
   explanation of, 463–64
   influence of social condition on, 463–64
   naturalism and, 463–80
   Steinbeck and, 475–79
Vivas, Eliseo, 40, 135
Von Rosk, Nancy, 303, 416

Waisbrooker, Lois, 244
Walcutt, Charles C., 3, 4, 7, 11, 82, 83, 84, 85, 124, 127, 406, 407, 414, 461
   divided-stream argument and, 453
   poetry and, 445–46
Walden (Thoreau), 300
Walker, Margaret, 384
Walker, Nancy, 228, 237n3
Wallace, Alfred Russel, 53, 140
The Walls of Jericho (Fisher), 59, 62–63
Ward, Joseph A., 303
Ward, Lester F., 244
War Is Kind (Crane), 447, 449
Warren, Kenneth, 257, 413
Washington, Booker T., 259
Washington, George, 217
Wasserstein, Wendy, 441
"The Wasteland" (Eliot), 115, 446
Waterloo, Stanley, 114
Watson, H. B. Marriott, 76
Watt, Ian, 95, 420
Weber, Max, 41
Weber, Myles, 302
Weeds (Kelley), 235, 246–47, 248
Weissman, August, 63
Wellek, Rene, 85
Wells, Ida Barnett, 261–62, 280
Wertheim, Stanley, 363
Wertime, Richard A., 332
West, James L. W., 399–400
Westermarck, Edvard, 225
Wharton, Edith, 3, 74

commodity culture and, 301, 302, 303
determinism, naturalistic authors and, 135
drama and, 438
feminism and, 218
French origins and, 21
ironic plotting and, 230
literary marketplace and, 357, 360, 370
marital infidelity plot and, 246
mastering literary marketplace, 367–6
morality and, 140, 145–147, 149
naturalism, women writers and, 223–36
nature in naturalism and, 56
Plato's cave and, 296
sexual selection and, 60–61
sexy son hypothesis and, 204–6
social mechanism as monster and, 33–34
on tragedies with happy endings, 427–28
unromantic machines and, 32
as writer in initial group of 1890s naturalists, 241
What Is Man? (Twain), 132, 133
What the Social Classes Owe to Each Other (Sumner), 172
What Was Naturalism?, 3
wheat, 87
   economic symbology of, 41, 45, 47, 316
   as force of nature, 31–32, 44, 148, 166
   mystical power of, 231, 408
White, Andrew Dickson, 155
White, Barbara, 206
"White Angel Bread Line" (Lange), 476, 478
Whited, Lana A., 419
White Fang (London), 167, 177–78, 318
Whitman, Walt, 160
Wiebe, Robert, 409
"The Wife of His Youth" (Chesnutt), 260
Wilde, Oscar, 427
Wilder, Billy, 486, 490, 491
Wilder, Thornton, 438
Williams, James, 366
Williams, Raymond, 296–97, 418
Williams, Tennessee, 433, 434, 436, 437
Williams, Tony, 496
will to power/to seem, 191
Wilson, August, 441
Wilson, Christopher, 101, 261, 358, 361, 371, 412, 414
Wilson, E. O., 218
The Wind (Scarborough), 246
Winesburg, Ohio (Anderson), 183, 191–93, 451
Wingfield, Amanda, 434
"Winter on Fifth Avenue" (Stieglitz), 465, 479n6
Winther, Sophus, 436
Winton, Tim, 99, 100
Wister, Owen, 285
Witherow, Jean, 237n3
Without God, Without Creed: The Origins of Unbelief in America (Turner), 155
Witla, Eugene, 466–68
"The Witness" (Petry), 296

Witschi, Nicolas, 230
Woman's Christian Temperance Union, 163, 164
The Woman Within (Glasgow), 193, 225
women
   body as spectacle, 231–33
   California described as, 455–57
   childbirth and, 235, 245
   courtship plot and power of choice by, 56, 59–63
   Darwin on role of sexual selection and, 211
   demeaned by men's contempt, 192
   evolutionary feminism and, 206–8
   extra-pair copulation and, 205
   female objectification and, 33
   femme fatales and, 49, 345
   intelligentsia and African Americans, 262
   Machiavellian intelligence and competition for mates between men and, 208–11
   marital sexual relationships, entrapment and, 246–47
   men's atavism and power over, 279
   mermaid's voices and, 57
   naturalism and characteristics of writing by, 229–36
   as naturalist writers, 226, 245–46
   poetry and identity of, 451
   prostitution and, 164, 251, 316, 317, 324, 340, 342–43, 432, 436, 470–71
   rural/wilderness landscapes and place of, 230–31
   sexy son hypothesis and, 204–6
   singing vulgar blues, 59
   as trapped baby-making machines and nurturer, 460
   valuing knowledge gained from fiction, 100
   as vamps in film noir, 490
   writers and naturalism, 223–36
Women, Compulsion, Modernity: The Moment of American Naturalism (Fleissner), 4, 257
Women and Economics: A Study of the Economic Relation between Men and Women as a Factor in Social Evolution (Gilman), 243–44
Wood, Michael, 100
Woodhull, Victoria, 244
Wordsworth, William, 126, 449, 455, 458
The Word and Its Witness: The Spiritualization of American Realism (Jackson), 94
World Almanac and Book of Facts 2002, 336n1
The World of Goods (Douglas and Isherwood), 301
The World Republic of Letters (Casanova), 98
Wright, Richard, 3, 74, 111, 135, 212, 241, 250–51, 258, 289, 310, 346–47, 348
   altruism and, 215, 216, 218
   city of excess and, 331
   factual research and, 113, 115
   plagiarism and, 111
   popular reception of naturalist texts and, 383–87
writers. *See also specific writers*
   determinism and naturalistic, 131–36

human courtship and pre-Darwinian, 56–57
identifying American literary naturalist, 72–74
inartistic skills of naturalist, 29–30
initial group of 1890s naturalist, 241
literary marketplace and naturalist, 357–71
marginalization of African American, 92
naturalism and African American, 257–71
naturalism and characteristics of women, 229–36
naturalism and women, 223–36
originality and, 115–16
pessimistic determinism and naturalistic, 81–82
Pizer on naturalist, 258
plagiarism and, 111–16
sexual selection and African-American, 269, 270
as solely responsible for unique work, 114
truth and, 266
women as naturalist, 226, 245–46

Yang, Seokwon, 303
Yates, Richard, 319
Yeazell, Ruth Bernard, 302
"The Yellow Wall-Paper" (Gilman), 244
Yerkes, Charles, 45
Young, Egerton, 109, 112, 113

Zabarella, Jacopo, 157
Zangwill, Israel, 76
Zayani, Mohamed, 419, 420
Zimbardo, Rose A., 434
Zitkala-Ša 74, 416
Zola, Émile, 3, 4, 80, 87, 100, 259, 278, 288, 298, 301, 376, 405, 430, 433, 437, 445
   commodity culture and, 291–292
   on crime, 340
   on determinism, 182, 340
   determinism, naturalistic authors and, 134
   dialogism and, 414, 415, 419
   evolution of literary naturalisms and, 38
   on fatalism, 127
   film noir and, 496n3
   influence on Chopin, Kate, 224–25
   as literary architect, 23
   man-made monsters in England, U.S., and, 27–29
   Medan group and, 22
   monster machine and, 24–32
   narrative distinctions between Tolstoy and, 105
   naturalism's origins in France with, 21–24, 54, 77–78, 98
   nature in naturalism and, 52
   obscenity and, 21–22
   as originator of naturalism, 98
   romanticism and, 22–23, 78–79
   sad endings and, 428, 429
   silent cinema influenced by, 496
   slice of life and, 296
   unromantic machines and, 34